Sponsoring Editor: George A. Middendorf
Project Editor: Karla B. Philip
Designer: Rita Naughton
Senior Production Manager: Kewal K. Sharma
Photo Researcher: Myra Schachne
Compositor: Progressive Typographers Inc.
Printer and Binder: Halliday Lithograph Corporation
Art Studio: Vantage Art Inc.
Chapter opening and cover illustrations: Bill Greer

PSYCHOLOGICAL DEVELOPMENT: A LIFE-SPAN APPROACH

Library of Congress Cataloging in Publication Data

Main entry under title:

Psychological development, a life-span approach.

Includes index.
1. Developmental psychology. I. Mussen, Paul Henry.
BF713.P78   155   78-11977
ISBN 0-06-044692-7

Psychological Development
A Life-Span Approach

Paul Henry Mussen
University of California, Berkeley

John Janeway Conger
University of Colorado School of Medicine

Jerome Kagan
Harvard University

James Geiwitz

HARPER & ROW, PUBLISHERS
New York   Hagerstown   San Francisco   London

Contents

PREFACE   *ix*

Chapter 1   THEORY AND RESEARCH IN DEVELOPMENTAL PSYCHOLOGY   *1*

Some Historical Perspectives   *4*
Developmental Psychology as a Scientific Discipline   *11*
Theory in Developmental Psychology   *17*
Basic Conditions of Learning   *34*
Concerns of Developmental Psychology   *38*
Summary   *39*

Chapter 2   BIOLOGICAL FACTORS IN EARLY DEVELOPMENT   *42*

Hereditary Transmission   *44*
Biological Influences During Pregnancy and Childbirth   *53*
Biological Factors in Infancy   *64*
Summary   *82*

Chapter 3   COGNITIVE AND SOCIAL DEVELOPMENT IN INFANCY   *88*

Perceptual Development   *89*
Mental Development: Piaget's Theory   *95*

Social Development   *98*
Summary   *120*

Chapter 4 LANGUAGE AND COGNITION   *124*

Theories of Language Development   *125*
The Beginnings of Speech   *129*
The Relationship Between Language and Cognition   *143*
Language and Social Class   *146*
Basic Cognitive Activities   *151*
Summary   *165*

Chapter 5 INTELLIGENCE   *171*

Piaget's Stages of Intelligence   *173*
Intelligence Tests   *178*
Environmental and Genetic Factors in Intelligence   *187*
Summary   *199*

Chapter 6 PRESCHOOL PERSONALITY DEVELOPMENT   *202*

Sex   *204*
Aggression   *204*
Dependency   *211*
Fear and Anxiety   *215*
Mastery and Achievement   *220*
Identification   *222*
The Home Environment   *230*
Summary   *234*

Chapter 7 MIDDLE CHILDHOOD   *239*

Influence of the Family in Middle Childhood   *240*
Relations with Peers   *247*
Adjustment to School   *249*
Family, Peers, and School Achievement   *256*
Development of Conscience   *259*
Psychological Problems of Middle Childhood   *262*
Problems of Minority-Group Membership   *267*
Summary   *270*

Chapter 8 ADOLESCENCE: BASIC DEVELOPMENT   *279*

Personality Development in Adolescence   *281*
Psychological Effects of Mental Growth   *288*

Biological Development in Adolescence   *291*
The Development of Independence   *298*
Adolescents and Their Peers   *303*
Moral Development and Values   *309*
Summary   *316*

Chapter 9   ADOLESCENCE: SOCIAL ISSUES   *322*

Sexual Attitudes and Behavior   *324*
Alienation and Commitment   *333*
Adolescents and Drugs   *343*
Juvenile Delinquency   *350*
Summary   *359*

Chapter 10   YOUNG ADULTS   *366*

Personality Development in Young Adulthood   *367*
Marriage   *373*
Parenthood   *384*
Careers   *389*
Summary   *401*

Chapter 11   THE MIDDLE YEARS   *407*

Personality Development in the Middle Years   *410*
Intellectual Development   *419*
Biological Concerns in Middle Adulthood   *428*
The Family in the Middle Years   *434*
Summary   *440*

Chapter 12   OLD AGE   *446*

Personalities, Ordered and Disordered   *448*
Social Factors in Aging   *454*
The Family in Old Age   *461*
Intellectual Development   *466*
Biological Concerns in Old Age   *472*
Death and Dying   *478*
Summary   *480*

INDEX   *487*

Preface

Our knowledge of human development, much like the individuals we study, is continually growing and changing. Systematic scientific investigation of psychological development is less than 100 years old. Astonishing progress has been made in the last 50 years, and particularly in the last 25 years. Initially, the subject matter of developmental psychology was largely confined to the discovery and description of age trends in physical, psychological, and social characteristics. Increasingly, however, we have become concerned with the processes underlying human growth and development—with a theoretical synthesis of observed phenomenon that can provide us with an understanding of how and why behavior originates and changes. Significant advances have been made in many areas, including sensory and perceptual ability, cognitive and language development, behavioral genetics, and the effects of socialization agents, such as parents, peers, and society itself.

Until very recently most of our concern has been with early development, and it is still true today that the greatest scientific progress has been in our knowledge of development during infancy and early childhood. However, in the past 10 years or so, research in adolescence has expanded greatly, both in quantity and quality. Currently, greatly increased attention is being paid to the developmental problems of early, middle, and late adulthood, and research in aging —biological, psychological, and social—is particularly active at present. In part, this expansion of research interest beyond childhood reflects improved methods for studying later developmental stages. But it also reflects important social changes. People are living longer today and the percentage of older people in the population is growing steadily. Thus, by their sheer numbers, they call for increased attention.

There is also another equally important set of social forces at work. Beginning with the growth of the civil rights movement in the 1950s and 1960s, we have seen a rapid increase in concern for individual human rights generally, manifested most recently in the development of the women's movement and activist groups of the elderly, such as the Gray Panthers. Increasingly, people are determined to make their own lives more meaningful and rewarding, regardless of the age group into which they currently fall. There is a growing realization, too, that age separation in our society has gone too far. As Maggie Kuhn, founder of the Gray Panthers, has stated, we need to recognize that life is "all of one piece," from birth to death, and that children, adolescents, adults, and old people need, and can benefit from, continuing interaction with each other.

Much of the recent research into the so-called *life crises* of early and middle adulthood—into the biological, psychological, social, and economic problems of aging, and, indeed, into the phenomenon of death and dying—has stemmed from a desire to help us better understand the developmental needs and problems of *all* age groups, in order to find better ways of meeting the needs and helping to solve the problems of each. We still have much to learn, but we have taken the exciting and challenging first steps—we are trying. This text is a small part of that effort.

One advantage of the life-span approach to development is that the skills, concepts, and theories of the child psychologist can be enormously useful in guiding the research into the newer areas of adult development. For example, the notion of personal identity can be used for an individual of any age, and the techniques developed for the investigation of memory and perception in children have found many applications in the study of these same processes in adults, particularly among the aging.

Another advantage of the life-span approach is that it rectifies the imbalance of a focus on children alone. Too often we emphasize the effects of parents on children, without a balancing picture of the effects of children on parents. It helps to know that while children are growing and changing, the parents are too. As an adolescent struggles to develop his or her identity, the parents may be in the throes of their own mid-life crises. Similarly, where a child-centered text might describe the parents primarily in terms of interactions with the child, those interactions are, in real life, significantly affected by the parent's career activities and goals, and by the relationship between spouses.

Psychological Development: A Life-Span Approach is essentially an alternative version of the Mussen, Conger, and Kagan *Child Development and Personality* text, with the themes and emphases of that book extended through young adulthood, the middle years, and old age. The first nine chapters of this text are, in fact, a condensed and somewhat less-detailed version of the child development textbook, modified to anticipate the discussion of adult development. The last three chapters are entirely new.

A word about sexist language: We have struggled mightily with the problem of the generic *he*, which is especially problematic in textbooks on human development. We have tried to avoid the "he-she" dilemma through various means such as the use of plurals and rephrasing, but there remains a certain percentage of pronouns that defy alteration. Because we believe that use of the generic *he* in such instances is no longer justifiable, we have alternated *he* with the generic *she;* both meaning "he or she." Some readers may find the generic *she* slightly distracting, but we feel the issue involved is worth it.

We have many people to thank. The authors gratefully acknowledge the constructive criticisms of reviewers Carol Dero, Kay Van Hover, and Margaret Lloyd. For secretarial and bibliographical assistance, we thank Jane McAfee, Pat Stubblefield, Vivien March, Dorothy Townsend, Doris Simpson, and Carole Lawton. William Putnam reviewed and suggested illustrations for the book, and we thank him, too.

P.H.M.
J.J.C.
J.K.
J.G.

CHAPTER 1
Theory and Research in Developmental Psychology

Susan Jenkins is a young girl, age 5, about to enter kindergarten. She was born and raised in an urban ghetto; she is a member of a minority group and the lower socioeconomic class. She has taken an intelligence test and has scored below the average of the children who will soon be her classmates. She is not looking forward to school; she sees little reason for it.

Developmental psychologists want to understand this girl. They want to understand the events in her infancy and early childhood that have influenced her present personality. They want to alter the course of future events so that she might lead a more effective life as an adult. For example, why are her test scores lower than those of middle-class children? Is it because of the learning experiences in Susan's home? Does it have something to do with the attitudes of her parents? Is Susan genetically disadvantaged in intelligence? Is she "disadvantaged" by intelligence tests and schools that are culturally biased in favor of the middle and upper social classes?

What does Susan's future hold? Is she determined to fall further and further behind her classmates in academic performance? Will her self-esteem decrease, until finally she turns to drugs to lessen the pain of failure? Will her status as a female keep her from aspiring to certain occupations?

We do not yet have complete answers to such complicated questions. Through research, however, developmental psychologists contribute to understanding and, ultimately, to solving these problems. In this book we will review the evidence that an impoverished environment contributes to poor performance in tests of intellectual functioning. We will look at studies that suggest that many of the items on "intelligence" tests involve vocabulary and information more familiar to members of the middle class than to those of the lower class. Values also vary. The lower class generally does not emphasize competition and intellectual achievement to the extent that the middle class does, and consequently lower-class children are often less motivated to perform well in tests or in school.

And what of the future? Do comprehensive programs of remedial education enable lower-class children to catch up to their middle-class peers? Systematic evaluation of a number of such programs suggests that certain kinds of training, if maintained long enough, can have significant long-term effects. Being a female presents social, political, and psychological problems which psychologists by themselves cannot solve. But developmental psychologists can study sex roles and investigate the ways in which biological and environmental factors contribute to established notions of "masculine" and "feminine."

George Coleman is approaching the age of 65 and is about to retire from his job as an executive at a bank. He likes his job; he is not looking forward to retirement. He wonders about "old age," whether his health will be good, whether his finances will hold out. He is beginning to consider his own death, and he wonders if there is really life after death, as his church teaches.

Developmental psychologists want to understand this man, too. They want to understand the relationship between George's personality and his job and how this relationship affects his attitude toward retirement. They want to trace his personality and intellectual development in the later years of his life. How do cultural attitudes toward old age affect his self-concept? Is it realistic for him to expect some decline in vision and hearing after the age of 65? How about reasoning ability? What is "aging," as distinct from the diseases that so often afflict the elderly? How is personal adjustment in the last years of life affected by experiences in childhood or in early adulthood?

Developmental psychologists are interested in changes that occur with age (Figure 1.1). In the past, the field has focused primarily on childhood and adolescence, but recently interest has expanded to the entire span of life, including young adulthood, middle age, and old age. In this introductory chapter, we will first look at some historical perspectives on child psychology, the psychology of adolescence, and adult development and aging. Then we will briefly consider developmental psychology as a scientific discipline and review a few of the major theoretical approaches. Some of the basic conditions of learning will be treated in more detail. Finally, there is a note on three basic concerns of developmental psychology. This done, we will be ready to explore the scientific evidence relating to the problems and the potentialities of our young girl and our old man, and to all the dangers and opportunities that face human beings as they develop from birth to death.

●Figure 1.1   Being young and being old can create psychological problems in our society. The youngster faces the problems of being an underachiever in an academically oriented world, and the elder faces the threat of aging in a society that is basically youth-oriented.

SOME HISTORICAL PERSPECTIVES

Child Psychology

Most people take it for granted that the events of early childhood affect an individual's later social and psychological adjustment. Moreover, almost everyone seems to be interested in children and their welfare; in their growth and development; and in their acquisition of skills, abilities, personality, and social characteristics. We live in a child-centered culture. This special emphasis on childhood is a relatively recent development in the history of the family.

Until the seventeenth century, children in many Western European countries were not treated in very distinctive ways. Obviously infants needed special care and attention, but children over 6 or 7 years of age were typically considered "small adults." They mingled, worked, and played with mature people, hindered only by their relatively small size and weak strength (1). Their clothing was not distinctive; rather, they dressed like the men and women of their social class. Children were not thought to be particularly "innocent" and in need of protection from verbal reference to sexual matters. Indeed, most parents viewed their children as "inherently evil" and punished them severely (by today's standards) for sexual and aggressive behaviors and for disobedience to authority (12).

The seventeenth century produced a marked change in attitudes toward children. They began to be viewed as individuals, and parents began to value independence and autonomy in their offspring. Gradually there appeared a whole new family attitude, oriented toward the child and his or her education. With the new attitude, the concept of the innocence of childhood won acceptance, and from that time on, children were to be spared all references to sexual matters lest their innocence be corrupted. As "special" people, children were dressed in special clothing reserved for their age group.

About the same time, the love relationship between parent and child began to be perceived as vitally important to the normal, healthy development of the child. Again, it may be difficult for us to imagine a time when parental love was considered *less* than vitally important. We are prone to attribute a wide range of problems in adolescence and adulthood—unhappiness, failure, mental disorders—to an early childhood without love. But prior to the mid seventeenth century, Europeans rarely referred to parental affection as a factor in child development. "The child needed a good education and faith in God; parents provided physical care, consistent discipline, and a model for proper behavior" (12, p. 42).

Probably the new attitudes toward childhood and parental love had their roots in the industrial revolution and, in particular, in the rise of an urban middle class. In an agricultural economy, children have clear economic value; even the younger children can help with chores and tend to the needs of infants. In an industrial economy, children have less value and may even become an economic burden. The responses to this changing role of children in the family were varied. Some parents, especially the very poor, simply abandoned their

● Figure 1.2 Children have become less important economically, more important as objects of sentiment.

children; the children who survived filled the orphanages of the day. Other parents set their children to work. But working in factories and mines was too difficult for young children, and finally child-labor laws were required to protect the children, many of whom had been forced to work 16 hours a day from the age of 5 upward (6).

The most benevolent response to the decreasing economic value of children was to treat them less as objects of utility and more as objects of sentiment (12) (see Figure 1.2). Children, particularly in the middle class, were accorded special status—set free from the requirement to contribute immediately to the family fortune—and carefully "nurtured" (loved and educated) so that they might eventually enhance the family's prestige by their accomplishments later in life. In analogy, the child was now more like a prized thoroughbred and less like a valuable plowhorse.

How does one proceed if the goal be that of raising a beloved child to be autonomous and creative (without being unnecessarily rebellious)? Questions such as this fueled the development of child psychology, as parents and teachers sought to understand the nature of the young child and the best means of guiding him or her to a happy and productive future.

Philosophers and child psychology   The earliest writers on child psychology were philosophers, clergy, educators, and reformers—not scientists—but the issues discussed are still important today. For example, the issue of *nature versus nurture* was frequently debated: To what extent were the behaviors of adults part of their inherited nature and to what extent the result of their experiences during childhood (their nurture)? The British philosopher John Locke, writing at the end of the seventeenth century, viewed the child's experiences and education as the fundamental determinants of development. The infant's mind, he wrote, is a *tabula rasa*—a blank slate—receptive to all kinds of learning.

Jean Jacques Rousseau, a French philosopher, believed that the child is endowed with an innate moral sense. He spoke of the child as a "noble savage" having intuitive knowledge of right and wrong. Left alone, "the child will become increasingly fit to live in the world . . . because nature has endowed him with an order of development that ensures his healthy growth. More than that, the typical interventions of parents and teachers mar and distort the natural succession of the changes of childhood. . . ." (13, p. 74).

Locke's and Rousseau's views of how children develop contrast sharply. In Locke's view, children are essentially passive and receptive, molded by pressures from the environment—rewards and punishments. In Rousseau's view, children respond actively to the world around them, using it to suit their purposes. The child is a "busy, testing, motivated explorer" (13, p. 75). As we shall see, this distinction between views of the child as active and searching and the child as passive and receptive is still very much with us.

Baby biographies   The first careful observations of children began to be published in the late eighteenth century. Frequently these "baby biographies" were notes on the development of the author's own child. The most eminent writer of such a biography was Charles Darwin, who published a diary of his observations of his son's early development (7). Darwin made the study of children respectable, not only because he published a baby biography but also because he

believed that "by careful observation of the infant and child, one could see the descent of man" (13, p. 115).

The early biographies were generally poor sources of scientific data. Too often the observations were unsystematic and biased by the observer's special theory about development of education. The bias of proud parents led them to emphasize the positive while neglecting the negative features of child development. Nevertheless, the early biographies defined many of the major problems in child psychology and excited widespread interest in the observation of children. Darwin was particularly influential "in his assignment of scientific value to childhood" (13, p. 115).

The Psychology of Adolescence

Although the ways in which societies have viewed their young people have varied enormously over the centuries, there are some general trends worth noting. Society's view of childhood, as we have seen, changed significantly during the seventeenth and eighteenth centuries, and one of the effects of this change was to set off young children below the age of puberty from older children or adolescents. Child-labor laws, for example, were designed to protect the younger children; the provisions for "able-bodied" adolescents were typically much milder or nonexistent. Adolescents were considered more like adults than children.

"Adolescence" and "youth" were not usually distinguished as stages in development until quite recently. Most of the earlier writings, usually by clergy or educators, commented on youth only when their "lack of wisdom" and their "unruly and undependable" behavior seemed to call for a treatise on helping adolescents control their impulses. Not until the declining years of the nineteenth century do we encounter more balanced views of the adolescent:

> The first typical adolescent of modern times was Wagner's *Siegfried:* the music of *Siegfried* expressed for the first time the combination of . . . purity, physical strength, naturism, spontaneity, and [love of life] which was to make the adolescent the hero of our twentieth century. . . . Youth gave the impression of secretly possessing new values capable of reviving an aged . . . society (1, p. 30).

"Youths as reformers" was a notion that blossomed into widespread currency, especially among youths themselves, only after World War I. It reached full flowering during the 1960s, when youth tried various means to convince the older generations of the wisdom of their opposition to the Vietnam War and of their liberalized standards of sexual behavior and drug use. These values marked "youth" as clearly different from typical older people.

As in the case of younger children, "adolescence" and "youth" probably owe their distinction to the industrial revolution. A simple, primarily agricultural economy can usually use the strength and stamina of relatively immature workers who lack developed skills but who are willing to learn in an apprentice or helper position. The decreasing need for unskilled labor that characterizes a growing idustrial economy meant that young people became more and more disadvantaged in the job market. To put it in more modern terms, unemploy-ment among youth became a chronic problem. Today, for example, unemploy-ment rates among youth typically run two to three times the rates among adults, and for inner-city minority youth the rates reach 70 percent and more (6).

The sons and daughters of the middle and upper class often use the period of youth for further preparation, increasing their skills in college and graduate schools. For youth unable to take advantage of such a moratorium on work, en-forced leisure is more likely to mean crime, drugs, and despair. From the point of view of many adults, "youth" became an important period of development when it became a problem. Crime, drugs, and despair among some adolescents might have been problems sufficient to stimulate government interest and sup-port for research, but their effect was compounded in the 1960s by the social activism of the more advantaged youth in high schools and colleges. We began to speak of "alienated youth," including social dropouts like the hippies and political revolutionaries who seemed willing to try any manner of terrorism to gain their ends.

Adult Development and Aging

Although an occasional philosopher and scientist exhibited an interest in the aging process, most of the history of the study of adult development is quite re-cent. In the United States, the first important psychological studies in this area were published in the 1920s, and barely more than a trickle of research can be noted until 1950 (5). In a review published in 1961, the author noted, "More research seems to have been published in the decade of 1950–1959 than had been published in the entire preceding 115 years the subject may be said to have existed" (3, p. 131). Since 1950, the trickle of research has become a steady stream, as the investigation of developmental processes in adults has become one of the more rapidly growing areas in psychology.

There are many reasons for this increasing interest in adult development. Interest in old age has grown as the number of old people in our population has increased. In the twentieth century alone, the percentage of people aged 65 or more has risen from 4 percent in 1900 to over 10 percent today, and it should approach 20 percent by the year 2000 (4). By the time people born during the so-called baby boom—in the decade following World War II—reach old age, the number of old people will reach 52 million, more than double the number today, and the median age (half the people are older, half are younger) will be 40. Today it is slightly less than 30 (see Figure 1.3). Much of the psychological research on old people has been motivated by a concern for their adjustment problems. How do they respond to retirement? What psychological processes (e.g., memory) and abilities (e.g., intelligence) show deficits in old age, and how do old people respond to such losses? How do old people relate to their families? How do they cope with illness and the anticipation of their own death?

A second major source of research on adult development emerged almost

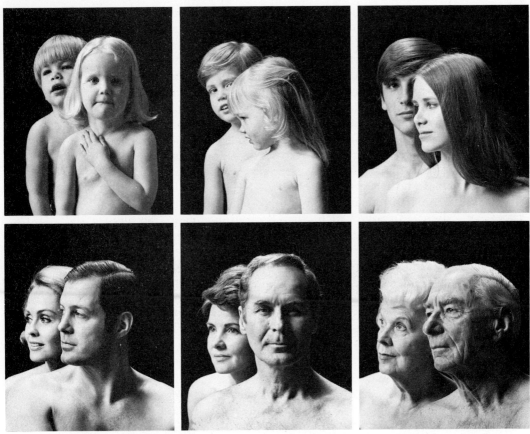

● Figure 1.3 Recently psychologists have been interested in development through the entire span of life. In the decade after World War II, 43 million babies—one-fifth of the present population—were born. Birth rates then fell, and the baby boom population is growing older.

by accident. In the 1920s and 1930s, several groups of psychologists began long-term studies of the same children, observing, testing, and interviewing the same children every few years or so to assess their physical, intellectual, and personality development. By the 1940s and 1950s, these subjects had reached adulthood. There seemed no good reason to discontinue the studies simply because the subjects were no longer children; indeed, there was the promise of interesting data on many questions. What happens in adulthood to children who are intellectually gifted? How stable over the years are personality traits first assessed in early childhood? What are the childhood experiences of people who later marry and then divorce, compared to those who remain married? A good deal of research on adult development owes its existence to the fact that adult subjects about whom much was already known became available for study (5).

There were many specific issues in psychology that required research in adult development. One of the earliest (and most enduring) concerned the course of intellectual development over the life span. Early research suggested that the growth of intelligence, as measured by standard IQ tests, was essentially complete by the age of 13 (23). Most adults, including most adult psychologists, found this result startling, and a number of studies soon followed testing the intelligence of people ranging in age from 10 to 80 (18). The peak of intellectual ability was moved up a bit, to around 20, but the apparent subsequent decline of mental ability among adult subjects spawned new controversy. The still-not-completely-resolved issue is discussed in detail in Chapter 12; the point here is simply that the issue itself was responsible for a considerable amount of research on one aspect of adult development.

Recently there has been a surge of interest in what psychologists call "normative life crises" (8) and what a bestselling author calls "passages" (20). Choosing a career and a spouse are major decisions everyone has to consider, usually during the period of young adulthood, between 20 and 30. Retirement is another life crisis faced by nearly everyone, even if the decision is not to retire. Because such events are normative—faced by nearly everyone in our society— and usually occur at defined periods of the lifespan—first marriage in young adulthood and then retirement in the middle sixties—they form the basis of an approach to adult development, much as normative events in childhood—toilet training, entering school—are important in child developmental psychology.

The exploding population of old people, the aging subjects of what were initially long-term studies of children, specific issues like intellectual development over the lifespan, and the recent interest in adult life crises—all these and many more reasons lie beneath the rapid increase in research and theory in adult development. It was not so long ago that "developmental psychologist" and "child psychologist" were more or less synonymous, but no more. Developmental psychology today involves the study of age-related changes over the entire span of life, from birth to death—or, as the more facetious put it, from womb to tomb.

DEVELOPMENTAL PSYCHOLOGY AS A SCIENTIFIC DISCIPLINE

The systematic study of children has burgeoned in the twentieth century. During the early part of this century, child psychology was limited primarily to the description of age trends, that is, the measurement of age changes in physical, psychological, and behavioral characteristics. Research efforts were devoted to the child's acquisition of such behaviors as walking, handling objects, and talking, providing detailed information on the age at which the average child first stands alone without support, picks up a cube with thumb and forefinger, or says his or her first word.

Precise description is one of the goals of any scientific discipline, but there are other goals as well. As scientific child psychology matured, researchers became increasingly concerned with the processes underlying human growth and development. For example, the early research on language development focused on the growth of vocabulary. Contemporary research on language development is more concerned with factors that influence the acquisition of grammar and the evolution of meaning. Similarly, early research in intelligence sought to determine how intelligence test scores changed with age. Current attention is centered on the factors that affect intellectual growth. Does social class membership affect intellectual performance? If so, why? Can special training overcome the effects of inadequate environmental stimulation? How does anxiety, achievement motivation, or impulsiveness affect measures of intelligence?

The scientific investigation of development in the adult years has followed similar lines. The first studies tended to define age trends in physical abilities (e.g., vision) and psychological characteristics (e.g., intelligence), and more recent investigations have been more concerned with underlying processes: Why do the mental abilities of some adults decline, while those of others increase? Simple description is being replaced in child, adolescent, and adult studies by explanation and theory.

Explanation and Theory

Explanation involves stating the factors (or antecedent conditions) that determine the outcomes (or consequents) we are interested in explaining. For example, what kinds of childhood experiences (antecedents) enhance the development of dependency, curiosity, or logical thinking (consequents)? How does an adult's relationship with fellow workers (antecedent) affect his or her reaction to forced retirement (consequent)?

In their search for antecedent–consequent relationships, scientists formulate theories, hypotheses, or educated guesses about the determinants of the phenomena under study. Scientific theories and hypotheses stimulate research and guide all phases of investigation, determining the variables to be studied, the methods of collecting relevant data, and the analyses of the results. Suppose a team of developmental psychologists hypothesize that a high level of aggression toward peers (children of the same age) is the outcome of a frustrating home situation, such as living with cold, restrictive, and rejecting parents. To test this hypothesis, the researchers must make meaningful assessments of children's aggressiveness. Perhaps they will systematically observe children's behavior in the classroom or on the playground, or perhaps they will use teachers' ratings. Data on the home situation could come from interviews with the children's parents or, if possible, from direct observation of parent–child interactions at home. From such information, the psychologists could evaluate the degree of parental warmth, restrictiveness, and rejection. Then they could assess the relationship between these home variables and the children's aggressiveness.

In a typical experiment, the data pose many new questions as they provide partial answers to the original ones. The data may point to new relationships that modify the hypothesis being investigated. In the example given, a frustrating home situation may appear in the data as a necessary condition for high levels of aggressiveness in children, but not as a sufficient condition by itself. In this case, high aggressiveness would be found only when a frustrating home environment exists, but frustration would not always lead to increased aggressiveness. Why does frustration in the home sometimes lead to aggression by children, and sometimes not? The data might suggest other important variables, such as the use of physical punishment, that could be explored in subsequent studies.

A good scientific theory enables us to predict events. Because we have a theory (a set of interrelated principles) explaining planetary motion, we can predict when the next eclipse of the sun will occur. If we had a good theory about children's learning in classrooms, we could predict many school failures before they occurred; we might then be able to take effective steps to reduce or eliminate such failures.

Research Methods

As in all scientific research, controlled observation and objective measurement are the fundamental tools in the psychologist's attempt to understand human development. Scientists strive to free their observations from subjective bias, such as the biases of pride that colored the observations of one's own child in the first baby biographies. If possible, scientists use instruments to measure and record events, standardized units of measurements, and mathematical descriptions of the data. If these are not possible, the methods used for observation and the resulting data should be described completely. These descriptions allow other scientists to judge the possible biases or distortions and even to repeat the experiment in detail if they so wish. Several replications of a basic study often provide confidence in an observed relationship that would not be possible from a single investigation alone.

As a scientific discipline matures, new methods and tools of observation and measurement are invented and old ones are improved or discarded. In recent years, there have been marked advancements in many research techniques in developmental psychology; examples are improved methods for measuring visual perception and attention in infants, for recording physiological responses such as heart rate and brain activity, and for separating the effects of motivation and ability in learning in old people. As would be expected, some previously accepted "facts"—generalizations from earlier studies when inadequate research techniques were the only ones available—are no longer accepted or, at best, seem to have only limited value. They are being replaced by conclusions based on more accurate, more systematic investigations using better research methods.

Experimental and nonexperimental methods   An *experiment* is a most desirable kind of observation because the factors affecting the phenomenon we are interested in can be controlled. In its simplest form, an experiment is designed to investigate the effects of changes in one variable (the antecedent or *independent variable*) on another variable (the consequent or *dependent variable*). The experiment itself consists of holding constant all but one of the variables presumably related to the event or behavior of interest and then manipulating this variable in accordance with the experimenter's plans. The purpose of the experiment is to observe whether, and how, the dependent variable changes as the variable being manipulated (the independent variable) is changed.

Suppose, for example, that psychologists want to investigate the effects of competition on children's performance in arithmetic tests. Do children who compete with each other do better than children who are not competing? The psychologists might attempt to answer this question by forming two groups of children matched (equated, approximately) in intelligence, arithmetic ability, health, and other factors that might affect performance. One group of children —the experimental group—would be placed in a competitive situation by informing them that the child with the highest score on the test would receive a prize. For the children in the control (comparison) group, no special instructions would be given. Both groups would be given the same arithmetic test (Figure 1.4).

In this experiment, the independent variable is the degree of competition, regulated by the experimenter's instructions. The dependent variable is the score on the arithmetic test. If the original hypothesis, that competition enhances performance, is valid in this situation, we would expect the children in the experimental group to score higher, on the average, than the children in the control group. If the investigators have been careful to match the groups on other important variables (which can be done by simply assigning children randomly to the two groups, if the groups are large enough), then we can be fairly certain that the difference in average test score between the two groups was due to the independent variable—degree of competition.

The unique advantage of the experimental method is that it is possible to control for the effects of antecedent variables other than the one being studied; this permits precise and accurate assessment of the effects of the experimental treatment. But there are problems of profound interest to developmental psychologists for which the experimental method is simply not appropriate or feasible. For example, suppose we are interested in testing a hypothesis about the relationship between early deprivation of affection and emotional adjustment during the adult years. We could hardly expect parents to reject their children for purposes of our experiment. But we might be able to find a group of people who had suffered a lack of love and warmth during childhood and compare their emotional adjustment (using personality tests and structured interviews) with a group who had normal, affectionate parents. We would want to control for the effects of other variables, of course, by matching the two groups as closely as possible on age, physical health, social class, and other factors that might affect emotional stability.

● Figure 1.4   Schematic drawing of an experiment.

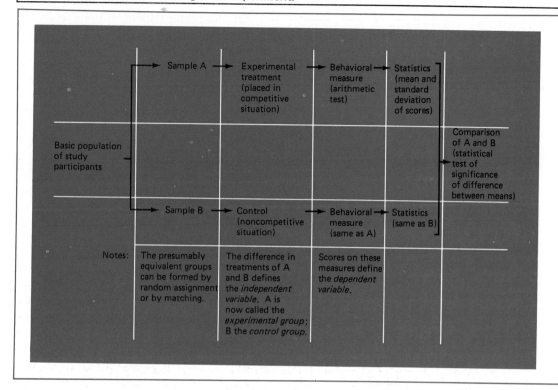

It is sometimes difficult to match groups on all relevant variables other than the independent variable; in early stages of research, it is often the case that we do not even know what the relevant variables are. Thus, the results of such studies are not quite as clearcut as those in which the experimenter manipulates the independent variable. But the problems investigated using "nature's" manipulations (already existing differences) are often of critical social importance, and, with care, these studies add much to our knowledge of human development.

Longitudinal and cross-sectional approaches   There are two contrasting broad approaches to the study of the changes that occur with age. The more common *cross-sectional* approach involves selecting subjects of different ages and collecting data all at one time. Thus, to trace the growth of reasoning ability in children, investigators might select 20 children at each of six ages—2, 4, 6, 8, 10, and 12—and administer reasoning tests to all of them. By comparing the average test performances of the different age groups, the investigators could describe age trends in reasoning ability. Using the *longitudinal* approach to investigate the same ability, investigators would study the same 20 children at two-year intervals, first when they were 2, then when they were 4 and 6 and 8 and 10 and 12. By comparing the average test performances of the children at different ages, the investigators could describe age trends in reasoning ability.

Each of these two approaches has distinct advantages and disadvantages. An obvious disadvantage of the longitudinal approach is that it requires several years to complete one study—ten years in the example above, while the children age from 2 to 12. The long time it takes has several indirect effects as well. For example, as the years pass, psychologists develop new and better measures, but the investigators involved in longitudinal studies are stuck with the ones they used at the beginning; they cannot change their intelligence test or their personality test in midstream. Similarly, theoretical interests change, so that what began as a "valuable" longitudinal study of the growth of vocabulary might become viewed as a relative waste of time when psychologists shift their interests to the grammar and the meaning of children's sentences. Another problem with longitudinal studies is that some subjects "drop out"—they die, leave town, or refuse to participate. The subjects who drop out are frequently different in many regards from those who are retested, so the results of the study are sometimes distorted. If you began a longitudinal study with a representative sample of the population in this country, chances are great that the sample would be nonrepresentative by the end of the study; subjects of lower intelligence and lower social class tend to drop out more frequently than the brighter and more advantaged people.

Despite its disadvantages, the longitudinal approach produces data that are invaluable in understanding developmental processes. This approach is especially valuable for assessing the stability of personal characteristics (intelligence, achievement motivation) over time. It is also favored for studies of the effects of early experience on later behavior. For example, if we believed that early maternal rejection leads to later problems for a child in his or her relationships with peers, the straightforward way of testing this hypothesis would be to find a group of infants whose mothers are rejecting them and then, years later, assess the children's social behavior. The only real alternative to a longitudinal study for a hypothesis like this is to interview the mothers of older children with interaction difficulties. The mothers would be asked about their relationships with their children when the children were infants, to determine whether or not "early maternal rejection" was present. In effect, this procedure tries to gather the same type of data as a longitudinal study, relying on the memories of the mothers to assess the early mother–infant relationships. Memories are not the best source of information, especially when searching for something negative in the informant's past.

The advantages of the cross-sectional study lie primarily in the shorter time required to complete it; one can obtain results on the most current hypothesis using the best available measures. The disadvantages lie primarily in the assumption that differences between groups of different ages reflect only the changes that occur from one age to another. Thus, if a cross-sectional study shows children at age 4 to be more logical than children at age 2, the assumption is that children *become* more logical as they age from 2 to 4. Usually this assumption is reasonable, but occasionally it can lead theorists astray. In adult studies in particular, cross-sectional data are often misleading. For example, you might compare groups of people aged 20, 45, and 70 on attitudes toward sex and war. The older people would appear more sexually inhibited and more war-mongering, but one would be foolish to conclude that people *become* more inhibited and aggressive with age. These are most likely generational differences, differences in attitudes engrained in children who grew up in different eras. As we shall see in Chapter 11, the early cross-sectional data on intellectual decline during the adult years were highly misleading for the same reason; they reflected generational differences in education, nutrition, and other factors—not true age changes in intelligence.

THEORY IN DEVELOPMENTAL PSYCHOLOGY

The aim of every scientific discipline is to construct a set of principles that will explain events. For example, one such principle in physics is that the momentum of an object is equal to the product of its mass and its velocity. That principle helps us understand what happens when a moving truck hits a standing telephone pole. In mature sciences such as chemistry and physics, the principles are related to one another and involve the same set of concepts.

Unfortunately, psychology is not as mature a science and has not as yet generated a large set of interrelated principles. Different psychologists use different concepts to explain a given phenomenon, and there are even disagreements about which phenomena should be alloted the major share of research attention. There is no single theory in developmental psychology; rather, there are a number of theories, each with a slightly different focus and a slightly different approach to understanding. We will briefly discuss a few of the broadest theories, those that integrate large bodies of data and generate considerable amounts of research on developmental processes. These are, first, the theory of Jean Piaget, which deals primarily with cognitive development. Then we will consider the psychoanalytic theory constructed by Sigmund Freud and extended by Erik Erikson; psychoanalytic theory deals primarily with personality development. Finally we will consider some basic principles of learning and the social learning theories of development that have emerged from the basic research.

Piaget's Theory of Intellectual Development

Jean Piaget, the Swiss psychologist (see Figure 1.5), views the child as trying to make sense of her world by dealing actively with objects and people. From encounters with events, she moves steadily through a series of stages toward the

● Figure 1.5   Jean Piaget observing children.

goal of abstract reasoning. One of the important features of Piaget's theory is the notion of active encounters between the child and her environment. Unlike many theories which view the child as passive, molded by environmental forces, Piaget's theory views the child as an investigator, a kind of very primitive scientist, who is always trying to understand puzzling events and to fit her ideas into a coherent whole.

Operations   The central concept in Piaget's theory is the *operation* (19). An operation is a special kind of rule that enables a person to appreciate the reciprocal relationship between two sets of events or ideas. In other words, one of the key characteristics of an operation is that it is *reversible*. Thus the child's understanding that six balls and two balls can be transformed into one group of eight balls or two groups of four each is based on an operation. The knowledge that dogs and cats can be grouped into the category of living things or that the category "living things" can be dismantled into separate dogs and cats also involves an operation. The role of reversibility is seen in the problem called "conservation of volume" in which the child has to appreciate the fact that the amount of water in one tall glass does not change when the water is transferred to a glass of a different shape or to two smaller glasses. The child knows that the amount of water does not change because she can restore the original state of affairs by pouring the water back into the original tall glass. The operation allows the child to return mentally to where she began. A child under the age of 6 or 7 usually does not have this ability. When she perceives the level of water to increase when it is poured from a wide to a tall, thinner glass, she believes the amount of water has increased (Figure 1.6).

According to Piaget, the acquisition of operations is the heart of intellectual growth. The two major mechanisms that allow the child to acquire operations and to modify and elaborate them are assimilation and accommodation.

Assimilation and accommodation   *Assimilation,* in simple terms, is the use of habitual ways of relating to the world in new situations. An infant may relate to small objects in his world by shaking and biting them. When he is presented with a small object he has never seen before, he is likely to shake it and bite it. An adult will resort to his typical mental routines or operations when faced with a new object; he might try to classify it by analyzing its features, for example.

Accommodation is the tendency to adjust to a new object, to change one's approach to it when assimilation is inadequate. The 2-year-old child who is presented with a magnet may initially interact with it in old familiar ways by banging it, bouncing it, or trying to make it produce a noise. But once he discovers the unique qualities of the magnet, that it attracts metal, he will accommodate to that quality and begin to touch the magnet to a variety of objects to see if they will adhere to it.

Intellectual growth occurs when a conflict between assimilation and accommodation is resolved in favor of accommodation. Initially children assimilate an event, even when a new response would be more advantageous. If father

● Figure 1.6   Conservation of volume.

and child are playing a game in which the child must guess which of the father's hands contains a small toy, the child may adopt a strategy of always guessing the right hand, even though the father is alternating the toy from right to left. Eventually the child accommodates to the new event and learns the rule the father is using.

Each time the child accommodates to a new event or problem, his knowledge grows and matures, for he has changed his ideas about the world and generated a more adaptive scheme. Initially the child attempts to understand a new experience by using old ideas and solutions. When they do not work, he is forced to change his understanding of the world so that eventually the new event is in harmony with his prior beliefs. One day his intellectual functioning will have matured to a point where he will be capable of a new way of thinking about old problems. At this point, he passes from one stage of intelligence to the next.

Developmental stages Piaget's theory describes four major stages of intellectual development: sensorimotor (0 to approximately 18 months), preoperational (18 months to age 7), concrete operations (age 7 to 12), and finally formal operations (age 12 onward). These stages will be described in detail in Chapters 3 and 5. Each stage is built upon and is a derivative of the earlier one. According to the theory, a child cannot skip a stage because each new stage borrows from the accomplishments of the earlier ones.

Stage theories are popular in developmental psychology, for they provide neat conceptual "handles" for major periods in the growth of intellect or, as we will see in the following discussion of psychoanalytic theory, personality. They suggest a progression but with rather abrupt changes, so that each major period of development is related to, but also distinct from, periods that precede or follow it. It is useful, for example, to consider the period of life before a child begins to speak as a separate stage from those that follow; although there is certainly intellectual growth during infancy, it is useful to consider it separately from the changes in intelligence that come after language has been acquired.

The stage approach, however, is not the only one possible. It is possible, for example, to view development as more continuous, with fewer abrupt changes. Indeed, some psychologists would argue that stage theories tend to fragment processes that have no distinct dividing lines, much as the arbitrary letter grades "A" and "B" might magnify the miniscule, one-point difference between two students on a final examination. Still another approach might view development in terms of periods of progress and "self-improvement" followed by periods of consolidation. For example, development in young adulthood is characterized by bold decisions about career and spouse, followed by periods of consolidation, in which the person focuses on "getting it together"—working at the chosen job, having children, "rooting." Finally, some view development as even more discontinuous than the stage approach. There may be stages, but they are quite distinct, something like those in the metamorphosis of a butterfly.

Stage theories usually imply (and sometimes explicitly assert) that stages cannot be skipped. This hypothesis may be true of many developmental progressions, but it may not be the case that all "stages" must necessarily follow one another in order. Most skiers have a "snow plow" stage and, later, a "parallel" stage, but some newer teaching methods have beginners skiing with their skis parallel, skipping the snow plow stage. Thus, the hypothesis that all stages in a developmental sequence occur in an invariable succession must be evaluated by research—even if one accepts the stage approach in general.

Psychoanalytic Theories of Development

Sigmund Freud (Figure 1.7), the originator of the psychoanalytic theory of personality, had a specific conception of the healthy, mature individual. The characteristics of such a person included the ability to enter into sexually gratifying love relationships, productive use of one's talents, and relative freedom from the conflicts and anxiety that lead to personal anguish and behavioral symptoms (9). Thus, while Piaget saw the ability to reason abstractly as a primary "goal" of development, Freud focused on the goal of emotional maturity.

According to Freud, the infant and the young child are more or less helpless in the face of powerful biological and social forces over which they have little control. These forces include an instinctual energy, which is biological in origin, and the social experiences that are part of family life. All children, Freud believed, develop sexual and aggressive feelings toward their parents which lead to conflict, anxiety, and, in a few, to mental illness.

Unconscious sexuality   Freud described two basic "instincts" or drives in humans: sex and aggression. Control of these instinctual forces is what constitutes socialization of the child, in Freud's theory, as society tries to motivate the child to "delay gratification" and to channel sexual and aggressive energies into more useful and less disruptive pursuits than overt sexual or aggressive behaviors. Parental punishment for such behaviors leads not only to suppression of the behaviors but also to *repression* of the ideas associated with instinctual urges. Repressed ideas are not available to consciousness—the person is not aware of them—although they often find expression in dreams, slips of the tongue, and neurotic symptoms. For example, Freud stated that all young children experience intense sexual desires for the parent of the opposite sex. These ideas become too threatening, too anxiety-provoking, so they are repressed; they become part of the *unconscious mind,* still exerting an influence on behavior, even though the individual is unaware of their influence.

Id, ego, and superego   The basis for the emotional difficulties of his patients, according to Freud, was conflict. In many cases, the conflict was between what the individuals wanted and what they felt they could achieve, or between these ideas (desires or potential actions) and internalized moral standards. Freud con-

● Figure 1.7 Sigmund Freud.

ceptualized these various aspects of personality as the *id*, the *ego*, and the *superego*. The id seeks immediate gratification of sexual and aggressive impulses, as well as self-preservation needs like hunger and thirst. In the newborn infant, presumably there is only id, but it soon becomes apparent that immediate gratification is rarely possible and a new psychological structure, designed to deal with reality, develops. Using logical thought and planful action, the ego strives to satisfy the desires of the id. Gradually a third structure also emerges, the superego, which represents the notions of "right and wrong," as originally enforced by parents and society, but eventually accepted and incorporated (internalized) by the child himself. The superego includes what is commonly known as the conscience, dealing out guilt for wrongdoing, and it also includes an ego-ideal and provides praise for "right-thinking" thoughts and actions. According to the theory, by the age of 5 or 6, the id, ego, and superego have all emerged to some degree in most children; emotional stability depends largely on whether or not they function harmoniously.

Conflicts among the id, ego, and superego are inevitable and lead to feelings of *anxiety* (10). The ego continually tries to reduce anxiety by realistic measures. When the ego is unsuccessful, either because the anxiety is too intense or because the ego's skills are not sophisticated enough, anxiety becomes a threat to the existence of the ego, and the ego will typically be forced to rely on unrealistic measures of defense. One such ego *defense mechanism* is denial. To illustrate, a young child whose mother has just died will sometimes totally deny the fact of her death and act as if the mother were still alive—making plans to take Mom to school or buying her a birthday present. To face the loss directly would provoke too much anxiety. Defense mechanisms can sometimes be useful, but if the child (or adult) relies on them too often and too rigidly for a long enough period of time, they can become *symptoms* of a serious neurosis.

Psychoanalytic developmental stages Freud believed that the important sources of pleasure for a child vary with age. In the first year or so, much of the infant's interaction with her environment involves her mouth: feeding, burping, spitting up, biting. The infant often explores objects by putting them in her mouth. Hence, in psychoanalytic theory, this stage of personality development is called the *oral stage*.

Freud suggested that what the child learns in these mouth-related activities are some very basic habits, attitudes, and personality traits. For example, if a baby is frustrated because of too few or too small feedings, she may develop an unusually strong desire to suck on things—her thumb at first, and later in life, perhaps cigarettes. More generally, as psychoanalyst Erik Erikson has said, the child learns the meaning of the verb "to get" (5). According to psychoanalytic theory, if the child gets what she needs most of the time, she learns to *trust* the world as an essentially benevolent environment.

The second year of life, roughly speaking, constitutes the *anal stage*. Toilet training is the major learning situation of the anal stage. In toilet training, the child is asked to do something she would rather not do—control her bladder and bowels. It is a case of what her parents want versus what she wants; it is a battle of wills. Thus toilet training is viewed by psychoanalysts as a critical situation for the development of personal independence and autonomy in the child.

Roughly between the ages of 2 and 5, the child supposedly enters the *phallic stage*. (As the name implies, this stage was more thoroughly worked out for the development of male children.) The major learning situation in the phallic stage is called the *Oedipus complex*, after the tragic Oedipus Rex, who in Sophocles' play unknowingly killed his father and married his mother. In the Freudian view of personality development, the young child has fantasy wishes for sexual affection from the parent of the opposite sex. The child is unconsciously afraid that the same-sex parent will learn of these desires and become angry with the child; in boys these fears are called *castration anxiety*, which is meant to suggest that they fear their powerful fathers will render them incapable of continuing the battle for their mother's affections. Because of these fears, the child represses the sexual desires for the opposite-sex parent and identifies with the same-sex parent, trying to gain some of that parent's power in a manner not dissimilar to an adult's joining a powerful group or organization to overcome his or her own feelings of inferiority.

One of the outcomes of the child's identification is that it leads him or her to adopt the values of the parent; since many of these values are the do's and the don'ts of society, the child's superego is born.

After the phallic stage, the sexual urgings of the child are supposedly not much of a problem until puberty; Freud called this the *latency period*. Erik Erikson views this period, running roughly from the age of 6 until puberty, as one of preparing for the adult world of work. The child typically enters school or, in less developed countries, begins an apprenticeship.

Adolescent and adult stages   Eventually, according to Freud, a *genital stage* of psychosexual development can be reached by those who have successfully mastered the emotional conflicts of earlier stages. The genital stage is a sort of ideal stage in which two people experience mutually gratifying sexual love for one another.

Erik Erikson was one of the few developmental psychologists to extend his stage theory to the adult years. In his view, years of adolescence and early adulthood involve the continuing search for personal *identity*, as the person tries to determine who he or she is. In young adulthood, one also faces the problem of establishing *intimacy* with another human being; it is a time for marriage (see Figure 1.8).

In the middle adult years, Erikson views the person as trying to deal with the issue of *generativity* versus *stagnation*. Generativity refers to those activities by which we usually judge lives to be meaningful or not—having children and educating them, being productive and creative in life. The danger is stagnation, a barren existence without meaning or growth. And finally, in old age, as the

● Figure 1.8 Erikson's Stages of Psychosocial Development. By this method of illustrating his stages, Erikson meant to emphasize the fact that the major issues in each stage were important at all stages of the life span, but particularly important at certain stages. For example, the issue of "trust versus mistrust" is critically important in infancy, but it is obviously an important issue throughout life.

Erickson's Stages of Development								
Stage	1	2	3	4	5	6	7	8
Maturity								Ego integrity vs. despair
Adulthood							Generativity vs. stagnation	
Young adulthood						Intimacy vs. isolation		
Puberty and adolescence					Identity vs. diffusion			
Latency				Industry vs. inferiority				
Locomotor/ Genital			Initiative vs. guilt					
Muscular/ Anal		Autonomy vs. shame						
Oral/ Sensory	Trust vs. mistrust							

individual considers his or her life as a whole, the battles won and lost, there is a sense of life well-lived, a sense of *integrity*, or there is a sense of *despair*, that time is running out and not much has been accomplished.

The validity of psychoanalytic theory   We have presented a very brief and general description of a few key concepts in psychoanalytic theory, but still the question arises: Is psychoanalytic theory correct? The reader may wonder if psychologists generally accept the notion of the Oedipus complex, or if there is any evidence that toilet training is critical in the development of willpower.

It is not easy to answer these questions. Psychoanalytic theory has been widely criticized in recent years. From the scientific point of view, it is severe criticism to say that most psychoanalytic hypotheses are so poorly defined that empirical tests are difficult or even impossible. What kind of toilet training procedures result in an overly submissive child? An overly rebellious child? The theory does not answer in sufficient detail to permit adequate tests. How would one test the hypothesis that all adults have repressed sexual desires for the parent of the opposite sex? Thus, one often finds the statement that there is no experimental evidence, pro or con, on many specific Freudian hypotheses.

More generally, the heavy emphasis on sexual motivation in psychoanalytic theory has been questioned. In this view, Freud was misled by the frequency of sexual conflicts among his patients in late nineteenth-century Vienna, where sexual standards were unusually severe. The permissive sexual standards of today have resulted in less guilt about sexual desires, but there appears to be no corresponding decrease in the incidence of neurosis and other mental disorders.

In spite of its faults, psychoanalytic theory has had a significant impact on the way psychologists view personality development. Modern psychologists and psychiatrists continue to believe that unconscious motives and conflicts can influence action and thought and that children have sexual desires that may lead to anxiety and guilt. The concept of defense mechanisms has been especially durable, helping both research scientists and clinical psychotherapists understand behaviors that, on the surface, often seem illogical. Current notions that early childhood experiences can significantly affect adult personality and that development proceeds through several relatively distinct stages were influenced by Freud's conceptualizations. Perhaps no modern developmental psychologist accepts Freud's theory without some reservations, but, then too, perhaps no one interested in human development can ignore completely Freud's insights.

Learning Theories of Development

Learning plays a major role in every developmental theory, so it is surprising to many students to find one approach explicitly designated a "learning theory" of development. What this label means is that the approach so designated is based on learning research and theory, an area of experimental psychology that derives most of its principles of carefully controlled laboratory studies on subhuman animals like rats. The concepts are not as "rich" perhaps as those in Piagetian or Freudian theory, but they are typically more precise and more clearly defined. Compared to the observations of a psychoanalyst, which are often unsystematic, the research on children done by a learning theorist is usually more rigorous; often the child and parent are brought into the psychologist's laboratory to enable even more careful control over the experimental variables.

Stated more simply, *learning* is the process by which behavior is modified as a result of experience (11, 14). Learning refers to both the acquisition of a new response or set of responses and the change in the frequency of an action that is already in the child's repertoire. For example, we speak of learning to play tennis, which involves a new set of motor coordinations, and we also speak of learning "not to cry" when things go wrong, which is a change in the frequency of a "natural" response.

Figure 1.9 Ivan Pavlov.

Classical conditioning   Many types of learning, especially that involving reflexive behaviors and primitive emotions like fear, can be understood as instances
of *classical conditioning*. First investigated by the Russian scientist Ivan Pavlov
in the early 1900s (Figure 1.9), the procedures of classical conditioning begin
with a stimulus that produces a response naturally, innately, without learning.
These are termed the *unconditioned stimulus* and the *unconditioned response*.
Pavlov used the stimulus of food, which automatically elicited the response of
salivation in the dogs he studied. Then Pavlov chose a neutral stimulus—one
that did not elicit the unconditioned response before learning—and paired it
continually with the unconditioned stimulus–response pair. This neutral stim-

ulus, usually a light or a buzzer, eventually elicits the unconditioned response by itself, that is, without the unconditioned stimulus. In Pavlov's experiments, the dogs heard a buzzer and were then given food, and they salivated. After several "trials" of this type, the sound of the buzzer alone produced salivation. At this point, conditioning is said to have occurred. The previously neutral buzzer stimulus is now called the *conditioned stimulus* and the salivation response is now called the *conditioned response* (see Figure 1.10).

Pavlov's principles have been applied to many cases of learning in infants and children. John B. Watson, the "father of behaviorism," was able to demonstrate that many childhood fears are probably the result of classical conditioning (3); a previously neutral stimulus (like a dog) is paired a few times with a fear-provoking stimulus (like a loud noise), and the child begins to show the fear response to the sight of the dog. In a more recent study of feeding responses

● Figure 1.10 Pavlov's dog. The dog is strapped into a harness in which it has grown used to standing. A tube attached to the dog's salivary gland collects any saliva secreted by the gland, and the number of drops from the tube is recorded on a revolving drum outside the chamber. A laboratory attendant can watch the dog through a one-way mirror and can deliver food to the dog's feedpan by remote control. Thus, there is nothing in the chamber to distract the dog's attention except the food, when it is delivered, and any other stimulus that the attendant wishes to present, such as the sound of a metronome. (After R. M. Yerkes and S. Morgulis. The method of Pavlov in animal behavior. *Psychological Bulletin,* 1909, *6* (8), 257–273.)

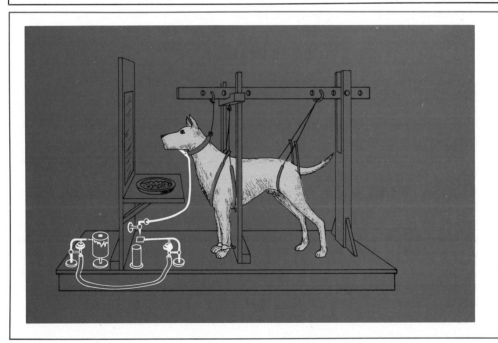

(17), the unconditioned stimulus was the stimulation of a nipple during the feeding of infants 2–9 days old. After frequent pairings of the neutral stimulus, a buzzer, with the feeding situation, the buzzer alone elicited sucking and mouth-opening responses in eight of the ten infants tested.

The use of a buzzer as the stimulus to be conditioned is convenient from a scientific point of view because its onset and duration can be controlled, but similar, more "natural" associations can be noted in almost every infant. The sight of a baby bottle, for example, does not originally elicit mouth movements, but after a month or two, the bottle-fed infant will show definite signs of a conditioned response to this stimulus (15, 17).

Operant conditioning *Operant* (or instrumental) *conditioning* involves a change in the likelihood of a response on the basis of what follows the response. If a response is followed by a reward or reinforcement, the probability that the response will occur normally increases; if the response leads to nothing (no reward) or to a negative state of affairs (punishment), the likelihood of the response normally decreases. Operant conditioning—the name is meant to imply that the person "operates" on the environment in order to gain the reward—was first described by the American psychologist B. F. Skinner (21, 22) (Figure 1.11).

Children obviously learn many new responses by operant conditioning, that is, they act in many instances to gain a reward or to avoid a punishment. Parents commonly use attention, affection, and praise as rewards for "successful" responses during toilet training, just to cite one example among many. Children learn to perform many responses that are "instrumental" in achieving a reward—opening a door, turning on a faucet, holding a baseball bat, writing with pen or pencil, ringing doorbells.

In a deliberate program of operant conditioning, severely withdrawn (autistic) children were taught to speak, to become more socially responsive, and to stop behaving in self-destructive ways (16). Many of these children had been in treatment using other methods for several years with no improvement. The children did not respond well to other people, ignoring them for the most part; some were so oblivious to their surroundings they appeared to be blind and deaf. They did not speak, although they occasionally made sounds having no discernible communicative intent; a few engaged in a speech behavior called "echolalia," which consists of simply repeating whatever sounds they hear. Self-destructive acts such as head-pounding were common. Some children had pounded their heads so severely they had broken their bones or injured their eyes, and others had bitten large chunks of flesh from their own bodies.

Using a systematic, carefully controlled program of rewards (food and attention) and punishments (removal of food and withdrawal of affection), the investigators were able to increase meaningful speech ("I want a cookie") and to reduce meaningless speech ("spaghetti Irene," "helicopter pillow"). By similar methods, they were able to increase social responsiveness, so that the children

● Figure 1.11   B. F. Skinner.

began to interact with (for example, to play with) adults and other children. Self-destructive behaviors turned out to be responsive to mild punishments— that is, a mild electric shock or a slap to the behind was usually sufficient to get a child to stop banging his or her head—and once the self-destructive behaviors were suppressed, social behaviors could be rewarded in their place.

Observational learning   Learning many of the complicated skills that humans possess by the time they reach adulthood would be extremely difficult if only classical and operant conditioning were involved. Many human activities are learned by watching another person—by observation and imitation. The nature of observational learning has been illuminated by the extensive research of

American psychologist Albert Bandura (Figure 1.12) and his associates (4). In a typical experiment, children observe the behavior of a *model,* either an adult or another child. The model performs a series of actions, such as pummeling an inflated doll as in Figure 1.13. Later the children were given an opportunity to play with the doll themselves, and they showed a high frequency of precisely imitative behaviors as you can see. They had acquired a rather complex behavior quickly, with no assistance from unconditioned stimuli or rewards.

Observational learning has been demonstrated over a wide variety of behaviors, and research has uncovered some of the determinants of the tendency to imitate. Do models have to be alive? No. Models on film and even cartoon characters are effective. Whom will children imitate? High status, well-liked models are generally better than models with less prestige and popularity. Children will

● Figure 1.12   Albert Bandura.

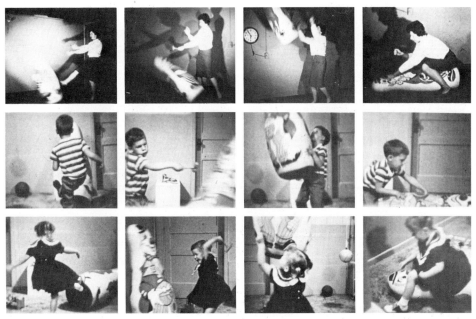

●Figure 1.13 Photographs of children reproducing the aggressive behavior of the female model they observed on film. (From A. Bandura, D. Ross, and S. A. Ross. Imitation of film-mediated aggressive models. *Journal of Abnormal and Social Psychology,* 1963, *66* (8). © 1963 by the American Psychological Association. By permission.)

also imitate models whom they perceive as similar to themselves more than models seen as dissimilar.

Children are also more likely to imitate the behavior of models who are rewarded for their actions than those who are punished. To demonstrate this tendency, children were shown films of a model displaying aggressive behavior under various conditions (2). In one condition, the model was severely punished for the aggressive behavior; in another, the model was generously rewarded; and in a third condition, no consequences of the aggressive behavior were shown. Children who watched the model being punished made many fewer imitative responses than children who observed rewards or no consequences.

At this point, one can ask: Did the children who observed a model being rewarded learn more than the other children? Or did the three groups learn equally well, with only the children who anticipated rewards willing to exhibit what they learned? To answer these questions, the experimenters offered children in all three groups highly attractive rewards to produce imitative responses. The previous differences among groups disappeared, revealing an equivalent amount of learning in the three groups. Thus, it is clear that children learn a considerable amount from observations of adults and other children, but they may not *demonstrate* their new skills until they find themselves in a situation in which they anticipate that the learned behaviors will result in a reward.

Observational learning and operant conditioning often supplement each other. To learn tennis, for example, the beginner learns both by watching the correct moves demonstrated by the instructor and by trying to perform on the tennis court in such a way as to elicit a word of praise from the instructor. Relationships between observational learning and classical conditioning are also common, as shown in the use of models to reduce fears of children. For example, many children have exaggerated fears of dogs. The sight of a dog is a conditioned stimulus that elicits an intense fear reaction; the fear, in turn, prevents them from the friendly interaction with dogs that might quell their fears. The children are willing to watch another child playing with a friendly dog, however, and observational learning of this sort has been shown to reduce significantly the children's own fears.

BASIC CONDITIONS OF LEARNING

The basic concepts of learning are emphasized in "learning theories" of development, but all theorists use learning concepts in one form or another. An understanding of the basic conditions of learning is essential to the understanding of development in humans, a species whose members are so adaptable to their environments, so free of compelling instinctive behaviors. What do we know about the nature of human learning? As parents and teachers know, learning is not inevitable; it does not always occur even in situations when we most expect it. What are the basic conditions of learning?

Stimulus Factors in Learning

There are many ways in which a stimulus plays a role in learning. Perhaps the most obvious is by its attracting the child's *attention*, for one cannot learn unless he or she pays attention to the stimulus. Material to be learned, for example, should be interesting, vivid, and distinctive, a fact that is recognized and used to advantage by the educational television program, *Sesame Street*. The learning difficulties of some children seem to reside primarily in their inability to attend properly. Autistic (severely withdrawn) children, for example, sometimes seem preoccupied with their own internal, private world; they pay little heed to external stimulation—as, for instance, words to imitate—to which they are exposed.

Stimuli also provide information about a situation. Children must often learn that behavior that is appropriate in one situation is inappropriate in another—that boisterous play is encouraged on the playground but punished in church. The stimuli that allow children to predict the probable outcome of their behavior are called *discriminative stimuli*. They do not control behavior in the sense that a stimulus (conditioned or unconditioned) elicits a response in classical conditioning; rather, they function to provide information about the likelihood of reward in operant conditioning situations.

A response made to a particular stimulus may be made also to similar stimuli, a phenomenon called *stimulus generalization*. Thus when a girl learns to fear one particularly noisy neighborhood dog, her initial reaction to other dogs is likely to be fear. If a boy has been rewarded for whiny, "childish" behavior with his parents, he is likely to try the same tactics on grandparents, teachers, and other adults. Although these two examples depict maladaptive responses, stimulus generalization is usually adaptive; most refrigerators, despite superficial variations in appearance, contain food for the hungry, most hot stoves, gas or electric, should be avoided, and most adults will punish whiny, "childish" behavior, even if one's parents are exceptions.

Language plays an important role in stimulus generalization among humans. The "similarity" of two stimuli may be physical—perceptual—or it may be conceptual. For example, if a girl is frightened by a dog, she may generalize her fear response to all animals of approximately the same size and shape and color of the one that frightened her; in this case, the similarity is perceptual. She may also generalize her fear on the basis of the word "dog," which she has learned to apply to a wide variety of animals, some of which are perceptually quite dissimilar to the fear-provoking dog. In like fashion, we call both a stack of a hundred pennies and a crisp green bill "a dollar," and we would respond to them in similar ways despite the radical dissimilarity in their physical appearance. Language-aided generalization of this type is sometimes called *mediated generalization*.

Initially, generalization is likely to be extensive. A child's first encounter with four-legged animals other than dogs may show evidence that he expects the cow or the horse to bark and fetch balls. New information, however, enables him to correct his overgeneralizations and instead to make appropriate *discriminations*. Children who generalize to playmates the whiny, dependent responses they make to their parents soon discover that whiny behavior doesn't work as well with playmates. When responses that had led to rewards in some situations lead to punishment or to no rewards in new, similar situations, the child makes discriminations, and learns to identify the discriminative stimuli that enable him to predict the probable outcome of his behavior.

Outcomes and Behavior

Much human behavior is obviously intended to gain a reward or to avoid negative consequences, and thus outcomes are among the most important factors in learning and performance. A *positive reinforcement* (reward) generally means that the behavior it follows will become more frequent (see Figure 1.14). If the behavior learned with positive reinforcement suddenly brings no reward, the behavior will ordinarily become less and less likely until it either disappears or returns to some baseline level. This process is called *extinction*. *Punishment* in-

● Figure 1.14 Behavior that is followed by a reward is more likely to be repeated in the future.

volves a negative outcome, but its effects are generally quite complicated; behaviors that a parent might punish, for example, are often those that also lead to rewards—for example, masturbating or dominating a younger sibling—and thus we have to consider the joint outcomes of reward *and* punishment. Sometimes a child learns discriminative stimuli—masturbating or dominating only when no parent is around.

Parents sometimes create behavior problems by unconsciously reinforcing undesirable responses. For example, a child who sleeps poorly, crying and fussing, often elicits the concern and attention of her parents. They may unintentionally increase the probability of sleep problems by coming to her and comforting her, thus rewarding her poor sleep habits. In one such case (23), a therapist suggested extinction as a treatment for a sleep-resistant boy. The parents put the child to bed (with loving attention), then closed the door to his room and ignored all crying, no matter how long or how loud. The first night the child cried almost an hour. The second night was much better, and by the end of the week, the child no longer cried when left in his room but instead played happily until he dropped off to sleep.

Schedules of reinforcement Rarely in real life do people receive a reward every time they make a response. Usually the reinforcements are *intermittent,* coming now and then. Laboratory studies with both animals and humans indicate that behavior that is intermittently reinforced persists for a long time without reinforcement; in contrast, behavior learned with constant reinforcement extinguishes quickly when it is no longer rewarded. Intermittent reinforcement explains why some old habits, even bad ones, are often so hard to break. The thrill of a few long-shot victories in a horse race is enough to keep many compulsive gamblers at the track for a long time.

B. F. Skinner and his colleagues (22) have described several patterns of intermittent reinforcement called *schedules of reinforcement. Interval schedules* are based on time intervals since the last reinforcement; this time interval can be *fixed* (always the same) or variable (varying around some average value). An example of a fixed-interval schedule is the way most of us are paid on our jobs; we receive a check every week, two weeks, or month. *Ratio schedules* are based on the number of responses per reinforcement. Slot machines in Nevada are on variable-ratio schedules; they pay off once every so many responses, but the ratio is variable, so players cannot predict the next reinforcement. The variable-ratio schedule produces a very high rate of responding, as anyone who has watched slot-machine players can testify.

Parents often put their children on very complicated combinations of these basic schedules. For example, parents busy working near their children might have them on a basic variable-interval schedule, rewarding them with love and attention on the average of every two hours or so. But if the child makes a certain number of responses of a certain type—screams are effective—the parent interrupts work and delivers the reward of attention on this ratio schedule. The result of this unintentional pattern of reinforcement is predictable: a highly vocal child who responds at a high and steady rate.

Performance Factors in Learning

Children learn quickly, so that in most new situations they are capable of making a variety of responses. They have a repertoire of responses, each with a slightly different strength, a slightly different probability of occurring. Arranged from the strongest to weakest, these responses form what psychologists call a *response hierarchy*. One of the chief advantages of thinking in terms of a response hierarchy is that one can view development as shifts in this hierarchy —some "childish" responses moving down and some more mature responses becoming more probable—rather than as "either-or" changes, where the infantile behaviors disappear completely and are replaced by the mature forms.

Consider a boy of 5 who has learned that the best way of attracting his parents' attention is to ask questions. This response is high in his hierarchy of responses when he desires their attention. However, suppose his parents suddenly become too busy to answer his questions. Unrewarded, the question-asking tactic falls to a lower position in the child's hierarchy. Older responses that had been rewarded earlier in life, such as crying and temper tantrums, may then return to their formerly high positions in the hierarchy and become more probable. A return to earlier, more "childish" forms of responding is called *regression*.

Ability is a factor in learning that is often overlooked or confused with other factors. Retarded children, for example, lack certain abilities and usually need special attention if they are to learn "to the best of their abilities." Abilities may also lead to motivation; if a child discovers he is good at the piano or tennis or schoolwork, if he finds the exercise of these "talents" leads to praise and approval, he is likely to become motivated to polish these talents and spend a lot of time involved with them. Ability and motivation are often confused, too. A ghetto child who shares few of the middle-class values of his teachers may be poorly motivated to perform well in school; his poor performance may be mistakenly inferred to indicate the lack of ability. In old people, low scores on certain tests reflect not so much declining ability as increasing cautiousness, a motivational factor.

CONCERNS OF DEVELOPMENTAL PSYCHOLOGY

All three major theoretical views—Piaget, Freud, and learning theory—have something important to contribute to our understanding of development. Since each concentrates on different aspects of development, they are not actually as contradictory as they may appear on the surface. By the same token, no single approach is sufficiently complete to explain all that is important about the development of the child, the adult, and the aged person. Hence we borrow in this book from all theories, attempting to integrate their contributions into a more complete picture of human development.

This book has no single theoretical orientation. At times we will view the child as changing as a result of conditioning, exposure to models, and administration of rewards and punishments. At other times he or she will be viewed as actively selecting experiences and altering beliefs because of inconsistency. Personality development and intellectual development—and the relationships between the two—at all stages of the life span will be discussed.

The major concerns of developmental psychology, regardless of the theoretical approach used to define and explain them, fall into three broad categories. The first involves *sequences* that most or all children and adults pass through as they grow and develop. The course of language development in children is a good example, and studies of the development of perception, motor skills, and reasoning ability usually fall into this category. The nature of intellectual development in the adult years is another good example—Is there a decline with age? When, if ever, does it begin? If decline occurs, what is the cause?

A second set of problems concerns *individual differences* rather than the individual similarities examined in more or less universal sequences. The psychologist wants to understand the reasons for variations in characteristics like school achievement, dependency on parents, social aggression, or successful aging (Figure 1.15).

A third set of problems is concerned with differences among children, adults, and old people in *different cultures* around the world. The effect of variations in child-training techniques—in parental responses to aggressive behavior, for example—is helpful in understanding the effect of parental practices within a culture. Often what is thought of as a "natural" or "universal" phenomenon turns out to be not so at all. In Western cultures, for example, it was widely assumed that between the ages of 5 or 6 and puberty children were in a "latent stage" of sexuality (see p. 25), that is, they were not very active sex-

● Figure 1.15 Developmental psychologists want to understand individual differences.

ually. In some other cultures, however, children are sexually active all their lives. What was perceived as a universal (and probably biological) stage of development turns out to be culturally determined.

Despite the huge contributions of many research efforts, our knowledge and understanding are incomplete. Indeed, scientific inquiry is often likely to raise more questions than it answers. As you read of the theories and the research on developmental sequences, individual differences, and cultural variations, you will see many gaps in our knowledge. But the scientific study of human development has come a long way in less than a century, and this book is a record of current progress. We hope you will find the review interesting and informative.

SUMMARY

Developmental psychologists are interested in changes that occur with age across the entire span of life. Interest in childhood emerged in the seventeenth century. Many of the basic issues were defined by philosophers such as John Locke and Jean Jacques Rousseau; for example, the nature vs. nurture issue began a debate about the relative contribution of hereditary and environmental factors in behavior that continues to this day, and whether children are primarily active and searching or passive and reactive is another durable issue. Baby biographies published in the late eighteenth century contained the first careful observations of child behavior.

Interest in adolescence and youth, which emerged in the late nineteenth century, increased sharply in the 1960s when some alienated youth began "dropping out" and others began protest actions against war, racism, and other social problems. Interest in the intellectual and personality development of adults is even more recent, spurred by significant increases in the number of people over 65 and a rapidly changing technology, which means frequent adjustments and crises (career changes, divorce, etc.) for many adults.

In scientific studies of children, adolescents, and adults, the first systematic investigations described age trends in physical, cognitive, and behavioral characteristics. More recently, however, researchers have become increasingly concerned with explanation and theory, with the processes underlying human development. A typical study involves a hypothesis which states a possible effect of one variable (the independent variable) on another (the dependent variable). When age is the independent variable, one can either use a longitudinal approach, investigating the same subjects at different ages, or a cross-sectional approach, comparing subjects of different ages.

As representatives of influential theories in developmental psychology, we discussed the theories of Piaget, Freud, and learning psychologists. Piaget's theory views the child as an active "investigator" who develops new mental operations through experience with the world. Typically the child tries to assimilate new experiences with habitual modes of acting and thinking; accommodation involves a change in response to a new object or event, usually because assimilation was inadequate. Primarily through a series of accommodations, the child moves through several stages of intellectual growth.

Freud's psychoanalytic theory describes children in conflict because of sexual and aggressive feelings toward their parents. In Freud's terms, the id, which represents these basic urges, is in conflict with the ego, the part of the personality that tries to cope with reality, or with the superego, which represents moral standards. In the infant the conflicts between what is desired and what is realistically possible often occur in feeding situations; hence, Freud called this the oral stage. In the anal stage, toilet training is a prominent situation. In the phallic stage, Freud describes the Oedipus complex: the young boy competes with his father for his mother. But the boy fears his father's power and eventually identifies with him. The psychoanalytic theory of adult development, as proposed by Erik Erikson, is based on a series of social "accomplishments": personal identity and the ability to be intimate in young adulthood, generativity in the middle adult years, and a sense of integrity in old age.

Learning theories of development emphasize the principles of classical conditioning, operant conditioning, and observational learning.

Stimuli elicit the response in classical conditioning, and they can also command attention or serve as "discriminative stimuli" to indicate when rewards are likely. Outcomes are important in operant conditioning; positive reinforcement supposedly makes the response more likely while extinction (no reinforcement) decreases response probability. Common schedules of intermittent reinforcement are ratio (based on the number of responses per reward) and interval (time between rewarded responses), and they can be fixed or variable. Learning is sometimes best viewed as a shift in a response hierarchy; in regression, for example, immature response can reappear if responses above it in the hierarchy are frustrated.

Drawing on the insights of Piagetian, Freudian, learning and other theories, we will discuss the differences in behavior of people at different stages of a sequence of development, individual differences at the same stage, and differences among the various cultures in the world.

References

1. Aries, P. **Centuries of childhood.** New York: Knopf, 1962.

2. Bandura, A. & Walters, R. H. **Social learning and personality development.** New York: Holt, Rinehart & Winston, 1963.

3. Birren, J. E. A brief history of the psychology of aging. Part II. **Gerontologist,** 1961, **1,** 127–134.

4. Butler, R. N. **Why survive?** New York: Harper & Row, 1975.

5. Charles, D. C. Historical antecedents of life-span developmental psychology. In L. R. Goulet & P. B. Baltes (Eds.), **Life-span developmental psychology: research and theory.** New York: Academic Press, 1970.

6. Conger, J. J. **The changing perception of children in society over the years.** Paper presented at the Worlds for Women Conference, Denver, Colorado, March 11, 1977.

7. Darwin, C. A. A biographical sketch of an infant. **Mind,** 1877, **2,** 285–294.

8. Datan, N. & Ginsberg, L. H. **Life-span developmental psychology: normative life crises.** New York: Academic Press, 1975.

9. Freud, S. **Introductory lectures on psychoanalysis.** (Standard ed.) Vol. 7. London: Hogarth, 1953.

10. Freud, S. **The problem of anxiety.** New York: Norton, 1936.

11. Hilgard, E. R. **Theories of learning.** New York: Harper & Row, 1954.

12. Kagan, J. The child in the family. **Daedalus,** 1977, 106(2), 33–56.

13. Kessen, W. **The child.** New York: Wiley, 1965.

14. Kimble, G. A. **Hilgard and Marquis' conditioning and learning (2nd ed.)** New York: Appleton-Century-Crofts, 1961.

15. Lipsitt, L. P. Learning in the first year of life. In L. P. Lipsitt and C. C. Spiker (Eds.), **Advances in child development and behavior.** New York: Academic Press, 1963, pp. 147–195.

16. Lovaas, O. I. A behavior therapy approach to the treatment of childhood schizophrenia. In J. Hill (Ed.), **Minnesota symposium on child psychology.** Minneapolis: University of Minnesota Press, 1967.

17. Marquis, D. P. Can conditioned responses be established in the newborn infant? **Journal of Genetic Psychology,** 1931, **39,** 479–492.

18. Miles, W. R. Measures of certain human abilities through the life-span. Proceedings of the National Academy of Sciences, 1931, 17, 627-632.

19. Piaget, J. **The origins of intelligence in children.** New York: International Universities Press, 1952.

20. Sheehy, G. **Passages.** New York: Dutton, 1976.

21. Skinner, B. F. **The behavior of organisms.** New York: Appleton-Century-Crofts, 1938.

22. Skinner, B. F. **Science and human behavior.** New York: Macmillan, 1953.

23. Yerkes, R. M. (Ed.) Psychological examining in the United States Army. **Memoirs of the National Academy of Sciences,** 1921, **15,** 1–890.

CHAPTER 2
Biological Factors in Early Development

Each child is a joint product of heredity and environment, a mixture of the forces of nature and nurture. Heredity (nature) is fixed at the moment of conception. The genes of the mother and father combine to produce a new and unique individual, predisposing her or him toward a certain look, perhaps a type of personality, and perhaps a profile of mental abilities. Although determined at conception, many genetic influences are not evidenced until later in life, when they manifest themselves physically or behaviorally. This "running off" of an individual's genetic program or schedule is called *maturation*. For example, after birth some senses become more acute. Roughly around the age of 18, a person reaches a maximum height, a height that is determined primarily (but by no means exclusively) by heredity. After the age of 50 or 60, gray hair sprouts where black hair had been, and other signs of "normal" aging become apparent; these, too, have been attributed to a genetic program, a genetic schedule for aging, a genetic clock running out.

But from the moment of conception, environmental factors (nurture) have their own effects. The first environment is the uterus where the maturing fetus develops in the protective fluid of the amniotic sac—an environment we tend to think of as peaceful and constant. This image is not inaccurate, especially when the uterine environment is compared with the outside world. Uterine environments do vary from mother to mother. Some mothers are healthy; others are malnourished or on drugs. These differences in mother's health can profoundly affect the uterine environment and, ultimately, some characteristics of the newborn child. For example, the child of the drug addict may not receive sufficient nourishment from the mother (through the umbilical cord) and is likely to be born underweight and sickly. In addition, because drugs can be transmitted from mother to fetus, the child may be born addicted. These characteristics are not genetically determined, although they are present at birth.

Once the child is born—already a mix of both genetic and environmental factors—the effects of inheritance and experience become even more difficult to untangle. A child's behavior changes significantly in many respects during the first year of life; some of this change is due to maturation (the running off of the genetic program) and some is a result of experience with objects and people. It is impossible to tell if a given behavior is "learned" or "matures" because genetic and environmental factors *interact*. That is, the influence of each depends on the quality of the other. To use an extreme example, there is a species of coral fish that lives off the coast of Australia in which the male has a harem of five or six females. If the male dies, the dominant female becomes biologically masculine: aggressive in defense of its harem and capable of fertilizing the eggs of the females.

There are many less extreme examples of such interrelationships between social conditions and biology. For example, a person with a constitutionally high level of anxiety might lead a productive and satisfying life in a nonthreatening environment; but if her parents are unloving and distant, if her world is hostile and stressful, she might have to spend most of her time and energy trying to reduce painful feelings of anxiety; she might even develop the symptoms of severe neurosis and require hospitalization. In a similar manner, genetic factors often determine the social environment to some extent: A child who is constitutionally hyperactive might create a world of adults who constantly try to slow her down, keep her quiet, inhibit her, frustrate her. A less active child might find the same people reacting quite differently and thus find the same environment much less frustrating.

Although the influence of *nature* (inborn factors) and that of *nurture* (environmental factors) are inextricably bound together, psychologists have traditionally distinguished between biological and environmental variables in discussions of child development. It can be useful to think about these factors separately as long as we remember that they do not *act* separately.

In this chapter we will consider three categories of biological factors in early development: First we will briefly consider genetic factors and try to understand how and what we inherit from our ancestors. Then we will discuss variables that influence development during pregnancy and birth, variables such as the diet and the health of the mother-to-be. Finally our attention will focus on the biological maturation of the child after birth, that is, on those behaviors, sensory capacities, needs, and temperamental characteristics that seem to emerge simply because the biological equipment of the infant continues to mature after birth as long as the child is in a reasonably normal environment.

HEREDITARY TRANSMISSION

The life of each individual begins when a sperm cell from the father penetrates the wall of an ovum, or egg, from the mother. The tiny tadpole-shaped sperm releases 23 minute particles called *chromosomes,* which combine with 23 chromosomes from the ovum to form 23 pairs in the first body cell of a new individual (Figure 2.1). This initial cell then divides, and each new cell divides again. As the cells divide and thus multiply, the same 23 pairs of chromosomes are duplicated in each one (Figure 2.2). Each chromosome is composed of around 20,000 *genes.* Each gene, in turn, is composed of a chemical called *deoxyribonucleic acid,* or *DNA* for short. DNA is the molecule of heredity; it contains the genetic code that determines what is transmitted from one generation to the next.

Genes also form pairs, one from the male chromosome and one from the female. Some genes are *dominant,* and some are *recessive.* When gene pairs have one dominant and one recessive gene, the individual manifests the characteristic determined by the dominant gene but also carries the recessive gene, which may be manifested in his or her offspring. Recessive genes determine traits only when two of them are paired. For example, eye color is determined by a single gene; "brown" is dominant, and "blue" is recessive. An individual who inherits two "brown" genes or one "brown" and one "blue" will have brown eyes; only someone with two "blue" genes will have blue eyes. But brown-eyed parents

●Figure 2.1   Chromosomes of the human male, magnified. (Courtesy of Dr. Theodore Puck.)

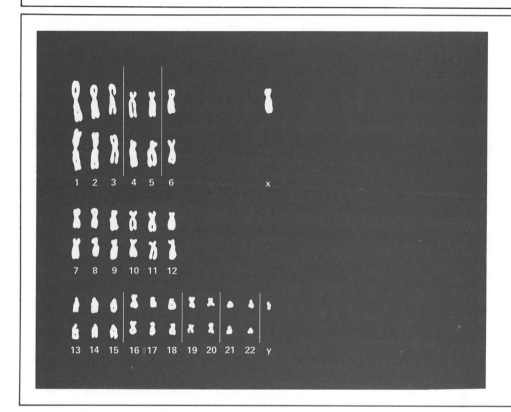

may carry the recessive "blue" genes, producing a certain (predictable) number of blue-eyed children.

The children of the same parents have somewhat different heredities, unless they are identical twins formed from the same ovum. It has been estimated that the total number of combinations of sperm and ovum chromosomes could produce 64 billion different children, and complex chemical reactions in the sperm and ova further increase the likelihood that each individual child will be unique.

Determining the Extent of Genetic Influences

The critical role played by genetic factors is clear in the case of eye color. Similarly, the importance of a single gene or set of genes in certain diseases is obvious. Huntington's chorea, a degenerative disease of the nervous system, de-

●Figure 2.2   How a fertilized egg cell multiplies. (From Amram Scheinfeld. *The New You and Heredity*, 1950, p. 12. Copyright 1950 by Amram Scheinfeld. Published by J. B. Lippincott Company. Also reprinted by permission of Paul R. Reynolds, Inc.)

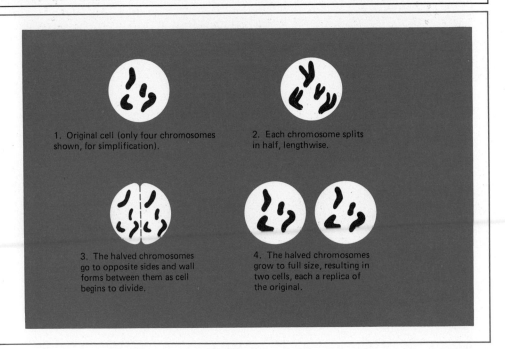

1. Original cell (only four chromosomes shown, for simplification).

2. Each chromosome splits in half, lengthwise.

3. The halved chromosomes go to opposite sides and wall forms between them as cell begins to divide.

4. The halved chromosomes grow to full size, resulting in two cells, each a replica of the original.

pends on the presence of a single dominant gene. But what about complex personality traits or psychological disorders in which no such specific gene can be isolated and in which environment may play an important part? In such cases, the only sure way of determining whether either set of factors plays an important part is to find some way of holding one set of factors as constant as possible while varying the other. If the personality trait or disorder then also varies, we know the factor we have varied plays an important role.

In humans, one way to do this is to compare identical with fraternal twins. *Identical twins* are, in a sense, biological oddities. When the fertilized egg begins splitting in the process that normally produces a single, multicelled individual, these two identical cells somehow separate and form two genetically identical individuals (Figure 2.3). Any differences in the behavior of these twins must be attributed to environmental factors (although these factors may be prenatal, before birth).

In contrast, *fraternal twins* (which result from two ova being fertilized at the same time) are no more similar genetically than other siblings, though they are likely to have been subjected to more similar environmental influences by

●Figure 2.3 Identical twins and fraternal twins. Identical twins (*left*) develop from a single ovum (egg) and are genetically identical. Fraternal twins (*right*) develop from two different ova and are no more similar genetically than other siblings.

virtue of having been born and reared at the same time. Thus, if a particular personality disorder or other condition occurs more often in the identical twins of persons with the disorder than it does in the fraternal twins of such persons, the likelihood that genetic factors play an important role is increased.

Another method is to compare children who have been adopted very early in life with both their biological parents and their adoptive parents. If these children, despite early separation, are more like their natural parents than their adoptive parents, the relative importance of genetic factors is suggested; if the opposite is the case, the importance of environmental influences is highlighted. Other methods are also employed; for example, identical twins can be compared with nontwin siblings, siblings can be compared with nonrelated children. But in each instance, the same basic principle is involved: Either genetic factors are varied while attempting to hold environmental factors constant, or the reverse.

What Is Transmitted?

Sex Of the 23 pairs of chromosomes, one pair is called the *sex chromosomes* and determines the sex of the child. In the normal female, both members of the pair are called *X chromosomes* (X for "unknown," because the existence of the chromosome was established before its function was known). The normal male has one X chromosome and a smaller Y chromosome. When a male's germ cells

Figure 2.4 Members of this Sicilian family each have extra fingers and toes, a condition believed to be hereditary. The man would like to play the part in a movie of a thief who leaves six fingerprints for detectives to ponder.

(which, like body cells, originally contain 46 chromosomes) split to form sperm, half of the sperm have an X chromosome and half have a Y chromosome. If an "X" sperm fertilizes the egg, the child will be a girl; a boy will result from the union of a male's "Y" sperm chromosome with the female's "X" egg.

A number of the genes that determine human characteristics, either physical or mental, are carried by the sex chromosomes and, for this reason, are called "sex-linked." One characteristic determined by a sex-linked gene is color blindness, which is more frequent in males. It is usually very difficult to determine the contribution of sex-linked genetic factors to more complex behaviors or traits in which the sexes differ, such as aggressiveness and timidity, for example. The observed differences may well be the result, in whole or in part, of learning and social expectations. Such issues lie at the heart of many debates in the feminist movement.

Physical features   An individual's physical features depend heavily upon heredity. Eye color, the shape of a nose, and the curliness of one's hair are typically determined by genes. How tall is she? How much does he weigh? Genetic factors play a major role in such characteristics (Figure 2.4) although environmental influences such as nutrition and disease are also important.

Mental defects   The vast majority of children classified as mentally retarded are probably *not* the victims of genetic disorder. But in certain cases, gross defects in intellectual ability can be traced to heredity. One of these, called *infantile amaurotic family idiocy,* results from a genetic defect in the nerve cells of the brain and spinal cord. The cells swell and fill with fat, causing blindness, paralysis, and mental deficiency. Because this disorder is caused by a recessive gene (73), it occurs most often when the parents are closely related. Marriage between close relations—cousins or even brother and sister—greatly increases the likelihood that both parents will pass on the recessive gene.

Another mental defect we know to be inherited is *phenylketonuria,* or *PKU* (36). People with this genetic defect cannot convert a chemical found in many foods to a harmless form. The toxic chemical accumulates and eventually damages the nerve cells of the central nervous system. Mental retardation is the result.

Although PKU is inherited, its effects can be minimized by control of the environment. The diagnosis of PKU involves rather simple blood or urine tests which can be administered in the first few weeks of life. If PKU is indicated, the child can be placed on a strict diet with foods low in the chemical the child's body cannot handle. Apart from a rather lackluster gastronomic regimen, these children then can lead a normal life.

Another mental defect with a genetic basis is called *Down's syndrome.* The children so afflicted are born with an Oriental cast to their facial appearance; therefore the defect was called *mongolism* in the past. Most of these children function at a very low level of intelligence. For many years it was thought that Down's syndrome was inherited, but recent studies suggest that it results from an extra chromosome in one of the 23 pairs; one of the "pairs" has three rather than two chromosomes. This abnormality occurs because of imperfect formation of sperm or egg cells, probably because of ill health or old age in one of the parents. Thus, while Down's syndrome is caused by genetic imperfections, it is not inherited in the usual sense; a parent who had a brother or sister with Down's syndrome is not more likely than average to have a Down's child.

Mental disorder   The role of genetic factors in the development of mental disorder has been, and continues to be, a source of controversy in the field of psychiatry. Some specific forms of mental illness are unquestionably inherited. We have already mentioned that Huntington's chorea is known to result from a single dominant gene. The illness is characterized by a progressive deterioration of mental and physical capacities which typically begins between the age of 30 and 40; before that there is no indication. Although this affliction is rare, many of us have heard of it because of Woody Guthrie, the folksinger who died of it. Woody's son, Arlo Guthrie, also a folksinger, has a 50 percent chance of seeing the symptoms develop in himself; either he got the chorea gene from his father or he inherited the other, normal gene in the pair.

There is much less agreement on the role of genetic factors in the more common mental disorders. Many disorders are known to be environmental in origin, involving brain damage because of injury, disease, or poison. The debate centers on the "functional" psychoses (severe mental illnesses with no apparent bodily cause) and the neuroses (milder forms of maladjustment). Some experts view these disorders as primarily genetic, but others claim that environmental factors, especially early life experiences, are more important.

Let us consider one of the most common functional psychoses, *schizophrenia*. This disorder is characterized by severe defects in logical thinking, emotions, and social responsiveness and, occasionally, hallucinations. Schizophrenia probably comes closest to what most people think of as being "crazy."

A few decades ago, many psychologists and psychiatrists believed that traumatic experiences in childhood were the major determinants of schizophrenia. Recent research indicates that hereditary factors are also important. If one member of a pair of identical twins is diagnosed schizophrenic, the chances that the second twin is (or will become) schizophrenic is around 42 percent; the comparable percentage for fraternal twins is 9 percent (43). Moreover, if children of schizophrenic parents are adopted during infancy and raised in a normal family, they still stand a better than average chance of becoming schizophrenic (41, 61).

Evidence of a genetic influence on schizophrenia does not mean that children of schizophrenic parents will necessarily become schizophrenic. A complex pattern of behavior such as schizophrenia is not like eye color; a child is not schizophrenic or normal in the same sense that his or her eyes are brown or blue. Instead, what is inherited is probably a *vulnerability* to schizophrenia; if the environment is benign, the symptoms of mental disorder may not develop at all. Conversely, a particularly horrifying family situation may induce severe mental disorder in all but the least genetically vulnerable (Table 2.1). Furthermore, there is increasing evidence that there are different kinds of schizophrenia and that genetic influences are strong in some types, weak in others (9, 20, 70).

Personality   Research on the role of heredity in personality is hampered by the lack of a specific set of behaviors to study. Personality traits (e.g., stubbornness,

●Table 2.1   Genetic and environmental factors in schizophrenia

Genetic constitution	Quality of the environment		
	Good	Average	Poor
Prone to schizophrenia	Slight possibility of schizophrenia	Moderate possibility of schizophrenia	Strong possibility of schizophrenia
Not prone to schizophrenia	No possibility	No possibility	Slight possibility

shyness, dominance) are global characteristics that are presumed to affect a number of behaviors; no specific behavior can contain the general definition of the trait. So investigations of inherited personality traits are difficult.

One personality dimension that is probably affected by genetic factors is *introversion–extraversion*. Introverts are shy and inhibited in social situations, while extraverts are more active and outgoing. Identical twins have been found to be more similar than fraternal twins with respect to such traits as soberness versus enthusiasm, avoidance versus enjoyment of social contact, and inhibition versus spontaneity (8, 62, 63); all of these traits are considered aspects of the more general introversion–extraversion dimension. Even as infants, identical twins are more alike than fraternal twins in the tendency to smile and to show fear of strangers (23).

Intelligence   Is intelligence inherited? This question has generated more controversy than almost any other in psychology. The major support for the view that intelligence is at least partly determined by genetic factors comes from research in which intelligence is defined by scores on IQ tests. (This definition is itself controversial). When the IQs of parents and children, or of brothers and sisters, are correlated, values around 0.50 can be expected. These correlations can be compared with those from pairings of genetically unrelated people—zero correlations in most cases. See Table 2.2. Although the difference between 0.50

Table 2.2 Correlations for intellectual ability

Correlations between	Number of studies	Average correlation
Unrelated persons		
Children reared apart	4	−.01
Foster parent and child	3	+.20
Children reared together	5	+.24
Collaterals		
Second cousins	1	+.16
First cousins	3	+.26
Uncle (or aunt) and nephew (or niece)	1	+.34
Siblings, reared apart	3	+.47
Siblings, reared together	36	+.55
Fraternal twins, different sex	9	+.49
Fraternal twins, same sex	11	+.56
Identical twins, reared apart	4	+.75
Identical twins, reared together	14	+.87
Direct line		
Grandparent and grandchild	3	+.27
Parent (as adult) and child	13	+.50
Parent (as child) and child	1	+.56

SOURCE: From A. R. Jensen, How much can we boost IQ and scholastic achievement? *Harvard Educational Review*, 39 (1969), pp. 1–123. Reprinted by permission.

and 0.00 may seem sufficient to implicate genetics, one must not forget that in most of these studies the parents and children (or brothers and sisters) lived in the same home, neighborhood, and community. Similar IQ scores could result from this similarity in their environments; heredity need not be involved. So we cannot tell from these correlations alone whether heredity is a significant determinant of IQ.

A better test of the extent of genetic influence comes from comparisons of the IQ scores of identical twins with those of fraternal twins, who all have similar environments but different heredities. In identical twins, IQ scores correlate 0.87, averaged over 14 different studies (38). For fraternal twins, the comparable figure (11 studies) is 0.56, about the same as the average correlation between siblings, 0.55. These comparisons suggest a strong genetic component in IQ scores. Particularly interesting are the few studies of identical twins reared apart. In these cases, the twins were separated because of family misfortune and raised in different families. Their environments were therefore considerably less similar than if they had been raised together. The IQs of such twins still correlate 0.75. Again, a sizable component of IQ seems to be inherited.

In dealing with a highly valued quality like intelligence, one must be very careful that conclusions be drawn only when the evidence is strong; also, care must be taken that these conclusions not be misinterpreted. There are many warnings to be appended to the conclusion that IQ is probably affected by genetic factors. For example, the environment of identical twins reared apart might not be as different as one might imagine. Typically the officials responsible for placing children in foster homes try to place them in similar families. Thus many of the twin pairs separated early in life went to families of similar social and educational backgrounds; in some cases they went to two branches of the same family. To attribute the correlation between the IQ of identical twins reared apart solely to heredity, therefore, is clearly unwarranted.

Another question can be raised. Is an IQ test a reasonable estimate of basic intelligence? The studies we reported suggest genetic influence on IQ scores; there are some psychologists who doubt the relevance of such measures, and no psychologist would argue that IQ tests are perfect. For a particular individual, the IQ score can be a very poor estimate of his or her true intellectual ability, because of poor background, inadequate motivation, or other environmental considerations.

Finally, the conclusion that IQ might be in part inherited does not imply that there are racial differences in intelligence. Typically there are differences between the average IQs of different races; blacks, for example, have lower average IQ scores than those of whites. To suggest that blacks are therefore genetically inferior to whites in intelligence is totally unwarranted. To conclude that there are racial differences in intelligence requires an assumption that race differences in opportunity do not exist, or are unimportant, or are not sufficient to explain the differences in IQ scores. None of these assumptions is supported by research data. (For a more complete discussion of this and other issues in intelligence, see Chapter 4.)

BIOLOGICAL INFLUENCES DURING PREGNANCY AND CHILDBIRTH

In traditional Chinese cultures, a person is considered to be 1 year old at birth (11). This system of age reckoning is perhaps more realistic than ours, in which a baby receives no credit at all for the nine months between conception and birth. Certainly the time of pregnancy is a significant period of development, as the fertilized egg becomes a human being. A number of factors affect the uterine environment and thus the biological development of the fetus. Let us consider some of these influences during pregnancy and childbirth.

How Conception Occurs

The occasions on which such conception is possible are strictly limited by the biological characteristics of the female reproductive system. Once every 28 days (in the average female) an ovum ripens in one of the two ovaries and is discharged into the corresponding Fallopian tube, which leads to the uterus. If a sperm penetrates and thus fertilizes the ovum during this journey from the ovary to the uterus, a new life begins (see Figure 2.5). If not, the ovum disintegrates in the uterus and is expelled, along with blood from a uterus that finds it doesn't need to nourish a fertilized egg, in the menstrual flow.

If a sperm has penetrated the ovum, a process begins in which the 23 chromosomes of the male cell allign themselves with the 23 chromosomes of the

●Figure 2.5   Schematic diagram of female reproductive system showing how conception occurs.

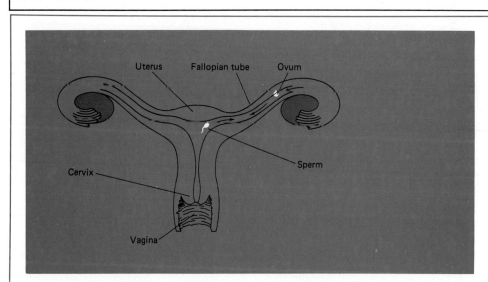

egg. Between 24 and 36 hours later, this single body cell splits into two. These 2 become 4 in another division and then 8, 16, and so on. Meanwhile the fertilized ovum attaches itself to the uterine wall and "plugs into" the mother's blood supply, its food supply. Technically the ovum becomes an *embryo*. Three membranes surround the embryo; they are filled with a watery fluid which shields the embryo from trauma experienced by the mother, provides an even temperature, and in general constitutes the placid environment glorified in hypotheses about the desire to return to the womb.

The umbilical cord is the lifeline of the embryo. Through it, blood from the mother is carried in, and "used" blood is transported out. However, the relationship between the embryo's bloodstream and the mother's is not a direct one. Various barriers and screens allow certain substances in but *not* others. In general, the valuable nutrients get in, and the dangerous waste products get out; the embryo has some protection against germs and bacteria carried in the mother's blood, but certain diseases—notably measles, influenza, and, later in development, syphilis—pass through and affect the development of the embryo. Various drugs—notably heroin, alcohol, and nicotine—also get through and affect embryonic development. Physicians invariably advise pregnant women to avoid unnecessary drugs and exposure to disease, especially during the first three months of pregnancy.

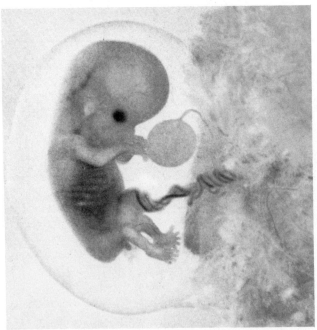

● Figure 2.6 Embryo at five weeks. The eye is seen as a dark-rimmed circle.

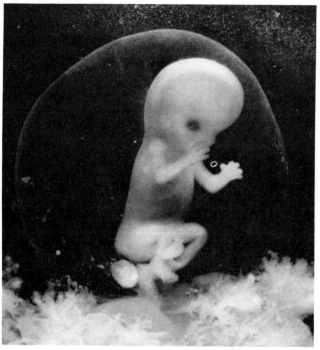

● Figure 2.7   Fetus at ten weeks. Hands and figures are now clearly observable.

Development of the Embryo

During the period of the embryo, development is extremely rapid (Figure 2.6). By the end of the third week, top and bottom, front and back, and right and left sides are discernible; a primitive heart has begun to beat (28). By 8 to 9 weeks, the embryo is about an inch long. Face, mouth, eyes, and ears have begun to form. Arms and legs and even tiny hands and feet with stubby fingers and toes have appeared (27). The nervous system develops rapidly during this early period, too, and it is particularly susceptible at this time to harmful influences from injury, drugs, and disease. For example, if the mother should contract German measles during this period, the chances of her having a mentally retarded child are significantly increased.

From the end of the second month until birth, the developing organism is called a *fetus*. The nervous system begins to function, at least in simple fashion; the fetus at 9 weeks is capable of responding to tactile (touch) stimulation (58) (Figure 2.7). Males and females become differentiated as hormones that came from the male's testes stimulate the beginnings of a male reproductive system. If the testes are damaged or otherwise fail to perform properly, the baby that is born will have a primarily female reproductive system, although it is genetically male. Failure of the female ovary to produce female hormones has no such effect. It appears, therefore, that the anatomy of the female reproductive system is basic: It is the form that will develop if either testes or ovaries fail to function.

The development of the fetus is rapid in the following weeks. At 12 weeks eyelids and nails have begun to form, and spontaneous movements of the arms and legs can be observed; the weight of the fetus, however, is not yet an ounce. At 16 weeks, the mother can feel the fetus' movements (Figure 2.8). Skin has developed to fairly adult form by 20 weeks and, by 24 weeks, the fetus is capable of crying should it be prematurely born.

The age of 28 weeks is generally taken as the time at which the fetus, if prematurely born, has a reasonable chance of survival. The nervous, circulatory, and other bodily systems have become sufficiently well structured to function, although, of course, special care is required. Typically the premature baby is placed in an incubator because the brain regions responsible for the control of body temperature and other functions are not quite adequate. Sensitivity to pain is either absent or less than that in babies born nine months after conception; in some respects, this decreased sensitivity is a blessing, since the premature infants experience less pain than a full-term baby would, but it is also a danger, for reactions to pain—crying, writhing—alert doctors and nurses that something is wrong (7).

● Figure 2.8   Sixteen-week-old embryo. The mother can now feel the fetus' movements.

Between 28 weeks and full term (about 40 weeks), physical development proceeds along the lines we have indicated. Muscle tone increases, and motor movements become more refined and sustained. The nervous system becomes more integrated and complex. Eventually the fetus is expelled—a child is born. Characteristics of a normal newborn baby will be discussed in more detail later, after a description of some of the more important prenatal influences.

Prenatal Environmental Influences

Ordinarily we think of the prenatal environment as constant and similar for all fetuses. Certainly the fetus' environment is simple in comparison with the complex world to be encountered after birth. Nevertheless, there are many variations in the prenatal environment, and these variations may result in significant physical and psychological differences among children.

Age of the mother   There is some evidence that mothers younger than 20 or older than 35 have a slightly greater probability of giving birth to children with physical defects. This may be due to the inadequate development of the reproductive system in some younger women and to progressive decline in reproductive functioning in some older ones. Older people in general are more susceptible to disease, and this may play a role in the case of the older mother.

Very young and relatively old mothers have a somewhat higher incidence of infant mortality. The probability of a mentally retarded child is also somewhat greater than for mothers between 20 and 35. Women who deliver their first infant when they are 35 or over are more likely than younger women to experience difficult pregnancies and longer and difficult periods of labor before birth. They are slightly more likely to require Caesarean sections for delivery. These facts may help us to understand human development after conception and before birth, but there is no reason for panic by the 37-year-old female reader who happens to be pregnant. The probability of serious complications in older mothers is only *slightly* increased. The doctor of such a reader can combat many of the difficulties that might arise, and improved medical techniques can lessen the chances of infant mortality and difficult pregnancies.

Diet of the mother   The expectant mother should have an adequate diet if she is going to maintain her own general good health during her pregnancy and deliver a healthy infant. In a study of the effects of nutrition during pregnancy, 90 pregnant women, whose diet through the first four or five months was deemed inadequate, were given dietary supplements. By comparing these women to other women who did not receive the nutritional supplements, the researchers (18, 78) determined that "good-diet" mothers were less likely to have complications such as anemia, toxemia, threatened and actual miscarriages, premature births, and babies dead at birth. Compared to the infants born to "poor-diet" mothers, the babies of women with better nutrition during pregnancy were generally healthier after birth. During the first six months of life, these babies had fewer major illnesses (e.g., pneumonia) and minor illnesses (e.g., colds).

The effect of the mother's diet during pregnancy on the child's later *mental* development is difficult to determine. An inadequately nourished mother is almost invariably a person who lives in a community marked by poverty, and the stressful conditions of being raised in such a community are additional obstacles faced by her child. A study of rats has shown that the pups of mothers kept on a very low protein diet had defects in the central nervous system (12), but no such relationship has been demonstrated conclusively with humans. Nevertheless, most psychologists believe that a very poor diet for the mother during pregnancy must have some adverse effect on the mental capacities of the child that is born. At the very least, a good diet is a wise precaution.

Drugs   During the last decade or so, doctors and parents have become increasingly concerned about the potentially harmful effects of drugs on the developing fetus. Since there has been a dramatic rise in the use of drugs, both legal and illegal, drugs now constitute one of the major threats to normal fetal development.

Different drugs have different effects on the fetus, of course, and a number of other factors, such as the stage of pregnancy when the drug is taken, are also influential. The first three months of pregnancy are the most risky. In the most famous case of drug damage, a tranquilizer called *thalidomide* was taken by a large number of women during the early months of their pregnancy; these women delivered a large number of babies with gross anatomical deformities such as no hands or no feet (Figure 2.9). Other drugs can be shown to affect the fetus at least temporarily. For example, newborn babies delivered from mothers who were given sedatives to calm them before delivery were noticeably less alert and attentive than the newborns of mothers who were not sedated (71). Although such effects generally seem to disappear in a few days, it is possible to "overload the fetal bloodstream (so) as to produce asphyxiation of the fetus at birth, with permanent brain damage of such a kind as to lead to mental impairment" (51, p. 162).

Heroin is believed by many to pass from the mother's bloodstream to the fetus'; the result, according to this view, is a baby who is born addicted to heroin. These babies are unusually irritable, and they tremble and may vomit—withdrawal symptoms. However, this view is controversial; some scientists believe that heroin is blocked by the blood barrier between mother and fetus, and that the "withdrawal symptoms" result from other factors such as the generally poor nutrition of mothers addicted to heroin (6). There is a danger that doctors will administer opiates needlessly to the babies of addicts in an attempt to ease withdrawal symptoms. There is no controversy, however, over recommending good nutrition during pregnancy and total abstinence of all drugs not prescribed by a physician.

It has been known since the early 1970s that chronic heavy drinking by a

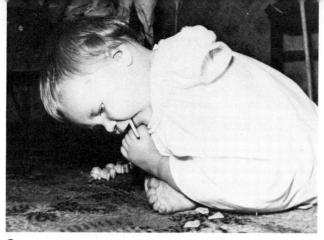

●Figure 2.9 "Thalidomide baby," born without arms, learns to substitute use of its feet.

pregnant woman can produce what is known as "fetal alcohol syndrome." The symptoms of this syndrome include: premature birth, microcephaly (abnormal smallness of the head), eye and ear problems, heart defects, extra fingers and toes, and disturbed sleep patterns (39, 40). Current research suggests slightly increased risk of fetal alcohol syndrome in mothers who drink as little as two–four ounces of hard liquor daily (54). It is estimated that as many as 6000 infants a year born in the United States suffer from fetal alcohol syndrome, more than the total number of "thalidomide babies" born over several years.

Irradiation   Radiation from X-rays, atomic bombs, and other sources is generally injurious to the fetus. Small amounts of irradiation, such as those used in an X-ray photograph or two, are not known to affect the fetus, but larger amounts, such as those used to treat cancer of the ovary or pelvis can have disastrous effects. In one study, over a third of 75 full-term infants whose mothers had therapeutic irradiation during pregnancy manifested mental or physical abnormalities that could not be attributed to anything but the treatments. Severe disturbances of the central nervous system were common; 16 infants were classified as microcephalic (which means "small brain"), a condition marked by feeble-mindedness, an abnormally small, pointed skull, and a very small brain; another 8 infants were extremely small, physically deformed, or blind (52, 53).

The most dramatic illustration of the effects of irradiation on the fetus is the experience of pregnant women who lived through the atomic bomb dropped on Hiroshima, Japan. If the woman had been pregnant 20 weeks or less and had lived within a half mile of the center of the explosion, she was very likely to have given birth to a physically or mentally abnormal child (55).

Maternal diseases and disorders   The barrier between the mother's and the child's bloodstream is only partially effective in screening out viruses and germs, and thus a mother's illness can affect the fetus. There have been reports of infants born with smallpox, measles, chickenpox, and mumps (30). A particularly serious threat to the fetus is syphilis, which affects the fetuses of about 25 percent of syphilitic mothers (16). If there is no miscarriage, the fetus may suffer marked damage to bones, liver, blood vessels, and lungs. If not treated soon after birth, the child may eventually develop eye damage, deafness, and brain damage. In some cases, the child may not show symptoms of the disease for several years.

Rubella, or as it is more commonly known, German measles, is dangerous during the first three or four months of pregnancy, during the early period of fetal development. About 12 percent of the mothers with rubella early in their pregnancy have defective children (32). The defects include deafness, obstructed vision (cataracts), and various degrees and forms of mental deficiency.

Rh factors   The Rh factor is a protein found in the red blood cells of some people, people who are called "Rh positive." Other people, called "Rh negative," do not have this substance. The body of an Rh-negative person will react to the Rh factor as if it were an invading germ by forming antibodies that attack and destroy the Rh-positive blood cells. For this reason, transfusions of Rh-positive blood into someone without the Rh factor can be extremely dangerous. For the same reason, if the fetus is Rh positive and the mother is Rh negative, there is danger that her antibodies will destroy the fetus' blood cells, leaving it without oxygen. If a fetus under such attack survives at all, the baby may be paralyzed or mentally deficient, probably because of damage to a brain starved of oxygen (50).

It takes time for the Rh-negative mother's blood to build up antibodies, so usually the first Rh-positive baby is delivered without complication. The second and third "mismatches" are more likely to involve serious reactions. Similarly, the Rh-negative fetus is no threat to an Rh-positive mother, because the fetus does not build up sufficient antibodies in time to injure her blood cells.

There are medical techniques now available that can minimize the consequences of Rh incompatibility.

Maternal emotional states   There are no direct connections between the mother's and the fetus' nervous systems. Nevertheless, the mother's emotional state can influence the fetus, because emotions result in the release of hormones and other chemicals into the bloodstream. Diffused into the bloodstream of the fetus, these chemicals can stimulate or depress its nervous system or parts of it. Thus emotional upset in the mother can irritate the fetus as well. One study noted that body movements of fetuses increased several hundred percent while their mothers were undergoing emotional stress. If the mother's stress lasted several weeks, fetal activity continued at an exaggerated level throughout the entire period. Even with a very brief emotional upset, the heightened irritability of the fetus usually lasted several hours (67, 68, 69).

The long-term effects of maternal emotional states on the development of the fetus are unclear. Mothers who were tense and anxious during pregnancy tend to have "colicky" infants, with distended abdomens, apparent pain, and

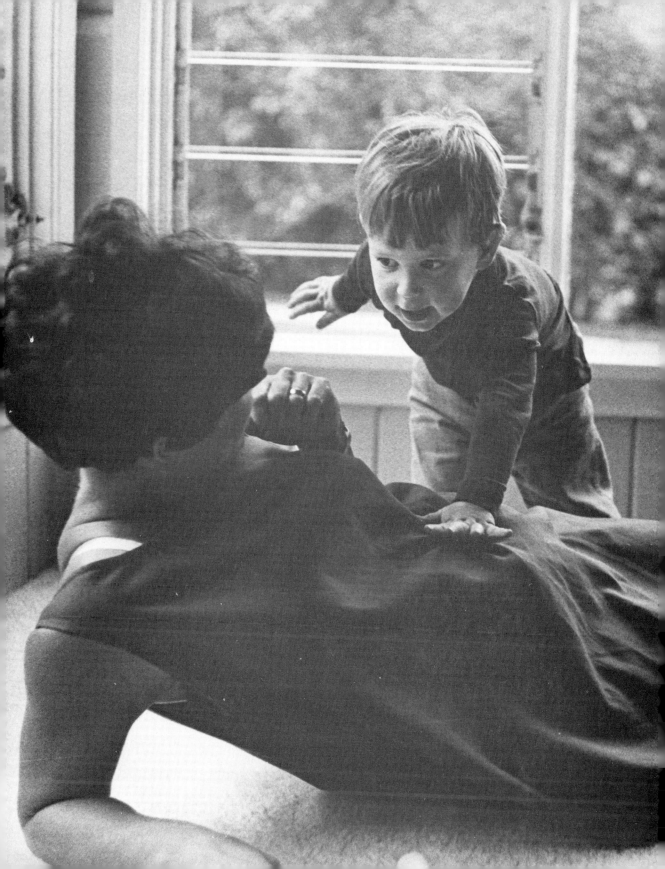

frequent crying (46). Of course, mothers who were anxious during pregnancy tend to be anxious after birth, too, and the tension in early mother–child interactions may be responsible for the colic; we cannot choose one explanation over the other without more research.

The Birth Process

In addition to events that occur during pregnancy, what happens during the process of delivery can affect the physical and psychological well-being of the baby. Two major dangers are rupturing of blood vessels in the brain caused by intense pressure on the head of the fetus during delivery and a lack of oxygen due to the failure of the newborn to breathe properly. In both cases, the brain is deprived of oxygen, and the result may be brain damage or even death. The brain stem, which controls many of our integrated motor behaviors, is particularly susceptible to this sort of injury, and thus the oxygen-deprived baby is most likely to show paralysis of legs or arms, tremors of the face or fingers, or an inability to use vocal muscles properly (which may interfere with speech).

There is some evidence that infants who experienced slight oxygen deprivation during birth are more easily distracted during the first two or three years (10) and possibly up to seven years (22), but there is no firm evidence of serious permanent intellectual damage.

Premature Births

An infant born at less than 37 weeks after conception is classified as premature. However, often it is difficult to obtain accurate information on the precise time the egg and sperm meet, so birth weight is more commonly used as the index of

●Table 2.3   Degree of handicap by birth weight

Birth weight (gm)	Degrees of handicap							
	Moderate/ Severe		Some		Little/None		Total	
	No	%	No	%	No	%	No	%
1250 and under	23	64	6	17	7	19	36	100
1251–1500	16	34	10	21	21	45	47	100
1501–1750	5	19	6	23	15	58	26	100
1751–2000	8	12	20	30	39	58	67	100
2001–2250	2	4	13	23	42	74	57	100
2251–2500	3	3	19	16	94	81	116	100
2501 and over	2	1	20	12	143	87	165	100

SOURCE: C. M. Drillien. School disposal and performance for children of different birthweight born 1953–1960. *Archives of Disease in Childhood*, 1970, 44, 562–570. By permission.

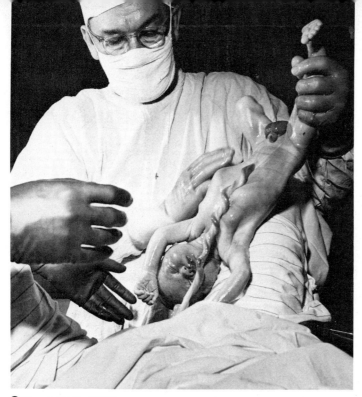

●Figure 2.10   Birth.

prematurity (Figure 2.10). An infant under $5\frac{1}{2}$ pounds is regarded as premature, and one under 4 pounds is "severely premature." A little less than 8 percent of hospital births fall into these categories, the vast majority weighing between 5 and $5\frac{1}{2}$ pounds.

Premature babies face a somewhat increased risk of various handicaps, including cerebral palsy, major defects in vision or hearing, and mental retardation; sometimes there are less severe handicaps, such as below-average IQ, perceptual disorders, learning problems, and behavioral symptoms (like hyperactivity), which do not become apparent until later in childhood. The risk of such dangers is highly correlated with the degree of prematurity, as shown in Table 2.3. Note that, in this study, 64 percent of children whose birth weight was below 1250 grams (2.75 lbs) and 34 percent of those with birth weights between 1250 and 1500 grams (3.3 lbs) showed moderate to severe handicaps. In contrast, most infants with birth weights over 2000 grams (4.4 lbs) showed little or no handicap. Other studies (2, 47, 59) show that intensive, expert care of premature babies in special medical centers can reduce the incidence of handicaps substantially, even among the smallest babies.

The fate of premature babies is influenced significantly by the quality of the home life they experience after birth. Those born into a loving, caring environment usually show little or no permanent handicap, unless they were very premature or did not receive proper medical treatment at birth. But in homes with poor parental care and living conditions, both physical and psychological difficulties are far more frequent than with full-term children living in the same environment. In this connection, it is sobering to discover that approximately 30 percent of "battered children" (beaten, usually by one of their parents) were born prematurely (2, 47, 72).

Socioeconomic Class

Problems associated with pregnancy and delivery are three or four times more frequent among families of lower socioeconomic classes than among middle-class families. According to the U.S. Public Health Service (49), the factors involved in the higher risk of infant damage or death occurring in the lower social classes include an impoverished environment, parental ignorance about child care, and failure to seek professional help. It is estimated that at least half of the newborn deaths in the lowest socioeconomic class were preventable.

On the average, the children of parents in the lower socioeconomic classes do poorly on IQ tests throughout their lives. There are many exceptions, of course, but the question arises, why do so many children of poor parents score low on IQ tests? One answer holds that some people are poor because they are not intelligent; the children of these unintelligent poor people inherit a low degree of intelligence. Another answer points out that the life experiences of most poor families do not encourage the kind of academic striving and achievement fostered by middle-class environments. The genetic and environmental factors are often pitted against one another in nature versus nurture arguments, but there are other factors, too, the ones we have just been discussing. Poor nutrition, exposure to mind-damaging poisons and irradiation, and poor medical care during pregnancy and birth are all more prevalent in lower-class than in middle-class families.

BIOLOGICAL FACTORS IN INFANCY

Flat-nosed, with red and wrinkled skin, the newborn child begins his or her life with major needs. A caretaking person must bring food and water or the child will die. The infant needs protection from extreme temperatures, and discomfort is among his or her first experiences. The infant's ability to communicate these needs consists largely of crying, thrashing, and other behaviors that attract the attention of a parent. These communications and the parent's response to them are important aspects of development in infancy, and they will be covered in the next chapter. Here we will focus on biological maturation during infancy and biological factors that can affect development.

The period of time we are discussing here and in the next chapter—the period we call *infancy*—lasts from birth to 18 months. At the age of $1\frac{1}{2}$ years, most children have begun to speak and are able to understand the speech of others. (The word "infancy" comes from a Latin word that means "not speaking.") The advent of speech marks one of the most significant changes in one's life; the stage of life we call infancy, the period of life without language, without the ability to attach symbolic meaning to experiences, is clearly defined and clearly different from later stages of development.

Body Growth in Infancy

Babies vary in size at birth and in rate of growth, and even sizable differences from the average may not be considered abnormal. With that word of caution for readers who may be comparing their children to the norms in this book, we can present a general picture of body growth in infancy. To begin with, the average full-term male baby is about 20 inches tall and weighs $7\frac{1}{2}$ pounds at birth. Females are slightly smaller on both dimensions.

The first year of life is one of remarkable growth. By the age of 1, the average baby is about 28 or 29 inches tall—an increase of over a third—and weighs about 20 pounds, almost tripling its birth weight. But "the body does not grow as a whole and in all directions at once" (76, p. 299). At birth, the head constitutes about one-third of the total body length; it is disproportionately large compared to an adult's head, which is about a tenth of total height (Figure 2.11).

● Figure 2.11 Changes in form and proportion of the human body during fetal and postnatal life. (From C. M. Jackson. Some aspects of form and growth. In W. J. Robbins, S. Brody, A. F. Hogan, C. M. Jackson, and C. W. Green (eds.), *Growth*. New Haven: Yale University Press, 1929, p. 118. By permission.)

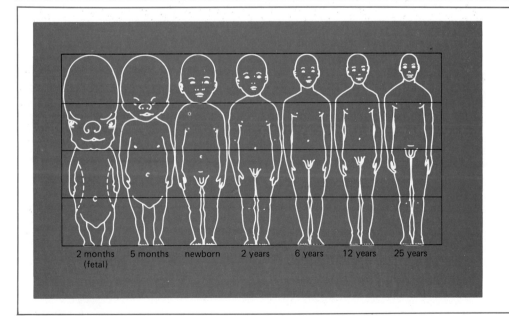

| 2 months (fetal) | 5 months | newborn | 2 years | 6 years | 12 years | 25 years |

The face of the infant is characterized by chubby cheeks, a high and protruding forehead, relatively large eyes, and a small mouth. Some ethologists (who study animals in their natural habitat) believe these characteristics trigger innate tendencies in adults to care for and protect the infant (19), but such notions are difficult to prove.

The bones of the infant are softer than those of an adult. Bones begin as soft cartilage tissue which becomes hardened into bone material by mineral deposits. This process of hardening starts before birth and continues, in the case of some bones, until late adolescence. The result is that the bones of the infant are pliable, more susceptible to deformity than those of older children, but less subject to breakage.

The newborn child has all the muscle fibers he or she will ever have, but the muscles are, of course, smaller than they will be. There is continuous growth in muscle length, breadth, and thickness until, in adulthood, the weight of the muscles is about 40 times what it was at birth (76).

There are a number of consistent sex differences in body growth. The average male has a greater proportion of muscle tissue than the average female, at infancy and at all other ages (24, 25). Females develop at a faster rate. One of the most intriguing sex differences is that physical growth among girls is less variable than among boys. For example, if we choose a particular aspect of growth, say the number of teeth at age 2, and examine a thousand children of each sex, there would be more boys with many teeth and more boys with few teeth; the number of teeth among girls would not vary as much (26). In addition, the growth of girls is more stable. The rate of skeletal development in a 2-year-old girl is a better predictor of her future rate of skeletal development than it is in a 2-year-old boy (1).

There is less variability and more stability among girls in intellectual development as well as in physical development. For example, if we know a 3-year-old girl's vocabulary, we are in a fairly good position to predict the number of words she will be able to use fluently when she is an adult; such predictions are less accurate with boys. Why do these sex differences exist? Is there some biological explanation why the course of development, both physical and intellectual, is more regular among females? Is the parallel between physical and intellectual development significant or merely a coincidence? As yet we do not know the answers to these questions.

The Newborn Baby: Initial Equipment

The newborn human is remarkably capable, at least compared to the newborn of some other mammals. Dogs, for example, are blind and deaf at birth. Human babies can see, hear, and smell, and they are sensitive to pain and touch. From the moment they are born, they are biologically ready to experience most of the basic sensations of their species. The only sense that may not be functioning at birth is taste, but it develops rather quickly after birth.

With most of the infant's sensory apparatus operating, many psychologists have assumed, with William James, that the world of the baby is "a blooming, buzzing confusion." The stimuli impinge but do not form organized percepts, which requires learning. Recent research on attention, however, suggests that the infant's world may actually be quieter than our own. Humans typically attend to one sensory "channel" at a time. When we are listening intently to a bird's song, we may not feel a touch, smell a flower, or see a deer. It is possible, therefore, that the child may not hear sounds around him when he is watching his mother; a baby focused on his hunger pangs may not feel his mother's touch.

On the behavioral side, the newborn comes equipped with a variety of reflexes, many of which are quite complex (Table 2.4). A 2-hour-old baby can follow a moving light with his eyes if the speed of the light is just right; his pupils dilate in darkness and constrict in light. The ability to suck and swallow has obvious survival advantages for the newborn and is present at birth. If you touch an infant's cheek on the corner of his mouth, he will turn in that direction; this is called a "rooting" reflex, and, along with sucking and swallowing, it makes breastfeeding a fairly integrated behavior pattern (Figure 2.12). Newborns can cough, sneeze, and vomit, to rid themselves of irritants. They can flex and extend their limbs, lift their chins from a prone position, and grasp an object placed in their palms (15) (see Figure 2.13).

Some reflexes have no obvious practical value for the newborn but tell in-

● Table 2.4　Reflexes of the newborn

Effective stimulus	Reflex
Tap upper lips sharply	Lips protrude
Tap bridge of nose	Eyes close tightly
Bright light suddenly shown to eyes	Closure of eyelids
Clap hands about 18 inches from infant's head	Closure of eyelids
Touch cornea with light piece of cotton	Eyes close
With baby held on back turn face slowly to right side	Jaw and right arm on side of face extended out; the left arm flexes
Extend forearms at elbow	Arms flex briskly
Put fingers into infant's hand and press his palms	Infant's fingers flex and enclose finger
Press thumbs against the ball of infant's feet	Toes flex
Scratch sole of foot starting from toes towards the heels	Big toe bends upward and small toes spread
Prick soles of feet with pin	Infant's knee and foot flex
Tickle area at corner of mouth	Head turns toward side of stimulation
Put index finger into mouth	Sucks
Hold infant in air, stomach down	Infant attempts to lift head and extends legs

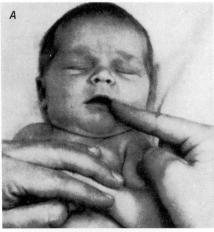
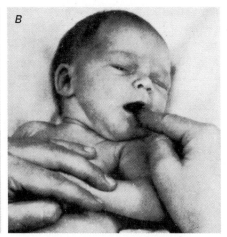
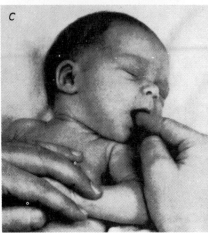

● Figure 2.12   The rooting reflex. *A.* Stimulation. The examiner tickles the side of the infant's mouth with a finger. *B.* Head turning. The infant turns his head in the direction of the finger. *C.* Grasping with the mouth. The infant tries to suck the stimulating finger. (From H. Prechtl and D. Beintema. The neurological examination of the fullterm newborn infant. *Little Club Clinics in Developmental Medicine,* 1964, *12,* 31. London: Spastics Society Medical Information Unit and William Heinemann Medical Books, Ltd. By permission.)

teresting tales about the development of his nervous system. In response to a sudden change in head position, a newborn exhibits the *Moro reflex:* The infant throws his arms out to the side and extends his fingers, then brings his arms and hands back to the midline, as if he were embracing someone (Figure 2.14). The Moro reflex begins to vanish when the child is 3 or 4 months old, and by 6 months it is difficult to elicit. Why does the Moro reflex disappear? Many psychologists believe the reflex is controlled by the brain stem, a part of the brain which is responsible for a number of basic biological functions like breathing. The reflex cannot be elicited in a normal adult because the cerebral cortex, the most "advanced" portion of the brain, inhibits the processes in the brain stem which are responsible for the reflex. According to this view, the cortex of the newborn is not fully functioning, and only gradually, over a period of months, gains normal control over brain-stem activities. Thus the presence of the Moro

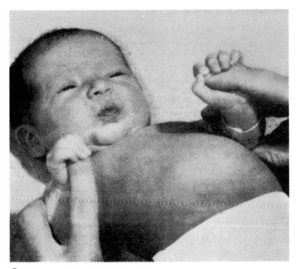

Figure 2.13 Testing the grasping reflex. The examiner presses a finger into the infant's palms and the infant's fingers flex around the examiner's finger. (From H. Prechtl and D. Beinmann. The neurological examination of the fullterm newborn infant. *Little Club Clinics in Developmental Medicine*, 1964, *12*, 35. London: Spastics Society Medical Information Unit and William Heinemann Medical Books, Ltd. By permission.)

reflex in newborns and its gradual disappearance indicate the developmental state of the infant's brain; if a 10-month-old was still showing the reflex, his doctor would have cause for alarm, for it would suggest a malfunction in his central nervous system.

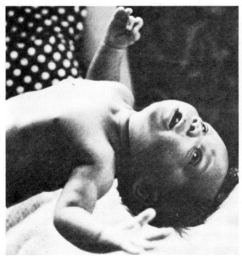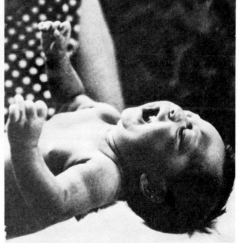

Figure 2.14 The Moro reflex.

Maturation in Infants

In the first year and a half of life, the child develops in many ways, and behavior becomes more coordinated and intentional.

Some of the behavior patterns that emerge in infancy are a result of learning, and some a result of *maturation*. Maturation implies that behaviors will appear when the child is ready for them; no special training or experience is necessary, just a reasonably normal environment.

Sensory Capacities

At birth infants can see fairly well. They can see light, dark, and color, and their visual acuity—visual "sharpness," as measured by common eye charts—is quite good. By observing the reflexive responses of day-old infants to patterned stimuli, one group of scientists estimated the newborn's acuity as 20/150, which means that a newborn can distinguish at 20 feet what the normal adult can see at 150 feet (13). The *pupillary reflex*—opening or closing of the pupil in response to changing illumination—is present but somewhat sluggish at birth; it is perfected in the first few days (56, 57).

Infants as young as a few days are capable of *visual pursuit*, following moving lights with their eyes. The two eyes do not consistently focus or *converge* on the same stimulus, however, until the child is 7 or 8 weeks old (80). Maturation of the ability to *accommodate* to the distance of a stimulus from the eyes takes about four months. We turn our eyes in for near objects—looking rather cross-eyed if the stimulus is very close—and out for distant objects; infants less than 2 months old appear to have a relatively fixed focus at about 8–9 inches from the face (33).

Infants can hear well at birth. For some reason not well-understood, low-frequency tones are calming, while high frequencies (like a whistle) seem to startle infants, producing an alert, "What's happening?" reaction (21). These built-in responses to different sounds are similar to those in other animals, where high-pitched cries indicate danger and low murmurings accompany feeding and pleasant social interaction such as grooming.

Infants show an equally curious differential reaction to sounds with different *rise times*. Rise time is the time required for a tone to reach maximum loudness. In one study (42), rise times were varied from "immediate" to two seconds. The fast rise times produced closing of the eyes, as if the startled infants were defending themselves, while the slow rise times produced the opposite, opening of the eyes, in the manner of someone wondering about and searching for the source of the sound. Explosions and other fast developing events may be dangerous enough to elicit the defensive behavior, but why the eye opening to slow rise times? "Something's coming (slowly)?"

Another quality of sound known to affect infants from birth is its *rhythmicity*. Rhythmic sounds have a calming effect, especially if they are also low in frequency. Perhaps this is why parents often quiet their distressed infants by repeating some word—"There, there . . ."—in a low voice.

Psychologists, members of a species that depends mostly on vision and hearing to get around, study the other senses perhaps less than they should. We know that the newborn is capable of responding to odors, because he or she will turn away from a particularly objectionable smell like ammonia (17). But it is hard to detect discrimination among less distinctive aromas. Pain sensitivity, as defined by a withdrawal response to a pin prick, appears to be present at birth, but the sense is initially dull, becoming considerably sharper by the end of the first week of life (64, 65). As we shall see later, pain plays a role in the child's acquisition of fear; constitutional differences in the sensitivity to pain may be one factor in determining differences in fearfulness in older children.

Response Capabilities

Sitting, crawling, and standing are good examples of behaviors that emerge as a result of maturation, that is, as a consequence of the increased complexity of the central nervous system and the growth of bones and muscles. Given the general opportunity to use limbs and body, every normal child will exhibit these behaviors at roughly the same time. No special training is necessary, although the behaviors become better coordinated, more precise, and more accurate with practice.

Locomotion   A child must crawl before she creeps, and creep before she walks. There are great individual differences in the ages at which infants reach the various stages of locomotion (moving about), but practically all infants go through the same sequence. The first stage, thrusting one knee forward beside the body, appeared by 28 weeks in about half of the infants in one study (4). By 34 weeks, half of the children were crawling, that is, moving with their stomachs on the floor; the muscles of the trunk, arms, and legs were not yet strong enough to support the body. Creeping on hands and knees began, on the average, at 40 weeks.

Walking depends on a series of preliminary achievements. The average child can stand if holding onto furniture at 42 weeks; walk while being held at 45 weeks; pull herself up to a standing position at 47 weeks. Ten weeks into her second year, she can stand alone, and two weeks later, she walks by herself (66) (see Figure 2.15).

Although these behaviors typically develop without any teaching by adults, severe restriction of the opportunity to practice new skills may retard their appearance or delay the development of more complex behaviors. Of three institutions studied in Iran (14), only one provided infants with opportunities to sit or to play in a prone position; these children walked at an earlier age than those in the more restricted environments. There is also some evidence that while early practice in walking is not necessary, it may help (82). Babies at 1 week have a

● Figure 2.15   The development of posture and locomotion in infants. (From *The First Two Years* by Mary M. Shirley. Institute of Child Welfare Monograph No. 7. Minneapolis: University of Minnesota Press. Copyright © 1933, renewed 1961 by the University of Minnesota. By permission.)

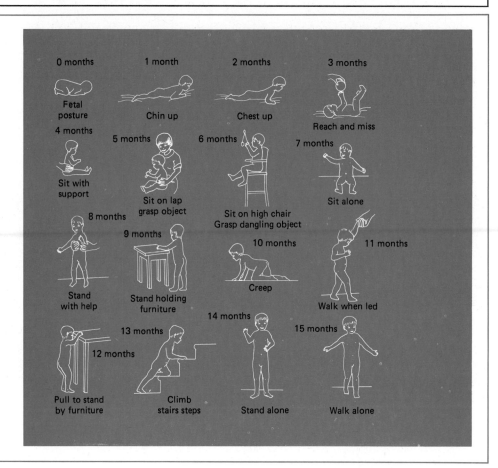

"walking reflex"—they make very primitive walking movements if held by the arms with their feet on the floor or a table. This reflex usually fades at about 2 months. A group of mothers spent 12 minutes a day letting their babies "walk," from 2 to 8 weeks of age. These infants began to walk alone $2\frac{1}{2}$ months earlier than children without the earlier special experience.

While many parents are eager to see their children develop faster than average, many children mature slower than average. Unless the discrepancies are quite large or there are other signs of abnormal physical development, such slowness should be of no concern. Many parents are afraid that even slightly

delayed physical maturation during infancy means slow intellectual development later, but within the normal range, there is no correlation between the two variables.

Reaching and grasping   If you place an attractive object in sight of a 1-month-old baby, she will stare at it but make no attempt to grab it. By $2\frac{1}{2}$ months, she begins to swipe at objects, but she is invariably far off target. By 4 months, the infant demonstrates a sort of tortured eye–hand coordination in which she puts her hand in the vicinity of the object and then alternates her glance between hand and object, gradually moving the hand closer; perhaps she will manage to make contact. The aim of the 5-month-old infant is nearly perfect. The response psychologists call this *visually directed reaching*.

The development of this response can be altered by impoverished or enriched environments. Infants raised in unstimulating institutions with few objects suitable for reaching are typically retarded in this skill. Infants provided with attractive mobiles and other toys develop visually directly reaching up to a month early (79).

Although providing an opportunity to display and polish a response that the child is mature enough to make can be beneficial, "enriching the environment" may not always be wise. The child must be ready for the more complex situation. At 3 or 4 months of age, the infant normally studies and swipes at attractive objects, and thus providing her with some will be stimulating. But babies of 5 weeks or less are more irritable and fussy in such an enriched environment than babies without attractive mobiles; the stimuli seem to be distressing to infants of this age. It is possible that a stimulus to which the baby cannot yet respond is distressing and that she is better off without it. Consider, as an analogy, a bicycle too big for her. The early frustrations may result in a dislike for cycling when she is physically more mature.

Basic Needs

It sometimes seems to busy parents that a baby is nothing but a collection of needs. It needs to be fed and protected, and it doesn't even have the decency to control its own bowel movements. These needs seem especially prominent in infancy because the child is unable to fill many of his or her needs without the aid of an older person. We will consider one need, for sleep, that is more or less self-regulatory and another, for food, that typically requires parental help. Both are needs that motivate adult behavior too, of course, although in a slightly different manner.

Sleep   Why do humans sleep? Psychologists do not have a satisfactory answer to this question. "There is little significant change in energy consumption by the body between quiet waking and sleep," asserts one noted physiological psychologist (77, p. 413). "We have yet to discover any metabolic poisons or toxins that require the occurrence of sleep to be dissipated. In short, the reasons for sleep to occur at all and to seem necessary remain a complete mystery."

Whatever its function, infants engage in more sleep than do adults. Newborns sleep about 80 percent of the time, while 1-year-olds sleep about 50 percent. The rhythms and depth of sleep also change rapidly during the first year. For the first three or four weeks, the average infant takes seven or eight naps a day. By six weeks, the number of sleep periods is down to two–four. By 28 weeks, most children will sleep through the night (thereby giving their parents a well-deserved rest of their own). From then on, until they reach 1 year of age, most infants require only two or three daytime naps (29).

Not only is the quantity of sleep in infants different from that in adults, the quality differs too. There are at least two different kinds of sleep. In one, considered a deep sleep, the sleeper exhibits rapid eye movements (REM); in the other, lighter sleep, no REM are observed. Infants spend from 30 to 50 percent of their sleep time in the REM sleep, while this percentage rarely exceeds 25 percent in adults; even within the 18 months of infancy there is a clear decrease in the amount of REM sleep (60) (see Figure 2.16). No one knows why this is so. In adults, REM sleep is associated with dreaming, but psychologists find it hard to imagine that the infant is dreaming. Dreaming? Of what? In what forms? Another mystery of sleep.

Hunger and thirst   The infant is notable for voracious consumption of a liquid food called milk. Hence it is difficult to distinguish hunger from thirst in the infant, and most often the two are discussed together. These needs must be satisfied by someone other than the infant; the infant needs help. If these needs are not satisfied quickly, tension mounts and results in a great deal of bodily activity. For this reason, hunger and thirst play an important role in an infant's earliest learning experiences, as we will see in Chapter 3.

The feeding patterns of American infants on "demand schedules" (feeding whenever hungry) indicate that newborns, on the average, like seven or eight meals per day. In a month, the number is reduced to five or six. At this time the average infant's food intake per day is between 18 and 25 ounces, rising to 35 ounces when he or she is 6–8 weeks old. Within the next few weeks, the number of feedings is further reduced, but total food intake does not change significantly (29).

In American culture, solid foods are often introduced into the diet when the infant is about 8 weeks of age, and by 20 weeks, cereals and vegetables may be regular items on the menu. By the time the American child is 1 year old, the three-meal regime has at least been introduced and in most cases stabilized.

Individual Differences Among Infants

Thus far we have been considering general developmental milestones in the *average* child. We have mentioned individual differences: Some children walk at

● Figure 2.16 Changes (with age) in amounts of total sleep, REM sleep, and non-REM sleep. (From H. P. Roffwarg, J. N. Muzio, and W. C. Dement. Ontogenic development of the human sleep-dream cycle. *Science*, 1966, *152*, 608. Revised since publication in *Science* by H. P. Roffwarg. By permission of the author.)

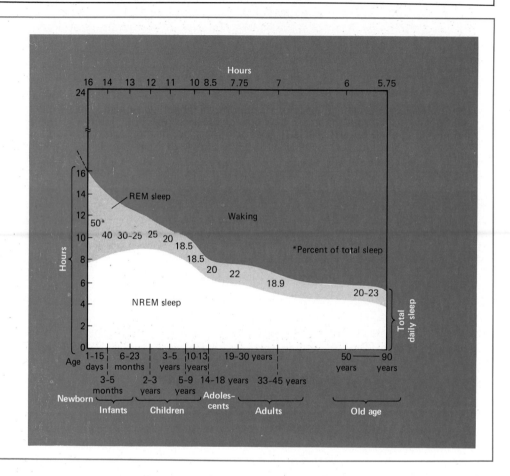

10 months, others at 18. For the most part, these differences are inconsequential; that is, they are unrelated to later differences—in intellectual ability, for example. Some may affect personality development at later stages, but whether they do or not depends on the reaction the characteristic elicits from parents.

One individual difference most parents notice quickly when comparing their child with others (or with an earlier child of their own) is the degree of spontaneous motor activity. Some infants thrash a lot, while others are relatively still and quiet, both awake and during sleep (37, 81). Boys may be slightly more active than girls (45, 74). These early differences in motor activity might influence later development in some cases. An extremely energetic infant might get into more closets and upset more dishes, thereby incurring parental restric-

tions and punishments more often than the less active child. On the other hand, athletic parents might be upset with a placid child, forcing him or her into rough and tumble play that runs counter to the child's basic nature.

Some infants are more irritable than others. They find numerous occasions to cry, whine, and fret, and they are not easily placated. At the other extreme is the imperturbable infant who seems to have an almost infinite tolerance for frustration.

Activity level and irritability are two of many characteristics on which in-

Temperamental quality	Rating	2 Months	6 Months
Activity Level	HIGH	Moves often in sleep. Wriggles when diaper is changed.	Tries to stand in tub and splashes. Bounces in crib. Crawls after dog.
	LOW	Does not move when being dressed or during sleep.	Passive in bath. Plays quietly in crib and falls asleep.
Quality of Mood	POSITIVE	Smacks lips when first tasting new food. Smiles at parents.	Plays and splashes in bath. Smiles at everyone.
	NEGATIVE	Fusses after nursing. Cries when carriage is rocked.	Cries when taken from tub. Cries when given food she does not like.
Approach/Withdrawal	POSITIVE	Smiles and licks washcloth. Has always liked bottle.	Likes new foods. Enjoyed first bath in a large tub. Smiles and gurgles.
	NEGATIVE	Rejected cereal the first time. Cries when strangers appear.	Smiles and babbles at strangers. Plays with new toys immediately.
Rhythmicity	REGULAR	Has been on four-hour feeding schedule since birth. Regular bowel movement.	Is asleep at 6:30 every night. Awakes at 7:00 A.M. Food intake is constant.
	IRREGULAR	Awakes at a different time each morning. Size of feedings varies.	Length of nap varies; so does food intake.
Adaptability	ADAPTIVE	Was passive during first bath; now enjoys bathing. Smiles at nurse.	Used to dislike new foods: now accepts them well.
	NOT ADAPTIVE	Still startled by sudden, sharp noise. Resists diapering.	Does not cooperate with dressing. Fusses and cries when left with sitter.

Table 2.5 Nine dimensions of infant temperament

1 Year	2 Years	5 Years	10 Years
Walks rapidly, eats eagerly. Climbs into everything.	Climbs furniture. Explores. Gets in and out of bed while being put to sleep.	Leaves table often during meals. Always runs.	Plays ball and engages in other sports. Cannot sit still long enough to do homework.
Finishes bottle slowly. Goes to sleep easily. Allows nail-cutting without fussing.	Enjoys quiet play with puzzles. Can listen to records for hours.	Takes a long time to dress. Sits quietly on long automobile rides.	Likes chess and reading. Eats very slowly.
Likes bottle; reaches for it and smiles. Laughs loudly when playing peekaboo.	Plays with sister: laughs and giggles. Smiles when he succeeds in putting shoes on.	Laughs loudly while watching television cartoons. Smiles at everyone.	Enjoys new accomplishments. Laughs when reading a funny passage aloud.
Cries when given injections. Cries when left alone.	Cries and squirms when given haircut. Cries when mother leaves.	Objects to putting boots on. Cries when frustrated.	Cries when he cannot solve a homework problem. Very "weepy" if he does not get enough sleep.
Approaches strangers readily. Sleeps well in new surroundings.	Slept well the first time he stayed overnight at grandparents' house.	Entered school building unhesitatingly. Tries new foods.	Went to camp happily. Loved to ski the first time.
Stiffened when placed on sled. Will not sleep in strange beds.	Avoids strange children in the playground. Whimpers first time at beach. Will not go into water.	Hid behind mother when entering school.	Severely homesick at camp during first days. Does not like new activities.
Naps after lunch each day. Always drinks bottle before bed.	Eats a big lunch each day. Always has a snack before bedtime.	Falls asleep when put to bed. Bowel movement regular.	Eats only at mealtimes. Sleeps the same amount of time each night.
Will not fall asleep for an hour or more. Moves bowels at a different time each day.	Nap time changes day to day. Toilet training is difficult because bowel movement is unpredictable.	Food intake varies: so does time of bowel movement.	Food intake varies. Falls asleep at a different time each night.
Was afraid of toy animals at first, now plays with them happily.	Obeys quickly. Stayed contentedly with grandparents for a week.	Hesitated to go to nursery school at first; now goes eagerly. Slept well on camping trip.	Likes camp, although homesick during first days. Learns enthusiastically.
Continues to reject new foods each time they are offered.	Cries and screams each time hair is cut. Disobeys persistently.	Has to be hand led into classroom each day. Bounces on bed in spite of spankings.	Does not adjust well to new school or new teacher; comes home late for dinner even when punished.

(Continued on page 80)

Temperamental quality	Rating	2 Months	6 Months
Threshold of Responsiveness	LOW	Stops sucking on bottle when approached.	Refuses fruit he likes when vitamins are added. Hides head from bright lights.
	HIGH	Is not startled by loud noises. Takes bottle and breast equally well.	Eats everything. Does not object to diapers being wet or soiled.
Intensity of Reaction	INTENSE	Cries when diapers are wet. Rejects food vigorously when satisfied.	Cries loudly at the sound of thunder. Makes sucking movements when vitamins are administered.
	MILD	Does not cry when diapers are wet. Whimpers instead of crying when hungry.	Does not kick often in tub. Does not smile. Screams and kicks when temperature is taken.
Distractibility	DISTRACTIBLE	Will stop crying for food if rocked. Stops fussing if given pacifier when diaper is being changed.	Stops crying when mother sings. Will remain still while clothing is changed if given a toy.
	NOT DISTRACTIBLE	Will not stop crying when diaper is changed. Fusses after eating, even if rocked.	Stops crying only after dressing is finished. Cries until given bottle.
Attention Span and Persistence	LONG	If soiled, continues to cry until changed. Repeatedly rejects water if he wants milk.	Watches toy mobile over crib intently. "Coos" frequently.
	SHORT	Cries when awakened but stops almost immediately. Objects only mildly if cereal precedes bottle.	Sucks pacifier for only a few minutes and spits it out.

1 Year	2 Years	5 Years	10 Years
Spits out food he does not like. Giggles when tickled.	Runs to door when father comes home. Must always be tucked tightly into bed.	Always notices when mother puts new dress on for first time. Refuses milk if it is not ice-cold.	Rejects fatty foods. Adjusts shower until water is at exactly the right temperature.
Eats food he likes even if mixed with disliked food. Can be left easily with strangers.	Can be left with anyone. Falls to sleep easily on either back or stomach.	Does not hear loud, sudden noises when reading. Does not object to injections.	Never complains when sick. Eats all foods.
Laughs hard when father plays roughly. Screamed and kicked when temperature was taken.	Yells if he feels excitement or delight. Cries loudly if a toy is taken away.	Rushes to greet father. Gets hiccups from laughing hard.	Tears up an entire page of homework if one mistake is made. Slams door of room when teased by younger brother.
Does not fuss much when clothing is pulled on over head.	When another child hit her, she looked surprised, did not hit back.	Drops eyes and remains silent when given a firm parental "No." Does not laugh much.	When a mistake is made in a model airplane, corrects it quietly. Does not comment when reprimanded.
Cries when face is washed unless it is made into a game.	Will stop tantrum if another activity is suggested.	Can be coaxed out of forbidden activity by being led into something else.	Needs absolute silence for homework. Has a hard time choosing a shirt in a store because they all appeal to him.
Cries when toy is taken away and rejects substitute.	Screams if refused some desired object. Ignores mother's calling.	Seems not to hear if involved in favorite activity. Cries for a long time when hurt.	Can read a book while television set is at high volume. Does chores on schedule.
Plays by self in playpen for more than an hour. Listens to singing for long periods.	Works on a puzzle until it is completed. Watches when shown how to do something.	Practiced riding a two-wheeled bicycle for hours until he mastered it. Spent over an hour reading a book.	Reads for two hours before sleeping. Does homework carefully.
Loses interest in a toy after a few minutes. Gives up easily if she falls while trying to walk.	Gives up easily if a toy is hard to use. Asks for help immediately if undressing becomes difficult.	Still cannot tie his shoes because he gives up when he is not successful. Fidgets when parents read to him.	Gets up frequently from homework for a snack. Never finishes a book.

fants can differ. In the view of one group of investigators (75), there are at least nine dimensions of temperament that can be identified in infants and which continue to be reflected in behavior as the child grows older. These traits and their manifestations at various ages are summarized in Table 2.5; what we have been calling irritability is most closely aligned with the "quality-of-mood" dimension.

Using these nine dimensions to rate the personalities of 141 children in New York City, psychologists found most children fell into one of three categories: the "easy child," the "difficult child," or the "slow to warm up" child (**75**). The easy children—about 40 percent of the total—were cheerful, had regular sleep patterns, approached new situations with interest, and adapted readily to changes in the environment. The difficult child—about 10 percent of the group—is very irregular in sleep and feeding, reacts intensely to frustration, is generally negative in mood, and withdraws passively from unusual events or people. Difficult children were likely to develop behavioral problems requiring psychiatric attention by the preschool years.

The third group of children (15 percent) were called "slow to warm up." These children are relatively inactive and quiet, likely to withdraw, at least initially, in the presence of novel objects or people. If allowed to adapt to the environment at their own pace, they can function quite well. A demanding parent, however, might push them into new situations too often or too quickly; the child's natural tendency to withdraw in such situations might result in a lonely child with few interests.

Many psychologists believe that temperamental traits such as the ones described are partially the result of biological factors. But the reaction of people to the infant's natural tendencies is important in determining the consequences of a temperamental quality. In the words of the authors of the New York study, "The paramount conclusion from our studies is that the debate over the relative importance of nature and nurture only confuses the issue. What is important is the interaction between the two—between the child's own characteristics and his environment. If the two influences are harmonized, one can expect healthy development of the child; if they are dissonant, behavioral problems are almost sure to ensue (75, p. 109)."

The above quotation is perhaps a good note on which to end a chapter on "nature." Biological influences do not end with infancy, of course; genetic, prenatal, and postnatal effects continue to interact with social, environmental factors, but later intellectual and personality development of the child involves the benefits of experience to a greater degree. In the next chapter, we begin our consideration of human "nurture" and learning during infancy.

SUMMARY

Behavior is a joint product of heredity and environment. Genetic influences are determined by 23 chromosomes from the father's sperm and an equal number from the mother's ovum (egg). Chromosomes are composed of genes, and genes, in turn, contain DNA. To estimate the contribution of heredity to a physical or behavioral trait, psychologists often compare closely related people (e.g., identical twins) with less genetically similar people (fraternal twins). Sex-linked genes are the basis of genetic differences between men and women. They account for the fact that many more men than women are color blind, but do they explain, even in part, differences in achievement motivation? A touchy and difficult question.

Some human characteristics and behavior patterns depend heavily upon heredity. Physical features and certain types of mental retardation (e.g., Down's syndrome) have a fairly clear genetic basis, but mental disorders like schizophrenia, personality traits like introversion–extraversion, and mental abilities like intelligence are more complex and the evidence is not as definitive.

There are a number of (nongenetic) biological influences during pregnancy and childbirth that affect the "equipment" and abilities with which the child begins life. If the mother is very young or very old, if her diet is particularly poor, if she takes certain drugs, if she is exposed to irradiation or certain diseases, or if her Rh factor is incompatible with that of the baby, there is a slightly increased risk of various complications ranging from minor and temporary difficulties to major and severe handicaps. At birth, oxygen deprivation and prematurity present problems, many of which have been lessened in recent years by medical advances.

After birth, the child grows quickly. Some of the behaviors that emerge are the result of maturation and require no special training or experience. Examples are crawling, creeping and walking, and reaching and grasping. Although normal infants vary considerably in the ages at which they exhibit these behaviors, the sequence of development is typically uniform—first crawling, then creeping, then walking, for example. Infants can see and hear fairly well at birth, although some improvement occurs in the first year. For some reason, infants find low-frequency, rhythmic sounds to be calming. Newborns sleep a lot, around 80 percent of the time, and their sleep is apparently deeper than that of adults. In the first six months or so, infants wake in the night for a feeding, but by the end of the first year, both feeding and sleeping schedules have stabilized into a more nearly adult pattern.

Individual differences among infants include degree of activity, irritability, and a number of other characteristics; taken together, these traits define, roughly, three "types" of infants. "Easy children" are cheerful, adaptive and interested in new situations. "Difficult children" are negative in mood, withdraw from new situations, and react intensely to frustration. Children who are "slow to warm up" are relatively passive. If allowed to adapt to novel situations at their own pace, they function quite well, but if pressed, they might withdraw. Their temperament, which may have a biological basis, interacts with their environment. If pushed too much they might withdraw; if not pushed, they may be less likely to do so. Whether the interaction between nature and nurture is harmonious or discordant is generally more important than debates on the relative influence of heredity and environment.

References

1. Acheson, R. M. Maturation of the skeleton. In F. Falkner (Ed.), **Human development.** Philadelphia: Saunders: 1966. Pp. 465–502.

2. Alden, E. R., Mandelkorn, T., Woodrum, D. E., Wennberg, R. P., Parks, C. R., & Hodson, W. A. Morbidity and mortality of infants weighing less than 1000 grams in an intensive care nursery. **Pediatrics,** 1972, **50,** 40–49.

3. Allport, G. **Personality: A psychological interpretation.** New York: Holt, Rinehart & Winston, 1937.

4. Ames, L. B. The sequential patterning of prone progression in the human infant. **Genetic Psychology Monographs,** 1937, **19,** 409–460.

5. Apgan, V., & Beck, J. **Is my baby all right?** New York: Pocket Books, 1974.

6. Brecher, E. M., & the editors of Consumer Reports. **Licit and illicit drugs.** Boston: Little Brown, 1972.

7. Carmichael, L. The onset and early development of behavior. In L. Carmichael (Ed.), **Manual of child psychology.** (2nd ed.) New York: Wiley, 1954.

8. Cattell, R. B., Stice, G. F., & Kristy N. F. A first approximation to nature-nurture ratios for eleven primary personality factors in objective tests. **Journal of Abnormal Social Psychology,** 1957, **54,** 143–159.

9. Clinical Psychiatry News, 1977, **5,** No. 5, 1, 40.

10. Corah, N. L., Anthony, E. J., Painter, P., Stern, J. A., & Thurston, D. Effects of perinatal anoxia after 7 years. **Psychological Monographs,** 1965, **79,** 1–34.

11. Corner, G. W. **Ourselves unborn: An embryologist's essay on man.** New Haven: Yale University Press, 1944.

12. Davison, A. N., & Dobbing, J. Myelination as a vulnerable period in brain development. **British Medical Bulletin,** 1966, **22,** 40–44.

13. Dayton, G. O., Jones, M. H., Aiu, P., Rawson, R. H., Steele, B., & Rose, M. Developmental study of coordinated eye movements in the human infant: I. Visual acuity in the newborn human: A study based on induced optokinetic nystagmus recorded by electro-oculography. **Archives of Opthamology,** 1964, **71,** 865–870.

14. Dennis, W. Causes of retardation among institutional children: Iran. **Journal of Genetic Psychology,** 1960, **96,** 47–59.

15. Desmond, M. M., Franklin, R. R., Vallbona, C., Hilt, R. H., Plumb, R., Arnold, H., & Watts, J. The clinicial behavior of the newly born: I. **Journal of Pediatrics,** 1963, **62,** 307–325.

16. Dippel, A. L. The relationship of congenital syphilis to abortion and miscarriage, and the mechanisms of intrauterine protection. **American Journal of Obstetrics and Gynecology,** 1944, **47,** 369–379.

17. Disher, D. R. The reactions of newborn infants to chemical stimuli administered nasally. **Ohio State University Studies in Control Psychology,** 1934(12), 1–52.

18. Drillien, C. M., & Ellis, R. W. B. **The growth and development of the prematurely born infant.** Baltimore: Williams & Wilkins, 1964.

19. Eibl-Eibesfeldt, I. **Love and hate.** New York: Holt, Rinehart & Winston, 1972.

20. Eisenberg, L. The intervention of biological and experiental factors in schizophrenia. In D. Rosenthal & S. Ketty (Eds.), **The transmission of schizophrenia.** London: Pergamon, 1968. Pp. 403–412.

21. Eisenberg, R. B., Griffin, E. J., Coursin, D. B., & Hunter, M. A. Auditory behavior in the neonate. **Journal of Speech and Hearing Research,** 1964, **7,** 245–269.

22. Ernhart, C. B., Graham, F. K., & Thurston, D. Relationship of neonatal apnea to development at three years. **Archives of Neurology,** 1960, **2,** 504–510.

23. Freedman, D. An ethological approach to the genetic study of human behavior. In S. G. Vandenberg (Ed.), **Methods and goals in human behavior genetics.** New York: Academic Press, 1965. Pp. 141–161.

24. Garn, S. M. Roentgenogrammetric determinations of body composition. **Human Biology,** 1957, **29,** 337–353.

25. Garn, S. M. Fat, body size, and growth in the new born. **Human Biology,** 1958, **30,** 265–280.

26. Garn, S. M., & Rohmann, C. G., Variability in the order of ossification of the boney centers of the hand and wrist. **American Journal of Physical Anthropology,** 1960, **18,** 219–229.

27. Gesell, A. **The embryology of behavior.** New York: Harper & Row, 1945.

28. Gesell, A. & Amatruda, C. S. **Developmental diagnosis: Normal and abnormal child development.** New York: Hoeber, 1941.

29. Gesell, A., Halverson, H. M., Thompson, H., Ilg, F. L., Costner, B. M., Ames, L. B., & Amatruda, C. S. **The first five years of life: A guide to the study of the preschool child.** New York: Harper & Row, 1940.

30. Goodpasture, E. W. Virus infection of the mammalian fetus. **Science,** 1942, **95,** 391–396.

31. Gottesman, I. I., & Shield, J. Genetic theorizing and schizophrenia. **British Journal of Psychiatry,** 1973, **122,** 15–30.

32. Greenberg, M., Pelliteri, O., & Barton, J. Frequency of defects in infants whose mothers had rubella during pregnancy. **Journal of the American Medical Association,** 1957, **165,** 675–678.

33. Haynes, H., White, B. L., & Held, R. Visual accommodation in human infants. **Science,** 1965, **148,** 528–530.

34. Hirsch, J. Behavior genetic analysis. New York: McGraw-Hill, 1967.

35. Honzik, M. P. Developmental studies of parent-child resemblance in intelligence. **Child Development,** 1957, **28,** 215–228.

36. Horner, F. A., & Streamer, C. W. Phenylketonuria treated from earliest infancy. **American Journal of Diseases of Children,** 1959, **97,** 345–347.

37. Irwin, O. C. The amount and nature of activities of newborn infants under constant external stimulating conditions during the first ten days of life. **Genetic Psychology Monographs,** 1930, **8,** 1–92.

38. Jensen, A. R. How much can we boost IQ and scholastic achievement? **Harvard Educational Review,** 1969, **39,** 1–123.

39. Jones, K. L., & Smith, D. W. Recognition of the fetal alcohol syndrome in early infancy. **Lancet,** 1973, **2,** 999.

40. Jones, K. L., Smith, D. W., Ulleland, C. N., & Streissguth, A. P. Pattern of malformation in offspring of chronic alcoholic mothers. **Lancet,** 1973, **1,** 1267.

41. Kallmann, F. H. **Heredity in health and mental disorder.** New York: Norton, 1953.

42. Kearsley, R. B. **The newborn's response to auditory stimulation.** Unpublished doctoral dissertation, Harvard University, 1972.

43. Kessler, S. Psychiatric genetics. In D. A. Hamburg and H. Keith, H. Brodie (Eds.), **American handbook of psychiatry, Vol. VI: New psychiatric frontiers.** New York: Basic Books, 1975. Pp. 352–384.

44. Klaus, M. H., & Fanaroff, A. A. **Care of the high-risk neonate.** Philadelphia: Saunders, 1973.

45. Knop, C. A. The dynamics of newly born babies. **Journal of Pediatrics,** 1946, **29,** 721–728.

46. Landis, C., & Bolles, M. M. **Textbook of abnormal psychology.** New York: Macmillan, 1947.

47. Lubchenco, L. O. **The high risk infant.** Philadelphia: W. B. Saunders Company, 1976.

48. Maccoby, E. E., & Jacklin, C. N. **The psychology of sex differences.** Stanford: Stanford University Press, 1974.

49. MacMahon, B., & Feldman, J. J. Infant mortality rates and socio-economic factors. National Center for Health Statistics, United States Public Health Service, 1972.

50. McGraw, M. B. Motivation of behavior. In L. Carmichael (Ed.), **Manual of child psychology.** New York: Wiley, 1946. Pp. 332–369.

51. Montagu, M. F. A. Constitutional and prenatal factors in infant and child health. In M. J. E. Senn (Ed.), **Symposium on the healthy personality.** New York: Josiah Macy, Jr. Foundation, 1950, Pp. 148–175.

52. Murphy, D. P. **Congenital malformation.** (2nd ed.) Philadelphia: University of Pennsylvania Press, 1947.

53. Murphy, D. P. The outcome of 625 pregnancies in women subjected to pelvic radium roentgen irradiation. **American Journal of Obstetrics and Gynecology,** 1929, **18,** 179–187.

54. New York Times, May 31, 1977.

55. Plummer, G. Anomalies occurring in children exposed in utero to the atomic bomb in Hiroshima. **Pediatrics,** 1952, **10,** 687.

56. Pratt, K. C. The effects of repeated visual stimulation on the activity of newborn infants. **Journal of Genetic Psychology,** 1934, **44,** 117–126.

57. Pratt, K. C. The neonate. In L. Carmichael (Ed.), **Manual of child psychology.** (2nd ed.) New York: Wiley, 1954. Pp. 215–291.

58. Rand, W., Sweeney, M., & Vincent, E. L. **Growth and development of the growing child.** Philadelphia: Saunders, 1946.

59. Rawlings, G., Stewart, A., Reynolds, E. O., & Strang, L. B. Changing prognosis for infants of very low birth weight. **Lancet,** 1971, **1,** 516–519.

60. Roffwarg, H. P., Muzio, J. N., & Dement, W. C. Ontogenetic development of the human sleep-dream cycle. **Science,** 1966, **152,** 604–619.

61. Rosenthal, D. **Genetic theory and abnormal behavior.** New York: McGraw-Hill, 1970.

62. Scarr, S. Genetic factors in activity motivation. **Child Development,** 1966, **37,** 663–673.

63. Scarr, S. Social introversion as a heritable response. **Child Development,** 1969, **40,** 823–832.

64. Sherman, M., & Sherman, I. C. Sensorimotor responses in infants. **Journal of Comparative Psychology,** 1925, **5,** 53–68.

65. Sherman, M., Sherman, I. C., & Flory, C. D. Infant behavior. **Comparative Psychology Monographs,** 1936, **12**(4).

66. Shirley, M. M. The first two years: A study of twenty-five babies. Vol. I. Postural and locomotor development. **Institute of Child Welfare Monographs,** Ser. No. 6. Minneapolis: University of Minnesota Press, 1933.

67. Sontag, L. W. The significance of fetal environmental differences. **American Journal of Obstetrics and Gynecology,** 1941, **42,** 996–1003.

68. Sontag, L. W. War and fetal maternal relationship. **Marriage and Family Living,** 1944, **6,** 1–5.

69. Sontag, L. W., & Wallace, R. F. The effect of cigarette smoking during pregnancy upon the fetal heart rate. **American Journal of Obstetrics and Gynecology,** 1935, **29,** 3–8.

70. Special report: Schizophrenia, 1976. **Schizophrenia Bulletin,** 1976, **2,** 509–565. (U.S. Department of Health, Education, and Welfare, Alcohol, Drug Abuse, and Mental Health Administration, 1976)

71. Stechler, G. Newborn attention as affected by medication during labor. **Science,** 1964, **144,** 315–317.

72. Steele, B. F., & Pollock, C. B. A psychiatric study of parents who abuse infants and small children. In R. E. Helfer and H. Kempe (Eds.), **The battered child.** Chicago: University of Chicago Press, 1968. Pp. 103–147.

73. Stern, C. **Principles of human genetics.** (2nd ed.) San Francisco: Freeman, 1960.

74. Terman, L. M., & Tyler, L. E. Psychological sex differences. In L. Carmichael (Ed.), **Manual of child psychology.** (2nd ed.) New York: Wiley, 1954.

75. Thomas, A., Chess, S., & Birch, H. G. The origin of personality. **Scientific American,** 1970, **223,** 102–109. Reprinted by permission.

76. Thompson, H. Physical growth. In L. Carmichael (Ed.), **Manual of child psychology.** (2nd ed.). New York: Wiley, 1954.

77. Thompson, R. F. **Introduction to physiological psychology.** New York: Harper & Row, 1975.

78. Tompkins, W. T. The clinical significance of nutritional deficiencies in pregnancy. **Bulletin of the New York Academy of Medicine,** 1948, **24,** 376–388.

79. White, B. L., & Held, R. Plasticity of sensory motor development. In J. F. Rosenblith & W. Allinsmith (Eds.), **Readings in child development and educational psychology.** (2nd ed.) Boston: Allyn and Bacon, 1966.

80. Wickelgren, L. W. The ocular response of human newborns to intermittent visual movement. **Journal of Experimental Child Psychology,** 1969, **8,** 469–482.

81. Wolff, P. H. Observations on newborn infants. **Psychosomatic Medicine,** 1959, **21,** 110–118.

82. Zelazo, N. A., Zelazo, P. R., & Kolb, S. Walking in the newborn. **Science,** 1972, **176,** 314–315.

CHAPTER 3
Cognitive and Social Development in Infancy

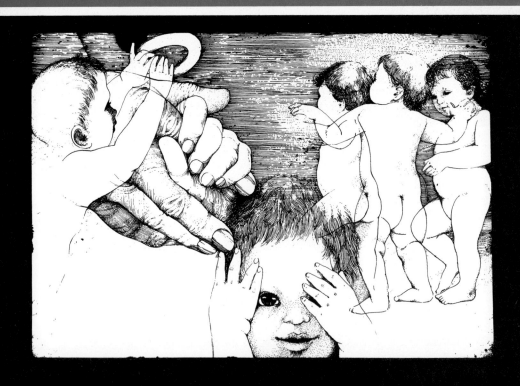

The infant's cognitive and social development is the focus of this chapter. We will consider basic aspects of perceptual development—what aspects of the environment attract the infant's attention, what ideas develop from new experience, and why infants sometimes interrupt their play to watch a TV commercial, even though they do not understand one word of its message.

As the infant develops perceptual and intellectual skills, she also begins her social development. As she interacts with her mother, father, brothers, and sisters, she develops attachments to these people. She becomes anxious in the presence of strangers or when her parents leave her alone. In the second half of this chapter, we will consider some basic features of social interaction between infants and the people around them. The course of normal social development will be described, and we will also look at the effects of atypical social environments—the effects of being raised in an institution rather than in a home, for example.

PERCEPTUAL DEVELOPMENT

What does an infant look at and what idea does he or she take from that encounter? We are beginning to accumulate answers to this question. The area of visual perception is the most thoroughly studied, and we know something about the characteristics of a visual stimulus that attract the infant's attention. A baby girl may be drawn to a large black circle on a white background because of its size and dark color. Since the infant's first knowledge of the world depends on her attention to outside events, the principles that determine what she looks at and for how long are of great interest to developmental psychologists (see Figure 3.1).

Stimulus Determinants of Attention

Movement, intensity, and contour   From the first day of life, the infant responds to moving stimuli and to variations in light intensity. A 5-day-old baby sucking on a nipple will momentarily stop sucking if a light begins to move in his or her visual field (23); a newborn will spend different amounts of time looking at lights of different brightness (27). Newborns study the contrast created by a contour or "outline" of a form, where the difference between light and dark is typically sharp and abrupt. If newborns are shown a black triangle on a white field, their eyes will be directed at the sides and especially at the points of the triangle, where the contrast between black and white is greatest (43). They will detect a black vertical bar in a white field, and their attention will remain near that vertical stripe, attracted by the high contrast at the contour (24, 42).

The strong attraction to contour can be used to assess the infant's visual skills. For example, you may have wondered how psychologists could estimate

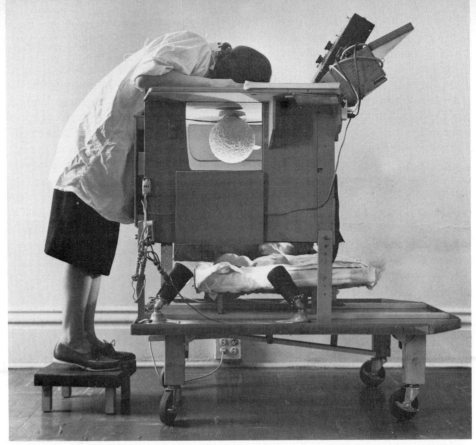

● Figure 3.1 A device used to study infant perception. (From R. L. Fantz. The origin of form perception. *Scientific American*, May 1961, *204*, 66. Photograph by David Linton. By permission.)

visual acuity in the newborn (p. 70); certainly we cannot use the ordinary eye-chart! One way of measuring acuity in infants is to present them with two different stimuli at the same time. One stimulus is a solid patch of gray or white and the other is identical in size but composed of stripes, say $\frac{1}{8}$ of an inch wide. If the infants cannot see the stripes, the striped patch looks identical to the solid patch. But if they can, they will spend more time looking at the striped patch, because it has more contour than the solid patch. Thus we can vary the width of the stripes and determine how wide they must be before the infant can see them; in so doing, visual acuity can be assessed. A 2-week-old infant can usually distinguish stripes $\frac{1}{8}$ inch apart at a distance of 9 inches from the face and, by 3 months, stripes $\frac{1}{64}$ inch wide 15 inches away (14, 15, 16).

There is such a thing as too much or too little contour, however, if the figure is too large to perceive in one glance or if it is too finely grained, the infant will be less attentive to it than to a figure with moderate amounts of contour.

Bull's-eyes and other patterns In addition to movement, intensity, and contour as important determinants of attention, other qualities also play a role. For example, most infants prefer to look at concentric and curved patterns over non-concentric and noncurved ones, and infants older than 8 weeks will look longer at a bull's-eye than they will at a striped pattern. Many subhuman animals show a similar response (5). Often the attention response is combined with a fear reaction. Monkeys are very attentive and fearful in response to a pair of staring eyes—in effect, two bull's-eyes. There may be some instinctive reaction to stimuli with concentric circles, even in humans.

Meaning and the Formation of Schemata

In addition to the physical qualities of movement and contour, the meaning or familiarity of a stimulus influences the amount of attention an infant will pay to it. In one study (22), 4-month-old children were shown the four faces in Figure 3.2. The infants spent most of their time viewing the face that looked most like a face (A), even though others (B, D) have more contour and more complexity. The comparison between face B and face D is significant, because the number

● Figure 3.2   Differences in fixation time for four different facial stimuli. (From F. A. Haaf and R. Q. Bell. A facial dimension in visual discrimination by human infants. *Child Development*, 1967, *38*, 895. Copyright 1967 by The Society of Research in Child Development, Inc. By permission.)

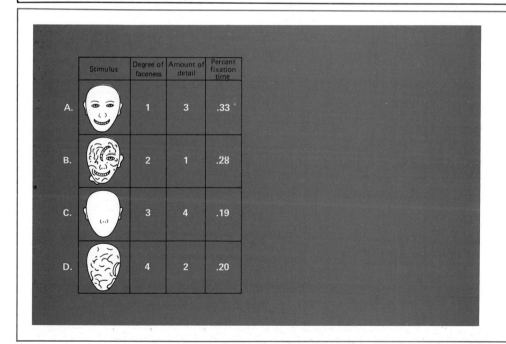

Stimulus	Degree of faceness	Amount of detail	Percent fixation time
A.	1	3	.33
B.	2	1	.28
C.	3	4	.19
D.	4	2	.20

of elements in each stimulus is about the same but B is more facelike than D. Infants looked at B longer than at D, and thus meaningfulness outranked complexity and contour.

The fact that meaning and familiarity affect an infant's distribution of attention means that he or she is building some sort of mental representation of experiences. We call such a representation a *schema* (plural: *schemata*). A schema is a basic memory trace, not necessarily in the form of mental images and—clearly, in the case of infants—not in terms of language. In fact, the nature of schemata is currently a vigorous area of research, and controversy abounds.

The ability to form schemata appears early, perhaps soon after birth. One sign of this ability is *habituation,* the gradual loss of interest to a stimulus that accompanies repeated exposures. For example, infants will look at a checkerboard or a face presented to them. The same stimulus can be presented again and again. Prior to 8 weeks of age, infants typically attend to the sixteenth presentation as long as they do to the first showing; after 8 weeks they seem to lose interest and may look away after 16 repetitions. Habituation implies that the infant is forming a schema of the stimulus; in order to look less at a face on a later trial, one must remember what has been seen earlier.

These first memories last at least as long as 24 hours, as shown by a study of 10-week-old infants (46). One group of infants looked at an orange ball moving up and down on a stage for only a few minutes. One day later these infants, together with another group who had never seen the orange ball before, were shown the same moving ball. The infants who had seen it before became bored more quickly (became inattentive sooner), an indication that something was remembered.

Another indication that the infant is creating some sort of representation or schema for what he or she sees is the phenomenon called *dishabituation*—the tendency to show renewed interest when a new stimulus event follows many repetitions of the same event. This occurs when, for example, an infant is shown a face on ten presentations and then on the eleventh presentation a checkerboard is substituted for the face; the child's attention increases dramatically. Because infants react to the new stimulus, dishabituation implies the memory of the old stimulus.

The Effects of Discrepancy

As infants experience the world around them, they build up schemata. By the age of 2 or 3 months, we note that the infant is more attentive to stimuli that are moderately different from those he or she usually encounters than to either the "same old" stimuli or radically different ones. From these and related observations, we can identify another major characteristic of a stimulus that will attract and hold the attention of the infant: The stimulus is slightly *discrepant* from the infant's established schema.

A discrepant stimulus differs a little from a schema but it is not totally dissimilar; the stimulus is related to the schema in some way. A picture of a table is not discrepant from a schema of a face, it is totally different. A picture of a face with no eyes would be discrepant from someone's schema of a face. Similarly, the face of a stranger is slightly discrepant from an infant's schema of the face of each of his or her parents.

A moderately discrepant stimulus is more likely to recruit and hold an infant's attention than a totally novel stimulus. In one investigation of the effects of discrepancy on attention (32), four groups of infants around 8 months of age listened to four different, distinctive spoken phrases—for example, "ba loo kee nay"—repeated eight times. Then all the infants heard the same test phrase, which was identical to the previous eight for one group, moderately different for two other groups, and markedly different for the fourth group. The infants in the middle two groups were more attentive to the test phrase than those who experienced either an identical phrase or one that was considerably different from the earlier eight stimuli.

Further support for the moderate-discrepancy hypothesis was obtained in a study of 4-month-old infants and mobiles (30). All the infants were first shown an arrangement of three colored objects in a mobile. Some mothers were then given the same mobile to take home to hang above the child's crib for half an hour a day for three weeks. Other mothers were given different mobiles, some of them slightly discrepant, some moderately discrepant, and some extremely discrepant from the original mobile. Each infant then returned to the laboratory to see once again the original arrangement of three colored objects. The infants who paid the most attention were those who, in the interim, had viewed a moderately discrepant arrangement. Those who had been seeing the same mobile and those who had seen the radically different arrangement were less attentive.

The Enhancement of Memory

Sometime around the end of the first year of life, infants' durations of attention to certain events and objects changes rather dramatically. For example, from the age of 2 months until 7–9 months, the duration of an infant's attention to masks of human faces decreases, but thereafter, from 10 months to 3 years, the duration of attention to the same masks typically increases. This sequence of events is observed not only in American children but also in Guatemalan children who live in rural villages and in African children living in the Kalahari desert (30). The initial decrease in attention can be explained by the discrepancy hypothesis: as the infant's schema for the face becomes better formed, the masks become less discrepant and recruit less attention. But why does attention to masks suddenly begin to increase after 10 months?

One factor appears to be a significant improvement in the ability of older children to retrieve knowledge from memory. That is, they can recall their schemata for faces more effectively. Additionally, they can keep two ideas in mind—

schemata (recalled images) and perceptions (present stimuli)—in a sort of "working" memory. This ability enables them to construct primitive *hypotheses* about the masks, crude attempts to explain why the masks, especially those of scrambled faces, are different from their schemata. They are able to compare the information in front of them with their knowledge of what a face should look like. They try mentally to transform the discrepant face into the form (the schema) with which they are familiar; it is as if they were asking, "What happened to this poor face? Who hit him? Where did his nose go?" Often such questions are explicitly asked by those children who have achieved speech. One child asked, "Who threw the pie at him?" Another remarked, "His nose is broken, Mommy. Why is it broken?" While the child is trying to resolve the discrepancy between what he sees and what he remembers, he remains attentive.

Perception of Depth

Does the human infant *learn* to see things in three dimensions? Or does he or she have this capacity from birth? These questions are not fully resolved; there is evidence on both sides. The interaction between inborn capacities and learned abilities is perhaps of greatest interest.

On the side of the learning position is evidence such as this: Infants prior to 10 weeks of age attend equally long to a two- or three-dimensional black circle; after 10 weeks, they prefer the three-dimensional circle. Up to 10 weeks of age, most infants will react in a similar fashion to faces that are two- or three-dimensional—a color photograph of the face versus the actual face of a person—but at 3 months they will smile and vocalize more to the actual face (38). These data support the hypothesis that the perception of depth may develop gradually through learning.

However, other evidence suggests that the infant is born with the capacity to perceive depth. One of the most provocative demonstrations of depth perception during infancy involves an apparatus called the *visual cliff* (Figure 3.3). Infants are placed on a center runway with a sheet of strong glass extending outward on either side. On one side, a textured pattern is placed far below the glass, giving the illusion of a cliff or drop-off. On the other side, the same pattern is placed high, up against the glass, giving the appearance of no cliff at all. In a typical experiment, the infant is called by his or her mother to cross over to her, first over the deep side and then over the shallow side. In the original study with this apparatus, 27 infants were willing to crawl onto the shallow side, but only 3 crawled over the visual cliff, even though the heavy glass (which they were able to touch) would have made the crossing safe (21). The young infant who cannot crawl shows a marked decrease in heart rate—indicating attention —when placed on the deep side (10).

The age of the infants tested in the original study—from 6 to 14 months— makes it impossible to conclude that depth perception is innate. But a series of experiments with animals (21) suggests that animals that rely on vision for sur-

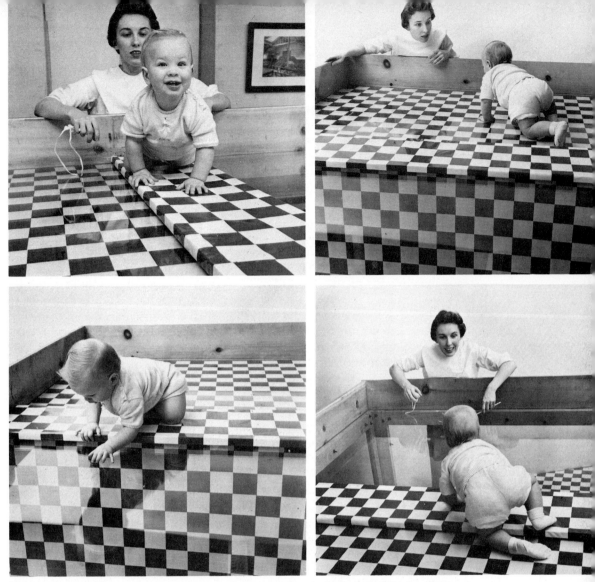

● Figure 3.3 The visual "cliff." (From E. J. Gibson and R. R. Walk. *Scientific American*, April 1961, *202*, 65. Photograph by William Vandivert. By permission.)

vival—a description that fits humans—avoid the visual cliff from birth. We should note, however, that human infants are clumsy creatures; even with good depth perception, they should be discouraged from crawling along the edge of a real cliff!

MENTAL DEVELOPMENT: PIAGET'S THEORY

Most psychologists agree that there are stages in the mental development of the child, that is, clusters of skills emerging at different times. As described briefly in Chapter 1, the developmental theory of Swiss psychologist Jean Piaget describes the intellectual progress of the human child toward the ultimate ability to reason abstractly. In Piaget's view, there are four major stages of intellectual development: sensorimotor (roughly 0–18 months), preoperational (18 months to 7 years), concrete operations (age 7–12), and finally formal operations (age 12 onward). These stages and the general theory will be discussed in detail in Chapter 5. Here we want only to describe the earliest stage, the *sensorimotor stage*, which covers the entire period of infancy (37).

Intellectual Development in Infancy

In the sensorimotor stage of development, a child's intelligence is manifested in his actions. When a 1-year-old wants a toy that is resting on a blanket but out of reach, he pulls the blanket toward him. This act of reaching for and pulling an object can be used to solve a number of different problems. Hence Piaget calls the action a sensorimotor scheme. Another sensorimotor scheme of action might be bouncing the crib in order to make toys and other attached objects shake or shimmer. The infant can suck, hit, bang, and shake, and when a new toy is presented to him, he will typically suck, hit, bang, or shake it. The sensorimotor schemes are viewed as knowledge that is used to solve problems. Within the sensorimotor period of infancy Piaget sees intellectual advances in the increasingly adaptive actions of the child. An infant of 4–6 months, for example, might be detected trying to produce a swinging motion in a mobile by kicking the crib. A little later in life (around 1 year), curiosity rears its delightful head. The infant begins to experiment—trial and error—with different solutions to the same problem. To get a toy behind a pillow, he or she might try using another toy rather than a fist to knock down the obstacle; or perhaps the feet might be used to get the prize.

The most advanced substage of the sensorimotor period is achieved at approximately 18 months. The child shows "invention of new means through internal mental combinations" (37). In more homely terms, the child is able to use imagery to solve problems; he or she is able to imagine "what it would be like if . . ." As Piaget observed of one subject, "Lucienne tries to kneel before a stool but, by leaning against it, pushes it further away. She then raises herself up, takes it and places it against a sofa. When it is firmly set there she leans against it and kneels without difficulty" (17, p. 119). This is clearly a creative solution to her problem. Lucienne was able to imagine what would happen to the stool if it was placed against the sofa and, because of such imagery, was able to solve her problem.

The ability to form internal representations of events, even of events not yet enacted, is a tremendous advance in intellectual capacity. Among the practical benefits gained is the child's ability to "defer imitation," that is, to reproduce behavior witnessed at an earlier time. Piaget described the temper tantrum of Jacqueline, his daughter: She saw another child throw a temper tantrum; the next day she tried it herself, producing an obvious imitation of the tantrum she had seen hours earlier.

The advent of the capacity to imagine behaviors rather than simply to perform them marks the end of the sensorimotor period. "The child is ready for an analogous but even more extended and tortuous apprenticeship in the use of symbols. . . . This does not, of course, mean that the child no longer continues to develop in the sensory-motor sphere. But it does mean that henceforth the most advanced *intellectual* adaptations of which a given child is capable will take place in a conceptual-symbolic rather than purely sensory-motor area" (17, p. 121).

Object Permanence

One of the major intellectual accomplishments of the sensorimotor period is the idea that objects are permanent and do not disappear even though they are not visible. We as adults don't find it hard to believe that a book moved from one place to another is the same book as before or that a book is not gone forever simply because it is hidden under a newspaper. But such notions of object permanence develop only gradually as the infant interacts with objects in her environment. During the first two or three months of life, according to Piaget, the child's visual universe is made up of a series of fleeting images without permanence. It is as if the child were on a train watching the world pass before her. She follows a stimulus until it passes out of her line of vision, and then she abandons any search for it, as if it had ceased to exist.

Infants between the ages of 3 and 6 months can coordinate what they are seeing with the movements of their hands and arms, enabling them to reach objects. But they will not reach for objects outside their immediate field of vision; they lose interest in hidden objects, for example (Figure 3.4). Piaget interprets the failure of children of this age to search for an object out of sight as indicating that they do not realize the object still exists.

Searching for a hidden object, in the infants Piaget observed, appeared in the last three months of the first year. If the infant sees her mother place a bottle under a blanket, she will search for the bottle there. Moreover, she will show surprise if the blanket is removed and no bottle is to be seen (due to a little sleight-of-hand by the mother); the surprise indicates she expected the object to be there. She believes in the permanence of the object (12).

In a still later development, the child will search for objects that she has not actually seen being hidden. For example, suppose the father shows the child a toy in a box, puts the box under a blanket, and then removes the toy, and shows the child an empty box. The child will search for the toy under the blanket when she does not find it in the box. The concept of a permanent object is now quite sophisticated.

Mental Development in the First Year

Piaget's view of mental development in the first year emphasized the fact that the child's knowledge is contained in actions. The child's knowledge of a bot-

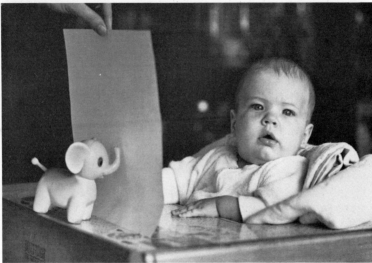

● Figure 3.4 Infants between the ages of 3 and 6 months lose interest in hidden objects, and will look away. They do not yet possess the concept of object permanence.

tle, therefore, is contained in actions with the bottle. An adult's intelligence, on the other hand, is typically viewed in terms of the manipulation of symbols, concepts, and rules in order to reason and to solve problems. These processes are aided by language, the development of which marks the end of infancy. The significant difference between action and thought is probably one reason why precocious development of sensorimotor schemes in infancy is not correlated with later estimates of conceptual intelligence. Marked retardation in sensorimotor development may in some cases forecast later mental retardation but the psychological significance of advanced sensorimotor development is still largely a mystery.

SOCIAL DEVELOPMENT

So far we have discussed biological factors in early development, perceptual development, and the course of intellectual growth during infancy. Infants also develop ideas of and responses to people. The infant requires other human beings, usually parents, to satisfy his or her needs; this aspect of interpersonal interaction is necessary for survival. Parents are objects to be perceived—the face, as we have seen, is an important stimulus for the infant. Parents also can be formidable obstacles to an infant's goal-directed behavior, if for example he or she has decided that the interior of the fireplace is an interesting place to be explored. And infants and adults can enjoy each other, play and hug-kiss-love each other.

Social Responses

From the moment the baby is born, he acts and reacts. Some of his responses are spontaneous; others are reactions to needs. Some of the behaviors are necessary for survival; others are not. As we have already discussed, the young baby scans the environment, vocalizes, sucks, smiles, cries, and thrashes. As he approaches the third and fourth months of life, he begins to cling to objects and to manipulate things—his fingers, his parents' hair, and toys. How does the caretaker—the mother, the father, the day-care teacher—respond to this limited set of responses?

Looking   The infant's attention is attracted to stimuli that have high black and white contrast and move. The eyes of the primary caretaker, usually the mother, fit these two requirements well. Moreover, the entire face is rather interesting. In addition to the eyes, the lips and tongue move, and the voice contributes stimulation in a different modality—it is an attractive mobile that makes sounds! Observations of infants older than 7 weeks show that they frequently spend long periods of time simply looking at their mother's face.

Vocalizing   Vocalizing in several forms is a universal response during infancy. From birth, infants cry. Before six–eight weeks of life, the infant begins to *coo* (35). The cooing sound is different from earlier crying sounds in that, in cooing, the infant uses its tongue to modulate the sounds, producing a variety of "vowel" sounds like "oo" and "ah." A short time later some consonant sounds are added, and we call it *babbling*. In normal children there is no strong relationship between the amount of early babbling and the time of onset or quality of speech during the second year. In an infant under 6 months of age, babbling usually indicates general excitement; the child will babble when he sees or hears something interesting or when he is doing something. Later, during the second half of the first year, the opposite is often the case; the child will be quiet and still while listening to a sound and, when the sound ends, begin babbling. The babbling seems to be reflexive to the excitement generated by processing information.

The cooing and babbling sounds of the infant older than 8–10 weeks can be influenced by the actions of the environment. American infants, who are spoken to 25–30 percent of the time they are awake, vocalize about 25 percent of the time they are awake. In contrast, the infant children of Guatemalan Indians are spoken to very little; mothers in this culture do not believe there is much value in such interactions. The Guatemalan infants vocalize only about 7 percent of the time they are awake (29).

Similarly, babies living in unstimulating orphanage environments vocalize less frequently and with less variety than do infants raised in normal families (8). Infants between 6 and 12 months old raised in middle-class homes show more frequent and varied sounds than do children of working-class families, presumably because middle-class mothers do more vocalizing to their infants. Observations of mother–child interaction in the home revealed minimal social class differences in cuddling, physical contact, and general nurturance. However, middle-class mothers were much more likely to talk to their infants and to respond to their babbling with reciprocal speech than were working-class mothers (48).

There are several other studies we could cite, but perhaps they are unnecessary. Vocalizing, usually babbling, is clearly a response that is affected by social interaction. Mobiles and other toys do not respond when the child vocalizes, but caretakers often do. The infant babbles, the mother smiles and babbles back; the infant babbles again and the mother repeats her actions, too.

Smiling   An infant's smile is a powerful positive reinforcer for the mother or father. Parents typically interpret the smile as a sign that their baby is happy and content. And if their baby is happy and content, they must be good parents—so their reasoning goes. If the infant smiles infrequently, the parents may begin to worry about the child's mental state and about their own competence as caretakers.

Obviously, happy and healthy babies smile more, on the average, than unhappy, unhealthy babies. In addition, smiling becomes more frequent if parents respond to it, by picking the infant up, for example (5). But there are also individual differences in smiling that are noticeable even among newborns. Some premature babies are consistently frequent smilers; others rarely smile (10). These differences in the inborn readiness to smile, which can exist even among different children in the same family, may play an important role in the dynamic interactions between parent and child. Parents may feel more comfortable with and attracted to an infant who often smiles during their times together. The baby who is biologically predisposed to smile less frequently may elicit undue worry or, worse, negative reactions from the parents.

Smiling at a human face is a common response in infants, and it has an interesting developmental history. As we mentioned above, the face is an attention-recruiting stimulus for babies, who spend a significant amount of time simply looking at it. It appears that by 4 months the infant has acquired a schema for the face, and he or she shows this achievement with a smile of recognition. At 4 months most infants will smile at a mask of a human face. No movement or sound is necessary, although a face with movement and a voice is more likely than a still representation to elicit the smile.

The peak age for smiling at a face is close to 4 months in a wide variety of cultures and is only slightly affected by experience with a mother's face. In one study (20), three groups of Israeli infants were compared in their frequency of smiling. Institutionalized infants rarely saw their parents and received routine institutional care. Kibbutz infants lived in collective settlements. They were raised in large houses with professional caretakers but were fed frequently during the first year by their own mothers. Family-reared children were raised by their mothers in modern apartments much like those found in the United States. Figure 3.5 graphs the frequency of smiling to a strange woman's face while the baby lay in the crib. The peak for smiling was delayed a few weeks for the infants raised in institutions, compared to kibbutz- and family-reared infants, but the peak for all infants was very close to 4 months. Later smiling behavior shows the effects of experience much more clearly than the onset of smiling.

Smiling can reflect the infant's growing knowledge, for the smile and laugh occur when the child understands a new event following some mental effort. At

Figure 3.5 Frequency of smiling among infants raised in three different environments. (From J. L. Gewirtz. The cause of infant smiling in four child-rearing environments in Israel. In B. M. Foss (ed.), *Determinants of Infant Behavior,* Vol. 3. London: Methuen, 1965. By permission of the publishers and The Tavistock Institute of Human Relations.)

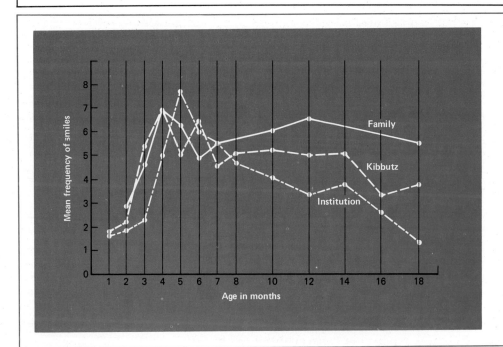

4 months infants smile to a face; at 8 months they will laugh at unusual auditory and tactile events; and 1-year-olds laugh most at discrepant visual and social events. Of course, smiling does not always indicate the act of cognitive understanding.

Distress   Crying, thrashing about, and other behaviors indicating distress are available to the infant from the first hours of postnatal life. The cry of the human infant has the same effect as the cries of other young animals—puppies, kittens, chicks: It signals the mother to retrieve and attend to her baby. The infant usually cries in response to either internal distress or a strange event. When the caretaker comes to relieve the distress, the human infant typically relaxes his muscles and, when held upright, rests his head on the caretaker's shoulder and holds the caretaker's neck.

Feeding   Sucking and the posture assumed when being held are two important responses found in feeding situations. These responses are obviously part of the experience of children who are nursed. But even the bottle-fed child is often cradled in the arms of the parent, and the sucking and the relaxed posture are part of this social interaction, too.

The feeding situation is a very significant one in the social development of the infant. The internal stimuli associated with hunger regularly mount to a high level of intensity several times a day, and the infant is almost completely dependent on someone else for gratification of this need. Delays in feeding are unavoidable and occur frequently, so hunger is the biological need most likely to result in sustained discomfort. Thus, many of the child's earliest learning experiences will involve hunger, the reduction of hunger, and the people who are associated with the gratification of this need.

Consider a 4-month-old baby boy and his mother in a typical hunger–feeding sequence. First the infant begins to feel uncomfortable and begins to cry and thrash. After several minutes, his mother comes to feed him. As she feeds him, he gradually becomes less active. He studies her face as he feeds. As hunger and pain abate, he feels his body cradled against hers; he smells her; and he hears her. The infant learns to associate pleasant sensations and the reduction of discomfort with the visual, tactile, olfactory, and auditory stimuli of the mother, and he learns to direct the responses of scanning, babbling, smiling, and clinging toward her.

The general pattern of learning we describe is not affected significantly by the particular feeding practices of the mother, such as whether she nurses or uses a bottle. In recent years, psychologists have deemphasized the importance of the specific manner of feeding. Instead, they believe the kind of social interaction that occurs during feeding is the critical factor. It is possible that some women feel that nursing is more personal and intimate and that this indirectly affects their attitude toward their babies. It is possible that nursing results in closer body contact with greater opportunities for mutual stimulation by sight, sounds, and smells; but these qualities can be present in bottle feeding, too, if

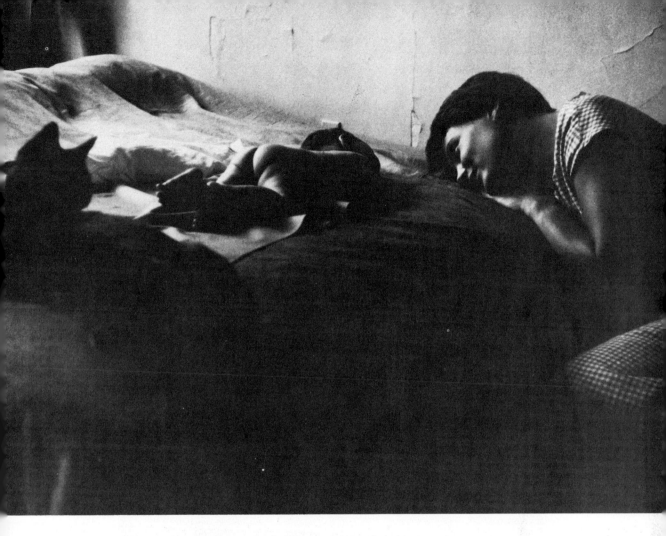

the child is held securely, talked to, and played with. One of the potential benefits of bottle feeding is that the father can do it.

Another feeding controversy that has been deemphasized concerns whether the baby should be fed on demand—whenever he or she cries for food—or on a schedule. Demand feeding prevents the buildup of painful hunger tensions. And scheduled feeding may mean that sometimes a child is fed before he or she desires food, sometimes when hunger pains have become so intense that eating is uncomfortable. On the other hand, babies are capable of adapting to reasonable feeding schedules. Again, the specific feeding routine is less important than the general quality of the parent–child interactions. Feeding should be a pleasant time, a loving time, and a time for the child to develop trust in a generally benevolent world. It should be a time for the development of attachment.

The Concept of Attachment

What do we mean when we say a child is attached to his or her mother? As the concept of *attachment* is used by psychologists, it means that the infant directs many of his or her behaviors—smiling, babbling, crying, clinging, following—toward the mother. Being separated from her leads to distress, especially in unfamiliar environments, while being reunited is calming. The infant is unlikely to become afraid when with the target of attachment, is most easily soothed by the target of attachment, and is most likely to seek the target of attachment when hungry, tired, bored, or afraid.

Not too many years ago, attachment was believed to be primarily due to the mother's presence during feeding. According to this view, the mother became a reward or reinforcement for the child—in technical terms, she become a secondary reinforcer—because of constant association with food, a primary (unlearned) reinforcer. Troubled by the pain of hunger, the infant would look to his or her mother for aid. And other motivating pains such as illness, cold, and injury are similar enough to hunger to elicit similar approach behavior to the mother.

A number of lines of research have complicated this simple view of attachment. In a series of experiments, Harry Harlow and his colleagues placed infant monkeys with "mothers" constructed of wire mesh. Some of these infants were

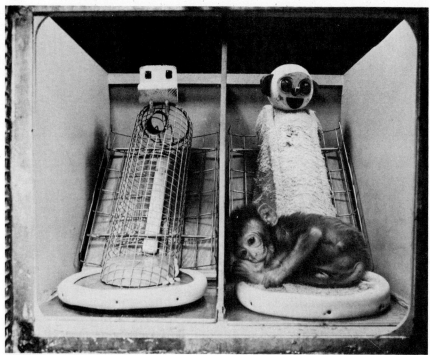

●Figure 3.6 Wire and cloth mother surrogates. (From H. F. Harlow and R. R. Zimmerman. Affectional responses in the infant monkey. *Science*, 1959, *130*, 422. By permission.)

● Figure 3.7 Typical response to cloth mother in the modified open-field test. (From H. F. Harlow and R. R. Zimmerman. Affectional responses in the infant monkey. *Science*, 1959, *130*, 430. By permission.)

fed from a bottle attached to the "chest" of a plain wire-mesh mother. Another wire-mesh mother in the room differed in just one respect from the other mother—it was covered with terrycloth (see Figure 3.6). When the monkeys were given the choice of going to either mother, the animals characteristically chose the terrycloth mother and spent more time clinging to her than to the plain wire-mesh mother, even though they were fed only by the wire mother. They would go to the wire mother when hungry, feed until satisfied, and then return to the terrycloth mother for most of the day (25, 26). In another experiment, a large wooden model of a spider (a fear-provoking stimulus) was placed in the cage with the infant monkeys. The monkeys ran for comfort to the terrycloth mother rather than to the wire-mesh mother (Figure 3.7). When the terrycloth mother was present, the young monkey was more likely to explore, later, the stimulus that had aroused its fear (Figure 3.8).

Harlow's studies not only deemphasize the importance of the feeding situation in mother–infant attachment, they also increase our appreciation of the importance of physical contact and the "clinging response," especially in threatening situations. The infant monkey's clinging when fearful is similar to the behavior of a 1-year-old child who runs to her mother or father and clings to a leg if she spots a stranger approaching or if she hears an unexpected loud noise.

Another facet of attachment behavior in infants is suggested by investigations of *imprinting* in animals (4). This remarkable phenomenon was first studied by ethologist Konrad Lorenz (Figure 3.9), who hatched some goose eggs in an incubator. The first live object the goslings saw after birth was Lorenz, and they followed *him* around the yard, even when their true mother was present; they also ran to Lorenz and not to their mother when frightened. This "attachment" of the goslings to Lorenz was called imprinting.

● Figure 3.8 Rhesus infant, raised with a cloth surrogate mother, displaying security and exploratory behavior in a strange situation in the mother's presence. (From H. Harlow and M. H. Harlow. Learning to love. *American Scientist*, 1966, *54*, (3), 251. By permission.)

One explanation of imprinting is that the newborn of each species are provided with a special set of responses that are established at birth or very shortly afterwards. Examples of these responses are the following behavior of Lorenz's goslings and also the clinging behavior of Harlow's monkeys. The objects that elicit these responses are likely to become objects of attachment for the young animals. In almost all natural circumstances, these objects are the mothers of the animals; only artificial manipulations of the environment allow us to observe the effect of responding to terrycloth "mothers" or inquisitive ethologists.

How does this apply to the human infant? As we have indicated, the human infant smiles, babbles, cries, looks, manipulates, and holds, among other things. In the natural course of events, the mother is the stimulus for these responses. The mother talks and stimulates the baby to babble: The mother moves her face and stimulates the child to scan it; the mother allows the baby to play with her hair and permits the manipulative responses to appear. By the time the infant is 4 or 5 months old, she has differentiated her mother from other people. She will not allow just anyone to pick her up when she cries, rock her when she is sleepy, or feed her when she is hungry; only her mother and a few other caretakers have earned that privilege. And the infant is more likely to approach, smile at, and play with these caretakers and less likely to be apprehensive and inhibited with them than with other adults. These behaviors reflect the infant's attachment to these caretakers (Figure 3.10).

Attachment and stranger anxiety   The gradual distinction between familiar people who are targets of attachment and all others depends, in part, on the formation of schemata for the infant's caretakers. When these schemata are finally established, the infant will detect the difference between familiar caretakers and strangers, and strangers may elicit fear and anxiety.

The anxiety of an infant in response to an unfamiliar person is a clear example of a discrepancy reaction. Imagine a child at 8 months sitting in her high chair, playing with her cereal. A strange woman enters the kitchen and stands facing the baby. The infant studies the stranger for ten seconds; her face tightens, and suddenly she begins to cry. If the stranger leaves, the child will calm down; if the stranger returns, it is likely that the child will cry again. We call this kind of reaction *stranger anxiety*.

● Figure 3.9   An example of imprinting. Here Konrad Lorenz is followed by goslings.

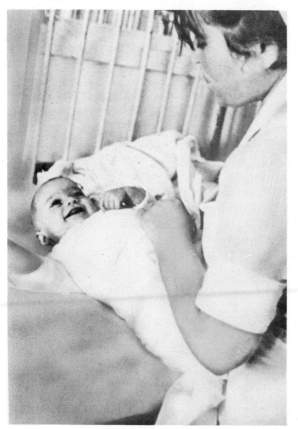

● Figure 3.10   Four-month-old institution infant smiling at caretaker while being dressed. (From J. L. Gewirtz. The cause of infant smiling in four child-rearing environments in Israel. In B. M. Foss (ed.), *Determinants of Infant Behavior*, vol. 3. London: Methuen, 1965, p. 217. By permission of the publisher and The Tavistock Institute of Human Relations.)

In American children stranger anxiety typically appears at about 6 months of age. It reaches a peak at about 8 months, and gradually disappears by the time the child is 12–15 months old. In isolated rural areas where infants have less frequent contact with strangers, the fear reaction lasts much longer. But all infants are less likely to show fear if they are sitting on their mothers' laps than if they are sitting a few feet away—much as Harlow's monkeys were less fearful if they were holding the terrycloth mother than if they were separated from it. Proximity to an object of attachment inhibits fear.

The human infant approaches familiar people, the people encountered most regularly. After a firm schema for a person has developed, the child shows fear to stimuli that resemble but are discrepant from the original person; stranger anxiety of this type usually occurs in a period from 6 to 15 months of age. But why does stranger anxiety occur at all? And why is it temporary? One reasonable hypothesis is that an infant's reaction to a discrepant event depends on whether or not he can make some response to it, in other words, has some way of interpreting it or acting on it. If the infant has an "appropriate" response to a situation, even if the situation is novel or never before encountered, he may not show fear at all; he may in fact, signify his feelings of mastery by smiling or laughing. According to this hypothesis, the emergency of stranger anxiety indicates that the 6- to 8-month-old infant has developed such a good schema for the mother's appearance and behavior that the stranger is discrepant. The infant is alerted. But he is too immature to make any constructive response to this discrepant event. He cannot deal with this strange event and, as a result, he cries. Only when he is older and more mature will he be able to do something about it. He can then ask for information: "Who is that, Mommy?" He can run to his parents. In some instances he may have been exposed to so many strangers in the interim that he will be able to "understand" their appearance and actions. A new person is now a less discrepant event than it was several months earlier.

Separation anxiety A second form of anxiety makes its appearance in American infants at about 8–12 months of age and begins to disappear at 20–24 months (1, 2, 3, 18). The event that elicits this fear is different from the one that causes stranger anxiety. Suppose a 12-month-old boy is playing in the living room with some toys; he sees his mother go out the front door; as the door closes he begins to cry. This is *separation anxiety*. A 5-month-old infant typically would not cry in this situation.

On the surface, separation anxiety does not seem to involve a discrepancy from an acquired schema, as was true for stranger anxiety. The child has seen his mother leave the house many times; so this event should not seem unusual. However, the infant is much more likely to cry if his mother or father leaves him in an unfamiliar place than if he is left in a familiar location. Even in his own home, he is more likely to cry if his parent leaves from a rarely used door (cellar, closet) than if the parent uses a typical exit like the front door. Thus, the degree of discrepancy of the total event from more typical events does appear to be a factor in separation anxiety.

The effect of a caretaker leaving is much less if a familiar person stays with the infant, as shown by the following experiment (34): Infant boys, 12–18 months, were placed, one by one, in an unfamiliar room, each with his mother, his father, and a female stranger. Each of the three adults left the room, one at a time, on a prearranged schedule. The children were rarely upset by the leaving of one parent, if the other parent remained. But when the second parent left too, leaving the infant alone with the strange woman, he was likely to cry and stop playing—both signs of fear.

Another factor that seems to reduce separation anxiety is the opportunity to respond in some way, usually to bring the infant into closer contact with the caretaker. For example, when 10-month-old children were placed in a strange room without their mothers, they cried. But when other infants were placed with their mothers in a room with an open door that led to the strange empty room, they often crawled into the strange room, but they did not cry. They looked around and then crawled back to their mothers. Thus two groups of infants were alone in a strange room; one cried and the other did not (41). The difference was that the babies in the second group could do something effective if they became apprehensive—they could crawl back to their mothers. There was nothing the other infants could do about their predicament; they were helpless and therefore anxious.

Separation anxiety seems to involve several major factors. The child is now able to recognize that he or she is in an unusual situation but is not able to interpret that situation or do anything constructive about it. This competence requires the child to retrieve or remember the situation when the mother was present and to compare that with what is happening now. These abilities require a certain level of cognitive maturity. Hence young infants do not show separation anxiety. The age when separation anxiety appears (8–12 months) is also the time when the child begins to show an enhancement in memory and evidence of the attempt to compare or relate events and to form hypotheses about them. It is possible that the child will not show separation anxiety until these cognitive competences have matured, that is, until the child is able to generate questions such as "What's happening? Where is Mother? Will she return?" If the infant can formulate the questions but cannot yet answer them he or she will be vulnerable to separation anxiety.

Regardless of the culture studied, the majority of children 10–24 months of age will cry following the experience of separation. There are, or course, individual differences among infants in the frequency and intensity of crying. Some infants are more prone to become afraid in uncertain situations. In addition, the interaction between child and parent might lead a particular child to become disposed to cry. For example, if a mother has always rewarded the child's crying by coming to him or her, then crying would be more likely to occur.

Separation anxiety disappears when the caretaker's absence is no longer a puzzle and when the child can do something about the separation. As children grow, they experience more frequent separations from their mother and become increasingly capable of interpreting her absence and reassuring themselves of her return. It is important to distinguish separation anxiety from later, similar phenomena. For example, a 3-year-old child may cry when her parents leave her at a nursery school for the first time, but this is not the simple separation anxiety we have been discussing; it is much more complex. The child may be afraid her parents will not pick her up at dismissal, or she may be afraid of the teachers and other children.

Interaction with Caretakers

Attachment is just one of the many important consequences of the interaction between the infant and his or her caretakers. Another, related outcome of a close and mutually interesting parent–child relationship is generalization of approach responses from the parents to other people. This phenomenon was clearly demonstrated in a study of monkeys raised under a variety of conditions. The monkeys in one group were raised by a human for three weeks and then placed alone in wire cages; they had no contact with other monkeys until they were 1 year old. A second group was reared by their natural mothers during the first year. The monkeys in a third group were placed in isolation at birth and could neither see nor touch monkeys or humans until they were 6 months old; then they were put in wire cages until they were 1 year old. During the second year of life, all the monkeys lived in cages and had regular opportunities to play with other monkeys each day.

The effect of early interactions—or the lack of them—was assessed when the monkeys were between 2 and 3 years of age. Each monkey was placed in a circular chamber with a human on one side and a monkey on the other. Thus the monkey could approach the other monkey, the human, or, if it chose to stay in the center, neither. The monkeys raised by a human for the first three weeks of life spent more time with the human, on the average, than the animals in the other groups did. The brief early experience had a remarkably strong effect and apparently led to a preference for human company. The mother-reared monkeys spent most of their time with the other monkey. The monkeys who were completely isolated for six months spent most of their time sitting alone in the center of the chamber, approaching neither monkey nor human (45).

The human infant, too, tends to approach people similar to his or her earliest caretakers. The generalization of social responses from a "mother substitute" to other people was shown in a study of 16 infants in an institution (40). For eight of these infants (the experimental babies) the investigator herself played the role of mother—eight hours a day, five days a week, for eight consecutive weeks. She bathed them, diapered them, played with them, smiled at them, and in general tried to be a "good mother." The other eight infants (the control group) were not given special treatment, although they were not deprived; they received typical institutional care, with several women performing caretaking duties in a more routine fashion. The experimental babies were different in two respects: they had a single caretaker during the eight-week period, and they received *more* nurturance.

All infants were tested each week during the eight-week experimental period and for four additional weeks afterward. These test situations were designed to measure social responsiveness to three people: the experimenter, an examiner who gave them other tests as well, and, at the end of the eight-week period, a stranger. In addition, systematic observation of posture and manipulative skills was included to determine the effect of the experimental treatment on nonsocial aspects of development. The results revealed that the experimental babies, who had been nurtured by the "mother-experimenter," showed much more social responsiveness to the experimenter than did the control children; this is no great surprise, of course. But the experimental babies were also more responsive to the examiner and the stranger. Specifically, if these people smiled at or talked to the children, the experimental babies were more likely to smile back or show some facial reaction than were the normally treated infants. These results suggest that social responses to a nurturant caretaker are often generalized to other people.

There were no significant differences between groups in the development of motor skills, as assessed by the posture and manipulation tests. Apparently the mother figure stimulated social behavior but had minimal effect on simple motor skills, at least over the brief period of the experiment.

The effect of minimal interaction   Interaction with adults is an extremely rich source of the varied experiences required for optimal perceptual, intellectual, and social development. It is illuminating, therefore, to examine the fate of young animals and human infants who have minimal interaction with adult caretakers. A monkey raised in isolation, without contact with humans or other monkeys, for the first six months of life, shows extremely abnormal behavior when removed from isolation (25). It avoids all social contact; it appears afraid of everything; and it spends much of its time crouching and clutching itself (see Figure 3.11). If the period of isolation is less than six months, there is a good

● Figure 3.11   The monkey raised in isolation shows unusual posture in the cage. (From H. Harlow and M. H. Harlow. Learning to love. *American Scientist,* 1966, *54* (3), 264. By permission.)

chance of eventual recovery, but monkeys isolated for more than six months often display unusual social and sexual behavior for the rest of their lives unless special therapy is introduced.

Even monkeys who are raised with terrycloth mothers (see p. 104) and who seem secure with them are initially fearful with other monkeys. When they grow up, their social and sexual behaviors are sometimes abnormal. For example, they appear eager to engage in sexual intercourse but they are strangely inept; the males may mount females from the side—"at cross purposes," as the investigators described it. Why are the monkeys raised by terrycloth mothers abnormal? Obviously, terrycloth mothers are different in several respects from real mothers. One simple difference is that the terrycloth mothers never move. In an effort to determine the effect of having a stationary mother, monkeys were raised with a terrycloth mother with a motor, which moved "her" irregularly around the cage (36). Compared to monkeys with motionless mothers, these monkeys were less fearful and more socially responsive when later allowed to interact with other monkeys.

No human child has been raised in such total isolation, but the effects of minimal interaction can be studied in infants raised in traditional kinds of institutions. Typically, each adult caretaker in such settings is responsible for 10–20 babies, which allows very little time for interactions other than essential feeding and maintenance duties; there are few toys; the hospitallike environment is typically clean, white, and uninteresting; and the infants are confined to their cribs.

In one study 75 babies were observed in an institution in the United States. They were not physically ill, but interpersonal interactions and opportunities to explore were inadequate. Each child "lived" in a crib in a glass-partitioned cubicle. They were fed with bottles propped; when cereals, fruits, and vegetables were added to their diets, the holes in the nipples were simply enlarged. A few toys—stuffed animals, rattles—were available. Seven to nine infants shared an attendant; during the remaining 16 hours, the nursery was empty of adults, except for a single caretaker who entered to feed the babies and change their diapers.

Prior to 3–4 months of age, these insitutionalized infants did not appear different from babies raised in families. After four months, however, several differences became evident. The institutionalized babies vocalized very little; they didn't babble; and they rarely cried. Adults who picked them up described them as feeling like "sawdust dolls." By 8 months, most of these infants were markedly less interested in toys than were normal babies. During the second half of the first year, sustained body-rocking, usually an indication of emotional disturbance, became very common. The infants seemed to lose interest in anything in their environment; their facial expressions were bland and unvarying; stranger anxiety was rare. Frustration was met passively, by crying or turning away; rarely would the infants actively attempt to solve a problem. Finally, language was delayed. One of the babies is described at 45 weeks of age:

Outstanding were his soberness, his forlorn appearance, and lack of animation. The interest that he showed in the toys was mainly for holding, inspecting and rarely mouthing. When he was unhappy he now had a cry that sounded neither demanding nor angry—just miserable—and it was usually accompanied by his beginning to rock. The capacity for protest which he had earlier was much diminished. He did not turn to adults to relieve his distress or to involve them in a playful or pleasurable interchange. He made no demands. The active approach to the world, which had been one of the happier aspects of his earlier development, vanished. As one made active and persistent efforts at a social interchange he became somewhat more responsive, animated and motorically active, but lapsed into his depressed and energyless appearance when the adult became less active with him (39, pp. 134–135).

"The light in Teddy has gone out." This description of one of the children summarizes well their unfortunate fate. All of the behaviors that are most likely to be learned in interaction with a loving adult—clinging, crying, approaching adults for play, and vocalization—were most clearly retarded or absent in the institutionalized children.

The presence of a single, consistent caretaker, however, is not, in itself, enough to guarantee a happy, alert baby. In Indian villages in Guatemala, where infants are continually with their mothers and nursed regularly, some of the listless, apathetic behaviors seen in institutionalized babies can be observed. In both the American institution and the Indian village, children had very little variety in their intellectual and emotional experiences; they had very few chances to explore their environments, to poke around while practicing new skills like reaching, manipulating, crawling, and creeping. Attractive toys were absent, and there was very little conversation between children and adults. For these reasons, it appears that the critical factors in the retarded development of these infants were the lack of variety in experience and the lack of opportunity for exploration and action during the first year, not lack of a close relationship with the mother.

When we say that slow intellectual development may be due to the lack of proper stimulation, we must be careful not to confuse *quantity* of stimulation with the more important *quality* of the environmental events. For example, some psychologists have suggested that lower-class children from economically poor environments may not have the kind of sensory stimulation that promotes maximal intellectual development. What does this mean? Compare the quiet bedroom of a middle-class home in the suburbs with a one-room apartment in an urban ghetto. In sheer quantity of stimulation, certainly the apartment exceeds the middle-class bedroom. But the middle-class environment is more varied and, partly because the quantity of stimulation is less, each stimulus is more distinctive. The middle-class baby typically has more toys, many of them designed to promote perceptual and mental development, and the distinctiveness of events in her environment makes it more likely that each will recruit her attention and that she will learn something from it. If her parent's instructions break the relative quiet of a middle-class home, she is likely to make some re-

● Figure 3.12   Israeli children raised in a kibbutz develop at the same rate as comparable children raised at home.

sponse; the lower-class child hears a voice yelling in a sea of noise coming from
the street and the apartment and is less likely to respond.

Even the habits of middle-class mothers make the stimulation they give
their babies more distinctive than that received by some lower-class babies. Observations of mothers with their 4-month-old daughters showed that when
middle-class mothers talked to their children, they were likely to be face-to-face
with them and not providing any other stimulation. The lower-class mother was
apt to talk to her baby while she was feeding, diapering, or burping the infant
(28). As a result, the vocalization was less distinctive. It is not surprising that
the average middle-class girl produces more varied sounds and is more advanced in language development than the average lower-class girl during the
first two years of life.

Institutional care does not always have to result in motor and intellectual
retardation. If the infant consistently receives care from an adult, she will become attached to this caretaker; if the infant also has an opportunity to move
around in an environment with a variety of stimuli, she will probably develop
like home-reared children (47). Infants who attend good day-care centers develop attachments to both their mother and the person who cares for them at the
center; they show stranger and separation anxiety at the normal times. A comparison of children reared at home and in day-care centers found no difference
between the groups in their attachment to adults at 30 months of age (9). Similarly, Israeli children raised in the group-care context of a kibbutz develop at the
same rate as middle-class Israeli infants reared at home (33) (see Figure 3.12). A
report on a well-run infant institution in the Soviet Union takes special note of

. . . the nursery's program for verbal-motor stimulation of its children. This is regarded by the staff as a matter of great importance and something that merits their sustained efforts. As part of the overall plan, every nurse has specific duties that she performs ecah day with all infants individually. As an example of "verbal duties," the task for Nurse A might be to ask each infant in turn, "Where is the cat?", "Where is the visitor?", "Show me your ear.", "Show me your hand.", and so on. In each case, the child's answer is followed by appropriate reinforcement. When the mother visits—and she is urged to visit often—she has access to the nurse's list of stimulants and is encouraged to further the verbal and motor training herself.

Attention to verbal and motor development is carried over to the toddler group. But in addition, a new goal is added to their program of upbringing. Staff efforts are now also focused on the child's development of self-help and independence. . . . The one to three year olds are shown how to pick up their toys before midday dinner, how to feed themselves, how to get along socially with their three table companions at dinner time, how to prepare themselves for a nap after dinner (7, pp. 10–11).

These Russian children show no adverse effects of institutionalization. In fact, they are better off than infants reared in inadequate homes. We must be careful when we speak of the potentially damaging effects of "institutionalization" to specify the important factors involved: little interaction between the infant and an adult caretaker, few chances to play and explore, and little variety in stimulation. These factors can be found in some homes, and thus the damaging effects of "institutionalization" can be found there too.

The capacity for recovery   A poor environment can impair the mental and social development of an infant, but humans have a remarkable capacity for recovery if the environment later becomes more benevolent. For example, some Guatemalan Indian infants are raised in dark huts; social interaction with adults is minimal; and they are not allowed to crawl about the hut. By the time they are a year old, they are listless and apathetic and have not yet attained the milestones of infancy. But at about 13 or 14 months, when they are able to move about on their own, they leave the dark huts and begin to explore the variety of the world outside. Their listless orientation and apparent mental dullness gradually fade. By the age of 10, they are cheerful, alert, and intellectually competent (31). An equally dramatic recovery was observed in children who lived in a Lebanese institution in which personal care was minimal (13). Tested between the ages of 2 and 12 months, these children fared quite poorly, compared to normal children. But by the age of 5 years, very little retardation could be detected.

The recovery of the Guatemalan and Lebanese infants is similar to that reported in an important study of isolated monkeys (45). Removed from isolation after six months, these monkeys showed the typical, abnormal behaviors we associate with such deprivation. They withdrew in fear, attacked novel stimuli, and displayed a number of bizarre habits. These monkeys were placed with infant monkeys, who did not approach or attack the isolates as adults often do; it was hoped that these interactions would constitute a sort of therapy for the disturbed animals. Slowly the older monkeys approached the nonthreatening infants and began to interact. After 26 weeks of such "therapy," the isolated monkeys had recovered significantly; their behavior was not very different from that of normal monkeys.

It seems fair to conclude that human infants whose development is slow or deviant due to conditions of rearing in the first year of life retain a considerable capacity for recovery. Early retardation because of an impoverished environment need not mean permanent incompetence; there may be more resilience in early development than psychologists have traditionally believed. However, recovery requires some change in the circumstances of the child; living continually in impoverished surroundings may add further insults to the child's developing personality, as he or she grows and tries to cope with a hostile and disorganized environment.

Cultural Differences in Child Rearing

In rural Guatemala the infant spends his or her time in a dark hut with no toys for the first ten or eleven months. In Israel the kibbutz infants live with a nurse and many other children. In a residential nursery in Czechoslovakia the infant has a cot in a large room with about 25 other children and experiences a regimented day. No two cultures rear their children in exactly the same way, and often there are sizable differences.

The skills and values older children learn also vary with culture. American children learn how to read and write; Guatemalan children learn to make tortillas, weave cloth, and plant corn. Children in northern India learn to be respectful and obedient; Danish and American children learn to be autonomous and individualistic. Differences in values lead to differences in behavior; the Indian child is quiet, while American children are boisterous.

Despite the rather obvious differences among cultures, there are also important similarities in development. Language, reasoning, and laughter develop in similar ways and at similar times, suggesting that there are some basic characteristics of human beings that develop in any culture. Differences among children of different cultures are most pronounced during the first five years of life and again after adolescence. Children around the world appear to be most similar between 5 and 12 years of age. The reason for this is that social play among age mates is remarkably similar in all cultures, and these behaviors are prominent during the middle years of childhood.

One important determinant of how the young child is handled is the parents' belief about the basic nature of children and their personal theory of how one molds a child into the ideal adult. In India parents believe a child is basically uncontrollable and therefore must never be allowed to be disrespectful. In America it is assumed that a child is relatively helpless and should be stimulated and encouraged. An intriguing study compared 30 Japanese and 30 American mothers and their 3- to 4-month old, first-born infants (11). The Japanese

● Figure 3.13 Parents in other cultures often have different beliefs about human nature and consequently use different techniques in raising children.

child typically lives and sleeps in the same room as the parents, and the Japanese mother is always close to her infant. When the infant cries, the mother is apt to respond quickly, and she feeds him soon after he begins to fret. In contrast, the American child usually has a room of his own, and the mother often lets him cry for a few minutes before she comes to feed him. The Japanese mother feels the need to soothe and quiet her baby, while the American mother more often wants to stimulate him and make him vocalize or smile. It is not surprising that the Japanese baby is less active than the American baby and much less vocal.

The differences in maternal practices seem to reflect differences in cultural philosophies about the nature of the human infant (Figure 3.13). The American mother believes that her child is basically passive and that it is her job to mold the child—to make him or her active and independent. As a result, she feels she must stimulate the child. The Japanese mother believes that her infant is basically independent and active and that it is her job to soothe the child—to make him or her dependent on the family. She sees the child as "a separate biological organism, which from the beginning, in order to develop, needs to be drawn into interdependent relations with others" (11).

Even within American society there have been major changes in how parents view and therefore handle their infants. In the early 1900s, government pamphlets advised American parents to avoid all excessive stimulation of the child because he or she had an extremely sensitive nervous system. Lately these pamphlets instruct the parents to allow their infants to experience as much stimulation as they wish, for this is the way babies learn. In the early part of this century, the parents were told not to feed or play with the baby every time he or she cried, for this was a sure way to spoil a child. Now we are told that we should not be so concerned about spoiling our children and that it is important to respond to a child's cry so that he or she will feel secure and develop trust in other people. Early pamphlets urged toilet training before the end of the first year and stern measures to prevent thumb-sucking and handling of the genitals. A little more than 50 years later, parents are being told to wait until their child understands the purpose of toilet training (at least until the middle of the second year) and not to worry about thumb-sucking or genital-touching.

These changes in "official" advice to parents reflect dramatic changes in philosophy regarding ideal traits and child development. American is less Puritan today than it was in the early 1900s, and "a capacity for joy" is considered as important as "good habits of character." The way young children are handled is intimately related to the values and beliefs of their culture. Since the available evidence suggests no major difference in the adjustment of young children then and now, it is reasonable to conclude that children develop adequately under a wide variety of environmental routines; it is not possible to write the perfect recipe for child rearing. However, we are learning some of the factors that adversely affect the optimal development of children, regardless of culture, and notions of "cultural relativity" should not blind us to this fact.

SUMMARY

Intense, moving stimuli with a lot of contour attract the attention of infants, and special patterns such as the bull's-eye have their own peculiar attraction. Gradually "meaningful" stimuli like faces elicit interest, as the child develops schemata (mental representations) for familiar objects. Stimuli that are moderately discrepant from an established schema are most likely to attract and maintain attention. The older infant often seems to be trying to resolve the discrepancy between a schema and a perception—forming crude "hypotheses" about why the perception is discrepant—probably because the ability to hold both schema and current perception in "working memory" has improved.

Piaget's theory of intellectual development describes infancy as the "sensorimotor stage." One of the major intellectual achievements during the sensorimotor stage is "object permanence," illustrated by the search for hidden objects.

The infant interacts with other human beings primarily through the behaviors of looking, vocalizing, smiling, distress reactions, and feeding. Social interactions with parents lead to attachment; the child directs most of his or her behaviors toward the parents, feels discomfort when they are not around, and is calmed by their presence.

Stranger anxiety occurs because the infant (6–15 months of age) has a good schemata for his or her parents, but cannot make a constructive response to recognized strangeness. Similarly, infants (8–24 months) show separation anxiety, probably because they can recognize the separation from their parents as an unusual event, but cannot yet understand it or do anything about it.

Even though infants are sometimes afraid of strangers and separation from their parents, they also tend to relate to relative strangers as they relate to their parents or primary caretakers. Infants who are raised in institutions with little or no interaction with adults are likely to become unusually passive and "lifeless." Studies suggest that the critical factors in minimal social interaction are the lack of variety in experience and the lack of opportunity for exploratory behavior. If an institution provides infants the chance to play and explore in a rich and caring environment, they appear to develop normally—better in fact than in inadequate home environments. Also, infants subjected to unstimulating environments show a surprising capacity for recovery if there is a significant change for the better in their circumstances.

Different cultures have different "theories" about the basic nature of children and how to rear them. Even in American culture, views of children and child-rearing practices vary from one era to another. In the matter of stimulation, for example, parents in the early 1900s tried to keep their infants from "excessive" amounts, while parents today are careful to provide "enough."

References

1. Ainsworth, M. D. S. **Infancy in Uganda.** Baltimore: Johns Hopkins Press, 1967.

2. Ainsworth, M. D. S. Object relations, dependency and attachment. **Child Development,** 1969, **40,** 969–1026.

3. Ainsworth, M. D. S., & Bell, S. M. Attachment, exploration and separation: Illustrated by the behavior of one year olds in strange situations, **Child Development,** 1970, **41,** 49–67.

4. Bateson, P. P. G. The characteristics and context of imprinting. **Biology Review,** 1966, **41,** 177–220.

5. Blest, A. D. The function of eyespot patterns in the Lepidoptera. **Behavior,** 1957, **11,** 209–256.

6. Brackbill, Y. Extinction of the smiling response in infants as a function of reinforcement schedule. **Child Development,** 1958, **29,** 114–124.

7. Brackbill, Y. **Research and clinical work with children.** Washington, D.C.: American Psychological Association, 1962.

8. Brodbeck, A. J., & Irwin, O. C. The speech behavior of infants without families. **Child Development,** 1946, **17,** 145–156.

9. Caldwell, B. M., Wright, C. M., Honig, A. S., & Tannenbaum, J. Infant day care and attachment. **American Journal of Orthopsychiatry,** 1970, **40**(3), 397–412.

10. Campos, J. J., Langer, A., & Krawitz, A. Cardiac responses on the visual cliff in prelocomotor human infants. **Science,** 1970, **170,** 196–197.

11. Caudill, W., & Weinstein, H. Maternal care and infant behavior in Japanese and American urban middle class families. In R. Konig & R. Hill (Eds.), **Yearbook of the International Sociological Association,** 1966.

12. Charlesworth, W. Development of the object concept. Paper presented at the meeting of the American Psychological Association, New York City, 1966.

13. Dennis, W., & Najarian, P. Infant development under environmental handicap. **Psychological Monographs,** 1957, **71**(Whole No. 436).

14. Fantz, R. L. The origin of form perception. **Scientific American,** 1961, **204,** 66–72.

15. Fantz, R. L. Visual experience in infants: Decreased attention to familiar patterns relative to novel ones. **Science,** 1964, **146,** 668–670.

16. Fantz, R. L. Visual perception from birth as shown by pattern selectivity. **Annals of the New York Academy of Science,** 1965, **118,** 793–814.

17. Flavell, J. H. **The Developmental psychology of Jean Piaget.** New York: Van Nostrand Reinhold, 1963.

18. Fleener, D. E., & Cairns, R. B. Attachment behaviors in human infants: Discriminative vocalization on maternal separation. **Developmental Psychology,** 1970, **2,** 215–223.

19. Freedman, D. G. The Effects of kinesthetic stimulation on weight gain and on smiling in premature infants. Paper presented at the annual meeting of the American Orthopsychiatric Association, San Francisco, 1966.

20. Gewirtz, J. L. The cause of infant smiling in four child-rearing environments in Israel. In B. M. Foss (Ed.), **Determinants of infant behavior.** Vol. III. London: Methuen, 1965. Pp. 205–260.

21. Gibson, E. J., & Walk, R. R. The "visual cliff." **Scientific American,** 1960, **202,** 2–9.

22. Haaf, R. A., & Bell, R. Q. A facial dimension in visual discrimination by human infants. **Child Development,** 1967, **38,** 893–899.

23. Haith, M. M. The response of the human newborn to visual movement. **Journal of Experimental Child Psychology,** 1966, **3,** 235–243.

24. Haith, M. M. Visual scanning in infants. Paper presented at the Regional Meeting of the Society for Research in Child Development. Clark University, Worcester, Mass., March, 1968.

25. Harlow, H., & Harlow, M. H. Learning to love. **American Scientist,** 1966, **54**(3), 244–272.

26. Harlow, H. F., & Zimmermann, R. R. Affectional responses in the infant monkey. **Science,** 1959, **130**(3373), 421–432.

27. Hershenson, M. Visual discrimination in the human newborn. **Journal of Comparative Physiological Psychology,** 1964, **58,** 270–276.

28. Kagan, J. **Change and continuity in infancy.** New York: Wiley, 1971.

29. Kagan, J. Crosscultural perspectives in human development. Paper presented at the meeting of the American Association for the Advancement of Science, Washington, D.C., December, 1972.

30. Kagan, J. Do infants think? **Scientific American,** 1972, **226**(3), 74–82.

31. Kagan, J. The plasticity of early intellectual development. Paper presented at the meeting of the Association for the Advancement of Science, Washington, D.C., 1972.

32. Kinney, D. K. Auditory stimulus discrepancy and infant attention. Unpublished doctoral dissertation, Harvard University, 1971.

33. Kohen-Raz, R. Mental and motor development of the kibbutz, institutionalized and home reared infants in Israel. **Child Development,** 1968, **39,** 489–504.

34. Kotelchuck, M. The nature of the child's tie to his father. Unpublished doctoral dissertation, Harvard University, 1972.

35. Lenneberg, E. H. **Biological functions of language.** New York: Wiley, 1967.

36. Mason, W. A. Motivational aspects of social responsiveness in young chimpanzees. In H. W. Stevenson, E. H. Hess, & H. L. Rheingold (Eds.), **Early behavior.** New York: Wiley, 1967.

37. Piaget, J. **The construction of reality in the child.** New York: Basic Books, 1954.

38. Polak, P. R., Emde, R. N., & Spitz, R. R. The smiling response: II. Visual discrimination and the onset of depth perception. **Journal of Nervous Mental Diseases,** 1964, **139,** 407–415.

39. Provence, S., & Lipton, R. C. **Infants in institutions.** New York: International Universities Press, 1962.

40. Rheingold, H. L. The modification of social responsiveness in institutional babies. **Monographs of the Society for Research in Child Development,** 1956, **2**(2, Serial No. 63).

41. Rheingold, H. L., & Eckerman, C. O. The infant separates himself from his mother. **Science,** 1970, **168,** 78–90.

42. Salapatek, P. Visual scanning of geometric figures by the human newborn. **Journal of Comparative and Physiological Psychology,** 1968, **66,** 247–248.

43. Salapatek, P., & Kessen, W. Visual scanning of triangles by the human newborn. **Journal of Experimental Child Psychology,** 1966, **3,** 113–122.

44. Sroufe, L. A., & Wunsch, J. P. The development of laughter in the first year of life. **Child Development,** 1972, **43,** 1326–1344.

45. Suomi, S. J., & Harlow, H. F. Social rehabilitation of isolate reared monkeys. **Developmental Psychology,** 1972, **6,** 487–496.

46. Super, C. M. Longterm memory in early infancy. Unpublished doctoral dissertation, Harvard University, 1972.

47. Tizard, B., Cooperman, O., Joseph, A., & Tizard, J. Environmental effects on language development. **Child Development,** 1972, **43,** 337–358.

48. Tulkin, S. R., & Kagan, J. Mother-child interaction in the first year of life. **Child Development,** 1972, **43,** 31–42.

CHAPTER 4
Language and Cognition

Our language is uniquely human and our most distinctive and complex achievement. It is impossible to conceive of even the most primitive and isolated human society functioning without language. This arbitrary system of symbols "make it possible for a creature with limited power of discrimination and a limited memory to transmit and understand an infinite variety of messages and to do this in spite of noise and distraction" (7, p. 246). Language enables us to communicate. Poets use language in beautiful and novel ways, yet the messages are understood. Words can excite or calm; they can express joy or sorrow, hope or despair, anger or caring. Language affects all aspects of human behavior; most of what we have learned has been transmitted to us through words or symbols, and language plays a definite, although not completely understood role in thinking, memory, reasoning, and problem-solving.

The study of language development in the child has become a rapidly growing area of theory and research. The psychologist who studies language must know both psychology and linguistics—the study of language, including phonology (sounds), syntax (structure), and semantics (meaning). Such a multitalented scientist is often called a *psycholinguist,* and he or she studies many aspects of adult language usage—for example, what kinds of sentences are hardest to understand, and why—as well as child language development. We will of course focus on child language. Even by themselves, studies of language acquisition constitute a very large and rapidly changing body of research. "All over the world the first sentences of small children are being as painstakingly taped, transcribed, and analyzed as if they were the last sayings of great sages. Which is a surprising fate for the likes of 'That doggie,' 'No more milk,' and 'Hit ball'" (8, p. 97).

In this chapter we will begin with a brief consideration of the two major theoretical approaches to language development—learning theory and linguistic theory. Then we will summarize some of the major research findings on the beginnings of speech in children. Following this we will take up two recurring questions about language: What is the relationship of language and thought? And how do differences in language—between social classes, for example—affect other aspects of intellectual life?

In the last major section of the chapter, we will begin our consideration of human cognitive development, which often parallels language development and is probably related to it in intricate ways. Here we discuss some basic cognitive units (including words) and some of the basic activities involved in thinking and problem-solving: perceiving, remembering, generating and evaluating ideas, and reasoning.

THEORIES OF LANGUAGE DEVELOPMENT

Because language is so unique and important, psychologists have tried to understand how it develops and functions. Much of what we know about language development comes from the analysis of what children say and when. These analyses, to be described shortly, are influenced by various theories of language development. In particular, theories that stress the effects of learning on language can be contrasted with theories that emphasize innate dispositions toward language supposedly characteristic of the human species. Our discussion of the empirical studies of child language will be aided by a brief overview of these important theories of language development. As we shall see, no single theory can provide an entirely satisfactory explanation of the emergence of human speech, and some integration of the two points of view will eventually be necessary.

Learning Theories

Many learning theorists have attempted to explain language acquisition in terms of stimulus–response associations and reinforcements. The most comprehensive effort of this type is that of B. F. Skinner, who published his major work in the subject, *Verbal Behavior,* in 1957 (53). Skinner maintained that language, like other behaviors, is learned through operant conditioning. The basic principle of operant conditioning is that any response that is followed by a reinforcement or reward is more likely to occur in the future. In the case of language, infants utter sounds spontaneously (as in babbling) or in imitation of someone. Parents and others in the environment reinforce certain sounds and ignore (or even mildly punish) others. For example, during the period of babbling, some sounds resemble adult forms more than other sounds; these speech-like sounds attract the attention and praise of the parents. Through selective reinforcement, the sounds become more like adult speech. At first, sounds like "kuh" may be reinforced with a cookie, "wa" with some water, and "da" with a smile from Daddy (see Figure 4.1). As the child matures, closer approximations to the actual words receive more immediate reinforcements, and thus ". . . more and more precise . . . speech responses may be gradually shaped up through successive approximation until the child readily emits the speech units involved in everyday language . . ." (58, p. 121).

Skinner's theory also maintains that children learn to imitate the speech of their parents through reinforcement. When the mother says "Say cookie," a response that approximates "cookie" will be reinforced immediately. If the child makes some other sound, however, the mother will repeat her request, withholding the reward until the child makes a more appropriate sound. In this way, the child comes to discriminate matched or imitated sounds from unmatched sounds.

We have described a few ways reinforcement might affect the learning of language, according to Skinner. Other learning approaches to language acquisition concentrate on a child's natural tendency to observe and imitate the people in his or her environment (3). Learning by observation has been shown to be a significant factor in the development of many social behaviors—children learn many of their sex-role behaviors by observing the parent of the same sex,

Figure 4.1   At first sounds like "kuh" may be reinforced with a cookie, "wa" with
some water, and "da" with a smile from Daddy.

for example. Language behavior, by this view, is acquired in similar fashion.
Reinforcement may not be necessary for learning, but rewards often determine
when new language skills will be exhibited. Children may learn how to say
something by hearing others, but they may not use their new knowledge—how
to form the past tense, for example—unless there is some incentive to do so—a
shade of meaning they can use for their benefit, for example, or a parent or
grandparent who will be pleased by the show of new skills.

Theories that stress observational learning have the advantage of being
able to account for one of the most impressive features of language acquisition
—how *rapidly* children acquire their native tongue. Most children begin to
speak around the age of 1 year, and, by the age of 4, are accomplished speakers
of a quite complex language. It is difficult to imagine such rapid acquisition in
terms of reinforcement alone, that is, in terms of a child uttering words or
sounds that the parent carefully selects for praise and approval. Learning by observation and imitation, on the other hand, can proceed rapidly.

Imitation, which is clearly observable in young children, may permit the
child to practice words he or she already understands. However, numerous attempts to improve children's grammar through imitation—by having them repeat more sophisticated sentences than they ordinarily use, for example—have

met with failure. One reviewer (16) concludes that imitation will not affect sentence construction unless the constructions modeled have already occurred in spontaneous speech; then imitation may result in increased usage of the improved forms.

Both the imitation and reinforcement approaches have trouble explaining the obvious *creativity* of children learning to speak. From very early on, children construct completely novel sentences, sentences that could not have been imitated or previous rewarded—for example, "Allgone sticky" after handwashing. Such original sentences show that the child is learning rules, not specific words and sentences. Thus, imitation (at least in the sense of repeating adult utterances) and reinforcement do not seem adequate to explain language acquisition in children. In fact, learning theories have not had much influence in experimental investigations of language development.

Linguistic Theories

In contrast to learning theories of language development, a number of theories stress the innate language abilities of the human species. Most of these theories are influenced by the writings of Noam Chomsky, a linguist at the Massachusetts Institute of Technology. In 1957, Chomsky's *Syntactic Structures* was published (13)—the same year Skinner's *Verbal Behavior* came out. In Chomsky's view, "there must be fundamental processes at work quite independently of 'feedback' from the environment." The child must have the ability "to generalize, hypothesize, and 'process information' in a variety of very special and apparently highly complex ways . . . which may be largely innate . . ." (12, p. 52). In other words, humans are born with a certain amount of "prewiring" related to language, and these inborn capacities make it almost inevitable that they will acquire language. Of course, although there may be built-in capacities for language, the child must have contact with language—must be exposed to the specific vocabulary and rules of a particular language—to acquire it.

The emphasis on basic, possibly innate, mechanisms in language behavior has encouraged studies different in kind from those influenced by learning theories. For example, the search for *linguistic universals*—characteristics of language found in all languages in the world—is a prominent area of inquiry. Many psycholinguists believe that certain features such as the essential relation of "subject" to "predicate" are universal, and some theorists suggest that beneath the surface structure of any language, there is a deep, underlying structure that all languages have in common.

The terms "surface structure" and "deep structure" are part of Chomsky's theory about the nature of language. While the theoretical constructs have very technical definitions, we can say that the surface structure is related to the actual sounds and words that make up a spoken sentence, while the deep structure is related to the underlying meaning of the utterance. The necessity of such a distinction is indicated by ambiguous sentences like "Visiting relatives can be a nuisance." The meaning of this sentence is not clear from its surface structure; we want to know if the speaker means (down deep) that he or she dislikes going to the home of relatives or that relatives who come to his or her home are a nuisance.

The linguistic approach to language acquisition also provides support for biological investigations of brain areas involved in language behavior. Obviously, if one is interested in prewired circuits, biological evidence is relevant. As one psycholinguist put it, the "massive regularities of (language) development remind one more of the maturation of a physical process, say, walking, than of a process of education, say, reading" (44, p. 1062). If speaking is more like walking than reading, then speaking should be inevitable and controlled by specific brain areas (as walking is).

There is evidence indicating that speech production and comprehension are controlled by specific areas of the brain, as the "innateness" theories would suppose. Damage to *Broca's area,* a brain area named after the neurologist who discovered its function, results in difficulties in *producing* speech; people with such damage know what they want to say, but somehow they cannot say it. Damage to *Wernicke's area,* another part of the brain, leads to difficulty in *comprehending* speech. On the other hand, the brain of the child is quite resilient, a fact learning theorists may find comforting. The brain has two hemispheres, and speech is usually more completely represented in the left than in the right hemisphere. If there is damage to the left hemisphere, through injury or disease, some loss of the ability to produce or comprehend speech can be expected. But if the damage occurs in infancy, before speech, the language function is taken over with little or no deficit by the right hemisphere. Even in the early years of speech, the right hemisphere can (with training) replace the left without much loss of capacity. This plasticity decreases with age, however, and recovery from brain damage to speech centers after adolescence is likely to be limited or absent.

Although learning theorists and linguist theorists may argue about the relative contribution of biological factors and experience, none doubts the interaction between these two influences. Ultimately we want to know the effects of both innate and environmental factors, and the nature of their interaction. The facts of child language development, discovered in empirical research, will help us construct a more encompassing theory of language acquisition. Let us turn, then, to the investigations of the beginnings of speech.

THE BEGINNINGS OF SPEECH

After their first words, around the age of 1, children's language capacities develop at a fairly regular pace—a remarkably fast pace, if one considers the complexity of the grammatical items and rules the child must learn. *Comprehension* generally precedes *production;* that is, the child can understand words and sentences he or she cannot yet create. Your study of foreign languages no doubt was similar; it was easier to read the language than it was to perform in class. Children understand questions and commands long before they can produce them.

Characteristics of Early Speech

The raw materials of spoken language are elementary sounds. In adult speech, these basic vowel and consonant sounds correspond roughly to the letters of the alphabet. During the early stages of babbling, babies produce all the sounds that form the basis of all languages, including German gutterals, French trills, and Hebrew *ch* sounds. The early babbling of an Indonesian baby cannot be distinguished from that of a Russian or English infant. The range of babbled sounds narrows at 9 or 10 months. The baby seems to stop vocal play and concentrates on the elementary sounds of his or her own language.

Regardless of the language to which infants are exposed, their earliest meaningful sounds are the consonants produced with the tongue in the front of the mouth—*p, m, b,* and *t*—and the vowels produced with the tongue in the back—*e, a.* An English child says *tut* before *cut;* Swedish children say *ta-ta* before *ka-ka;* and Japanese children say *ta* before *ka* (44). The early appearance of *m* and *p* in speech sounds may be the reason that *mama* and *papa* are among the first words acquired by all children—and why these words mean "mother" and "father" in a wide range of cultures.

At first, speech is very primitive, consisting mostly of one-word utterances. This kind of speech has been called *holophrastic* (44), which means simply that each word may stand for a complex idea; the single word is used where an adult might use a long sentence. The child might say "ball" and mean "That is a ball." In a different context the same word might mean something quite different. "Ball" might mean "Give me the ball" or "I am throwing the ball." (See Figure 4.2.)

Children begin to combine words at 18–24 months, beginning with simple, two-word sentences like "More milk." By the age of 48–60 months (4–5 years), most children have acquired the basic rules of grammar of their language. Think of a 5-year-old you know, and compare the complexity of his or her speech to that of a child of 1½–2 years. The differences are enormous. In a period of approximately 30 months, a child progresses from the primitive combinations of two words to near-mastery of a very complex system of grammar. The speed and ease of this transition is one of the facts supporting linguistic theories of innate abilities; how can one learn so fast if not prewired to do so?

First Sentences

As we mentioned, simple sentences of two words or more begin at 18–24 months. These early sentences have been called *telegraphic,* which means they

● Figure 4.2 One-word speech is holophrastic, that is, each word may stand for a complex idea. Thus "ball" in one context (*A*) may mean "Give me the ball," and, in another context (*B*), "I am throwing the ball."

seem like the sentences adults compose for telegrams, where each word costs money. "Where hat?" "Throw ball." These sentences are largely made up of nouns and verbs and an occasional adjective. Eliminated are prepositions (e.g., in, on), conjunctions (and, or), articles (the, a), auxiliary verbs (have, did), copular verbs (am, was), and inflections (endings to indicate plurals—dog*s*—or tense —walk*ed*).

Even the imitative speech of children is telegraphic. If you ask a child between 2 and 3 to repeat a simple sentence like "I can see a cow," he is likely to respond with "See cow" or "I see cow." He omits words, but he does not confuse word order, preserving the order of the model. This suggests that "the model sentence is processed by the child as some kind of construction and not simply as a list of words" (8). At this stage, the child has a limited capacity; he produces only a few words, but these are the most important ones.

Word order, which is important in the English language, is regular even in the child's first two-word sentences. If the 18-month-old observes his father going out of the house, he says "Daddy go"; he never says "Go Daddy." Apparently the child has a simple set of rules for formulating sentences, which allows him to put the subject, verb, and object of the sentence in proper order. "I getting ball" is not perfect, but when you consider the knowledge about language involved, it is quite remarkable.

When children begin to produce strings of more than two words, their sentences become more complex and take on a *hierarchical structure* which can be analyzed in terms of units and subunits. For instance, a child may begin a short sentence and then expand it immediately with a longer sentence, as though he first prepared one component and then plugged it into a more complex construction. Here are some examples: "Hit ball . . . Jeff hit ball." "Go car . . . Jeff go car." A little later, the child may expand his sentences into even more complex forms: "Sit down . . . Jeff sit down . . . Jeff sit down (pause) chair." Here he seems to have analyzed his sentence into its major grammatical units. The sentence has a subject ("Jeff") and a predicate ("sit down chair"), and the predicate is further divided into an action ("sit down") and a location ("chair"). Consider the sentence "Put . . . the red hat . . . on." In this sentence, "the red hat"—a noun phrase—seems to be used as a single unit, placed between the two parts of the verb, "put on." The child pauses either before or after the noun phrase, or both, but he never says "Put the red . . . hat on" or "Put the . . . red hat on." The noun phrase seems to function as a unit (9). "Sentences . . . are not mere strings of words but hierarchies of units organized according to grammatical principles. The child apparently operates on these basic and universal principles even when composing short, idiosyncratic childish utterances" (55, p. 48).

Semantic Development

Analysis of the structure or syntax of a young child's speech gives us no information about the meaning or semantics of what the child says. Yet it is obvious that in their two- and three-word sentences, youngsters are usually attempting to communicate something meaningful; only rarely do they passively parrot sounds without meaning to them or make verbal responses for no purposes other than to gain a reward. One bit of evidence for this is the child's proper use of word order from the beginning, word order that is almost always correct for the meanings intended. A child will say "See Mama" when the context of the remark indicates she wants us to look at her mother, but she will say "Mama see" when she wants her mother to look at us. In English, where much meaning is conveyed by word order, the proper use of word order is important.

The early, telegraphic sentences of children in all cultures are intended to express a broad range of meanings. Analysis of many samples of early speech, taken from children speaking widely different languages—English, German, Russian, Finnish, and Turkish—indicates that "there is a striking uniformity across children and across languages in the kinds of meanings expressed in simple two-word utterances, suggesting that semantic development is closely tied to general cognitive development" (56, p. 199). The following semantic relations are typical of early speech:

Identification:	see doggie
Location:	book there
Repetition:	more milk
Nonexistence:	allgone thing
Negation:	not wolf
Possession:	my candy
Attribution:	big car
Agent-Action:	mama walk
Action-Object:	hit you
Agent-Object:	mama book
Action-Location:	sit chair
Action-Recipient:	give papa
Action-Instrument:	cut knife
Question:	where ball? (56)

By the time she is 2 years old, the average child has an effective vocabulary of over 300 words. By 3, the number of words she can use or understand has increased to about 1000. Between the ages of 3 and 5, the child adds over 50 words to her vocabulary each month, on the average. As we would expect, the child's vocabulary is generally more concrete than the adult's; she uses few abstract words like *action, article,* and *quality,* all of which are common in adult speech (6). It could be argued, however, that even though the words seem concrete, they are actually used by the child in rather general ways. One linguist, Eve Clark, maintains that the meanings the child assigns to many of her first words are *overextensions* or *overgeneralizations;* that is, her definitions are broader than an adult's (14). For example, she may say "doggie" not only to dogs but also when she means cats, cows, horses, rabbits, or other four-legged animals. According to Clark, this kind of overextension reflects the child's tendency to define her terms on the basis of only one or two perceptual features of the stimulus, such as four-leggedness or movement. The adult's definitions, in contrast, are usually based on combinations of many features. The child gradually narrows the meaning of her overextended terms as new words are introduced into her vocabulary and take over parts of the more general definition. When the child learns the word *cow,* she adds features like moo-sounds and udders to the criteria of four-legged and movement; she can separate the meaning of *cow* from the meaning of *dog* (Figure 4.3).

Although there are many instances of overgeneralization in the child's early vocabulary, there are also *underextensions* or *overdiscriminations,* that is, definitions that are more narrow than an adult's (1). Between the ages of 2½ and 6, both overextensions and underextensions are common. There are at least two sources of underextensions. One is failure to include instances in a class be-

Figure 4.3   A hypothetical example of how an infant overextends and restructures the meaning of the word *bow-wow*. (Adapted from E. V. Clark, What's in a word? On the child's acquisition of semantics in his first language. In T. E. Moore (ed.), *Cognitive Development and the Acquisition of Language*. New York: Academic Press, 1973, pp. 65–110. By permission.)

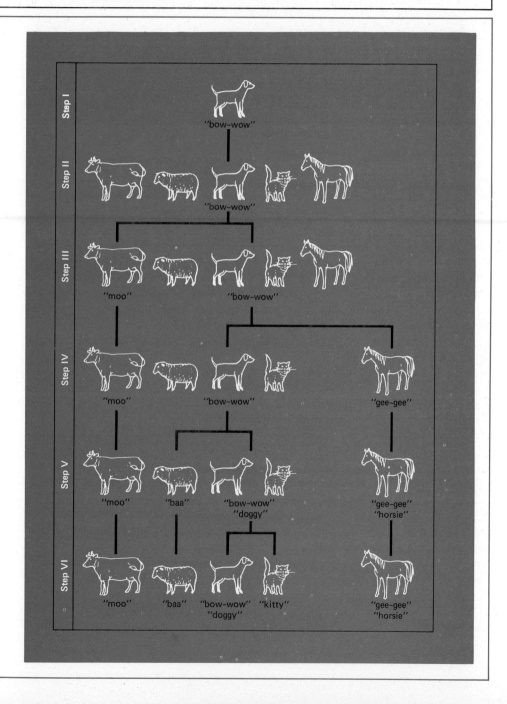

cause they are unfamiliar and perceptually different from a typical instance of the concept; thus, a praying mantis or a worm may not be included in the category "animal," and caviar may be excluded from the category "food." There are also cases in which very familiar objects are not considered instances of a general class. A dog is a "dog"; it's not an "animal," at least not to many young children.

As the child develops beyond the one- and two-word stages of language acquisition, the structure of his or her language increases in complexity. In most cases, this means that different or more complex meanings can be expressed.

One of the changes that occur as language develops is the appearance of a set of new words and word endings (inflections). The child begins to use a few prepositions, especially *in* and *on;* an occasional article such as *an;* forms of the verb "to be," such as *is* and *are;* endings that indicate plurals and possessives; and some inflections for tense, such as the *-ed* ending for past tense. The use of these words and inflections improves gradually over a period of two or three years. It may be a year or two between first correct use and constant correct use; one young girl was using the ending *-ing* in about half of the instances where it was required when she was 30 months old, but she was not correct all of the time until 16 months later (8).

Children vary in the *time* and *rate* they acquire these forms, but the *order* of acquisition seems to be remarkably uniform. In one intensive study of the spontaneous speech of three children, a study that continued over several years (8), one child consistently developed new forms sooner than the other two. But all three children mastered *-ing* before they could handle the past tense of irregular verbs (e.g., *go, went*), and irregular verbs were less difficult for them than *is, was,* and *were. In* and *on* were the first prepositions learned, but only as they applied to locations—*in* a box, *on* a table. The same prepositions indicating time—*in* June, *on* Wednesday—were not observable until later.

What accounts for the constant order of language acquisition and for the other regularities discovered? At present there is no answer to this question. Perhaps there are some built-in mechanisms that enable children to process what they hear and somehow, from this, to infer or construct the rules of grammar—a basic assumption of most linguistic theories of language development. But if there are such mechanisms, we know very little about how they work. The basic hypothesis of learning theorists is that something in the environment — rewards, adults to imitate—controls the development of language; the available data do not lend strong support to this hypothesis. For example, it might be hypothesized that the forms acquired earliest are the ones used most frequently by the child's parents and, therefore, most frequently heard by the child. In the intensive longitudinal study discussed above (8), samples of speech were available for both children and their parents. It was possible to correlate the frequency of parental use of the small words and endings we described—*in, on, -ing,* and so on—with the children's order of acquisition. The correlation was essentially zero; children did not acquire the more frequently used words and endings first.

Some other possible factors include the *perceptual salience* of the form—does it have some distinctive or attention-getting perceptual qualities, such as an unusual sound or high intensity?—and *informational value*—is the form necessary to communicate meaning? These factors are likely to be important but, again, they do not seem to operate in any simple fashion.

Various procedures used by parents to teach language have been analyzed, without much evidence of strong effects. For example, as they interact with young children, parents often model the language by *expanding* a child's telegraphic sentences to well-formed speech. If the child says "Nancy walk," her father might respond "Yes. Nancy is going for a walk." Such expansions provide the child with "relevant data" from which she can derive some general grammatical rules. Moreover, expansions are given at the ideal time, right after the child has made the abbreviated statement. Yet an experimental test of the effect of expansions yielded no evidence that such procedures increase grammatical knowledge (10). One group of children under $3\frac{1}{2}$ years of age received 40 minutes of intensive and deliberate expansion every school day for three months. A control group received no special treatment. At the end of the experiment, the expansion group did not differ from the control group on any of the measures of linguistic competence.

Similarly, it is difficult to discover a major effect of parental rewards and punishments on the language behavior of their children. In the first place, very few parents reward better grammar. In one analysis of parent–child interactions, all instances where a child's utterance was followed by approval ("That's right," "Very good") or disapproval ("That's wrong," "No") were examined.

> Most commonly . . . the grounds on which an utterance was approved or disapproved . . . were not strictly linguistic at all. When Eve expressed the opinion that her mother was a girl by saying He a girl, her mother answered That's right. The child's utterance was ungrammatical, but her mother did not respond to that fact; instead, she responded to the truth of the proposition the child intended to express. In general, the parents fitted propositions to the child's utterances, however incomplete or distorted the utterances, and then approved or not according to the correspondence between proposition and reality. Thus, Her curl my hair was approved because the mother was, in fact, curling Eve's hair. However, Sarah's grammatically impeccable There's the animal farmhouse was disapproved because the building was a lighthouse, and Adam's Walt Disney comes on on Tuesday was disapproved because Walt Disney came on on some other day. It seems, then, to be truth value rather than syntactic well-formedness that chiefly governs explicit verbal reinforcement by parents—which renders mildly paradoxical the fact that the usual product of such a training schedule is an adult whose speech is highly grammatical but not notably truthful (10, p. 70).

What if parents decide to note carefully and reward the better pronunciations and word choices of their children? The evidence is that such attempts have no effect other than to frustrate and anger the children (5); one study found that children rewarded for good grammar developed more *slowly* than control-group children without such treatment (48).

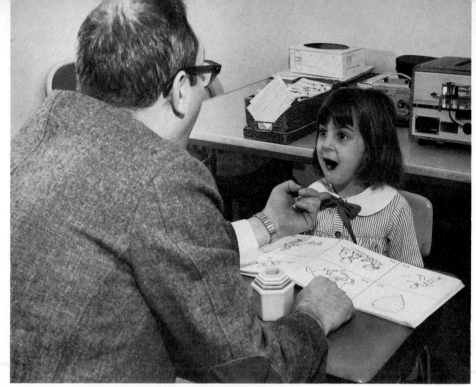

● Figure 4.4   Child being tested for language skills.

The evidence, then, does not show marked effects of expansions or rewards on the development of grammatical competence. The search goes on for environmental factors and kinds of training that facilitate the acquisition of this competence. It is clear that the environmental influences are not simple ones.

Are there linguistic variables, relatively independent of environment, that can explain the constancies in the order of language development? Roger Brown (8) suggests that grammatical or semantic complexity may be a critical factor. On the level of semantics (meaning), plural forms refer only to the number of a thing and the past tense of most verbs means only that something happened earlier. The word *were,* however, is more complex; it indicates both number (it is a plural form) and time (it is a form used for past tense). By arranging a number of words and endings on a scale of complexity, Brown discovered a significant correlation between complexity and order of acquisition; in general, simpler forms appear first. This suggests, in turn, that the child's grammatical competence is closely linked with the development of cognitive and intellectual capacities. As these capacities increase, the child can learn and use more complex rules appropriately. (See Figure 4.4 for an illustration of how children are tested for language abilities.)

Language Universals

Most of the findings we have discussed were based on data from English-speaking children. How general are these findings? Are there "universals of language development," that is, "similar developmental processes in different sorts of languages?" (54, p. 176). And we would like to know if it is possible "to trace out a universal course of linguistic development on the basis of what we know about the course of cognitive development" (54, p. 180). To answer such questions, we need to compare language acquisition in children of many different cultures; studies of languages radically different from English are the most valuable.

The first stage of speech, in which almost all utterances are one or two words long, is strikingly similar all around the world. Dan Slobin, a psycholinguist who has been responsible for a number of excellent cross-cultural studies, describes the similarities this way: "If you ignore word order and read through transcriptions of two-word utterances in the various languages we have studied, the utterances read like direct translations of one another" (57, p. 177). A list of the semantic relationships expressed in these two-word sentences, with examples from English, has been presented on page 133. Evidence such as this supports the notion that the first linguistic forms to appear in the child's speech are those that express meanings consistent with the child's level of cognitive development.

What children want to communicate is clearly related to their cognitive level, that is, to their understanding of the world and of the relationships among objects and events in it. But children must have linguistic means of communicating what they want to say, and such means are not always available. Forms used to express a particular meaning vary from language to language. In English the form for plurals is relatively simple, and American children learn and use this form early. In Arabic, however, the plural form is extremely complex and Egyptian children do not master it until quite late in their language development. American and Egyptian children probably *understand* the concept of plurals at the same time, but their ability to produce plurals differs greatly.

A more compelling example of the influence of grammatical complexity on the child's rate of language acquisition is found in data on young bilingual children who speak both Serbo-Croatian and Hungarian. These children are able to express directions and positions like *into, out of,* and *on top of* in Hungarian long before they can express these locations in Serbo-Croatian, which has a much more complex grammar. Obviously these children understand the meanings of direction and position, for they can express them in grammatically acceptable ways in one of their languages, although not in the other, more complex one.

By comparing the course of language acquisition in several cultures, certain general principles emerge about how children learn (56). For example, in some languages (including English), words indicating location—*in, on, at*—generally follow a verb or a noun—"Sit *on* the chair. Put the toy *in* the box." In other languages, these forms generally precede verbs and nouns. A universal feature of language development is that forms indicating locations that are placed *after* nouns and verbs are acquired earlier than forms placed *before* nouns and verbs. This in turn suggests that children find it easier to learn forms that *follow* such critical parts of the sentence as the action (verb) and the object (noun).

Children also seem to pay attention to word order when they are learning their native language. In many languages, word order conveys some of the meaning, and alterations in word order change meaning. In English, for example, changing the word order of "Mary hit John" to "John hit Mary" changes our understanding of the sentence. Children learning languages where word order is important use consistent word order from the very first. Many languages, however, permit more flexibility in word order (because they use more inflections)—German, Finnish, and Turkish are examples. We know, in English, that "Mary hit John" means that John got hit because of the order of words; in other languages, the words themselves are altered to indicate who is the hitter and who is the "hittee," so scrambling the order—"hit hitter hittee" —doesn't affect our knowledge of who got hit. In these languages, children do not use consistent word order in their first sentences. Furthermore, when imitating adult speech, these children frequently change the order of the words, something American children practically never do. Apparently even very young children make judgments about whether or not their language requires a fixed order of words; if it does, they use a fixed order; if it doesn't, they permit themselves the freedom of the language.

Language Development During the School Years

As we have seen, the young child makes dramatic progress in language competence between the time he or she begins to speak, at approximately the age of 1, and the ages of 4 or 5. This achievement is so impressive that language development in the later years of life has been ignored or slighted until recently. In 1963 a psycholinguist maintained that "all the basic structure used by adults to generate their sentences can be found in the grammar of nursery school children" (45, p. 419). This statement seems too strong in the light of recent research, which suggests that the child makes important syntactic and semantic advances long after the nursery school years.

A number of important grammatical forms are only incompletely developed between the ages of 5 and 7 and are not always used appropriately until later. These include the use of *have* as an auxiliary or "helping word"—as in "I have gone"—and nominalization, that is, using a verb as a noun—as in "Walking is good exercise." In addition, there are some forms used only by children and not by adults; for example, the kind of redundancy manifested in "She picked it up the penny."

Certain types of sentences cause trouble for younger school children (around 6 years old). Consider, for example, "Lucy is easy to hurt." This means that it is easy to hurt Lucy; that is, in the sentence's underlying structure, Lucy is the *object* of the verb "to hurt." Children find this hard to understand, and they interpret the sentence to mean that Lucy is the one doing the hurting, as if the sentence were structurally the same as "Lucy is eager to hurt." Another, similar type of sentence that children find difficult is the passive sentence, such as "John was hit by Mary." Again, the subject of the sentence (John) is the person affected by the action, instead of the one doing the hitting, as is the case in the active-sentence equivalent, "Mary hit John." At 5 years, children are just beginning to comprehend passive sentences, and they almost never use such constructions in their own spontaneous speech. When children were presented pictures and encouraged by an experimenter to describe them with passive sentences—by focusing their attention upon the acted-upon object rather than on the actor—young children still did not use the passive form. Not until about the age of 7 could children be induced to give more than 50 percent passive sentences, even after an example was given and the acted-upon object was shown first in the picture (59).

Longitudinal studies of language development during the years from kindergarten to ninth grade show a general and gradual improvement in language skills. Vocabulary increases (Figure 4.5), speech performance improves, and sentences increase markedly in length and grammatical complexity (41). There are also some relatively abrupt shifts. Between kindergarten and first grade and between the fifth and seventh grade, for example, there is evidence of large increases in the use of new or previously infrequent grammatical constructions (50).

Vocabularies increase as children learn the meanings of new words. In some cases, children define a word in a way quite different from an adult's definition, at least for a while. For example, until the age of 8, many children misinterpret the verb *ask,* responding to it as if it meant the same as *tell.* When instructed to "Tell X (another child) what to feed the doll," a child at this age will say, correctly, "A banana." However, when told to "Ask X what to feed the doll," the child doesn't ask a question at all but instead simply tells the other child, "A banana" (11, 36).

Children increase rapidly in comprehension and use of prepositions during the first years of school. To test the understanding of prepositions, two methods have been used (50). In one, children are presented with pictures and asked to choose the one that, say, "shows the girl *behind* the car." Performance on this measure improves steadily with age. Only 73 percent of the responses of the 3- and 4-year-old children, but about 97 percent of the 10-year-olds, were correct. The greatest increase occurred between 5 and 6 years. A second procedure asks for a preference: The child is asked, "Which sounds better: 'He is holding the door *to* his friend,' or 'He is holding the door *for* his friend?'" Nursery school and kindergarten children performed at a chance level (50 percent) on a test composed of such questions, but at the age of 6 performance jumped to a level that indicated full understanding of the correct prepositions.

Piaget has pointed out that the meanings of words indicating relationships like *brother* and *sister* develop gradually. At the earliest stage, children tend to

● Figure 4.5 Average vocabulary size of children at various ages. The child's vocabulary increases rapidly in the years from 2 to 6.

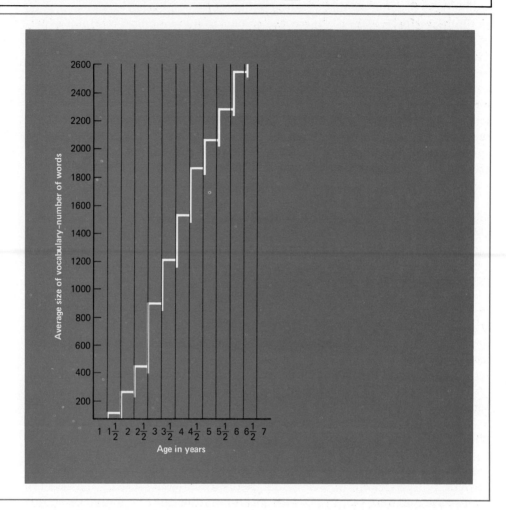

equate *brother* with *boy* and *sister* with *girl.* "What is a sister?" a 5-year-old was asked. "A sister is a girl you know." At the next stage, the children recognize that the use of these terms requires other children in the family. One of Piaget's 9-year-old subjects defined *brother:* "When there is a boy and another boy, when there are two of them." Finally children realize that *brother* and *sister* refer to a relationship among members of the same family. Apparently the first meanings are derived from perceptual data—"I see that brothers are always boys and sisters always girls." Later, with increased cognitive development, the child adds social criteria—brotherhood and sisterhood are interpersonal relationships shared by two people with the same parents.

Double-function words are words such as *bright, hard, sweet,* and *cold,* which have both a physical and a psychological meaning. Before the age of 7, children apply these words properly to physical objects, but they do not believe that these words can be used to describe people—with the possible exception of *sweet*. With 7- and 8-year-olds, some of the words are used appropriately to refer to people, although children this age cannot relate the "people meaning" to the physical meaning. By 9–10 years of age, about half of the children can use the words in both a physical and a psychological context, and they can explain the relationship between the two uses (2). "Children first master the object reference of double function words and then the psychological sense of these terms as independent meanings, and finally, the dual or relational aspects of the words are acquired" (50, p. 424).

THE RELATIONSHIP BETWEEN LANGUAGE AND COGNITION

Are processes like perception, learning, and memory affected by our linguistic capabilities? Does language influence thought, concept formation, reasoning ability, and problem-solving? Does increased verbal ability enhance mental development? In short, are cognitive functions dependent on language?

These are ancient questions, but there are still no definitive answers. Verbal ability undoubtedly aids thinking and problem-solving, but not all cognitive processes are based on language. The child's language abilities increase by leaps and bounds between infancy and the ages of 3 or 4, and, at the same time, cognitive abilities also increase dramatically. The 3- or 4-year-old learns, perceives, thinks, reasons, and solves problems in ways that are vastly different from those of the 1- or 2-year-old. However, many deaf children who are very deficient in language solve cognitive problems as well as hearing children do. This suggests that thought and problem-solving are not entirely dependent on language.

Russian psychologists, notably Vygotsky and Luria, have tried to describe a course of events in which a child's thought processes and language abilities become interdependent, at least in the typical case. Vygotsky (60) believed that thought and language are initially distinct: "In the speech development of the child, we can with certainty establish a preintellectual stage, and in his thought development, a prelinguistic stage." For a time, these two processes develop independently, but "at a certain point these lines meet, whereupon thought becomes verbal and speech rational" (60, p. 44). As Luria put it, "in the early stages of child development, speech is only a means of communication with adults and other children. . . . Subsequently, it becomes a means whereby he organizes his experience and regulates his own actions. So the child's activity is mediated through words" (42, p. 116).

This course of events, as it is observed in the child's behavior, is viewed as a process whereby thought becomes more and more like "inner speech." As the child's language capacities improve, she discovers that language is useful in organizing one's activities—through labeling and similar means. The child then begins to use language *for herself,* that is, not to communicate but to organize. At this stage, a parent will often find a child "speaking to herself"—out loud—explaining things to herself and directing herself to do certain things—"Martha's toy." "Don't touch." Gradually this kind of speech "goes underground"; that is, it becomes inner speech, and thought becomes more and more like language.

Verbal Mediation

The influence of words on behavior, as in a child's self-instruction, is called *verbal mediation,* a distinctively human ability. As a simpler example, words can be used to generalize from one set of objects to another—six nickels and three dimes are rendered equivalent by the words "thirty cents." In a similar fashion, most 4-year-old children have learned to apply the word *candy* to certain stimuli. Because candy means to them something good to eat, they are apt to behave in a predictable way toward all things they label candy. When an adult

● Figure 4.6 Once a child has learned the meaning of the word *candy*, the world is filled with difficult choices between equivalent values.

introduces a new object children have never seen and says, "Have a piece of candy," the children will transfer the behavior they have learned for the word candy to this novel stimulus. In all probability they will take this new object and pop it into their mouth. Thus, verbally mediated generalization is usually adaptive and allows the child to behave appropriately to new stimuli on first contact (Figure 4.6).

Verbal mediation has been shown to be of major help in a number of learning and problem-solving tasks. In one study (37), children were rewarded for choosing the largest of three black squares. Then three new squares were presented, the smallest of which was the same size as the largest of the previous trio; again the choice of the largest was rewarded. Preschool children with limited language ability find it difficult to learn to make choices on the basis of relationships among stimuli—"always choose the largest"—rather than on the basis of an absolute quality like size. They continue to select the square that was previously rewarded, even though it is now the smallest square and therefore incorrect and unrewarded. Kindergarten (and older) children can tell themselves to choose "the largest one," regardless of the actual size of the stimuli (37). They can use words (verbal mediators) to help them solve the relational problem.

Language and Problem-Solving

The use of language in general, and labels in particular, has a tremendous influence on the process of problem-solving. One function of labels is descriptive, as shown in a Russian study of picture matching (40). Children were shown pictures of butterfly wings and instructed to match them with similar ones in a large sample. The matchings were to be made on the basis of the patterns of wing marking. The children at first found this task difficult and perplexing because they had trouble separating the pattern from the color of the wings. An experimental group was then given labels (the Russian words for spots and stripes) to describe the various patterns, while a control group was not given any descriptive words. After they had learned these labels, the experimental group improved markedly. Even the younger members of the experimental group performed better than the older children of the control group. Clearly, attaching labels to these stimuli gave them some distinctiveness that made the matching task easier.

Furthermore, if young children do not spontaneously use words or labels as mediators in solving cognitive problems, they can learn to do so with very little training. For example, in simple recall tests, children were first shown a series of pictures of objects (e.g., a vase, a spoon, a hammer). Later they were presented with a large group of pictures and asked to pick out the ones that had been presented earlier. Some children spontaneously called the first pictures by name, and they could recall them much better than the children who did not label the stimuli. These latter children, however, can be instructed to label the pictures and to rehearse the labels; their performance then improves significantly (35).

More complex and difficult problems are also easier to solve if verbal mediators are used. In one experiment (23), one group of 9- and 10-year-olds was instructed to verbalize while trying to solve difficult problems (moving discs from one circle to another in the smallest number of moves). A control group did not receive these instructions. The verbalizers solved the problems more quickly and efficiently than did the subjects who did not verbalize. The experimenters noted that verbalization had the effect of making subjects think of new reasons for their behavior and thus facilitated the discovery of correct solutions.

Verbal mediation can help bridge time gaps in memory, and formulating verbal rules helps guide performance in reasoning and problem-solving tasks. Nevertheless, we cannot state conclusively that language is necessary for memory, thought, or problem-solving. For some children, mediators such as images or other nonverbal representations may serve the same purpose that words do for verbal children. Deaf children who do not learn to speak until rather late in life perform as well as children with normal hearing on many intellectual tasks. Though they are generally deficient in verbal skills, deaf children follow the average child's course of cognitive development, though in some instances the rate of development may be slower. The high level of performance on intellectual tasks "by deaf persons implies an efficient functioning of a symbolic system other than verbal" (22, p. 160). Words and labels may be the most commonly used mediators in thinking and problem-solving, but they are not the only possible ones. "Versatile creatures that we are, other symbolic means are apparently exploited when language is denied us, as with the young deaf" (21, p. 17).

Some cognitive psychologists, notably Piaget, have concluded that language more often *reflects*, rather than *determines*, the child's level of cognitive development. Attempts have been made to accelerate young children's cognitive development by teaching them new ways to talk about problems, tasks, and concepts. These efforts have not proven successful, generally speaking. The children do not seem to be able to *integrate* the "informational units"—words and concepts; their cognitive abilities are too undeveloped (28).

The relationship of language development to cognitive development is controversial, and it is likely to remain so until we have much more research. At this point, it is clear that language and thought are related. But we are far from a satisfactory understanding of that relationship.

LANGUAGE AND SOCIAL CLASS

People speak in a variety of tongues, even within a shared language system such as American English. The "Southern accent" is not merely a soft pronunciation, it is also a slightly different way of speaking—a different grammar. People in the Midwest speak in language slightly different from that of people on the east or west coasts. People in the lower socioeconomic classes, in any location, speak a somewhat different language from those in the middle classes. Recently psychologists have become interested in the implications of such variations in language for possible differences in cognitive development.

A number of years ago an English sociologist named Basil Bernstein began to study what he called the *restricted language codes* of the lower class and the *elaborated language codes* of the middle class (4). In dealing with their children, Bernstein noted, lower-class parents use short, simple sentences that describe immediate events and objects. Lower-class communication codes emphasize the concrete, here-and-now reality, with very little abstraction or reference to general principles. In addition, lower-class codes are more "communal"; that is, they assume you share the experience, the assumptions, and the definitions of the speaker. In this respect, lower-class codes are like those of "in-groups" such as adolescents with their almost spy-code language systems. In contrast, parents in the middle class rely on language to teach their children about the broader implications of what they do—to teach them moral standards, to help them understand that other people have the same feelings and emotions they do. According to Bernstein, the middle-class child becomes interested in universal meanings which transcend the given context, while the lower-class child's language ties him or her closely to the context. The lower-class code is restrictive; it does not elaborate.

As a result of learning a restricted language code, according to Bernstein, lower-class children are more likely to think in concrete, less conceptual terms. This in itself will cause them problems in school. In addition, lower-class children try to communicate with their teacher in a code the teacher may not understand. The restricted code is understood only by those who know; the elaborated code is designed to be understood by anyone. Lower-class children are thus likely to experience difficulty in school. They think "wrong"; they say the wrong things.

Bernstein's work has been severely criticized by a number of researchers in language development. One fault they find is that he does not distinguish between language *performance* and language *competence*. The critics maintain that lower-class children may possess the ability (competence) to use the elaborated code, but they do not ordinarily use this code (performance) because it is viewed as overly "fancy" and too closely associated with school and the values it represents. They may feel that they must uphold the values of their own group, and this requires use of the "tough," restricted code, even though they know and understand the elaborated code (see Figure 4.7).

Do lower-class children know the elaborated code? To answer this question, one study (52) had lower- and middle-class boys write two letters, one informal and one formal. The informal letter was to be written to "a close friend," while the formal letter was an application for funds to a school official; only the writers of the best letters would be granted the money they needed for an important trip. It was virtually impossible to distinguish the social class of the writer in the formal-letter condition. "When a formal situation made it necessary for

● Figure 4.7 Children from different social backgrounds often express themselves in different ways.

the children to use the elaborated code, they [the lower-class children] could do so; the necessary competence is available" (25, p. 74). In the informal letters, the lower-class children could revert to their favored, restricted code, and they did so. But it was clear that their performance in the informal context did not mirror their competence, as shown in the formal situation.

In America, some psychologists have suggested that black ghetto children have difficulties in school because of restricted language codes they learn at home. Black children, it is claimed, suffer from "verbal deficits"; their grammar is simpler, less differentiated, and more concrete than that used by middle-class whites. Again, such judgments may reflect a failure to differentiate between language competence and performance. The speech of black children in their homes and neighborhoods, with family and friends, is rich and fluent, showing none of the "verbal deficits" that sometimes appear in speech at school. Linguistic analysis of the language spoken by black ghetto children shows that it is slightly different but no less complex or logical than "standard" English (38). The deficiencies of school speech are largely motivational, not linguistic. In many cases, black children view the school system as hostile and threatening. Hence in school they behave defensively, talking very little and mostly in monosyllables. Unfortunately, such performance in school and in interviews is often considered evidence of low levels of linguistic competence and even inadequate intelligence. These conclusions are unwarranted.

The following interview illustrates the differences in speech performance in different social situations. The interviewer was Clarence Robins (CR), a black man raised in Harlem, where the research was conducted. Leon was an 8-year-old black child.

> CR: What if you saw somebody kickin somebody else on the ground, or was using a stick, what would you do if you saw that?
> LEON: Mmmm.
> CR: If it was supposed to be a fair fight—
> LEON: I don' know.
> CR: You don' know? Would you do anything? . . . huh? I can't hear you.
> LEON: No.
> CR: Did you ever see somebody got beat up real bad?
> LEON: . . . Nope . . .
> CR: Well—uh—did you ever get into a fight with a guy?
> LEON: Nope.
> CR: That was bigger than you?
> LEON: Nope.
> CR: You never been in a fight?
> LEON: Nope.
> CR: Nobody ever pick on you?
> LEON: Nope.
> CR: Nobody ever hit you?
> LEON: Nope.
> CR: How come?
> LEON: Ah 'on' know.
> CR: Didn't you ever hit somebody?
> LEON: Nope.
> CR: (incredulously) You never hit nobody?
> LEON: Mhm.
> CR: Aaa, ba-a-be, you ain't gonna tell me that!" (38, p. 159)

The researchers did not believe that Leon's defensive and inarticulate speech performance gave a valid picture of his verbal ability. So in the next interview they changed the social situation in several ways. Robins, the interviewer, brought along a supply of potato chips, making the interview more like a party. He also brought along Leon's best friend, 8-year-old Greg. Robins got down on the floor of Leon's room, so he was closer to Leon's height, and while interviewing, he used taboo words and introduced taboo topics.

> CR: Is there anybody who says your momma drink pee?
> LEON: (Rapidly and breathlessly) Yee-ah!
> GREG: Yup!
> LEON: And your father eat doo-doo for breakfas'!
> CR: Ohhh!! (laughs)
> LEON: And they say your father—your father eat doo-doo for dinner!
> GREG: When they sound on me, I say C.B.S. C.B.M.

CR: What that mean?

LEON: Congo booger-snatch! (laughs)

GREG: Congo booger-snatcher! (laughs)

GREG: And sometimes I'll curse with B.B.

CR: What that?

GREG: Black boy! (Leon crunching on potato chips) Oh that's a M.B.B.

CR: M. B. B. What's that?

GREG: 'Merican Black Boy.

CR: Ohh . . .

GREG: Anyway, 'Mericans is same like white people, right?

LEON: And they talk about Allah.

CR: Oh yeah?

GREG: Yeah.

CR: What they say about Allah?

LEON:Allah-Allah is God.

GREG: Allah—

CR: And what else?

LEON: I don' know the res'

GREG: Allah i—Allah is God, Allah is the only God, Allah . . .

LEON: Allah is the son of God.

GREG: But can he make magic?

LEON: Nope.

GREG: I know who can make magic.

CR: Who can?

LEON: The God, the real one.

CR: Who can make magic?

GREG: The son of po'—(CR: Hm?) I'm saying the po'k chop God!* He only a po'k chop God! (Leon chuckles).

If you had heard only the first interview, you would have grossly underestimated Leon's verbal competence. In the second interview, the monosyllables and defensiveness disappeared; the two boys had so much to say that they kept interrupting each other. The discussion was clearly not restricted to concrete events; some of the concepts (the pork chop God) were so abstract that they are difficult to define.

You can note a few of the purely grammatical differences between Leon's home language and standard English. Where standard English would prescribe "He *is* only a pork chop God," Leon and Greg do not use "is," and Robins knows the Harlem language well enough to leave the word "do" out of "What

---

* The reference to the *pork chop God* condenses several concepts of black nationalism current in the Harlem community. A *pork chop* is a Negro who has not lost the traditional subservient ideology of the South, who has no knowledge of himself in Muslim terms, and the *pork chop God* would be the traditional God of Southern Baptists. He and His followers may be pork chops, but He still holds the power in Leon and Gregory's world (38, pp. 160–161).

they say about Allah?" Linguists have found black ghetto English to be a highly structured language, related to but different from standard English. A number of educators have proposed that standard English be taught in inner-city schools as a second language or dialect, not as a refinement or superior form of a language that these children already speak. In other words, black ghetto children have to be, to all intents and purposes, bilingual, speaking one language in the schools and another in their neighborhoods.

> Linguists believe that we must begin to adapt our school system to the language and learning styles of the majority in the inner-city schools. They argue that everyone has the right to learn the standard languages and culture in reading and writing (and speaking, if they are so inclined); but this is the end result, not the beginning of the educational process. They do not believe that the standard language is the only medium in which teaching and learning can take place, or that the first step in education is to convert all first-graders to replicas of white middle-class suburban children (39, p. 67).

BASIC COGNITIVE ACTIVITIES

What are the basic units of cognitive activity? What are the essential processes? As we summarize some of our present knowledge of how a child thinks, you might consider the role of language in the various abilities.

The word *cognition* refers to things that go on in one's mind. Cognitive activities include perception; encoding, storage, and retrieval processes in memory; the manipulation of schemata, images, symbols, and concepts in creative thinking, reasoning, evaluation, and problem-solving; and the acquisition of knowledge and beliefs about the environment. Stated more concisely, cognition includes perception, memory, generation of ideas, evaluation, and reasoning. These five basic processes will be our focus of discussion following a brief description of the major cognitive units involved in cognitive processing.

The Units of Cognitive Activity

The *schema* (plural: *schemata*) is probably the young child's first cognitive unit. The schema is the mind's way of representing the most important aspects, or critical features, of an event. The schema is neither a photographic copy nor an image, but is rather like a blueprint. Like blueprints, schemata preserve the arrangement of and relations among significant features. Think of an old childhood friend or a playground area near your elementary school. These memories will be marked by a few important elements—the chum's hair, a broken swing in the playground. For most people, their schemata of Abraham Lincoln emphasize his beard and rugged face and perhaps his stovepipe hat; one's schema of the Capitol building in Washington has the dome as its most outstanding feature. A schema can also be likened to a cartoonist's caricature of a face, which exaggerates distinctive features.

An *image* is a more detailed and conscious representation created from a schema. The schema is the skeleton from which the more elaborate image is built. A few children (and even fewer adults) can maintain an almost complete visual image of a picture; when the picture is taken away, they can describe it in detail, as if they were still looking at the picture itself (26). This unique ability is called *eidetic imagery.*

Symbols (including words) are *arbitrary* ways of representing events, characteristics, or qualities of objects and actions. A skull-and-crossbones is a symbol for a potentially dangerous substance (to adults at least; see Figure 4.8), and a yellow light at an intersection is a symbol for caution. Letters, words, and numbers are the most frequently encountered symbols. The schema and the image preserve at least parts of a specific perceptual experience, but the symbol does not. Kindergarten children already know many symbols—many of the letters of the alphabet, the skull-and-crossbones, and the red, octagonal street sign that symbolizes "stop."

A *concept* is a higher-order cognitive unit. It stands for or represents a set of attributes held in common by a group of schemata, images, or symbols. The major difference between a symbol and a concept is that the symbol stands for a specific single event, while a concept represents something common to several events. A word may be a symbol or a concept, depending on how it is used. "The house" or "my house" indicates a particular house and is thus a symbol; "a house" or simply "house" may refer to houses in general and is thus a concept. Children usually learn words as symbols first and then, if appropriate, as concepts. "Man" may at first mean nothing more than the child's father; it is being used as a symbol. When it is later used to refer to all males, it is being used as a concept. Similarly, a 2-year-old may say "Bad!" and mean only that his pants

● Figure 4.8   This symbol for poisons and dangerous medicines has been criticized by authorities, who report that some children think it means "pirate's drink" and consequently are attracted to it.

are wet. When he begins to regard a variety of transgressions like hitting, stealing, and lying as bad, we assume he has acquired the concept.

Concepts change with age in many respects. A child may use a concept in a highly personal way when he first learns the word for it; "dog," for example, may mean "all friendly, live things." Whatever the initial distortion, concepts become more "valid" with time; that is, they are used more and more frequently in the ways other people use them (19). One obstacle to the young child's effective use and understanding of concepts is his tendency to regard all concepts as absolute, without relative meaning. For example, when a 4-year-old learns the concept "dark," he thinks it is descriptive of an absolute class of colors—black and other dark hues. If two shades of yellow are presented and he is asked, "Which is darker?" he will probably not understand the question. Similarly, most young children believe that 1, 2, and 3 are "small" numbers and that 99 and 100 are "large" numbers. They cannot make sense of a question like "Which is smaller? 1 or 2?"

One of the difficulties in teaching the young child to see the relative qualities of concepts is that relative qualities do not stand still; they constantly shift. The number 6 is bigger than 5 but smaller than 7. Often the dimension of comparison shifts: An orange is a good thing to eat, but a bad thing to bounce. Often the context is different: A child may be the smallest in his family but the tallest in his class. All of this is confusing to children at first, but experience with the relative qualities of concepts is a great teacher.

A *rule* is another important cognitive unit. Rules are essentially statements about relationships between concepts. "Water" and "wetness" are related; this simple, descriptive relationship is part of the definition of the concept of water. "Water can be used to extinguish fire" is a somewhat more complicated rule. In many respects, rules are developed like the hypotheses and laws of a scientist; through experience, the child notes that concepts are related, and through more experience, he may modify the initial statement of the relationship. "All dogs are friendly" may, with experience, become "Most dogs are friendly." With experience, he may discover that, some fires cannot be extinguished with water (grease fires, for example). Rules are the outcome of the child's developing career as a kind of informal "scientist," who makes his best guess on the basis of his considerable but unsystematic experience with the real world.

Cognitive Activities

Cognitive activities can be divided, at a very general level, into two broad types: directed and undirected. Undirected cognition—uncontrolled, with no conscious purpose—has been less thoroughly studied, although it is an important aspect of many personality theories—Freud's, for example. Dreams, "free associations," and other relatively undirected cognitions are useful in therapy because they often reveal more about the person's emotional conflicts than directed cognitive activities do. Directed cognitions are subject to inhibition

and control by an *executive process*—the ego, in Freud's terms—which seeks to emphasize the positive and downplay the negative.

The executive process gives direction to cognition. It functions to give the person the ability to cope with his or her environment—to solve problems—by organizing other cognitive processes in some logical fashion. The executive process involves monitoring and coordinating perceptions, memories, and reasoning processes; integrating past experiences, future possibilities, and present circumstances; selecting the best strategies to solve a problem; permitting some self-conscious awareness of one's own thought processes. Developmentally, the higher-order abilities that we are calling the executive process emerge around the age of 4 or 5 and are in firm control of cognitive functioning by the age of 10 or 11.

The basic cognitive activities that are coordinated by the executive process are perception and interpretation, memory, generation of hypotheses, evaluation, and deductive reasoning. We will discuss each of these basic activities in turn.

Process 1: Perception and interpretation

Perception is the process by which people extract meaningful information from the mosaic of physical stimulation. The goal of perception is to understand events in the world by matching what is sensed to some cognitive unit. The very young child usually represents experience by schemata; the older child is more likely to use symbols and concepts, especially words. Consider the following figure: ⊂⊃. If this figure were shown to a 1-year-old, she would most likely represent it as a schema, in picturelike form. A 6-year-old is likely to use language: "It's a finger" or "It's a pencil." If asked later to draw it or select a figure from a set of similar ones, she might make an error that would reveal she perceived it as resembling a finger or a pencil. She might draw it as ⊂⊳, transforming the pencillike figure to one even more closely resembling the word she has used to interpret the finger.

Several important changes in the nature of perception occur between early childhood and adolescence. Increasing knowledge about the world affects perception. To use a simple example, written words are nothing more than a collection of lines to a very young child, but as she learns how to write, the letters, words, and eventually phrases become meaningful perceptual units. Similarly, units of perception that adults take for granted—houses, cars, even people—become more distinct to the child as she learns more about the environment and culture.

The older child is able to focus attention in a systematic way for a longer period of time. Developmental changes on a variety of intellectual tasks suggest that between 5 and 7 years of age there is a dramatic increase in a child's ability to solve problems requiring sustained attention. Children under 5, in all cultures, are more easily distracted. Some psychologists have speculated that an important reorganization of the central nervous system occurs between 5 and 7 years of age and that this reorganization is partly responsible for the dramatic increase in the child's capacity for sustained attention (62).

The general course of perceptual development, according to Eleanor Gibson (24), begins with undifferentiated responsiveness to stimulation. Gradually simple patterns and objects are differentiated from background stimuli and, most importantly, *distinctive features* of these patterns and objects are noticed and abstracted. These distinctive features allow the child to form more and more complex and realistic schemata, images, and symbols as he or she gains more experience with the environment.

Support for Gibson's view of perceptual development comes from a variety of sources. Studies of how children learn to read, for example, suggest that the child's first task is to detect the distinctive features of each letter: vertical lines, horizontal lines, open curves, closed curves, etc. They learn to discriminate a "b" from an "e" quickly enough, although they may confuse a "b" with a "d," which has the same features but differs in orientation. Adults know that orientation is critical, but it is easy to show that distinctive features are important in letter and word recognition. Study the sentence below:

Tⴑ⊖ ℘iⴑl wⴂnt ⴑom⊖ ⴂn ⴑouⴈ ⴂℓⴂ

It probably took you less than a minute to read the seven-word sentence, even though you've never seen the words printed that way before. Why was it so easy? Because you have learned a set of rules for letters and letter sequences and can detect the distinctive features of an "e" even if it is printed backwards or upside down.

A second type of evidence for Gibson's distinctive-feature theory is a child's ability to identify objects from pictures. A photograph or a drawing of an object is quite different from the object itself, but the picture resembles the object in its distinctive features. If children actually learn the distinctive features of objects, then they should be able to recognize a schematic picture of a familiar object even though they have had no previous contact with pictures. In one investigation (32), isolated Indian children living in the mountainous area of Guatemala, who had no access to photographs, pencils, or paper, were shown line drawings that merely suggested familiar objects (see Figure 4.9). Children 7–11 years of age named 79 percent of the objects correctly. American children, who have unlimited access to television, photographs, books, and magazines, could do only a little better—85 percent. Moreover, when these same Indian children were asked to find the triangles embedded in larger pictures (see Figure 4.10), they were correct 80 percent of the time—the same score earned by American children of the same age. It seems, therefore, that the ability to ana-

● Figure 4.9   Children were asked to guess the object from its incomplete form.

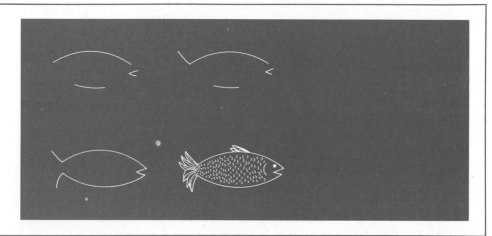

● Figure 4.10   Children were asked to locate the triangles embedded in the drawing.

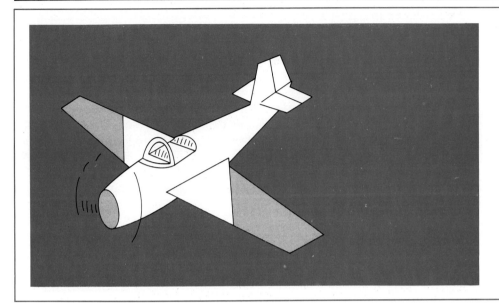

lyze two-dimensional pictures and to detect the distinctive features of objects does not require specific exposure to pictures.

In sum, development brings increased perceptual skills. With age, the child becomes more adept at focusing attention on an event without being distracted. As a result, the child's perceptions become more efficient, more selective, and more accurate. As the child gains experience, he or she learns more of the distinctive attributes of events and acquires the ability to detect an object from partial information, as in pictures.

Process 2: Memory   *Memory* refers to the retention of experiences for a period after they have ended. This period may be short, as in the case of trying to hold on to a phone number long enough to dial it, or it may be very long: A word definition may never be forgotten, although it may not always be easily retrievable.

Memory is usually measured in one of two ways. The person is asked either to *recall* an event or to *recognize* it. In recall, the child must retrieve all the necessary information from memory; she may be asked to define "rabbit" or to state her mother's birthday. In recognition the child is given possible answers which she must recognize as correct or incorrect; she may be asked if a rabbit is an animal or a plant, or to say "true" or "false" to "Your mother's birthday is in

January." Recognition is generally much easier than recall for everybody, but there is some evidence that the difference between the two methods is more pronounced in younger children. A group of 4-year-olds could recognize photographs they had been shown previously as well as 10-year-olds, but they were much less adept at trying to recall the dozen pictures they had seen (33).

Social class and cultural differences in recall are also greater than class and cultural diffferences in recognition. When middle-class children from an urban area in Guatemala were compared with isolated village children from the same country, the middle-class city children recalled longer strings of numbers and sentences than did the rural children, but the difference between the city and rural children in recognition memory was less dramatic (33). In the recall task the city children used various strategies for rehearsing, organizing, and retrieving the material. The rural children had not learned these strategies, and hence performed more poorly (32). These strategies were of less value on the test of recognition memory.

The use of strategies like rehearsal (repeating or reviewing the item after presentation), grouping items that are similar in some sense, and systematic search of memory probably account for the superior recall of the older child (20). This conclusion is supported by an experiment in which children of different ages were shown 24 pictures of objects (47). Each object belonged to one of four categories: transportation, animal, furniture, clothing. The pictures were scattered on a table, and the children were given three minutes to study them; they could move the pictures around or do anything else that might help them remember. They were not told about the four categories. The experimenter wanted to determine which children would rearrange the pictures into categories and whether children who did this would recall more. None of the first-graders and only a few of the third-graders rearranged the pictures by category. However, from the fourth through the sixth grades, there was an increasing tendency to rearrange (and recall) by category with a corresponding increase in the number of pictures recalled (47).

The younger child's memory can be helped if material is organized. If the objects are clustered into categories by the experimenter, the child can use these categories to improve his or her recall performance (15). In another experiment (27), children in the second, fourth, and sixth grades were shown lists of nine numbers to memorize. The numbers were presented either in a standard way—731246589—or in sets of threes—731 246 589. The older children performed equally well on both presentations; most of them spontaneously imposed their own groupings of triplets on the standard set. But the younger children, who did not typically group the standard set, remembered more numbers when they were presented in triplets.

Motivation often affects memory. In both children and adults, a strong desire to learn improves recall, possibly because of more careful and extensive use of the strategies we have been discussing. Anxiety usually impairs memory; children are often affected more than adults because their ability to organize,

store, and retrieve information is not as well learned or as well practiced. In one study (46), third-grade boys were divided into three groups. One group was made anxious by causing them to fail on a word problem; a second group was allowed to succeed on the same problem; and a third group was not given the problem at all. Each child was then read the following short story:

> The American horse known as Man of Wars was a very fine horse. He ran in races in the United States, in France and in Germany. He was brown with a red mane and had very strong legs. Five times a year, he was in horse shows in Boston, where children came to see him trot and run. After watching him, the children were served hot chocolate, biscuits and fudge (46).

Immediately after hearing the story, the children had to recall as much of it as possible. The children who were made anxious had markedly poorer memory for the elements of the story than the other two groups, who were equal in their recall scores.

In sum, better techniques to store and retrieve information, richer concepts and schemata to aid storage and retrieval, increased ability to focus attention and to avoid the distracting effects of anxiety all lead to better recall during the school years. The basic developmental change, evidenced particularly in recall measures, appears to involve the ability to organize larger amounts of incoming information and self-consciously transfer it to long-term memory. By contrast, the simple ability to remember whether or not something has been experienced previously, as evidenced by recognition tests, may not improve very much from the preschool years to preadolescence.

Process 3: Generation of hypotheses   The perception and interpretation of events and their storage in memory are typically the first two processes activated when the child solves a problem. The third process is the generation of hypotheses or possible solutions, in other words, the production of alternative ideas to solve the problem. This process is called the *induction phase* of problem-solving and is related to the notion of creativity.

The most common intellectual problem a child has to solve is to categorize new objects. The child of 6 has learned a basic set of concepts for the objects most frequently encountered—animals, food, clothing, planes, cars, furniture, homes, money, women, men. When he encounters a new object—a helicopter, for example—he wants to know to what category it belongs. The helicopter is large; perhaps it is a truck. The helicopter flies; perhaps it is a bird. The category in which the object is placed makes a difference in behavior: A child would not respond to a very large, noisy bird, which might be frightening, in the same way he would to a colorful flying machine, which might be very attractive.

Hypotheses and decisions about "what something is" are not generated by adding up the total number of similarities between the new object and a representative of a known category. Instead a few special or critical characteristics determine the child's judgment that two objects are similar—that a helicopter and an airplane are similar because they both fly and are both mechanical, even though they don't look very much alike. Many experiments have been designed to discover the critical features children use in categorization. In one (43), 4-year-olds were given a line drawing of a house (Picture A in Figure 4.11) and then shown two other drawings of houses, one of the same size and color but upside down (Picture B) and the other right side up but of different size and color (Picture C). When asked, "Which is most like Picture A?" the children were most likely to choose Picture B, even though they knew the house was upside down. They chose to regard orientation as a less critical feature than size and color.

The child with a rich and varied storehouse of schemata, images, symbols, and concepts is typically regarded as *intelligent*. Obviously a rich storehouse of knowledge is valuable in generating possible solutions to problems, but intelligence is not the only important factor; another is *creativity*, which may be defined as the ability to *use* one's intelligence in an original and constructive way. Intelligence and creativity are related, for it is difficult to be creative without a reservoir of knowledge, but intelligent children can be creative or not. There are many tests of creativity. Among the simplest and most straightforward are those that request the child to generate as many ideas as possible on a given

● Figure 4.11   Test item to determine whether orientation or size-color is used as the primary basis for similiarity.

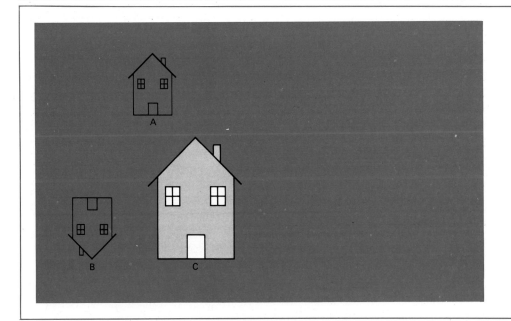

Figure 4.12 Drawings used to test creativity. (From M. A. Wallach and N. Kogan. *Modes of Thinking in Young Children.* New York: Holt, Rinehart & Winston, 1965, figures 2 and 3. By permission.)

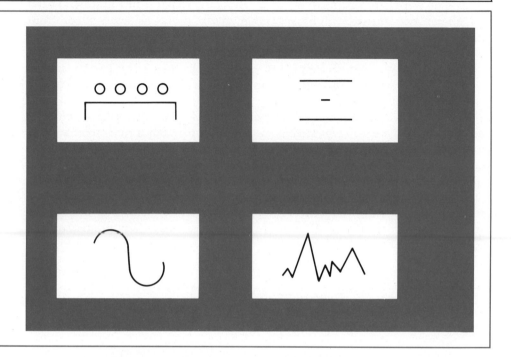

topic. How many different ways can you use a newspaper? A shoe? Name all the things you know that are sharp. In what ways are a train and a tractor alike? The children can be shown line drawings and asked to name all the things each drawing might be (Figure 4.12, top), or all the things each design makes them think of (Figure 4.12, bottom). The children who give the most answers (or the most unique answers) are classified as creative. This measure of creativity is essentially uncorrelated with standard tests of intelligence (50).

A creative, intelligent child is outstanding at generating possible solutions to a problem, but there are still obstacles to consider. One is *failure to understand the problem.* Many times young children do not understand the vocabulary used in a question. If they are asked, "What must you do to make water boil?" they might not answer because they are unaccustomed to the grammatical form "must you do." If the question is rephrased, "What do you do to make water boil?" they can answer correctly—"Put it on the stove." Similarly, children 6 or 7 years old and younger are often confused by questions involving hypothetical, make-believe objects or events. "If a three-headed fish met a four-headed fish, how many heads would there be all together?" 6-year-olds may refuse to consider this question, even though they can add 3 and 4 correctly, because they know there are no fish with more than one head.

A second obstacle to problem-solving is *failure to remember the problem*. In one of Piaget's famous problems, the examiner places six blue buttons and four red buttons on the table and asks, "Are there more blue buttons or more buttons?" There are many reasons why a child might answer incorrectly: One is that he or she might forget the question—was it "more blue or more buttons," or was it "more blue or more red buttons?"

A third obstacle is *lack of knowledge*. Isolated Indian children living in poor Guatemalan villages where illness is common had trouble with a test item that required finding an acceptable explanation for "why a man was so happy (for the last few weeks) that he has been singing." American 8-year-olds can generate several possible reasons; perhaps he has just been promoted in his job. But the poor Guatemalan 8-year-old is perplexed. "He is crazy, for no one can be happy for that long a time."

A fourth barrier to problem-solving is *possession of other hypotheses*. As scientists are well aware, strong belief in old, established theories can discourage creative new integrations. A fifth obstacle is *fear of error*. The fear of criticism from others and the desire to avoid self-generated feelings of shame and humiliation for making a mistake often keep children from expressing or even thinking about new ideas.

Each of the five conditions that inhibit the generation of possible solutions to a problem is particularly dominant at different stages of development. Most preschool children have trouble understanding and remembering the problem, and they may lack sufficient knowledge. School-age children may lack knowledge, too, and they are particularly susceptible to fears of failure. Older children and adults have trouble with strong preconceptions and beliefs that lead them to reject new, insightful solutions that contradict their older views. The truly creative child is rare. He or she must be intelligent, knowledgeable, open to new ideas, and willing to take chances, without excessive fear of criticism.

Process 4: Evaluation   Evaluation pertains to the degree to which the child pauses to consider and assess the quality of his or her thinking. This process influences the entire spectrum of mental work: initial perception, recall, and the generation of hypotheses.

Consider the generation of hypotheses. Some children accept and report the first hypothesis they produce and act on it without stopping to think about its appropriateness or accuracy. These children are called *impulsive*. Other children are *reflective*. They devote a longer time to the consideration of the merits of their ideas before reporting or acting; they censor poor hypotheses and generate new ones. This difference among children is evident as early as 2 years of age and seems to be relatively stable over time (29, 30, 31).

One of the tests used to assess the tendency to be reflective or impulsive is called Matching Familiar Figures (see Figure 4.13). The top figure is the stan-

●Figure 4.13   Sample items from the Matching Familiar Figures Test for reflection-impulsivity in the school-age child.

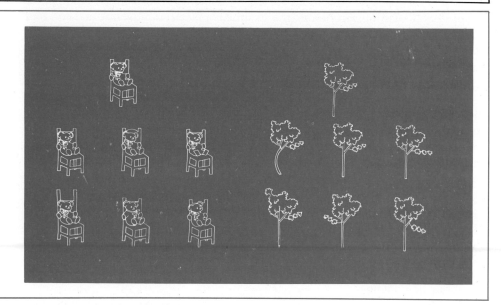

dard; the child is asked to decide which of the six test figures matches the standard. The time required to decide and the number of errors are recorded. Those children who respond quickly and make many errors are considered impulsive, while the slower, more accurate children are considered reflective. Among American children there is a dramatic decrease in errors and a corresponding increase in response time from 5 to 12 years of age; so children in general become more reflective. They tend to keep their relative standing in their age group, however—the most reflective 5-year-olds become the most reflective 10-year-olds; the individual differences remain, in spite of the general trend.

Reflective children, in contrast to impulsive children, wait longer before they describe a picture or answer a question, and they are less likely to recall words that did not appear in a previous list or to make errors in reading or reasoning tests. In short, they are more cautious and, as a result, more accurate. In tests like Matching Familiar Figures, studies of eye movements show that the reflective children scan the stimuli more efficiently and are more likely to look at every variant before offering a choice (18). The impulsive children adopt a much riskier strategy and answer before they have examined every variant carefully.

Impulsive children can be taught to be more reflective (15, 51). They can be given rewards for being more cautious and more accurate and punishments for impulsive behavior. Watching other children behaving reflectively is also effective, as is simply instructing the impulsive children to inhibit their quick responses. And having a teacher who is reflective can be a significant factor among young school children (63).

Although the disposition to be impulsive or reflective is modifiable, the usual stability of this trait in several situations over many years of life suggests that there may be innate factors involved. There is reason to believe that some children are born with a temperament that makes it easier for them to become reflective or impulsive (see pp. 76–82). Observation of infants' play with toys reveals that some children flit from toy to toy, while others play with one toy for longer periods. There is a tendency for the more deliberate infants to become reflective school children and for the more impulsive children to remain so. As in most human traits, environmental and innate biological factors probably interact in producing the final result.

Process 5: Deductive reasoning   In the *deductive phase* of problem-solving, the generated hypotheses are tested for appropriateness in a process that involves deductive reasoning. Deductive reasoning is "if–then" reasoning. It may proceed entirely in the mind—for example, solving a problem in geometry with logic—or it may entail gathering empirical evidence, much as a scientist does. Suppose a child sees a large animal lying by a tree. She might first assume the animal is sleeping. After several minutes of observation, however, she may decide that the animal could be dead. She's not sure. She reasons roughly as a scientist would. "If the animal is asleep and I hit it with a stone, it will wake up. If it is dead, the stone will have no effect." She gathers empirical evidence with her "death test"—a thrown stone—and thereby enables herself to deduct which of two reasonable hypotheses is more probably correct.

The use of complicated mental routines and empirical hypothesis testing increases dramatically during the school years, especially after the age of 12 or so. It is possible that the "overseeing" function we have called the "executive process" is the most important factor in the development of these abilities. As we shall see in the next chapter, these behaviors are characteristic of Piaget's "formal operational stage" of intellectual development.

SUMMARY

Although children often use speech to gain rewards, reinforcement theories do not seem to explain adequately the extreme rapidity of language acquisition. Similarly, while children often imitate the speech of older children and adults, imitation theories have difficulty explaining the startling creativity of children's language. Direct attempts to reinforce children for more sophisticated grammar or to have children repeat more complex sentences have failed to show any increased capacity over children without such experience. It appears that children do not easily learn forms until they have achieved an appropriate level of cognitive development, and then they seem to acquire the forms without much effort. Linguistic theories suggest innate capacities for language that make language acquisition nearly inevitable, once the proper neurological "equipment" has matured. Although the rapidity and creativity of children's language acquisition are in accord with such theories, we know very little about the biological development of language abilities and even less about the nature of the interaction between the "built-in capacities" and the "specific language environment"—the actual vocabulary and detailed rules of grammar in the children's native tongue.

Most children utter their first word around the age of 1. Six months to a year later they begin forming simple two-word sentences, expressing a limited set of meanings found in cultures around the world. Examples are location—"book there"—and possession—"my candy." The average child's vocabulary increases rapidly, but many of his or her words are either "overextended"—"dog" refers to all four-legged animals—or "underextended"—"dog" refers only to the family pet. As children develop, their sentences lose their "telegraphic" quality; words such as prepositions, articles, and inflections (to indicate plurals, tense, etc.) are added. The order of acquisition of grammatical forms, remarkably uniform among children, does not seem to be correlated with the frequency of adult usage; explicit expressions presented for imitation and direct rewards for improved grammar similarly have little effect. There is a tendency, however, for children to acquire less grammatically complex forms sooner than more complex forms. This tendency appears to reflect a general principle of language acquisition found in several cultures; another general principle is the tendency to attend to the aspects of grammar that convey meaning, for example, word order, but only in languages where changing word order changes meaning.

Language abilities continue to develop in the school years. The understanding (comprehension) and use (production) of forms like the passive sentence—for example, "John was hit by Mary"—increases. Words that express complex social relationships, such as "sister," and double meanings, such as "bright" in reference to both light and intelligence, are mastered.

What is the relationship between language and thought? Piaget suggests that language development follows cognitive development, while Vygotsky suggests that thought and language, initially independent, become interdependent. Certainly words influence behavior, as in verbal mediation of generalization: a quarter and a stack of nickels are "the same" because they are both "twenty-five cents." Labeling very often helps memory, and verbalization in problem-solving tasks seems to aid in generating possible solutions.

Some scholars have suggested differences among social classes in the degree of elaboration (general meaning) in their typical sentence construction. While people from the lower social classes, who tend also to be from ethnic minorities, often use words and sentence forms understood only by their "in-groups," most can use "elaborated codes" if necessary.

As a brief introduction to the ways psychologists view cognition, we discussed five basic units of cognitive activity—schemata, images, symbols, concepts, and rules—and five cognitive activities—perception, memory, generating hypotheses, evaluation, and deduction. Cognitive activity that is "intentional" or "directed" is supposedly guided by some higher-order process that Freud called the "ego" and we call the "executive process."

Perception and interpretation are the processes by which people extract meaningful information from environmental stimuli. As children develop, they learn distinctive features of common patterns; this allows them to perceive objects in uncommon orientation or in two dimensions, as in drawings or photographs. Memory improves as children develop better strategies for storing and retrieving information. Generating hypotheses about possible solutions to problems is aided by the use of analytic and superordinate concepts and by the creative ability to generate many possibilities. Obstacles to problem-solving include failures to understand or remember the problem and lack of knowledge—characteristic of younger children—fear of error, and the interfering effects of a firmly held but incorrect hypothesis—characteristic of older children and adolescents. Reflective children tend to evaluate their information and hypotheses before acting or deciding; impulsive children tend to act more quickly but less accurately. Finally, deductive reasoning is used to test hypotheses in an "if–then" manner.

References

1. Anglin, J. Studies in semantic development. Unpublished manuscript, Harvard University, 1972.

2. Asch, S. E., & Nerlove, H. The development of double-function terms in children: An exploratory investigation. In B. Kaplan & S. Wapner (Eds.), **Perspectives in psychological theory: Essays in honor of Heinz Werner.** New York: International Universities Press, 1960. Pp.47–60.

3. Bandura, A. **Principles of behavior modification.** New York: Holt, Rinehart & Winston, 1969.

4. Bernstein, B. A sociolinguistic approach to socialization: with some reference to educability. In F. Williams (Ed.), **Language and poverty: Perspectives on a theme.** Chicago: Markham, 1970. Pp. 25–61.

5. Braine, M. D. S. On two types of models of the internalization of grammars. In D. I. Slobin (Ed.), **The ontogenesis of grammar.** New York: Academic Press, 1971.

6. Brown, R. How shall a thing be called? **Psychological Review,** 1958, **65,** 14–21.

7. Brown, R. **Social psychology.** New York: Free Press of Glencoe, 1965.

8. Brown, R. **A first language.** Cambridge: Harvard University Press, 1973.

9. Brown, R., & Bellugi, U. Three processes in the child's acquisition of syntax. **Harvard Educational Review,** 1964, **34,** 133–151.

10. Brown, R., Cazden, C., & Bellugi-Klima, U. The child's grammar from I to III. In J. P. Hill (Ed.), **Minnesota symposia on child psychology.** Vol. 2. Minneapolis: University of Minnesota Press, 1969, Pp. 28–73.

11. Chomsky, C. **The acquisition of syntax in children from 5 to 10.** Cambridge: MIT press, 1969.

12. Chomsky, N. A review of **Verbal behavior** by B. F. Skinner. **Language,** 1959, **35,** 26–58.

13. Chomsky, N. **Syntactic structures.** The Hague: Mouton, 1957.

14. Clark, E. V. What's in a word? On the child's acquisition of semantics in his first language. In T. E. Moore (Ed.), **Cognitive development and the acquisition of language.** New York: Academic Press, 1973. Pp. 65–110.

15. Cole, M., Frankel, F., & Sharp, D. Development of free recall learning in children. **Developmental Psychology,** 1971, **4,** 109–123.

16. Dale, P. S. **Language development.** (2nd ed.). Hinsdale, Ill.: Dryden, 1976.

17. Debus, R. L. Effects of brief observation of model behavior on conceptual tempo of impulsive children. **Developmental Psychology,** 1970, **2,** 22–32.

18. Drake, D. M. Perceptual correlates of impulsive and reflective behavior. **Developmental Psychology,** 1970, **2,** 202–214.

19. Flavell, J. H. Concept development. In P. H. Mussen (Ed.), **Handbook of child psychology.** New York: Wiley, 1970. Pp. 983–1060.

20. Flavell, J. H. Developmental studies of mediated memory. In H. P. Reese & L. P. Lipsitt (Eds.), **Advances in child development and behavior.** Vol. 5. New York: Academic Press, 1970. Pp. 182–211.

21. Flavell, J. H., & Hill, J. P. Developmental psychology. **Annual Review of Psychology,** 1969, **20,** 1–56.

22. Furth, H. G. Research with the deaf: implications for language and cognition. **Psychological Bulletin,** 1964, **62,** 145–164.

23. Gagné, R. M., & Smith, E. C. A study of the effects of verbalization on problem-solving. **Journal of Experimental Psychology,** 1964, **63,** 12–18.

24. Gibson, E. J. **Principles of perceptual learning and development.** New York: Appleton-Century-Crofts, 1969.

25. Ginzburg, H. **The myth of the deprived child.** Englewood Cliffs. N.J.: Prentice-Hall, 1972.

26. Haber, R. N., & Haber, R. B. Eidetic imagery. **Perceptual Motor Skills,** 1964, **19,** 131–138.

27. Harris, G. J., & Burke, D. The effects of grouping on short term serial recall of digits by children: developmental trends. **Child Development,** 1972, **43,** 710–716.

28. Inhelder, B., Bovet, M., Sinclair, H., & Smock, D. C. On cognitive development. **American Psychologist,** 1966, **21,** 160–164.

29. Kagan, J. Individual differences in the resolution of response uncertainty. **Journal of Personality and Social Psychology,** 1965, **2,** 154–160.

30. Kagan, J. Reflection impulsivity and reading ability in primary grade children. **Child Development,** 1965, **36,** 609–628.

31. Kagan, J. Generality and dynamics of conceptual tempo. **Journal of Abnormal Psychology,** 1966, **71,** 17–24.

32. Kagan, J. Cross cultural perspectives on early development. Paper presented at the meeting of the American Association for the Advancement of Science, Washington, D.C., December, 1972.

33. Kagan, J., Klein, R. E., Haith, M. M., & Morrison, F. J. Memory and meaning in two cultures. **Child Development,** 1973, **44,** 221–223.

34. Kagan, J., Rosman, B. L., Day, D., Albert, J., & Philips, W. Information processing in the child. **Psychological Monographs,** 1964, **78**(1, Whole No. 578).

35. Keeney, T. J., Cannizzo, S. R., & Flavell, J. H. Spontaneous and induced verbal rehearsal in a recall task. **Child Development,** 1967, **38,** 953–966.

36. Kessel, F. S. The role of syntax in children's comprehension from ages six to twelve. **Monographs of the Society for Research in Child Development,** 1970, **35**(6, Whole No. 139).

37. Kuenne, M. R. Experimental investigation of the relation of language to transportation behavior in young children. **Journal of Experimental Psychology,** 1946, **36,** 471–490.

38. Labov, W. The logic of nonstandard English. In F. Williams (Ed.), **Language and poverty: perspectives on a theme.** Chicago: Markham, 1970. Pp. 153–189.

39. Labov, W. Academic ignorance and black intelligence. **Atlantic Monthly,** 1972, **229**(June), 59–67.

40. Liublinskaya, A. A. The development of children's speech and thought. In B. Simon (Ed.), **Psychology in the Soviet Union.** Stanford, Calif.: Stanford University Press, 1957. Pp. 197–204.

41. Loban, W. D. **Problems in oral English.** (Research Report No. 5.) Champaign, Ill.: National Council of Teachers of English, 1966.

42. Luria, A. R. The role of language in the formation of temporary connections. In B. Simon (Ed.), **Psychology in the Soviet Union.** Stanford, Calif.: Stanford University Press, 1957. Pp. 115–129.

43. McGurk, H. The salience of orientation in young children's perception of form. **Child Development,** 1972, **43,** 1047–1052.

44. McNeill, D. The development of language. In P. Mussen (Ed.), **Carmichael's Manual of child development.** Vol. 1. New York: Wiley, 1970. Pp. 1061–1161.

45. Menyuk, P. Syntactic structures in the language of children. **Child Development,** 1963, **34,** 407–422.

46. Messer, S. B. The effect of anxiety over intellectual performance on reflective and impulsive children. Unpublished doctoral dissertation, Harvard University, 1968.

47. Neimark, E. D., Slotnick, N. S., & Ulrich, T. The development of memorization strategies. **Developmental Psychology,** 1971, **5,** 427–432.

48. Nelson, K. Structure and strategy in learning to talk. **Monographs of the Society for Research in Child Development,** 1973, **38,** No. 149.

49. Olver, R. R., & Hornsby, J. R. On equivalence. In J. S. Bruner, R. R. Olver, & P. M. Greenfield (Eds.), **Studies in cognitive growth.** New York: Wiley, 1966. Pp. 68–85.

50. Palermo, D. S., & Molfese, D. L. Language acquisition from age five onward. **Psychological Bulletin,** 1972, **78,** 409–428.

51. Ridberg, E. H., Parke, R. D., & Hetherington, E. M. Modification of impulsive and reflective cognitive styles through observation of film mediated models. **Developmental Psychology,** 1971, **5,** 369–377.

52. Robinson, W. P. The elaborated code in working class language. **Language and Speech,** 1965, **8,** 243–252.

53. Skinner, B. F. **Verbal behavior.** New York: Appleton-Century-Crofts, 1957.

54. Slobin, D. I. Cognitive prerequisites for the development of grammar. In C. A. Ferguson & D. I. Slobin (Eds.), **Studies of child language development.** New York: Holt, Rinehart & Winston, 1973. Pp. 175–208.

55. Slobin, D. I. **Psycholinguistics.** Glenview, Ill.: Scott, Foresman, 1971.

56. Slobin, D. I. Seven questions about language development. In P. C. Dodwell (Ed.), **New horizons in psychology, No. 2.** Baltimore: Penguin, 1972. Pp. 197–215.

57. Slobin, D. I. Universals of grammatical development in children. In G. B. Flores d'Arcais & W. J. M. Levelt (Eds.), **Advances in psycholinguistics.** New York: American Elsevier, 1970.

58. Staats, A. W., & Staats, C. K. **Complex human behavior.** New York: Holt, Rinehart & Winston, 1963.

59. Turner, E. W., & Rommetveit, R. Experimental manipulation of the production of active and passive voice in children. **Language and Speech,** 1967, **10,** 169–180.

60. Vygotsky, L. S. **Thought and language.** Cambridge, Mass.: M.I.T. Press, 1962.

61. Wallach, M. A., & Kogan, N. **Modes of thinking in young children.** New York: Holt, Rinehart & Winston, 1965.

62. White, S. H. Changes in learning processes in the late pre-school years. Paper presented at the meeting of the American Education Research Association, Chicago, 1968.

63. Yando, R. M., & Kagan, J. The effect of teacher tempo on the child. **Child Development,** 1968, **39,** 27–34.

CHAPTER 5
Intelligence

Human societies have varied widely in the personal characteristics they value most highly. A society that depends on wild animals for food might consider hunting skill to be the most important ability one can develop. The people of another society, farmers faced with poor and rocky soil, might value physical endurance and sheer perseverance, for the willingness to work hard and try again after frustration is the quality that marks the successful person in such conditions. The people of a small island might honor sailing skills above all others.

In our society, intelligence is perhaps the most highly valued trait. We live in a highly technological society, one in which the person who can understand and apply the highly abstract concepts of mathematics, physics, chemistry, and economics is the person who is likely to gain the greatest wealth and status. In a rapidly changing society like ours, the person who can learn new information quickly and who can adjust quickly to new situations is the person who will "keep ahead of the game."

The ability to learn quickly, adjust rapidly, and to solve problems efficiently is a large part of what many people mean by "intelligence." Beyond such general definitions, however, there is much controversy about the theoretical construct of intelligence. Is intelligence a single, general ability, or are there a number of relatively distinct abilities involved? Is intelligence a "native ability," determined primarily by education and other experiences? Do the so-called "IQ tests" measure intelligence adequately? Is a person with high intelligence apt to be highly successful in our culture? None of these questions can be answered unequivocally, and—perhaps befitting the importance of "intelligence" in our culture—the disputes are among the most heated in all of psychology.

Psychologists have typically approached the topic of intelligence in one of two ways. One is to explore the process of intellectual development in children. An 8-year-old is obviously more intelligent than a 3-year-old, but how? In what ways? What new intellectual abilities has the 8-year-old developed? The French psychologist Jean Piaget has been most prominent in the study of the intellectual development of children, and we begin this chapter with his views on age-related changes in a child's cognitive abilities.

The second major approach focuses on the measurement of intelligence. In the later part of this chapter, we will concentrate on intelligence tests: What do they measure? What factors affect intelligence test scores? Here the question of heredity versus environment will be explored, and both sides of the exceptionally controversial issue of race differences in intelligence will be discussed.

One of the issues related to the "native ability" versus "environment" question concerns the effects of remedial education for disadvantaged children. Some critics of government programs say these projects are ineffective; children of limited "native ability" are being pushed to equal the performance of children with considerably better genetic endowment; such environmental interventions, they assert, are fruitless, perhaps damaging. Other psychologists suggest that intelligence cannot be separated from "education," broadly defined as environmental experiences; if the "education" of disadvantaged children is improved early enough and extensively enough, there will be remarkable benefits. We will look at the research evidence on the effects of remedial or compensatory education in the last section of this chapter.

PIAGET'S STAGES OF INTELLIGENCE

Although intellectual growth continues from birth to adulthood and beyond, there are a few major periods in which significant changes in the nature of intelligence occur. For example, at about the age of $1\frac{1}{2}$ years, the advent of language ends the developmental period called "infancy" and the stage of intelligence Jean Piaget called the "sensorimotor stage" (discussed in Chapter 3). Now we will consider three later stages defined by Piaget's research: preoperational, concrete operational, and formal operational.

The Preoperational Stage (Ages $1\frac{1}{2}$–7)

Intelligence in the sensorimotor stage, from birth to $1\frac{1}{2}$ years, is manifested in action (motor behavior); children increase in their ability to solve simple problems, such as regaining a toy placed out of reach or out of sight. Toward the end of the sensorimotor period, there is evidence of a primitive ability to imagine or predict the effects of various actions, so that a certain amount of trial-and-error experimentation can go on inside the child's head. There is a kind of internal representation and manipulation of reality, and this development marks the end of the sensorimotor period as clearly as the development of language. From then on, asserts Piaget, intellectual development proceeds in the "conceptual-symbolic rather than purely sensory-motor arena" (18, p. 121).

The child in the preoperational stage has language. Schemata (mental representations) are now symbolic. The 2-year-old will treat a stick as if it were a candle and pretend to blow it out, or treat a block of wood as if it were a car and move it around, with dramatic sound effects. This ability to treat objects as symbolic of other things is an essential characteristic of the preoperational stage. Piaget offers an illustration in which a doll is treated as a live baby. "At 2 years 1 month, J put her doll's head through the balcony railings with its face turned toward the street and began to tell it what she saw, 'You see the lake and trees, you see a carriage or houses.' The same day she seated her doll on a sofa and told it what she herself had seen in the garden" (22, p. 127).

Piaget believes that preoperational children are incapable of true categorization or classification. Although a 2- or 3-year-old will occasionally collect similar objects (say, all the red blocks in a pile), the child presumably has no mental representation of a category and cannot define a characteristic that unites all members of the class.

The preoperational child is generally egocentric. This does not mean he is selfish; it means that he has difficulty taking another person's point of view. For example, suppose you hold a playing card between yourself and a young child, so that he sees the face of the card and you see the back. If you ask him what *you* are seeing, he will most likely describe the face of the card, that is, what *he* is seeing. The preoperational child tends to think that everyone sees what he sees, that everyone feels what he feels, and that everyone thinks as he does. Even his speech is egocentric, difficult to follow if one doesn't know the situation and approximately what the child is trying to say; he isn't able to take into account the requirements of the listener.

The Stage of Concrete Operations (Ages 7–12)

There are several important differences between children in the preoperational stage and those, age 7 and older, who have reached the stage of concrete operations. An *operation,* in Piaget's terms, is a mental routine that transforms information for some purpose. Examples are mathematical operations—adding two numbers to get a third—and classification schemes—putting all spotted objects together. The differences listed below reflect mental operations an older children can perform and a preoperational child cannot.

Mental representations   One major difference between the preoperational and the operational child is that the younger child cannot create a mental representation of a series of actions. The 5-year-old can learn to walk four blocks from her home to a neighborhood store, but she cannot sit at a table with pencil and paper and trace the route she takes. She does not have a mental representation of the entire sequence of movements; she walks to the store successfully by making correct turns at certain places along the way, just as a rat runs a maze, but she has no overall plan or cognitive map.

Conservation   One of Piaget's most notable contributions to developmental psychology has been his investigations of the concept of *conservation,* another mental operation that emerges around the age of 7. "Conservation" is used in the sense of something that does not change in spite of other transformations. For example, suppose we show you a ball of clay, then hammer it into a pancake shape; has the amount of clay been changed? Obviously not. But children under 7 are likely to answer "Yes," because the pancake *looks* like less than the ball. Similarly, if a 5-year-old is shown two identical glasses of water and then watches as one is poured into a wider glass, so that the water level does not rise as high, she is likely to say that now the amount in the wider glass is less than that in the narrower glass. She cannot consider all the dimensions simultaneously—height and width—nor can she mentally reverse an action—"If you poured it back, it would be the same again." She cannot perform the mental manipulations necessary to understand the concept of conservation of amount.

The preoperational child has trouble with the notion of conservation in many dimensions. If two sticks of equal length are placed side by side so that

● Figure 5.1 Child engaged in Piagetian conservation task. Changing the shape of a ball of clay does not change the amount of clay.

their endpoints coincide, all children will admit they are equal. If one stick is moved forward an inch, the average 5-year-old will say that it is now longer, while the 7-year-old will acknowledge that they are still the same length. Similarly, the preoperational child does not appreciate the fact that if the number of objects in two collections is equal, changing the shape of the collections does not affect the equality in number. If two rows of five buttons are arranged in equal lengths, all children will admit there is an equal number. If one row is then spread out, made longer, the 5-year-old is likely to assert that it now contains a greater number of buttons: The 7-year-old is unimpressed by the mere regrouping (Figure 5.1).

In general, preoperational children are swayed by appearance: The higher level and the longer row *look* like more. Even adults are influenced by such perceptual tricks; witness the manipulations of merchandisers to create boxes that appear to have more of their product than their competitors have, even though the amounts are in fact equal. When the child develops the ability to transform perceptions according to some *conceptual* rule—the width of a glass can compensate for the height—he or she can understand the notion of conservation in the face of obvious change.

Relational terms   The preoperational child has difficulty with relational terms such as "darker," "larger," and "bigger." She tends to think in absolute terms. A house is big; if compared to a large apartment building, it is still big. Similarly, a brother might be tall, since he is taller than she; he is tall even in the company of adults, for how can a tall person suddenly become short? The comparison of two people, objects, or events is a mental operation that few young children can perform well. After the age of 7, however, these comparisons give adult meanings to relational terms.

Classifications   According to Piaget, the preoperational child cannot think simultaneously about part of a whole and the whole. If a 5-year-old is shown eight yellow candies and four brown candies and asked, "Are there more yellow candies or more candies?" she is likely to say, "More yellow candies." Piaget believes this reply means that the child cannot reason about parts and wholes at the same time.

Serializations   Children who have reached the level of concrete operations can arrange objects on some dimension such as weight or size. The 5-year-old typically cannot arrange eight sticks of differing lengths in a row according to length. Such an ability is probably necessary for understanding numerical relationships of various kinds and, therefore, for the learning of arithmetic.

The Stage of Formal Operations (Age 12 On)

In this final stage of intellectual development, children begin to function somewhat like scientists. They are capable of thinking abstractly, of generating hypotheses, of spinning a "grand" theory or two. They begin to use systematic, formal routines (formal operations) to evaluate all the possible solutions to a problem. Consider the following question put to a 7-year-old and a 13-year-old: "A man was found dead in the back seat of a car that had hit a telephone pole. What happened?" The younger child thinks up a satisfactory answer and reports it: "The pole knocked the man into the back seat and killed him." The older child generates a host of possible answers: "The pole knocked him into the back seat." "He was riding in the back seat when the car hit the pole." "He was placed in the back seat after the crash to make his murder look like an accident." This child is interested in more information, that is, evidence that will enable him or her to reduce the number of plausible hypotheses.

Children who are capable of formal operational reasoning do much better than younger children on tasks that require systematic organization. In games like Twenty Questions, older children can carefully eliminate possibilities and "zero in" on the correct answer, while younger children tend to ask questions that are unrelated to one another and that seem to be asked simply because they occur to the child. Another example of a task in which formal operations greatly aided the problem-solver is one in which children were asked to pair colors (21). Given six piles of squares of different colors, children were told to make all possible pairs. The older children could generate a rule that would enable them to make these pairings in a systematic way; for example, they might start with one color—red—and pair it with each of the other colors—green, yellow, blue, orange, purple: then they would repeat this process with the second color—green—and so on. The younger child might succeed in pairing all colors but only with a laborious trial-and-error routine.

Formal operations are more concerned with the form than the content of a problem, and thus formal-operational thought is less distracted by unusual or impossible elements in a problem. An older child can solve a problem such as "If a banana can eat two rocks in one day, how many rocks can it eat in three days?" Younger children cannot imagine a banana eating a rock, so they will refuse to solve the problem; they cannot disregard the content of the problem and reason in a purely hypothetical way.

Formal, abstract rules that apply to whole classes of problems, such as those in mathematics, are used to advantage by children in the formal operational stage. Formal thought reflects a generalized orientation toward problem-solving. The basis of this orientation is the tendency to isolate the important elements of a problem and systematically explore all the possible solutions, evaluating each in a rational and objective way. This description sounds like a definition of the scientific method, and it is meant to; formal operations are basic to scientific thinking.

Adolescent children are in a sense budding scientists; they are also in a sense budding philosophers. Intrigued by abstract ideas, adolescents may drive their parents to distraction with their endless debates on the nature of truth and the implications of reincarnation. Older children become capable of thinking about thinking; they can reflect on *how* they solved a problem—on the rules and processes they used—and they can judge the general effectiveness of a procedure for solving problems independently of the solutions it may generate in a particular case. The child in the stage of concrete operations tends to deal largely with the present, with the here and now; the adolescent becomes concerned with the hypothetical, the future, and the remote. One adolescent was overheard to remark, "I was thinking about my future, and then I began to think about why I was thinking about my future, and then I began to think about why I was thinking about why I was thinking about my future!" Piaget believes that this kind of preoccupation with thought is one of the prime characteristics of the stage of formal operations (Figure 5.2).

INTELLIGENCE TESTS

"Intelligence" is undoubtedly one of the most mysterious, elusive, confused, and controversial words in the English language. Clearly we need some term or

● Figure 5.2 Preoccupation with abstract ideas and the process of thinking are prime characteristics of the stage of formal operations.

concept to refer to a person's mental capacity to solve problems; to learn, remember, and utilize information; and to reason and make inferences. We have just discussed the approach of Jean Piaget. Focusing on the processes involved in intellectual development, Piaget notes the differences in the quality of intelligence at different ages, culminating in the adult abilities to reason abstractly and, in general, to perform formal operations.

Now we will turn to another more quantitative approach, one that centers around the "mental test." The explicit emphasis of this approach has been practical—a concern with *individual differences* in intellectual ability and the *measurement* of these differences. There is less concern than in Piaget's approach with age-related differences and in underlying cognitive processes. Psychologists who use intelligence tests are usually trying to determine an individual's relative standing in his or her age group; they are less interested in whether people have developed new kinds of intellectual abilities that they did not have five years ago than they are in whether they have more or less intelligence than other students in their class. These rankings on intelligence tests are used for practical purposes—to make predictions about scholastic achievement and, often, to make decisions about who is admitted to a school or special program.

The Stanford-Binet

The first widely accepted test of intelligence was published in France by Alfred Binet (with Theodore Simon) in 1905. The intelligence test was invented to solve a practical problem. At the turn of the century, the public schools in Paris were overcrowded, and there were many mentally retarded children who could not profit much from the kind of schooling offered. The French Ministry of Public Instruction asked Binet, a psychologist, to devise some means of identifying mentally retarded youngsters, a way of discriminating between children of low ability and children of adequate ability but low motivation. The French educators wanted to know which students could be expected to profit from academic instruction. The test that Binet developed not only did the job for which it was intended, it also provided a model for all later tests; the tests used today are remarkably similar to Binet's "first edition." One intelligence test widely used today is a direct descendant, a revised version, of Binet's.

Binet did not start with a preconceived idea of an entity called "intelligence." He started more simply with the observation that, on a number of tasks, children generally regarded as bright did better than others. These tasks involved simple questions or problems: The child might be asked to build something with blocks or to explain why we have houses. Thirty such tasks, ranging in difficulty from very simple to very difficult, made up Binet's first intelligence test. In his opinion, the items on his test were tapping the functions of "reasoning, judgment, and imagination."

Binet's test was translated and adapted for use in the United States in 1916 by psychologist Lewis Terman of Stanford University. In America, the test is known as the *Stanford-Binet Intelligence Test*. Terman introduced the notion of the *intelligence quotient*—the *IQ*. By 1916, the items on the Binet test had been arranged into age scales, so that the average child should be able to answer all the questions up to and including those for his age. From these age scales, the concept of *mental age* was derived. A child who could answer all of the questions through the 10-year-old scale was considered to have a "mental age" of 10; if he was in fact 8 years old, he would be considered brighter than average; if he was in fact 12 years old, he would be considered duller than average. Terman simply divided mental age by real (chronological) age to obtain the IQ: The child with a mental age of 10 and a chronological age of 8 would have an IQ of 10/8 or 1.25. The result is multiplied by 100 to eliminate decimals; so this child's IQ would be 125. The average IQ, by definition, is 100. The child with a chronological age of 12 and a mental age of 10 would have an IQ of $10/12 \times 100$, or 83.

The Stanford-Binet was revised in 1937 and again in 1960 (27). In 1960, the scoring procedures were changed so that the literal meaning of IQ—that is, mental age divided by chronological age—no longer applies. But the average IQ—the score earned by the average child at his or her age—is still 100; higher scores still indicate relative brightness, and lower scores still suggest dullness. The term "IQ" is still used, although it is not strictly appropriate.

The Stanford-Binet includes a wide variety of items. The 2-year level of the 1960 version has the following tasks: placing simple blocks properly in a three-hole form board; identifying models of common objects, such as a cup, by their use; identifying major parts of a doll's body; and repeating two digits. The 4-year level items rely more on language: naming pictures that illustrate a variety of common objects; naming objects from memory; discriminating visual forms such as squares, circles, and triangles; defining words such as "ball" and "bat"; repeating a ten-word sentence; and counting four objects. At the 6-year level, the child must define at least six words such as "orange," "envelope," and "puddle"; state the differences between a bird and a dog, between a slipper and a

● Figure 5.3   Distribution of IQs in the Terman-Merrill standardization group. (From L. M. Terman and M. A. Merrill. *Measuring Intelligence: A Guide to the Administration of the New Revised Stanford-Binet Tests of Intelligence.* Boston: Houghton Mifflin, 1937. By permission.)

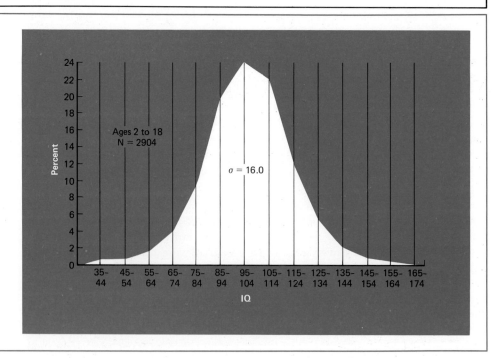

● Figure 5.4   Administering the Wechsler Intelligence Scale for Children. (By permission of The Psychological Corporation.)

boot; recognize parts that are missing in pictures of a wagon, a shoe, a rabbit; count up to nine blocks; and trace a correct path through a simple maze.

The distribution of Stanford-Binet IQ scores among American children is shown in Figure 5.3. Most children have average IQs, around 100. About 68 percent are within one standard deviation, that is, between 84 and 116. A little over 2 percent of the population have IQs over 132, two standard deviations above the mean, and an approximately equal number have IQs under 68, two standard deviations under the average.

Other Intelligence Tests

Two other individual intelligence tests for children, both designed by the American psychologist David Wechsler, are also widely used. These are the Wechsler Intelligence Scale for Children—usually called the "WISC"—for children between the ages of 7 and 16, and the Wechsler Preschool-Primary Scale of Intelligence (WPPSI) for ages 4–6½ (see Figure 5.4). While the items in the Stanford-Binet are grouped by age levels, the items in the Wechsler tests are divided into two scales—one verbal and one performance. The verbal scale includes tests of information ("How many weeks are there in a year?"), comprehension ("Why should we keep away from bad company?"), digit span (repeating digits forward and backward), similarities ("In what way are air and water alike?"), arithmetic, and vocabulary. The performance scale has five subtests. In picture arrangement, the child must order three or more cartoon panels in a way that tells a story; in picture completion, the child must tell what is missing from each picture presented; object assembly is like a jigsaw puzzle. In block design, the child arranges small blocks to recreate a design shown by the examiner. In the coding subtest, the children learn a symbol for each number up to 9 and are required to write the code symbol in blank spaces under a series of numbers. A Verbal IQ and a Performance IQ are derived from scores on the verbal and performance scales, and a Full-Scale IQ is derived from the combination.

Although there are differences in the test items and in the methods of scoring, IQs determined by the Wechsler and the Stanford-Binet are highly correlated. The Stanford-Binet IQ correlates about +.80 with the Verbal IQ of the WISC, +.65 with the Performance IQ, and +.80 with the Full-Scale IQ (20).

The intelligence tests described thus far must be individually administered. There are a number of group tests available, tests that can be administered to several children at one time. These tests have obvious advantages; in particular, they are economical of time. They also have limitations—one such being that the examiner has no idea why a child might be performing poorly. Practical decisions about children who deviate on group intelligence tests should not be made without individual follow-up testing, together with an investigation of other factors that might be affecting their performance, such as poor health or family problems.

Infant Tests

The individual and group tests we have been discussing cannot be used with children under 2 or 3 years of age. Yet many believe it would be useful to be able to evaluate the intelligence of infants. An infant intelligence test would aid adoption agencies in placing infants with adoptive parents of approximately the same intellectual level. A valid test would help in detecting mental retardation early, so parents could make better plans for handling their retarded children. In addition, most parents are anxious to have some authoritative reassurance that their children are "normal."

As a result of these considerations, a number of infant intelligence tests have been developed. In principle, these tests are constructed by the same methods used for all intelligence tests. A large number of items are selected that presumably measure important aspects of intellectual ability. A large number of infants drawn from all U.S. culture groups—that is, a representative sample—take the test. Some items are eliminated because they do not discriminate among infants as well as others; the remaining items make up the final version of the test. The test is "standardized" by trying it out on a representative sample of infants; "standards" (or "norms") of average performance are calculated.

These norms might be phrased in terms of average scores for infants of various ages, or the age at which half the infants pass an item—the median age—might be listed. It is then possible to assess the rates of progress of individual children as relatively rapid, average, or slower than average.

One of the newest and most carefully standardized infant tests, Bayley's Scale of Mental Development, consists of 163 items (2). The following list taken from the scale illustrates the kinds of items used in infant tests. The numbers in parentheses give the median age in months, that is, the age at which 50 percent of the children tested passed the items.

Blinks at shadow of hand (1.9)
Head follows vanishing spoon (3.2)
Recover rattle, in crib (4.9)
Picks up cube deftly and directly (5.7)
Manipulates bell; interest in detail (6.5)
Fingers holes in peg board (8.9)
Stirs with spoon in imitation (9.7)
Imitates words (12.5)
Builds tower of two cubes (13.8)
Says two words (14.2)
Uses gestures to make wants known (14.6)
Attains toy with stick (17.0)
Imitates crayon stroke (17.8)
Places two round and two square blocks in a board (19.3)
Names two objects (21.4)
Points to five pictures (21.6)
Names three pictures (22.1)
Builds tower of six cubes (23.0)
Names three objects (24.0)
Names five pictures (25.0)

Clearly most of the items tap sensorimotor and perceptual functions, although some involve an elementary understanding and use of language.

How well do infant tests of intelligence work? Unfortunately, they have proven to have limited practical utility for most children, although they can be of value in distinguishing between defective and normal babies. A well-trained, sensitive baby tester may be able to use the tests to diagnose specific disabilities such as deficient social responsiveness or inadequate vision or learning. On the basis of extensive experience, one clinical researcher concluded that these tests "can succeed in detecting the mentally deviant at a very early age, often before pathology becomes manifest through pediatric or neurological examinations" (5, p. 20).

However, a broader and more important question must be asked: Does performance on infant intelligence tests predict scores on later tests of intelligence for children in general? This is the issue of constancy or stability of IQ.

The Constancy of IQ

For most infants, scores on infant tests of intelligence do not forecast their future mental status. Bayley's Scale was given to infants who later, at ages 6 and 7, took the Stanford-Binet. The correlations between the early and later scores were low and insignificant, and Bayley concluded that "scores made before 18 months are completely useless in the prediction of school age abilities" (1, p. 100). Test performance at 21 months did not predict scores at 6 or 7 years much better (11). These findings emphasize the difficulty of making an accurate determination of intelligence before the age of 2.

Why are infant test scores uncorrelated with later measures of intelligence? Most psychologists believe that the lack of relationship is due, in large part, to the vastly different kinds of abilities sampled at earlier and later ages. Infant tests are made up primarily of items measuring motor skills and sensorimotor development—for instance, placing pegs in a peg board, building towers of cubes, obtaining toys that are out of arm's reach with a stick, and imitating gestures. In contrast, intelligence tests for older children and adults emphasize verbal ability, cognitive functioning, and abstract thinking. To expect these quite different sets of skills to be correlated is like expecting college professors to be excellent mechanics.

Tests given to infants under 2 have little value for the prediction of future intelligence test scores, but tests given to older children are more highly predictive. In one extensive study (11), children were given intelligence tests periodically beginning at age 21 months. Three different tests were used: the California Preschool Schedule in the preschool period; the Stanford-Binet in the school years; at 18, the Wechsler Adult Intelligence Scale. Table 5.1 shows the correlations of scores at each age from 2 to 12 with scores at 10 and 18 years of

Table 5.1   Correlations between Stanford-Binet IQ during the preschool and middle-childhood years and IQ at ages 10 and 18 (Wechsler-Bellevue)

Age	Correlation with IQ at age 10	Correlation with IQ at age 18
2	.37	.31
3	.36	.35
4	.66	.42
6	.76	.61
7	.78	.71
8	.88	.70
9	.90	.76
10	—	.70
12	.87	.76

SOURCE: Adapted from M. P. Honzik, J. W. Macfarlane, and L. Allen, The stability of mental test performance between two and eighteen years. *Journal of Experimental Education*, 1948, 17. By permission.

age. As you can see, scores at and after the age of 6 are quite good predictors of later performance—even of the IQ score earned on an adult scale during early adulthood.

Intelligence test scores are more stable over short than over long periods of time; the shorter the interval between tests, the higher the correlation between the IQ scores. For example, the correlation between IQs obtained at ages 3 and 5 is higher than the correlation between IQs measured at 3 and 7. Moreover, the IQ becomes more stable—less likely to change—with increasing age. Thus, the correlation between IQs at ages 3 and 5 is 0.72; the correlation between IQs at ages 8 and 10 is 0.88 (15).

Despite these relatively high correlations, we must be cautious in using test scores for predicting the future status of individual children. High correlations do not preclude the possibility of quite significant changes in the IQ scores of a particular child. In one longitudinal study of children between the ages of 6 and 18 (11), repeated testing showed that over half the children varied by 15 or more points at different times.

Three specific cases give some human reality to such statistics (11). The IQ scores for these three children are plotted in Figure 5.5 in "standard" scores, which means that zero is average for all the children tested. Notice that the three children are quite similar in IQ scores around the ages of 4 and 5; they score slightly above average. After that point, one child is relatively stable (783); one shows a dramatic decline (946); and one shows dramatic increases (567). We will tell you some things about the lives of these three children that might have been influential in the stability or changes in their IQ scores, but it is often difficult to be sure of the cause of change in any particular case; the major point is that IQ scores can change, often markedly, for a number of reasons.

Case 783, a boy, maintained a relatively stable IQ from ages 2 to 18. He had a poor health history and difficulties in school; he was considered insecure and he showed some symptoms of emotional disturbance. Many psychologists would consider these factors predictive of a variable IQ score, but in this case they were not. Case 567, a girl, was also sickly and, when young, was shy; after the age of 10 her social life expanded and she became more interested in music and sports. These changes in her situation were—perhaps—reflected in improved intelligence test scores.

Case 946, a girl, varied in IQ between 142 and 87. Her lowest score was obtained at 9 years, "a period of acute body concern and excessive modesty. Immigrant parents of grammar school education . . . were divorced when the girl was 7. This child was acutely uneasy around her young stepfather for the first years of her mother's new marriage. Much internal as well as external turmoil has characterized her life" (11, p. 314).

On the basis of their analysis of the test records of 252 children, the investigators "were impressed by the fact that the children whose scores showed the greatest fluctuations were children whose life experiences had also fluctuated between disturbing and satisfying periods" (11, p. 314).

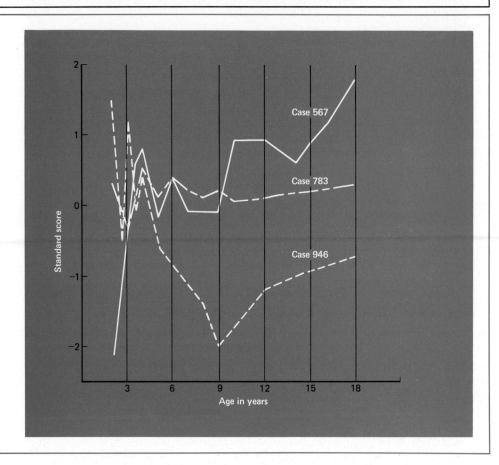

● Figure 5.5   Records made by three children on successive mental tests. (From M. P. Honzik, J. W. Macfarlane, and L. Allen. The stability of mental test performance between two and eighteen years. *Journal of Experimental Education*, 1948, *17*, 454–455.)

The Usefulness of IQs

What do we actually know when a child obtains an IQ of, for example, 132 on the Stanford-Binet? At the very least, we know that he or she can do the items better than most children; a score of 132 is better than or equal to the score earned by 97 percent of the children in the standardization sample. But is this performance on the Stanford-Binet related to other behaviors? Does the child who scores high on intelligence tests also do better in reading, writing, and arithmetic?

   In general, IQ scores have been found to be related to academic performance. One investigator (4) lists the following correlations between the Stanford-Binet test and school grades:

IQ and reading comprehension .73
IQ and reading speed .43
IQ and English usage .59
IQ and history .59
IQ and biology .54
IQ and geometry .48

Clearly, intelligence test scores are good predictors of academic achievement. This should come as no great surprise, since the tests have been designed for this purpose. Test items are selected on the basis of their ability to predict success in traditional school subjects. In addition, high test scores and good grades depend on similar skills, knowledge, and motives—good vocabulary, test-taking abilities, self-confidence, high motivation to succeed in intellectual tasks, an ability to reflect on an answer rather than to give it impulsively, and other such characteristics.

ENVIRONMENTAL AND GENETIC FACTORS IN INTELLIGENCE

The marked shifts in some individuals' intelligence test scores from one time to another suggest that life experiences have significant effects on test performance. This is to be expected, for the intelligence test does not assess "native ability" directly. More than anything else, such tests reflect a child's knowledge of his or her culture. Also, test scores are strongly influenced by motivational factors, such as the need to achieve. Since middle-class children are more consistently encouraged than lower-class children to learn to read, add, and write, one expects that IQ, social class, and school grades will all be positively correlated, and they are. Moreover, the personality characteristics that are consistently related to school success—persistence, responsible behavior, nonaggression—are characteristics fostered by middle-class environments.

In one major study of the relationship between personality and IQ change (16, 26), the children who showed the greatest increase in IQ during the ages 6–10 were compared to the children who showed the greatest decrease during these years. Compared to children who decreased in IQ, those who increased were more independent, more competitive, and more verbally aggressive. While there was no relation between the pattern of IQ changes and the degree of friendliness with age-mates, those who gained in IQ worked harder in school, showed a strong desire to master intellectual problems, and were not likely to withdraw from difficult problem situations.

Heredity Versus Environment

In our discussion of genetic influences on development in Chapter 2, we noted several kinds of evidence supporting the widely prevalent notion that genetic factors play an important role in determining intelligence. You will recall that the correlation between IQs of parents and their natural children is about 0.50, but the correlations between parents and their adopted children is much lower, about 0.25. The IQs of identical twins, who have the same heredity, correlate about 0.90. Even the IQs of identical twins who are reared in different environments correlate about 0.75, which is higher than the correlation for fraternal twins (different heredities) who are reared together—0.55. On the basis of these data and other evidence, many psychologists believe that there are genetic factors that affect intelligence.

How much of intelligence is contributed by genetic factors and how much by environmental influences? Most psychologists are unwilling to make a definite statement about the relative contributions of heredity and environment, and many believe the question, when phrased in this either–or way, is unanswerable. Intelligence, like most human traits, is the product of complex interactions of numerous hereditary and environmental forces, interactions that cannot be described in terms of the simple addition of the two factors.

We have already discussed, in several places, the effects of various environmental factors on intelligence. Injury or disease during pregnancy may affect the environment of the fetus and result in temporary or permanent retardation. The infant's diet during the first few months of life, particularly the adequacy of protein intake, also appears to be important for later intellectual development.

Social class is a broadly defined variable that is related to many environmental factors that may affect intelligence test performance. Compared to middle-class families, lower-class mothers are more likely to become ill during pregnancy, and lower-class infants are more likely to have deficient diets. Child-rearing practices differ between social classes. Middle-class parents, on the average, value intellectual development and achievement more than do lower-class parents. Middle-class parents consistently use more words in responding to their preschool children's questions and in teaching them how to solve problems. They also offer greater cognitive challenges, more "opportunities for labeling, for identifying objects and feelings," and they provide "adult models who . . . demonstrate the usefulness of language as a tool for dealing with interpersonal interaction and for ordering stimuli in the environment" (10, p. 875). Furthermore, in contrast with lower-class parents, middle-class parents use sentences with much more subtle and complex grammar, and their talk contains more abstractions and concepts.

Typically, what the middle-class child learns at home is of more use on an intelligence test than what the lower-class child learns. This does not mean that the knowledge of the lower-class child is inferior; it may indeed be superior for coping with a lower-class environment. But when it comes to coping with a question on an IQ test, middle-class children are more likely to find their experience of value. For instance, in tasks such as sorting pictures (10), both lower-class children and their mothers differed from their middle-class counterparts. The middle-class subjects were more likely to use categorical responses ("all handicapped people"), while the lower-class children and their mothers used relatively more relational responses ("a husband and a wife"). Categorical re-

sponses are not inherently superior to relational responses, but they are decidedly more useful when faced with a test question such as "In what way are book, teacher, and newspaper alike?" In general, the middle-class child is more likely to be taught to analyze a problem carefully, withholding judgment until various possibilities are considered, and these tactics are conducive to high scores on IQ tests.

Racial Differences in Intelligence

There is evidence that both genetic factors and environmental factors influence intelligence. Most psychologists believe we have just begun to untangle the complex interactions between the two types of factors. Others believe, however, that we can determine the relative contribution of heredity and environment for at least some groups in some environments. A small minority of psychologists believe that one can even compare groups and make educated guesses about the genetic endowment for intelligence of different races. The most notable and provocative writings on race differences in intelligence are by Arthur Jensen, an educational psychologist at the University of California.

Race, IQ, and heredity   Here is the gist of Jensen's position (13): First, complicated (and controversial) statistical analyses of the correlations between the IQs of blood relatives, some of which we have discussed, suggest that heredity accounts for 80 percent of the variation in IQ scores. Thus Jensen believes that genetic factors are far more important than environmental factors in determining intelligence. The second, related point is Jensen's review of research on compensatory or remedial educational programs designed to increase the cognitive skills and IQ scores of disadvantaged children (mostly black). These programs, Jensen claims, have failed; he implies that they have failed because genetic factors are so important in determining intelligence. Third, numerous studies show that, on the average, blacks score 10–15 points below whites on most standard tests of intelligence. From these three lines of evidence, Jensen suggests, we may conclude that it is a distinct possibility (not a fact) that blacks are genetically inferior to whites in intelligence. It is a possibility, he claims, that warrants research and that, if true, has wide-ranging implications for education and other fields.

A response to Jensen   Like most psychologists, we disagree with Jensen's interpretations of the data and with his conclusions. In our opinion, the evidence does not support the genetic superiority of any race. We will present a few of our reasons, but our brief discussion can be no more than an overview. We strongly recommend that interested students read Jensen's original article (13) and a book entitled *Race Differences in Intelligence* (19) which is probably the best statement of the position of the majority of psychologists.

Examination of the data on identical twins shows that IQ scores are significantly influenced by environmental factors. Identical twins reared in drastically different environments do not resemble each other as closely as those reared in more similar environments. In one study (7), identical twins reared in different environments were found to have an average difference in IQ of 14 points, roughly the same average difference found between black and white populations. On the basis of these data, I. I. Gottesman, a leading behavioral geneticist, concluded, "The differences observed . . . between whites and Negroes can hardly be accepted as sufficient evidence that with respect to intelligence the Negro American is genetically less endowed" (7, p. 28).

As we noted earlier, most psychologists reject Jensen's conclusions that 80 percent—or, for that matter, any specific proportion—of the variation in intelligence is attributable to heredity. But even if we were able to estimate accurately the contribution of heredity to the determination of intelligence test scores in one group—for example, in the white, middle-class group from which most of the subjects in the twin studies come—we could not assume that the same estimate holds for other ethnic groups or other social classes. Consider, as an analogy, the trait of skin color. In a mixed population like that of the United States, genetic factors account for much of the variation in skin color. But in a homogeneous population such as Norway's, environmental factors—whether or not the person works outdoors, for example—account for much more of the variation in skin color. Thus genetic factors might play a greater role for whites than for blacks, who suffer more, on the average, from environmental obstacles like poor diets and discrimination. Recent estimates suggest that, indeed, environmental influences on IQ are stronger in socioeconomically disadvantaged families (24). Perhaps if "all children had optimal environments for development, then genetic differences would account for most of the variance of behavior" (23, p. 1294). But this is not the situation today.

Suppose it were the case that genetic factors accounted for a sizable percentage of the variation in the IQs of whites and also for a similarly large percentage of the variation in those of blacks. Even then, it could not be concluded that the difference between the average white's score and the average black's is due to genetic differences between races. To clarify this point, consider some data on height, a physical trait that is determined largely by genetic factors. In white middle-class populations, heredity is estimated (from twin studies) to account for about 90 percent of the variance in height—an estimate higher than even the most extreme figures for intelligence. With that in mind, we can compare the average height of two groups: Indian children living in rural areas of Central and South America and Indian children living in towns and cities in the same countries. The rural children are, on the average, significantly shorter than the urban children. Is this difference genetic? It is very unlikely, since both groups come from the same racial stock and have approximately the same average genetic endowment. *Within* each group, there are some tall and some short children, and this variety is probably 90 percent genetic in origin; but the difference *between* groups is probably close to 100 percent environmental. The rural children do not grow as tall as those in the cities because they suffer more from disease and malnutrition, not because they are genetically inferior. Thus, in intelligence, one need not conclude that racial groups differ in genetic endowment even if there is evidence of significant genetic influence on intelligence within each group. As one prominent psychologist put it, "The essential error in Jensen's argument is the conclusion that if a trait is under genetic control, differences between two populations in that trait must be due to genetic factors. This is the heart of Jensen's position, and it is not persuasive" (14, p. 275).

Finally, we cannot agree with Jensen's verdict that compensatory education is without value. Even if a trait is in part genetically determined, it does not mean that environmental changes will have little effect. We can use the analogy of height: The average height of children in the United States and in many other countries has increased considerably during the past 200 years, as a function of better nutrition and immunization against disease. Suppose some scientist had estimated the relative contribution of genetic factors to height as 90 percent in the year 1800. "Would it then have been safe to conclude that height cannot be increased through environmental influences? If that conclusion had been drawn, it would have been wrong" (6, p. 302).

The traditional preschool, oriented primarily toward children's play, has not been effective in raising the intelligence levels of children from poor families, but other, more intensive programs have been quite successful. The effective programs are the ones that make concerted efforts to train children directly in cognitive skills and in languages; in some of the programs, parents are instrumental in the training. We will consider a few of these programs in the following section.

Improving Cognitive Functioning

As we noted earlier, many economically deprived families do not or cannot provide the intellectual stimulation that promotes good performance on intelligence tests. Children need interesting, challenging, and rewarding experiences beginning at a very early age if they are to realize their full intellectual potential, and many do not get such experiences at home. There is no evidence of marked differences in intelligence among infants of different races or social classes. By the time they enter school, however, poor white and black children earn significantly lower IQ scores, on the average, than do middle-class white children. In addition, the disadvantaged children frequently fall further and further behind in tests of intellectual functions as they progress through the schools.

In recent years many governmental and social agencies have tried to reverse this unfortunate trend with remedial educational programs for disadvantaged children. The goal is a very broad one: to improve the conditions of poor children so that they can develop intellectual competencies and motivational patterns that will enable them to share more fully in the economic and social rewards our complex society has to offer. Despite their high-sounding purpose, remedial programs have been criticized—by Jensen, for example—as ineffective. Are there effective programs? Or are disadvantaged children doomed by heredity and/or the irreversible effects of an unstimulating infancy to a life in which their relative standing on intellectual measures progressively worsens?

Some effective projects Fortunately, a number of studies provide dramatic evidence that radical changes in environment, especially if instituted early in life, can be effective in raising a child's level of cognitive functioning. In one study (25), seriously retarded babies were transferred from an orphanage to institutions for the mentally retarded before they were 3 years old. Each child was assigned to a "mother"—an older, mentally retarded girl who was put in charge of raising the child. A comparison group of children matched on age, intelligence, and medical history remained in the orphanage until adoption at a later age. After two and a half years, the children individually reared by the mentally retarded "mothers" showed great increases in IQ—an average gain was 32 points. The control-group children showed significant losses, with an average loss of 21 points.

The two groups were studied again 20 years after they left the orphanage or the institution for the mentally retarded. All who had been in the experimental group with individualized mothering—even though that mothering was given by mentally retarded girls—were self-supporting. They had completed an average of 12 years of school, and about one out of three had a year or more of college. In contrast, the average educational level attained by the control group was the fourth grade. Many of the control-group children were in state institutions, and none was really self-supporting. Clearly the individual attention given the experimental children when they were very young had highly significant and enduring positive results.

In another major study (9), investigators gave tests of intelligence to all mothers of newborns in a black ghetto. Those with a measured IQ of 75 or less and their infants were assigned at random to either the experimental or control group. The control group was given no special treatment; the children were simply tested at the same times as the experimental children. Children in the experimental group were assigned to teachers who were in charge of them for most of the day, five days a week, from the age of 3 months on. Most of the teachers lived in the same neighborhood as the children and shared their cultural background.

The general educational program included an attempt to make the child's general routine—eating, sleeping, and activity—interesting, exciting, and varied during the first year and a half of life. Then the learning experiences became more structured. After the children reached the age of 2 years, their daily curriculum included activities designed to promote the development of skills in language, including reading, mathematics, and problem-solving.

The infant's mother was not ignored in this program. The teacher had the major responsibility for establishing rapport with the mother. For the first six to eight weeks of the program, the teacher worked with the child in the home—until the mother had enough confidence in the teacher to allow the child to go to the research center. The teachers maintained continuous contact with the parents, reporting on progress. While the children were having stimulating experiences at the research center, efforts were made to improve the mothers' homemaking and child-rearing skills and to prepare them for better employment opportunities. It was hoped that increased earnings and increased self-confidence would lead to positive changes in the home environment.

As even this sketchy outline indicates, this was a complex, comprehensive, and multifaceted program, extremely difficult and expensive to implement, and follow-up studies of these children will continue for many years. The preliminary results are most encouraging. At various ages between 6 and 22 months, the children were tested on an infant scale that measured sensorimotor abilities and general cognitive development. At ages 6, 10, and 14 months, the experimental and control children performed at a comparable level. At 18 months, the experimental group began to show superior performance. The difference between the groups was even greater at 22 months: The experimental children scored well above the norm for their age, while the control group was at or slightly below the norm.

Beginning at the age of 24 months, intelligence tests such as the Stanford-Binet were administered at regular intervals. Figure 5.6 shows the results. At 24 months, the experimental children were already outscoring the control-group

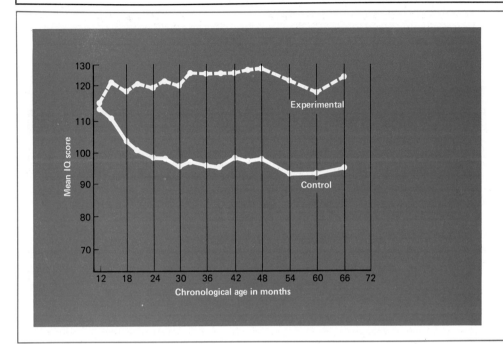

●Figure 5.6   Mean IQ performance with increasing age for the experimental and control groups. (From R. Heber, H. Garber, S. Harrington, and C. Hoffman. *Rehabilitation of Families at Risk for Mental Retardation*. Unpublished progress report, Research and Training Center, University of Wisconsin, Madison, Wis., December, 1972, p. 107.)

children by an average of 25 points, a difference maintained through the age of 66 months (5½ years). The average IQ of the children with special training hovered around 120, while the untreated children averaged between 90 and 95. The improvement in the intellectual performance of the experimental children was uniform; not one scored below 100 in the later IQ tests.

These are indeed impressive findings. Clearly the intensive infant stimulation program resulted in remarkable increases in cognitive abilities.

Intervention later in childhood   In both of the programs we have discussed, children began receiving remedial treatment very early in life. What about children who have passed through the important period of infancy in unstimulating environments? Can compensatory projects increase the intellectual talents of these children? Can enrichment later, during the preschool years, offset early cognitive deficiencies? It is impossible to answer these questions definitively at this time, but several studies suggest that with conscientious effort, such goals can be achieved.

The Early Training Project of Peabody College (8) is one of the most successful attempts to work with disadvantaged preschool children. The stated purpose of the project was "to see whether it is possible, by specially planned techniques, to offset the progressive retardation in cognitive development and school achievement that characterizes the culturally deprived child as he passes through his years of schooling" (8, p. 887). The investigators worked with black children around the age of 3 who came from poverty-stricken families. One group of children attended three special summer sessions of preschool, and another group attended two such sessions. Control groups received no special training.

In the special sessions, the experimental children participated in a concentrated program designed to stimulate the motivation to achieve and to foster the development of behaviors correlated with achievement, such as persistence, ability to delay gratification, and interest in school materials like books and puzzles. In addition, the mothers of the children met weekly with a specially trained teacher who tried to make them aware of their children's motives and to encourage them to reward strivings for achievement.

At the end of the training period, the trained children were superior to the controls in tests of vocabulary, language ability, and reading readiness. Follow-up studies 27 months later and again after five years, when the children had finished two years of public school, showed that the experimental group continued to demonstrate their early established gains, although the positive effects were somewhat less marked. The control-group children, on the other hand, showed the usual phenomenon of progressive retardation with increasing age. In short, without special training, children from deprived backgrounds are likely to fall further and further behind in intellectual skills as they become older. The cognitive functioning of specially trained children, however, is likely to improve, and at least some of their gains are likely to be maintained (17).

The active participation of parents who reward intellectual efforts is extremely helpful, but not absolutely necessary. Among disadvantaged nursery-school children, daily individual tutoring sessions, 15–20 minutes a day, have produced marked gains in cognitive functioning (3). In the tutoring sessions, designed to generate an "abstract attitude," the child became actively involved with stimuli in order to "comprehend their significance." The training tasks tried to improve the child's "ability to organize thoughts, to reflect upon situations, to comprehend the meaning of events, and to structure behavior so as to be able to choose among alternatives" (3, p. 380). In each task the child had to understand and use language, to produce relevant responses independently, and to discuss hypothetical situations related to the task—for example, past, future, and alternative courses of action. "By structuring the teaching time in this way, the teacher made maximum use of every opportunity to aid the child in developing his budding ability to think and to reflect" (3, p. 382).

The children in this study, 3–4½ years old, were divided into four groups, matched as closely as possible with respect to IQ, age, and sex. One group was tutored five times a week, and another group received the same training three times a week. There were two control groups: One of them had daily individual sessions with the teacher but no tutoring, and the other experienced only the regular nursery-school program. The study lasted four months; all children were tested before and after the training period.

The average IQ gain for the group that had five days of tutoring a week was 15. The group that had three days of tutoring per week averaged a seven-point IQ gain. The children in the two control groups showed very slight gains — 2.0 and 1.3 points. Thus, tutoring clearly resulted in improvement in intelligence test performance, and the amount of improvement was related to the amount of training.

Some of the children in the tutored groups manifested other dramatic changes in behavior. Several children who originally were excessively withdrawn opened up; they had before spoken incoherently, but now they became more articulate; and the symptoms of emotional upset they exhibited diminished.

> The most striking gains in the program were the apparent joy in learning and the feeling of mastery which the children displayed as the tutoring progressed. The untutored children, even those who received individual attention, showed none of these attitudes. This result is extremely important in that it strongly suggests that exposure to materials, a school-like situation, and an interested adult is not sufficient for learning. Both mastery and enthusiasm for learning will come only when the child can be shown how to become actively involved in the learning process (**3**, p. 388).

To summarize our discussion of successful remedial programs, we can say, at the very least, that projects such as these can give children from poor environments a "head start"—some cognitive abilities they would not ordinarily have when they began school. As a result of special training, these children are better prepared to deal with schoolwork, and they perform at a higher level in tests and in tasks related to school achievement (see Figure 5.7). We are therefore inclined to agree with the following statement, written by J. McV. Hunt in response to Jensen's negative appraisal of remedial programs.

> Compensatory education has not failed. Investigations of compensatory education have now shown that traditional play school has little to offer the children of the poor, but programs which made an effort to inculcate cognitive skills, language skills, and number skills, whether they be taught directly or incorporated into games, show fair success. A substantial portion of this success endures. If the parents are drawn into the process, the little evidence available suggests that the effect on the children, and on the parents as well, increases in both degree and direction. All this . . . sounds to me like substantial success. . . . Thus, Jensen's opening statement ["compensatory education has apparently failed"] is a half-truth, and a dangerous half-truth . . . (12, p. 298).

● Figure 5.7   The most striking gains in successful programs of remedial education are in the apparent joy of learning.

SUMMARY

Studies of intellectual development in children have been greatly influenced by the theory and research of Jean Piaget. Piaget's ideas about the nature of intellect in infancy, in the stage he called "sensorimotor," were discussed in Chapter 3. The second stage, roughly covering the years from $1\frac{1}{2}$ to 7, is called "preoperational." Although the intellect now develops in conceptual-symbolic ways, the child's thinking tends to be egocentric. In the stage of "concrete operations" (ages 7–12), operations (mental routines) enable the child to form plans and other mental representations, to understand the concepts of conservation, to think in relational terms, to classify, and to serialize. After the age of 12 or so, the child begins to think more logically, more systematically—using more "formal operations."

Attempts to estimate individual differences in intelligence led to the development of intelligence tests, sometimes called "IQ tests." The Stanford-Binet test once used a measure of "mental age" divided by real or "chronological age" called the "intelligence quotient," which is the basis of the term "IQ"; although more sophisticated statistical techniques are now used, an IQ of 100 is still the average score of children in any age group. Other commonly used intelligence tests include the Wechsler Intelligence Scale for Children (WISC) and the Wechsler Preschool-Primary Scale of Intelligence (WPPSI).

Although it would be useful to be able to estimate the intelligence of infants, infant test scores do not correlate highly with scores later in childhood. Many psychologists attribute these low correlations to the fact that infant tests focus on sensory-motor abilities rather than the verbal and conceptual abilities tapped by intelligence tests designed for children who can use language. Beyond infancy, however, IQ scores tend to be stable for most children, and they predict reasonably well the performance of these children in school subjects. In individual cases, unstable home environments can result in varying IQ scores at different ages.

High correlations between the intelligence test scores of closely related individuals suggest significant genetic influences in intelligence, but close relations typically share similar environments too. The differences in average IQ scores between whites and blacks have been attributed by some psychologists to genetic differences between the races, but the evidence for such a conclusion is weak, especially considering the sizable environmental differences between the average white and black person. It is clear that the values and child-rearing practices of middle-class parents (disproportionately white) tend to stress the verbal and intellectual skills that allow children to do well on IQ tests (and in school). One of the main supports of the arguments that blacks are genetically inferior in intelligence is the "failure" of remedial educational programs for disadvantaged children. While it is true that many such programs seem to provide too little and too late, several more intensive programs have been shown to have profound and durable effects. Improvement tends to be greater the earlier the child is helped, and the active participation of the parents is highly desirable. But carefully designed compensatory programs seem to benefit children of all ages.

References

1. Bayley, N. Mental growth during the first three years. In R. G. Barker, J. S. Kounin, & H. F. Wright (Eds.), **Child behavior and development.** New York: McGraw-Hill, 1943. Pp. 87–106.

2. Bayley, N. **Bayley's scales of infant development.** New York: The Psychological Corporation, 1968.

3. Blank, M., & Solomon, F. A tutorial language program to develop abstract thinking in socially disadvantaged preschool children. **Child Development,** 1968, **39**(2), 379–389.

4. Bond, E. A. **Tenth grade abilities and achievements.** New York: Bureau of Publications, Teachers College, Columbia University Press, 1940.

5. Escalona, S. The use of infant tests for predictive purposes. In W. E. Martin & C. B. Stendler (Eds.), **Readings in child development.** New York: Harcourt Brace Jovanovich, 1954. Pp. 95–103.

6. Gage, N. L. I.Q. heritability, race differences, and educational research. **Phi Delta Kappan,** 1972 (January), 297–307.

7. Gottesman, I. I. Biogenetics of race and class. In M. Deutsch, I. Katz, and A. R. Jensen (Eds.), **Social class, race, and psychological development.** New York: Holt, Rinehart & Winston, 1968. Pp. 11–51.

8. Gray, S. W., & Klaus, R. A. An experimental preschool program for culturally deprived children. **Child Development,** 1965, **36**(4), 887–898.

9. Heber, R., Garber, H., Harrington, S., and Hoffman, C. Rehabilitation of families at risk for mental retardation. Unpublished progress reports, Research and Training Center, University of Wisconsin, Madison, Wis., (a) October, 1971; (b) December, 1972.

10. Hess, R. D., & Shipman, V. C. Early experience and the socialization of cognitive modes in children. **Child Development,** 1965, **36**(4), 869–886.

11. Honzik, M. P., Macfarlane, J. W., & Allen, L. The stability of mental test performance between two and eighteen years. **Journal of Experimental Education,** 1948, **17,** 309–324.

12. Hunt, J. McV. Has compensatory education failed? Has it been attempted? **Harvard Educational Review,** 1969, **39,** 278–300.

13. Jensen, A. R. How much can we boost I.Q. and scholastic achievement? **Harvard Educational Review,** 1969, **39,** 449–483.

14. Kagan, J. Inadequate evidence and illogical conclusions. **Harvard Educational Review,** 1969, **39,** 274–277.

15. Kagan, J., & Moss, H. A. **Birth to maturity: A study in psychological development.** New York: Wiley, 1962.

16. Kagan, J., Sontag, L. W., Baker, C. T., & Nelson, V. L. Personality and I.Q. change. **Journal of Abnormal and Social Psychology,** 1958, **56,** 261–266.

17. Klaus, R. A., & Gray, S. The early training project for disadvantaged children: A report after five years. **Monographs of the Society for Research in Child Development,** 1968, **33**(4).

18. Lester, B., & Klein, R. E. Unpublished manuscript, Institute Nutrition Central America and Panama, Guatemala City, 1972.

19. Loehlin, J. D., Lindzey, G., & Spuhler, J. N. **Race differences in intelligence.** San Francisco: Freeman, 1975.

20. Mussen, P. H., Dean, S., & Rosenberg, M. Some further evidence on the validity of the WISC. **Journal of Consulting Psychology,** 1952, **16,** 410–411.

21. Neimark, E. D. Longitudinal development of formal operational thought. Unpublished manuscript, 1972.

22. Piaget, J. **Play, dreams, and imitation in childhood.** New York: Norton, 1951.

23. Scarr-Salapatek, S. Race, social class and IQ. **Science,** 1971, **174,** 1285–1295.

24. Scarr-Salapatek, S. Unknowns in the IQ equation. **Science,** 1971, **174,** 1223–1228.

25. Skeels, H. M. Adult status of children with contrasting early life experiences: A follow-up study. **Monographs of the Society for Research in Child Development,** 1966, **31**(3, Whole No. 105).

26. Sontag, L. W., Baker, C. T., & Nelson, V. L. Mental growth and personality: A longitudinal study. **Monographs of the Society for Research in Child Development,** 1958, **23**(68), 1–143.

27. Terman, L. M., & Merrill, M. A. **Measuring intelligence: A guide to the administration of the new revised Stanford-Binet tests of intelligence.** Boston: Houghton Mifflin, 1960.

CHAPTER 6
Preschool Personality Development

The preschool years, from the age of 2 or 3 to the age of 5 or 6, are years of widening social experience and rapid personality development. A walking, talking, relatively competent girl of 2 encounters her culture—interpreted for her by her parents, her nursery-school teachers, even her playmates—and by the time she enters school, she has become "socialized" in many important ways. She knows she is a girl, and she knows what that is supposed to mean; she feels a sort of kinship with her mother. She has a rudimentary set of moral standards. She has learned when aggressive behaviors can be exhibited without getting a slap or a frown from her parents—and when they cannot. She thinks "little children" are funny; they cry and run to Mommy or Daddy when frightened, and they seem to be frightened by everything; to be called a "baby" herself is an insult like no other. She views herself as much more mature and competent than she was just a few years ago—and she is right.

The development of these important social behaviors is the topic of this chapter. *Socialization* is a general term we use for the process by which an individual acquires behavior patterns, motivations, attitudes, and values that her culture considers important. At birth the infant has an enormously wide range of behavioral potentialities open to her. She can, theoretically, become either an aggressive adult or one who is self-effacing with others; she may turn out to be selfish or generous, honest or dishonest, achievement-oriented or lazy, sexually inhibited or free. Yet ordinarily the individual adopts only those personality characteristics and behaviors considered to fall within the range of what is appropriate, or at least acceptable, by her own social, ethnic, and religious group. Children of the American middle class are encouraged to be independent, assertive, socially responsive, achievement-oriented, and competitive. Zuni and Hopi Indian children in America and youngsters on Israeli kibbutzim are trained to be relatively less competitive and more cooperative. Japanese adults, compared to adult Americans, are generally more group-oriented and more self-effacing and outwardly passive.

Most of the research that we will report in this chapter has used middle-class children in the United States as subjects. This is essentially a chapter on American socialization patterns, a description of how these children in the United States learn what their culture values. Every culture has to deal in some way with the behaviors and motives to be discussed: sex, aggression, dependency, fear and anxiety, achievement. But cultures differ widely in their view of these behaviors: Some cultures are very restrictive about the expression of sex and aggression, others are very permissive.

Cultures also vary in their methods of child-rearing—the means of socialization. Again, every culture uses the same basic processes—learning by rewards and punishments, imitation, and identification—but some use harsh punishment to bring what they consider "uncivilized, evil" children into line with cultural norms, while others prefer employing rewards to encourage what they consider to be "innocent" small persons; still other cultures rely largely on imitation to socialize their children. In some respects, the large and complex society of the United States is a good one to study, for the range of values and the variety in child-rearing techniques is greater here than in most other countries. After considering the behaviors, motives, and basic processes of socialization, we will examine some global characteristics of the home environment (warmth, democracy in disciplinary policies) that affect preschool personality development in many general ways.

SEX

Sigmund Freud (in 1905) was scorned and ridiculed when he suggested that children have sexual desires and fantasies, but today the notion of sexual motivation in children is widely accepted. Indeed, many sexual behaviors can be readily observed, now that the strict Victorian prohibitions on their display have been eased. Masturbation and sex-play occur in very young children of both sexes, and these activities, if permitted, typically increase during the preschool period. The preschool child is also likely to have opportunities to notice the differences between his or her own genitals and those of adults and of the opposite sex. The discrepancies elicit curiosity and a desire to understand the differences. Questions about sex, particularly about anatomical sex differences, are common between the ages of 2 and 5 (37). Also frequent are questions about the origin of babies.

In spite of relatively greater acceptance of children's "natural" sexual motives, there are still many parents who feel they should suppress all of the child's sexual activity, interest, and curiosity. The child may be scolded or spanked for masturbating or even for asking questions about sex (67). If this occurs, the genitals may become the focus for conflict because they supply uniquely pleasant sensations and, at the same time, evoke the anticipation of punishment and anxiety. In more permissive cultures, children are much more open and spontaneous in their sexual behaviors. For example, in the Trobriand Islands, sexual exploration is not punished and, as a result, preschool children are very active sexually; in fact, a large proportion of their play is sexually oriented (50).

Punishment for early sexual activity or curiosity may be a major source of adolescent and adult anxiety about sex. It may lead to misunderstanding and attitudes that hamper not only adult sexual enjoyment but also interpersonal interactions in general. Such adverse effects could be avoided if parents would handle their child's sexual curiosity frankly and realistically, acting neither embarrassed nor secretive about questions or, on the other hand, overwhelming the child with too much information.

AGGRESSION

Aggressive behaviors are actions that are intended to cause injury or anxiety to others, and include hitting, kicking, destroying property, quarrelling, attacking others verbally, and resisting requests. Many of these behaviors derive from *hostility,* the motive or desire to hurt someone, but other motives also produce ag-

gression. For example, a child may hit or threaten another child in order to obtain a toy the other child has; in this case, the aggressive behavior has an instrumental, not a hostile, purpose. Preschool children sometimes hit playmates as a sign of affection, as a way of greeting; in this case the motivation is friendly, not hostile. Conversely, hostility might find expression in acts that are not generally considered aggressive. For instance, a girl who is hostile toward her academically oriented parents may do poorly in school because she knows her performance will disturb her parents.

Frustration and Aggression

Why are people aggressive? According to one popular formulation, the *frustration-aggression hypothesis,* aggression is a common and perhaps inevitable reaction to frustration. Frustration was originally defined as encountering an obstacle to achieving some desired goal (24), but most psychologists interpret this definition rather liberally. A threat to self-esteem can be considered frustrating, for example, if we view it as an obstacle to the goal of achieving high self-esteem. An internal conflict that prevents or delays the gratification of an important desire can be as frustrating as an externally imposed barrier. Feelings of inadequacy or anxiety can also lead to frustration.

There is abundant evidence that aggression is a common reaction to frustration. To cite just one experiment among many, preschool children were observed at play for 30 minutes to establish a baseline level of aggressive behavior. Then one group was given difficult tasks to do, frustrating the subjects. In a second 30-minute period after the frustrating event, these subjects displayed significantly greater increases in aggressive behavior than subjects in a control group, who had no intervening frustration (84).

The child's *interpretation* of the frustrating situation, rather than the absolute amount of frustration, is the most important factor in determining his reaction. He may encounter many situations that seem to be frustrating from an adult observer's point of view, but to him the events are inconsequential, producing little or no reaction of any kind. Careful observation of children in their natural habitats (home, nursery school, playground) indicated that the average preschool child experienced more than 90 "goal blockages" per day (27). Most of these interferences did not disturb the child much at all, and if he or she did respond, the reaction was typically very mild and of short duration.

This is not to say that children do not react aggressively to frustration, of course; they do. But one must take care in identifying what is frustrating to a child. Indeed, children differ among themselves in their assessments of how frustrating a particular interference is. A highly dependent child may be very upset by the brief absence of his mother, but frustrated little by a domineering playmate; a more independent child would find the conflict with a dominant playmate more disturbing than his mother's absence. Some children seem to have generally high "frustration tolerance"—nothing seems to displease them—while others are upset by every little thing.

Situational factors also affect the child's reaction to a frustrating event. Ordinarily frustration leads to aggressive behavior and, if the child is playing after frustration, a corresponding reduction in the creativeness and constructiveness of play (9). If children are frustrated in the presence of close friends, however, their play may become more constructive. In one study (71), close friends became more cooperative and more creative when frustrated, joining forces against the experimenter, the source of their frustration.

Learning and Aggression

Why are people aggressive? Frustration is one answer; another is that they have learned aggressive behaviors. Psychologists interested in learning and aggression in children have studied such topics as the effects of rewards; the effects of little or no punishment for aggressive behaviors (permissiveness); the effects of observing an aggressive model, especially on imitation; and the effects of punishment and parental influences in general.

The effects of rewards   Rewards for aggressive responses lead to increases in those responses and also to generalization of the behaviors to other situations. In one experimental study (8), preschool children received trinkets as rewards for verbal aggression while playing with dolls (calling the dolls "dirty," "bad"); a control group was rewarded, too, but for nonaggressive verbal responses. All children were then observed in another play situation with different toys. Compared to the control group, the children who had been rewarded for verbal aggression made significantly more of these responses both while they were being rewarded and also later, when no rewards were given to children in either group. In the later play period, the children in the experimental group also displayed more *nonverbal* aggression—hitting dolls, destroying toys.

Playmates are frequently sources of rewards for the aggressive behavior of children. Many parents complain that their children are more aggressive after they have attended nursery school than before. An aggressive child in the nursery school is frequently rewarded for her aggression by the victim, who gives up the desired toy or place on the swing more readily than an older child or parent would have. In fact, the nursery school may provide an effective setting for the increase in aggressive behavior in even relatively passive children. At first the passive child is a frequent victim of aggression, but eventually she may counterattack. If her counterattack is successful, her aggression is rewarded, and it becomes more probable. Later she begins to initiate aggressive actions, and if these are rewarded too, the passive child may become a holy terror (59). Children who are passive and, in addition, do not interact with other children do not show significant increases in aggressive behavior; neither do passive children who are unsuccessful in their counterattacks against aggressive peers.

Rewards can be used to reduce aggression in children if they are used with understanding. To illustrate, psychologists set out to control aggression in a nursery-school class by having teachers consciously ignore aggressive acts—which at least removes the reward of a teacher's attention—while deliberately rewarding, through attention and praise, cooperative behavior (19). This "training period" lasted for two weeks. The number of acts of physical and verbal aggression decreased significantly during the training period. The teachers were amazed at the results, commenting in particular on cases of some extremely aggressive boys who had become "friendly and cooperative to a degree the teachers had not thought possible."

Permissiveness   The effects of permissiveness toward aggression—allowing the child to express aggression openly and freely—are comparable to the effects of direct reward. In one study (8), the effect of a permissive adult could be observed in increased aggression from the first five minutes to the second half of a ten-minute doll-play session.

A permissive adult, however, seems to do more than simply *allow* aggression. Adult permissiveness seems actually to *encourage* aggression, as shown by an experiment in which children participated in two free-play sessions with a young friend (68). For half of the children, a permissive adult was present throughout, but for the other half, no adult was present. Two-thirds of the children observed with the permissive adult showed more aggression in the second session than they had in the first. However, in the adult-absent group, all the children showed *less* aggression in the second session. Apparently, the accepting adult was seen as granting permission for aggressive expression. In the absence of an adult, the child's own internalized standards (prohibitions against aggression) were more in control.

Modeling and imitation   Observing an adult or another child behaving aggressively is likely to lead to imitative aggression in young children. In one of many pioneering experiments on this topic by Albert Bandura and his associates (7), preschool children observed an adult attempting to solve a problem. During the trials of the problem-solving task, the model made many incidental, irrelevant responses that had nothing to do with the problem. These irrelevant responses included aggressive behavior toward dolls in the room. When the model was with the control group, she did not behave in aggressive ways. Later the children were asked to solve a similar problem. Of the children in the experimental group, 90 percent imitated the aggressive responses of the model. Not one of the control children displayed such behavior (see Figure 1.12).

Children imitate the aggressive behavior of people they have seen on film, too, and even aggressive cartoon characters can elicit imitation. In one of Bandura's classic studies (6), nursery-school children were assigned to one of five groups. One group saw adults behaving aggressively toward a large inflated plastic doll. A second group saw a film of the same models and actions. A third group saw a film of a model costumed as a cartoon cat behaving aggressively in the same way. There were, in addition, two control groups, one which saw no models and another which observed filmed models behaving nonaggressively.

After the exposure, children in all groups were mildly frustrated and then allowed to play individually in a room with a number of toys, including the inflated plastic doll. The results are shown in Figure 6.1. The live model elicited the most imitative responses, but the children who had seen film or cartoon models also displayed more aggression than did the control groups. The children who had seen aggression also displayed more aggressive behavior in general; that is, they spanked dolls, shot toy animals, and crashed toy cars more frequently than did the control groups, even though these forms of aggression had never been demonstrated by the models.

Modeling of *nonaggressive* behavior can reduce the amount of aggression in preschool children. Domineering and aggressive children in one study (20) observed dolls (representing preschool children) in little playlets depicting both aggressive and cooperative behavior. For example, one playlet concerned the use of a desired toy; the doll-children, in one circumstance, fought over it and

● Figure 6.1   Mean imitative and total aggressive responses by children who were exposed to aggressive models, nonaggressive models, or no models. (Adapted from A. Bandura. *Aggression*. New York: Prentice Hall, 1973. Data from Bandura et al., 1963.)

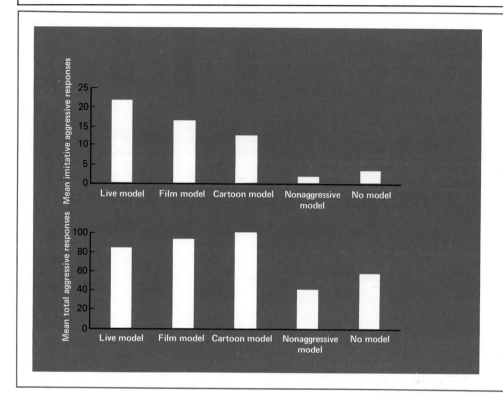

broke it and, in another circumstance, cooperated by taking turns. This modeling "therapy" had a significant and enduring effect, reducing the children's aggressive behavior (Figure 6.2).

Punishment and other parental influences   Punishment is another means to reduce aggressive behavior, one commonly used by parents. Numerous studies attest to the value of punishment for at least suppressing undesirable behavior (58), but many psychologists have argued that punishment has few long-term effects—the child becomes aggressive again as soon as the adult leaves the scene. In addition, punishment may have bad side-effects, such as causing the child to hate the parent. These criticisms are often justified: "In everyday use punishments are typically excessive, ill-timed, erratic, and administered vengefully without providing positive direction (3, p. 298)." On the other hand,

Figure 6.2   Cooperative and aggressive behavior by hyperaggressive children before and after receiving modeling therapy in which cooperative coping styles were favored over aggressive ones. (Adapted from A. Bandura. *Aggression*. New York: Prentice-Hall, 1973. Data from Chittenden, 1942.)

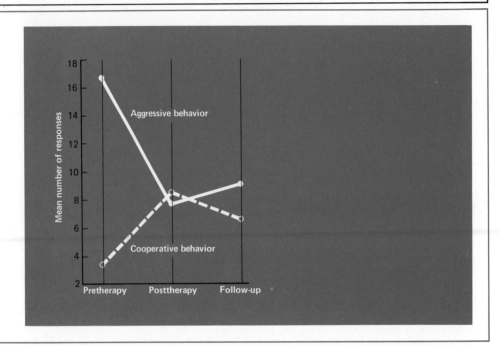

thoughtful use of mild punishment may be an effective means of modifying aggressive behavior in some circumstances.

A parent may punish a child either by withdrawing or withholding rewards or by doing something unpleasant (physical punishment). In the latter case, exemplified by hitting or spanking the child for some wrongdoing, the child may become hostile toward the parent or she may begin to avoid the parent. Reward withdrawal is, generally speaking, a more effective punishment. If, for example, the child is temporarily denied some privilege or possession, she is not likely to avoid the parent who, after all, is the one who can reinstate the reward. If reinstatement of the privilege or possession is made contingent on some constructive behavior such as cooperation, desirable changes may occur quite rapidly (3).

A parent who employs physical punishment to inhibit a child's aggressive behavior may reduce the incidence of such behavior, at least in the home. But the parent is also serving as an aggressive model, demonstrating to the child the potential usefulness of aggression and how to use it effectively (4). Hence the long-term effects of physical punishment may be to enhance aggression rather than to inhibit it.

Inconsistent handling of the child's aggression may also stimulate aggressive expression. Mothers who permit aggression on some occasions and punish it at other times are likely to have very highly aggressive children (67). When the child *is* able to behave aggressively, she is rewarded by the release of her hostility; when she is *not* allowed expression of hostility, the frustration becomes all the more intense because of the inconsistency of the discipline. This frustration, of course, may itself instigate increased aggressive behavior.

The Stability of Aggressive Expression

Can we predict the amount of a child's later aggressive behavior from his or her aggressiveness at an earlier period? Or is aggression so variable from one situation to another that there is little consistency for individuals over time? The research evidence indicates that aggressiveness is a relatively stable trait, at least during the preschool years. According to ratings by nursery-school teachers, a child who is prone to aggressive behavior at age 3 is usually also prone to aggressive behavior at age 5, and the children who have many "aggressive outbursts" are essentially the same ones at each age (25). Furthermore, the amount of aggression expressed while in nursery school is a good predictor of how much aggressive behavior the child will display in kindergarten (41).

One major longitudinal study included ratings of aggressive behavior during several periods of childhood, based on observations made in the children's homes, in nursery and elementary schools, and in day camps. Assessments of adult personality also included information on aggressiveness. Aggressive behavior was found to be more stable for boys than for girls during childhood and adolescence (44). Rage and tantrum behaviors during preschool were predictive of adolescent and adult irritability and aggression for males, but not for females. Boys who showed extreme degrees of aggressive expression during the early school years became men who were relatively easily angered and were verbally more aggressive when frustrated.

DEPENDENCY

The dependency motive is the wish to be nurtured, aided, comforted, and protected by others or to be emotionally close to or accepted by other people. This motive is likely to be directed to a specific person, that is, a 3-year-old who wants love and comfort from her mother may not want affection from her older sister, her nursery-school teacher, or her playmates. Preschool children manifest numerous types and forms of dependent behavior with different people: seeking assistance, attention, recognition, approval, reassurance, contact; clinging to adults or other children; resisting separation from adults; soliciting affection and support from a teacher. Of course, strong dependency motivation does not always result in dependent behavior, especially when the parents indicate that they consider such actions "babyish." Many young children experience considerable conflict between their desire to ask for help and comfort and their desire to please their parents, who are demanding independence. In the preschool years, this conflict is particularly intense (15, 35).

Changing Forms of Dependent Behavior

Sometime in the second year of life, children in Western cultures begin a process of "spontaneous progressive detachment" from their mothers, who are typically the first objects of the children's dependency motives. In one careful short-term longitudinal study (48), children's dependency behaviors were observed in a series of episodes with and without their mothers—in an unfamiliar room, in the presence of a stranger, and in a reunion with their mothers—at the ages of 2, $2\frac{1}{2}$, and 3. The children's protests when separated from their mothers declined substantially in intensity between the ages of 2 and 3. At the age of 3, the children were much less likely to cry and more likely to accept comforting from a stranger; they were less likely than the younger children to ask for their mothers. Furthermore, in the unfamiliar room, remaining near the mother and touching her or clinging to her also decreased with age. But even the 3-year-old children retreated toward their mothers when a stranger entered the room, using them as "security bases" in much the same way they had done at the age of 2.

Comparisons of the dependent behavior of 2-, 4-, and 5-year-olds show that the forms of dependent expression change with age (32). Of the three age groups, the 2-year-olds cling and seek affection most frequently, while the 5-year-olds are most likely to seek both reassurance and positive attention from adults (Figure 6.3). Attention- and approval-seeking are relatively mature forms of dependency expression, while direct bids for affection by clinging, touching, and crying are immature forms.

Intercorrelations among various types of dependency expression also change with age (25). Among 3-year-olds, *instrumental dependency* (seeking out the teacher for assistance in obtaining a goal) was highly correlated with *emotional dependency* (clinging and seeking affection); that is, a child who exhibited a lot of one type of behavior also exhibited a lot of the other. By the age of 4, however, this correlation had disappeared; the two types of dependent behavior were not significantly related. On the other hand, there was no association between instrumental dependency and another variable, *autonomy* (independent behaviors), among 3-year-olds, but by the age of 4, these variables had become significantly negatively correlated. Apparently by the age of 4, self-reliance and help-seeking had become alternative problem-solving strategies; if the child used one frequently, he or she was not likely to employ the other very often.

Situational Factors Affecting Dependency

Although dependency is fairly pervasive during the preschool period, the incidence of dependent behaviors is strongly affected by the situation. Children are

●Figure 6.3   A nurturant adult can be source of comfort and protection.

particularly likely to express dependency in situations that make them fearful and anxious. In a study of nursery-school girls (61, 62), half were observed with their mothers in a "frightening" room where there was a slow-burning alcohol lamp and pictures of sad faces on the wall, and where scary noises were heard, including a long banging, a child crying, and a high-pitched shriek. The other children were observed in a room full of toys, with happy pictures on the walls, while a phonograph played children's songs. Immature dependency behaviors (clinging, staying close) were observed much more frequently in the "frightening" situation. But anxiety did not affect the frequency of the more mature forms of dependency such as seeking attention, approval, and help.

A situation in which the child is not receiving what is perceived to be the due allowance of attention is another one that elicits dependency behaviors. Children make frequent bids for attention to a busy teacher (29) or a busy mother (66). Their desire for attention can be used to make them learn. In one study (31), a female experimenter played and talked with each of several children individually. In one group, this attention was suddenly withdrawn, presumably increasing the children's need for nurturance. The child in this group learned a simple task, with successful performance earning attention and praise, more rapidly than children who had not experienced the withdrawal of attention. Moreover, highly dependent boys were more strongly influenced than relatively independent boys by this treatment. Apparently the child's need for attention and nurturance was heightened by the withdrawal of nurturance, making praise and approval a particularly effective reward in the learning task.

Child-Rearing Practices

Parents, of course, have a profound influence on the amount of dependent behavior their children will exhibit. A child who is frequently rewarded for such behavior and rarely punished is not likely to give it up. Rewards for independent actions, together with discouragement of "babyish" dependency, will probably reduce the incidence of dependent behaviors. Most parents begin to encourage self-reliance during the preschool period. By the time children are 5 years old, they are expected to be able to dress themselves, to attend to themselves in the bathroom, to solve minor problems without help, and to play alone without constant supervision. If the parents are warm and accepting of the occasional failures and lapses into immature emotionality, development is normal: The child gradually matures as an independent individual.

Unusual child-rearing practices often produce abnormal behavior patterns. For instance, unusually high levels of early maternal protection of boys are associated with abnormal dependency in later childhood and adulthood. "A protective mother prevents the child from learning how to deal with environmental crises on his own and facilitates the development of a feeling of helplessness in the child" (44, p. 214).

Another child-rearing practice that has been found to be related to dependent behavior is excessive use of love and withdrawal of love to control the child's behavior—giving love, affection, and approval when the child behaves "properly," but withholding affection when the child behaves in unacceptable ways. This gratification-deprivation sequence can apparently increase the child's need for parental attention and approval. Another problematic child-rearing practice is inconsistent discipline. Clinical studies of overdependent youngsters (27) show many of them to be uncertain about the consequences of dependency overtures; sometimes the behavior is irritably punished, but sometimes the acts elicit a soothing, affectionate response. These findings are consistent with those of a study of kindergarten children. According to interviews with the mothers of these children, punishing dependent behavior but ultimately giving the child the attention or help he or she demands is likely to increase the frequency of dependent behavior.

> The situation in which the mother sometimes loses her temper over the child's dependency and sometimes responds sweetly and nurturantly, or in which she becomes irritated but nevertheless turns her attention to the child and gives him what

he wants, is one ideally calculated to produce conflict in the child. On the one hand, he anticipates unpleasant consequences to his behavior, and this anticipation produces anxiety. On the other hand, he simultaneously anticipates reward. When he has an impulse to be dependent, the impulse makes him both anxious and hopeful; the fear of the mother's irritation may make him inhibit his impulse temporarily, but the hope of getting the mother's attention through dependent behavior is still there. If eventually the dependent behavior does show itself, it will be exceptionally intense, doubly irritating to the mother, and impossible to ignore (67, pp. 173–174).

FEAR AND ANXIETY

Anxiety and fear, often classified as *affects* or *emotions,* also play an extremely important role in human motivation. They are unpleasant states that evoke behaviors designed to reduce the uneasiness and discomfort. Many normal problem-solving behaviors are motivated by the desire to relieve anxiety or fear. Sometimes, however, the source of fear is deliberately avoided; if the source is the child's nursery school or the neighborhood playground, this can mean serious self-restrictions of the child's activities. Both children and adults employ various cognitive distortions called *defense mechanisms* to relieve fear and anxiety, as we shall see (Figure 6.4).

Fear is generally considered the more specific emotion; the child is afraid of a definite "something"—fast-moving vehicles or large animals, for example. Anxiety is presumably more diffuse, less focused, "free-floating," a general state of discomfort that is less easily traced to one particular source. This distinction is difficult to maintain in real life, especially with young children. As Freud pointed out, a child with free-floating anxiety tends to find an object to which to attach it. For example, general anxiety about separation from parents may express itself in a specific fear of the building in which the child is supposed to attend nursery school or engage in other activities apart from the parents.

Preschool Children's Fears

Every child develops a variety of fears and anxieties. Some of these serve a self-preservation function, keeping children off busy streets with fast-moving vehicles and away from fierce animals and dangerous tools. Moreover, fears may serve as the basis for learning new, adaptive responses. The fear of speeding cars can motivate the child to learn the where and when of crossing streets safely. Fear of animals or natural events such as thunderstorms may stimulate the child's interest in learning more about nature and about natural science. However, extensive, overly intense, and frequent fear reactions, such as crying, retreating, cringing, trembling, and cowering, are incompatible with constructive behavior. If the child is to develop adequate emotional adjustments, extreme fear responses must be replaced by mature, purposeful reactions.

● Figure 6.4   Sometimes fear or anxiety can seem overwhelming.

Fears such as those of unexpected movements and strange objects, settings, or people—fears of real objects or real stimuli—decline with age during the preschool years. But fears of anticipated, imaginary, or supernatural dangers, such as the possibility of accidents, darkness, dreams, and ghosts, increase. Apparently the child's cognitive development—his increased understanding of the world and greater use of representations and symbols—influences his emotional reactions. In spite of general trends such as these, specific childhood fears are highly unpredictable, and there are marked individual differences in susceptibility to fear (40). A child may fear something in one context—when he is alone, for example—and pay no attention to it in another context—when his parents are present.

According to parents' reports, half of the average preschool child's fears disappear "spontaneously" about a year or two after they first appear, and only a third persist in their original form. Many fears, especially intense ones, seem to spread or generalize to objects or situations similar to the original source. A child who is frightened by a mouse running through his bedroom may become fearful of all scratching noises or all noises at night. There is a marked tendency for a child to adopt the fears of his parents—particularly fears of dogs, insects, and storms (30)—either by identification with the parents or by observational learning.

Eliminating Fears

When we say many childhood fears disappear "spontaneously," we mean "without any deliberate attempts to eliminate them." We do not mean that nothing happens or that the fears simply dissolve. In most cases, further exposure to the fear-invoking stimulus together with increased cognitive development allows the child to learn more effective responses to the stimulus. One can never assume that children will "outgrow" their fears automatically. Indeed, some fears are particularly resistant to change. Consider a young girl who, because of one bad experience or because she has observed a fearful parent, is afraid of dogs. If she were able to interact with several dogs, she would find most of them friendly, not in the least frightening. But her response to the sight of a dog is fear and, because of the fear, avoidance. Each time she avoids a dog—walking away, running into the house—her fears gradually subside, providing reinforcement for the avoidance response and making her *more* likely to avoid dogs in the future. And the avoidance response ensures that she will not have the experiences—contact with friendly dogs—that would allow her to overcome her fears. Thus many fears are very persistent, unlikely to "go away by themselves."

The principles of learning theory may be applied with success in reducing children's fear. For example, something the child fears, such as a snake, may be presented at the same time the child receives something pleasant, such as candy. After several such pairings, the child may begin to have more positive reactions to the object previously feared (42). In an experimental attempt to overcome fears (39), youngsters who were afraid of the dark were accompanied into a dark room by a friendly adult or were encouraged to become active explorers in dark places where they found valuable prizes. In these situations the connections between the feared stimulus (the dark) and the fear responses are weakened. Encouraged by the attractive, positive features of the situations, the children experience darkness with little or no anxiety; in technical terms, their fear responses are *extinguished*.

As children grow older and use language with more facility, verbal explanations can supplement conditioning techniques. Explanations alone are not often successful, but confrontations with the feared situation are aided considerably by encouraging words and gentle explanations (30). Often when children change their interpretation of an event, their response to it changes; explanations often remove some of the mystery and uncertainty in a frightening situation, allowing the child to view it more positively, eliminating or reducing his or her fear response.

Observing a playmate calmly approaching feared stimuli can also reduce the fears of preschool children. In one experimental demonstration (5), 2- and 3-year-olds who were afraid of dogs were assigned to one of four groups. Group 1, the *model plus positive context* group, attended a series of eight enjoyable parties. During each party, a 4-year-old child—the model—interacted with a dog. The interactions became gradually more intense and involved, from party session to session, from simply petting the dog to climbing into a playpen with it. Group 2, the *model plus neutral context* group, observed the same peer model performing the same sequence of interactions with the dog, but without parties. A third group—*exposure plus positive context*—attended parties during which a dog was brought into the room, but did not observe any modeling, and the fourth, the *positive context* group, participated in parties but saw neither the dog nor the model.

On the day after completion of the treatment series and also a month later, the strength of the children's fears were measured by their responses to an experimenter's request for more and more fear-provoking interactions with a dog. The higher the score, the more intense the interactions the child would permit before refusing. Figure 6.5 shows the results on a pretest, the posttest, and the follow-up. The influence of the model is apparent. The children in both modeling conditions displayed significantly greater increases in approach responses (indicating less fear) than did the children without models. Simple exposure to the dog was not enough; the positive context had a slightly beneficial effect—perhaps the children tried a little harder to please their new friends, the experimenters—but modeling was clearly the most important factor in the large and lasting reduction of fear. Of the children who observed a fearless model, 67 percent were willing to get into the playpen with the dog, even with no one else in the room; very few of the children in the other groups were able to do so.

Anxiety and Defense Mechanisms

At low levels, anxiety can serve constructive purposes, acting as a spur to creativity and problem-solving. However, strong anxiety may be emotionally crippling, evoking a deep sense of helplessness and inadequacy, rendering the person ineffectual and desperate.

Excessive anxiety may have its roots in harsh, punitive, or inconsistent child-rearing practices. Parents might impose standards of behavior that are too high; they might be too critical, never praising the child's efforts; or they might change frequently and inconsistently in their moods and discipline (45, 63). The child begins to distrust her own impulses, anticipating punishment or rejection. She becomes anxious and insecure. She may have nightmares or wet her bed (27).

Because anxiety is so unpleasant, the child develops *defense mechanisms* to avoid or reduce the painful feelings. Defense mechanisms are "cognitive tricks" in which some aspect of reality is distorted, although the child is not

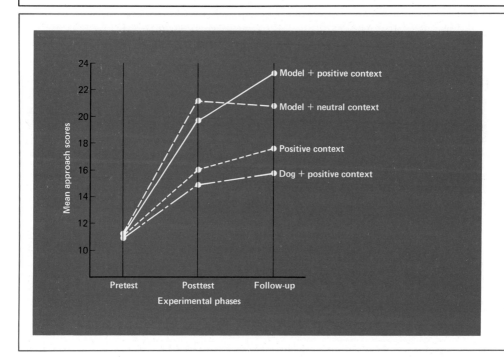

● Figure 6.5   The willingness of fearful children to approach a dog after four kinds of experience. (From A. Bandura, J. E. Grusec, and F. L. Menlove. Vicarious extinction of avoidance behavior. *Journal of Personality and Social Psychology*, 1967, *5*. Copyright 1967 by the American Psychological Association. By permission.)

consciously aware of the distortion. For example, a child may have provoked a friend's anger by attempting to dominate her. Because it would make her too anxious to admit that she was responsible for what happened, the child may blame the friend. *She* is not trying to dominate; her friend is, and with hostility at that! This defensive technique is called *projection;* the child attributed her own undesirable thoughts and impulses to someone else.

Other defense mechanisms include *denial,* the insistence (and belief) that an anxiety-provoking event or situation, such as the death of a beloved pet, is not true. A related defense mechanism, *repression,* involves excluding from consciousness wishes, impulses, or ideas that cause anxiety. A child may appear to forget an embarrassing event or, because of repression, be unaware of a desire to dominate or hurt another child. In *regression,* the child reverts to less mature behaviors—acts "babyish"—hoping to elicit parental attention. In *displacement,* the original object of an impulse is repressed and a new one substituted. The child may want to hurt her mother, but the idea elicits anxiety; so she decides it is a neighborhood friend on whom she wants to vent her frustrations.

Many children of preschool age have imaginary playmates to whom they turn for solace in times of crisis—after being punished, for instance. Children vary considerably in the degree to which they see their ficticious playmates as imaginary; for some, the "pals" are quite real. By creating a friendly, comforting, and compatible playmate, the child achieves in fantasy what is missing in reality. Unless the attachment to the playmate is very intense and the distortion of reality extreme, the fantasy need not be a matter of great parental concern.

Everyone uses unconscious defense mechanisms at times. Defense mechanisms are not always harmful; indeed, they are sometimes helpful. In the case of children, defense mechanisms may prevent anxiety from disrupting or overwhelming the weakly organized personality structures we call the "self" or the "ego." Reduction of anxiety may also be necessary if the child is to cope with the problems that are the source of anxiety. However, when a child's distortions of reality are frequent and when the child uses a small number of defensive techniques in a rigid manner, much of his or her behavior will be inappropriate to the situation—and, therefore, maladaptive. For example, consider a young girl who uniformly projects her hostile impulses onto her parents, constantly accusing them of hating her and of treating her badly. This inflexible use of projection will probably cause problems in her relations with her parents. In addition, the girl will not learn how to cope with feelings of anger, since she will not acknowledge them in herself. Such inappropriate and inflexible use of defense mechanisms may require counseling from a clinical psychologist or psychiatrist (65).

MASTERY AND ACHIEVEMENT

The behaviors and motives we have discussed so far—sex, aggression, dependency, and fear—must be modified and, to some extent, controlled for the sake of the individual's emotional and social adjustment. Mastery behavior and achievement motivation, on the other hand, typically bring benefits to both individual and society. Parents are usually concerned with encouraging and developing these traits (unless of course "achievements" take an antisocial direction, e.g., stealing), not in controlling them. Some psychologists believe that the child is born with motivation to deal effectively with the environment (69). She seeks out challenging tasks, such as crawling down stairs as an infant or "walking a tightrope" on a curb when older, and she takes pleasure in successful performance.

While the desire to master problems and to increase one's skills and abilities at culturally valued tasks may be derived in part from a basic mastery motive, it must be recognized that achievement behaviors may also gratify other motives. Achievement in our culture brings recognition, status, and, often, power, even in the nursery school. Parents love a child who does well, or at least many children believe that to be so. If achievement comes at the expense of another child, as often happens in competitive games, aggressive motives might be involved.

Preschool children who are highly motivated to achieve in intellectual

tasks are also likely to be relatively independent and self-reliant. For example, among the preschool children in one study (21), those who spent most of their time in "intellectual" activities, such as reading books, exhibited less dependent behavior toward adults than did peers who were not very interested in these activities. When children motivated for achievement did act in dependent ways, they were more likely to seek attention or help in solving a problem than emotional support. These children often played adult roles with playmates and were likely to be accepted as leaders.

Parents play a key role in stimulating achievement motivation. Studies of high-achievement children show that their parents encouraged achievement from infancy onward (21). The parents ignored excessive requests for help and expected age-appropriate, self-reliant behavior at an early age. For example, the mothers of high-achievement children were found to have encouraged early mastery of such basic skills as walking and talking (70).

It is interesting to note that there are no sex differences in intellectual achievement during the preschool years (22), and variations among children of different social classes are less than the differences later in life. In our culture, middle-class boys eventually become the most achievement-oriented. These boys receive greater encouragement to achieve and more approval when they do than do girls and lower-class children. Most of the successful "role models" in our society are male and middle class. Indeed, many middle-class boys are under extreme pressure to "succeed"; failure means not only a loss of self-esteem but often physical or emotional punishment as well.

In spite of the differences among groups, achievement motivation, especially in the intellectual area, is one of the most stable aspects of a child's personality. Girls and boys who show a strong desire to perfect intellectual skills during the preschool years tend to retain this motivation through adolescence and early adulthood (51).

IDENTIFICATION

We have frequently used the concepts of reinforcement, punishment, and imitation in explaining preschool personality development. But not all behavior and personality characteristics can be explained in these terms. In fact, many significant and complex patterns of personality traits, behaviors, personal idiosyncracies, motives, attitudes, and moral standards appear to be acquired by the child "spontaneously," without direct training or reward—without anyone's teaching and without the child's intending to learn. In short, some acquired characteristics do not seem to yield readily to analysis in terms of reward, punishment, or imitation. A more subtle process, *identification,* is involved.

Identification, a concept introduced by Freud, refers to the process that leads the child to think, feel, and behave as though the characteristics of another person—usually a parent in the case of a young child—belong to him or her. A 6-year-old boy feels proud as he watches his mother defeat a rival in tennis. A young girl helps an even younger child cross the street and feels very grown-up; she has identified with her mother or father—thought, acted, and felt, as they would have or, at least, as she perceives they would have. Identification, however, is not ordinarily a consciously initiated process; it is not like learning to ride a bicycle.

Identification is not concerned with why and how children learn isolated acts from their parents (17). Identification is a more sweeping and intense phenomenon: The child takes on a *pattern* of parental behavior, and does so with an emotional intensity that suggests strong underlying motivation. Identification with a parent may be a very important source of security for a young child. By means of identification, the child "takes on" the parent's strength and adequacy. As a result, the child feels more competent and self-controlled. Any sign of weakness or inadequacy on the part of the parent might be met with great alarm on the part of the child, whose own self-esteem is threatened rather directly because of identification.

The Development of Identification

Two conditions are basic to the development of identification. Identification begins with the child's perception that he and the person with whom he identifies—the model—are *similar* in some ways—that they share physical, psychological, or social attributes. Once the identification is formed, it will be either strengthened or weakened depending on how psychologically *attractive* and *desirable* the model is.

A child comes to feel similar to a parent in a number of ways. Parents and children often share physical characteristics such as hair and eye color and general facial appearance. Psychological characteristics, especially temperaments and abilities, are often similar—"You have a temper just like your father!" Other people typically respond to a family, in some respects, as a unit—"The Tashmans are growing some fine vegetables" or "Those Verburgs are an industrious lot." In addition, as the child adopts the parent's behaviors and gestures, the perception of similarity increases. Each time the child perceives some similarity with the model, the identification is strengthened.

When both parents are perceived in a positive light, say, as nurturant and competent, the child will be motivated to increase the shared similarities with them. Typically, however, the child will perceive greater similarity to the parent of the same sex and will therefore identify more strongly with that parent.

If the model is attractive, the child is motivated to become increasingly identified with him or her. Most children feel that their parents have numerous desirable characteristics, skills, and privileges. Most parents are seen as strong and powerful, and they have abilities and access to pleasures the child envies. Perceiving his own lack of capabilities and privileges, the child seems to assume that if he were similar to his parents, he would also possess the parents' desirable psychological characteristics and command of resources. Therefore, the more attractive the parent, the more intense is the child's desire to acquire the parent's attributes, and the greater the identification. For example, a nurturant parent is more likely to be taken as a model than is a rejecting one.

Identification is not an all-or-none phenomenon. The child does not identify 100 percent with one model and not at all with another. As we mentioned, each child identifies, to some degree, with both parents. As his social contacts widen, he identifies with other adults and children outside the family. Behavior patterns that originate in identification may flourish because of external rewards later, as when the child strives to achieve because his mother is an achiever and later earns rewards from teachers for his academic achievement.

Two major consequences of parental identification begin to develop rapidly during the preschool period. The first is *sex-typing,* which refers to the adoption of behavior, values, attitudes, and interests generally considered appropriate to the masculine or feminine role in the child's culture. The second is the formation of the *superego* or *conscience,* the internalization of the culture's standards of moral conduct, values, beliefs, and self-control. Both of these are broad, pervasive, multifaceted aspects of the individual's personality.

Sex-typing

During the preschool years, sex-typing generally figures prominently in the socialization of the child, and most parents pay attention to the sex appropriateness of their children's behavior. The topics of masculine and feminine behavior and roles have come under careful scrutiny in psychology in recent years, as the related issue of discrimination against women in jobs, finances, and other areas has become prominent in society at large. Are there sex differences in behaviors such as achievement, competitiveness, and dependency? If so, are these differences determined by underlying biological differences, or are they produced by differing methods of child-rearing and different social expectations for the two sexes? These are not easy questions to answer. In most instances, sex differences seem to be largely the products of socialization (Figure 6.6), although biological factors may also be involved (in aggression, for example).

● Figure 6.6   Sex roles are typically learned by observation and identification.

In most (but not all) cultures, girls are socialized in ways that encourage the development of nurturance to children and obedience to males, while boys are pressured toward self-reliance and leadership (10). These practices are designed to prepare the children for their adult roles, in which men typically "win the bread" by hunting or work at the Bank of America, while women care for children and cook food. In most primitive societies and in earlier times in our own culture, physical strength and speed were the major determinants of the assignment of important roles in the community. Since men, on the average, are stronger and faster than women, they typically were given the tasks of hunting, heavy agriculture, and group defense; women—the child bearers—were assigned to care for the children, too, and to do those housekeeping tasks such as cooking that fit in with their primary task of child-rearing.

In a technologically developed society such as ours, physical strength and speed are less important in work and defense. In most jobs, women can perform as well as men; it takes no brawn to program a computer or to file legal petitions with a court. Child-rearing practices are gradually changing to reflect the changes in the labor market. Many families make an effort not to "sex-type" their children, and instead try to raise children of both sexes to be self-reliant *and* nurturant.

Nevertheless, most parents still have rather firm notions about appropriate masculine and feminine behavior; they share the stereotypes of their culture. They encourage their young son to fight back if attacked by a playmate, but they are likely to punish this response in a daughter (67). If a preschool girl cries after losing a game, her reaction is likely to be accepted as appropriate for girls, but a boy who shows tears is likely to be reminded that "Boys don't cry." In general, in American society, women are supposed to inhibit aggressive and sexual motives; to be friendly, sensitive, and nurturant; to be attractive but poised; to be passive, dependent, and emotional, especially in the presence of men (42). Men are supposed to be active, aggressive, independent, strong in the face of adversity, and unemotional, except when watching pro football games. These notions of sex-appropriate interests and behavior are well known to children by the age of 5. Most 3-, 4-, and 5-year-olds prefer toys, objects, and activities (e.g., guns vs. dolls, hunting vs. cooking) that are considered appropriate for their own sex (18).

Aggression   Sex differences in children's aggressive responses have been more intensively studied than many other behaviors. There is some evidence of possible biological bases for these differences. As one would expect with a biologically based trait, sex differences in most forms of aggressiveness are almost universally found in studies of aggression in our culture and in almost all other cultures as well. The differences are apparent very early in life, at least by the age of 2. Similar sex differences are found in other animals (e.g., monkeys and apes) closely related to homo sapiens.

But any effects of biological differences in the potential for aggression interacts with the effects of social experience—social learning and identification —which clearly plays a major role in the expression of aggression. In American culture, as in almost all cultures (23), boys have traditionally received more encouragement (reward) and less punishment for aggressive behavior than have girls. In addition, the models for identification for boys (fathers, sports heros) typically manifest more aggression than do models for girls (mothers, artists). Hence, boys are generally less anxious about expressing aggression than are girls and during the preschool years, show more aggression in both play and fantasy. Fights, quarrels, insults, destructive behavior, and tantrums are all more common among nursery-school boys than girls (47).

Some sex differences become more marked with increasing age during the preschool period. At the age of 2, both boys and girls scream and hit, but by the age of 4, boys do more hitting and less screaming than do girls (41). Instead of hitting, an act that frequently brings punishment, girls are more apt to scold or insult another child (28). And, of course, socialization of sex differences continues throughout childhood. As a result, the average woman in our society is much less aggressive in the direct, physical, overt style of men.

Parental influence   There are strong parental pressures that foster sex-typing in general patterns of behavior. According to the data of one study (16), parents in our culture try to instill the Protestant ethic in boys: The boys are taught to achieve, to compete, to control their emotions. For little girls, on the other hand, emphasis is placed on developing and maintaining close interpersonal relationships (eventually with husbands and children). Little girls are encouraged to talk about their troubles (boys are not). Parents are more likely to give their daughters comfort and reassurance when in doubt or in trouble; their sons are expected to cope. Parents of girls said that it was important to give them "time to daydream and loaf."

The process of identification also promotes the development of sex-typed behaviors. The little boy in the typical American family identifies primarily with his father; the little girl identifies primarily with her mother. Each takes on the behavior patterns and attitudes of the like-sexed parent, with the approval and encouragement of both parents. Boys who experiment with being "like mother" and, to a lesser extent, girls who try to be "like father" soon discover that this is not their "proper destiny" (60). It should be noted that this process of identification with the parent of the same sex does not necessarily lead to stereotyped masculine or feminine behavior. Cultural stereotypes result only when the father and mother themselves personify these extreme images of what a man and a woman should be.

Several circumstances can alter the picture of the typical family. The sex of older siblings has some effect on identification behaviors, for children typically also identify to some extent with older brothers or sisters. Girls with older brothers display more masculine behaviors than do girls without older brothers, and boys with older sisters manifest more feminine characteristics than do boys without such models (60). Boys who were separated from their fathers for long periods of time—their fathers were at sea for several months at a time or away because of commitments to the armed services—were found to be less firmly established in their sex-role behavior than were boys whose fathers were continually available (46).

The degree to which the child adopts a parent's behavior is in part a function of the parent's nurturance (54, 55, 56, 57). The ten most "masculine" boys in one group of 5-year-olds (who presumably had stronger identifications with their fathers) perceived their fathers as more nurturant and rewarding than the ten least masculine boys perceived theirs. Analogously, femininity in preschool girls seems to be related to warm, nurturant mother–daughter relationships. Highly feminine girls consider their mothers to be warmer, more nurturant, affectionate, and gratifying. According to mothers' reports, highly feminine girls have more intense and warmer interactions with their mothers than do less feminine girls.

The Development of Conscience

During the preschool years the child begins to show evidence of conscience development—acquisition of a set of values and moral standards of behavior. He is pleased or praises himself when he acts in accordance with these standards, and he feels guilty if he violates them, even if no adult is present to shame him. These moral standards are learned primarily from the parents and accepted because they are important to the parents; conscience is largely a product of identification (52).

Guilt   Guilt about "doing something wrong" is often used as an index of conscience development (Figure 6.7). Parental practices such as frequent use of praise and affection and infrequent use of physical punishment and threats are one influence on the degree to which the child accepts responsibility and experiences guilt when misbehaving (14). Among 5-year-old girls in one study, those who actively sought adult approval and nurturance were most likely to imitate adult moral standards. This was demonstrated in the ways they instructed another child about the rules of a game, in showing interest in another child's safety, and in becoming upset when they committed acts of which adults might disapprove. Older boys with internalized standards of morality reported that their parents were affectionate and did not use force or threats in disciplining them, but instead emphasized the effects of the child's misbehavior on the parents' feelings (38). The use of withdrawal of love as a technique of punishment (compared to physical punishment) has been associated with a strongly developed conscience, but only if strong affectionate relationships between parent and child already exist (78).

Altruism   The concept of a conscience has two aspects: learning the prohibitions of society, which leads to guilt about "immoral" behavior, and learning the ideals of society (Figure 6.8). Altruistic behaviors—generous, unselfish acts—fall into the latter category. Parental warmth and nurturance are also related to generosity and socially oriented actions among children. For example, nursery-school boys were presented with a bowl of candies and told they could share any or all of them with friends. Those who shared a substantial portion of

●Figure 6.7 Guilt is often used as an index of conscience development.

● Figure 6.8   Altruistic behavior is often used as an index of conscience development.

their candies perceived their fathers as warmer, more nurturant, and more rewarding than did boys who kept almost all the candies for themselves (64).

.This finding is generally supportive of the hypothesis that conscience development is influenced by the strength of the child's identification with his or
her parents. But it must be recognized that identification is only one of many
factors affecting the child's moral judgments. Most parents attend closely to
their children's moral behaviors, punishing them when they "do wrong" and
praising them for altruistic acts. The mood of the child is also a factor. In one
experiment, the investigators manipulated events so that children experienced
either success or failure in a game. Later asked to contribute money to poor
children, the successful subjects were more likely to give and in greater average
amounts than were children who had experienced failure. Finally, observation
of playmates or adults who are behaving generously also enhances children's
generosity (33).

THE HOME ENVIRONMENT

Up to this point we have centered our attention on the development of particular
behaviors—aggression, dependency—and the major processes involved—
learning, imitation, identification. We will conclude this chapter by examining
some broad aspects of the social environment of the home, including parent–
child relationships, as they affect the development of traits, motives, behaviors,
and the general structure of personality.

Investigations of early parent–child interactions can focus on quite specific variables, such as the mother's role in satisfying the infant's basic needs. As the child matures, relationships with his or her parents become more extensive, more complex, and more subtle. Thus, many investigations of parent–child interactions during the preschool years focus not on specific interactions in restricted situations, but on broad, global characteristics of the home and parental behavior. Examples are parental warmth, permissiveness, and democracy and authoritarianism in the home.

These general, comprehensive dimensions are difficult to measure objectively. *Interviews* with parents and *questionnaires* about parent–child relations are frequently used, but parents are not always the best people to ask about their own or their children's behavior. Their reports are likely to be biased, and important information may be forgotten, withheld, or distorted (consciously or unconsciously). If care is taken to separate opinion and interpretation from description, however, parental reports can be useful (36, 37).

A *home visit* involves a trained observer who goes to the child's home and records the interactions of family members as they go about their customary activities. In *structured observation,* parents and children are presented with a standard task; for example, the mother may be told to teach her child how to use an educational toy. These spontaneous interactions presumably provide an opportunity to assess the way the mother habitually instructs her child, the way she motivates and rewards him or her, the way she deals with failure, frustration, and dependency, and a number of other important aspects of the parent–child relationship (11). These methods suffer to the extent that parents exhibit only their "best" behavior when they are being observed, but with careful preparation and many observations over time, valuable data can be gathered.

Democratic and Controlled Home Atmospheres

Two global characteristics of the home environment that have been extensively studied involve the general nature of parental discipline. From careful observations in the home, researchers identified one dimension which they called *democracy* and another called *control* (1, 2). The home environment high in democracy is characterized by the avoidance of arbitrary decisions and a high level of verbal contact between parents and children (consultations about decisions, reasons for family rules). Controlled homes emphasize clear-cut restrictions on behavior and, consequently, friction over disciplinary procedures is low.

The different home atmospheres are associated with strikingly different personalities in the children. Nursery-school children from democratic homes were rated as generally active, competitive, creative, and outgoing. They also ranked high in leadership, playfulness, and aggressiveness—though not in underlying hostility. They tended to be more curious, disobedient, and nonconforming, especially if (in addition to democracy) the home was characterized by a great deal of parent–child interaction.

Children from homes rated high in control presented a quite different picture. They showed relatively little quarrelsomeness, negativism, disobedience, aggression, playfulness, tenacity, or fearfulness. In the cases of children from homes where discipline was very strict and the parents ruled with an iron hand —high control together with low democracy, sometimes called *authoritarian control*—the result was quiet, well-behaved, nonresistant youngsters who were socially unaggressive. In these homes, conformity was obtained at the expense of curiosity, originality, and freedom of expression.

Democratic parents run the risk of being overly permissive and producing too little conformity to cultural demands in their children. Fortunately, in the homes investigated in these studies, most of the democratic parents practiced enough control to avoid the pitfalls of extreme nonconformity.

Home Environments of Competent Children

Somewhat similar studies of the home environment by Diana Baumrind (13) began by rating the competence and maturity of preschool children. In one large study (9), competence was defined by high ratings in the following areas: *self-control; approach tendencies*—the tendency to approach "novel, stressful, exciting, or unexpected situations in an explorative and curious fashion"; *vitality; self-reliance* or independence; and *peer affiliation*—the "ability and desire to express warmth" toward playmates. Three groups of children were selected for further study. Pattern I children were the most mature, competent, content, independent, realistic, self-reliant, self-controlled, explorative, affiliative, and self-assertive. Pattern II children were rated as moderately self-reliant and self-controlled, but relatively discontented, insecure, withdrawn, distrustful, and uninterested in peer friendships. Pattern III children were the most immature; they were highly dependent, with less self-control than the other children, and they tended to withdraw from novel or stressful situations.

Now, what are the parents of these three types of children like? Using interviews, home visits, and structured observations, the parents were evaluated on four child-rearing dimensions: *control; maturity demands*—pressures on the child to perform at a high level intellectually, socially, and emotionally; *clarity of parent–child communication*—for example, giving reasons, asking the child's opinions; and *parental nurturance,* including both warmth and involvement (pleasure in the child's accomplishments).

The average scores of the parents of the three groups of children, assessed in the home visits, are shown in Figure 6.9. The parents of mature, competent, Pattern I children scored uniformly high on all four dimensions. Compared with the other parents studied, they were warm, loving, supportive, and they communicated well with their children. At the same time, they were controlling and demanded mature behavior from their children. Although they respected their youngsters' independence and decisions, they generally held firm in their own positions, being clear and explicit about the reasons for their directives.

● Figure 6.9 Average scores of parents of children with different patterns of behavior on four child-rearing dimensions. Pattern I parents were called *authoritative;* Pattern II parents were called *authoritarian;* and, Pattern III parents were called *permissive.* (From Diana Baumrind. Child care practices anteceding three patterns of preschool behavior. *Genetic Psychology Monographs,* 1967, *75.* By permission.)

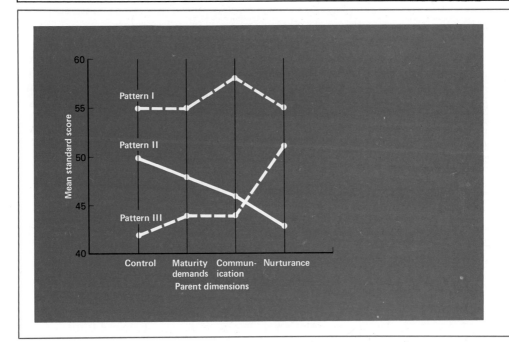

This combination of high control and positive encouragement of the child's independent strivings was called *authoritative* parental behavior.

The parents of children who were somewhat self-reliant but relatively discontented and withdrawn (Pattern II) were rated very low on nurturance; they were not very warm, affectionate, or sympathetic with their children. But they were highly controlling and used power freely; they used coercion rather than reason; they did not encourage the child's expression of disagreement. These parents were called *authoritarian.*

The parents of the immature children (Pattern III) were quite warm and loving, as compared with authoritarian parents. But they were not well organized; they were lax in both discipline and praise; they made relatively few demands for mature behavior. These nurturant but noncontrolling and nondemanding parents were labeled *permissive.*

In a later study (12), Baumrind reversed the procedures of her earlier investigation. She began with the three basic patterns of parental authority—authoritative, authoritarian, and permissive—and then investigated their effects on preschool children's competence and maturity. Authoritative parents were found to be the most effective in promoting the development of competence, independence, purposiveness, and achievement orientation in girls and social responsibility in boys. Both authoritative and authoritarian parents preached socially responsible behaviors but only the authoritative parents modeled this kind of behavior for their children; the authoritarian parents did not practice what they preached. Hence the children of authoritative parents behaved more responsibly.

Permissive parents did not demand much of their children. They did not reward self-reliant or responsible behavior, and they did not discourage immature behavior. Their sons were relatively low in achievement orientation. Neither permissive lack of control nor rigid, authoritarian control provided the child with the knowledge and experience necessary to act in independent, self-reliant ways.

As a whole, these studies indicate that competence, maturity, independence, friendliness, self-control, and self-reliance are fostered by nurturant, warm home environments in which independent actions and responsible behavior are encouraged and rewarded. Parental control or firmness and high maturity demands are equally important. The children of warm but overly indulgent parents and the children of firm but aloof parents do not fare as well.

SUMMARY

During the preschool years, many new behaviors and attitudes develop as children interact with their social environment in a general process called *socialization*. Parents and other social agents attempt to teach the children how to control their sexual and aggressive urges, in accord with the prevailing cultural attitudes toward these behaviors.

Aggression develops for many reasons. Children may react to frustration with aggression, or they may imitate the physical or verbal attacks of their playmates. Permissive adults seem not only to allow but often to encourage it. Once the child attacks, he may find his aggression rewarded by compliant playmates. Of course, rewards can also be used to promote nonaggressive responses, and modeling of nonaggressiveness behavior can also reduce aggression. Punishment to control children's aggression must be used carefully to avoid undesirable side-effects; sometimes, for example, children begin to hate their parents because of the punishment, and sometimes parents become models of aggressive behavior (e.g., spanking) to effectively suppress their children's unwanted behavior—roughly the opposite of what the parents are trying to teach.

Preschool children have particular conflicts between their desires to be aided and comforted by others—dependency motives—and their interests in independent actions, which parents have begun to encourage. Dependency behaviors change with age: The youngest of the preschoolers tend to cling, cry, and seek affection quite directly; older preschoolers seek attention and approval or, in what is generally considered an even more mature type of search, aid in solving problems. Dependency behaviors are more common when the child is frightened or when the parent or teacher is too busy to pay the "proper" amount of attention. Inconsistent discipline, in which dependency behaviors are sometimes lavishly rewarded and sometimes irritably punished, is likely to lead to "overdependent" children.

Every child develops fears and less specific anxieties. In a few cases, the fears require minor "therapy," such as letting the child observe a nonanxious model. Also there is some danger that anxious children will adopt inflexible defense mechanisms to control their anxiety; examples are projection, denial, repression, regression, and displacement.

Identification is a process by which the child takes on the general patterns of behaviors and values of emotionally significant adults, usually the parents. Sex-typing develops in part through identification with the like-sexed parent, although society also encourages "masculine" behavior in boys and "feminine" behavior in girls through direct rewards and punishments. Similarly, conscience develops in part through identification with parents. Children of warm, nurturant parents, with whom identification is likely, tend to show more guilt when they misbehave, and they are also more likely to exhibit altruistic behavior such as sharing.

Broad characteristics of the home environment also influence the personality development of preschool children. The children who seemed best adjusted came from homes relatively high in "democracy" and moderate in "control." A distinction was made between "authoritarian" parents, who allow little democracy in family decisions and are also very restrictive, and "authoritative" parents, who are relatively restrictive although they solicit and respect the opinions of their children. The children of authoritative parents were the more mature and well-adjusted. "Permissive" parents, who are nurturant but not controlling and not demanding, had children who seemed driftless and immature.

References

1. Baldwin, A. L. The effect of home environment on nursery school behavior. **Child Development,** 1949, **20,** 49–62.
2. Baldwin, A. L., Kalhorn, J., & Breese, F. H. The appraisal of parent behavior. **Psychological Monographs,** 1949 **63**(299).
3. Bandura, A. **Aggression.** Englewood Cliffs, New Jersey: Prentice-Hall, 1973.
4. Bandura, A. The role of modeling processes in personality development. In W. W. Hartup and N. L. Smothergill (Eds.), **The young child.** Washington, D.C.: National Association for the Education of Young Children, 1967. Pp. 42–58.
5. Bandura, A., Grusec, J. E., & Menlove, F. L. Vicarious extinction of avoidance behavior. **Journal of Personality and Social Psychology,** 1967, **5,** 16–23.
6. Bandura, A., Ross, D., & Ross, S. A. Imitation of film-mediated aggressive models. **Journal of Abnormal and Social Psychology,** 1963, **66,** 3–11.
7. Bandura, A., & Huston, A. C. Identification as a process of incidental learning. **Journal of Abnormal and Social Psychology,** 1961, **63,** 311–318.
8. Bandura, W., & Walters, R. H. Aggression. In H. W. Stevenson (Ed.), **Child Psychology.** (62nd Yearbook of the National Society for the Study of Education.) Chicago: University of Chicago Press, 1963. Pp. 364–415.

9. Barker, R. G., Dembo, T., & Lewin, K. Frustration and regression. In R. G. Barker, J. S. Kounin, & H. F. Wright (Eds.), **Child behavior and development.** New York: McGraw-Hill, 1943. Pp. 441–458.

10. Barry, H., Bacon, M. K., & Child, I. L. A cross-cultural survey of some sex differences in socialization. **Journal of Abnormal and Social Psychology,** 1963, **67**, 527–534.

11. Baumrind, D. Child care practices anteceding three patterns of preschool behavior. **Genetic Psychology Monographs,** 1967, **75**, 43–88.

12. Baumrind, D. Current patterns of parental authority. **Developmental Psychology Monographs,** 1971, No. 1, 1–103.

13. Baumrind, D. Socialization and instrumental competence in young children. In W. W. Hartup (Ed.), **The young child: Reviews of research.** Vol. 2. Washington, D.C.: National Association for the Education of Young Children, 1972. Pp. 202–224.

14. Becker, W. C. Consequences of different kinds of parental discipline. In M. L. Hoffman & L. W. Hoffman (Eds.), **Review of child development research.** Vol. 1. New York: Russell Sage Foundation, 1964. Pp. 169–208.

15. Beller, E. K. Dependency and independence in young children. **Journal of Genetic Psychology,** 1955, **87**, 25–35.

16. Block, J. H. Conceptions of sex role: Some cross-cultural and longitudinal perspectives. **American Psychologist,** 1973, **28**, 512–529.

17. Bronfenbrenner, U. Freudian theories of identification and their derivatives. **Child Development,** 1960, **31**, 15–40.

18. Brown, D. G. Sex-role preference in young children. **Psychological Monographs,** 1956, **70**(421), 1–19.

19. Brown, P., & Elliott, R. Control of aggression in a nursery school class. **Journal of Experimental Child Psychology,** 1965, **2**, 103–107.

20. Chittenden, G. E. An experimental study in measuring and modifying assertive behavior in young children. **Monographs of the Society for Research in Child Development,** 1942, VII, No. 1.

21. Crandall, V. J. Achievement. In H. W. Stevenson (Ed.), **Child psychology.** (62nd Yearbook of the National Society for the Study of Education.) Chicago: University of Chicago Press, 1963. Pp. 416–459.

22. Crandall, V. J., & Rabson, A. Children's repetition choices in an intellectual achievement situation following success and failure. **Journal of Genetic Psychology,** 1960, **92**, 161–168.

23. D'Andrade, R. G. Sex differences and cultural institutions. In E. E. Maccoby (Ed.), **The development of sex differences.** Stanford, Calif.: Stanford University Press, 1966. Pp. 173–203.

24. Dollard, J., Doob, L. W., Miller, N. E., Mowrer, O. H., & Sears, R. R. **Frustration and aggression.** New Haven: Yale University Press.

25. Emmerich, W. Continuity and stability in early social development: II. Teacher ratings. **Child Development,** 1966, **37**, 17–28.

26. Fawl, C. L. Disturbances experienced by children in their natural habitats. In R. G. Barker (Ed.), **The stream of behavior.** New York: Appleton-Century-Crofts, 1963. Pp. 99–126.

27. Ferguson, L. R. **Personality development.** Belmont, Calif.: Brooks-Cole, 1970.

28. Feshbach, N., & Feshbach, S. Children's aggression. In W. W. Hartup (Ed.), **The young child: Reviews of research.** Vol. 2. Washington, D.C.: National Association for the Education of Young Children, 1972. Pp. 284–302.

29. Gewirtz, J. L. A factor analysis of some attention-seeking behaviors of young children. **Child Development,** 1956, **27,** 17–36.

30. Hagman, R. R. A study of fears of children of preschool age. **Journal of Experimental Education,** 1932, **1,** 110–130.

31. Hartup, W. W. Nurturance and nurturance-withdrawal in relation to the dependency behavior of preschool children. **Child Development,** 1958, **29,** 191–201.

32. Hartup, W. W. Dependence and independence. In H. W. Stevenson (Ed.), **Child psychology.** (62nd Yearbook of the National Society for the Study of Education.) Chicago: University of Chicago Press, 1963. Pp. 333–363.

33. Hartup, W. W., & Coates, B. Imitation of a peer as a function of reinforcement from the peer group and rewardingness of the model. **Child Development,** 1967, **38**(4), 1003–1016.

34. Hattendorf, K. W. A study of the questions of young children concerning sex: A phase of an experimental approach to parental education. **Journal of Social Psychology,** 1932, **3,** 37–65.

35. Heathers, G. Emotional dependence and independence in nursery-school play. **Journal of Genetic Psychology,** 1955, **87,** 37–58.

36. Hoffman, M. L. An interview method for obtaining descriptions of parent-child interaction. **Merrill-Palmer Quarterly,** 1957, **3**(2), 76–83.

37. Hoffman, M. L. Parent discipline and the child's consideration for others. **Child Development,** 1963, **34,** 573–588.

38. Hoffman, M. L., & Saltzstein, H. D. Parent discipline and the child's moral development. **Journal of Personality and Social Psychology,** 1967, **5,** 45–57.

39. Holmes, F. B. An experimental investigation of a method of overcoming children's fears. **Child Development,** 1936, **7,** 6–30.

40. Jersild, A. T., & Holmes, F. B. **Children's fears.** New York: Bureau of Publications, Teachers College, Columbia University, 1935.

41. Jersild, A. T., & Markey, F. V. Conflicts between preschool children. **Child Development Monographs,** 1935, No. 21.

42. Jones, M. C. A laboratory study of fear: The case of Peter. **Pedagogical Seminary,** 1924, **31,** 308–315.

43. Kagan, J. Acquisition and significance of sex-typing and sex-role identity. In M. L. Hoffman & L. W. Hoffman (Eds.), **Review of child development research.** Vol. 1. New York: Russel Sage Foundation, 1964. Pp. 137–167.

44. Kagan, J., & Moss, H. A. **Birth to maturity: A study in psychological development.** New York: Wiley, 1962.

45. Kessler, J. W. **Psychopathology of childhood.** Englewood Cliffs. N.J.: Prentice-Hall, 1966.

46. Lynn, D. **The father's influence.** Belmont, Calif.: Brooks-Cole, 1973,

47. Maccoby, E. E. (Ed.) **The development of sex differences.** Stanford, Calif.: Stanford University Press, 1966.

48. Maccoby, E. E., & Feldman, S. Mother-attachment and stranger-reactions in the third year of life. **Monographs of the Society for Research in Child Development,** 1972, **37**(1).

49. Maccoby, E. E., & Jacklin, C. N. **The psychology of sex differences.** Stanford: Stanford University Press, 1974.

50. Malinowski, B. Prenuptial intercourse between the sexes in the Trobriand Islands, N. W. Melanesia. **Psychoanalytic Review,** 1927, **14,** 20–36.

51. Moss. H. A., & Kagan, J. The stability of achievement and recognition seeking behaviors. **Journal of Abnormal and Social Psychology,** 1961, **62,** 504–513.

52. Mowrer, O. H. **Learning theory and personality dynamics.** New York: Ronald, 1950.

53. Murphy, G. **Personality.** New York: Harper & Row, 1947.

54. Mussen, P. & Distler, L. Masculinity, identification and father-son relationships. **Journal of Abnormal and Social Psychology,** 1959, **59,** 350–356.

55. Mussen, P., & Distler, L. Child rearing antecedents of masculine identification in kindergarten boys. **Child Development,** 1960, **31,** 89–100.

56. Mussen, P., & Parker, A. Mother nurturance and girls' incidental imitative learning. **Journal of Personality and Social Psychology,** 1965, **2,** 94–97.

57. Mussen, P., & Rutherford, E. Parent-child relations and parental personality in relation to young children's sex-role preferences. **Child Development,** 1963, **34,** 589–607.

58. Parker, R. D., & Deur, J. The inhibiting effects of inconsistent and consistent punishment on children's aggression. Unpublished manuscript, University of Wisconsin, 1970.

59. Patterson, G. R., Littman, R. A., & Bricker, W. Assertive behavior in children: A step toward a theory of aggression. **Monographs of the Society for Research in Child Development,** 1967, **32**(5), 1–43.

60. Rosenberg, B. G., & Sutton-Smith, B. **Sex and identity.** New York: Holt, Rinehart & Winston, 1972.

61. Rosenthal, M. K. The effect of a novel situation and anxiety on two groups of dependency behavior. **British Journal of Psycology,** 1967, **58,** 357–364.

62. Rosenthal, M. K. The generalization of dependency behavior from mother to stranger. **Journal of Child Psychology and Psychiatry,** 1967 **8,** 117–133.

63. Ruebush, B. K. Anxiety. In H. W. Stevenson (Ed.), **Chld psychology.** (62nd Yearbook of the National Society for the Study of Education.) Chicago: University of Chicago Press, 1963. Pp. 460–516.

64. Rutherford, E., & Mussen, P. Generosity in nursery school boys. **Child Development,** 1968, **39,** 755–765.

65. Sarason, S. B., Davidson, K. S., Lighthall, F., Waite, R. R., & Ruebush, B. K. **Anxiety in elementary school children.** New York: Wiley, 1960.

66. Sears, R. R. Dependency motivation. In M. Jones (Ed.), **Nebraska symposium on motivation.** Lincoln: University of Nebraska Press, 1963. Pp. 25–64.

67. Sears R. R., Maccoby, E. E., & Levin, H. **Patterns of child rearing.** New York: Harper & Row, 1957.

68. Siegel, A., & Kohn, L. Permissiveness, permission and aggression: The effect of adult presence or absence on children's play. **Child Development,** 1959, **30,** 131–141.

69. White, R. Motivation reconsidered: The concept of competence. **Psychological Review,** 1959, **66,** 297–333.

70. Winterbottom, M. R. The relation of need for achievement to learning experience in independence and mastery. In J. W. Atkinson (Ed.), **Motives in fantasy, action and society.** New York: Van Nostrand Reinhold, 1958. Pp. 453–478.

71. Wright, M. E. The influence of frustration upon the social relationships of young children. Unpublished doctoral dissertation, State University of Iowa, 1940.

72. Yarrow, L. J. The effect of antecedent frustration on projective play. **Psychological Monographs,** 1948, **62**(6).

CHAPTER 7
Middle Childhood

The age of 5 or 6 marks the end of the preschool years and the beginning of "middle childhood," a period vaguely defined by its position between the beginning of school and the onset of adolescence. This rather negative definition (*not* preschool, *not* adolescence) does little justice to the many important developments of these years. The average child of 6 has already mastered the stage of cognitive development Piaget called "preoperational" (see Chapter 3). His thinking is not as simplistically egocentric; he is beginning to see points of view other than his own, and sometimes he even lets them influence his judgments and behaviors. He uses mental routines or "operations" to think about things in relatively logical and organized ways. It is well that he has developed these new cognitive skills, for he is about to begin his "formal" education. He enters the first grade.

During the years of middle childhood, the child's social environment expands enormously. The number of interactions with peers—playmates and classmates of the same age—increases greatly, and so does the frequency of encounters with adults other than parents—most notably, teachers. The child struggles with school tasks, learning how to read and write, discovering where he stands among the students in his class and experiencing what it is like to succeed or fail in front of a large group of friends and potential adversaries. He tries to "get along" with his peers. He develops a few basic ideas about what is ethical and what is not. Throughout these early years of school, he is sometimes triumphant and confident, but often puzzled, confused, or scared—anxious of what his teacher will think, wondering what his parents will think, disturbed by conflicts with his peers, uncertain of his impulses, mystified by life. He struggles on, and, in the process, begins to develop a self concept, an embryonic notion of who he is, what he can and cannot do, who likes him and why.

In this chapter, we will begin with a look at the influence of the family, which is still crucial in middle childhood. The following sections will deal with two other important aspects of the child's expanding social environment: relations with peers and adjustment to school. Then we will turn to a consideration of conscience, how it develops and why. In the final sections we will discuss some of the major psychological problems that can develop in the struggles of middle childhood.

INFLUENCE OF THE FAMILY IN MIDDLE CHILDHOOD

Parent Behavior

Although no two sets of parents are exactly alike, certain general dimensions of parental behavior have been found to be important in understanding parent–child relationships in the middle years of childhood. (For a discussion of such dimensions in the behavior of the preschool child's parents, see pp. 230–234.) One major dimension that consistently emerges from studies of young children and their parents is *acceptance–rejection*, which is characterized by warmth and affection at one extreme and aloofness and outright hostility at the other. As one would expect, a parent–child relationship characterized by parental hostility and rejection creates severe problems for the child. The result may be academic difficulties (99), poor relationships with playmates (87), ill health (103), delinquency, or neurotic disorders (3). The rejected child is often hostile and aggressive toward the parents, either consciously or unconsciously (35).

A second major dimension of parental behavior may be broadly termed *control–autonomy*. Control in this sense has two aspects: (1) setting and enforcing rules of behavior, and (2) restricting the child's development of individuality and autonomy. It has become increasingly clear (26) that these two aspects of control need to be differentiated, for they do not always go together. For example, we have described a pattern of parental behavior called *authoritative* (p. 233) in which reasonable rules and standards are strictly enforced but, within these limits, the child's personal autonomy is respected, even encouraged.

Parents rated high on *psychological control*—unwillingness to let the child develop as an individual separate from the parents—promote infantile, dependent behavior in their children. In addition, their children often lack direction in developing life goals and seem to have difficulty forming mature relationships with their peers (5, 110). Parents rated high on the rule-making, standard-setting aspect of control have children who tend to be inhibited, while lax control fosters impulsive behaviors.

The democratic parent

Although the general dimensions of parental behavior we have described can be considered by themselves, more meaningful generalizations are possible when we consider these dimensions in interaction. For example, many parents are accepting and warm and also low on the dimension of psychological control; that is, they allow their children considerable freedom and autonomy. Such parents have been labeled "democratic"; they are in many respects the parents idealized in stories of the "typical" American family. The children of such parents are likely to be rather outgoing, socially assertive, and independent, as well as friendly, creative, and lacking in hostility toward others or themselves (8, 74). Democratic parents can be either firm or lax in the rule-making kind of control (Figure 7.1). Firm control seems generally preferable. When combined with parental warmth, it tends to produce responsible and purposive children (24); if control is lax, the child may be somewhat aggressive, overly assertive, disobedient, and unable to deal with frustration (21).

The rejecting parent

The parent who is rejecting, cold, and hostile has an unhappy child, needless to say. Parents who lack warmth and also restrict their children's behavior severely—*authoritarian parents,* as they have been called—tend to promote hostility in their children, but they do not allow the hostility to be expressed. Their children may not even be able to admit their hostile feelings to conscious awareness; neurotic disorders may result (117). The children may

● Figure 7.1 Democratic parents may exercise firm control, but they are interested in their children's opinions.

hate themselves, even attack themselves; that is, they may be "accident-prone" or suicidal (2). Shyness and the lack of self-confidence are more common consequences (74).

Parents who are rejecting but who also are lax in their control of the child —*neglectful parents*—are likely to maximize "aggressive, poorly controlled behavior" (12). In other words, the child has a much better than average chance of becoming a "delinquent." When the parents do "discipline" the child, they are often arbitrary, inconsistent, and overly severe, expressing hostility more than a concerned attempt to guide the child's development.

Influences on the Child's Self-Concept

A favorable conception of oneself is essential to personal happiness and effective functioning. According to one large-scale study (42), children with high self-esteem approach tasks and social interactions with the expectation that they will be well received and successful. They have confidence in their own judgments and opinions, which permits them to express their views when there is controversy and even when they expect a hostile reaction to their opinions. High-esteem children lack the self-consciousness and self-preoccupation of low-esteem children. Though they are forceful, they are straightforward, not devious or "personal"; thus other children respect and like them and accept them as leaders.

Children with low self-esteem, according to the results of this study, are apprehensive about expressing their opinions. They do not want to anger others or even to attract attention. Preoccupied with "personal problems," they tend to withdraw from social interactions and thus add to their problems by denying themselves friendly and supportive relationships.

How do parents influence the self-concept of their children? One way is to exhibit or model the self-confidence and self-reliance they expect in their children (42). Another way is to be consistently encouraging and supportive of their children. Parents of children high in self-esteem, for example, like to do things with their children. They are not impatient with "unimportant" problems that their children bring to them, even if the problems are made up to gain attention. In contrast, parents of children low in self-esteem are more likely to withdraw from their children, to be inattentive and neglectful. They tend to view their children as a "burden."

Although the parents of high-esteem children encourage self-reliance and independent behavior, they also see a need to protect their children from tasks that might be too difficult and too frustrating (42). They set carefully defined limits on their children's behavior and enforce these established rules carefully and consistently. *Within these limits,* the child's rights and opinions are *emphasized.* The child's views are sought, his or her opinions are respected, and concessions are often granted to the child in case of disagreement.

Parents of children low in self-esteem, on the average, are likely to be rather indifferent to their offspring. They see less need to protect them from difficult tasks; they see very little value in the opinions of their children; and they seek to control obnoxious behavior with harsh, disrespectful, and inconsistent punishments. There are times when the results of psychological research sound like characterizations from melodramatic novels, with clearly defined good guys and bad guys; this, perhaps, is one such time.

Response to Children's Predispositions

By emphasizing the influences of parental behavior on the child's personality development, we sometimes make it sound as if children are like balls of clay, to be molded this way or that by their parents' shaping techniques. As any parent can testify, however, children vary in a number of characteristics from birth, and these characteristics affect parental treatment. It is difficult to be consistently warm and accepting of a chronically cranky and irritable baby, for example.

In one major longitudinal study (25), children were observed from early childhood (age 5) through middle adolescence (age 16). Two basic dimensions of enduring behavioral predispositions were found: *emotional expressiveness-reserve* and *placidity-explosiveness*. How these predispositions were manifested in specific behaviors appeared to be a function of parental reaction and also societal standards of appropriate behavior for boys and girls at various developmental stages. For example, a boy who was placid as a child and who had calm, stable parents had in many respects an optimal situation during this period. But there appeared to be some "long-term limitations of such an apparently ideal experience, since the boy who had been explosive . . . in early childhood appears as an adult to be more interesting, perhaps even a more creative individual than his placid contemporary" (25, p. 69). This was not true for girls, however; the placid girl appeared to receive even more rewards as she reached adolescence. She was viewed "as calm and relaxed, intellectually alert, and socially charming; a generally likable, competent, and successful individual" (25, p. 69). Similarly expressiveness tended to meet with more social approval in boys; in girls it was met with ambivalence.

Characteristics exhibited early in life by the child influenced the parents' treatment of him or her. Parents tend to prefer expressive children (of either sex), viewing reserved children as withdrawn and unloving. The typical result is that parents interact with (and thereby reinforce the behavior of) expressive children, making them even more assertive. Similarly, their negative attitude toward reserved children creates in the children an even greater tendency to withdraw.

Parental Absence

In ever increasing measure, families are being broken up by death, divorce, and separation. Even in intact families, many parents find their jobs pulling them away from the family for days, months, and even years. What are the effects of prolonged parental absence on the child's adjustment in the middle-childhood years?

Father absence, generally speaking, increases slightly the probability of the son showing feminine patterns of behavior. Boys without fathers, compared to boys with fathers, have patterns of scores on tests of intellectual and conceptual performance more like those of girls (9, 29); they are more "intuitive," for example, and less analytical. They also rank somewhat lower, on the average, on ratings of masculine aggressiveness, preference for the male sex role, and interest in competitive, physical-contact games (65). However, in what may seem to be contradictory evidence, boys without fathers sometimes show "exaggerated toughness, aggressiveness, and cruelty"; they are more likely than other boys to become involved in delinquent activities (24).

If we assume that the absence of a father can lead to problems with a young boy's identity as a male, both the feminine behaviors and the extreme masculine posturing make sense. Most father-absent boys, it should be noted, develop quite normally, but those who have identity problems tend to fall at the extremes. Either they are more "feminine" than the average boy or, in a desperate effort to establish their masculine credentials, they are extremely "male." Similar observations have been made of boys whose fathers are present but ineffective, passive, and neglecting (29). There is evidence that father-substitutes such as Big Brothers and supportive groups like the Boy Scouts can help to reduce the impact of an absent father (16).

The effects of father absence on girls have not been studied as extensively as in the case of boys, and, in general, the effects do not seem as pronounced. Perhaps the fact that girls identify more strongly with their mothers protects them to some extent. Girls without fathers, however, sometimes have difficulties interacting with males during adolescence. Daughters of widows tend to be more anxious with boys, more shy and withdrawn than average. As a group, they tend to start dating later and to be sexually inhibited. Daughters of divorced women, on the other hand, tend to start dating earlier than father-present girls, and they tend to have sexual intercourse at an earlier age (64).

The Influence of Siblings

More than 80 percent of American children have at least one sibling (brother or sister). In the child's interactions with her siblings, she learns patterns of sharing and cunning, cooperation and competition, dominance and submission. One of the important variables in determining the influence of siblings is the child's *ordinal position* among them. For example, the first-born child is greeted by eager but inexperienced parents. Her arrival on the scene may precipitate a crisis in the relationship between spouses (see pp. 385–386). Parents may expect too much from a first-born child and, later, the older child may have to care for her younger siblings before she is ready for such responsibility. The oldest child may see her favored position in the family usurped by the birth of other children, and she may feel threatened and insecure (Figure 7.2).

Research on first-born children has shown them to be more achievement-oriented but also more subject to stress than later-born children (1, 10, 74, 111). Also befitting their "leading" role among the children of the family, they are generally more adult-oriented, more socially responsible, more conforming to social pressures, more subject to feelings of guilt and inadequacy; they are inclined to choose occupations involving a parentlike realtionship with children, such as teacher.

In general, the sex of the sibling has a predictable effect: The children with brothers have more "masculine" traits than children with sisters (79, 80, 81). The girls with brothers, compared to girls with sisters, are more ambitious and more aggressive and do better on tests of intellectual ability. Girls with older brothers have more "tomboyish" traits than girls with older sisters. Boys with older sisters are less aggressive than boys with older brothers.

● Figure 7.2   Birth order may have an effect on the developing child's personality.

Sibling rivalry   Spacing between siblings makes a difference in how the older child feels about his or her younger sibling, the degree of threat felt, and the amount of competition and rivalry between siblings (79, 80, 81). A two- to four-year difference between siblings seems to be the most threatening to the older child. If she is only a year or so older than her sibling, her self-image is still diffuse and unclear when her brother or sister is born, and she probably will not regard the newcomer as a major competitor for the parents' affection. If she is 5 or 6 years older than her sibling, her self-image is more established, and she is less threatened; she can play the role of identification model—"hero"—for her younger brother or sister.

Sibling death in childhood   In view of the important role that siblings play in the life of a child, particularly during middle childhood, it should come as no great surprise to learn that the death of a sibling from accident or illness has a significant effect on the child (19). Sibling death may precipitate grief and mourning, depression, anxiety, withdrawal, regression, or delinquent behavior (13, 57). There are likely to be exaggerated feelings about the lost sibling—either hostility or overidealization (19). Death of a child imposes on the parents an important responsibility to see that the remaining siblings are helped to work out their often complex, confusing, and anxiety-producing feelings before longer-term psychological problems are created.

RELATIONS WITH PEERS

The child of school age moves out of the home and beyond the family for a sizable percentage of his or her waking hours—a percentage that increases steadily from kindergarten to high school (27). As might be expected, the influence of people other than parents and siblings—notably teachers and peers—also increases during middle childhood.

The peer group (classmates, playmates) provides many of the same opportunities for socialization experiences that siblings do—how to deal with hostility, dominance, and other motives and behaviors—but peers are different in several important respects. First, siblings are arranged in an age hierarchy, while peers are usually the same age as the child. Comparisons of physical prowess, intellect, courage, and other attributes are made with equals, not with children significantly younger or older. Comparisons among peers thus provide a clearer measure of one's relative status and, more generally, a clearer basis for one's self-concept. A second difference between the home and the playground or school is that love and affection are major factors in the home, while on the playground, the child must prove herself worthy of respect. "It is a sharp strain for many children when they pass from the atmosphere of a child-centered home into the competitive realities of even a friendly play group. . . . The penalties for failure are humiliation, ridicule, rejection from the group" (122, p. 145).

Peer Subcultures

The influence of the peer group appears stronger in American culture than in many other societies (or even in our own society in earlier eras). Mexican youth (91) and Chinese youth living in Hawaii (68) are far less involved in peer subcultures than is the average American child, and the same is true of many European youth. On the other hand, children living in an Israeli kibbutz or within the Soviet educational system are reared with even more peer contact than American children experience (114).

In Israel and Russia, peer influences are more likely than they are in America to reflect traditional adult standards. In America, talk of "generation gaps" reflects a concern about *different* values in adult and child peer groups. Many scholars have suggested that these differences are, in part, a function of rapid social change; the social and physical environment of an 8-year-old today is much different from that experienced by parents when they were the same age. Compared to parents in slow-changing societies, American parents have a more difficult time instructing, advising, or even empathizing with their children, and thus the influence of the peer group is greatly enhanced (77).

During the early years of middle childhood, informal groups or "gatherings" of children are most common. These groups have no formal rules, and membership is a now-and-then thing. Later in middle childhood, at the age of 10 and thereafter, some children's groups are more structured—Boys' Clubs, Campfire Girls, and the like. There is a clear tendency to segregate on the basis of sex, much more so than among preschool children or adolescents (27). Partly this segregation reflects the different interests of boys and girls during middle years of childhood, but adults also encourage separate activities and groups in their efforts to promote sex-typed identification. It may or may not be true that 10-year-old boys instinctively like rough-and-tumble games more than do girls of the same age, but it is certainly true that boys are more likely than girls to receive parental support and approval for playing football.

Social Status Among Peers

Why are some children popular and others not? (See Figure 7.3). The most popular children tend to be more socially aggressive, outgoing, and enthusiastic (22, 23). They have more cheerful dispositions; they are more friendly, better looking, and more tidy than the least popular children. Social acceptance and status have also been related to creativity and intelligence (27), self-confidence (28), and the ability to get along with other children—to share, to cooperate, to be a "good sport" (62). The particular attributes that lead to popularity vary somewhat with age and sex. Fifth-grade children, for example, value good looks more than do first-graders. Body size, muscular strength, and athletic ability are correlated with popularity among boys (119).

The attributes of low-status or rejected children include anxiety, excessive emotional dependence on adults, uncertainty, social indifference, withdrawal, rebelliousness, aggressiveness, and hostility (62). Physical liabilities such as obesity or facial disfigurement are also associated with rejection (108).

The consequences of social status among children are many, but a good summary statement is simply that high-status children are usually the leaders of the gang. High-status boys and girls in a summer camp were able to sway the behavior of others by both direct and indirect means (101). Others followed their leads, thus rewarding their leadership activities. Children with high status were less likely than the average child to accept others' commands and suggestions, but they were more attuned to and responsive to group trends in mood and behavior. Because they felt secure and self-confident, they felt free to accept or reject other children's attempts to influence them. Their peers, aware of the high-status children's position in the social hierarchy, usually made indirect approaches to them—"offhand" suggestions, subtle indications of preference.

Conformity to Peers

Conformity—the tendency to adopt the values and behaviors of others—increases in the early years of middle childhood. A common method of testing

●Figure 7.3   Why are some children popular while others are not?

conformity is to have the child make perceptual judgments—for example, judging which of three lines is equal in length to another, comparison line. Several other children, acting on instructions from the experimenter, deliberately choose incorrectly. The question is whether the child will choose the line favored by the other children, thus conforming to "group norms," or the line he or she perceives to be correct. Preschool children are "generally impervious to normative pressure from their peers" (62, p. 407), and only a small minority (12 percent) of kindergarten children show any shift in the duration of group norms (69). In contrast, children in the early grades of school, almost without exception, show a tendency to "go along" with the experimenter's confederates in the line-judging task (14).

ADJUSTMENT TO SCHOOL

Once children enter the first grade, school becomes the center of their world apart from their family, occupying almost half of their waking hours for at least a decade. For many children, school entrance marks the first extended separation from the mother, and thus school plays a major role in reducing (or reconstructing) dependency behaviors. School presents the child with new adults to obey, new grown-ups whose acceptance must be courted. The primary purpose of school is to increase the child's intellectual skills, but it is clearly a time of personal and social development as well. Teachers and classmates play their roles, and even intellectual tasks have effects on personality, affecting the student's motivation to study and learn and, more generally, master the task at hand.

The Role of the Teacher

Among the factors affecting the child's adjustment to school, probably none is as important as the teacher–pupil relationship. This is especially true when the child enters school for the first time. The teacher is likely to be the first adult outside the immediate family to play a major role in the child's life and teachers continue to have significant influences on development throughout the school years. They may help the child overcome handicaps and develop talents and interests; or they may add to his or her difficulties and frustrations. Most adults remember at least one teacher who stimulated their intellectual interest or who seemed at the time as the "most nearly perfect human being." They can also recall at least one teacher who "turned them off" or who seemed mean and insensitive, with no apparent interest in their pupils' welfare.

Teachers as substitute mothers   As adults in a position of authority, first grade teachers function in many respects as substitute parents. And children usually perceive them in this light: School beginners tend to have similar perceptions of their mothers and their teachers, who are usually women in the early grades. If the mother is viewed as a strict disciplinarian, so is the teacher. This correlation between perceptions persists at least through the first year of school (55).

Although more and more men are teaching in the elementary grades, it is no accident that most teachers in the early years of school are women. Society (as well as the child) tends to view these teachers as substitute mothers, more nurturant and less fear-arousing than men, and thus well-equipped to facilitate the child's entry into the educational system (Figure 7.4). There has been very little research on this assumption. There are some indications of negative as well as positive effects. Many children, because of the preponderance of women in the elementary school system, begin to see education as "feminine" (73, 76). In addition, teachers tend to reward neatness, obedience, and the inhibition of aggressive behaviors—a program similar to the one young girls experience at home but different from that experienced by young boys. As a result, many young boys, especially those strongly influenced by sex-role stereotypes, belittle and avoid academic work. The academic motivation of young girls, on the other hand, may be increased; perhaps this attitude helps to account for girls' consistently greater achievement in the early grades (20). However, the female student who identifies with women teachers in the early grades may encounter problems later, in high school and college, where the majority of teachers are often male. Probably children of both sexes would be better off if both male and female teachers could be found in approximately equal numbers at all levels of the educational system.

●Figure 7.4   In the early grades the teacher tends to be seen as a substitute mother.

Teacher characteristics and student progress   The characteristics of a good teacher are not dissimilar to those of a good parent, as described in the first part of the chapter. For example, many of the best teachers can be described as authoritative—but not authoritarian (11). They set clearly stated, reasonable, and consistently-enforced limits on the child's behavior, but within these limits, they encourage independence and creativity. They provide guidance and direction, standards and goals, and yet they are "democratic," interested in the views of the student.

If the teacher is warm, flexible, and encouraging of initiative and responsibility, his or her pupils are more likely to be involved in class activities and to be constructive when faced with possible failure (118). In contrast, teachers who are strict disciplinarians and who do not encourage students in independent activities foster negative attitudes toward school and teachers; their students show increased tension and hostility, and they have a greater chance of later difficulties in school adjustment.

However, the same teacher may not be equally effective with all kinds of students. A student's performance is related to his or her view of the teacher, although it is difficult to say which is cause and which is effect. Overachieving students, those whose school performance is greater than expected from IQ tests, tend to perceive their teachers as warm, friendly, and concerned (123). Underachievers, who do worse than expected on tests of intellectual ability, are likely to perceive the same teachers as cold, unfriendly, and unconcerned.

Teachers also influence their pupils in other ways. First-grade children

taught by impulsive teachers tend to become more impulsive and hasty themselves, while those taught by more reflective teachers tend to become more careful, orderly, and less hasty in responding to school tasks (126). Such teacher characteristics may also have different effects on different kinds of students. For example, *conforming* children, who were already self-controlled and orderly, performed slightly better with *turbulent* (impulsive) teachers than with *self-controlled* teachers, although most of the fourth-, fifth-, and sixth-graders did better with the self-controlled teachers (63).

The characteristics of the teacher may be especially important for the socioeconomically disadvantaged student, who may have less adult warmth and support at home than the average middle-class student does. Unfortunately, teachers of disadvantaged children are more likely than teachers of middle-class children to display rigid attitudes toward child control and to be negative and dominating (127). This pattern of interaction is likely to duplicate the negative, punishing control the disadvantaged child too often receives at home.

Variations in Teaching Methods

The effectiveness of different teaching methods also varies from one child to another. In general, anxiety tends to impair academic achievement, but the teaching methods are important, too. Highly anxious students generally do better with a more structured approach. In formal, teacher-centered classes, such children may even exceed the academic performance of less anxious students, but in informal, student-centered classes, the less anxious students usually function better (47). Similarly, relatively compulsive children, who depend more on order and predictability, do better with structured teaching methods (60).

How do traditional schools with more formal classes compare in general to the more informal, student-oriented schools? In the traditional school, the primary emphasis is on imparting established knowledge, and teachers function as authority figures; order and discipline are heavily stressed. Student motivation is assumed to rest on teacher approval and competition among peers. In the student-oriented school, there is greater emphasis on the child's "total development"—intellectual, social, and psychological. Instructional methods encourage the child's independent exploration, experimentation, and discovery. Motivations are assumed to be an innate curiosity and a desire for mastery and competence.

In a study comparing the effects of these two types of schools, few consistent differences in cognitive skills were found, but there were differences in the pupils' self-images. Children from the student-oriented schools had more complex, differentiated perceptions of themselves. They were more accepting of negative impulses and less stereotyped in their conceptions of social sex roles. In contrast, the experimenters found their "traditionally schooled counterparts to be more consistently impersonal, future-oriented, and conventional in their images of roles and development" (93, p. 373). Some of the brightest children in the student-oriented schools reacted to the freedom by doing very well; others "floundered unproductively." Freedom is apparently an opportunity for some students. For others it is a source of stress.

Textbooks

While the teachers and classmates probably exert a more profound effect on the child's development, textbooks can also play a more important role than many people realize. It is, of course, obvious that textbooks contribute to the development of the child's academic skills. What has probably been less evident, at least until recently, is that textbooks may also influence the child's social attitudes and emotional development (39, 40, 58). In recent years, many groups and individuals have complained to school boards about textbooks which, they claimed, were racist or sexist or which allegedly encouraged sexual or aggressive behavior.

The general tone of most children's early readers—with a few notable exceptions—is still primarily of the "Dick and Jane" variety.

> Dick and Jane's world is a friendly one, populated by good, smiling people who are ready and eager to help children whenever necessary. Strangers, therefore, are not to be mistrusted but are viewed as potential helpmates. Human nature and physical nature are also cooperative and friendly rather than competitive and conspiring. There are no evil impulses to be controlled. Instead, free rein and encouragement is given for seeking more and more fun and play. Life in general is easy and comfortable; frustrations are rare and usually overcome quite easily. Combining work with play, seeking out new friends, and giving generously are all amply rewarded by nature, adults and one's peers (129, p. 331).

Many educators complain that this "fantasy world" fails to satisfy the growing need for children to gain understanding of, and sympathy for, cultural diversity and real-life problems. For example, "despite the fact that 60 percent of Americans now live in cities, city life is largely ignored in these readers" (70). Not only are urban, lower-class, and nonwhite children ignored, but also "kids from large families, or one-parent homes, children who wear glasses, youngsters who are short, tall, slim, or stocky" (92).

Recently some publishers have tried to overcome the obvious liabilities of traditional readers for urban, racially mixed schools by producing texts that "focus on the life of a working-class family, living in a typical, racially mixed, urban neighborhood" (90, p. 305). With a few notable exceptions, these attempts have not been strikingly successful. As one reviewer put it, in most of the "new" books, "what is depicted is a Negro family living in a happy, stable, white suburban neighborhood" (20, p. 179).

The readers for the early grades still tend to present rigid stereotypes of masculine and feminine behavior (20, 34). Boys are active and aggressive; they are either playing pranks or industriously working on some adultlike activity (e.g., building a clubhouse). Girls, in contrast, are quieter, more interested in school activities; their stories generally have "Pollyannaish" themes; that is, they are likely to involve warm, positive emotions. Females are more frequently portrayed as sociable, kind, timid, unambitious, and uncreative. Adults of both sexes play mostly family roles: father, mother, uncle, aunt. Many psychologists have suggested that describing adult careers—without sexual bias—would be one worthwhile change; another, of course, would be to eliminate the sexual bias in descriptions of childhood activities as well (128).

Effects of School Size

Many people today are concerned about the effects of "bigness" on the quality of contemporary life. Does school size affect the personality and academic achievement of children and adolescents? The answer seems to be that school size *per se* is not the important factor, but that bigger schools tend to have more students in a class; teachers in large classes spend more time controlling and restraining their students, while teachers of a smaller number of students can interact with them in a freer and more personal atmosphere (102). Similarly, the average student in a small school participates in more extracurricular activities and holds more positions of responsibility (124). These students reported that the opportunity and experience of school activities had helped them to develop skills and increase self-confidence; they gained a sense of accomplishment and an ability to work closely with others. This was especially true of "marginal" students—those with lower-than-average IQs and social skills. In large schools, these students were "outsiders," relatively uninvolved in academic or extracurricular activities. In small schools, on the other hand, marginal students were pressured to participate—because they were needed—and thus they became more involved in the general student subculture (125). Perhaps for this reason, they were less likely to "drop out" of school, compared to their counterparts at large schools (61). It appears that the slogan "bigger is better," at least as it applied to the educational setting, is open to considerable question.

School Dropouts

In a society characterized by rapid technological change, a person without education is likely to be seriously disadvantaged. Since the school dropout rate is higher among the poor than among the well-to-do and highest of all among ethnically segregated youths living in urban and rural slums, the typical dropout is adding to his or her other problems with the lack of a formal education (15). At the bottom of the socioeconomic ladder, one of every two lower-lower-class youths drops out prior to completing high school (32). Nevertheless, a number of studies show that economic need is not ordinarily the major factor in dropping out (36, 41, 120). For example, in a large urban community, only 3 percent of the young people withdrew from school because of financial need or because they were needed at home (30).

A greater number of dropouts than graduates are below-average in intelligence test performance; almost 33 percent of dropouts, but only 10 percent of high school graduates, have IQ scores below 85 (120). Nevertheless, well over half the dropouts have average or above-average IQ scores, which indicates that academic ability is not a decisive factor in most cases. Problems show up early. The typical dropout, even though of average IQ, is already behind his or her peers by the second grade in reading and spelling (30). By the seventh grade, the students who will eventually drop out are, on the average, two years behind their classmates in reading and arithmetic. Their grades in general are below average, and many have failed one or more school years (120).

Children with deprived backgrounds are often disinterested in academic activities and, as a result, often do poorly in school; they are the most likely candidates to become dropouts. But the majority of lower-class children eventually complete high school, and many of the dropouts are from the middle and upper classes. If dropouts are compared with graduates matched on family social class and minority-group membership, we discover that communication tends to be poor in the families of the students who eventually withdraw from school (31, 32). Mutual understanding and acceptance is often lacking. Dropouts also tend to have fewer friends outside the family than do graduates, and their few friendships are often superficial. In all respects, the typical dropout is socially isolated.

Perhaps not surprisingly, the typical dropout is more troubled emotionally, lower in self-esteem, and less likely to have clear personal, social, or occupational goals than is the average graduate (7, 32). Dropouts tend to be hostile and resentful of authority in any form—parents, teachers, bosses. They are likely to be impulsive, viewing the world as an unpredictable place characterized by violence, conflict, cheating, faithlessness, and exploitation.

Many of the dropouts' later problems—higher unemployment rates, more personality problems, lower aspiration levels, an increased possibility of criminal behavior—are reflections of the kinds of problems that led them to drop out in the first place. The act of dropping out itself does not appear to aggravate their problems (6, 98); that is, dropping out is basically a result, not a cause, of their problems. Most psychologists agree that the greatest challenge is to improve the conditions that lead eventually to dropping out (and a host of other difficulties), beginning as early as possible in the child's life.

FAMILY, PEERS, AND SCHOOL ACHIEVEMENT

Not surprisingly, the socioeconomic status of a child's family is significantly related to his or her level of educational aspiration and to school achievement. Children of the higher social classes have traditionally aspired to higher educational levels than have their lower-middle-class and lower-class peers. They conceive of themselves as having better-than-average "school ability," even compared to lower-class classmates matched in intelligence (6). And they do better in school, on the average, at all grade levels (46). These differences are partly a function of broader cultural and educational opportunities in the upper social classes and fewer health and nutritional problems (17). But other, more subtle factors also operate to restrict the educational aspirations and accomplishments of lower-class youngsters, including the influence of parents and peers.

Parental Values and Academic Motivation

From school entrance on, middle- and upper-class parents typically display a marked interest in their children's academic careers—urging greater efforts, praising indications of progress, and not infrequently providing tangible rewards, such as a bicycle or money, for academic accomplishments (97) (see Figure 7.5). These parents are likely to view education as important not only intel-

Figure 7.5 Parents who encourage academic striving tend to have children who are successful students.

lectually but socially and economically as well. They view school (perhaps quite accurately) as a way of preparing new generations of young people for life in a society that is dominated by the upper social classes. As one psychologist has noted, "schools succeed relatively well with upper- and middle-class youngsters. After all, schools are built for them, staffed by middle-class people, and modeled after middle-class people" (88, p. 295). Economically deprived and minority-group parents are often suspicious of schools because of their middle-class orientation. Many of them believe in education as a means of advancement, but they are disenchanted with the kind of education their children receive in schools—an education that they see as irrelevant and even damaging to the real needs of their children.

Social class is a very broad variable, however, and within each social class there are parents who encourage academic achievement and parents who are indifferent. In fact, the particular values of a child's parents are generally more important than the child's social class. For example, a study of high-school boys (75) showed that lower-class boys whose parents encouraged and supported educational and occupational mobility had higher aspirations than did middle-class boys whose parents did not encourage such striving. In a similar investigation (6), boys who had positive and rewarding relations with their parents— were close to them, interacted and consulted with them—had good attitudes about school and about their own scholastic abilities, even if their family was classified as lower class.

Parents of academically motivated, achieving children are likely to place a high value on autonomy and independence (4) and, of course, on mastery, competence, and achievement (89). These parents tend to be democratic and to encourage an active "give-and-take" relationship with their children; they demonstrate curiosity and a respect for knowledge (94). In contrast, parental dominance or parental submissiveness adversely affects the development of academic motivation (50).

It is possible, of course, to make children overly concerned about scholastic success. Some parents create a high level of anxiety in their children about failing to "measure up" in school, with the result that the anxiety interferes with clear thinking or leads to withdrawal from school activities as a kind of defense mechanism. A number of very bright children do poorly in school for these reasons. Many times in such cases, the parents push even harder, and severe emotional problems may result (18). It should be noted, however, that mild or moderate anxiety is normal and, in fact, usually increases scholastic performance; decrements in performance occur only when the level of anxiety is high (113).

Peer Values Versus Parent Values

Acceptance by peers is one of the strongest needs of children in the middle years of childhood. If the child's friends value education and aspire to high levels in the educational system, the child is likely to do the same; if school is scorned by the child's friends, he or she, too, is likely to place a negative value on it (75). In most middle- and upper-class groups, scholastic success (or at least the absence of scholastic failure) is positively valued and explicitly rewarded not only by teachers and parents but also by young people themselves. Lower-class children are less likely to be encouraged in academic striving by either parents or peers.

While peer influences may dominate in certain customs and fads, parental values are likely to have greater influence in more fundamental areas such as life goals, including educational aspirations. Thus, if parental and peer values happen to conflict, the child's educational goals are more likely to reflect the values of the parents, even compared to his or her best school friend (75). The majority of students, however, have educational plans that are in line with *both* parental and peer expectations.

Obviously there are exceptions to these general conclusions, as in cases where deviant peer-group pressures are unusually strong and homogeneous. Similarly, where communication between parents and their children has broken down, parental influence is correspondingly weakened.

DEVELOPMENT OF CONSCIENCE

While the beginnings of a personal conscience and moral standards may be seen in the preschool years, middle childhood represents a critical period during which conscience develops at a rapid rate. Piaget believes that from age 5 to 12 the child's morality passes from a rigid and inflexible notion of right and wrong to a sense of justice that takes into account the situations in which the "immoral" act occurred. For example, a 5-year-old is apt to view lying as bad, regardless of circumstances. With increasing age, the child becomes more flexible and is willing to admit exceptions to the general rule (100). He can conceive of situations in which lying might be justified—for example, to spare someone's feelings.

In the earlier stage, called the stage of "moral realism," rules are considered sacred and unchangeable. This is true not only of moral rules but also of other rules as well; younger children believe, for example, that rules for games are also unchangeable and are often upset by suggestions of minor variations. Typically this "moral reality" is described to children by their parents, and thus "obedience to adults" is a prime factor in moral behavior during this stage. Gradually, during middle childhood, children become less liberal-minded, and they are more and more able to take the feelings of other people into account. Rules become more and more a matter of mutual agreement; that is, they can be changed if everyone agrees. And morality begins to involve intentions, not simply behaviors and consequences.

Research tends to support Piaget's hypothesis that older children view rule violations in a broader context. When students in the second, fifth, and eighth grades were questioned about the correct thing to do when one child hits another, the older children were more likely to ask about the circumstances of the aggressive act and the motive for it (49). In another study (117), only 7 percent of the children in the middle grades of school expressed the view that a rule should never be broken (compared to a majority of primary-grade children); the older children said it depended on the circumstances—or even the morality of the rule itself. As one psychologist summarized the changes, "Moral realism yields gradually during childhood to an ethics of reciprocity; what is right is now defined not in terms of self-evident and inherent necessity but in terms of a sense of balance or justice. Rightness is a matter of mutual consideration of needs" (95, p. 386).

Kohlberg's Stages of Moral Reasoning

Piaget's approach to the study of moral judgments was to tell children short stories involving morality and then to ask them questions about the story and their reaction to it. Lawrence Kohlberg has used a similar approach to explore further, and more systematically, the stages in the development of moral reasoning. Kohlberg constructed a set of moral dilemmas in story form for his subjects to consider. In one, a man's wife is dying. A druggist has discovered a drug that might save her, but he is charging too much and is unwilling to finance the husband's purchase. The husband steals the drug. The subjects are asked, "Should the husband have done that?" Other dilemmas involve a doctor faced with a patient soon to die, in great pain, and begging for a mercy killing; and another a military leader in battle who must send someone (himself?) on a probably fatal mission.

A careful analysis of the responses to the moral dilemmas led Kohlberg and his associates to define three levels of moral reasoning, with two stages within each level. At the lowest level—the *premoral* or *preconventional level*—children are very concerned about their needs and about the possible consequences of behaviors designed to fill those needs. In stage 1, children have an *obedience and punishment orientation:* They believe that people should act morally because, if they don't, they will be punished. In stage 2, moral reasoning is still based on self-interest, but the "logic" is slightly more sophisticated. Acts that bring bad consequences are still bad, but acts that are rewarded are good, according to this "naive hedonism." There is, in stage 2, a primitive notion of the value of cooperation and exchange with another person—"I'll scratch your back if you'll scratch mine." But the emphasis is on satisfying personal needs with a minimum of trouble. Stage 2 is said to involve an *instrumental-relativist orientation* because everything is viewed as "relative" to personal desires and morality resides in what is "instrumental" in satisfying those desires.

Preconventional reasoning is the most common level of moral thinking throughout most of middle childhood and corresponds to Piaget's cognitive stage of concrete operations (83). The child's notions of what is good or bad—right or wrong—are initially very concrete and simplistic. Gradually, as conscience develops, the child begins to internalize moral standards—to feel that disapproved behavior is "bad" and to feel guilty about it even if it goes unpunished. Eventually, toward the end of the middle years, most children—in countries around the world—reach the conventional level of moral reasoning.

The *conventional level* of morality is marked by descriptions of "proper" social roles and the value of traditions and laws. Stage 3 involves a *good boy, good girl orientation*, in which moral value is seen in conforming to stereotyped images of how a "good boy" or "good girl" should behave. The child is concerned with approval from others; pleasing and helping others is "nice to do." Stage 3 morality is common in preadolescence and early adolescence giving way in many cases to Stage 4 as progress in formal operational thinking continues. Stage 4 involves a *law and order orientation*, in which the person recognizes the need for obedience to rules, even if the rules are not the best; the world is something like a baseball game, where one may complain mightily about an umpire's decision but still recognize that without the umpire there would be chaos.

Moral reasoning in its most sophisticated form is found at the *postconventional* or *principled level* (see pp. 369–370). In stage 5, *the social contract orientation* emphasizes morality as respect for the rights of others and democratic agreements as the basis for laws. Stage 6 involves a *universal ethical principle orientation:* morality is defined by abstract principles like the golden rule. Few adults, and even fewer older adolescents ever reach stage 6.

Parent–Child Relationships and Conscience Development

Both Piaget and Kohlberg stress the relationship between cognitive maturation and moral development. As Kohlberg points out, without some facility in abstract thinking, the development of generalized standards would be difficult, perhaps impossible (82). However, while improved cognitive abilities may allow the child to be aware of moral values, commitment to following these rules will depend largely on other factors. In particular, the quality of the parent–child relationship is of critical importance.

A variety of studies indicate that parental warmth and love foster the development of conscience, as shown by guilt reactions and the adoption of personal moral standards (12). Love-oriented patterns of discipline are especially effective if affection is combined with instruction in moral reasoning (66). Instructive parents give explanations and reasons for requiring certain behaviors; they might point out the practical realities of a situation, for example, or how inappropriate behavior may be harmful to the child or others. Children of such parents, therefore, are more likely to have a clear understanding of right and wrong. And, more generally, they are shown how to reason about moral questions—a skill they eventually develop on their own.

In power-oriented patterns of discipline, parents use direct commands, threats, and physical force. They do not rely on their children's inner emotions (guilt, shame, love) or provide instruction in moral reasoning. The result is typically children who develop weak internal standards of morality, who instead continue to be influenced by the likelihood of "getting caught" or being punished (66).

PSYCHOLOGICAL PROBLEMS OF MIDDLE CHILDHOOD

Anxiety, frustration, and conflict are part of the human condition, and all children will encounter some psychological problems at one time or another. There is some evidence that psychological problems are more frequent at certain ages than at others. For example, referrals to psychiatric and psychological clinics tend to peak in the periods 4–7 years and 9–11 years, as well as 14–16 for adolescents (2, 109). It has been suggested that these periods represent transition stages that "interrupt the course of development and give rise to temporary imbalances" (2, p. 704). There may be a sudden acceleration in physical or cognitive development—during puberty, for example—or a change in parental expectations and social demands. The problems of children aged 4–7 are frequently related to beginning school.

Psychological problems are more common among young boys than among girls. During the first grade, boys are referred for clinical help eleven times as often as are girls, for problems such as "social and emotional immaturity, a syndrome characterized by a high rate of absenteeism, fatigability, inability to attend and concentrate, shyness, poor motivation for work, underweight, inability to follow directions, slow learning, infantile speech patterns and problems in the visual-motor and visual-perception areas" (2, p. 723). In all of the early grades, boys are more likely than girls to have severe speech and reading difficulties, personality and behavioral problems, school failure, and delinquency. When girls are referred for help with emotional problems, it is more often because they are overly anxious or fearful; boys are more often destructive and out of control.

Fears and Phobias

Many of the young child's psychological problems involve fear and anxiety, either directly, as in the cases of children who are overly anxious, or indirectly, as with children who try to disguise their fears by acting tough. The importance of fears in the mental life of 10-year-old children was shown by a study (51) in which the children were asked to draw the most important events in their lives. Almost one-third of the drawings illustrated fear experiences. Although many childhood fears are a function of direct experience with frightening events (being bitten by a dog, being hit by a car) or a product of parental warnings (stay away from fire, watch out for snakes), there are also many fears that are symbolic in nature. About 20 percent of children's fears are unrealistic and concern imaginary creatures, the dark, and being alone (71). Children between 9 and 12 said they were only moderately afraid of immediate, possible dangers, such as get-

●Figure 7.6 Children may be more afraid of impossible events, such as an attack by a tiger or by ghosts, than of realistic dangers.

ting hit by a car, but were very afraid of remote or impossible events, such as a lion attack or a visit from ghosts (Figure 7.6).

Fear of ghosts, lions, witches, and other unlikely adversaries, which are usually imagined as hurting or killing the child, may be symbolic substitutes for the fear of parental punishment (48). For this reason, rational attempts to reduce a child's fear of ghosts by pointing out that ghosts do not actually exist, are not likely to be successful. If the fear of ghosts symbolizes fear of punishment, then only reassurance about the love of his or her parents will reduce it.

Nightmares and sleepwalking   Sometimes childhood fears are expressed in "bad dreams" or nightmares. Nightmares tend to reach a peak between the ages of 4 and 6 (78), but more than a quarter of the 6- to 12-year-olds still have these frightening dreams (85). An occasional nightmare, of course, is not cause for parents' worry, but frequent and severe nightmares, especially if a particular theme seems to be recurring, indicate mental conflict and anxiety in a degree that requires attention. Some children experience an extreme form of nightmare, called "night terror." In such cases, the child is hard to waken, and wakening does not relieve the fears; the child is still in a state of panic, and has difficulty reorienting to reality. It is believed that in night terrors the child is reliving some traumatic event (78).

Other sleep disturbances that occur more frequently among children than among adults include the puzzling phenomenon of sleepwalking. Sleepwalking children are not insensitive to their environments, for they avoid obstacles in their paths and often respond to authoritative commands to return to bed. But it is evident that they are not really awake or alert (54). Many psychologists have likened sleepwalking to hypnosis. Both involved altered states of consciousness that most people have trouble remembering later, and suggestible children are somewhat more susceptible to sleepwalking than is the average child. In other respects, sleepwalking may be like nightmares—a way of working out the conflicts and anxieties of the day. Both nightmares and sleepwalking occur at the deepest stage of sleep (as do night terrors, bedwetting, and sleeptalking), when conscious control of thoughts and behavior may be at a very low level. Unless sleepwalking is both frequent and a serious problem, investigators recommend that the child should *not* be treated for it. The child will outgrow the condition eventually, and, in addition, most treatments are ineffective, making the child anxious about his or her "problem" for no good reason (44).

School phobias   One of the relatively common childhood fears of greatest concern to parents is *school phobia*—a fear, which may approach panic, of leaving home and going to school. Most children are occasionally reluctant to go to school, but persistent and intense fear of school is a symptom of underlying conflicts which should be treated. School phobias are more frequent among girls than among boys.

School phobias may result from a number of different factors, but the most widely observed pattern involves a fear of separation from a mother who has unconsciously created an abnormal dependency on her (78). She is threatened by the child's independence, often because her own dependency problems with her own mother were never resolved (72). She perceives school as a cold, forbidding place, and the child usually develops similar fears and perceptions. Another common pattern involves the child who comes to school with an inflated sense of his value and abilities. He is threatened by reactions and evaluations that do not correspond with his unrealistic self-image and retreats to home and mother, where he receives "higher grades" (86). One factor that does not seem important in school phobias, interestingly enough, is intelligence, for most children with such problems have at least average ability (33).

Obsessions and Compulsions

During the middle-childhood years, the child's desire to do what he wants to do when he wants to do it remains strong. On the other hand, his developing conscience dictates that many of these impulses are wrong. Under these circumstances, he becomes anxious. To ward off the unacceptable impulses—and thus control his anxiety—the child may develop obsessions and compulsions. (See also the discussion of defense mechanisms, pp. 219–220). Obsessions are repetitive, constantly intruding thoughts; compulsions are acts that the person feels compelled to perform, even though he may recognize them as unrealistic. Many people have obsessive thoughts and compulsions when they are realistically worried about something; for example, when a severe storm is brewing, parents may constantly go over, in their minds or in actual behavior, what they will do if a tornado is reported. Children sometimes develop similar obsessions and compulsions to deal with their unrealistic (and often unconscious) worries and anxieties.

Many young children have intense conflicts between the desire to be messy and dirty—which may also be associated with masturbation—and the cleanliness required of all "good children." To ward off the anxiety created by the desire to be dirty, the child may develop compulsive cleaning rituals, washing hands constantly and arranging his or her room in a mysterious but sacred order. Obsessive thoughts of germs and poisons may supplement the compulsions. If these problems are persistent and severe, psychological or psychiatric help may be necessary. Mild obsessions and compulsions, however, are common among children between 8 and 10 (117) and usually should not be a matter of great concern (Figure 7.7). Most adults can remember periods when they had "foolish" recurrent thoughts they could not get out of their heads or when they engaged in such activities as touching every third picket in a fence, avoiding cracks in the sidewalk, or having to do some other activity in a special way.

Serious obsessions and compulsions are a form of neurosis. Not unexpectedly, these severe manifestations are more frequent in the children of overly strict, fastidious parents, who hold their child to extreme standards of thought and behavior and allow little room for the expression of normal childhood impulses (78). If such parents are otherwise affectionate and withhold love as their primary means of punishment, the situation is highly conducive to the development of guilt and anxiety in the child; obsessions and compulsions may be his or her reaction to these troubling emotions.

Physical Symptoms

Psychological problems of the school-age child may be reflected in real or imagined physical symptoms. *Hypochondriasis*—excessive concern about imaginary or minor symptoms—usually occurs in children who are preoccupied with their bodies (112). The families of these children are likely to be extremely "illness-conscious"; the emphasis on health problems apparently moves the children to express their fears and anxieties in physical symptoms, which gain attention and sympathy (121).

Tics are involuntary muscle movements, such as eyeblinks or head movements, which often appear or increase in times of stress (52). Many tics are no more than "leaks" of general anxiety and restlessness. Others appear to give their own clues to the nature of an underlying conflict (78). A facial grimace may represent (unconsciously) "making a face at somebody." Some head shakes look as if the child is saying "No" to some unconscious wish. Similarly, nose

●Figure 7.7 Common compulsive rituals among school age children include touching every third picket in a fence, or avoiding cracks in the sidewalk.

wrinkling may indicate the child doesn't like "the smell of things," and eye blinking may represent an attempt to keep herself from seeing something she feels she shouldn't. Tics are most common in tense children with fairly strict parents (115). These children have to bottle up their irritations and impulses, and they are only partially successful; the tension bubbles out now and then in the form of a tic.

Usually the child is unaware of her tic, or if she is conscious of it, she finds it difficult or impossible to stop. Scolding, therefore, has little effect, except to make the child more anxious. Efforts should be made to reduce pressure on the child and to make her home life as relaxed as possible. Most tics disappear eventually, and only particularly persistent and troubling ones need be treated by professional therapists.

Psychosomatic illnesses are real, physical disorders that are caused or aggravated by psychological problems. Anxiety and conflict are often the chief determinants of childhood headaches, stomach aches, lack of appetite, obesity, diarrhea, tiredness, and allergies (112). The complex interactions of physiological and psychological factors is apparent in children with asthma (104). In some asthmatic children, the psychological component seems to be paramount; as soon as they leave home and family, presumably the source of their anxieties, to live in a children's residential treatment center, their symptoms are significantly reduced—to the point where no medication is necessary. Other children require lengthy treatment with strong drugs; their asthmatic responses are believed to be primarily physiological. Compared to these children, the children whose asthma problems are essentially solved when they leave home are signifi-

cantly more likely to report that emotions such as anger, anxiety, and depression trigger their asthma. Furthermore, their mothers and fathers display authoritarian and punitive attitudes to a greater degree than do the parents of the children with "physiological asthma."

PROBLEMS OF MINORITY-GROUP MEMBERSHIP

Children of all ethnic groups encounter problems of adjustment in middle childhood, but some children carry an additional burden—membership in a minority group that is subject to hostility and discrimination from majority-group peers and adults. Such children may become understandably resentful and bitter. Worse still, they may consciously or unconsciously begin to accept derogatory views of themselves and their own group (37). The result may be alienation from society and the development of what Erik Erikson calls a *negative* identity, marked by low self-esteem (53).

Self-Images in Minority Groups

The child's awareness of his racial or ethnic status develops early in childhood, usually by about age 4 or 5 (37). In the past at least, the child tended to accept society's negative stereotypes of his group. For example, in 1939, some black children aged 2 to 7 were shown a variety of black and white dolls and asked such questions as "Which doll looks nice?", "Which doll looks bad?", and "Which doll is a 'nice' color?" Most of the children picked the white dolls as looking nice, of a "nice" color, and picked the black dolls as the ones that looked bad (38). In another early study, black children between the ages of 3 and 7 perceived children of their own race as aggressive, bad, and those "whom other children fear" significantly more often than white children saw whites as possessing these characteristics (116). Similarly, Mexican-American children born in the United States were found to perceive themselves as significantly more lazy and uneducated, poorer, and of lower social status, compared to the way Mexican-Americans born in Mexico perceived themselves (45).

Fortunately, this picture is now changing, with increasing racial and ethnic pride ("black is beautiful," the concept of La Raza). In a 1969 replication of the doll study reported above, most of the black children preferred the black dolls to the white ones (67). Similarly, a number of recent studies show that the self-esteem of preadolescent and adolescent blacks often equals or exceeds that of whites (43). A lot depends on the child's relationship with his parents, which is more important for self-esteem than minority-group status, social class, and all other influences combined (6). The child with warm, understanding parents who are proud of him and actively involved in fostering his development is likely to develop a high regard for himself, even in a society where discrimination is still widely prevalent.

The Development of Prejudice

Significant numbers of children develop hostile attitudes toward minority groups before they enter kindergarten. During the early school years more children acquire these prejudices, which become more crystallized and conform more closely to adult patterns of prejudice (105, 107). Children's prejudices are rarely based on their own experiences; instead, they reflect the direct or indirect teaching of adults (Figure 7.8). Even parents who preach democratic values may convey underlying prejudices by disapproving of "certain kinds" of friendships and social relationships.

Children who are hostile to blacks, Jews, or members of other racial or ethnic groups tend to have certain personality characteristics. Compared to tolerant children, prejudiced children tend to reject people whom they consider "weak" or "different"; they have rigid, stereotyped conceptions of masculine and feminine behavior; they admire strong and powerful people; they feel a need to conform rigidly to approved social values and moralistically condemn those who do not (56, 59). In addition, intolerant children seem to fear and distrust others; they feel insecure, even helpless, in what they consider to be a chaotic world. In discussing relationships with parents, tolerant children frequently mentioned affection, cooperation, and companionship, but prejudiced children complained of lack of affection and harsh, punitive treatment.

The prejudiced child tends to be rather rigid and think in discrete categories, and thus his or her approach to intellectual tasks is less effective than that of a less prejudiced child. In one investigation (84), prejudiced 7-year-old

Figure 7.8 Children's prejudices are often based on the attitudes of others, rather than their own experiences.

children had more difficulty solving problems than did tolerant children because they were more likely to persist with an incorrect hunch; they also showed an inability to make use of hints the examiner gave them. The prejudiced children tended to look for simple solutions, and they performed poorly with ambiguous problems that required them to provide their own organization and structure. In brief, the rigidity of attitude that helps maintain prejudice was also reflected in the intolerant child's approach to intellectual tasks.

Prejudicial attitudes can be changed and racial tolerance increased if children of different races are allowed to interact in democratic circumstances (96). Many intolerant children are prejudiced because they live among bigots, and they have adjusted to that environment. If they are given direct experience with children of other races, they discover that many of their beliefs are incorrect or exaggerated—that "kids are kids," no matter what their background. A well-liked teacher or camp counselor who is unprejudiced also can affect the racial attitudes of young children (106). It is worth noting, however, that the prejudice of some children grows from deep-seated hostilities. These children expect the world to be cruel and unpleasant; they expect to be treated "unfairly," and they can usually find "evidence" that their perceptions are accurate. Interactions with children of other races are not likely to reduce this kind of prejudice and, in fact, may increase intolerance (96).

SUMMARY

Although the child in middle childhood is exposed to an ever-increasing number of influences outside the family, relationships with parents remain of major importance. One major dimension of parental behavior involves the parents' degree of control over their child's behavior, which has at least two aspects: setting and enforcing rules of behavior and restricting the child's autonomy. Democratic parents are loving and accepting of their children and encourage autonomy, although they may set and enforce strict rules; their children are typically well-adjusted. Rejecting parents who also restrict their children's behavior—authoritarian parents—have unhappy, hostile offspring, while rejecting parents who are lax in controls—neglectful parents—have unhappy, undisciplined children.

Children with high self-esteem are self-confident and assertive, while children with low self-esteem tend to be preoccupied with their own personal problems. Parents influence their children's self-concept by setting a good example and by encouraging self-confidence and self-reliance, although they may protect their children from tasks that promise to be too frustrating.

Children's temperamental characteristics, such as emotional expressiveness and "explosiveness," affect the way parents treat them. Parents generally prefer a child who expresses affection, but explosiveness is sometimes disapproved in girls and in younger boys.

Although most children with an absent parent develop normally, some boys without fathers are less "masculine" than average and some, in apparent overreaction, are "super-masculine." Girls without fathers sometimes have difficulty relating to boys.

Birth order and the sex and age of siblings can influence personality development. First-born children tend to be more adult-oriented and more motivated to achieve than later-born children. Sisters increase slightly the likelihood of feminine traits, and brothers increase masculine tendencies. The typically strong involvement of siblings with one another sometimes results in sibling rivalry. The death of a sibling is confusing and threatening to a young child.

Peer groups become increasingly important as the child begins school. Popular children, who are also leaders in the group, are enthusiastic, cheerful, friendly, intelligent, and self-confident. Unpopular children are anxious, dependent, and hostile. Conformity, infrequently observed in preschoolers, is more common among children in the early grades.

The teacher is one of the most important factors in a child's adjustment to school. In the early grades, teachers are often women who are viewed as a substitute mother. Like good parents, good teachers set and enforce reasonable rules and, within these limits, encourage independence and creativity. Pupils often take on characteristics of their teachers, becoming more impulsive with an impulsive teacher or more reflective with a cautious teacher.

Structured teaching methods often work better for anxious or compulsive children. Some children seem to flounder in informal, student-oriented schools, but others find the relative freedom a spur to creativity and self-understanding. Similarly, some children seem to "get lost" in very large schools and do better in smaller schools, where they are more likely to participate in school activities. Textbooks have recently come under criticism for failing to depict urban life and minority groups realistically.

Many children who eventually drop out of school are having difficulties by the first or second grade, performing below their intellectual capabilities. Dropouts are typically isolated from family and friends; they tend to view the world as unpredictable, violent, and exploitative.

Middle- and upper-class parents encourage academic excellence in their children, but many lower-class parents see education as irrelevant. Similarly, middle- and upper-class children find support for their intellectual strivings from their peers, while many lower-class children are discouraged by their friends.

Children in the early school years make rapid and significant advances in the development of conscience. Preschool children are apt to consider rules unchangeable, but this "moral realism" soon gives way to a sense of justice that considers the circumstances of the action. Kohlberg hypothesizes a "preconventional" level of moral reasoning in which children have either an "obedience and punishment" orientation (stage 1), characteristic of preschoolers, or an "instrumental-relativist" orientation (stage 2), characteristic of middle childhood. Toward the end of middle childhood, some children reach the "conventional" level of morality, with a "good boy, good girl" orientation (stage 3) or a "law and order" orientation (stage 4). The final or "principled" level of moral reasoning, according to Kohlberg, is found in some adults and includes stage 5, the "social contract" orientation, and stage 6, the "universal ethical principle" orientation. The development of conscience is facilitated by affectionate parents who take the time to explain rules and prohibitions.

Children in middle childhood are subject to a variety of fears and anxieties, including those that stem from beginning school and those that emerge with improved cognitive abilities to imagine frightening creatures and events. Obsessions and compulsions and physical symptoms such as tics and pyschosomatic illnesses sometimes develop because of conflicts between, for example, a desire to be messy and a desire to be a "good, clean child."

Minority-group children have special burdens. Increasing racial and ethnic pride has raised their levels of self-esteem, but the prejudice of a few intolerant classmates continues. Some children are able to change their views when they discover, through interaction with minority group children, that their stereotypes are inaccurate, but other children are prejudiced because of personal insecurities that are relatively immune to facts.

References

1. Altus, W. D. Birth order and its sequelae. **International Journal of Psychiatry,** 1967, **3,** 23–39.

2. Anthony, E. J. The behafior disorders of children. In P. H. Mussen (Ed.), **Carmichael's Manual of child psychology.** (3rd ed.) Vol. 2. New York: Wiley, 1970. Pp. 667–754.

3. Anthony, E. J., & Benedek, T. **Parenthood: Its psychology and psychopatholgy.** Boston: Little, Brown, 1970.

4. Argyle, M., & Robinson, P. Two origins of achievement motivation. **British Journal of Social and Clinical Psychology,** 1962, **1,** 107–120.

5. Armentrout, J. A., & Burger, G. K. Children's reports of parental child-rearing behavior at five grade levels. **Developmental Psychology,** 1972, **7,** 44–48.

6. Bachman, J. G. **Youth in transtition.** Vol. 2. **The impact of family background and intelligence on tenth grade boys.** Ann Arbor: Institute for Social Research, University of Michigan, 1970.

7. Bachman, J. G., Green, S., & Wirtanen, I. **Dropping out—problem or symptom.** Ann Arbor: Institute for Social Research, University of Michigan, 1972.

8. Baldwin, A. L. The effect of home environment on nursery school behavior. **Child Development,** 1949, **20,** 49–61.

9. Barclay, A. G., & Cusumano, D. Father-absence, cross-sex identity, and field-dependent behavior in male adolescents. **Child Development,** 1967, **38,** 243–250.

10. Barry, H., Jr. Birth order: Achievement, schizophrenia and culture. **International Journal of Psychology,** 1967, **3,** 439–444.

11. Baumrind, D. A critique of radical innovation as a solution to contemporary problems of education. Unpublished manuscript, University of California, Berkeley, March, 1972.

12. Becker, W. C. Consequences of different kinds of parental discipline. In M. L. Hoffman & L. W. Hoffman (Eds.), **Review of child development.** Vol. 1. New York: Russell Sage Foundation, 1964.

13. Bender, L. Children's reaction to the death of a sibling. In **A Dynamic Psychopathology of Childhood.** Springfield, Ill.: Thomas, 1954.

14. Berenda, R. W. **The influence of the group on the judgments of children.** New York: King's Crown Press, 1950.

15. Bertrand, A. L. School attendance and attainment: Function and dysfunction of school and family systems. **Social Forces,** 1962, **40,** 228–233.

16. Biller, H. B., & Davids, A. Parent-child relations, personality development, and psychopathology. In A. Davids (Ed.), **Abnormal child psychology.** Belmont, Calif.: Brooks Cole, 1973, 48–76.

17. Birch, H. G., & Gussow, J. D. **Disadvantaged children: Health, nutrition and school failure.** New York: Grune and Stratton, 1970.

18. Birney, R. C., Burdick, H., & Teevan, R. C. **Fear of failure.** New York: Van Nostrand Reinhold, 1969.

19. Blinder, B. J. Sibling death in childhood. **Child Psychiatry and Human Development,** 1972, **2,** 169–175.

20. Blom, G. E. Sex differences in reading disability. **Reading Forum.** 31–46 (NINDS Monographs No. 11). Washington, D.C.: National Institute of Neurological Diseases, National Institute of Health, 1970.

21. Blom, G. E., Waite, R. R., & Zimet, S. G. Ethnic integration and urbanization of a first grade reading textbook: A research study. **Psychology in the Schools,** 1967, **4,** 176–181.

22. Bonney, M. E. Sex differences in social success and personality traits. **Child Development,** 1944, **15,** 63–79.

23. Bonney, M. E. The constancy of sociometric scores and their relationship to teacher judgments of social success and to personality self-ratings. **Sociometry,** 1943, **6,** 409–424.

24. Bronfenbrenner, U. The psychological costs of quality and equality in education. **Child Development,** 1967, **38,** 909–925.

25. Bronson, W. C. The role of enduring orientations to the environment in personality development. **Genetic Psychology Monographs,** 1972, **86,** 3–80.

26. Burger, G. K., & Armentrout, J. A. A factor analysis of fifth and sixth graders' reports of parental child-rearing behavior. **Developmental Psychology,** 1971, **4,** 483.

27. Campbell, J. D. Peer relations in childhood. In M. L. Hoffman & L. W. Hoffman (Eds.), **Review of child development research.** Vol. 1. New York: Russell Sage Foundation, 1964. Pp. 289–322.

28. Campbell, J. D., & Yarrow, M. R. Perceptual and behavioral correlates of social effectiveness. **Sociometry,** 1961, **24,** 1–20.

29. Carlsmith, L. Effect of early father-absence on scholastic aptitude. **Harvard Educational Review,** 1964, **34,** 3–21.

30. Carrino, C. Identifying potential dropouts in the elementary grades. **Dissertation Abstracts,** 1966, **27,** 343.

31. Cervantes, L. F. Family background, primary relationships, and the high school dropout. **Journal of Marriage and the Family,** 1965, **5,** 218–223.

32. Cervantes, L. F. **The dropout: Causes and cures.** Ann Arbor: University of Michigan Press, 1965.

33. Chazan, M. School phobia. **British Journal of Educational Psychology,** 1962, **32,** 209–217.

34. Child, I. L., Potter, E. H., & Levine, E. M. Children's textbooks and personality development: An exploration in the social psychology of education. **Psychological Monographs,** 1946, **60**(3).

35. Chwast, J. Sociopathic behavior in children. In B. B. Wolman (Ed.), **Manual of child psychopathology.** New York: McGraw-Hill, 1972, Pp. 436–445.

36. Clark, K. B. Alternative public school systems. **Harvard Educational Review,** 1968, **38,** 100–113.

37. Clark, K. B. **Prejudice and your child.** Boston: Beacon, 1955.

38. Clark, K. B., & Clark, M. P. Racial identification and preference in Negro children. In T. M. Newcomb and E. L. Hartley (Eds.), **Readings in social psychology.** New York: Holt, Rinehart & Winston, 1947. Pp. 169–178.

39. Collier, M. J., & Gaier, E. L. The hero in the preferred childhood stories of college men. **American Imago,** 1959, **16,** 177–194.

40. Collier, M. J., & Gaier, E. L. Adult reactions to preferred childhood stories. **Child Development,** 1958, **29,** 97–103.

41. Combs, J. & Cooley, W. W. Dropouts: In high school and after school. **American Educational Research Journal,** 1968, **5,** 343–363.

42. Coopersmith, S. **The antecedents of self-esteem.** San Francisco: Freeman, 1967.

43. Dansby, P. G. Black pride in the Seventies: Fact or fantasy? In R. L. Jones (Ed.), **Black psychology.** New York: Harper & Row, 1972, Pp. 145–155.

44. Dement, W. C. **Some must watch while some must sleep.** San Francisco: Freeman, 1974.

45. Derbyshire, R. L. Adolescent identity crisis in urban Mexican Americans in East Los Angeles. In E. B. Brody (Ed.), **Minority group adolescents in the United States.** Baltimore: Williams & Wilkins, 1968. Pp. 157–204.

46. Deutsch, M. The disadvantaged child and the learning process. In A. H. Passow (Ed.), **Education in depressed areas.** New York: Columbia University Press, 1963, Pp. 163–179.

47. Dowaliby, F. J., & Schumer, H. Teacher-centered versus student-centered mode of college classroom instruction as related to manifest anxiety. **Proceedings, 79th Annual Convention of the American Psychological Association,** 1971, **6,** 541–542.

48. Dunlop, G. M. Certain aspects of children's fears. Unpublished doctoral dissertation, Columbia University, 1951.

49. Durkin, D. Children's concepts of justice: A comparison with the Piaget data. **Child Development,** 1959, **30,** 59–67.

50. Elder, G. H., Jr. Family structure and educational attainment: A cross-national analysis. **American Sociological Review,** 1965, **30,** 81–96.

51. England, A. O. Nonstructured approach to the study of children's fears. **Journal of Clinical Psychology,** 1946, **2,** 363–368.

52. English, O. S., & Finch, S. M. **Introduction to psychiatry.** New York: Norton, 1954.

53. Erikson, E. H. **Identity: Youth and crisis.** New York: Norton, 1968.

54. Finch, S. M. **Fundamentals of child psychiatry.** New York: Norton, 1960.

55. Franco, D. The child's perception of "The Teacher" as compared to his perception of "The Mother." **Dissertation Abstracts,** 1964, **24,** 3414–3415.

56. Frenkel-Brunswik, E. A study of prejudice in children. **Human Relations,** 1958, **1,** 295–306.

57. Furman, R. A. Death and the young child. **Psychoanalytic Study of the Child,** 1964, **19,** 321–333.

58. Gaier, E. L., & Collier, M. J. The latency-stage story preferences of American and Finnish children. **Child Development,** 1960, **31,** 431–451.

59. Gregory, I. Anterospective data following childhood loss of a parent: I. Delinquency and high school drop out. **Archives of General Psychiatry,** 1965, **13,** 99–109.

60. Grimes, J. W., & Allinsmith, W. Compulsivity, anxiety, and school achievement. **Merrill-Palmer Quarterly,** 1961, **7,** 247–269.

61. Gump, P. V. **Big schools, small schools.** Moravia, N.Y.: Chronicle Guidance Publications, 1966.

62. Hartup, W. W. Peer interaction and social organization. In P. H. Mussen (Ed.). **Carmichael's Manual of child psychology.** (3rd ed.) Vol. 2. New York: Wiley, 1970. Pp. 457–558.

63. Heil, L. M., & Washburne, C. Characteristics of teachers related to children's progress. **Journal of Teacher Education,** 1961, **12,** 401–406.

64. Hetherington, E. M. Effects of father absence on personality development in adolescent daughters. **Developmental Psychology,** 1972, **7,** 327–336.

65. Hetherington, E. M. Effects of paternal absence on sex typed behavior in Negro and white preadolescent males. **Journal of Personality and Social Psychology,** 1960, **1,** 87–91.

66. Hoffman, M. L. Moral development. In P. H. Massen (Ed.), **Carmichael's manual of child psychology** (Vol. 2). New York: Wiley, 1970.

67. Hraba, J., & Grant, G. Black is beautiful: A reexamination of racial preference and identification. **Journal of Personality and Social Psychology,** 1970, **16,** 398–402.

68. Hsu, F. L. K., Watrous, B. G., & Lord, E. M. Culture pattern and adolescent behavior. **International Journal of Social Psychiatry,** 1960–1961, **7,** 33–35.

69. Hunt, R. G., & Synnerdale, V. Social influences among kindergarten children. **Sociology and Social Research,** 1959, **43,** 171–174.

70. Jennings, F. Textbooks and trapped idealists. **Saturday Review,** January 18, 1964, 57–59, 77–78.

71. Jersild, A. T., Markey, F. V., & Jersild, C. L. Children's fears, dreams, wishes, daydreams, likes, dislikes, pleasant and unpleasant memories. **Child Development Monographs,** 1933, No. 12.

72. Johnson, A. M. School phobia. **American Journal of Orthopsychiatry,** 1941, **11,** 702–711.

73. Kagan, J. The child's sex role classification of school objects. **Child Development,** 1964, **35,** 1051.

74. Kagan, J., & Moss, H. A. **Birth to maturity: The Fels study of psychological development.** New York: Wiley, 1962.

75. Kandel, D. B., & Lesser, G. S. Parental and peer influences on educational plans of adolescents. **American Sociological Review,** 1969, **34,** 213–223.

76. Kellogg, R. L. A direct approach to sex-role identification of school-related objects. **Psychological Reports,** 1969, **24,** 839–841.

77. Keniston, K. Social change and youth in America. **Daedalus,** Winter 1962, 145–171.

78. Kessler, J. W. **Psychopathology of childhood.** Englewood Cliffs, N.J.: Prentice-Hall, 1966.

79. Koch, H. L. Attitudes of children toward their peers as related to certain characteristics of their siblings. **Psychological Monographs,** 1956, **70**(426), 1–41.

80. Koch, H. L. Sissiness and tomboyishness in relation to sibling characteristics. **Journal of Genetic Psychology,** 1956, **88,** 231–244.

81. Koch, H. L. Some emotional attitudes of the young child in relation to characteristics of his siblings. **Child Development,** 1956, **27,** 393–426.

82. Kohlberg, L. Development of moral character and moral ideology. In M. L. Hoffman & L. W. Hoffman (Eds.), **Review of child development.** Vol. I. New York: Russell Sage Foundation, 1964. Pp. 383–431.

83. Kohlberg, L. The development of children's orientations toward a moral order: I. Sequence in the development of moral thought. **Vita Humana,** 1963, **6,** 11–33.

84. Kutner, B. Patterns of mental functioning associated with prejudice in children. **Psychological Monographs,** 1958, **72**(460).

85. Lapouse, R., & Monk, M. A. Fears and worries in a representative sample of children. **American Journal of Orthopsychiatry,** 1959, **29,** 803–818.

86. Leventhal, T., & Sills, M. Self-image in school phobia. **American Journal of Orthopsychiatry,** 1964, **34,** 685–695.

87. Levin, H. Permissive child rearing and adult role behavior. In D. E. Dulany, R. L. DeValois, D. C. Beardsley & M. R. Winterbottom (eds.), **Contributions to modern psychology.** New York: Oxford University Press, 1958. Pp. 307–312.

88. McCandless, B. **Adolescents: Behavior and development.** Hinsdale, Ill.: Dryden, 1970.

89. McClelland, D. C. **The achieving society.** New York: Van Nostrand Reinhold, 1961.

90. Marburger, C. L. Consideration for educational planning. In A. H. Passow (Ed.), **Education in depressed areas.** New York: Columbia University Press, 1963. Pp. 298–321.

91. Maslow, A. H., & Diaz-Guerrero, R. Delinquency as a value disturbance. In J. G. Peatman & E. L. Hartley (Eds.), **Festschrift for Gardner Murphy.** New York: Harper & Row, 1960. Pp 228–240.

92. Michalak, J. City life in primers. **New York Herald-Tribune,** January 26, 1965.

93. Minuchin, P., Biber, B., Shapiro, E., and Zimiles, H. **The psychological impact of school experience.** New York: Basic Books, 1969.

94. Morrow, W. R., & Wilson, R. C. Family relations of bright high-achieving and underachieving high school boys. **Child Development,** 1961, **32,** 501–510.

95. Murphy, G. **Personality,** New York: Harper & Row, 1947.

96. Mussen, P. H. Some personality and social factors related to changes in children's attitudes toward Negroes. **Journal of Abnormal and Social Psychology,** 1950, **45,** 423–441.

97. Myerhoff, B. G., & Larson, W. R. Primary and formal aspects of family organization: Group consensus, problem perception, and adolescent school success. **Journal of Marriage and the Family,** 1965, **29,** 213–217.

98. Newsletter, Institute for Social Research, University of Michigan, 1971.

99. Peppin, B. H. Parental understanding, parental acceptance and the self-concept of children as a function of academic over- and under-achievement. **Dissertation Abstracts,** 1963, **23,** 4422–4423.

100. Piaget, J. **The moral judgment of the child.** London: Routledge & Kegan Paul, 1932.

101. Polansky, N., Lippitt, R., & Redl, F. An investigation of behavioral contagion in groups. **Human Relations,** 1950, **3,** 319–348.

102. Prescott, E., et al. Group day care as a child-rearing environment: An observational study of day care programs. Pasadena, Calif.: ERIC Research in Education, Pacific Oaks College, 1967.

103. Purcell, K. Assessment of psychological determinants in childhood asthma. In P. H. Mussen, J. J. Conger & J. Kagan (Eds.), **Readings in a child development and personality.** New York: Harper & Row, 1970 (2nd ed.).

104. Purcell, K. & Weiss, J. H. Emotions and asthma: Assessment and treatment. In C. G. Costello (Ed.), **Symptoms of psychopathology.** New York: Wiley, 1971.

105. Radke, M. J., & Trager, H. G. Children's perception of the social roles of Negroes and whites. **Journal of Psychology,** 1950, **29,** 3–33.

106. Radke-Yarrow, M. International dynamics in a desegration process. **Journal of Social Issues,** 1958, **14,** 3–63.

107. Radke-Yarrow, M., Trager, H. G., & Miller, J. The role of parents in the development of children's ethnic attitudes. **Child Development,** 1952, **23,** 13–53.

108. Richardson, S. Personal communication.

109. Rosen, B. M., Bahn, A. K., & Kramer, M. Demographic and diagnostic characteristics of psychiatric outpatients in the U.S.A., 1961. **American Journal of Orthopsychiatry,** 1964, **24,** 455–467.

110. Schaefer, E. S. A configurational analysis of children's reports of parent behavior. **Journal of Consulting Psychology,** 1965, **29,** 552–557.

111. Sears, R. R., Maccoby, E. E., & Levin, H. **Patterns of child rearing.** New York: Harper & Row, 1957.

112. Senn, M. J. E., & Solnit, A. J. **Problems in child behavior and development.** Philadelphia: Lea and Febiger, 1970.

113. Sharma, S. Manifest anxiety and school achievement of adolescents. **Journal of Consulting and Clinical Psychology,** 1970, **34,** 403–407.

114. Spiro, M. E. **Children of the kibbutz.** Cambridge, Mass.: Harvard University Press, 1958.

115. Spock, B. **Baby and child care.** New York: Pocket Books, 1970.

116. Stevenson, H. W., & Stewart, E. C. A developmental study of race awareness in young children. **Child Development,** 1958, **29,** 399–410.

117. Tapp, J. L., & Levine, F. J. Compliance from kindergarten to college: A speculative research note. **Journal of Youth and Adolescence,** 1972, **1,** 233–249.

118. Thompson, G. E. The social and emotional development of preschool children under two types of education programs. **Psychological Monographs,** 1944, **56.**

119. Tuddenham, R. D. Studies in reputation: III. Correlates of popularity among elementary school children. **Journal of Educational Psychology,** 1951, **42,** 257–276.

120. Voss, H. L., Wendling, A., & Elliott, D. S. Some types of high-school dropouts. **Journal of Educational Research,** 1966, **59,** 363–368.

121. Weiner, I. B., & Elkind, D. **Child development: A core approach.** New York: Wiley, 1972.

122. White, R. W. **The abnormal personality: A textbook.** New York: Ronald, 1948.

123. White, W. F., & Dekle, O. T. Effect of teacher's motivational cues on achievement level in elementary grades. **Psychological Reports,** 1966, **18,** 351–356.

124. Wicker, A. W. Undermanning, performances, and students' subjective experiences in behavior settings of large and small high schools. **Journal of Personality and Social Psychology,** 1968, **10,** 255–261.

125. Willems, E. P. Sense of obligation to high school activities as related to school size and marginality of student. **Child Development,** 1967, **38,** 1247–1260.

126. Yando, R. M., & Kagan, J. The effect of teacher tempo on the child. **Child Development,** 1968, **39,** 27–34.

127. Yee, A. H. Source and direction of casual influence in teacher-pupil relationships. **Journal of Educational Psychology,** 1968, **59,** 275–282.

128. Zimet, S. G. The messages in elementary reading texts. **Today's Education,** 1973, **62,** 43ff.

129. Zimet, S. G. American elementary reading textbooks: A sociological review. **Teachers College Record,** 1969, **70,** 331–340.

CHAPTER 8
Adolescence: Basic Development

Adolescence means growing up, both literally—the root word in Latin (*adolescens*) means "growing up"—and figuratively—it is the period from puberty to maturity, roughly speaking. It includes, most prominently, the "teen" years from 13 to 18 or 19, and perhaps a little beyond, depending on how rapidly the individual matures. Adolescence is a period of great biological changes, as young bodies are made ready for reproduction. Adolescence is also a period of significant social changes, as young minds are made ready for the important tasks of adult life—working, loving. In the few short years between childhood and normal adulthood, the adolescent must gradually establish a personal identity; he must adjust to the major biological changes he is undergoing; he must establish cooperative and workable relationships with his peers; he must gradually achieve independence from his family; and he must develop a set of guiding moral beliefs and standards which can lend some order and consistency to decisions and actions in a diverse and often confusing world. These basic developments will be covered in this chapter. In the following chapter, some of the major concerns of society regarding adolescents will be discussed: increased sex drives, which society attempts, not always successfully, to channel into socially approved forms of sexual behavior; drugs; alternative life-styles; criminal behavior (delinquency); and alienation in general.

One of our major aims in these chapters will be to examine the evidence of conflicting adult views of the values, attitudes, and behavior of today's adolescents. Some observers see the major developmental tasks as relatively unchanging from generation to generation, and thus see today's adolescent as much the same as always—except perhaps for a few superficial differences in dress and behavior. Proponents of this view may be tempted to quote Aristotle, who assessed the adolescent character over 2000 years ago:

> The young are in character prone to desire and ready to carry any desire they may have formed into action. . . . They are changeful too, and fickle in their desires, which are as transitory as they are vehement; for their wishes are keen without being permanent, like a sick man's fits of hunger and thirst.
>
> They are passionate, irascible, and apt to be carried away by their impulses. They are the slaves, too, of their passion, as their ambition prevents their ever brooking a slight and renders them indignant at the mere idea of enduring an injury. . . . They are fonder both of honor and of victory than of money, the reason why they care so little for money being that they have never yet had experience of want.
>
> They are charitable rather than the reverse, as they have never yet been witnesses of many villainies, and they are trustful, as they have not yet been often deceived. . . . They have high aspirations; for they have never yet been humiliated by the experience of life, but are unacquainted with the limiting force of circumstances. . . .
>
> If the young commit a fault, it is always on the side of excess and exaggeration for they carry everything too far, whether it be their love or hatred or anything else. They regard themselves as omniscient and are positive in their assertions; this is, in fact, the reason of their carrying everything too far (52, pp. 18–19).

Other observers of adolescents are alarmed, claiming that youth today is more rebellious, more troubled emotionally, and more critical of valuable traditions than were previous generations. Many of these observers see present adolescent behavior as a threat to the future of society. In contrast, a third group of observers tells us not to worry, that the adolescents of today are brighter and better informed than their parents; less sentimental, but more genuinely idealistic, more open and honest, but less hypocritical; and more tolerant of individual differences. Probably all of these views have elements of truth and elements of oversimplification. We will attempt to arrive at a balanced judgment about the problems confronting adolescents and their responses to these problems.

PERSONALITY DEVELOPMENT IN ADOLESCENCE

Identity

In many ways, the question "Who am I?" is the central problem of adolescence. Establishing a unique and "personalized" *identity* has been the subject of innumerable novels and biographies over many centuries, but only in recent decades has it become the focus of systematic psychological concern—principally through the writings of Erik Erikson (31, 32, 33). The adolescent or adult with a strong sense of identity (or *ego identity*) sees himself or herself as a distinctive individual—in some respects like no other person, even though one may share many motives, values, and interests with others. In addition to uniqueness, identity reflects a feeling of self-consistency; that is, one's identity is an integration of one's needs, capabilities, goals, and values into a (more or less) coherent whole that is (more or less) consistent over time. An identity need not be all positive; it can contain negative elements as well (34). But there must be some central core to the self—something to provide a frame of reference within which the person can view with some perspective the varied events of a rapidly changing, often chaotic, world.

The danger of this developmental period is *ego confusion—not* knowing who you are or having several conflicting identities. Many adolescents find themselves playing roles which shift from one situation to another and they worry about "Which, if any, is the real me?" They also self-consciously try out different roles in the hopes of finding one that seems right. One adolescent girl had three distinctly different handwriting styles. When asked why she did not choose one and stick to it, she replied, "How can I only write one way till I know who I am?" (66, p. 601).

The problem of identity becomes acute at adolescence for a variety of reasons. Without some sense of identity, of who he or she is and where he or she is headed, the adolescent faces virtually insurmountable odds in attempting to cope with the social demands made at this time—to be independent, to establish meaningful and workable relations with peers of both sexes, and to decide, at

● Figure 8.1 Forming a personal identity is one of the main developmental tasks of adolescence.

least in some preliminary respects, on life's goals and a life's work (Figure 8.1). These social demands come at the same time the body of the young boy or girl is rapidly changing size and shape, making feelings of self-consistency difficult. Sexual maturity "floods body and imagination with forbidden desires" (30, p. 9). Another factor in the development of personal identity is the newly developed cognitive capacity to reason abstractly (see pp. 176–178). This ability enables the adolescent to imagine different identities—which may hinder him or her in making necessary commitments—and conceptually to integrate and understand the "sameness" that remains amid the diversity of physiological and social changes.

Identifications and Identity

How does a sense of identity develop? Part of the answer lies in the people and groups with which the child identifies, that is, admires, desires to be like, imitates, sympathizes with. These childhood indentifications include individuals such as parents, high-status peers, teachers, folk heroes, and groups such as "our gang," "our generation," Americans, and ethnic groups (37). Each of these identifications provides a source of values and behaviors that can be "tried on for size," and each leaves some residue, some characteristics that seem to fit. Eventually these characteristics must be synthesized into a coherent, consistent, and unique whole—the "real me."

Perhaps the most critical identifications depend on the relationship the adolescent has had, and continues to have, with his or her parents. Establishing a strong ego identity will be greatly facilitated by a rewarding interaction with both parents (60, 61). Under favorable circumstances, the same-sex parent demonstrates most clearly the proper values and behaviors of the sex role, but the opposite-sex parent is also a competent individual who shares many of the values of his or her spouse. Adolescents with parents of this sort are likely to have positive and clearly defined self-perceptions. They are also likely to have fewer conflicts between their self-perceptions, on the one hand, and the internal demands of approaching sexual maturity and the external demands of society, on the other; and such conflicts as they do encounter are handled more effectively.

Adolescent boys with nurturant fathers perceive themselves as having greater role-consistency than sons of less nurturant men; that is, they perceive themselves as responding in similar ways to parents, friends, employers, casual acquaintances, young children, and members of the opposite sex (43). Thus, whether they view themselves as relaxed or formal, warm or aloof, they tend to view themselves as the same in a variety of interpersonal situations. Adolescent girls who score high in identification with their mothers tend to perceive themselves as "calm," "reasonable," "reserved," "self-controlled," "confident," and "wise." In contrast, those scoring low in identification tend to view themselves as "changeable, " "impulsive," "rebellious," "restless," "dramatic," "touchy," and "tactless" (5). In Erikson's terms, the boys with the nurturant fathers (with whom the boys presumably identify strongly) and the girls who identify strongly with their mothers show clear signs of emerging ego identity, while the inconsistent, restless adolescents without strong identifications reflect ego confusion.

Sexual Identity

A major part of one's personal identity is one's sex: "I am a man," or "I am a woman." Notions of what it means to be a man or a woman are in a state of flux, and controversy abounds, with the result that many young people experience conflict whether they accept traditional sex roles or the newer, less differentiated, "adrogynous" roles (combining both "masculine" and "feminine" characteristics). The stereotypes of the traditional sex roles—that is, widely held (but not necessarily correct) beliefs about which traits are masculine and which

● Table 8.1 Stereotypic sex-role items (responses from 74 college men and 80 college women)

Feminine	Masculine
COMPETENCY CLUSTER: MASCULINE POLE IS MORE DESIRABLE	
Not at all aggressive	Very aggressive
Not at all independent	Very independent
Very emotional	Not at all emotional
Does not hide emotions at all	Almost always hides emotions
Very subjective	Very objective
Very easily influenced	Not at all easily influenced
Very submissive	Very dominant
Dislikes math and science very much	Likes math and science very much
Very excitable in a minor crisis	Not at all excitable in a minor crisis
Very passive	Very active
Not at all competitive	Very competitive
Very illogical	Very logical
Very home oriented	Very worldly
Not at all skilled in business	Very skilled in business
Very sneaky	Very direct
Does not know the way of the world	Knows the way of the world
Feelings easily hurt	Feelings not easily hurt
Not at all adventurous	Very adventurous
Has difficulty making decisions	Can make decisions easily
Cries very easily	Never cries
Almost never acts as a leader	Almost always acts as a leader
Not at all self-confident	Very self-confident
Very uncomfortable about being aggressive	Not at all uncomfortable about being aggressive
Not at all ambitious	Very ambitious
Unable to separate feelings from ideas	Easily able to separate feelings from ideas
Very dependent	Not at all dependent
Very conceited about appearance	Never conceited about appearance
Thinks women are always superior to men	Thinks men are always superior to women
Does not talk feely about sex with men	Talks freely about sex with men

SOURCE: I. K. Broverman, S. R. Vogel, D. M. Broverman, F. E. Clarkson, and P. S. Rosencrantz, "Sex Role Stereotypes: A Current Appraisal," in *Journal of Social Issues*, vol. 28, 1972, p. 63. Reprinted by permission.

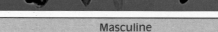

Table 8.1 *(continued)*

Feminine	Masculine
WARMTH-EXPRESSIVENESS CLUSTER: FEMININE POLE IS MORE DESIRABLE	
Doesn't use harsh language at all	Uses very harsh language
Very talkative	Not at all talkative
Very tactful	Very blunt
Very gentle	Very rough
Very aware of feelings of others	Not at all aware of feelings of others
Very religious	Not at all religious
Very interested in own appearance	Not at all interested in own appearance
Very neat in habits	Very sloppy in habits
Very quiet	Very loud
Very strong need for security	Very little need for security
Enjoys art and literature	Does not enjoy art or literature at all
Easily expresses tender feelings	Does not express tender feelings at all easily

are feminine—are shown in Table 8.1. Men are supposedly more independent and assertive, less emotional, more competitive and adventurous—a cluster of traits we tend to associate with competent people in the world of work (13). Women, according to views commonly held by both men and women, are gentler, more sensitive, more warm and loving, more nurturant—they make very nice mothers, in other words. Androgynous sex roles (2) allow both sexes to express both feminine and masculine traits, to be both nurturant and independent.

Adolescent boys with traditional, highly masculine interests are typically more self-confident than boys with relatively feminine interests (65). Masculine boys tend to be more carefree, more contented, more relaxed, more exuberant, happier, calmer, and smoother in social functioning than are less masculine boys. However, when the highly masculine boys reach young adulthood, they may suffer decreases in self-confidence and self-acceptance (64). Less masculine boys tend to change in a favorable direction, feeling more positive about themselves as they grow older.

How can these shifts be explained? Apparently masculine traits are highly rewarded in the culture of the adolescent peer group but less highly valued in adult society. One is reminded of men who seem happy only when recounting their daring exploits on the high-school football field, and of others who seemed "invisible" or even "sissyish" in high school but who went on to successful careers in one of the many fields that require interpersonal sensitivity and nurturant qualities—physician, psychologist, teacher.

In any case, stereotyped masculine identification does not guarantee a stable, long-term sense of ego identity. Perhaps the most desirable male identification under most conditions in contemporary society is one that, while basically masculine, allows for flexibility and avoids constricting stereotypes. Adolescent boys whose fathers provide a *moderately* masculine role model have less difficulty in establishing appropriate and effective behavior than do boys whose fathers are either extremely masculine or very low in masculinity (44).

The situation with respect to sex-typing and identity is even more complex for girls. The male sex role is generally more clearly and more rigidly defined; a girl is generally permitted to engage in "masculine" activities, more so than a boy is allowed to do "feminine" things (1). Since the female's sex role is less specific, there are more ways to establish a feminine ego identity—there is more diversity, especially today. While this diversity is not always desirable—it can lead to indecision and confusion—it does allow a relatively conflict-free sexual identity in the traditional mode, in the modern "self-assertive" mode, or any of several intermediate forms. A girl who identifies with a traditional mother and a girl who identifies with a more socially assertive, intellectual, highly independent mother can both develop a strong sense of identity. On the other hand, a girl whose sex-role behaviors are based on rejection of a nonnurturant mother (traditional or modern) will likely have identity problems.

The adolescent girls in one extensive study (21) fell into one of three categories. Girls with a strong, uncomplicated, traditional feminine sex-role identification were clearly identified with their mothers and had close and amiable relationships with strong, traditional parents. This type of girl:

> . . . gains self-esteem from helping others and playing a succorant role; she typically chooses an adult ideal on the basis of interpersonal warmth and sensitivity. She shows little motivation for personal achievement. She prefers security to success, she does not daydream about achievement, but rather exclusively about popularity, dating, marriage, and family goals (21, p. 244).

Another group of girls were also strongly feminine, but they recognized attractions in the masculine role. They were interested in marriage and motherhood, but they also maintained a lively interest in personal achievement and individual development. Like the more traditional girls, their relationships with their parents were positive and generally rewarding. Their mothers, with whom they identified, were likely to be ambitious and highly educated women who worked outside the home and encouraged their daughters' independence and self-reliance.

A third group of girls had antifeminine identifications. Their parents tended to be traditional, restrictive, and punitive, and family relationships were characterized by conflict. These girls rejected the feminine role model—which they perceived as restricting—but seemed to be unable to replace it with anything satisfactory. In general, the antifeminine girls were insecure, low in self-esteem, with few friends or activities. They had poorly defined identities.

Another major study (4) produced similar results. Men and women (aged 30–40 at the time of testing) who came from warm and rewarding families were generally well-adjusted and effective. Some were playing rather traditional sex

Figure 8.2 The parent of the same sex provides a model for sex-role identification.

roles, while others were more adrogynous: The men had more feminine qualities than average, and the women were slightly more masculine than average. These differences were related to the parents' sex roles, which were less traditional, less differentiated in the families of the children who also turned out to play less traditional roles. Thus identifications with different types of nurturant parents leads to different sexual identities, but in both cases the children developed into reasonably content and self-confident adults.

In marked contrast, however, were the men and women in two other groups. In one group, the least desirable values and behaviors of the traditional sex roles were honored, even exaggerated. The men were "hypermasculine," impulsive, aggressive, exploitative, and self-centered; the women were narcissistic, sexually preoccupied, uninterested in achievement. The families of these subjects tended to have a "like-sex parent who was neurotic, rejecting, and provided a poor model for identification. The cross-sex parent, on the other hand, was characterized, for both males and females, as somewhat seductive" (4, p. 524).

The second group of men and women scored very low on measures of traditional sex roles. The same-sex parent, with whom they normally would have identified, was typically "emotionally uninvolved," and the personalities of the subjects, perhaps as a result, were more like those of the cross-sex parent. Both men and women from this background seemed to typify the negative aspects of sex-role reversal. The men tended to be vulnerable, self-doubting, insecure, hypersensitive, and dependent. The women were described as critical, rebellious, and assertive, vigorously demanding autonomy and independence. These subjects, on the whole, were more conflicted and burdened by psychopathology than any other group in the study, the men slightly more so than the women.

Both of the studies we have described affirm the primary importance of growing up in a psychologically healthy, interacting, caring family, where both parents provide models for basic values and generally effective behavior and where the same-sex parent provides a workable and rewarding figure for sexual identification (Figure 8.2). In such a setting, whether the parental sex roles are traditional or modern, the adolescent seems to develop a strong sense of sexual identity that is nevertheless flexible enough to avoid the emotional conflicts and problems of adjustment that come with exaggerated, stereotyped sexual identities and desperate sex-role reversals.

PSYCHOLOGICAL EFFECTS OF MENTAL GROWTH

As we have seen in Chapter 5, the young person's cognitive abilities continue to develop during the adolescent years. The importance of the changes taking place during this period, most notably the advent of the stage of formal operations, would be difficult to overestimate. These changes, which involve the ability to reason abstractly, have widespread effects on the adolescent's performance in school, relationships with parents and friends, ideas about society and morality, and personality development.

An Age of Criticism

The intellectual development of adolescents affects school performance most directly. It would be virtually impossible to master such academic subjects as calculus or the use of metaphors without a high level of abstract thinking. Further reflection, however, should make it clear that many other aspects of adolescent development are also dependent on the cognitive advances occurring during this period. The adolescent's new-found ability "not only to grasp the immediate state of things but also the possible state they might or could assume" (27, p. 152) often leads the adolescent to compare the actual with the ideal and, on that basis, to criticize. Parents, for example, may be found wanting; their values are less than ideal and they may not always act in accordance with such values as they do hold. The parents of "other kids" are assumed to be more understanding and less provincial.

Existing social, political, and religious systems come in for similar criticism. The preoccupation of many adolescents with the construction of elaborate and highly theoretical alternative systems is dependent on their emerging capacity for formal theoretical thought; the "awareness of the discrepancy between the actual and the possible" makes the adolescent something of a rebel or even a revolutionary (27). The fact that such concerns tend to be most characteristic of our brightest young people appears due at least as much to their greater cognitive ability as to their more "permissive upbringing," "affluence," or other explanations favored by some politicians and journalists.

Cognitive Aspects of Personality Development

Adolescent cognitive development is reflected not only in attitudes and values with respect to parents and society, but also in attitudes toward the self and in the personality traits and defense mechanisms likely to become prominent during adolescence. With her increasing ability to consider hypothetical possibilities (and influenced by the rapid biological and social changes of this period), the adolescent is likely to become *introspective* and *analytical*. She may become concerned with such issues as whether the world she perceives actually exists and, indeed, whether she herself is "real"; perhaps even her body is a product of her consciousness, and nothing more.

Achieving a well-defined sense of personal identity is partially dependent on the capacity of the individual to conceptualize herself in abstract terms, at times almost like a spectator. Of course, this same capacity allows her to imagine herself in other roles, with other values, and thus, to some extent, decisions and commitments to one particular identity are made more difficult. In any case, the adolescent is typically "self-conscious" and "selfish"—preoccupied with her personal attempts to define herself. She often believes that other people are also monitoring the changes in her appearance and behaviors—she feels that she is "on stage"—and her self-consciousness often takes the form of shame or embarrassment (28). When the adolescent is feeling self-critical, she is likely to think her imaginary audience is also critical.

The adolescent's frequent use of irony—of the sometimes elaborate "put on" or "put down"—can be partly understood as an exercise of new talents for thinking at the symbolic level of the metaphor. Delight in the use of *double-entendres*—statements with two meanings, one of which is usually risqué—is not merely an exhilarating taste of forbidden fruit, it is also an opportunity to demonstrate a new cognitive skill. The same may be said of the older adolescent's appreciation of political and social satire and his or her skill "in making the apparently innocent yet cutting remark" (26).

The emerging awareness of how things might be, in contrast to the way they are, may help explain the depressive moods to which many adolescents seem prone. Personal programs of self-improvement may be hindered by excessive self-criticism (and recognition of how much improvement is possible),

and the young person may feel that trying to "get it all together" is a hopeless task. Handicapped and crippled children who previously have been generally cheerful are likely to experience depression at adolescence, and many adopted children develop a compulsive desire to find their real parents (27).

The psychological defense mechanisms (see pp. 219–220) employed by adolescents may also reflect their level of cognitive development. *Asceticism* is considered to be often a reaction to intense sexual conflicts developing after puberty (9) (Figure 8.3). In the name of religious dedication or simple self-discipline, a young girl might avoid all forms of sexual behavior; typically, she also avoids alcoholic beverages and other drugs, all but the most simple foods, and even the most basic creature comforts such as warm clothing and mechanical means of transportation, and she may even take a vow of poverty. The justification of asceticism is typically highly intellectual, with appeals to the "highest" (most abstract) principles of morality.

Intellectualization is another defense mechanism characteristic of adolescents. Intellectualization involves disassociating the intellectual aspect of an event from the emotional aspects. Thus, apparently impersonal, highly abstract discussions of sex, love, and marriage, of aggression in human affairs, of freedom versus responsibility, and of the existence of God may, in fact, more nearly reflect deep-seated personal concerns. If not used to extremes, intellectualization can be useful in the resolution of adolescent conflicts. By thinking about the implications of various actions (rather than experiencing the implications of real behavior) and by thinking about the sexual and aggressive impulses of "people in general" (rather than about personal desires), the adolescent may solve some of his or her problems without potentially overwhelming anxiety.

BIOLOGICAL DEVELOPMENT IN ADOLESCENCE

Among the most dramatic of the developmental events to which all young people must adjust is the host of interrelated biological changes occurring during the early adolescent period from about 11 to 15 years of age. The basic change is one in which the body readies itself for reproduction, in females with gradual enlargement of the ovaries and uterus and in males with the development of the prostate gland and seminal vesicles (76). This period of sexual maturation is called *puberty* (from the Latin word *pubertas*, meaning "age of manhood"). Related changes in sex characteristics include the enlargement of breasts and the beginning of menstruation in girls and the growth of facial hair and the lowering of the voice in boys—and, in both, a sharply increased sex drive. The adolescent's body also undergoes a *growth spurt*, a rapid acceleration in height and weight and quickly changing body proportions. Acne may become a problem, hampering adolescents' efforts to present themselves as sexually attractive.

●Figure 8.3   Asceticism is sometimes a defense against intense and confusing impulses and emotions.

There is a close correspondence between the age at which an individual reaches his or her maximum rate of growth and the age of puberty. Both growth and sexual maturation are due, in part, to an increased output of activating hormones by the pituitary gland, located at the base of the brain (63, 76). Pituitary hormone stimulates the sex glands (ovary, testes) to release increased amounts of *androgens*—the masculinizing hormones, including *testosterone*—and *estrogens*—the feminizing hormones. Both sexes produce both the male and female hormones, and variations in the relative proportions affect the masculinity or femininity of the body; it is not uncommon, for example, for a woman to have

● Figure 8.4   Average growth curves showing the adolescent's growth spurt. (From J. M. Tanner, R. H. Whitehouse, and M. Takaishi. Standards from birth to maturity for height, weight, height velocity, and weight velocity; British children, 1965. *Archives of the Diseases of Childhood*, 1966, *41*, 455–471. By permission.)

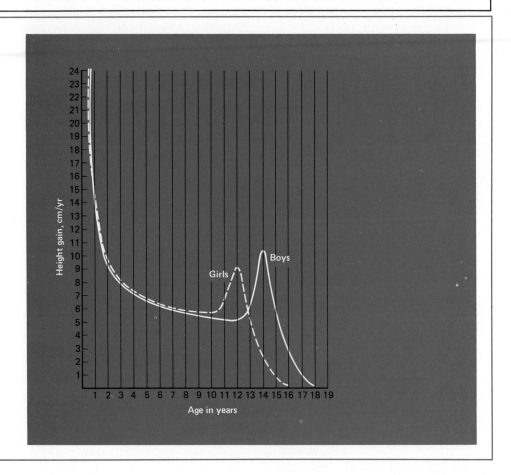

facial hair or for a man to have slightly enlarged breasts. The sex hormones act in conjunction with other hormones to produce growth of bone and muscle, which is one reason the growth spurt and sexual maturation are related.

Physical Maturation

The adolescent growth spurt varies widely in intensity, duration, and age of onset among perfectly normal children—a fact often poorly understood by ado-

●Figure 8.5   Diagram of sequence of events at adolescence in boys and girls. The average boy and girl are represented. The range of ages within which each event charted may begin and end is given by the figures placed directly below its start and finish. (From W. A. Marshall and J. M. Tanner. Variations in the pattern of pubertal changes in boys. *Archives of the Diseases of Childhood,* 1970, *45,* 13; and from J. M. Tanner. *Growth at Adolescence,* 2d. Philadelphia: Davis, 1962. By permission.)

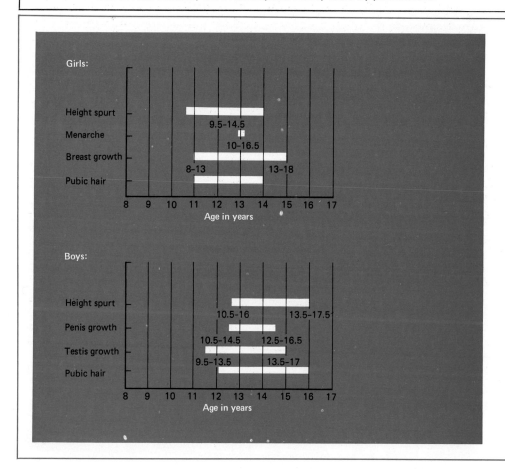

lescents and their parents and, consequently, too often a source of needless concern. In boys, for example, the growth spurt may begin as early as $10\frac{1}{2}$ years or as late as 16 years (76). For the average boy (see Figure 8.4), an accelerated growth pattern starts around the age of 13, reaches a peak growth rate around 14, and then decelerates, with slower growth for about four more years. In girls, age at onset of the growth spurt ranges from $7\frac{1}{2}$ to $11\frac{1}{2}$; the average girl begins her spurt slightly before the age of 11, reaching a peak at 13 before decelerating.

The rate of sexual maturation also varies significantly from child to child (Figure 8.5). The "bud stage" of breast development may occur as early as age 8 in some girls, as late as 13 in others (72). Menstruation may begin any time between 10 and 17. In boys, onset of penis growth ranges from age $10\frac{1}{2}$ to age $14\frac{1}{2}$; maturation of the penis may be complete in some boys by $13\frac{1}{2}$, while in others it may not be complete until the age of 17, or even later (44). In other words, this aspect of sexual maturation is finished in some boys before it has even begun in others; such variation is entirely normal (see Figure 8.6).

Although virtually all skeletal and muscular structures take part in the growth spurt, they do so to differing extents and according to different time tables (76). Head, hands, and feet reach adult status first, sometimes leading to adolescent complaints of having grotesquely large feet. Legs and arms reach maximum length before the trunk stops widening or lengthening, producing an early stage in which the gangling adolescent is "all arms and legs."

As height and weight increase during the growth spurt, other physical developments increase strength. Boys show greater overall gains in muscle tissue than do girls (76), which is one reason why they also show greater increases in strength (40). For the most part, prepubescent boys and girls are similar in strength, but after the growth spurt, boys are, and remain, much stronger. While this greater strength is principally a function of greater muscular development, it is due partly to a number of related developmental factors as well. Relative to their size, boys develop larger hearts and lungs, a higher systolic blood pressure, a greater capacity for carrying oxygen in the blood, a lower resting heart rate, and a greater ability "for neutralizing the chemical products of muscular exercise, such as lactic acid" (66, p. 95), which make themselves felt as fatigue.

Psychological Aspects of Maturation

As body parts change in size and function, the adolescent is simultaneously trying to establish a personal identity—some notion of who he or she is. As we have seen, part of this personal identity is a feeling of *self-consistency*, a feeling

●Figure 8.6   Different degrees of puberal development at the same chronological age. *Upper row:* three boys, all aged $14\frac{3}{4}$ years. *Lower row:* three girls, all aged $12\frac{3}{4}$ years. (From J.M. Tanner, Growth and endocrinology of the adolescent. In L.I. Gardner (ed.), *Endocrine and Genetic Diseases of Childhood and Adolescence*, 2d ed. Philadelphia: Saunders, 1975. By permission.)

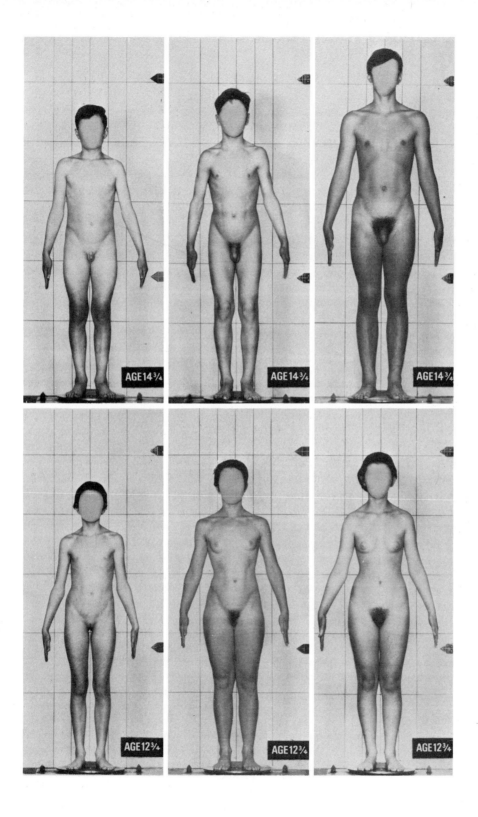

AGE 14¾ AGE 14¾ AGE 14¾

AGE 12¾ AGE 12¾ AGE 12¾

that one is the same person, in some essential sense, over time. Adolescents, particularly younger adolescents, are faced with rapid changes in physique and with biological and emotional changes due to sexual maturation, all of which threaten their feelings of self-consistency. They need time to integrate these changes into their developing ego identities.

Another factor influencing ego identity and related feelings of self-esteem is the reaction of other adolescents to one's changing body. Adolescence is a time when the peer group becomes a major source of security and status; and attractive appearance and physical skills are highly valued in adolescent society (66). While there have been recent, hopeful signs of greater tolerance of diversity among today's youth, deviation from group norms in rate of development or poor standing in the adolescent "beauty contest" is still an agonizing experience for many young people. The average adolescent is unusually sensitive to, and often critical of, his or her changing physical self. If adolescents are asked what they like and dislike about themselves, physical characteristics are typically mentioned more often than either social or intellectual ones (14). And mostly their personal characteristics are *disliked*, especially among younger adolescents.

The adolescent who perceives himself or herself as deviating physically from cultural ideals is likely to have an impaired self-concept. For example, chubby adolescent boys tend to score lower than average on measures of self-concept (58). It should be stressed, however, that the adolescent's self-perceptions do not always correspond to objective reality. An average-sized boy might have a "body image" of himself as small and weak, perhaps because he compares himself to an older brother instead of his peers. An attractive girl might think of herself as ugly, perhaps because she has been told repeatedly that she resembles an aunt whom she dislikes intensely.

Adolescent girls tend to be even more concerned about physical development than boys. In spite of recent changes in sex-role concepts, the self-esteem of most girls is still closely related to outward appearance (58). Girls are more likely than boys to interpret objective remarks about appearance—"you look awful"—as criticisms of their personalities—"You are awful" (22). On the other hand, extreme physical attractiveness, while generally a social asset that increases self-esteem, has its own special risks:

. . . older boys may exploit her youth and naiveté, especially if she matures early. She may be hurt by the discovery that boys are competing for her solely because of her glamour and sexual attractiveness. She may become used to receiving things she has not earned and would not receive if she were not so pretty. A further risk is that her parents may use her as a means of satisfying their pride and competitive ambition in the social area. They may overemphasize the importance of success in dating and underemphasize the need to establish competence in other areas of life as well (23, p. 97).

Psychological aspects of menstruation   Menstruation means much more to the adolescent girl than just a simple physiological readjustment. It is a sign of sexual maturity and the capacity for having children. It is a symbol of one's status as a female. Because a girl's reactions to menstruation may generalize so broadly, it is vital that her initial experiences be as favorable as possible.

Many girls look forward calmly to the onset of menstruation, and some receive it proudly, as an indication of increased status. Unfortunately, there are many young girls who fear menstruation or hate it for a variety of reasons. One realistic source of negative reactions is the physical discomfort (headaches, backaches, cramps) experienced by many girls in the first years of menstruation, when the menses are likely to be irregular (46). Few of the reasons for negative feelings, however, have much basis in fact. For example, among girls poorly prepared for the onset of menstruation, the flow of blood is sometimes assumed to mean serious internal injury (29). Much more pervasive is the view that menstruating women are somehow "unclean." Finally, some girls have problems with their sexual identity and may even want to be male; for them, menstruation is an undesirable demonstration that they are female and can do nothing about it (66).

Many of these negative reactions to menstruation can be avoided if the parents, perhaps with the aid of the family doctor or a sex education teacher, provide complete information and show pride and pleasure in their daughter's greater maturity. Not only will the parents' support help make the onset of menstruation a more pleasant event, but it will have consequent benefits for the girl's whole future sexual and social role as a woman.

Early versus late maturation   Although there are wide variations in the rate of physical maturation among normal adolescents, late maturing boys often find themselves at a social disadvantage among their peers. Compared to boys who mature relatively early, late maturers are typically rated as less attractive in physique. They tend to be seen as tense, bossy, and generally immoderate in their behaviors; they are often attention-seekers. As a result, they are usually less popular than early maturers, and fewer of them are leaders (47, 49). Late maturers often have negative conceptions of themselves and strong feelings of rejection (67). Although eventual physical development eases the plight of the average late-maturing boy, many of the personality differences between him and the average early maturer persist into young adulthood (48).

The psychological effects of early versus late maturation on girls are more complicated. Early maturing girls generally have a more favorable "total adjustment" than late maturers, a more positive self-conception, and a more relaxed and secure view of themselves (50). However, the differences between early and late maturers are not as pronounced for girls as they are for boys. In addition, in the youngest age groups (around the sixth grade), girls who have begun puberty may actually be temporarily in relative disfavor with their classmates, most of whom are still prepuberal (35). All things considered, early maturation is less of an advantage for girls than for boys, for whom greater size and strength are relatively unambiguous values.

THE DEVELOPMENT OF INDEPENDENCE

The development of independence is central to any discussion of the tasks of adolescence, especially in American society, with its relatively strong emphasis on self-reliance. Failure to resolve the conflict between a continuing dependence and the newer demands (and privileges) of independence will lead to difficulties in most other areas as well. Without the achievement of a reasonable degree of separation and autonomy, the adolescent can hardly be expected to achieve mature heterosexual or peer relationships or a personal sense of identity, which requires a positive image of oneself as separate, unified, and consistent.

Establishing true independence from parents is seldom a simple matter because motivations and rewards for independence and for continued dependence are both likely to be strong, thus leading to conflict and vacillating behavior. However, the degree of difficulty that adolescents will encounter in establishing independence will depend in large measure on the culture in which they live and on the specific child-rearing practices of their parents. There are wide variations in independence training from culture to culture and from one set of parents to another.

Independence in Other Cultures

In many cultures, especially in simpler societies, the task of establishing independence may be easier than it is in our own complex, fragmented, and rapidly changing culture. Among the Mountain Arapesh people of New Guinea, for example, there is a very gradual transition from a rather high degree of dependence and indulgent care in infancy and early childhood to increasing independence as the child grows older, with no discernible spurt during puberty or adolescence (62). For example, in marriage, which in this culture tends to occur during adolescence, the Arapesh girl does not suddenly leave home to go to live in a strange household with strange people in order to undergo the joint uncertainties of married life, sex, and childbearing. Typically she has been chosen as a wife by her husband's parents many years prior to the marriage, and she has been allowed during the interim to wander back and forth between her own home and her future husband's. By the time of her marriage, her parents-in-law are like an additional mother and father; she has known her husband almost as an older brother, whose responsibility it has been to look after her and to help her grow up. As time goes by, the Arapesh girl takes on increasing responsibility. There is none of the sharp separation from home and family that is likely to characterize marriage for an American girl. There is none of the atmosphere of

●Figure 8.7 In some cultures young people are expected to be self-reliant at an early age.

confusion, of a sudden break with parents, of moving into a new house or apartment, often in a distant city, and beginning a separate existence with a relatively unknown male, bearing and caring for her children largely by herself.

Similarly, the independence problems faced by the Arapesh boy are likely to be less severe than those faced by American boys. Once the Arapesh youth has passed through the initiation ceremony following puberty, he assumes added responsibility for helping to support his parents, grandparents, younger brothers and sisters, and the young girl to whom he is betrothed (62). But he does not need to go out into a new community on his own, obtain an unfamiliar job, and complete his emotional independence from his parents. He continues, but with new responsibilities, to till the family's garden. He still sees his parents daily, and when at last he marries, it is to a girl he has known and cared for over a long period of time. Figure 8.7 illustrates the self-reliance developed by adolescents in some cultures.

In contrast to societies like the Arapesh, children and adolescents in some other cultures may find the establishment of independence a stressful and anxiety-producing task. The Mundugumor adolescents of the South Seas, for example, must cope with a social organization "based on a theory of a natural hostility between all members of the same sex" (62, p. 176). Fathers and sons view each other almost as natural enemies, as do mothers and daughters. Moreover, relations between husbands and wives are notably poor. Fathers band together with daughters, while mothers form alliances with sons, and rivalry and distrust between the two family groups are typical.

Consequently, the Mundugumor boy approaches adolescence psychologically close only to his mother, hostile toward his father, and distrustful of girls his own age. The adolescent girl is close to her father, resentful of her mother, and suspicious of her male contemporaries. In addition, the girl's problem is magnified because of the jealous father's attempts to keep his hold on her as long as possible. Thus, the problem of orderly transition from dependence on the parents to the setting up of an independent household is extremely difficult. Independence also has few rewards, as the life cycle repeats itself; the adolescent goes on to become a parent, with unpleasant relationships with spouse and children of the same sex. In fact, the only really attractive aspect of independence for the Mundugumor youth seems to be escape from the hostility of the same-sex parent.

Independence in the United States

American adolescents, at least in most families, are spared the strife and hostility faced by young people in the Mundugumor society. On the other hand, they clearly encounter greater stress in establishing independence than do the Arapesh, and the task is a relatively difficult one in the United States, compared to most other cultures. The American adolescent is expected, in the limited period between puberty and adulthood, to pass from a state of relatively great dependence on the family to one of considerable independence. Strong societal demands for independent behavior, in the face of incompatible and well-established dependent responses, are likely to produce conflict. Furthermore, this conflict coincides with the other problems of adolescence—physical growth, sexual maturity, identity formation—which make the resolution even more difficult.

Our culture does not spell out a clear pattern for the transition from dependence to independence. In many cultures, major transitions that involve an increase in responsibility are marked by formalized procedures called *rites of pas-*

sage. These initiation ceremonies, which often occur at puberty, serve as guides to parents and adolescents alike as to when and how independence should be granted and assumed. One such ceremony for girls, for example, ends with the girl adopting the dress of a mature woman (36). Americans have few of these ceremonies to guide them. We do have a variety of laws that define adult status for one or another purpose, but even these are often inconsistent. For example, the ages at which a person can legally drive a car, drink alcoholic beverages, see pornographic movies, marry, vote, or own property vary from state to state.

As a consequence, the American adolescent who must face the problems of transition from childish dependency to adult independence is likely to be impressed, not with the solidarity of the expectations of adults, but with their confusion and divisiveness. In one instance, or with one set of people, the adolescent may find independent, self-reliant behavior rewarded, while in other instances, or with other people, the same behavior brings punishment. Some of his or her peers are allowed to earn and spend their own money, to own a car, to take trips by themselves or with friends, and to make their own educational and vocational plans. In contrast, other adolescents of the same age are allowed to do none of these things. Even within a family, one parent might be much more accepting of independent behavior than the other.

But not all problems of achieving independence stem from inconsistencies on the part of society or parents. Adolescents themselves are conflicted. They may really desire to be free agents, but they may just as strongly want the security and lack of responsibility associated with continuing dependence.

Parent–child relationships and the development of independence   The parent who provides a successful model of independence with which the child can identify and who balances controls and realistically age-graded opportunities for independent behavior will make the task of establishing independence a great deal easier. Adolescents from democratic families (in which the adolescents freely participate in family discussions about their behavior and may even make decisions, but where parents retain ultimate control) are likely to consider their parents fair and reasonable (25). Autocratic parents (those who simply tell their children what to do) usually rank lowest in ratings of fairness. These results are consistent with the general finding that communication between parents and children fosters identification, whereas unilateral exercise of power without communication is more likely to produce resentment (5).

Some parents attempt to make their exercise of power "legitimate," by explaining their rules of conduct and their expectations; other parents do not (24). Democratic and permissive parents who also provide frequent explanations are most likely to have adolescents who are *confident* of their own values and *independent* in their actions. The sons and daughters of autocratic, nonexplaining parents are more frequently dependent and low in self-confidence. Commenting on a study of several thousand American and Danish adolescents and their parents, the investigators noted the essential similarity of independence training in the two countries: "In both countries, feelings of independence are enhanced when parents have few rules, when they provide explanation for their rules, and when they are democratic and engage the child actively in the decision-making process. Furthermore, feelings of independence from parents in both countries, far from leading to rebelliousness, are associated with closeness to parents and positive attitudes toward them" (59, p. 357) (see Figure 8.8).

The democratic child-rearing structure provides opportunities for increasing independence, guided by interested parents who communicate with the

●Figure 8.8 Feelings of independence are associated with positive attitudes toward parents, rather than rebelliousness.

child and exercise appropriate control. This structure promotes positive identification with parents, based on love and respect, and provides models of reasonable independence—that is, autonomy within the framework of a democratic order. Autocratic and authoritarian patterns of parental behavior may have been more workable in simpler, slower moving societies, but they appear maladaptive for mastering the demands of a society in rapid transition.

Similarly, laissez-faire parenting—permissive but uncommunicative—does not provide the kind of support an adolescent needs. In one study (10), drug abuse and other forms of socially deviant behavior occurred most frequently among middle-class adolescents whose parents outwardly expressed the values of individuality, independence, and the need for equalitarianism in the family, but who were actually using these proclaimed values to avoid parental responsibility. By refusing to "control" their children, these parents ended up leaving them to drift essentially alone in an uncharted sea. They provided no models of responsible adult behavior. And—ironically, given their statements about parent–child "togetherness"—the equalitarian-permissive parents actually spent less time in family activities with their children, enjoyed their company less, and were less able to handle family problems than were the more traditional parents of low drug-risk adolescents.

Sex differences in independence conflicts   In general, girls in our culture appear to experience fewer and less stressful conflicts over the development of independence than do boys (1, 8, 21). Girls are more likely than boys to consider their parent's rules to be fair, right, or lenient (21). They are also more likely to progress from an initial childhood acceptance of parental authority to a more independent identification with that authority without an intervening phase of defiant assertion of their own values.

How can we explain the apparently lesser degree of conflict with parents and within themselves on the part of girls? Several factors may be involved. One may be the traditional cultural reinforcement, in the years prior to adolescence, of dependency and compliance in girls and of independence and self-assertiveness (and even limited aggression) in boys (20). As these cultural traditions change, providing more rewards and more models for female independence, we might expect more conflict among adolescent girls. Another factor in the degree of conflict, however, may be more biological than cultural: the somewhat greater and qualitatively different aggressive impulses that emerge, at puberty, in boys. Stronger drives generally result in more conflict between the individual and society, and aggressive impulses may play a direct role in assertive rebellion against parents (1).

ADOLESCENTS AND THEIR PEERS

Peers play an important role in the psychological development of most adolescents. That role is probably growing, as family influence declines, as entrance into adult society is increasingly delayed, and as communication among adolescents by means of television and specialized magazines increases. Nevertheless, many adults have exaggerated the influence of peer groups, attributing to them everything from changing standards of social and sexual behavior to alienation, drug use, and delinquency. The significance of other forces (parental, societal) is thus underestimated. In this section we will consider the kinds of influences that peers exert and the effects of such influences, and hopefully we will come to a more accurate and balanced view of the "youth culture."

Interactions with peers serve many of the same functions for the adolescent that they do for the child (see pp. 247–249). But the role peers play in adolescence is an even more important one for a variety of reasons. For one reason, relations with both same-sex and opposite-sex peers in this period come closer to serving as prototypes for later adult relationships. The young man or woman who has not learned how to get along with others in a work setting, how to relate socially to others of the same sex, and how to establish satisfactory heterosexual relationships—ranging from friendship to love—is likely to have difficulty in later social adjustment.

A friend of the same age is important to adolescents as someone with whom to share doubts and dreams, to discuss intense and often confusing feelings, and to evaluate strategies, plans, and outcomes. Parents seem better able to do some of this with younger children, but during adolescence the parent–child relationship is frequently so charged with conflicting emotions—love and hostility, dependent yearnings alongside strivings for independence, disagreements over values and behavior—that many adolescents find they cannot "communicate" with their parents. Parents may not take adolescent problems seriously enough, forgetting their own adolescent turmoil; they may even make fun of their adolescent boy or girl; or they may find adolescent problems uninteresting, too impractical, too . . . "adolescent." Peers, on the other hand, are engaged in the same struggle for identity and independence and thus are intensely interested in the same topics and problems.

Adolescence may provide an important opportunity, sometimes the last major opportunity, for repairing psychological damage incurred during the earlier years of childhood (6, 38). For example, a warm, supportive, and non-manipulative girl may sometimes do a great deal, both intellectually and emotionally, to show the son of a demanding, manipulative mother that relations with women can be rewarding and nonthreatening. A girl whose parents have acknowledged her worth only when she has accomplished some socially approved, external goal, such as high grades in school, may learn from her peers that she can be appreciated for herself alone—for who she is, rather than for what she can do. Of course, there is the other side of the coin: Peer influence can also be harmful. The boy or girl who is ridiculed or rejected may acquire anxious, avoidance responses to social situations that will prove difficult to extinguish. Group influences may pressure an insecure adolescent boy into destructive behavior he will later regret or into experiments with drugs or sex that he is poorly equipped to handle emotionally (15, 69).

Conformity to Peer Culture

The heightened importance of the peer group is an important factor in the increased conformity to the values, customs, and fads of peer culture characteristic of adolescence. Although peer-group conformity is observable in earlier childhood, most studies indicate a significant increase with the onset of adolescence (7, 17). Of course, some young people conform more than others; there are wide individual differences in the strength of this need (77). On the average, however, there appears to be a rather rapid rise in conformity during the preadolescent and early adolescent years, followed by a gradual but steady decline from middle through late adolescence (Figure 8.9).

Furthermore, findings in recent studies are generally similar to those obtained many years ago. In other words, although the particular manifestations of conformity change rapidly in our society, conformity among adolescents is always a significant phenomenon, in one form or another. There can be little doubt that the adolescent, particularly the younger one, has strong needs to conform to peer-group norms and pressures. According to a national survey of ado-

●Figure 8.9   Graph summarizing the results of children's conformity to the judgments of a peer group. The results for both females and males show that susceptibility to peer influence increases with age until early adolescence and then gradually declines. Such data are but one indicator of the importance of peer influences in later childhood. (Adapted from P. R. Costanzo and M. E. Shaw. Conformity as a function of age level. *Child Development*, 1966, 37, 967–975.)

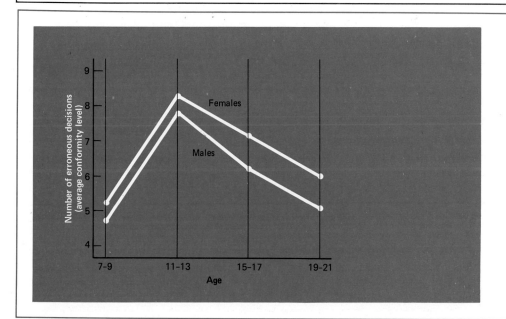

lescent attitudes conducted over many years, there are significant social-class differences among American adolescents in many aspects of values, needs, and behavior, but "in their desire for popularity and their conformist attitude they are as one: low-income or high-income, their concern is to be liked" (71, p. 267).

Parents are frequently mystified, and sometimes threatened, by the shifting external trappings of adolescent peer culture—the faddish fashions in appearance, music, and vocabulary. One of the principal reasons for adolescent fads, of course, is precisely to be "different." No longer children but not yet adults, adolescents are virtually forced to create an "interim culture" of their own. Actually, parents should probably take comfort from the presence of these outward signs of the separateness of adolescents. By achieving the semblance of a group identity in these relatively superficial ways, adolescents may satisfy some of the need to be different from their parents and therefore not strive to be different from their parents in more fundamental matters (21). As we shall see later, adolescent values and behavior are different to some degree—sometimes to an important degree—from those of adults, but most adolescents show a fundamental continuity in many of the values of their parents that is often overlooked.

Parental Versus Peer Influences

The widespread view that parental and peer-group values are necessarily incompatible and that there is inevitably a sharp decline in parental influence during adolescence is misleading in the case of most adolescents. There is usually considerable overlap between the values of the adolescent's parents and peers because of social, economic, religious, educational, and even geographic commonalities in their backgrounds. A white, Catholic, lower-middle-class, "ethnic," blue-collar adolescent's peers in one of our larger cities are likely to share more values with the adolescent's parents than with upper- or upper-middle-class WASP young people (17). In this sense, peers may actually reinforce parental values.

Parents, in return, often support the values of the adolescent peer group. Many parents, for example, place a great emphasis on popularity and social success and thus strengthen the adolescent's motivation to conform to peer expectations (66). Also, many parents are confused and threatened by a rapidly changing society and feel they cannot guide their children well (21); although they may bemoan adolescent conformity, they may foster the young person's turn to the peer group by their own use of peer-group "wisdom": "Well, are the other kids in your class allowed to do that?"

Neither parental nor peer influence extends to all areas of adolescent decision-making and behavior (11, 18). The weight given to either parental or peer opinion will depend to a significant degree on the adolescent's appraisal of its relative value in a specific situation. Peer influence is typically predominant

in such matters as tastes in music and entertainment, fashions, patterns of interactions with the same or opposite sex, and the like. Parental influence is more
likely to dominate in moral and social values (21).

An unusually dominant role of the peer group often reflects a lack of attention and affection at home.

> The peer-oriented child is more a product of parental disregard than of the attrac-
> tiveness of the peer group . . . he turns to his age-mates less by choice than by de-
> fault. The vacuum left by the withdrawal of parents and adults from the lives of
> children is filled with an undesired—and possibly *undesirable*—substitute of an
> age-segregated peer group (12, p. 96).

Typically the parents of extremely peer-oriented youth are not punitive or punishing; they are simply unconcerned and uninvolved, neither supporting nor
controlling their adolescent children, leaving them free to seek approval and affection elsewhere (16). This much freedom, of course, does not produce a happy
adolescent. Extremely peer-oriented adolescents tend to hold negative views of
themselves and of their peer group. Compared to young people who are more
adult-oriented, they are less dependable, "meaner," and less academically
oriented. Their peer-group activities are more apt to include such activities as
teasing and baiting other young people, "playing hooky," listening to records,
gossiping, going to movies or parties, and doing something illegal. They are
less likely than the more adult-oriented adolescents to make or build something, play a musical instrument, watch sports, or help someone. They have
generally low self-esteem and a relatively dim view of their future.

Parental influence is greatest where parental interest and understanding
and the amount of shared family activity is highest (57). The fortunate adolescents with such parents are significantly more likely than adolescents with poor
parent–child relationships to see the influence of their parents and their peers
as essentially similar.

Parental influence during adolescence appears greatest at the sixth-grade
level and least at the twelfth-grade level, perhaps not surprisingly. In the early
grades, the extent of parental influence is only minimally a function of the quality of the relationship between parent and child, but in the later grades, where
the potential impact of peers has increased significantly, the parent–child relationship is a major determinant of parental influence (57). In short, parents
need to maintain a relationship of love and respect with their adolescent children; without it, they might be able to influence them at the beginning of adolescence, but their role will be usurped by the peer group in the later years of
high school.

Let us reemphasize the fact, however, that the basic values of parents and
peers are typically similar, and thus the influence from the two sources tends to
be compatible, even reinforcing. Self-confident, autonomous adolescents are
able to profit from their interactions both with their parents and with their

friends, without being strongly dependent on either or unduly troubled by parent–peer differences (70). Ironically, the self-confident, independent adolescent —the one who is least concerned about social success—is likely to be among the most popular of all; he or she is considered a "tower of strength" (75).

Social Acceptance, Neglect, and Rejection

In general, adolescents of both sexes who are accepted by their peers are perceived as liking other people and being tolerant, flexible, and sympathetic; as being lively, cheerful, good-natured, and having a sense of humor; as acting "naturally" and self-confidently without being conceited; and as possessing initiative, enthusiasm, and drive (19). Adolescents who are viewed favorably tend to be those who contribute to others by making them feel accepted and involved, by promoting constructive interaction among peers, or by planning and initiating interesting and enjoyable group activities (51).

In contrast, the adolescent who is ill at ease and lacks self-confidence, who tends to be timid, nervous, or withdrawn, is likely to be neglected by his peers and thus to become a social isolate (66). If he reacts to his neglect with a compensating overaggressiveness and demands for attention, he courts active dislike and outright rejection. Similarly, the adolescent who is self-centered and insensitive to the needs of others (and thus tactless and inconsiderate) is likely to receive little consideration in return.

There are, of course, many other factors that might affect acceptance or rejection, including intelligence and ability, physical attractiveness, social class, and ethnic-group membership. Intelligence, for example, affects social acceptance in a number of ways, both directly and indirectly. Other facts being equal, intelligence is positively correlated with acceptance by peers (41). Indirectly, intelligence is related to self-confidence (especially in a school setting); low intelligence may therefore lead to insecurity, withdrawal, or compensatory demands for attention—behaviors that typically result in social neglect or rejection (66).

The adolescent who is rejected for whatever reason is likely to be caught in a vicious circle. If he is already insecure, emotionally troubled, and preoccupied with himself, he is likely to be rejected by his peers. This rejection further undermines his self-confidence and increases his sense of social isolation. In turn, the increasing troubles result in even more inappropriate behavior, and so on around the circle. There is encouraging evidence that today's adolescents are a bit more accepting and tolerant of individual differences. But to expect adolescents—unsure of their identities and unclear about the demands of a confusing society—to be immune to the favor of their peers is unrealistic. We can only hope to be sensitive to those young people whose emotional difficulties are compounded by their peer culture to provide some "external" support and perhaps some temporary psychotherapy.

MORAL DEVELOPMENT AND VALUES

At no time in life is the average person as likely to be concerned about moral values and standards as during adolescence. The adolescent's accelerated cognitive development makes him or her more aware of moral questions and values and more capable of dealing with them in a relatively sophisticated fashion. Furthermore, social demands upon the adolescent are changing rapidly, and this requires a continuing reappraisal of moral values and beliefs. To complicate matters further, the young person may engage in thinking about broad moral issues not simply for their own sake, but as a way of struggling with more personal problems. For example, probing the most abstract features of the concept of violence may serve as a way of helping the adolescent deal with his or her own aggressive impulses. In brief, increased adolescent concern with the problem of moral values and standards is likely to involve cognitive, social, and intimate emotional aspects.

Factors in Moral Development

Cognitive growth   The increasing cognitive abilities of adolescents is one major factor in their moral development. As they reach the stage of formal operational thought, they are better able to consider other people's points of view in a matter, and they are also able to reason logically and abstractly about the issues in question. In terms of Kohlberg's theory of moral development (see pp. 260–261), early adolescence is a time when most young people have shifted away from the simplistic *preconventional* modes of moral judgment to the more cognitively complex *conventional* modes (55).

At the preconventional level, the child acts morally for fear of punishment or because it is a more effective way than attempts at immediate gratification to get what she wants—at least in the long run. At the conventional level of moral reasoning, the views of other people are taken into account, and the reasoning is more abstract. Generally two stages at the conventional level are distinguished. The first, which occurs as the individual begins to approach formal operational thinking, involves a *good boy, good girl orientation;* a young person at this stage tries to understand what her parents would want her to do, or what her peers would want her to do. It is an approval-seeking kind or morality, but clearly an advance over the selfish morality of the preconventional level.

The second stage of conventional morality is a *law and order orientation:* "Right behavior consists of doing one's duty, showing respect for authority, and maintaining the given social order for its own sake" (54). Law and order orientations are characteristic of many adolescents and, indeed, many adults. The authority of parents and peers is abstracted to general rules and laws, which are seen as necessary if there is to be order in a society of individuals, each with his or her own point of view. Examples of this kind of moral reasoning are ubiquitous, often in the speeches of politicians and other public officials. "One should not take the law into his own hands."

Only with the development of an advanced stage of formal operational thinking does what Kohlberg calls *postconventional* morality become possible. The individual begins to examine the social utility of moral beliefs to see if they stand up under careful scrutiny. In its most developed forms, postconventional morality involves such concepts as being governed by conscience and "a higher law" or by abstract ethical principles. Some older adolescents and youth become capable of some forms of postconventional morality, but, for the most part, this orientation is considered an adult stage and will be discussed in Chapter 10.

Cognitive growth is a necessary but not a sufficient condition for moral development. Abstract reasoning and the ability to see other perspectives are necessary for the development of conventional and postconventional morality, but they do not ensure that the individual will achieve this degree of moral reasoning. Other factors in moral development are obviously involved, and chief among these are changing societal demands and personal conflicts.

Changing societal demands   Younger children face fewer demands than adolescents for making moral choices. The world of younger children involves rules, established largely by their parents, and many simple decisions that involve moral standards about stealing, sharing, and similar behaviors. Younger children are expected to internalize the basic morality of society and to establish internal controls of their "immoral" impulses.

But the demands on adolescents are greater. They are faced with a series of critical decisions that will affect their lives for years to come, and all of these decisions involve moral standards or personal values. Should I try marijuana? What are one's responsibilities in a "serious" relationship between members of the opposite sex? Many adolescent activities are a kind of preparation for the most important decisions of one's life, those concerning career and marriage. Is the world of work an opportunity to help others, or is it a "jungle," where the fittest survive (earn huge incomes)? Is a woman's primary responsibility in a marriage to raise the children? Can two-career marriages work? Is marriage valid in today's world? At least some thinking about such issues is required in adolescence, and often some preliminary decisions (such as selecting high-school classes) are made.

Personal conflicts   The increased cognitive ability to reason abstractly and the increasing societal demands to think about values result in much adolescent wrestling with broad questions of moral judgment. Reasoning abstractly about values and morals often gains significant impetus from still another source as well: the personal problems the adolescent faces in dealing with his or her own impulses. As we mentioned previously, adolescents are prone to intellectualize their emotional conflicts, discussing the abstract nature of "love" as a way of dealing with guilt over personal sexual impulses or debating war and peace as a way of coming to grips with their own aggressive urges. Conflicts with parents about moral or political values may reflect efforts to establish an independent identity or to express a deep resentment toward hostile or indifferent parents.

Religious Beliefs

Religious beliefs, like moral values generally, reflect the adolescent's accelerated cognitive development in their becoming more abstract and less literal between the ages of 12 and 18. For example, God comes to be considered more frequently as an abstract power and less frequently as a fatherly human being (56), and belief in the importance of religion, at least formal religion, declines.

Cultural changes in religious views also appear to be at work. There has been a steady erosion in the past decade in the percentage of adolescents and youth who hold religion to be "a very important personal value" (79). At least part of this decline in interest in religion is related to changing values among young people and a perception on the part of many of them that formal, institutionalized religion is failing to reflect these changes. For example, rightly or wrongly, approximately half of all adolescents in a national survey believed that "Churches teach that enjoyment of sex is sinful" and that churches are not doing their best to understand young people's ideas about sex (74). God is viewed as being more understanding than the officials of institutionalized religion. A number of young people also feel that institutionalized religion does not afford full status and recognition to women (3). And a majority of Catholic youth disagree with their Church's position on birth control, divorce, and the rights of priests to marry.

Today's adolescents seem to place a somewhat greater emphasis than have previous generations on personal, rather than institutionalized, religion. Many find more "spiritual benefit" in nature or in fellowship with others than in attending church services (42). An interesting recent development, although involving relatively few young people, is the emergence of religious sects such as Hare Krishna, Children of God, the Jesus Movement, and the Reverend Moon's Unification Church (Figure 8.10). Some of these groups are informal, loosely structured organizations held together principally by a concern for others, disillusionment with materialistic values, and the belief—often simple, direct, and fundamentalistic—in personal salvation (68). Other groups are highly authoritarian, requiring complete obedience to the rigid dictates of leaders (73). The "simple" faith that is characteristic of many of these sects seems an odd result of the increasing ability to reason abstractly that we have suggested as a major source of moral concern in adolescence. It seems likely that these sects recruit young people who have recognized the faults of society but whose intellectual searches for new meaning have failed. Many of the young people in the more authoritarian movements have experienced "total conversion" following a

● Figure 8.10 Some young people recently have been drawn to fundamentalistic religions.

period of rootlessness and identity confusion, often with extensive drug use and sexual exploration (3, 68). The simple, straightforward values and beliefs of the sects may appear a welcome relief in a chaotic world, and the authoritarian structure of the sects relieves the followers of the troubling necessity of making so many important decisions.

Society and Values

In the 1960s, much was made of a so-called "revolution" in the values of young people. They were, it was said, developing a "counterculture"—a set of values, beliefs, and life-styles so profoundly different from their elders that the term "generation gap" was no longer sufficient to describe the differences. In the 1970s, some social observers claim to have discovered a rush back to pre-1960s values, a new conservatism presumably reflected, for example, in the decline of political activism on high-school and college campuses. As we shall see, both assertions have distorted or oversimplified the facts in one way or another.

In looking at the changing values of young people, we will include studies of college youth as well as those of high-school students. The differences between college students and college-bound adolescents are less significant than the differences between college or college-bound young people and those who have no plans for college and who, after graduation from high school, go to work, often in "blue-collar" jobs. One of the principal errors of many social observers in the 1960s was a tendency to generalize the values and behaviors of college and college-bound youth to all young people. The views of noncollege youth remained markedly more conservative in many areas, ranging from attitudes toward sexual freedom, use of drugs, and conformity in dress to views on the Vietnam war, business and government, minority rights, and law and order. Clearly, in the 1960s, adolescents and youth had their own "silent majority" (77). Even among college students in the 1960s, many values—such as "competition encourages excellence"—were not very different from those held by their parents.

College and college-bound youth are a minority of all young people, but their value trends are important because it is from among these youth that leaders typically emerge. In addition, changes in the values of working-class youth tend to follow those of their advantaged peers, with a delay of only a few years. One trend of the 1970s among middle- and upper-class high-school and college students is, as many commentators have noted, a marked decline in political and social activism. The percentage of students classifying themselves as far left or far right, never large, has dropped still further (38, 77, 78). Demonstrations have virtually disappeared on most campuses. While there has been a significant increase since 1970 in the percentage of students entering the traditional two-party system (two to one as Democrats), enthusiasm for political parties is less than overwhelming: In 1973, 61 percent of college students stated that political parties needed fundamental reform or elimination. Perhaps the most telling recent finding is that only 24 percent of college youth consider altering society to be "a very important personal value"; this figure is down by a third since 1971 (79).

In spite of this decline in political activism, there is no evidence of an "across-the-board" retreat from the new values of 1960s. For example, there has been no return to a more traditional sexual morality; rather, previous trends in both values and behavior appear to be accelerating. In the late 1960s, a majority of college students still considered "casual premarital sexual relations" wrong, but by the early 1970s, only a third still held this view (79). Similarly, the percentages of students who consider abortion, homosexuality, and having children outside of marriage as morally wrong have all continued to decline. Such findings hardly support the hypothesis of a widespread return to traditional values in all areas of life.

Similarly, love and friendship, which emerged as the two most important personal values in the late 1960s, remained so in the middle 1970s, with slightly more than nine out of ten students citing them as "very important" (78, 79). Fulfilling oneself as a person and having an opportunity for self-expression (two other hallmarks of 1960s values) also have remained strong. Support of increased freedom, self-determination, and equality for women—an issue that was only beginning to emerge among young people in the 1960s—has received broad support in the 1970s.

On the other hand, college youth in the 1970s appear more willing to accept a number of social constraints than was the case in the late 1960s. Their attitudes appear more pragmatic; they apparently have adopted the view that they can go along with some constraints without unduly restricting their ability to pursue their own goals. And in the case of certain constraints, an increasing number feel that they are not only acceptable, but desirable. Although the percentage of those viewing prohibitions against marijuana as "easily acceptable" declined steadily from 1968 to 1973 (from 55 percent to 38 percent), the already substantial majority easily accepting prohibitions against mind-expanding drugs and heroin has increased. Opposition to the use of violence to achieve worthwhile ends has increased markedly, as has disapproval of destroying private property and taking things without paying for them. The number of those who feel that commitment to a meaningful career is a very important goal increased slightly (to 81 percent in 1973), and the percentage willing to accept the authority of employers in the work situation has also grown. None of these findings, however, means that young people today have suddenly become entranced with big business or government. Nine out of ten college youth still think that business is too concerned with profits and not enough with public responsibility, and more than half think that big business is in need of fundamental reform (up from 38 percent in 1969).

Basically, what appears to be happening is the development of a more pragmatic approach to life. More young people feel that it is not only possible but necessary to find a way to pursue their own personal goals and values without "taking on the system" at every turn. It is significant that privacy as a personal value has steadily increased in importance since the 1960s. Although few of these young people feel they will pursue the same kind of lives as their parents, a clear majority (60 percent) feel they will have no difficulty in accepting the kind of life society has to offer (78, 79). Fewer are interested in pursuing radically different alternative life-styles on a permanent basis than was the case in the late sixties. For example, although approximately one-third of students currently indicate an interest in living off the land or living in a commune, less than one in twenty would want to do so permanently.

Working youths   As we mentioned, the "working-class' youth of the 1960s—high-school students with no intention of going to college and college-age young people who had a fulltime job—were much more conservative, much more like the average American adult, in the 1960s. Since then, however, non-college youth have become considerably more liberal (79), to the extent that, in 1973, the values of working young people were very similar to the values held by college youth four years earlier (Figure 8.11). For example, in 1969, only 38

●Figure 8.11　Noncollege youth have adopted many of the values of college youth of the late sixties and early seventies.

percent of college students considered religion a very important value, compared to 64 percent noncollege youth; by 1973, however, the figure for noncollege youth had dropped to 42 percent. The traditional belief that "hard work always pays off" was held by 56 percent of college youth in 1969, but by 79 percent of noncollege youth; by 1973, the figure for noncollege youth was 56 percent. "Patriotism" was "very important" to 35 percent of the college youth and to 60 percent of the noncollege youth in 1969; by 1973, the figure for noncollege youths had dropped to 40 percent. Comparable changes have been found in values concerning premarital sexual relations, abortion, and homosexuality.

Most of today's youth, college and noncollege, appear to be reasonably happy and self-confident (78, 79). A great majority report that they enjoy life and feel in control of their future. They agree that, all in all, "my life is going well," and they anticipate no real problems in their future. The majority of all youth currently do not appear alienated, either from themselves or from society. A significant majority, however, still do feel alienated to varying degrees, as we shall see in the following chapter.

SUMMARY

One of the central tasks of adolescence is establishing a personal ego identity. Ego confusion—the absence of an identity or having several conflicting identities—is a significant threat during this period of rapid physical and social change. Identifications with parents, high-status peers, teachers, and folk heroes play a major role in the development of an individual's identity, as do affiliations with various groups—"our gang," ethnic groups, and the like. The children of nurturant parents tend to have better organized identities than do children of less nurturant parents, presumably because of stronger identifications.

Sexual identities—being a "man" or a "woman"—are influenced by cultural stereotypes and also by the models provided by parents. Research suggests that overly masculine identities, although favored during adolescence, create problems for young adult males. Generally, the adolescents who develop sexual identities ("traditional" or "modern") that provide security, self-confidence, and flexibility in adjusting to society are those whose parents are loving and competent; parents who are rejecting or neglecting tend to have unhappy, self-doubting children who either exaggerate their "normal" sex role or reverse it.

Intellectual development in adolescence accounts for a number of traits that emerge at this time. Because they can imagine other possibilities, adolescents are often highly critical of themselves, other people, and social institutions. They tend to "intellectualize" their personal conflicts; that is, they engage in highly abstract discussions of love, war, and God as if they themselves had no problems with sex, aggression, and spirituality.

Physical growth and change during adolescence is one of its most notable features. Sexual maturation during puberty results in child-bearing capabilities and in secondary sex characteristics like breasts and menstruation in girls and facial hair and deeper voices in boys. Sexual maturation and the related growth spurt vary considerably in time of onset; such variation is usually entirely normal. Psychologically, these rapid body changes make it difficult to gain a consistent image of onself. The adolescent's new abilities to analyze and criticize are used on his or her own body, which invariably is less than perfect. Adolescents who do, in fact, lie outside the "acceptable" range of shapes, weights, or heights may have problems in social interaction. Similarly, negative attitudes about menstruation or later-than-average maturation can affect self-esteem for many years.

Establishing independence in America is easier than in some other cultures (Mundugumor), harder than in others (Arapesh). Parents can aid their adolescent children by balancing realistic controls with opportunities for self-reliant behavior. Democratic parents who explain the few rules they have tend to have relatively independent offspring; the children of autocratic or overly permissive parents tend to be hostile or confused.

Peer relations are important during adolescence, as many of the basic social roles of life—friend, lover, co-worker—are encountered in adult forms for the first time. The natural desire to be liked and to be evaluated positively by peers leads to increased conformity. Usually the basic values of peers and parents are similar, and thus their influences are not often incompatible. Peer influence is greatest in music, dress, and other relatively superficial areas. Unusual peer influence in the area of moral standards often reflects troubles in the home. Social acceptance is highest among adolescents who are tolerant, cheerful, self-confident, and enthusiastic. Timid, insecure adolescents are typically ignored, unless, in reaction to neglect, they demand attention; then they may be rejected outright.

A time of changing societal demands and personal conflicts, adolescence is a period when the young person's moral beliefs are challenged and, hopefully, refined and strengthened. According to Kohlberg, adolescents typically develop "conventional" modes of moral reasoning; initially most of them adopt a "good boy, good girl" orientation, which emphasizes the approval of parents, teachers, and peers, followed by a "law and order" orientation, in which the role of law in society becomes the chief concern. Some older adolescents and youth become capable of a broader, more abstract "postconventional" morality. Although institutionalized religions are declining in popularity among today's adolescents, interest in the nature of God and morality remains high. There is a tendency for adolescents to think about religion in increasingly abstract terms. At the same time, however, many adolescents turn to authoritarian religions, perhaps in reaction to their own sense of rootlessness and confusion.

The values of college-bound adolescents and college youth have undergone many changes in the last two decades. Attitudes toward sexual behavior changed considerably in the 1960s and remain permissive in the 1970s; interest in altering society by protest and demonstration, relatively high in the 1960s, has lessened; concern for personal privacy and women's rights have emerged as significant values in the 1970s. Noncollege young people tend to have slightly more "traditional" values, but recently their attitudes have been changing in the direction of the more liberal values of their college-oriented peers.

References

1. Bardwick, J. **Psychology of women: a study of bio-cultural conflicts.** New York: Harper & Row, 1971.
2. Bem, S. L. The measurement of psychological androgyny. **Journal of Consulting and Clinical Psychology,** 1974, **42,** 155–162.
3. Bengston, V. L., & Starr, J. M. Contrast and consensus: a generational analysis of youth in the 1970's. In R. J. Havighurst & P. H. Dreyer (Eds.), **Youth: the seventy-fourth yearbook of the National Society for the Study of Education, Part I.** Chicago: University of Chicago Press, 1975. Pp. 224–266.
4. Block, J. H. Conceptions of sex role: some cross-cultural and longitudinal perspectives. **American Psychologist,** 1973, **28,** 512–526.
5. Block, J., & Turula, E. Identification, ego control, and adjustment. **Child Development,** 1963, **34,** 945–953.
6. Blos, P. **On adolescence: a psychoanalytic interpretation.** New York: Free Press, 1962.
7. Blos, P. **The adolescent personality: a study of individual behavior.** Englewood Cliffs, N.J.: Prentice-Hall, 1941.
8. Blos, P. The child analyst looks at the younger adolescent. **Daedalus,** Fall 1971, **100,** 961–978.
9. Blos, P. **The young adolescent: clinical studies.** New York: Free Press, 1970.
10. Blum, R. H., et al. **Horatio Alger's children.** San Francisco: Jossey-Bass, 1972.
11. Brittain, C. V. Age and sex of siblings and conformity toward parents versus peers in adolescence. **Child Development,** 1966, **37,** 709–714.
12. Bronfenbrenner, U. **Two worlds of childhood: U.S. and U.S.S.R.** New York: Russell Sage Foundation, 1970.
13. Broverman, I. K., Vogel, S. R., Broverman, D. M., Clarkson, F. E., & Rosenkrantz, P. S. Sex-role stereotypes: a current appraisal. **Journal of Social Issues,** 1972, **28,** 59–78.
14. Burgess, A. P., & Burgess, H. J. L. The growth pattern of East African schoolgirls. **Human Biology,** 1964, **36,** 177–193.
15. Campbell, J. D. Peer relations in childhood. In M. L. Hoffman & L. W. Hoffman (Eds.), **Review of child development research (vol. I).** New York: Russell Sage Foundation, 1964. Pp. 289–322.
16. Condry, J., & Siman, M. L. Characteristics of peer- and adult-oriented children. **Journal of Marriage and the Family,** 1974, **36,** 543–554.
17. Conger, J. J. A world they never knew: the family and social change. **Daedalus,** Fall 1971, **100,** 1105–1138.
18. Conger, J. J. A world they never made: parents and children in the 1970s. Invited address, American Academy of Pediatrics meeting, Denver, April 17, 1975.
19. Conger, J. J. **Adolescence and youth: psychological development in a changing world.** New York: Harper & Row, 1977.
20. Douvan, E. New sources of conflict at adolescence and early adulthood. In J. M.

Bardwick, et al., **Feminine personality and conflict.** Monterey Calif.: Brooks/Cole, 1970. Pp. 31–43.

21. Douvan, E. A., & Adelson, J. **The adolescent experience.** New York: Wiley, 1966.

22. Douvan, E. A., & Kaye, C. **Adolescent girls.** Ann Arbor: Survey Research Center, University of Michigan, 1957.

23. Dwyer, J., & Mayer, J. **Variations in physical appearance during adolescence. Part 2: Girls.** Postgraduate Medicine, 1967, **42,** 91–97.

24. Elder, G. H., Jr. Parental power legitimation and its effect on the adolescent. **Sociometry,** 1963, **26,** 50–65.

25. Elder, G. H., Jr. Structural variations in the child-rearing relationship. **Sociometry,** 1962, **25,** 241–262.

26. Elkind, D. **Children and adolescents: interpretive essays on Jean Piaget.** New York: Oxford University Press, 1970.

27. Elkind, D. Cognitive development in adolescence. In J. F. Adams (Ed.), **Understanding adolescence.** Boston: Allyn & Bacon, 1968. Pp. 128–158.

28. Elkind, D. Egocentrism in adolescence. **Child Development,** 1967, **38,** 1025–1034.

29. English, O. S., & Pearson, G. H. **Emotional problems of living.** New York: Norton, 1955.

30. Erikson, E. H. **Childhood and society.** New York: Norton, 1950.

31. Erikson, E. H. **A healthy personality for every child. A fact finding report: a digest.** (Mid-century White House Conference on Children and Youth.) Raleigh, N.C.: Health Publications Institute, 1951. Pp. 8–25.

32. Erikson, E. H. **Identity: youth and crisis.** New York: Norton, 1968.

33. Erikson, E. H. The problem of ego identity. **Journal of the American Psychoanalytic Association,** 1956, **4,** 56–121.

34. Evans, R. I. **Dialogue with Erik Erikson.** New York: Harper & Row, 1967.

35. Faust, M. S. Developmental maturity as a determinant in prestige of adolescent girls. **Child Development,** 1960, **31,** 173–184.

36. Ford, C. W., & Beach, F. A. **Patterns of sexual behavior.** Harper & Row, 1951.

37. Fox, D. J., & Jordan, V. B. Racial preference and identification of black, American Chinese, and white children. **Genetic Psychology Monographs,** 1973, **88,** 229–286.

38. Freud, A. Adolescence. **Psychoanalytic Study of the Child,** 1958, **13,** 255–278.

39. Gallup International, Inc. **The Gallup opinion index: political, social and economic trends, January–March.** June 5, 1970, 55–57, 60.

40. Garrison, K. C. Physiological changes in adolescence. In J. F. Adams (Ed.), **Understanding adolescence: current developments in adolescent psychology.** Boston: Allyn & Bacon, 1968.

41. Hallworth, H. J., Davis, H., & Gamston, C. Some adolescents' perceptions of adolescent personality. **Journal of Social and Clinical Psychology,** 1965, **4,** 81–91.

42. Harris, L. Change, yes—upheaval, no. **Life,** January 8, 1971, 22–27.

43. Heilbrun, A. B., Jr. Identification and behavioral ineffectiveness during late adolescence. In E. D. Evans (Ed.), **Adolescents: readings in behavior and development.** New York: Holt, Rinehart and Winston, 1970.

44. Heilbrun, A. B., Jr. Parental model attributes, nurturant reinforcement, and consistency of behavior in adolescents. **Child Development,** 1964, **35,** 151–167.

45. Heilbrun, A. B., Jr., & Gillard, B. J. Perceived maternal childbearing behavior and motivational effects of social reinforcement in females. **Perceptual and Motor Skills,** 1966, **23,** 439–446.

46. Israel, S. L. Normal puberty and adolescence. **Annals of New York Academy of Science,** 1967, **142,** 773–778.

47. Jones, M. C. A study of socialization patterns at the high school level. **Journal of Genetic Psychology,** 1958, **92,** 87–111.

48. Jones, M. C. The later careers of boys who were early or late maturing. **Child Development,** 1957, **28,** 113–128.

49. Jones, M. C., & Bayley, N. Physical maturing among boys as related to behavior. **Journal of Educational Psychology,** 1950, **41,** 129–148.

50. Jones, M. C., & Mussen, P. H. Self-conceptions, motivations, and interpersonal attitudes of early and late maturing girls. **Child Development,** 1958, **29,** 491–501.

51. Keislar, E. R. Experimental development of "like" and "dislike" of others among adolescent girls. **Child Development,** 1961, **32,** 59–66.

52. Kiell, N. **The universal experience of adolescence.** Boston: Beacon, 1967.

53. Kohlberg, L. Continuities in childhood and adult moral development revisited. In P. B. Baltes and K. W. Schaie (Eds.), **Life-span developmental psychology: personality and socialization.** New York: Academic Press, 1973.

54. Kohlberg, L., & Gilligan, C. The adolescent as a philosopher: the discovery of the self in a postconventional world. **Daedalus,** Fall 1971, 1051–1086.

55. Kohlberg, L., & Turiel, E. (Eds.). **Recent research in moral development.** New York: Holt, Rinehart & Winston, 1972.

56. Kuhlen, R. G., & Arnold, M. Age differences in religious beliefs and problems during adolescence. **Journal of Genetic Psychology,** 1944, **65,** 291–300.

57. Larson, L. E. The relative influence of parent–adolescent affect in predicting the salience of hierarchy among youth. Paper presented at the annual meeting of the National Council on Family Relations, Chicago, October 1970.

58. Lerner, R. M., & Karabenick, S. A. Physical attractiveness, body attitudes, and self-concept in late adolescents. **Journal of Youth and Adolescence,** 1974, **3,** 7–316.

59. Lesser, G. S., & Kandel, D. Parent–adolescent relationships and adolescent independence in the United States and Denmark. **Journal of Marriage and the Family,** 1969, **31,** 348–358.

60. Lynn, D. B. **Parental and sex-role identification: a theoretical formulation.** Berkeley: McCutchan, 1969.

61. Martin, B. Parent–child relations. In F. D. Horowitz (Ed.), **Review of child development research (vol. 4).** Chicago: University of Chicago Press, 1975. Pp. 463–540.

62. Mead, M. **From the south seas. Part III: Sex and temperament in three primitive societies.** New York Morrow, 1939.

63. Money, J., & Ehrhardt, A. A. **Man and woman, boy and girl: the differentiation and dimorphism of gender identity from conception to maturity.** Baltimore: Johns Hopkins University Press, 1972.

64. Mussen, P. H. Long-term consequents of masculinity of interests in adolescence. **Journal of Consulting Psychology,** 1962, **26,** 435–440.

65. Mussen, P. H. Some antecedents and consequents of masculine sex-typing in adolescent boys. **Psychological Monographs,** 1961, **75,** No. 506.

66. Mussen, P. H., Conger, J. J., & Kagan, J. **Child development and personality.** New York: Harper & Row, 1975 (4th ed.).

67. Mussen, P. H., & Jones, M. C. Self-conceptions, motivations, and interpersonal attitudes of late and early maturing boys. **Child Development,** 1957, **28,** 243–256.

68. Plowman, E. E. **The Jesus movement in America.** New York: Pyramid Books, 1971.

69. Polansky, N., Lippitt, R., & Redl, F. An investigation of behavioral contagion in groups. **Human Relations,** 1950, **3,** 319–348.

70. Purnell, R. F. Socioeconomic status and sex differences in adolescent reference-group orientation. **Journal of Genetic Psychology,** 1970, **116,** 233–239.

71. Remmers, H. H., & Radler, D. H. **The American teenager.** Indianapolis: Bobbs-Merrill, 1957.

72. Reynolds, E. L., & Wines, J. V. Individual differences in physical changes associated with adolescence in girls. **American Journal of Diseases of Children,** 1948, **75,** 329–350.

73. Rice, B. Messiah from Korea: honor thy father Moon. **Psychology Today,** January 1976, **9,** 36ff.

74. Sorensen, R. C. **Adolescent sexuality in contemporary America: personal values and sexual behavior ages** 13–19. New York: Harry N. Abrams, Inc., 1973.

75. Stone, L. J., & Church, J. **Childhood and adolescence: a psychology of the growing person.** New York: Random House, 1973 (3rd ed.).

76. Tanner, J. M., Physical growth. In P. H. Mussen (Ed.), **Carmichael's manual of child psychology (vol. 2).** New York: Wiley, 1970 (3rd ed.).

77. Tuddenham, R. D. Correlates of yielding to a distorted group norm. **Journal of Personality,** 1959, **27,** 272–284.

78. Yankelovich, D. **Generations apart.** New York: CBS News, 1969.

79. Yankelovich, D. **The new morality: a profile of American youth in the 1970s.** New York: McGraw Hill, 1974.

CHAPTER 9
Adolescence: Social Issues

This chapter is about sex and alienation and drugs and crime. These are topics stimulating enough to sell millions of newspapers and magazines, stimulating enough, perhaps, to interest you in this chapter, with no further introduction. But let us also point out that these topics are important social issues, issues that reflect variable relationships between individual adolescents and the society around them. How adolescents adjust to their sexuality, how they come to grips with the realization that they will have to make a living in a society that is far from perfect, how they deal with the widespread availability of drugs, and to what extent they are willing to control their behavior in accordance with current laws—these are problems of obvious importance to individual adolescents, but society cares, too, how they are resolved.

Every young person must adjust to an increased sex drive and a new biological ability to have children. Until quite recently, society's code of acceptable behavior did not include sex "before marriage," and sexual frustrations was a common adolescent problem. Although premarital sexual intercourse remains unacceptable in many geographic and cultural subgroups, in other areas and subgroups attitudes and behaviors are more liberal. Different problems arise when sex among young people is prevalent, not the least of which are unwanted pregnancies; several hundred thousand babies are born each year to teenaged, unwed mothers. Thus, there are problems both with stringent prohibitions and with uncontrolled sexuality. So it is no wonder that society monitors the sexual attitudes and behavior of adolescents with keen interest.

Alienation is another social issue in adolescence, affecting a sizable number of young people. Most young people are aware of differences between their values and those of "society in general," but for some, these differences are so intense that they feel set apart from the community. Some respond actively by becoming social reformers or political revolutionaries, and others react passively, "dropping out" to form new communities or to wander through life aimlessly. Although most adolescents who use drugs do so only occasionally and for recreational purposes, drugs may become the whole world for some unfortunate alienated adolescents. Criminal behavior is still another response to alienation; in the last section of this chapter we will examine the adolescent outlaws who roam our streets in the cities and, increasingly, in the suburbs as well. Society has an obvious interest in these topics.

Lest all this talk of deviancy and alienation set a depressing tone, however, we should preview some of our general conclusions. The vast majority of young people are making rational adjustments to their sexuality, adjustments that, in some respects, may be better than those made by their parents and grandparents. The vast majority of adolescents are not alienated from society. The vast majority of young people who use drugs do so in a responsible fashion, more intelligently than many adults. Adolescence is a time of many important and difficult adjustments, to be sure, but almost all young people do adjust adequately and enter adult life reasonably happy and optimistic. The misfortune of the few should not keep us from recognizing the achievements of the many.

SEXUAL ATTITUDES AND BEHAVIOR

Among the many dramatic developmental events surrounding puberty, few are more challenging to the adolescent's emerging sense of identity than the increase in the sex drive. Adjusting to one's sexuality with as little conflict and disruption as possible is a major developmental task for both boys and girls. The extent to which sexuality becomes a source of joy or despair, of challenge and success or failure and defeat, depends on many factors, including cultural standards and early parent–child relationships, and, in part, on whether the person is a boy or a girl.

Sex Differences in Sexuality

For most boys, the rapid increase in sexual drive that accompanies adolescence is difficult, if not impossible, to deny. The sex drive in young males is strong and specific; it is clearly a "drive," and what it is driving one toward is equally clear. An adolescent boy must confront his sexuality directly. He must find some means of satisfaction without excessive guilt and establish some internal controls without crippling inhibitions (21).

Among girls the sexual drive is likely to be more diffuse and ambiguous. Sexual impulses are more easily denied or transformed—"spiritualized, idealized, etherealized" (21, p. 111). As adolescence proceeds, girls become more consciously aware of their sexual urges, but, even then, erotic gratification is likely to remain secondary to the fulfillment of other needs such as self-esteem, affection, and love. The overall relationship with a boy—the extent to which trust, concern, and mutual interests exist—usually takes precedence over simple sexual release. The urges in girls seem less insistent than in boys, and thus control of impulses is generally much less of a problem.

Boys, on the average, are more sexually active than girls. They masturbate more frequently; they are more likely to have sexual intercourse; they have orgasms during dreams (nocturnal emissions); and they think about sex much more often (9). In one study (82), over half of the 13- to 15-year-old boys with some sexual experience agreed with the statement: "Sometimes I think I am addicted to sex, the way some people are addicted to drugs." Why is the sex drive apparently so compelling in boys compared to girls? A number of theories have been advanced, some primarily biological, others primarily cultural. Biological theories relate the greater sexual aggressiveness of young males to hormonal differences between the sexes. In particular, the male hormone testosterone has been shown to increase sexual and aggressive behavior (in both sexes) in laboratory animals. Both sexes have both male and female hormones to some degree, and variations in the level of male hormones in human females have been related to variations in sexual and aggressive behavior among "normal" women (22, 76).

While biological factors undoubtedly play some role in the amount and the kind of sexual activity displayed, the lesser activity of the average female adoles-

cent is also in part attributable to our society's traditionally more restrictive attitudes toward sexual gratification for girls (60). In Victorian times, it was simply assumed that normal women did not have strong sexual drives, and any woman who gave evidence of sexual passion was either "morally degraded or emotionally abnormal" (43, p. 96). Although less extreme in their views, many adults even today maintain that sex doesn't mean as much to a woman as to a man.

A majority of today's adolescent girls, however, do not subscribe to such views. In a recent survey, two-thirds of them expressed the belief that "Women enjoy sex as much as men," and only one of ten believed that "Women have innately less capacity for sexual pleasure than men" (43). Masters and Johnson, who have studied the human sexual response, lend scientific support to this view. Their research indicated that the woman's basic "physiological capacity for sexual response . . . surpasses that of man" (60, pp. 219–220).

Another complex question about sex differences in sexuality involves the circumstances in which the sex drive is likely to be aroused. Some authorities have argued that one of the reasons why adolescent boys manifest more sexual activity is because boys are more easily aroused by a greater variety of stimuli, such as erotic art, films, and literature (56, 57). However, a recent wide-ranging series of experimental investigations showed that while males still emerge as more responsive in an overall survey, the differences are considerably smaller than originally supposed (85). Furthermore, some groups of females—the younger, more liberal, and more sexually experienced females—reported greater sexual excitement in response to sexual stimuli than did some groups of males— the older, more conservative, more inhibited, or less experienced. Also of interest is the fact that although males more frequently reported *subjective* feelings of arousal, the sexes did not differ substantially in measured physiological response to the stimuli (86); this may suggest more conflict about responsiveness among females.

In sum, sex differences in sexual activity must be attributed at least partially to differing cultural standards for girls and boys. If present trends continue, the effect of the "double standard"—one moral code for males, another, more restrictive one for females—will be reduced, and we should expect smaller differences between the sexes in sexual behavior.

Cultural Influences on Sexuality

If cultural standards play a major role in the expression of sexuality, we should expect to find rather wide variations in sexual attitudes and behavior from one culture to another. Some cultures are quite restrictive. Among the Cuna of South America, children "remain ignorant of sexual matters (as far as adult information is concerned) until the last stages of the marriage ceremony. They are not even allowed to watch animals give birth" (29, p. 180). The Ashanti of West Central Africa believe that sexual intercourse involving a girl who has not undergone the puberty ceremony is so harmful to the community that the offense is punishable by death for both partners.

In contrast, sexual experience in some societies is carefully nurtured from early childhood on. The Chewa of Africa believe that unless children begin to exercise themselves sexually early in life they will never produce offspring. "Older children build little huts some distance from the village, and there, with the complete approval of their parents, boys and girls play at being husband and wife. Such child matings may extend well into adolescence, with periodic exchanges of partners until marriage occurs" (29, p. 190). Similarly, the Lepcha of India believe that girls "will not mature without benefit of sexual intercourse. Early sex play among boys and girls characteristically involves many forms of mutual masturbation and usually ends in attempted copulation. By the time they are 11 or 12 years old, most girls regularly engage in full intercourse" (29, p. 191).

Some cultures are permissive at one period of a child's development and restrictive at other periods. The Siriono of South America forbid intercourse before puberty but premarital relations after puberty are customary (29). Somewhat the reverse is true of the Alorese of Oceania. Alorese mothers often fondle the genitals of their infants while nursing them, and young boys and girls are allowed to masturbate freely; occasionally they may imitate intercourse. But as these children grow older, sexual activity is increasingly disapproved. By late childhood, sexual behavior is forbidden.

Societies also vary widely in the relative acceptability of various forms of sexual behavior—for example, heterosexual versus homosexual behavior. In some societies, such as the Rwala Bedouins of Eurasia, homosexuality is so strongly opposed that both male and female offenders are put to death. In other societies, such as the Mbundu of Angola, it is simply considered immature, and it is ridiculed. In still others, it is considered an essential part of sexual and social maturation. For example, among the Siwans of Africa, all men and boys engage in homosexual intercourse; although assuming a feminine role is strictly limited to sexual situations, "males are singled out as peculiar if they do not indulge in these homosexual activities" (29, pp. 131–132).

There are also distinctive, though generally less extreme, differences in cultural attitudes toward sexuality among the developed nations. The Danes, to cite just one example, are considerably more permissive than the Irish. Obviously, adolescent sexual attitudes and practices vary widely from one culture to another. These attitudes and practices have a marked influence on the ease with which the adolescent is able to adjust to adult heterosexuality.

Sexual Attitudes of Contemporary American Adolescents

One of the most prominent aspects of the youth culture of the 1960s—and clearly one of the more enduring—was the development of a "new sexual morality." Part of this new morality involves a desire for greater openness about sex. Thus, unlike some of their elders, adolescents are overwhelmingly in favor of sex education in the schools. In one study of middle-class girls, 98 percent endorsed the idea (43). There is also a growing tendency among young people to view decisions about individual sexual behavior as more a private and less a public concern. Thus there has been a steady increase from the middle 1960s to the present in the percentage of adolescents and youth who feel that premarital sexual relationships, interracial relationships, relations between consenting homosexuals, children born outside of marriage, and abortion are a matter for the individual to decide and are not *public* moral issues (82, 95).

"When it comes to morality in sex, the important thing is the way people treat each other, not the things they do together." This statement, endorsed by three-fourths of the American adolescents in one survey (82), reflects the emphasis in the new morality on the nature of the relationships, rather than on the sexual behavior per se. Eighty percent of adolescent boys and 72 percent of adolescent girls in this country agree with the statement: "It's all right for young people to have sex before getting married if they are in love with each other." Seventy-five percent of the girls maintain that: "I wouldn't want to have sex with a boy unless I loved him." Although only 47 percent of the boys endorsed

● Figure 9.1 In sexual attitudes, younger adolescents are likely to be more conservative than older adolescents.

this stringent a requirement, 69 percent agreed: "I would not want to have sex
with a girl unless I liked her as a person" (65). However, most adolescents oppose the use of pressure or force in sex, exploitation, and sex solely for the sake
of physical enjoyment.

Diversity of attitudes   While such findings reflect overall attitudes of contemporary youth, other data reveal that adolescents' sexual attitudes vary with age,
sex, social class, race, religion, and geographical area. For example (and contrary to much popular thinking), younger adolescents are generally more *conservative* than older adolescents (82) (Figure 9.1). Significantly fewer 13- to 15-
year-olds than 16- to 19-year-olds endorse premarital intercourse, and significantly more of the younger adolescents believe a girl loses respect if she has
sexual relations and that a girl should stay a virgin until marriage.

Girls as a group are generally more conservative than boys in attitudes,
values, and behavior. Girls are more likely to believe that partners in advanced
forms of petting or intercourse should be in love, engaged, or married (42, 66).
Part of this greater conservatism in girls can be attributed to the influence of
parental and community standards, but some of the conservatism appears due to
the greater tendency among girls to view sex in terms of a larger relationship
that involves love and commitment (96).

Economically privileged college-bound and college youth are generally more liberal in sexual attitudes than "working-class" youth, although the latter appear to be catching up very quickly (see pp. 314–316). In terms of geography, students from the east and west coasts are generally more liberal than students from the Midwest (63). Students at permissive, liberally oriented colleges are less conservative than those at more traditional colleges—a not surprising finding. Perhaps more interesting is the finding that at some of these permissive colleges, girls are more liberal in their views than boys (58, 66).

It would appear from these data that adolescent attitudes and values regarding sex are changing, although the extent of the change varies widely from one segment of the youth population to another. Indeed, as in other areas of social concern, the differences between some subgroups of youth appear wider than those between youth in general and adults in general. There is a real and often ignored danger in generalizing too widely from special subgroups (a particular college campus or a particular urban high school) to all youth.

Parent–child differences If adolescents have a "new morality," many parents tend to have the "old morality." Parents are more likely than their adolescent children to disapprove of sex education, of making birth control information and devices available to adolescents, and of premarital sexual relations (7, 82). Parents are more likely to view sexual behavior in terms of prevailing social codes and less likely to be influenced by the relationship between the persons involved. Among adolescents, there are many virgins who nevertheless do not disapprove of premarital intercourse; among adults, there are many hypocrites who indulged in premarital intercourse themselves but disapprove of it for others (56, 57). Only 36 percent of all adolescents (28 percent of boys, 44 percent of girls) believe that: "When it comes to sex, my attitudes and my parent's attitudes are pretty much the same" (82). Still, in most cases, there is mutual respect between parents and youth for each other's attitudes—as long as the discrepancies are not *too* great; only a small minority of adolescents feel hassled by their parents in this regard (82).

It should be recognized that parents and children stand in different relationships to one another and differ in their responsibilities. For one thing, "there is a significant difference between defining appropriate role conduct for others to follow and defining proper role conduct to be followed by one's self" (7, p. 34). Parents do not wish to see their children hurt, either by becoming involved in sexual and emotional relationships they may not be prepared to handle or by becoming pregnant or involved in early, ill-considered marriages. Thus they tend to be more cautious, not only in sexual attitudes, but in any matter that is potentially dangerous to the physical or psychological health of their offspring. Even among adolescents, feelings of responsibility are related to more conservative attitudes: First-born children, who generally take some responsibility for their younger siblings, are the least likely of any birth order to approve of premarital intercourse, while the youngest are the most likely to approve of it (73).

Sexual Behavior

How are the significant and continuing changes in sexual attitudes and values among contemporary adolescents reflected in their behavior? The answer to this question depends on what behavior one is referring to, among which adolescents, and how recently. For example, among boys the percentage who have engaged in masturbation by age 19 has remained fairly stable since their parents' generation at around 90 percent (16). The percentage for girls, however, has risen significantly, from about 30 to over 40 percent. For both boys and girls, the incidence of masturbation among younger adolescents is steadily increasing. One might be tempted to conclude that masturbation would occur most commonly among adolescents lacking other outlets, but such is not the case; masturbation occurs about three times as frequently among those engaged in sexual intercourse or petting to orgasm as among the sexually inexperienced (82).

The incidence of premarital intercourse has increased dramatically for some groups of adolescents but has not changed much for others. A national survey published in 1973 (82) found that 44 percent of boys and 30 percent of girls have had sexual intercourse prior to age 16. These figures increased to 72 percent of boys and 57 percent of girls by age 19. When compared with females of their mothers' generation in the famous Kinsey investigations (only 3 percent of whom had engaged in premarital intercourse by age 16, and less than 20 percent by age 19), the figures for girls represent a very large increase, particularly at the younger age level. When compared with males of their fathers' generation (39 percent by age 16, 72 percent by age 19), the figures for contemporary adolescent boys show a much smaller increase and reflect mainly a tendency to have first intercourse at a slightly younger age.

The small, overall increase among males, however, masks a sizable increase among certain males—those who go on to college. In the 1940s, 49 percent of this group reported having premarital intercourse (the figure for working-class youth was 84 percent), but, by the 1970s, 82 percent were sexually active before marriage. The percentage increase among females in the higher socioeconomic classes is similarly striking, from 27 percent in the 1940s to 56 percent in the 1970s (42, 56, 57). Of course, it was in the socioeconomically favored groups that most of the manifestations of the "youth revolution" were centered. In the case of sexual behavior, changes in attitudes and values have been followed by significant changes in behavior.

Pregnancy and Contraception

The new sexual morality among adolescents has many positive aspects, such as a greater emphasis on honesty and more concern with "the relationship" than with the sex act per se, but increased sexual activity also brings with it a host of potential problems. Many young adolescents find themselves involved in sexual relationships that they cannot handle without anxiety and guilt. Venereal dis-

● Figure 9.2   Number of out-of-wedlock births per 1000 unmarried females aged 14–17, 18–19, and 20–24, United States, 1961–1974. (Adapted from Guttmacher Institute. *11 Million Teenagers.* New York: Guttmacher Institute, 1976.)

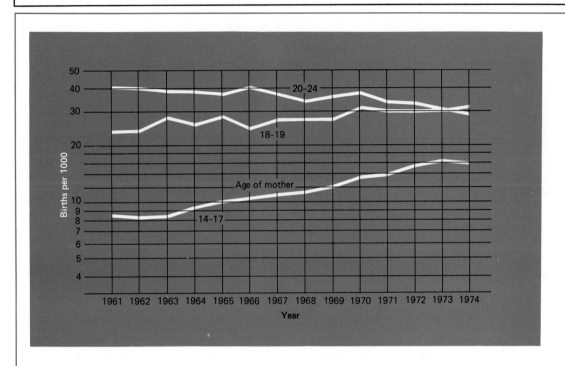

ease is an increasing problem among adolescents, as it is among all age groups. Perhaps the greatest potential problem, however, is an unwanted pregnancy. Every year about 10 percent of the teenaged girls in the United States get pregnant (2) (Figure 9.2). About 60 percent of these pregnancies result in the birth of a baby—over 600,000 babies are born each year to teenaged mothers (Figure 9.3)—while the remaining 40 percent of the pregnancies are terminated by abortion or miscarriage.

Not all of these teenaged pregnancies are unwanted, of course. Many (28 percent) occur *after* marriages involving a young girl. Many of these pregnancies *result* in marriages, at least some of which are happy ones, hastened perhaps by the pregnancies but not undesired. But most of the teenaged pregnancies are unwanted. Those terminated by abortion—one third of all abortions in the United States are obtained by teenagers—often involve expense and emotional conflicts (2). If a baby is born "out of wedlock," it is usually kept rather than given up for adoption or raised by relatives. Unwed mothers of all ages

● Figure 9.3   Outcome of pregnancies to teenage females, United States, 1974.
(Adapted from Alan Guttmacher Institute. *11 Million Teenagers.* New York: Guttmacher Institute, 1976.)

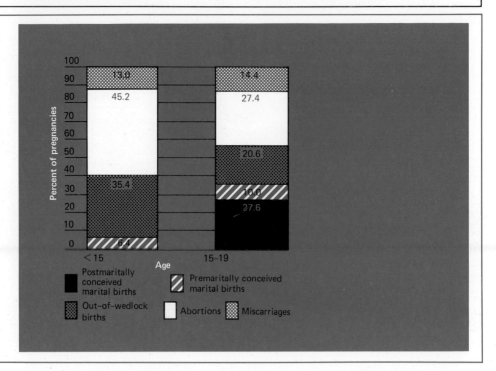

have problems; teenaged unwed mothers have the most of all, without the skills
or the experience necessary for a good job, without the "normal" social life of
an adolescent, without the ability to provide a "normal" environment for her
child.

Ignorance of contraceptive practices is a major factor in teenaged pregnancies. Less than 50 percent of the adolescent girls in one national study (50, 51)
reported using any contraceptive method in their most recent intercourse; four
out of five said they "sometimes" had sexual relations without using any contraceptive method; and one in six "never" used contraceptive devices. Although a
few young girls said they didn't care whether or not they became pregnant—indeed, some actively desired pregnancy—this was not the case for most. Some
claimed it was an "OK time of the month," although their knowledge of the
menstrual cycle hardly inspired confidence: the majority of these girls believed
that ovulation occurred during menstruation! Others felt they were too young to
become pregnant (although they were menstruating), and there were some who
were sure there was no danger because they had sexual relations so infre-

quently. This widespread ignorance of the biology of reproduction and the nature of contraception is aggravated by equally widespread notions that contraceptive devices take the spontaneity, romance, and pleasure out of sex. In the view of many adolescent boys, and even more girls, "If the girl uses birth control pills or other forms of contraception, it makes it seem as if she were *planning* to have sex."

It seems unlikely that the trend toward increasing sexual experience among adolescents will be reversed. What one must hope is that adolescents can be helped to become mature enough, informed enough, responsible enough, sure enough of their own identities and value systems, and sensitive and concerned enough about the welfare of others so that the casualties of the "sexual revolution" can be kept to a minimum. And so that sex, as a vital human relationship, can promote, rather than hinder, growth toward maturity and emotional fulfillment.

ALIENATION AND COMMITMENT

As we saw in the previous chapter, despite a lack of enchantment with many of the policies and values of government and other institutions, a majority of today's adolescents and youth are confident and optimistic about their personal lives. Although they favor a variety of social and political changes they see as desirable, they expect to be able to find a rewarding life within the existing order. These relatively optimistic feelings are not shared by all adolescents, however; there is a significant minority which is deeply dissatisfied with the state of society, or themselves, or both.

Alienation

It has become fashionable in recent years to speak of troubled young people as "alienated." By such labeling we may gain the illusion that we have explained their behavior, but, in fact, all we have done is to imply that "something is wrong somewhere," that some sort of relationship has been lost or broken. Until we specify what the person is alienated from, for what reasons, and with what consequences, we have accomplished little (53).

Some aspects of alienation tend to be relatively widespread in our culture, while others tend to be limited to particular subgroups. At present there is rather widespread alienation from religious faith and from the notion of a meaningful and orderly universe, with a personal God at its center. This feeling of "existential outcastness" (53), of the essential lack of any absolute meaning in the universe as a whole, can be painful indeed and may result in feelings of deprivation and outrage. Another widespread variety of alienation, common in societies undergoing rapid social change, involves an acute sense of historical loss. Tradition, customs, technology, tastes in music and in dress—they all change so quickly that it is inevitable that some people will mourn their loss.

Revivals, nostalgia, and simple yearnings for "the good old days" are manifestations of this sense of loss.

Most of the adolescents we will discuss in the remainder of this chapter share a disillusionment with the American culture; their alienation takes the form of a rejection of traditional societal values and practices. Although all of these young people can be called "alienated," the reasons for their disillusionment are quite varied. Economically favored middle- and upper-class youth may be reacting against what they perceive as an obsessive preoccupation with materialistic rewards and social status, and the shallowness and hypocrisy of many of the values and practices of contemporary society. In contrast, for lower-class minority youth who have suffered economic deprivation and ethnic discrimination, alienation is, to a great extent, imposed by society. These young people are prevented by the accident of birth and by discrimination from sharing in the affluent society they see all around them and on television. After an early childhood marked by inadequate nutrition and a lack of intellectual stimulation, many disadvantaged children enter overcrowded, run-down schools. Under these conditions, they may fail to make normal school progress and may drop out of school. Few jobs are available for unskilled, high-school dropouts, and disadvantaged young people may encounter discrimination even in jobs for which they are qualified. For such youth, the American dream becomes a nightmare.

Alienation Among Privileged Youth

Alienation of the poor, the unemployed, and the victims of racial or ethnic discrimination is not difficult to understand. More puzzling is the alienation of privileged youth, those middle- and upper-class young people who reject the very values and practices of which they are the apparent beneficiaries. In some instances, the alienation may be quite specific; it may involve rejecting a specific aspect of the culture (such as the war in Vietnam during the late 1960s and early 1970s) while still accepting society as a whole. Other young people experience alienation that is much deeper and more pervasive, feeling themselves at odds with a society "rotten to the core."

There are also differences in young people's responses to the alienating aspects of society. Some youth work within the established social order to modify the social structure in ways they deem desirable—in politics, for example, or in social services. Others may feel that slight modifications are useless and that something approximating a revolution is necessary. Still other youth may respond to their alienation by withdrawing from society; apathy and depression are characteristic symptoms. Delinquency can be another response to alienation, even in the privileged social classes. A more complex and deliberate response is to search for an "alternative life-style" in a separate subculture of like-minded individuals, in a religious sect (see pp. 311–312), in a rural commune, or perhaps in an urban neighborhood that becomes a "community," like the fabled Haight-Ashbury district in the San Francisco of the 1960s.

Despite individual differences in the forms their alienation takes, many alienated young people share a common disillusionment with our "technocratic" (77), "postindustrial" (32), or "mass" society. This society, in the view of these young people, is one in which the goals of technological progress and economic affluence are relentlessly pursued without regard for the human costs or the quality of the environment. This society seems to them to value things more than people, and it achieves affluence for a few at the expense of the many at the bottom of the socioeconomic ladder. "Big business" and "big government" are seen as impersonal organizations that act in ways inimical to the values these young people hold strongly.

What are these strongly held values? They include intimacy ("love," both individual and communal), individuality (freedom to know and to be oneself), autonomy (freedom from coercion and freedom to act independently), and honesty (lack of pretense). Conversely, these young people tend to question or reject such values and practices as relentless competition and status-seeking, "game playing" that involves manipulation of others, and respect for authority based on power or assigned status (rather than on talents, wisdom, or experience).

Activism

Active protest by high-school and college students reached its height in the 1960s and early 1970s. The issues were many—from "free speech" to civil rights to the war in Vietnam—and the means of protest varied from quiet demonstrations to violent and deadly clashes between students and police. Student activism spawned scientific controversy, too, as psychologists and sociologists sought to understand this relatively new social phenomenon. Some observers regarded student activists as immature, insecure, undisciplined, and deeply troubled young people who, though bright, were "fixated at the stage of the temper tantrum" (20, p. 23). Other observers considered the opposite to be the case. They found student activists to be unusually intelligent, mature, psychologically resilient, and socially effective (77).

Much of the initial research during the 1960s seemed to support the more positive view of the activists. In general, these studies suggested that activist students of this period were brighter than their nonactivist peers, more successful academically, more flexible, more individualistic, and more autonomous (81, 93). They also emerged as more imaginative; more concerned with abstract thinking in the areas of art, literature, music, and philosophy; and more liberal and less conventional in religious values (28, 41).

Activist students in these studies came largely from upper-status, often professional families (89). Their parents were less likely than the parents of nonactivist students to "intervene strongly" in the decisions of their adolescent sons and daughters. According to their activist children, these parents were milder, warmer, more lenient, and less strict in their child-rearing practices. The views of the activists, rather than being in opposition to those of their parents, tended to parallel them. For example, the attitudes of the fathers of activist sons, as reflected in their responses to questions on various social issues, were more liberal than those of the fathers of nonactivist sons. Activist sons appeared to share their fathers' liberal values, but to carry them further and to act on them in a more militant or radical fashion (28).

The activist students typically studied in these early investigations were college youth at one of the "elite" campuses (Berkeley, Chicago) who championed left-oriented or liberal policies. Later studies, involving a broader sample of activist young people on both the left and the right (conservative) ends of the political spectrum, led to some qualifications of the conclusions of the earlier work. For example, some traits seemed characteristic of activists, regardless of their political ideology. Both left-oriented and right-oriented activists were found to be more autonomous and assertive than nonactivist students and also more sociable and less in need of support and nurturance (54). Other traits

seemed characteristic of left-oriented students, whether or not they were activists. Liberal young people appeared more sensitive and manifested more concern for the welfare of others; they placed little value on conformity and recognition, compared to right-oriented students. Right-oriented students (activist or not) valued leadership more highly.

Among groups distinguished by degree of activism or political ideology or both, there were no significant differences on measures of intelligence, responsibility, seriousness of purpose, perserverance, or emotional stability. In short, these later studies did not support either the stereotype of left-oriented activists as members of an extraordinarily intelligent and compassionate "psychological nobility" or the contrary stereotype portraying them as maladjusted young people, acting out their personal authority conflicts in the real world. Both of these views were exaggerations and oversimplifications (55).

Similarly, the generally positive relationships left-oriented activists had with their parents should not be overemphasized. Undoubtedly many activist youth had rewarding parent–child relationships, and their activism may have reflected, in part, identification with and extensions of liberal parental values.

However, there is little justification for assuming that this was nearly always the case or that parent–child relationships were better among activists than among nonactivists. Several investigations (6, 94) found that conservative and middle-of-the-road youth were just as likely as activists to get along well with their parents, share their basic values, and report close childhood ties with them. Other studies found that while most left-oriented activists were psychologically healthy, there were some who had definite emotional problems—as one would expect in any heterogeneous group defined only by opposition to certain institutional values and practices (78).

Radical Dissent Versus Socially Oriented Activism

Another problem with many of the early studies was a tendency to lump together the *radical dissenters* (revolutionaries) and *moderate reformers*. The radical dissenters felt a need for extreme, even violent change, believing that the "social system is too rotten for repair" (94). Moderate reformers, in contrast, felt that most social institutions were badly in need of change, but that reform and repair was possible without the destruction of these institutions.

In a study comparing these two types of left-oriented activists (94), the radical dissenters rejected all traditional values of American culture. They opposed any interference with their personal freedom or social constraints imposed for "moral" reasons. They felt that dress and grooming were exclusively personal matters and that drug use, abortion, homosexuality between consenting adults, and premarital or extramarital sexual relations were private matters, not public issues.

Moderate reformers, like the revolutionaries, felt strongly that big business was "overly concerned with profits and not with public responsibility," that "economic well-being in this country is unjustly and unfairly distributed," and that we are basically "a racist nation." However, unlike the revolutionaries, the moderate reformers did not believe that traditional social institutions should be done away with. Their position on more personal values was also less extreme than those of the revolutionaries. While a majority felt that abortion and much sexual behavior were not public moral issues, they felt that extramarital relations were wrong, and they said they could "accept easily" prohibitions against LSD and other drugs (excluding marijuana).

Activism and Activists Today

The height of student activism was reached in the 1960s and early 1970s. Since the end of the war in Vietnam, active protests have declined. By 1973, less than 10 percent of college youth identified with the "New Left" (95). But despite a decrease in the visible manifestations of radical thought, many privileged youth continue to express attitudes and values that suggest that disenchantment with many social institutions persists. More than six of ten agree with the view that "this country is a democracy in name only and that special interests run things" (95). Two-thirds of the socioeconomically favored young people believe "we are a racist nation," and a majority (at least) believe that political parties, prisons, big business, and other institutions are badly in need of fundamental (radical) reform.

Why then the relative absence of radical behavior? Several answers have been proposed. One is that the war in Vietnam (and related issues such as the draft) elicited intense emotional responses and led to feelings of urgency and a need for personal involvement and action. With the war over, activism (but not the skeptical views) declined. A second answer is perhaps a reduction in the differences between the views of young people and the views of the adult community that has occurred for several reasons. In the sense that demonstrations and other protests were meant to be alarmist—to *inform* the public of danger and immoral government policies—one could say they were quite successful. Toward the end of the war in Vietnam, not only youth but the majority of adults wanted U.S. withdrawal. Startling revelations of widespread government deceptions, conspiracies, and violations of individual rights—collectively labeled "Watergate"—seemed to substantiate the cynical views of young people. The result was a degree of disillusionment in adults fully as deep and as pervasive as that in high-school and college students. Perhaps a third answer is the increasing violence by some of the more extreme activist groups such as the Symbionese Liberation Army. To many philosophically nonviolent protestors, such violence was intolerable (52).

There have been a few studies of people who were activists in the 1960s to see what they are doing today (25, 26). Compared to people who were non-activists, the former activists are more likely to hold left-oriented political views, to be active in politics, and to participate in organizations championing some cause, such as civil liberties, the environment, consumer advocacy, or population planning. In terms of career choice, former activists are disproportionately represented in such fields as education, politics, social services, health care, and government service (some as elected officials); they are underrepresented in business and industry. In general, most of the former student activists are still quite active in their attempts to better society, but the means are less intense, more traditional (Figure 9.4).

The Social Dropouts

In every society there have been those who do not share the values of the dominant social order and who, rather than trying to change the order (as the activists do) or even drifting along with it, have "dropped out." The alternative life-styles that result have been, in some cases, purposeful and well-defined (e.g., in some communes) and, in other cases, aimless and confused. The so-called "hippies" of the 1960s were certainly not the first to listen to a "different drummer." The history of the United States contains many accounts of separatist move-

● Figure 9.4   A protest leader in the 1960s, Tom Hayden made a favorable showing in the Democratic primary for U.S. Senator from California in 1976. Had he won the primary, he would have faced S. I. Hayakawa, who rose to prominence because of his stern treatment of student protestors at San Francisco State University.

ments, many of them religious and some quite successful (e.g., the Amish in Pennsylvania). The "beat" generation of the 1950s preceded the hippie movement and, in fact, played a significant role in its birth.

Hippies   The hippies were the social dropouts of the late 1960s and early 1970s. The hippie movement involved primarily children of white middle- or upper-class families (69); like social activism, it was primarily a manifestation of alienation among our more privileged youth. The parents of the typical hippie were socially active, politically moderate, and success-oriented—in short, "pillars of the community."

There was no single type of hippie. There were philosophically oriented young people interested in forming alternative communities, and there were aimless drifters. There were people interested only in drugs or easy sex, and there were very young adolescents rebelling against their parents. But despite their diversity, hippies showed a common aversion to what they perceived as the aggressive, highly competitive, conformity-demanding nature of society, with its emphasis on social status and material success. Not only did they view these values as hollow, neurotic attachments to meaningless goals ("hang-ups"), but also as in direct conflict with their own presumed values: love, gentleness, honesty; an immediate attitude of acceptance and sharing, with no questions asked, an emphasis on personal freedom and individual self-expression ("doing your own thing"); an antiintellectual appreciation of sensation and inner experience, typically aided by drugs; a presumed lack of social or sexual inhibitions.

Obviously many of these hippie values can be admired by anyone; that is, love and sharing are, in some sense, the most traditional of values. One could argue that the hippie movement was in part, at least, a reaction to an increasingly technocratic and impersonal world that had forgotten its most basic values. But there was a dark side of the hippie movement, too. It was essentially parasitic, depending for sustenance on part-time jobs in the "system," handouts gained "panhandling," or money from "square" parents back home (11). A few hippies made their own way, notably musicians and a few artists, and a few communes flourished, at least for a while. But most hippies were constantly short of cash (Figure 9.5). The drugs on which the hippie culture was based created problems, especially the paronoia-producing amphetamines ("Speed kills"). Also, there were too many hippies who believed in chemical shortcuts to creativity and meaningfulness through the use of hallucinogens such as LSD.

Many of the hippie participants in one major study were characterized by "ego deficits," manifested by an inability "to understand, organize, or integrate the events of their lives" (69, p. 22). Despite their relatively high intelligence (ranging from bright–normal to superior, with a mean IQ of 119) and generally good earlier academic records (69), many of these young people displayed difficulties in memory, attention, and thought, and they showed a marked lack of critical judgment (12). A majority showed little frustration tolerance, preferring to avoid "hassles" (often with the aid of drugs) rather than to face up to emotionally difficult situations.

Even more striking was the frequency of inadequacies in establishing interpersonal relationships: "A universally reported experience of our subjects is a profound sense of psychological distance from others which often dates back to their earliest memories of childhood" (12, p. 7). Despite their "normal," middle-class backgrounds, these young people had typically been subjected to unusually high degrees of stimulation, stress, and trauma (69, 84), particularly during middle childhood. There had been intense conflicts between parents; accidents and serious illnesses; a loss of parents or siblings through death, divorce, or desertion; chronic parental illness or alcoholism; frequent changes of residence; sexual molestation; exposure to violence. "What particularly characterizes their accounts of childhood . . . is their sense of living amidst great confusion, chaos, and disorganization, and their inability to escape for even brief periods to a calmer and more benign environment" (69, p. 15).

Where have all the flowers gone?   The original hippie movement began to disintegrate after its peak in the 1967 "summer of love." As the hippie "scene" became fragmented, disorganized, and crime-ridden and as the social climate of the nation changed in the declining days of the Vietnam War, most of the "true" hippies departed, and potential new "recruits" had no coherent scene to attract

● Figure 9.5   Most hippies were chronically short of cash.

or shelter them. This does not mean that young people with hippie inclinations no longer exist, although their numbers, particularly within the middle class, have been markedly reduced. Approximately half a million young people under 17 still run away from home each year (69), and a like number of 17- to 21-year-olds take to the road. Many of these troubled young people can currently be found in the ranks of the "street people" who live near universities or in urban ghettos (62). The fact that a hippie culture, in its original sense, no longer exists serves only to heighten their alienation and to leave them more powerless and vulnerable. Their need for human services—health care, shelter, protection, counseling—is often desperate.

What happened to the original hippies who are now young adults? Some, of course, have returned to the mainstream of society and the lives they once renounced. Some have become permanent casualties of a once hopeful revolution —victims of escalating drug use, "freaked-out" psychologically, drifting endlessly from one bleak "scene" to another, or even in jail (15). Most, however, appear to occupy a middle ground. In an investigation of the fate of San Francisco hippies (68, 70, 91), most had moved out of the Haight-Ashbury area, although a majority still lived in urban centers. Only 10 percent had married, but 45 percent reported living with a partner of the opposite sex; these relationships seemed relatively long-term, especially when compared to the transitory relationships they had reported in the past. Most (75 percent) were employed (in contrast to 17 percent at the beginning of the study), and about a third had returned to school either part- or full-time. Drug use had declined, particularly the use of mind-altering drugs.

It would be a mistake to conclude that these young adults had re-embraced the "establishment." Although most were employed, they tended to have minimally stressful jobs, below the level expected from their educational achievements. Most were still regular users of marijuana, hashish, and alcohol. The former hippies still refused to participate in traditional political activities; they viewed organized politics as "a farce." They rejected all Western forms of religion. Thus, although their life-styles appeared more conventional, "their ideology remained hip" (91, p. 9).

ADOLESCENTS AND DRUGS

Probably no other area during the past decade was subject to a "generation gap" as wide as that in attitudes toward drugs. Especially during the late 1960s and early 1970s, many adults expressed a genuine fear that adolescent use of marijuana, LSD, and other "mind-altering" drugs might result in serious, perhaps even permanent damage to physical health and psychological well-being. Concern for the welfare of individuals, however, was clearly only part of the picture, insufficient in itself to explain the extent of societal alarm and the frequently irrational and punitive measures adopted to deal with "the drug problem"; long prison sentences for marijuana use were far more likely than the drug itself to affect the young person's psychological well-being.

Clearly the gap between the attitudes of adolescents and adults toward drugs was a symbol of a deeper division on fundamental social values. Use of drugs (other than alcohol or nicotine, of course) came to symbolize to many adults an entire way of life, one that directly challenged the basic values of a society dedicated to the Protestant ethic, with its emphasis on activity, competition, aggressiveness, delayed gratification, and material success. To many adolescents, this was not an inaccurate characterization; to them, too, the use of drugs was at least partly symbolic. Drug use symbolized their personal freedom in an over-controlled society, a rejection of authority, and a personal statement that being "mellow" was more important than being competitive. Adolescents viewed societal attitudes (and laws) as hypocritical, endorsing drugs that were known killers (alcohol and nicotine) while disapproving marijuana, whose adverse effects, if any, were yet to be determined.

Fortunately the exaggerated early positions on drugs have become less extreme, for both adults and young people, in the later 1970s (79). Many adults have become better informed on the nature and effects of drugs, especially marijuana, and some of their fears have therefore decreased. Much of this information came from research studies, but some adults began to gain knowledge from personal experience as well, as illicit drug use increased, particularly among younger adults. There was also ample evidence that severe punishments instituted to control drug use were not working and served only to increase the alienation of young people (and to give many of them prison records). The views of most young people have also become more moderate. The dangers of some drugs, such as heroin, barbiturates, "speed" (amphetamines), and hydrocarbon vapors (obtained by, for example, sniffing glue) were more commonly recognized and admitted, and even the use of marijuana has become more "recreational" than "religious." Both adults and adolescents seem increasingly concerned with "responsible" use of drugs (including alcohol) and with help, rather than punishment, for those who misuse drugs.

Alcohol

Many psychologists are becoming concerned about increases in the adolescent use of alcohol, particularly among younger adolescents (Figure 9.6). Although few parents approve of adolescent drinking, disapproval is typically less intense than it is of the use of other drugs. Indeed, many adults do not even classify alcoholic beverages as "drugs." In addition, adolescent drinking is not likely to be viewed as a sign of rejection of parental or societal values.

The vast majority of young people have at least tried alcoholic beverages by the end of adolescence, with estimates ranging from 71 to 92 percent in various areas of the country—a higher overall average than for any other psychoactive drug, including marijuana (14). Alcohol use among adolescents is increasing. In a survey of high-school seniors (46), the percentage of those drinking (on three or more occasions) rose from approximately 70 percent in 1969 to nearly 90 percent in 1975—certainly a striking increase. Sex differences are declining. In a 1969 California survey (39), 52 percent of seventh-grade boys, but only 38 percent of the girls, had begun drinking; by 1973, the percentage of boys had risen sharply, to 72 percent, but this figure was nearly matched by the 67 percent of the seventh-grade girls who had begun to drink.

●Figure 9.6 Many psychologists are becoming concerned about increases in adolescent use of alcohol.

The great majority of drinking adolescents have only an occasional drink. Even by the twelfth grade, only about 12 percent drink hard liquor or wine once a week or more frequently (3). Beer drinking is more common among senior boys (42 percent, weekly), but half have only one or two beers when they do drink; among senior girls, less than 15 percent drink beer as frequently as once a week.

Unfortunately, however, a small (but increasing) percentage of adolescents are already serious "problem drinkers." In 1975, 6 percent of high-school seniors (8 percent of boys) reported drinking "almost every day" (46). Another study indicates that about 5 percent of the students in grades 7–12 drink to the point of intoxication ("get drunk") at least once a week (Figure 9.7). These figures are restricted to young people still in school; the incidence of problem drinking is known to be substantially higher among school dropouts (3). While the percentage of adolescents who are serious problem drinkers is small, the number of individuals involved is quite large and certainly cause for concern.

●Figure 9.7   Percentage of teenage drinkers who report getting drunk by frequency and school grade, 1974. (From *Alcohol and Health: New knowledge.* Second special report to the U. S. Congress, National Institute on Alcohol Abuse and Alcoholism, U.S. Department of Health, Education, and Welfare. Washington, D.C.: U.S. Government Printing Office, June 1974. No. 1724-00399, preprint edition.)

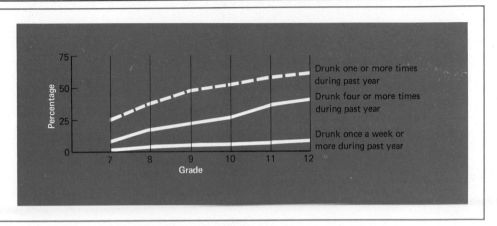

The health and welfare of these adolescents is one major concern; another—since most of these young people drink at night in cars (3)—is the health and welfare of pedestrians and other drivers on the road.

Marijuana

The use of marijuana is becoming widespread throughout the population of the United States. Among adults, for example, only 4 percent said, in 1969, that they had tried marijuana at least once; in 1973, that figure had tripled, to 12 percent; by 1977, the percentage doubled again, to 24 percent (34). Over half of all young adults (under the age of 30) had tried marijuana by 1977.

Similar increases can be noted among adolescents. For example, between 1972 and 1974, use among all young people aged 12 to 17 rose from 14 percent to 23 percent (46, 72). There are also significant tendencies for marijuana use to begin at younger and younger ages. In 1974, 22 percent of the 14- and 15-year-olds had tried "pot." However, there are wide variations in the extent of use from one school to another, with estimates in a 1973 study ranging from 6 percent of the students at one school to over 60 percent at another (59). Boys are typically more likely to use marijuana, but sex differences are declining, and sometimes junior and senior girls (who presumably are dating older boys) have a higher rate of usage than their male classmates (90). Marijuana use is higher among young people in the East and West, compared to the Midwest and South, and higher in urban areas, compared to rural.

The use of marijuana among college students is particularly common, although, again, there are significant variations from school to school and from one part of the United States to another. From various national surveys (14), the increase among college youth can be plotted: In 1967, 5 percent indicated they had tried marijuana; in 1969, 22 percent; in 1970, 42 percent; in 1972, 51 percent; in 1975, 63 percent. As with alcohol, most young people who use marijuana do so infrequently—maybe once or twice a month, or less (46).

Why do young people use marijuana? In a survey of 26,000 college students (64), the most frequently (58 percent of the respondents) cited reason for use of marijuana the first time was "curiosity." Only 6 percent volunteered the reason "for kicks." When asked why they continued to smoke marijuana, the most common (68 percent) answer was, simply, because "it's fun." Only 7 percent said that the drug helped them to gain a "greater insight" into themselves. Thus, although much is made in some quarters of neurotic needs for marijuana or of the deep, philosophical implications of drug use in our culture, the facts are that most current marijuana users are "normal" young people who try it because they are curious and continue because they find it pleasurable.

Parents and peers Both parents and peers play a role in youthful marijuana use. Parental use of tranquilizers, amphetamines, or barbituates, as well as alcohol and tobacco, is positively correlated with the use of marijuana and other illegal drugs by their children (8). Involvement with other drug-using adolescents, however, is an even stronger correlate of marijuana use. In a study in New York state, among secondary school students whose closest school-friends had never used marijuana, only 15 percent reported using the drug themselves; in contrast, among those whose closest school-friends smoked pot frequently, use increased to 79 percent (48, 49). The highest use rates of all were found among adolescents whose parents *and* closest school-friends were drug users.

Findings such as these seem to fit a theory of deviant behavior in which the parents can "prepare" the adolescent for drug use, either by engaging in the behaviors themselves, producing a tendency to imitate, or by creating a negative climate in the home from which the young person seeks to escape. Still, the young person will usually not engage in the deviant behavior unless drug use is common in the peer culture. "Peer behavior is the crucial determining factor in adolescent drug use; parental behavior becomes important when such behavior exists in the peer group" (48, p. 126).

Personal characteristics of marijuana users Young people who have tried marijuana a few times and then have either given it up or used it very infrequently (experimenters) are practically indistinguishable from nonusers, although they may be slightly "more open to experience" (80). Moderate or intermittent users, as a group, are clearly less conventional, more adventuresome, and more impulsive than either experimenters or nonusers (74). They are also likely to be more rebellious and nonconformist, and more likely to express "antiestablishment" views regarding politics, religion, and the "success ethic" (35, 75). Moderate users in college are more likely to be majoring in the arts and humanities than in the natural sciences or business; their grades tend to be about the same as those of nonusers (38). The picture of the moderate user, in general, is one of a relatively normal personality whose liberal political and social views extend to most areas of his or her life, including drug use.

Chronic heavy users, however, are likely to manifest indications of significant psychological disturbance. In a number of studies, heavy use of marijuana has been associated with poor social adjustment, poor work adjustment, a high level of hostility, and difficulty in problem-solving (90). Heavy users seem to have a desire for the "psychotomimetic" experience—to get so "stoned" that their experiences mimic those of psychotic individuals, for example, to have hallucinations—rather than a desire for simple tension-reduction or fun. On psychological tests, relative to nonusers, heavy users have been found to be anxious, restless, suspicious, depressed, negativistic, insecure, irresponsible, immature, and incapable of sustained intimate social or emotional relationships with others (63, 97). They are also, typically, multiple drug users. In short, the picture of the heavy marijuana user is of a disturbed personality. The evidence suggests that heavy drug use is primarily a result of psychological disturbance, rather than its cause, although obviously drug abuse adds to the individual's problems and probably contributes to the increasing deterioration in social behavior.

Other Drugs

Young people are considerably more wary of other drugs than they are of marijuana or alcohol. Many people feared that, as marijuana use spread, other drugs like LSD, "speed," and even heroin would also increase rapidly in popularity, but recent surveys indicate that these fears are largely unwarranted. In the period between 1968 and 1972, there were slight increases in the use of "other drugs" among high-school students (79). Experimentation with opiates (such as heroin) rose to approximately 5 percent. Use of hallucinogens (such as LSD), stimulants (like the amphetamines or "speed"), and depressants (such as barbiturates or "sleeping pills") also increased, but in no case was more than one adolescent in five involved. Since 1972, furthermore, use of these drugs appears to have stabilized (46). It should also be noted that a significant percentage of the students who have tried these other drugs either use them very infrequently or abandon them entirely after a period of experimentation. More than three-fourths of all high-school seniors in 1975 disapproved of even experimentation with amphetamines, narcotics, LSD, and barbiturates, and over 70 percent stated they would forbid their own children to use any illicit drug except marijuana (46).

None of this discussion is intended to indicate that use of these other drugs among young people is not a matter of serious and continuing concern. One can say that "only" 3–5 percent of junior and senior high-school students have ever tried heroin, but this adds up to over 1 million individuals. Younger adolescents, in particular, with their relative lack of judgement and knowledge, may be more susceptible to dangerous and ill-considered practices, including indiscriminate, multiple drug use.

Why Do Adolescents Take Drugs?

The reasons adolescents take drugs vary widely. Curiosity, as we mentioned in the case of marijuana, is a frequently reported reason among young adolescents; conformity to peer pressure and the desires to "be cool," to show-off, and to be popular are also commonly cited. In many respects, the reasons most adolescents take drugs parallel those of adults: Alcohol and other drugs promise relaxation, euphoria, loss of inhibitions, relief from stress and anxiety, or the feeling —however temporary—of mastery, insight, or power. Both adolescents and adults live in a drug culture where, as TV commercials constantly remind us, relief is "just a swallow away."

For a minority of young people, particularly heavy multiple drug users, reliance on drugs may reflect emotional disturbances of varying degrees of severity and an inability to cope with the demands of living or to find a meaningful personal identity. In some such cases, family relationships may offer clues to the difficulties. Some young people, who have been using drugs since preadolescence, must be given instruction in how to deal with anxiety and boredom— or, more positively, how to have fun—without drugs.

Finally, an indifferent society must share part of the blame. Disadvantaged adolescents often face a future without hope. They are confronted with economic, social, and racial discrimination, with impossible living conditions, often with untreated physical ills, and with a breakdown in their social environment and in their own families. Perhaps it is not too surprising that some of them give up the search for meaning and a sense of ego identity entirely and seek escape in the oblivion of hard narcotics.

JUVENILE DELINQUENCY

Delinquency is basically a legal concept, defined in different ways in different times and places. Thus, drinking, fighting, and some forms of sexual behavior might be considered delinquent at one time in a particular culture but may be sanctioned at another time or in another culture. In our society, the term "juvenile delinquent" is applied to young persons under 16 or 18 years of age who exhibit behavior punishable by law.

Incidence of Delinquent Behavior

The number of young persons who are detected, reported, or charged with delinquent behavior began to increase substantially in 1948, and the rate has con-

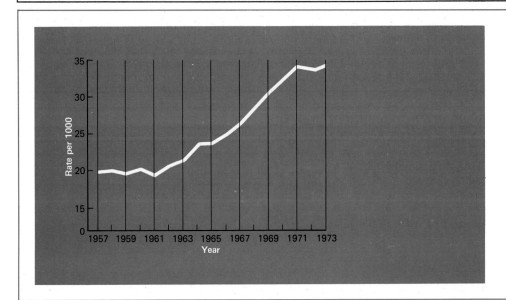

●Figure 9.8   Rate of delinquency cases disposed of by juvenile courts involving children 10 through 17 years of age. (From U. Bronfenbrenner. The challenge of social change to public policy and developmental research. Paper presented at the biannual meeting of the Society for Research in Child Development, Denver, April 2, 1975. By permission. Source: U.S. Office of Human Development and U.S. Office of Youth Development, *Juvenile Court Statistics,* annual.)

tinued to rise ever since (85), especially during the 1960s (23). (See Figure 9.8.) According to recent estimates, at least 12 percent of all young people (22 percent of boys) will turn up in juvenile court records before the end of adolescence.

Furthermore, since 1960 the incidence of more serious offenses among young people has been rising at a faster rate than delinquency in general, and twice as fast as comparable adult crimes. Although persons aged 10 through 21 constitute only 23 percent of the population, they account for a far higher percentage of many offenses (see Figure 9.9). This is particularly true in some of our largest cities; for example, in 1976 in Chicago, one-third of all murders were committed by people aged 20 or younger, a 29 percent increase over 1975.

There are clear sex differences in both the frequency and the nature of delinquent behavior. For many years the ratio of boy to girl offenses was four or five to one (36). The most frequent complaints against boys involved active or aggressive behaviors, such as joyriding, burglary, malicious mischief, auto theft, and, increasingly in the 1960s, illegal drug use (23, 85). Girls, on the other hand, were more likely to be reported for such offenses as running away from home, "incorrigibility" (parental inability to control the girl), and illicit

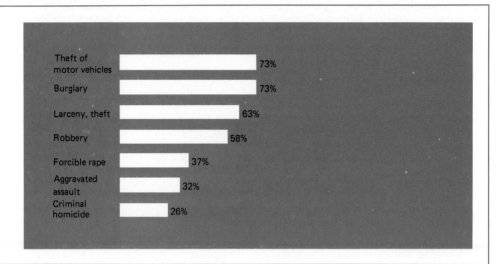

● Figure 9.9   Arrests of persons under 21 years of age as percentage of all arrests. (From Federal Bureau of Investigation, 1977.)

Theft of motor vehicles	73%
Burglary	73%
Larceny, theft	63%
Robbery	58%
Forcible rape	37%
Aggravated assault	32%
Criminal homicide	26%

sexual behavior. Boys are more likely to be apprehended by police, whereas girls are more likely to be reported by parents who claim they cannot cope with their daughter's behavior (44).

Sex differences, while still large, are narrowing. In recent years, the percentage increase in arrests of girls under 18 for all offenses was nearly three times that of boys (87). Furthermore, from 1970 to 1975, the arrest rate for girls under 18 for serious crimes, traditionally more common among boys, climbed 40 percent, compared to 24 percent for boys (88). At least part of the recent rise in girls' delinquency has been attributed to increased independence and assertiveness among females in our society, which, while generally a positive trend, is bound to have a few unfortunate side-effects (47).

Reported delinquency is high among youth of lower socioeconomic status, particularly those living in urban ghettos (33). Detailed interviews with adolescents of all social classes, however, suggest that official police records exaggerate the differences between lower-class youth and their middle- and upper-class peers (37). First, it should be noted that police apprehended the delinquent in only about 3 percent of his or her offenses; "the risk of being caught is in reality quite small" (37, p. 102). Using all delinquent acts the adolescents were willing to admit to (rather than those few that end up in the official statistics), the social classes were not very different: "For every two middle-class boys among the . . . most delinquent boys, there were about three lower-class boys" (37, p. 116). The much wider differences in the official records may result, in some cases, from discrimination against lower-status youth by juvenile authorities.

In other cases, the generally poorer home and neighborhood environment of the lower-class delinquent child may force the court to find legal solutions to his or her problems, while an upper-class youth guilty of a similar offense may be released to the parents' custody, without formal charges.

Social Change, Deprivation, and Delinquency

Increases in delinquency are most likely to occur when a sense of community solidarity and of the integrity of the extended family have been most seriously disrupted. Thus, in recent decades, the greatest percentage increases in juvenile crime have occurred in the suburbs (24), especially in communities characterized by high "turnover" of its socially and geographically mobile residents.

Nevertheless, delinquency rates are still highest in deteriorated neighborhoods near the centers of large cities (45). In some areas, marked by economic deprivation and general disorganization, delinquency is often an approved tradition, and there are many opportunities for learning antisocial behavior from delinquent peers. Delinquent gangs often provide a sense of personal worth, a social life, and peer-group acceptance—needs common to all adolescents—as well as protection from some of the evils that can befall people who live in socially disorganized ghetto areas. Rapid population turnover, a lack of family support, and insistent poverty promote a sense of despair. In the words of one 16-year-old boy, "Man, I've been on the outlaw trail most all my life. Can't help it. What else you got for me? . . . The only real world is what I got in my hand. Everything else is makeup" (83, p. 91).

Personality and Delinquency

Why does one child from a particular neighborhood, school, social class, and ethnic background become delinquent, while another, apparently subject to the same general environmental influences, does not? One factor that has been suggested is intelligence, and, indeed, the average delinquent scores somewhat lower on IQ tests than nondelinquents with the same general background (13). Nevertheless, most delinquents are at least of average intelligence, and there is considerable overlap in IQ scores between delinquent and nondelinquent groups. Low intelligence cannot be considered a major factor in most cases of delinquency (17).

More significantly, delinquents have been found more likely than matched groups of nondelinquents to be socially assertive, defiant, ambivalent to authority, resentful, hostile, suspicious and destructive, impulsive, and lacking in self control (17, 18). Many of these traits appear defensive in nature, reflecting poor self-concepts and feelings of inadequacy, emotional rejection, and frustration of the need for self-expression.

Delinquents are more likely than nondelinquents to perceive themselves, consciously or unconsciously, as "lazy," "bad," "sad," and "ignorant." According to their own self-concepts, delinquents are "undesirable people; they tend not to like, value, or respect themselves. In addition, their self-concepts are confused, conflictual, contradictory, uncertain and variable" (27, p. 81).

Delinquent boys   Personality differences between delinquent and nondelinquent boys emerged in the early school years, continuing and, indeed, expanding over the years. The data of one extensive longitudinal study (17, 18) showed that boys who became delinquents were viewed by their teachers as more poorly adjusted than their classmates as early as the third grade. They appeared less considerate and fair in dealing with others, less friendly, less responsible, more impulsive, and more antagonistic to authority. In return, they were less liked and accepted by their peers.

In their schoolwork, the future delinquents were much more easily distracted, daydreamed more, and, in general, had difficulty maintaining attention and sticking to the task at hand until it was completed. They were less likely to display special abilities or interests. Not surprisingly, these social and academic problems seemed to reflect underlying emotional problems. In the opinion of their teachers, future delinquents more often came from a disturbed home environment and were considered overly aggressive.

In the middle school years (grades four–six), inconsistent academic performance among future delinquents became increasingly evident. These boys also demonstrated less leadership ability and had a narrower range of general interests, and they became more and more attention-seeking. Surprisingly, however, resentment and rejection of school authority began to differentiate *less* clearly between delinquents and nondelinquents at this age. This appeared to be due to increases in rebelliousness among the nondelinquent boys, rather than to decreases among the delinquents; "problems with authority are *generally* more common at this age than among school beginners" (17, p. 186).

By the end of the ninth grade, when these boys were entering the period in which delinquent acts are most common, the delinquents manifested differences from their nondelinquent peers in virtually every area of personality functioning and behavior. At this age they showed a much greater antagonism toward authority in comparison with nondelinquent peers than was true in grades four–six. Apparently in the years between middle childhood and adolescence, the attitudes of nondelinquents toward authority improved considerably, while among delinquents the attitudes continued to deteriorate. Other notable differences that, like antagonism toward authority, probably underlie or support the disposition to commit delinquent acts were the delinquents' lack of consideration for the rights of others and their lack of cooperation in observing school regulations.

Peer relations remained significantly poorer among the delinquents in adolescence. The delinquents were less friendly and pleasant toward classmates and, in return, were less well liked and accepted by their peers. Their academic performance continued below average; their work habits were poor; and they

were careless, distractible, and given to daydreaming. Teacher ratings showed them to be less well adjusted generally; they lacked self-confidence and self-respect; they were less cheerful, more attention-seeking. Teachers again were more likely to note (without being asked) a "disturbed home environment" as a factor in the boys' problems.

The teacher impressions of poorer adjustment among the delinquents found support in the self-report personality questionnaires of the boys themselves. They described themselves as less capable of close personal ties with either peers or adults. They had fewer interests in life, and they shared few of the values and goals of American middle-class culture. The delinquents emerged in the testing as more egocentric, childishly demanding, inconsiderate, and "given to petty expressions of pique" (17, p. 188). They appeared more likely than nondelinquents to respond to pressures and demands with hostility, rejection, or withdrawal. They were not happy or proud of this adjustment to life; they acknowledged intense feelings of anxiety, depression, and discouragement, and they knew they took refuge in daydreams more than most of their classmates.

Delinquent girls   Somewhat similar results were obtained for girls, significant differences between future delinquents and nondelinquents becoming evident by the third grade or earlier. Increasingly it became evident that future delinquents were significantly less well adjusted socially, emotionally, and academically than their nondelinquent peers. They were less poised and more unstable emotionally; less likely to be cheerful, happy, or friendly; and less likely to possess a good sense of humor. They had more difficulty in relating to same- and opposite-sex peers. They were less likely to show respect and consideration for the rights of others and, in return, were less well liked and accepted by others.

The delinquent girls also displayed significantly more antagonism toward adult authority and were much less cooperative in observing school regulations. At the same time, they had difficulty learning to think for themselves and developing a clear set of values and realistic goals. They were less creative and displayed fewer special abilities and interests. Their work habits were poor.

Many of these differences are similar to those obtained for boys, but there were some variations in degree and emphasis. For example, the greatest differences between delinquent and nondelinquent girls appeared in the area of emotional adjustment; among boys, the greatest differences occurred in the areas of creative ability, self-reliance, and relations with peers. Delinquent boys showed much less leadership ability than did nondelinquent boys, but this trait was found in essentially equal measure in delinquent and nondelinquent girls. Unhappiness and moodiness differentiated delinquents from nondelinquents much more strongly for girls than for boys. On the self-report personality tests, many more differences of all kinds emerged for boys than for girls. This is consistent with the findings of other studies (40) that delinquent girls are more likely than delinquent boys to be aware of the "socially proper response" in various situations and to indicate these socially desirable responses on personality tests—even though their actual behavior, feelings, and attitudes may be quite different.

Parent–Child Relationships

The single indicator that most accurately predicts adolescent delinquency is the young person's relationship with his or her parents (5). The better an adolescent gets along with parents, the less likely he or she is to become delinquent. With remarkable consistency, investigations indicate that parents of young children who eventually become delinquent use lax, erratic, or overly strict disciplinary techniques; they also use physical punishment rather than reasoning with the child about misconduct (1, 36, 71). Parent–child relationships of delinquents are far more likely than those of nondelinquents to be characterized by mutual hostility, lack of family cohesiveness, and parental rejection or indifference. Parents of delinquents are more likely to have minimal aspirations for their children, to be hostile or indifferent toward school, and to have a variety of personal problems and police records of their own (1, 19).

Fathers of delinquents are more likely than those of nondelinquents to be rated by observers as cruel, neglecting, and inclined to ridicule their children (particularly sons) and less likely to be rated as warm and affectionate (61, 71). In return, the delinquent young, especially sons, are likely to have few close ties to their fathers and to consider them wholly unacceptable as models of conduct (36). Mothers of delinquents are more likely than those of nondelinquents to be rated as careless or inadequate in child supervision and as hostile or indifferent and less likely to be rated as loving (61, 71). Their daughters more frequently than nondelinquents acknowledge hostility toward their mothers and report that their mothers spent less time with them (92).

Broken homes are associated with a higher incidence of delinquent behavior (1). However, the likelihood of adolescent delinquency is far higher in *nonbroken* homes characterized by mutual hostility or indifference than in *broken* homes (usually mother only) characterized by family cohesiveness and mutual affection and support.

Prevention and Treatment of Delinquency

Efforts to treat delinquency have not been encouraging. The traditional approaches involving punishment or imprisonment have generally tended to make matters worse. These approaches subject the young person to psychologically traumatic and embittering experiences, while providing little or no psychological, educational, or vocational aid, and, in addition, "correctional institutions" too often serve as "finishing schools" for future criminal behavior. Other approaches—psychiatric treatment, work–study programs, family therapy, the use

of "street-corner" youth workers, foster-home placement, recreational programs, educational and vocational program, or various combinations of these techniques—have not had consistent or widespread success (14). It should be noted, however, that most of these "new" approaches have been tried on young people with the already serious problems; for the most part, the programs have been too little and too late.

Currently one of the most promising approaches to the treatment of delinquency is placement in small "group" homes in the community. The warm, intimate atmosphere in such homes stands in marked contrast to the cold sterility of the typical training school and permits close individual attention and supervision. In one such home, called Achievement Place, six to eight boys at a time lived with two professional "parents" (4, 67). Interactions were frequent, personal, and warm. If the boys assumed more personal and social responsiblity, they were rewarded with greater privileges. The results were dramatic. Achievement Place boys, compared to similar adolescents on probation or in a "training school," showed markedly lower rates of repeat offenses, higher school attendance, and better grades. The quality of the "parents," however, is a crucial variable; when the program was repeated with colder, less understanding directors, the success rate dropped significantly (67).

Future efforts to reduce delinquency will probably have to emphasize prevention more than treatment. Treatment would appear destined to have only limited success as long as our society does little to change the social conditions that breed delinquency. These include poverty, urban decay, discrimination, the breakdown of an effective sense of community among all classes of citizens, and the increasing paralysis of fundamental social institutions, such as the schools and the government. Without a real commitment to attacking such problems, we are likely to find that the rate of delinquency, already staggering, will rise still higher.

SUMMARY

The sexual drives of younger adolescent boys seem more insistent than the sexual drives of girls; consequently, boys have more problems adjusting to their sexuality and are generally more sexually active. While male hormones may play some role in these sex differences, differing standards for boys and girls are also involved. Standards vary not only for different groups within a culture but also among cultures.

The "new sexual morality" that emerged in the 1960s has endured into the 1970s. Elements of this new morality include greater openness about sex (e.g., more sex education), the notion that sex is mostly a private matter, and an emphasis on the nature of the relationship, rather than on the sexual behavior per se. Relatively conservative groups include younger adolescents (compared to older adolescents), girls (compared to boys), college youth (compared to blue-collar youth), and students in the Midwest and the South (compared to students on the coasts); often differences between groups of young people exceed those between young people in general and adults. Parents, as a rule, are more conservative in sexual attitudes than their adolescent children, but these differences do not seem to cause many problems.

Sexual activity has generally increased among young people in the last decade or two. Notable increases have been in masturbation among girls (always high among boys) and sexual intercourse among girls and among college students. Every year, over 1 million teenaged girls become pregnant, many of them because of ignorance about female biology and contraception.

A significant minority of young people are disillusioned with and alienated from American society; they reject many traditional values and practices. Some alienated youth respond by actively trying to change society, through either reform or revolution. Studies of activists in the 1960s showed them to be more independent, assertive, and sociable than nonactivists, but views of the activist as a brilliant and compassionate reformer or as a troubled child rejecting authority were both exaggerated. Many of today's college students remain disenchanted with societal values and practices, but they appear less likely to exhibit radical behavior. Perhaps the absence of a common cause like the war in Vietnam, the spread of disillusionment to other segments of the population, including adults, and distaste for violence can account for some of the reduction in active protests.

Some alienated youth respond by dropping out of the "competitive, materialistic rat race." In the 1960s the dropouts were called "hippies." The hippie values included love, honesty, and personal freedom; social and sexual "inhibitions" were deplored; the intellect was suspect, while sensations (often amplified by drugs) were glorified. Lack of money and drug abuse were significant problems. Studies of hippies found them to be intelligent but low in frustration tolerance and lacking in critical judgment. Their childhood experiences were characteristically chaotic and disorganized.

Activists of the 1960s are generally still active today, but their attempts to reform are more traditional: involvement in politics, education, and cause-oriented organizations. Hippies of the 1960s, generally speaking, are also more moderate, at least in their behavior, but they continue to avoid stressful jobs and to reject "establishment" values.

Another development of the 1960s was the surge in the use of marijuana, LSD, and other "mind-altering" drugs among youth. The reaction of parents and other adults to such drug use was often irrational and extreme. The dangers of continuing increase in the use of alcohol among adolescents, however, have probably been underestimated. About 90 percent of high-school seniors have had at least a few drinks, and between 5 and 10 percent drink almost every day. Marijuana, typically, is tried because of curiosity; those adolescents who continue to use it do so because "it's fun." Over 60 percent of college youth have tried marijuana. The use of other drugs such as LSD and heroin is nowhere near as widespread; in fact, current adolescent attitudes toward these "other drugs" are generally negative.

Why do adolescents use drugs? Although the vast majority of those who use drugs do so "recreationally, " chronic heavy users often have personality disturbances. Social characteristics of drug abusers include an unhappy home environment and friends who encourage and support drug use.

Juvenile delinquency is also increasing in this country. Rates for girls are increasing more rapidly than for boys, shrinking the usual sex differences. Although delinquency is highest in urban ghettos, it has become common in middle-class suburbs, too; middle-class children are less likely to be caught and less likely to be formally charged, compared to lower-class children, and thus police records tend to exaggerate social class differences. Children who eventually become delinquent are notably different from their peers as early as the third grade. The future delinquents perform poorly in school (although they are usually of at least average intelligence); appear inconsiderate, unfriendly, and impulsive; and are generally antagonistic to authority. Delinquent girls, compared to nondelinquents, are notably poor in emotional adjustment, while delinquent boys, compared to their nondelinquent peers, lack self-reliance and leadership ability.

The parents of delinquents are often hostile or indifferent to their children, using inconsistent and harsh disciplinary techniques. Such a home often "breaks up," but a broken home characterized by affection and family cohesiveness is not likely to produce delinquent children. Treatment of delinquents in similarly warm and cohesive "group homes," which provide opportunities for responsible behavior and rewards for achievement, has shown promise, but the roots of crime lie in social problems such as poverty and the breakdown in an effective sense of community.

References

1. Ahlstrom, W. M., & Havighurst, R. J. **400 losers.** San Francisco: Jossey-Bass, 1971.

2. Alan Guttmacher Institute. **11 million teenagers.** New York: Planned Parenthood, 1976.

3. **Alcohol and health: new knowledge.** Second special report to the U.S. Congress, National Institute on Alcohol Abuse and Alcoholism, Department of Health, Education, and Welfare. Washington, D.C.: Superintendent of Documents, U.S. Printing Office, No. 1724-00399, June 1974 (preprint edition).

4. Allen, J. D., Phillips, E. L., Phillips, E. A., Fixsen, D. L., & Wolf, M. M. **Achievement place: a novel.** Research Press (in press).

5. Backman, J. G. Youth in transition, vol. II: the impact of family background and intelligence on tenth-grade boys. Ann Arbor: Institute for Social Research, University of Michigan, 1970.

6. Balswick, J. D., & Macrides, C. Parental stimulus for adolescent rebellion. **Adolescence,** 1975, **38,** 253–259.

7. Bell, R. R. Parent–child conflict in sexual values. **Journal of Social Issues,** 1966, **22,** 34–44.

8. Blum, R. H., et al. **Horatio Alger's children.** San Francisco: Jossey-Bass, 1972.

9. Brecher, E. M. **The sex researchers.** New York: New American Library, 1971.

10. Bromberg, W. Marihuana intoxication. **American Journal of Psychiatry,** 1934, **91,** 303–330.

11. Brown, J. D. (Ed.), **The hippies.** New York: Time–Life Books, 1967.

12. Calef, V., Gryler, R., Hilles, R., Kempner, P., Pittel, S. M., & Wallerstein, R. S. Impairments of ego function is psychedelic drug users. Paper presented at the Conference on Drug Use and Drug Subcultures, Asilomar, Pacific Grove, Calif., February 11–15, 1970.

13. Caplan, N. S., & Siebert, L. A. Distribution of juvenile delinquent intelligence test scores over a thirty-four year period (N = 51,808). **Journal of Clinical Psychology,** 1964, **20,** 242–247.

14. Conger, J. J. **Adolescence and youth: psychological development in a changing world.** New York: Harper & Row, 1977.

15. Conger, J. J. Parent–child relationships, social change, and adolescent vulnerability. Paper presented at the eighth international conference of the International Association for Child Psychiatry and Allied Professions, Philadelphia, July 28, 1974.

16. Conger, J. J. Sexual attitudes and behavior of contemporary adolescents. In J. J. Conger (Ed.), **Contemporary issues in adolescent development.** New York: Harper & Row, 1975. Pp. 221–230.

17. Conger, J. J., & Miller, W. C. **Personality, social class, and delinquency.** New York: Wiley, 1966.

18. Conger, J. J., Miller, W. C., & Walsmith, C. R. Antecedents of delinquency, personality, social class and intelligence. In P. H. Mussen, J. J. Conger, & J. Kagan (Eds.), **Readings in child development and personality.** New York: Harper & Row, 1965.

19. Cressey, D. R., & Ward, D. A. **Delinquency, crime, and social process.** New York: Harper & Row, 1969.

20. Dempsey, D. Bruno Bettelheim is Dr. No. **The New York Times Magazine,** January 11, 1970, 22ff.

21. Douvan, E. A., & Adelson, J. **The adolescent experience.** New York: Wiley, 1966.

22. Ehrhardt, A. A. Maternalism in fetal hormonal and related symptoms. In J. Zubin and J. Money (Eds.), **Contemporary sexual behavior: critical issue in the 1970s.** Baltimore: Johns Hopkins University Press, 1973. Pp. 99–116.

23. Federal Bureau of Investigation, U.S. Department of Justice. **Uniform crime reports, 1960–1972.** Washington, D.C.: U.S. Government Printing Office.

24. Fendrich, J. M. Activists ten years later: a test of generational unit continuity. **Journal of Social Issues,** 1974, **30,** 95–118.

25. Fendrich, J. M., & Tarleau, A. T. Marching to a different drummer: occupational and political correlates of former political activists. **Social Forces,** 1973, **52,** 245–253.

26. Feuer, L. S. **The conflict of generations.** New York: Basic Books, 1969.

27. Fixsen, D. L., Montrose, M. W., & Phillips, E. L. Achievement Place experiment in self-government with pre-delinquents.

28. Fleck, S. Pregnancy as a symptom of adolescent maladjustment. **International Journal of Social Psychiatry,** 1956, **2,** 118–131.

29. Ford, C. S., & Beach, F. A. **Patterns of sexual behavior.** New York: Harper-Hoeber, 1951.

30. Freud, S. **Civilization and its discontents.** London: Hogarth, 1961.

31. Galbraith, J. K. **The new industrial state.** Boston: Houghton Mifflin, 1967.

32. Gallenkamp, C. R., & Rychiak, J. F. Parental attitudes of sanction in middle-class male adolescents. **Journal of Social Psychology,** 1968, **75,** 255–260.

33. Gallup, G. H., Jr., & Davis, J. O., III. Gallup poll, **Denver Post,** May 26, 1969.

34. Gallup, G. H., Jr., & Davis, J. O., III. Gallup poll. **San Francisco Chronicle,** May 16, 1977.

35. Gallup, G. H., Jr., & Davis, J. O., III. New breed of students. **American Institute of Public Opinion,** May 26, 1969.

36. Gold, M. **Delinquent behavior in an American city.** Monterey, Calif.: Brooks/Cole, 1970.

37. Gold, M. Undetected delinquent behavior. **Journal of Research on Crime and Delinquency,** 1966, **3,** 27–46.

38. Grossman, J. C., Goldstein, R., & Eisenman, R. Openness to experience and marijuana use: an initial investigation. **Proceedings of the 79th Annual Convention of the American Psychological Association,** 1971, **6,** 335–336 (summary).

39. Harris, L., & Associates, Inc. Public awareness of the National Institute on Alcohol Abuse and Alcoholism advertising campaign and public attitudes toward drinking and alcohol abuse. Phase One: Fall 1972, Study No. 2224; Phase Two: Spring 1973, Study No. 2318; Phase Three: Fall 1973, Study No. 2342; Phase Four: Winter 1974 and Overall Summary, Study No. 2355. Reports prepared for the National Institute on Alcohol Abuse and Alcoholism.

40. Hauser, S. T. **Black and white identity formation: studies in the psychosocial development of lower socioeconomic class adolescent boys.** New York: Wiley, 1971.

41. Horney, K. **Neurosis and human growth.** New York: Norton, 1950.

42. Hunt, M. **Sexual behavior in the 1970s.** Chicago: Playboy Press, 1974.

43. Hunt, M. Special sex education survey. **Seventeen,** July 1970, 94ff.

44. Johnson, A. M. Juvenile delinquency. In S. Arieti (Ed.), **American handbook of psychiatry.** New York: Basic Books, 1959. Pp. 840–856.

45. Johnson, A. M. Sanctions of superego lacunae of adolescents. In K. R. Eissler (Ed.), **Searchlights on delinquency.** New York: International Universities Press, 1949. Pp. 79–108.

46. Johnston, L., & Bachman, J. **Monitoring the future: a continuing study of the life styles and values of youth.** Ann Arbor: Institute for Social Research, 1975.

47. **Juvenile Court Statistics 1970. 30,** 107–135.

49. Kandel, D. The role of parents and peers in adolescent marijuana use. **Science,** 1973, **181,** 1067–1070.

50. Kantner, J. F., & Zelnik, M. Contraception and pregnancy: experience of young unmarried women in the United States. **Family Planning Perspectives,** 1973, **5,** 21–35.

51. Kanter, J. F., & Zelnik, M. Sexual experience of young unmarried women in the United States. **Family Planning Perspectives,** 1974, **4,** 9–18.

52. Keniston, K. The sources of student dissent. **Journal of Social Issues,** 1967, **22,** 108 –137.

53. Keniston, K. **Young radicals: notes on committed youth.** New York: Harcourt Brace Jovanovich, 1968.

54. Kerpelman, L. C. Student activism and ideology in higher education institutions. Unpublished manuscript, Department of Psychology, University of Massachusetts, 1971.

55. Kessner, D. S., et al. **Infant death: an analysis by maternal risk and health care.** Washington, D.C.: Institute of Medicine, National Academy of Sciences, 1973.

56. Kinsey, A. C., Pomeroy, W. B., & Martin, C. E. **Sexual behavior in the human male.** Philadelphia: Saunders, 1948.

57. Kinsey, A. C., Pomeroy, W. B., Martin, C. E., & Gebhard, P. H. **Sexual behavior in the human female.** Philadelphia: Saunders, 1953.

58. Luckey, E., & Nass, G. A. A comparison of sexual attitudes and behavior in an international sample. **Journal of Marriage and the Family,** 1969, **31,** 364–379.

59. **Marihuana and health.** Third annual report to Congress from the Secretary of Health, Education, and Welfare. Washington, D.C.: U.S. Government Printing Office, 1974.

60. Masters, W. H., & Johnson, V. E. **Human sexual inadequacy.** Boston: Little Brown, 1970.

61. McCord, W., McCord, J., & Zola, I. K. **Origins of crime.** New York: Columbia University Press, 1959.

62. Miller, J., & Baumohl, J. **Down and out in Berkeley: an overview of a study of street people.** Berkeley: University of California School of Social Welfare, 1974.

63. Mirin, S., Shapiro, L., Meyer, R., Pillard, R., & Fisher, S. Casual versus heavy use of marijuana: a redefinition of the marijuana problem. **American Journal of Psychiatry,** 1971, **127,** 54–60.

64. Mizner, G. L., Barter, J. T., & Werme, P. H. Patterns of drug use among college students. **American Journal of Psychiatry,** 1970, **127,** 15–24.

65. Packard, V. and the sexual behavior reported by 2100 young adults. In V. Packard,

The sexual wilderness: the contemporary upheaval in male–female relationships. New York: Pocket Books, 1970. Pp. 166–184.

66. Packard, V. **The sexual wilderness: the contemporary upheaval in male–female relationships.** New York: Pocket Books, 1970.

67. Phillips, E. L., Phillips, E. A., Fixsen, D. L., & Wolf, M. M. Achievement Place: behavior shaping works for delinquents. **Psychology Today,** 1973, **7,** 75–79.

68. Pittel, S. M. **The etiology of youthful drug involvement.** Berkeley: Berkeley Center for Drug Studies, The Wright Institute (unpublished monograph).

69. Pittel, S. M., Calef, V., Gryler, R. B., Hilles, L., Hofer, R., & Kempner, P. Developmental factors in adolescent drug use: a study of psychedelic drug users. **Journal of the American Academy of Child Psychiatry,** 1971, **10,** 640–660.

70. Pittel, S. M., & Miller, H. **Dropping down: the hippie then and now.** Berkeley: Haight Ashbury Research Project, The Wright Institute, 1976 (tentative title, manuscript in preparation).

71. Powers, E., & Witmer, H. **Prevention of delinquency: the Cambridge–Somerville youth study.** New York: Columbia University Press, 1951.

72. Press release, National Institute on Drug Abuse (NIDA), October 1, 1975.

73. Reiss, I. L. How and why America's sex standards are changing. In W. Simon & J. H. Gagnon (Eds.), **The sexual scene.** Chicago: Trans-action Books, 1970. Pp. 43–57.

74. Response Analysis Corporation. Survey on drug use, prepared for the National Commission on Marijuana and Drug Abuse. Washington, D.C., May 1972.

75. Robinson, L. Marijuana use in high school girls: a psycho-social case study. **Dissertation Abstracts International,** 1970, **31**(5-A), 2196.

76. Rossi, A. S. Maternalism, sexuality, and the new feminism. In J. Zubin & J. Money (Eds.), **Contemporary sexual behavior: critical issues in the 1970s.** Baltimore: Johns Hopkins University Press, 1973. Pp. 145–174.

77. Roszak, T. **The making of a counter culture: reflections on the technocratic society and its youthful opposition.** Garden City, N.Y.: Doubleday, 1968.

78. Sampson, E. E., & Korn, H. A. (Eds.). **Student activism and dissent: alternatives for social change.** San Francisco: Jossey-Bass, 1970.

79. Shafer, R. P., et al. **Drug use in America: problem in perspective.** Second report of the National Commission on Marijuana and Drug Abuse. Washington, D.C.: U.S. Government Printing Office, No. 5266-00003, 1973.

80. Shafer, R. P., et al. **Marijuana: a signal of misunderstanding. The official report of the National Commission on Marijuana and Drug Abuse.** New York: New American Library, 1972.

81. Somers, R. H. The mainsprings of the rebellion: a survey of Berkeley students in November, 1964. In S. M. Lipset, & S. S. Wolin (Eds.), **The Berkeley student revolt.** Garden City, N.Y.: Doubleday, 1965. Pp. 530–537.

82. Sorensen, R. C. **Adolescent sexuality in contemporary America: personal values and sexual behavior ages 13–19.** New York: Harry N. Abrams, Inc., 1973.

83. Stevens, S. The "rat packs" of New York. **The New York Times,** November 28, 1971, 29ff.

84. Stubbs, V. M. Environmental stress in the development of young drug users. Paper presented at the annual meeting of the California State Psychological Association, Coronado, Calif., January 31, 1971.

85. The American almanac: the statistical abstract of the United States (Bureau of the

Census, U.S. Department of Commerce). New York: Grosset and Dunlap, 1975 (95th ed.).

86. The report of the Commission on Obscenity and Pornography. New York: Bantam Books, 1970.

87. The world almanac and book of facts, 1975. New York: Newspaper Enterprise Association, 1975.

88. The youth crime plague. **Time,** July 11, 1977, p. 19.

89. Trent, J. W., & Craise, J. L. Commitment and conformity in the American college. **Journal of Social Issues,** 1967, **22,** 34–51.

90. Victor, H. R., Grossman, J. C., & Eisenman, R. Openness to experience and marijuana use in high school students. **Journal of Consulting and Clinical Psychology,** 1973, **41,** 78–85.

91. Wallach, A. Varying fates of young drug users. Paper presented at the annual meeting of the California State Psychological Association, Coronado, Calif., January 31, 1971.

92. Wattenberg, W. W. **The adolescent years.** New York: Harcourt Brace Jovanovich, 1955.

93. Watts, W. A., & Whittaker, D. N. Some socio-psychological differences between highly committed members of the Free Speech Movement and the student population at Berkeley. **Journal of Applied Behavioral Science,** 1966, **2,** 41–62.

94. Yankelovich, D. **Generations apart: a study of the generation gap.** New York: CBS News, 1969.

95. Yankelovich, D. **The new morality: a profile of American youth in the 1970s.** New York: McGraw-Hill, 1974.

96. Yankelovich, D., & the editors of **Fortune. Youth in turmoil.** New York: Time–Life Books, 1969.

97. Zinberg, N., & Weil, A. A comparison of marijuana users and nonusers. **Nature,** 1970, **226,** 119–123.

CHAPTER 10
Young Adults

When does a child become an adult? No one answer fits all cultures, all contexts, all individuals. In some cultures, young people barely into their teens achieve the full rights and privileges—and the responsibilities—of adulthood. In our society, the age of 18 has some legal status—an 18-year-old can vote, for example—and it marks the beginning of young adulthood in a number of other ways, too. At 18, most young people graduate from high school, and some choose jobs then. Others go off to college or take additional vocational training (sometimes in the armed services); specific job decisions may be delayed, but choices made then—about courses of study and training—directly affect the later occupational decisions. Decisions about marriage and children are also made by most people in the first five–ten years after graduation, if they have not been made already. Young adulthood is a time for "getting started in life."

Choosing a mate, getting a job, having children—settling down. These are the topics of this chapter on young adulthood; they are the topics that define adult status. In this regard it is worth quoting Sigmund Freud's famous answer to the question of what a "normal" adult should be able to do well: "Lieben und arbeiten." In English, "to love and to work." To be able to love and to be able to work without unnecessary anxiety and without despair—these are the primary goals of life.

Partly because of the important decisions made about marriage and career, the personality of the typical young adult stabilizes and matures. In the first section of this chapter, we will explore a few of the ways in which personality changes and grows in the 20s and early 30s. Then we will discuss marriage: choosing a mate and choosing a style. Children usually follow marriage; so we will examine next some of the joys *and* problems of adjustment that an enlarged family brings. Finally we will turn to the topic of careers, where the focus will be on the early stage: vocational choice.

PERSONALITY DEVELOPMENT IN YOUNG ADULTHOOD

The period of young adulthood is an exciting, interesting, and for most people a relatively happy time of life. It was the time most frequently chosen by a national sample of Americans as "the best years of a person's life." It is seen as a time "to develop ambitions and to set goals" (30). During this period an individual's life undergoes rapid and significant changes, and he or she has more independence, more responsibility, more status. At the same time, young adults are in a position to make some serious mistakes—choosing the wrong mate, starting a bad career—and this adds an element of danger and apprehension.

How do all these changes affect the individual's personality? Of course, the events that occur in the life of one individual may not occur in the life of another, and two people will differ in their response to the same event. But there is a similarity in the lives of most young adults. They become adults both legally and socially, and they encounter at least the possibility of a marriage and a career. These *normative life crises*—changes that occur in the lives of most people

(19)—allow us to examine a general course of personality development during the early years of adulthood.

Personal Growth

As young adults break away from their parents and assume more responsibility, often beginning careers and families of their own, most of them change in rather predictable ways. Psychologist Robert White has described these personality changes in terms of five major "growth trends," which were formulated largely from his own intensive study of the lives of "normal" college students (76).

The stabilizing of ego identity

As we have seen, the problem of determining one's personal *identity*—"who I am" as a unique individual—became especially acute at adolescence (pp. 281–288). Although many young adults are still having difficulty establishing themselves, there is a general trend toward stabilization of identity. A more stable identity is "not only more sharp and clear but also more consistent and free from transient influences" (76, p. 336). Young adults are more sure of themselves, partly because they have made many of the major decisions about marriage and career that help define adult identities. They know more about how they are likely to act in a given situation. White points out:

> To be called a coward by a kindergarten playmate may be an extremely upsetting experience; one is not sure to what extent the epithet may be deserved. To be called a coward at the age of thirty is quite another matter. . . . at thirty a person pretty much knows whether or not he is a coward; he can make a self-judgment on the basis of his accumulated experience, and he knows this judgment is sounder than the one arriving from the outside (76, p. 336).

Young adults become progressively less affected by a single success or failure; they know their abilities better than they did when younger. Even praise is sometimes rejected as unsuitable.

College students usually become more stable in their identities over their college years. In one sample, only 11 percent had "achieved identity" by the end of their freshman year, but 45 percent had done so by the end of their senior year (73). Unhappily, however, about one-third of the seniors still had little or no commitment to personal goals and beliefs and did not appear to be actively seeking alternatives in order to make choices; this state was termed "identity diffusion."

College students who have given a lot of thought to their personal commitments and achieved identity tend to be relatively independent of family influences (14) and high in self-esteem (44); they seem to be able to express affection easily (20). Young women who have achieved identity tend to be notably resistant to conformity pressures, especially when compared to women still in a state of identity diffusion (67).

The freeing of personal relationships As ego identity stabilizes, it becomes possible for the individual to relate to others as independent human beings with their own needs, desires, abilities, and foibles. Earlier interactions are characterized by anxiety—Will this person like me?—and defensiveness, a reluctance to be oneself, partly because the person is not sure what his or her self really is. The young adult is not so eager to get his or her point across; he or she is willing to listen to (is even interested in) other people's opinions. Interpersonal interactions "become more friendly, warm, and respectful. There may even be greater room for assertiveness and criticism" (76, p. 345).

Psychologist Carl Rogers has noted that healthy interpersonal relationships are marked by *unconditional positive regard* of each participant in the relationship for the other (71). Unconditional positive regard means that the other person is always highly valued, even if he or she does something embarrassing or malicious; the acts themselves can be criticized or condemned, but the positive regard for the person is not conditional on "proper" behavior. A second feature of a healthy relationship is *empathy*, the accurate perception of what the other person is thinking and feeling.

The deepening of interests Young children and adolescents often take a sudden interest in something, indulge that interest briefly until their curiosity is satisfied or some external reward is obtained, and then rapidly lose all interest. Young adults become more involved in their interests and spend more time and energy and money on them; some become vocations and others become avocations (see Figure 10.1). They more often do things "for their own sake." Joggers may begin jogging to lose weight or to run with friends but develop an intense interest in what they may call "the sheer beauty of running," selecting their routes with the same care a gourmet cook might use in selecting a menu.

The humanizing of values Moral development (see pp. 259–262 and 309–311) does not cease at adolescence. The further growth in ethical concerns that White has observed in young adults is called a *"humanizing"* of values. Two aspects of moral development that characterize this period are: "(1) the person increasingly discovers the human meaning of values and their relation to the achievement of social purposes, and (2) he increasingly brings to bear his own experience and his own motives in affirming and promoting a value system" (76, p. 355). White gives the example of a physician who has opposed "socialized medicine" throughout his life, but for different reasons at different times. In his earlier years, he was opposed "because the midwestern Republicans amongst whom he had grown up were generally opposed to socialization." Later his reasons were more personal—he had personally experienced the benefits of a system of individual freedom—and more social—he believed that patients would suffer under state-controlled medicine.

White's notions of humanized values correspond roughly to Kohlberg's notion of a "postconventional" or "principled" level of moral development. In Kohlberg's theory (36), as we have seen (see pp. 260–261), there are three levels

●Figure 10.1　Young adults become more involved in their personal interests.

of moral development—preconventional, found primarily in children; conventional, which includes a "law-and-order" stage of thinking that many people never progress beyond; and postconventional, which includes at least two stages. Stage 5, the *social-contract, legalistic orientation,* has been described as the official morality of the U.S. government. What is right is that which the majority of citizens agree on and set into law. If any aspect of this morality is later shown to be ill-advised, the social contract among citizens can be revised; the laws can be changed. Stage 5 reasoning has been found to increase dramatically in the college years (37, 65). In fact, after reanalysis of data that had shown some stage 5 reasoning in adolescents, Kohlberg concluded that no person under the age of 23 "displayed true stage 5 thought" (35, p. 192).

Similarly, stage 6 morality was identified as a development of adulthood. In stage 6, the *universal-ethical-principle orientation,* morality is based on abstract ethical principles defined by logic—for example, the golden rule (see Figure 10.2). Suppose a person is presented with a moral problem: A man needs a drug to save his wife's life but cannot afford it. Should he steal it? The person at stage 6 might answer, "Yes, because life is involved"; or the answer might be "No" for some equally principled reason. But the answer would *not* describe the man in the problem as acting because the dying patient is his wife. Personal (selfish) considerations are not important, only impersonal values, objectively defined. In Kohlberg's view, very few people ever reach stage 6 of moral development; but if they do, they do so in the adult years.

What are the events of adulthood that lead to principled morality? From limited evidence, Kohlberg has tentatively suggested two sorts of important personal experiences. The first is "the experience of leaving home and entering a college community with conflicting values in the context of moratorium, identity questioning, and the need for commitment" (35, p. 195). The term "moratorium" is used in the sense of a delay in making major life decisions, such as choosing a job. College affords the student a few years to explore values and to learn about himself or herself before facing the obligations of everyday life. The importance of this experience is suggested by the fact that *none* of the participants in Kohlberg's study who did not attend college—who went directly into an adult occupation—developed postconventional morality.

The second personal experience important for movement to principled thought is "explicit cognitive-moral stimulation." In other words, the person must have not only the time and the supportive environment to consider moral principles but also the stimulus to do so. A college "moral discussion program" is apparently effective stimulation for many students (8), leading 40 percent of

●Figure 10.2　In the late 1960s and early 1970s a number of young people went to jail because of their ethical principles.

the "conventional" participants to stage 5. For others, Kohlberg (35) suggests, the student-moratorium experience is ineffective until later in life, when the person experiences "sustained responsibility for the welfare of others and the experience of irreversible moral choice"—the kind of experiences one has when supervising people in an important job or when making important family decisions.

The expansion of caring   The humanization of values is correlated with the expansion of caring, that is, "increased caring for the welfare of other persons and human concerns" (76, p. 359). Increased interest in and concern for other people is one of the clearest indications of maturity, one noted by almost every personality theorist who has dealt extensively with development in the adult years. Alfred Adler (1) talked of increased "social interest," while Andras Angyal (2) wrote of "homonomy," a tendency to increase harmony and joint action with other individuals in a group; Abraham Maslow (45) spoke of "belongingness and love needs," while Carl Rogers (54) emphasized empathy and unconditional positive regard. As we shall see, the increase in the concern for others is apparent in differences in scores on vocational interest tests taken between high school and college. It is also apparent in the young adult's increased interest in civil rights, social welfare, and proselytizing religions.

Later Stages in Young Adulthood

If one becomes an adult by age 20, what does one become at age 30? Many people feel they pass a new threshold at 30.

> Men and women alike speak of feeling too narrow and restricted. They blame all sorts of things, but what the restrictions boil down to are the outgrowth of career and personal choices of the twenties. They may have been choices perfectly suited to that stage. But now the fit feels different. Some inner aspect that was left out is striving to be taken into account. Important new choices must be made, and commitments altered or deepened. The work involves great change, turmoil, and often crisis—a simultaneous feeling of rock bottom and the urge to bust out (58, p. 28).

Another investigator reports a similar feeling of transition in his study participants aged 29–34: Their earlier feelings of self-confidence began to waver. They began to question "what they were doing and why they were doing it. As they became more self-reflective, this group found deeper strivings that had been put aside during their 20s when building a workable life structure had been the most important task" (27, p. 74).

If the 20s is the time to make important decisions about marriage, parenthood, and career, the age-30 transition period (roughly 28–32) is the time for evaluation. Have I made the right choices? Did I choose the right career? (This may be my last chance for a meaningful change in my career!) Did I choose the right mate for me? Are we growing in different directions? (This may be my last chance for a meaningful change in my marriage!) These can be questions with a desperate, anxious quality, reflecting a great deal of inner turmoil. This turmoil can lead to unwise, hasty decisions to quit one's job or to file for divorce, and it can lead to psychological problems, such as alcoholism, neurosis, and impulsive extramarital affairs, that stem from attempts to reduce the anxiety without dealing with the basic problem.

Many of the normal growth trends described earlier relate to the age-30 transition crisis faced by many people. The stabilization of ego-identity and the deepening of interests, for example, may put the person in a position at age 30 to make far better career decisions than he or she could at age 20. Nevertheless, because these decisions had to be made earlier, age 30 may become a time of "agonizing reappraisal"; 30-year-olds are often dismayed by the shallow, "childish" reasons they used at age 20 to make critical choices in life. Similarly, a deepening sense of identity, a better defined set of personal interests, and more open and honest interpersonal relationships may allow an individual at age 30 to make a significantly better choice of a marital partner than the person could have made at age 20. Again, however, by age 30 the choice usually has already been made, and the decisions at age 30 are most likely to involve minor or major changes in an already existing relationship. Often, of course, no changes are made and, instead, there is a deeper commitment to original choices of both job and spouse.

MARRIAGE

Erik Erikson's pioneering efforts to describe the important stages of adult development portray young adulthood as a period in which the individual is faced with the dilemma of *intimacy versus isolation* (22). Intimate alliances may involve deep friendships, but the need for intimacy is most clearly expressed in the young adult's sexual relationships. "Strictly speaking, it is only now that *true genitality* can fully develop; for much of the sex life preceding these commitments is of the identity-searching kind, or is dominated by phallic or vaginal strivings which make of sex-life a kind of genital combat" (22, p. 264). That is, before a personal identity is established, sex is selfish; the individual cannot really allow himself or herself to make the sacrifices and compromises necessary for mature, mutual sexuality.

In "true genitality," according to Erikson, sexual energy is expressed without fear or guilt in an affectionate and sensual union between two people. While a truly satisfying sexual relationship is a prime characteristic of this highest form of intimacy, mutual trust is also required. An intimate alliance is formed "with a loved partner . . . with whom one is able and willing to regulate the cycles of work, procreation, and recreation" (22, p. 266). Thus, the characteristics of genital sexuality could as well be listed as the goals of an ideal marriage. In another perspective, they could be aspects of a definition of "love" (23).

The danger of this period of development, in Erikson's view, is isolation.

Intimacy involves risk and vulnerability, and some people are unwilling to take the chance of rejection or loss. They may still be struggling for identity or they may be incapable of a mature relationship because of previous, unresolved conflicts. Extremely narcissistic people, for example, cannot love another person nearly as much as they love themselves. Whatever the reason, isolated people face the rest of their lives alone, without love or even true friendship.

In young adulthood, the issue of intimacy or isolation is usually phrased in terms of the individual's questions about marriage. Is it time for me to get married and settle down? Whom should I marry? What does marriage mean to me? Can we make our marriage work? Some young adults of today claim they plan never to be married, but if the recent past is any indication, about 96 or 97 percent of them will marry eventually (13). Half of all men who marry are married by the age of 23, and the median age for women is 21. Almost everyone who does marry does so before the age of 35 (counting only first marriages). So the problems of marriage—choosing a mate and defining a style of intimacy both partners can live with—are among the major developmental tasks of the early years of adulthood.

Choosing a Mate

The notion that the potential bride or groom should have any say in the choice of a mate is a relatively recent development in human history, and one that even today many cultures view with alarm. How can one so young make such an important decision? Love, supposedly the basis for Western marriages, is viewed by many Eastern cultures as a threat to marriage; it causes the young people to act impulsively without consideration of the important social, religious, and economic factors in marriage. Love is fine, but it should come *after* marriage, not before (42).

In our society, the young person usually has the major say in the choice of a mate, although parents and friends can sometimes "make life difficult" if they disagree with his or her choice. What determines the choice of mate? A variety of factors have been suggested. The person will tend to choose someone with similar interests, for example, or someone with a similar background. Listing social characteristics and personality traits people prefer in a potential mate does not do justice to the complex interactions that develop and change over time as a couple moves through the various stages of courtship and mate selection. A factor that may be important in early dating—physical attractiveness, for example—may be less important in the final stages, when one is deciding whether or not to share a lifetime with another human being.

A number of recent theories (34, 40, 46, 69) have tried to describe the stages of mate selection in terms of the important decisions and developments that occur as the couple progresses toward greater intimacy and, presumably, marriage. Most of these theories view courtship as a continuing "filtering" process in which the individual progressively narrows his or her choice among all possible mates. One such filter theory includes most of the factors that have been shown to influence mate selection (69); while one may disagree with the sequence of decisions, this theory will help us organize the research on the major determinants of the choice of a spouse.

As shown in Figure 10.3, the initial screening of prospective mates occurs through a "propinquity filter." "Propinquity" means "closeness in space" and refers to the fact that people who marry are very likely to have been raised in families that lived relatively close together (69). More than half of the marriages surveyed in Columbus, Ohio, were of couples who lived within 16 blocks of one another when they first dated (15). One researcher (69) discovered that the likelihood of marriage decreases with the square of the distance, just as the physical attraction of a magnet does!

One of the main reasons propinquity is related to mate selection is simply that one is more likely to meet people who live close by—you can hardly marry someone you have never met. Having met, people who live closer together interact more frequently than those who live farther apart, and frequent interactions make friendship and love possible. Maintaining a relationship over great distances requires time, money, and energy. "Shrewd parents have known and used this principle for a long time to break up 'unfortunate' love interests of their children by moving away or encouraging their son or daughter to attend a college remote from home, perhaps 'to test the endurance of the relationship' " (70, p. 157).

Another filter in the process of mate selection is based on attractiveness. Just what is considered attractive often varies considerably from person to person and from culture to culture. The Hindu holy man, Manu, wrote: "The desirable woman to marry walks like an elephant." Westerners would probably place other qualities higher on the list of ideal characteristics, even when we understand that it is an unhurried and self-confident gait that many Indians admire (42). Also to be avoided in a woman, according to Hindu writings, are thick hair on the body, red hair, immoderate talking, and a family history of female offspring. The ideal man has a strong collarbone and a fine head of hair; his voice is full of vigor. These old, traditional prescriptions sometimes mix ancient superstitions with common sense, but they illustrate the fact that all cultures—and nearly all individuals—have definite ideas about the characteristics of an ideal mate.

In American society, the characteristics that determine attractiveness include height, weight, age, and the physical features we call beautiful (handsome) or ugly. Consider, for example, the factor of age. In the United States, the groom is expected to be slightly older than the bride, and in three out of four marriages, he is; the median age difference is generally between two and three years (13).

The relative age of the potential mate "is one of the most powerful screening devices in the process of marital selection" (13, p. 90), but only if certain limits are exceeded. The potential husband can be up to ten years older or three years younger without much problem. If he is much older or younger than this,

●Figure 10.3   A filter theory of mate selection. (Adapted from J. R. Udry. *The Social Context of Marriage.* 2d ed. Philadelphia: Lippincott, 1971.)

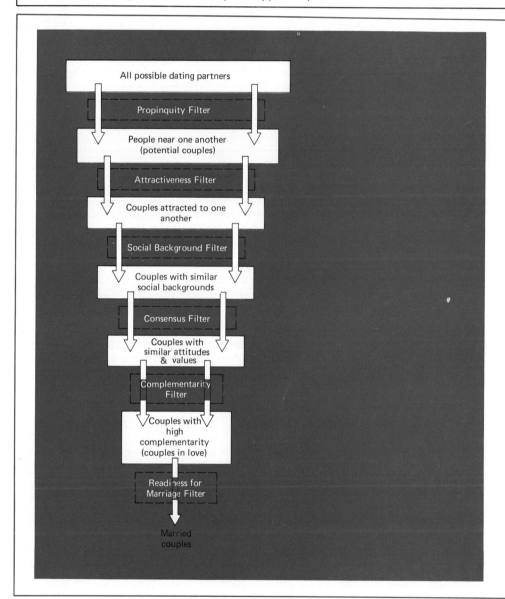

parents might become upset with the prospective match. More directly, many young men do not consider women who are more than three years older or ten years younger to be "eligible" mates, and many women similarly define age boundaries for potential husbands. Women whose marriages exceed these socially defined age limits rate their marriages as less satisfactory than those whose husbands are within the "proper" age range (5).

The basis of the social custom of older men marrying younger women includes the notion that the man is the head of the family and must establish himself as a responsible "breadwinner" before marriage. With more and more women developing careers of their own, we may expect to find this social custom waning. There are, in fact, good reasons encouraging marriages in which the wife is older. For example, if this were the case, the wife would not have to look forward to years alone, as a widow; now, typically, her older husband dies many years before she does.

Social factors in mate selection   The third filter in Figure 10.3 screens potential mates on the basis of social background. Marriage partners are typically similar in religion, race, political affiliation, and in that collection of variables —education, occupation, income, and status—that are typically considered to be the components of "social class." These background factors are often stressed by parents more than by the young people involved; in cultures where the marital partner is chosen by the parents with no input from the child, background factors are often the overriding considerations.

Parents in the United States have less influence on mate selection than parents in other cultures, but they do have concepts of the "correct" choice for their sons and daughters (61). If the child's choice of mate deviates significantly from the parents' ideal, especially on certain key characteristics such as religious faith, the parents may exert considerable pressure; they can argue, they can be inhospitable to the prospective spouse, and they can withdraw emotional and economic support. One researcher (62) found that 81 percent of the parents in his study admitted using pressure when their children dated people of whom they disapproved. The parents claimed that in the majority of cases their techniques were successful.

The race or religious faith of a potential mate is generally less important to young people today than in the past. Although interracial marriages are still rare, the number doubled between 1960 and 1970 (13). Similarly, the number of interfaith marriages has doubled in the last generation (10). Still, there remains widespread social disapproval of such unions. As recently as 1967, many states had laws prohibiting interracial marriages, and a 1970 survey showed that 40 percent of the parents of college students claimed they could "never accept" an interracial match for their child (61). Among the students themselves, 28 percent said they could "never accept" a spouse of a different race.

All three major religions strongly discourage interfaith marriages, feeling that a person's faith is weakened when his or her spouse does not share those beliefs. In addition, conflict between two different faiths is considered a threat to family life, both to the relationship between husband and wife and to the relationships between parents and children. Such fears appear to be justified. People who marry outside their religion tend to stop attending church or synagogue, and many lose all active interest in their religion (51). Interfaith marriages are also less stable (53). On the other hand, marriages between people of the same faith are not generally happier or more satisfying than interfaith marriages; they appear to be more stable simply because the partners are willing to endure more unhappiness and dissatisfaction before resorting to divorce or separation.

Unlike race and religion, factors that have become less important in mate selection, the influence of social class has increased slightly. College students are far more critical of marrying outside one's social class today than were students before World War II (53). Overall trends in interclass marriages are neither up nor down (56), but there is a decrease in the proportion of marriages in which the class discrepancy is large. "People are paying less attention to small differences and more attention to larger differences" (70, p. 158). Although such class consciousness may seem unusual in a democratic society, it is more understandable when phrased in terms of the "components" of social class: Young people are becoming slightly more wary of marrying someone who differs significantly in education, occupational goals, and life-style.

Attitudes and needs   One of the most solidly established facts of psychology is that people like people who share their opinions and attitudes (12). Generally speaking, political conservatives like other conservatives more than liberals; people who think bullfighting is a barbarous sport like other critics more than afficionados; and, to a martini drinker, a preference for gin and vermouth is a solid point in a person's favor. Within marriages, partners who share more interests like each other more than those with relatively dissimilar attitudes, and thus their marriages are generally more pleasant and satisfying. In addition, divergent attitudes may mean that the marrriage partners are often acting at cross-purposes—canceling each other's vote in presidential elections, for example—or that they cannot share in what one considers an important or satisfying activity—as when one spouse is fanatical about a particular sport and the other refuses to participate in it or even watch it on television. In any case, potential marital partners with similar attitudes are attracted to one another; they are more likely than pairs with less similarity to date, to enjoy the date, to proceed toward more serious courtship, and, finally, to marry (34, 69).

After the "consensus filter" screens out marriage candidates with widely discrepant attitudes and values (see Figure 10.3), the degree to which the potential partners *complement* one another in needs and personality traits may become important. In theory, complementary needs are not always similar (78). If one partner has a high need for achievement, perhaps it is preferable for the other to be low in achievement motivation; perhaps two achievers in the family will lead to conflict and hostility. Sometimes a high degree of one need is complemented by a high degree of another, different need; perhaps a highly dominant person should be matched with a highly submissive spouse.

The theory of complementary needs in marriage is appealing—it is one of the few theories that suggest that "opposites attract," in some respects at least—

but the empirical evidence is inconsistent (69), with perhaps the bulk of the research showing that marital partners have similar and not complementary needs. There is some evidence, however, that complementary needs play a small but critical role at later stages in the courtship process (34).

The readiness factor Although a person's age does not help us much in predicting whom he or she will marry, it is one of the best predictors of when the marriage will occur. There is considerable social pressure in our culture to marry and to do so within a certain age period. Marriages below the age of 18 or 20 are likely to be frowned upon—too young—and someone who has never been married by the age of 30 may be viewed with suspicion. (The U.S. Bureau of the Census defines "bachelor" as a never-married man over 35 and "spinster" as a never-married woman over 30.) Over three-quarters of all people who marry do so before the age of 25 (13).

A person's age is such an important factor in marriage that several theorists have concluded that trying to predict whom someone will marry is largely a matter of identifying whom the person is seriously dating at the time he or she is "ready" to marry:

> . . . the final, direct stimulus for selecting a particular mate may be largely due to chance, situational or idiosyncratic factors, or particularistic norms. For instance, experiences such as peer or family pressures to marry at a certain point in time, impending graduation from college, the death of a parent, an identity crisis, or some other unpredictable event may be more instrumental in crystallizing an actual marriage commitment than any general explanatory variable that yet has been identified (40, p. 16).

In a large-scale study of couples introduced by a computer-dating enterprise (59), the single best predictor of whether the couple would marry or not—among social variables, interests and attitudes, and personality factors—was the "strong desire to marry soon"! One young lawyer put it this way: "Within six months before or after our graduation from law school, all but one of my friends got married. I don't think it could be that everybody met the right girl by coincidence. There must have been an element of its being the right time. Not to take away from Jeanie . . ." (58, p. 101).

People rarely, if ever, go through a deliberate screening process like the one we have described, but the screening process occurs nevertheless. People marry "the person they love," but love is partially determined in subtle and indirect ways by such things as similarities in social background, attitudes, interests, and values. Once the decision to marry is made, by whatever means, the couple's next question arises: "What kind of marriage do we want?" (Figure 10.4).

Choosing a Style

A century ago, there was only one common form of marriage: Marriage was a lifetime contract; divorce was very rare. The husband was head of the family.

●Figure 10.4   What will marriage be like?

He earned the money and made most, if not all, of the major family decisions such as where to live, when the wife should become pregnant, and which children should go to college. The wife's role was that of "homemaker," that is, keeping a neat home, preparing meals, raising children. This *patriarchal* (father-dominated) family evolved in twentieth-century America to a more *dem-*

ocratic form (11). The democratic marriage is based on companionship—mutual affection—more than the older patriarchal form was. Typically the husband is still dominant, but the wife has more of a voice in family decisions; even the children participate as they grow older. In the patriarchal form of marriage, duty and tradition were the key reasons for doing things as one did, but the goals of happiness and personal growth became paramount in the democratic marriage. The democratic form of marriage and the family is the one most people today would call "traditional," as even newer forms develop to contrast with it.

There is no question that young people marrying today have more conscious decisions to make about their marriage—*after* marriage—than ever before. One of the most important decisions concerns the roles of husband and wife. Although they are frequently hampered by laws discriminating against women and, in a few cases, against men, many couples are trying to form a more nearly equal marriage. Each partner has a career, and each has responsibility for bringing in income. Both are homemakers; the husband is expected to share equally in cooking, cleaning, and other household tasks. Children are a joint responsibility. This *equalitarian* form of marriage may represent the next step in the process of evolution that replaced the rigid patriarchal family structure with the more flexible democratic marriage.

Alternatives to conventional marriage   Some young people feel that conventional marriages, even equalitarian ones, no longer suit the needs of the individual in today's society and that new forms of marriage should be explored. In support of their thesis, they point to the divorce rate, which has been rising dramatically since the late 1950s. A careful 1973 study of census data (25) led to the prediction that between three and four of every ten marriages contracted by women born between 1940 and 1944 would eventually end in divorce; for women born after 1955—the women who are now getting married—the chances of avoiding divorce are certainly slimmer, probably less than 50:50. From these facts, it has been suggested that, in the near future, the most common form of marriage will be the *serial marriage* (68), in which each individual marries more than one person—in a series, of course, not at the same time. Some young people have begun to anticipate at least the possibility of divorce by specifying the economic arrangements in the case of separation or by considering their union to be a short-term contract—say, five years—with options for renewal.

Group marriage is one of the most unconventional forms of marriage today. Typically involving three or four people, group marriage is based on an agreement to share incomes, living quarters, and the many rights and responsibilities of marriage (34). Women who express an interest in group marriage hope that the new interpersonal relationships will ease the sense of isolation they feel at home with their children, their dependence on their husbands for "adult contact," and their frustration at the underutilization of their talents. Men are impressed by the economic advantages of group marriage, with multiple incomes and reduced expenses. If one person loses his or her job or decides to begin a different career, the other marriage partners could support the group, at least for a time. Some groups have become legal corporations and enjoy striking tax advantages (50).

On the other hand, group marriage requires "a tremendous investment of time, effort, and emotional energy"; it is a "hot house" situation, with no "cultural support or guidelines" (17, 51). Most group marriages dissolve in a year or two.

Group marriage is a specific form of *communal living*. Other types of communes range from the structured and reasonably successful kibbutzim (collective settlements) in Israel to various loosely structured and usually unstable communes in the United States (Figure 10.5). Perhaps the most interesting aspect of these modern experiments, which are typically designed to achieve the advantages of a larger family group, is that they represent, in part, an attempt to return to a very old form of family life: the extended family. In earlier eras, grandparents, several siblings and their spouses, and often a few cousins lived together on the same farm or as close neighbors in a stable small town. In today's highly technological and mobile society, blood relatives are replaced by like-minded peers, chosen, to a large extent, by the same principles of mate selection that determine choice in the conventional marriage.

Cohabitation   For many young people, *cohabitation*—living together without a legal marriage—is an alternative form of marriage. About 25 percent of a nationwide sample of college students reported living, or having lived, with someone in a cohabitant relationship (6). A 1974 survey of American men between the ages of 20 and 30 found that 18 percent had at some time lived with a woman for six months or longer, although only 5 percent were cohabitating at the time of the study (16). Contrary to the view that "living together" is most prevalent among college youth, cohabitation was reported by more high-school dropouts (23 percent) than by either high-school or college graduates (each 17 percent).

Instead of an alternative form of marriage, however, most young adults consider cohabitation to be a kind of "intense dating," a way for people who are not yet ready for marriage to have a close sexual relationship. Most of the people involved in such relationships expect to marry in the future (6). Their future spouses will in some cases be the people they have been living with, but not necessarily; only rarely is cohabitation viewed as a "trial marriage." Nevertheless, cohabitation helps the participants clarify their ideas about marriage and the kind of person they would like to marry. Most people say that they also learn a lot about themselves in these intimate encounters, that they mature and gain a better sense of personal identity (43).

PARENTHOOD

The "script" for the typical American family begins with courtship, engagement, and marriage. After a year or so, the happy young couple begins thinking about "having a baby" or "starting a family." Thought turns to action and soon

● Figure 10.5 A communal family.

the wife is shopping for maternity clothes. Sometime in the second year of marriage, the "blessed event" occurs, and the couple becomes a trio. Not long afterward, a few "new brothers and sisters" are added to the growing family. Eventually the couple decides they have enough children; they settle back to watch their children grow; they cry during graduation ceremonies.

The typical American family described above is still typical—at least in terms of statistics—but variations on this theme are much more common than they were even a decade ago (71). For example, more couples are having no children at all. Although eight or nine out of ten women will have at least one child in their lifetime, the percentage of childless married women who expect to remain childless increased by 23 percent in the three years from 1971 to 1974. More couples are waiting longer to have their first child. Among women married between 1955 and 1959, 70 percent had their first child within the first two years of marriage; for women married between 1965 and 1969, this figure dropped to 60 percent. Families are also getting smaller. In 1955, 38 percent of the women aged 18–24 planned to have four or more children; in 1974, only 8 percent had such plans.

Thus, not all married couples become parents, and the timing is more variable. Still, most couples do have children relatively early in their marriages, and this new role—parenthood—involves a number of adjustments. It is on these developmental tasks, faced by most young adults, that we will focus now.

The Crisis of the First Child

It is impossible for the childless couple to anticipate fully the changes their first child will bring in their lives. There are profound joys and satisfactions in parenthood, and there are problems that require solutions and changed circumstances that require adaptation. In one survey (39), fully 83 percent of the middle-class couples interviewed were willing to call the arrival of their first child as an "extensive" or a "severe" crisis. The mothers complained of chronic tiredness, the loss of outside social activities, and the sharp increase in household duties; they were concerned, in many cases, with the loss of the satisfactions and the income of an outside job and with what they felt was an abrupt and significant decrease in sexual attractiveness. The fathers bemoaned many of the same things; they too were tired, they too missed the adventures and parties to which childless couples have greater access, and they too missed the income from the wife's job. They were dismayed by the decline in the wife's sexual responsiveness, and they were amazed by how much babies cost, both before and after birth. New fathers, 62 percent in a later study (22), felt neglected.

> With the birth of the first child, the amount of time the wife must spend in housework doubles, and the amount of time she spends in conversation with her husband is cut in half. Even when there is time, it is difficult for husband and wife to carry on an adult conversation when there are little children in the room. As the child becomes a social being, after about one year of age, he resents the attention which parents pay to each other which cuts him out. Toddlers are famous for screaming or upsetting milk when their parents are in conversation at the meal table and for pulling on one parent or trying to jam themselves between parents during a goodbye kiss. The intimate give-and-take of communication which helps to maintain the special feelings spouses have for each other may have to be limited to the time after the children are in bed, and by that time the young mother may be folded up on the

couch asleep. Having their lovemaking interrupted by an infant squall is an experience few young couples greet with enthusiasm. Husband and wife may come to think of themselves as parents first and husband and wife to one another only secondarily (69, pp. 430–431).

The changes in a person's life that come with parenthood are sharp and large and threaten the developing intimacy of the marital relationship. There may be conflicts between the spouses over child-rearing practices. One parent may feel that the discipline in the family is too strict, inhibiting the child's natural creativity, while the other feels that discipline is lax, allowing the child to dominate family activities. Many couples discover for the first time that their views on children are widely discrepant, even though strongly held; it was not something they talked about during the courtship.

In the average American family, parenthood affects the wife's life more than the husband's, as many of the complaints we have listed indicate. Figure 10.6 gives us some idea of the household burden; the amount of housework often doubles with the arrival of the first child, decreasing only slightly as the

●Figure 10.6　Amount of housework, by age of youngest child. (Adapted from E. Wiegand. *Use of Time by Full-time and Part-time Homemakers in Relation to Home Management.* Ithaca, NY: Cornell University Agricultural Experiment Station, 1954.)

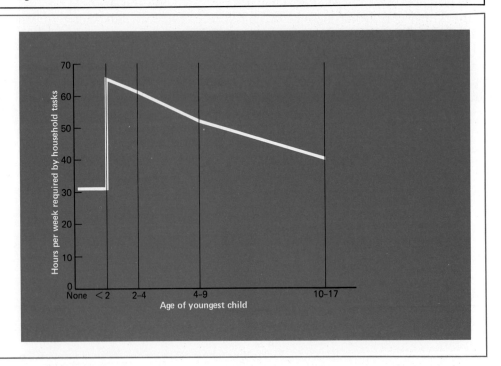

children grow older (77). Child care and household duties require so much time that the wife's career, social activities, friendships, and relationship with her husband all suffer. As one recent reviewer put it, the "data point to a substantial overload built into the mother role, even for women voluntarily choosing it" (38, p. 495). Nevertheless, many mothers feel guilty about not spending even more time with their infants and begrudge themselves the few hours they may take for themselves.

Parenthood typically alters the power relationship in the marriage (5). If the wife has been working and then quits—the most common case—she becomes increasingly dependent on her husband financially. More and more she becomes dependent on him for other needs, too: For one thing, he provides adult contact and indeed may become her chief source of news about the outside world. The sharing of activities decreases, while the division of labor increases. Often the wife stays home, minding the children, when the husband goes out— to a convention in a distant city or even to the store. The marriage which had been equalitarian becomes more like the husband-dominant forms. A number of studies (38) show that husbands do *less* housework after the birth of the first child than before: It has now become "women's work."

Alternative Styles of Parenthood

Focusing on the threats to intimacy posed by parenthood, we have obviously not done justice to the many rewards of having children. Although there are problems and realistic complaints, most parents derive great joy and satisfaction from their children. Children fulfill certain nurturant needs; they are "someones" to care for. Most parents live vicariously through their children, at least at times, taking great personal satisfaction from their accomplishments and sharing the sadness of life's minor defeats. Having children also fulfills most people's deeply ingrained expectations of life.

> A life cycle without parenthood is for most people an uncompleted life cycle. When adults do not have children it just does not 'seem right,' and it is assumed that they must be unhappy in their childlessness, even though this is often not the case. . . . Friends and neighbors expect young couples to have children, and parents usually relish becoming grandparents. It is surprising how many people one can make happy simply by having children (69, pp. 438–439).

In a study comparing 40 couples who were satisfied with their marriage with 40 dissatisfied couples (41), "children" was the most frequent answer to a question about the greatest satisfactions of marriage. There was no difference between the two groups in this regard; the dissatisfied couples liked their children, but they complained about the lack of companionship in their marriages. In fact, 63 percent of the dissatisfied couples listed children as the *only* satisfaction in their marriage.

Nevertheless, parenthood, if not a crisis, is a period of radical adjustment.

Many young couples have begun to consider alternatives to the traditional style of parenthood, and at least five of these are fairly common (69). First, many couples are waiting longer after marriage before having their first child. As we mentioned, there has been a sharp decline in the number of women having babies in the first two years of marriage, and this trend seems likely to continue. With a longer "prechild" period for the husband and wife to develop as a couple, they should be more resistant to many of the forces that tend to separate them when the child is born, and children can be more nearly a shared activity.

A second alternative is to have no children at all. The number of voluntarily childless couples is increasing at a rapid rate (71), and society is at least accepting, if not approving, of this alternative. Research evidence on the marital happiness of childless couples is inconsistent, probably for the reason that some couples are childless because the husband and wife dislike each other and others are childless because they love (and don't want to share) each other.

A third alternative is to redefine the roles of mother and father so that rigid differentiations and compartmentalizations do not divide the couple. The father can play a more active role in child-care and household work, and many new mothers are not giving up their careers to tend to the new baby.

A fourth alternative requires only minor changes in the traditional style of parenthood; it is to set aside definite times for husband–wife interaction. In some cases this is a financial consideration. The couple may have to choose between a new sofa and the expense of baby-sitters once or twice a week. In other cases parents define a "mother–father time" during the day, when children are told to "get lost" for a while. It may be the hour after work, when the couple relaxes together and shares their day's events. Older children may sometimes resent being excluded, but, as one thoughtful observer put it, "It is not unhealthy for a child to know that his parents' relationship to each other is important to them" (69, p. 436).

A fifth alternative is simply better education for parenthood. Parenthood is often a crisis because the parents are so ill-prepared for their new roles. There is very little training for these roles in our society (55, 69), nothing like, for example, the training one gets in dating, engagement, and "living together" for eventual marriage. "Not only is training for these roles impoverished, but there is no apprenticeship: The new parent starts out abruptly on a 24-hour schedule" (38, p. 494). Some scholars have even suggested that one be required to take a course and pass a test before being allowed to become a parent. It is clear that the present generation takes parenthood more seriously than before, and less for granted.

Single Parents

We should not leave the topic of parenthood without a brief note on single parents, a family situation that may pose problems for many women, families, and society in general. The divorce rate is rising, and so is the number of unmarried women having children. The result is a startling increase in the number of

Choosing a Career

In many respects choosing a career—or at least a first major occupation—is like choosing a mate. Social factors such as the social status of the job are important, and a person tries to "form a union" with a job that is in line with his or her interests and needs. Job selection is a reciprocal process, like mate selection. The company is trying to determine the kind of employee it wants, while the employee is trying to choose the right job. When the relationship between employer and employee turns out to be unsatisfactory, a "divorce" is likely, through dismissal or resignation.

"No meaningful data exist on how most young adults . . . start to work in particular places, industries, or vocational settings" (4, p. 220). This lack of research on vocational choice is puzzling if one considers the real-life importance of the topic; it reflects the paucity of scientific evidence on adult development in general. What little research evidence is available, however, enables us to identify some of the factors in vocational choice. "Propinquity," that high-sounding word meaning closeness in space, is important. Someone growing up in a coal-mining region is more likely to become a miner than someone growing up in a farming region. Similarly, background factors such as social class, ethnic origin, sex, and race enable us to predict a person's vocation with better than chance accuracy. Children from the working class can move up the social-class ladder with greater ease in the United States than in most other countries, but most choose occupations that are similar to those of their parents, perhaps one or two but not several steps up the ladder. Jewish culture, which places a high value on education, leads a large number of Jews to choose academic professions. Female workers are typically secretaries, clerks, nurses, or teachers, although this tradition is rapidly changing (see pp. 397–401). Black workers, often because of overt discrimination, have filled many of the lower jobs on the income–status scale, but this state of affairs is also changing. Apart from illegal discrimination, certain occupations are limited to people of a certain level of ability, regardless of race, sex, or age. In some cases, in occupations that require great strength, for example, many women and many people over 50 may be excluded; but exclusions should be on the basis of individual ability, not on the basis of group membership.

Personality factors are also important determinants of vocational choice—understandably so, since one's choice of career is often an expression of his or her personality. For example, researchers have found small but consistent relationships between achievement motivation and scientific careers, affiliation needs and sales careers, and power motivation and executive or supervisorial occupations (72).

Some investigators have tried to probe the underlying psychodynamics of career choice. One investigator hypothesized that professional actors would have a less firmly established identity than would an average person (31). The reasoning was that playing a role, in which the character's identity is established by the playwright, would be a very attractive profession for people who have problems with their own identity. Actors did indeed score lower on a measure of ego identity than did nonactors, and, in addition, the more "identity confusion," the more successful the actor!

Vocational interests   An individual's pattern of interests—activities the person likes and dislikes—is one of the most thoroughly studied personality factors in vocational choice. If one goes to a guidance counselor for advice on careers, chances are that the counselor will suggest taking a vocational interest test such as the Strong–Campbell Interest Inventory, which is the latest version of the famous Strong Vocational Interest Blank (SVIB), or one of the Kuder interest inventories. The general theory behind tests of this type is that people who have interests similar to those of successful members of a particular occupational group will probably enjoy work in that occupation (Figure 10.8).

The Strong inventories request a response of "Like," "Dislike," or "Indifferent" to several hundred items describing activities or topics such as economics, fishing, discussing politics, and being an actor. The pattern of responses that earns a high score for a particular occupation was initially determined by comparing satisfied people in that occupation to "people in general." More happy engineers than people in general liked the idea of being an author of a technical book; so an individual who marks "Like" in response to "Author of technical book" earns one point on the Engineer scale (18). If the individual marks many items in the way most satisfied engineers did, he will earn a high score on the total scale; presumably he has demonstrated the pattern of interests that have led engineers to enjoy their work. If he also has the *ability* to be an engineer, he might find engineering a rewarding career. A low score on the Engineer scale suggests that he might be unhappy in that occupation, even if he has the ability.

People tend to choose jobs predicted by high scores on the SVIB, Kuder, and other interest inventories. A study of men who had taken the SVIB 18 years previously (60) showed that five times as many had earned scores in the highest category ("A") for their occupation, compared to men in other occupations. Of college men with the highest scores on the Engineer scale, one-third became engineers, one-third entered related occupations, and one-third took unrelated jobs. For a psychological test, this is a very good prediction indeed.

Interest tests also predict who will be happiest in their work. In one study of clerks (48), satisfied workers averaged 48 on the SVIB Office Worker scale, while dissatisfied clerks averaged 21. Workers who try one occupation and then change to another tend to have lower SVIB scores for the first occupation than do workers who stay with that job. And workers who change jobs tend to choose a new one that could have been predicted from high scores on the SVIB (61).

Interests also predict job success, although to a lesser lower degree than job choice or satisfaction, probably because job success is determined largely by ability. As one reviewer put it, "Interest cannot save the incapable; lack of interest cannot spoil the chances of those with high aptitude" (18, p. 475). Still, in

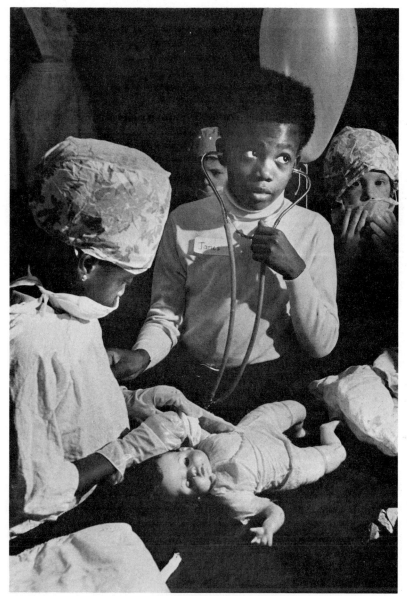

● Figure 10.8 Interests similar to those of successful members of a profession predict satisfaction with that profession.

certain occupations where success depends significantly on one's motivation—for example, in sales occupations—SVIB scores are predictive. Insurance agents with the highest scores on the Sales Interest scale wrote almost three times the dollar amount of insurance per year as did agents who had scored in the lowest ("C") category (61).

There are many reasons why the interests of a young adult might be a poor basis for job choice, in individual cases. A young woman might lack the ability for an occupation that interests her. In addition, her interests might change significantly in a short time, especially if she is attending college and living away from her parents for the first time. Although scores on interest inventories tend to be reasonably stable over the years—the SVIB correlates about 0.75 between two administrations to the same people 18 years apart (60)—some individuals change radically. Most of us know people who seemed extremely practical and "businesslike" at one period of their lives and extremely idealistic, self-sacrificing, and mystical at another time. More generally, certain experiences, such as attending college, can have a marked effect on interest patterns; most college students show a decline in business interests during their college years and an increased interest in "altruistic" occupations that involve helping others (social worker, nurse). Another factor to consider is the change in the occupations themselves. New jobs are created every year, some of which defy classification in terms of older job categories. And the interests of satisfied members of a profession may change. As the economic benefits of practicing medicine increase, for example, people with business interests might find this occupation more to their liking than before.

Intelligence and other abilities   Intelligence is related to job choice in a number of ways, some direct and some indirect (see pp. 178–187). Certain jobs require an above-average degree of intelligence for successful performance and thus are open only to people of relatively high IQ. Indirectly, a high level of intelligence predicts success in school, and many jobs require school training; physicians, for example, must be able to complete the scholastic program for the M.D. degree. In general, I.Q. scores correlate about 0.50 with "economic success," a variable composed of job income and the social prestige of the occupation (7).

In addition to intelligence, a number of other abilities are important in certain occupations. An artist must be creative. Certain assembly jobs require good motor ability—good manual dexterity and good reaction time. People with good spatial ability can manipulate things mentally; they can visualize what an object would look like from the back or the top; they understand the basic plan of a structure. Such an ability is presumably useful in fields such as drafting, architecture, and dress designing, to mention just a few. Two common ability tests used in vocational guidance are the Differential Aptitude Test and the General Aptitude Test Battery (18).

Vocational Values

Much has been made of a presumed revolution in the vocational values and goals of American young people. They are no longer interested in material success, it has been asserted, and they view business and industry as exploit-

ative, unjust, and concerned with profit at the expense of human need, social values, and the quality of the environment. In more personal terms, young people are said to consider many traditional occupations as too limiting of individual expression; they do not relish being a cog in a large, impersonal machine.

Such blanket generalizations should be viewed with great caution, as we have noted in Chapter 9. Although a limited number of young people are profoundly disenchanted with American society, most young people still believe in the traditional principles of the "work ethic"; they still believe, for example, that hard work leads to success and wealth and that these goals are worth striving for (79). On the other hand, it is true that young people today are less willing than their predecessors to "put up with" arbitrary, authoritarian, or impersonal treatment by employers, and they view the principles and practices of American business with considerable cynicism. Another reason it is difficult to generalize about youth is that values often differ considerably in different segments of the youth population. There is increasing evidence that while college youth are becoming more conventional in their vocational aspirations, at least compared to young people in the 1960s, the less advantaged noncollege majority are becoming more critical and dissatisfied.

College youth   Research indicates that there has been a recent increase in the percentage of "career-minded" college students, that is, in "those young people whose major purpose in going to college is to train themselves for a career" (80, p. 16), as contrasted with those who view their college experience primarily as a period of self-discovery and change (Figure 10.9). Similarly, the percentage of college youth viewing "the money you earn" as an important job criterion increased from approximately one-third in 1970 to almost two-thirds in 1973. Compared to previous college classes, the class of 1978 included significantly more students intending to major in such specific career fields as agriculture,

● Figure 10.9   Size of the "career-minded" group (college youth). (From D. Yankelovich. *The New Morality: A Profile of American Youth in the 70s.* New York: McGraw-Hill, 1974.)

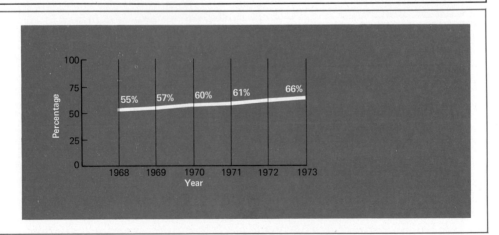

business, and the health professions; significantly fewer students chose such areas as humanities and fine arts (29).

These changes, while impressive, do not mean that today's college youth are returning to the vocational values of the 1950s, as some observers have suggested. Today's young people have strong preferences for work that is personally rewarding and that involves friendly co-workers.

> . . . they are trying to achieve a synthesis between the old and the new values by assuming that it is possible to seek and find self-fulfillment and personal satisfaction in a conventional career, while simultaneously enjoying the kind of financial rewards that will enable them to live full, rich lives outside of their work. The job criteria they stress put equal emphasis on challenging work, the ability to express one's self, and free time for outside interests, as well as on the money one can earn, economic security, and the chance to get ahead (80, p. 20).

Noncollege youth   While the evidence indicates that college youth are becoming more optimistic about the prospects of achieving both self-fulfillment and economic security in their work, the noncollege majority is apparently becoming more skeptical. For example, fewer blue-collar youth than college youth find their work interesting or feel their jobs have a "good future" (80). These findings suggest that noncollege youth in the 1970s have adopted the values of college youth in the 1960s, including a genuine desire for self-fulfillment and individual expression in work and in their lives as a whole. Unlike their more privileged peers, however, blue-collar youth are less likely to obtain jobs that provide such opportunities. One observer has expressed the problem:

> That the majority of noncollege youth face the prospect of growing difficulties with their jobs must be regarded as a matter of serious concern to the society. These young people, after all, represent the great bulk of the new labor force. The problem they face is compounded by the multiplier effect of higher expectations with lower opportunities: their New Values inevitably clash with the built-in rigidities and limited responses of the traditional work place.
>
> . . . We are reaching one of those critical turning-points in our social history where the options of the future and the opportunities to create new institutions are truly open. The die is not yet cast. The majority of young people continue to bring to their work a deeply rooted desire to do a good job and a hunger for work that will satisfy some of their deepest cravings—for community, for fellowship, for participation, for challenge, for self-fulfillment, for freedom, and for equality (80, p. 37).

Women and Work

We briefly mentioned sex as a factor in vocational choice: Women tend to choose certain jobs, notably teaching, nursing, and secretarial work. The occupations most women choose are "women's jobs"; that is, most of the people holding such jobs are women. "Women's jobs" are characterized generally by low prestige and especially by low pay. In the 1975 *Manpower Report of the*

President, published by the U.S. Department of Labor, it was noted that three of four male workers earned over $7000 in 1972, while two of three full-time female workers earned *less* than that amount. Even adjusting for differences in education, occupational status, length of employment, and other factors in income, a woman earns about 62 percent of the salary of a man (64). There is much overt discrimination against women in industry. For example, male tellers in banks are often paid more than female tellers, ostensibly because they are sometimes called upon to carry heavy sacks of money; if there are no male tellers, however, the women carry the sacks without noticeable strain *and* without additional compensation (3). Women scientists often have to be better qualified and more productive to receive the same professional rewards as men (75). Examples like these are easy to find in almost every occupational field.

Although attitudes are changing, employers have traditionally assumed that the female labor force consists of young women who work until marriage or the birth of their first child, plus a few older women who work to supplement their husband's income. This image of the female worker was not entirely inaccurate 50 years ago, but today most working women are married and most have children. The labor force participation of married women living with their husbands increased by 80 percent between 1950 and 1974. About half of the women in the so-called "child-rearing years"—ages 25–34—now work, representing an increase of nearly 40 percent since 1960 (71). In addition, a large number of women with children in high school or college, when child-rearing responsibilities have lessened but child-rearing costs have ballooned, have returned to the labor force they left many years ago.

In spite of these changes in the nature of the female labor force, most women are still found in "women's jobs." Such employment fills American industry's need for cheap skilled labor in which neither the employer nor the employee makes much of a commitment. If training is required, it is typically obtained before employment—for example, in a nursing school; extensive on-the-job training is rare. Without commitment (and without much advancement), the person doing women's work can easily quit and find an almost identical job in a new community—her "career" is not much of an obstacle to her husband's mobility (47). Many of these jobs are described as "glamorous," which refers to job characteristics such as the opportunities to dress stylishly and to meet men. To glamorize the job of bank teller, for example, some banks have provided free charm school lessons, free beauty treatments, and uniforms designed by high-fashion designers; there are even contests—"Miss Drive-In Teller"—in which candidates are judged on appearance, poise, and job efficiency (49).

Is occupational segregation—women in women's jobs, men in men's—decreasing? Yes, slowly, although some researchers (28) feel that much of the decrease is due to males entering traditionally female fields—nursing, for example, and teaching in elementary schools—rather than to an influx of women into traditionally male occupations. A common index of occupational segrega-

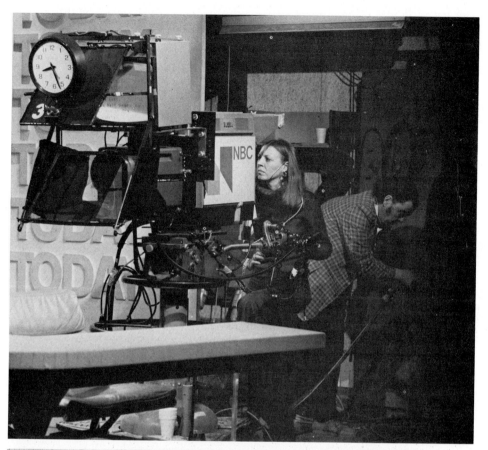

Figure 10.10 More women are entering traditionally male-dominated occupations.

tion by sex is essentially the percentage of people who would have to change to jobs commonly held by the opposite sex in order to eliminate segregation completely (24). In 1960, this index was 66 percent; by 1970, it had dropped slightly to 59 percent. In addition to males entering nursing and elementary teaching, significant numbers of females became engineers, accountants, and science technicians, jobs that men traditionally occupy. A third factor in the decrease of occupational segregation is rapid growth in certain occupations that have never been strongly dominated by one sex—secondary school and college teachers, computer specialists, health technology.

As more and more women choose and prepare themselves for less traditional, male-dominated occupations, differences between such "innovators" and women headed for more traditional women's jobs have been of interest (Figure 10.10). Innovators are more likely to have a working mother, for example, and the mother's job is likely to be innovative, too (66). There is very little evidence that innovative women identify more strongly than average with their fathers. Support and encouragement from others—parents, teachers, friends, boyfriends—is a very significant factor in innovative career choices (14, 66).

The influence of the mother on the career decisions of her daughter have been summarized succinctly: "The high-achieving woman has a high-achieving daughter" (32, p. 213). There are several reasons why this tends to be the case. First, the mother provides a good model of an achievement-oriented woman for her daughter. Furthermore, such mothers are more likely to encourage independence in their daughters. And, finally, the father in such a family is typically one who is proud of his wife's accomplishments while accepting her as a female. The daughters begin to realize that competition and achievement does not mean they will be less attractive to men, as many women fear (33); and that a relationship between two self-actualizing people can be very satisfying indeed (32).

Female medical students reported that both parents consistently reinforced their intellectual and achievement-oriented strivings.

> There is a father opening a savings account for his daughter's college education upon her birth; a mother beset by economic hardship who collects three full bookcases of secondhand classics for her children; wealthy parents planning . . . the living inheritance of providing (their offspring) with the best education money can buy; a father after being continuously active in his daughter's school projects (driving her home from her laboratory experiments at 2 A.M.) jokingly laments her medical school's activities since medical school has no PTA! (14, pp. 205–206).

These examples reflect an *unusual* degree of parental support, for daughters are rarely encouraged so strongly. Male physicians were asked "Should your daughter seek a career in medicine?" and approximately half said "No" (26). This should be compared to other sources that report "almost unanimous parental acceptance of medicine as a worthwhile career for sons" (14, p. 206).

Women entering medicine also cited their personal interests and motivations as important factors in their decisions. They liked the things doctors do, and they felt they could fulfill self-actualization needs—to be the best one can be—in this profession. Their "mission motives" were strong; they spoke often of altruism, humanitarianism, and idealism. Compared to male medical students, they were less interested in the economic aspects of a medical career.

Times are changing with respect to women and work, and they will be changing even more rapidly in the future:

> Because marriage is no longer an end in itself; because so many women spend time outside of marriage or in between marriages; because family/parental roles occupy a relatively short portion of a woman's total life in today's two-child society; because women are receiving the education and training (and with it the career aspirations) to cause them to plan for and expect employment opportunities parallel to those of men; and finally, because all of these conditions represent changes from the recent past, to note that the pattern of female labor force participation is likely to change is anticlimactic (71, p. 114).

SUMMARY

Young adulthood is a time of "pulling up roots"—of establishing independence from parents—while searching for one's own personal identity. Marriage and career decisions, among other factors, tend to stabilize one's identity. As ego identity stabilizes, interpersonal relationships become "freer"—another person can be appreciated without reference to one's own needs—and interests deepen. Moral development in young adulthood involves a general "humanizing" of values and often leads to a "social-contract, legalistic orientation" to ethics: What is right is that which most people agree on. Some young adults achieve a "universal-ethical-principle orientation," where morality is based on abstract principles such as the golden rule. Such principled morality is apparently facilitated by the opportunity to think about conflicting values without having to make immediate decisions—an opportunity typically afforded college students, for example. The humanizing of values often results in a related "expansion of caring," that is, an increased interest in the welfare of others.

In the later stages of young adulthood, around the age of 30, many people begin to question the important decisions made earlier. Sometimes they make changes in spouses or careers, but often there is simply a deeper commitment to the earlier decisions.

Marriage is, in part, an attempt to resolve the dilemma of intimacy versus isolation. Erik Erikson views a truly satisfying sexual relationship as one with mutual trust and love, without fear or guilt, and with a willingness to regulate the normal routines of "work, procreation, and recreation."

That the potential bride or groom should have any say in the choice of a mate is a relatively recent development in human history. The factors that determine the choice of a mate in our society are not always consciously considered, but they can be described as a kind of "filtering" process in which the choice is progressively narrowed. A propinquity filter accepts only those with whom the person commonly comes in contact. An attractiveness filter accepts only those whom the person finds physically attractive. A social background filter accepts only those who are similar in religion, race, political affiliation, social class, and so on. A consensus filter accepts only those who are similar in attitudes and values, and a complementary filter accepts people whose needs complement those of the prospective spouse. Finally there is a readiness filter reflecting the social pressure to marry at a certain age, usually within the young adult range of 18–35.

Once married, various styles of marriage are possible. The older patriarchal forms have given way to democratic and equalitarian styles in which the wife plays a more assertive role. Even newer forms include serial marriage, group marriage, communal living, and cohabitation (living together without legal marriage).

If the couple decides to have children, the arrival of the first child causes significant changes in the lives of the parents. Women typically have more child-rearing responsibilities; they find their housework increased and their contact with adults (including their husbands) decreased. Although children are usually a source of great pleasure and satisfaction, many couples are trying to relieve a few of the burdens of parenthood by: (1) waiting longer after marriage before having children, (2) having no children at all, (3) redefining the roles of "mother" and "father" so that the father takes on more child-care duties, (4) setting aside specific times for husband–wife interaction, apart from the children, and (5) preparing themselves for the potential problems of parenthood through better education. The problems of parenthood are especially numerous for single parents, who are typically women with small incomes.

Choosing a career is a difficult task in today's complex society. Vocational guidance tests can indicate interests shared with successful members of various occupations and specific abilities that may be important in specific jobs. Most young people today still believe that hard work will lead to material success, which they value, although they dislike impersonal treatment by large corporations, and they view the goals and practices of American business with cynicism. College youth are apparently becoming more "career-oriented," although they have not given up their desires to find work that is self-fulfilling. Noncollege youth are also interested in self-fulfilling work, but they are often frustrated in their attempts to find satisfying occupations.

Although occupational discrimination against women is decreasing, women have traditionally been relegated to "temporary" jobs (until they marry or have children) with low salaries and little chance of advancement. Women who enter less traditional fields typically have parents, teachers, and friends who support their strivings and applaud their accomplishments. An achieving mother can provide a model of a successful woman and, with the father, an example of an intimate relationship between two achievement-oriented individuals. In other words, she demonstrates the abilities to love without anxiety and to work efficiently, and these two abilities, according to Freud, mark the truly healthy adult personality.

References

1. Adler, A. **Understanding human nature.** Philadelphia: Chilton, 1927.
2. Angyal, A. **Foundations for a science of personality.** New York: The Commonwealth Fund, 1941.
3. Bird, C. **Born female.** New York: McKay, 1968.
4. Bischof, L. J. **Adult psychology** (2nd ed.) New York: Harper & Row, 1976.
5. Blood, R. O. **The family.** New York: Free Press, 1972.
6. Bower, D. W., & Christopherson, V. A. University student cohabitation: a regional comparison of selected attitudes and behavior. **Journal of Marriage and the Family,** 1977, **39,** 447–453.
7. Bowles, S., & Gintis, H. I.Q. in the U.S. class structure. **Social Policy,** 1972, **3**(4).
8. Boyd, D. A developmental approach to undergraduate ethics. Unpublished doctoral dissertation, Harvard University, 1973. Cited in (**35**).
9. Bronfenbrenner, U. The challenge of social change to public policy and developmental research. Paper presented at the meeting of the Society for Research in Child Development, Denver, April 2, 1975.
10. Bumpass, L. The trend of interfaith marriage in the United States. **Social Biology,** 1970, **17**(3), 253–259.
11. Burgess, E. W., Locke, H. J., & Thomes, M. M. **The family** (3rd ed.). New York: American Book Co., 1963.
12. Byrne, D. **The attraction paradigm.** New York: Academic Press, 1971.
13. Carter, H., & Glick, P. C. **Marriage and divorce** (2nd ed.). Cambridge: Harvard University Press, 1976.
14. Cartwright, L. K. Conscious factors entering into decisions of women to study medicine. **Journal of Social Issues,** 1972, **28,** 201–215.
15. Clarke, A. C. An examination of the operation of residential propinquity as a factor in mate selection. **American Sociological Review,** 1952, **27,** 17–22.
16. Clayton, R. R., & Voss, H. L. Shacking up: Cohabitation in the 1970s. **Journal of Marriage and the Family,** 1977, **39,** 273–283.
17. Constantine, L. L., & Constantine, J. M. Dissolution of marriage in a nonconventional context. **The Family Coordinator,** 1972, **21,** 457–462.
18. Cronbach, L. J. **Essentials of psychological testing** (3rd ed.) New York: Harper & Row, 1970.
19. Datan, N., & Ginsberg, L. H. (Eds.) **Life-span developmental psychology: normative life crises.** New York: Academic Press, 1975.
20. Donovan, J. M. Ego identity status and interpersonal style. **Journal of Youth and Adolescence,** 1975, **4,** 37–55.
21. Dyer, E. D. Parenthood as crisis: a re-study. **Marriage and Family Living,** 1963, **25,** 196–201.
22. Erikson, E. **Childhood and society** (2nd ed.) New York: Norton, 1963.
23. Erikson, E. **Insight and responsibility.** New York: Norton, 1964.

24. Fuchs, V. R. A note on sex segregation in professional occupations. **Explorations in Economic Research,** 1975, **2,** 105–111.

25. Glick, P. C., & Norton, A. J. Perspectives on the recent upturn in divorce and remarriage. **Demography,** 1973, **10,** 301–314.

26. Gosswiler, R. A. A girl becomes a doctor. **Today's Health,** 1969 (June), 29–33.

27. Gould, R. Adult life stages: growth toward self-tolerance. **Psychology Today,** 1975, **8**(9), 74–78.

28. Gross, E. Plus ca change . . . ? The sexual structure of occupations over time. **Social Problems,** 1968, **16,** 198–208.

29. Harris, L. Change, yes—upheaval, no. **Life,** January 8, 1971, **70,** 22–27.

30. Harris, L. & associates. **The myth and reality of aging in America.** Washington: The National Council on the Aging, 1975.

31. Henry, W. E. Identity and diffusion in professional actors. Paper presented at the meeting of the American Psychological Association, September, 1965. Cited in Kimmel, D. C. **Adulthood and aging.** New York: Wiley, 1974.

32. Hoffman, L. W. The professional woman as mother. **Annals of the New York Academy of Sciences,** 1973, **208,** 211–216.

33. Horner, M. S. Femininity and successful achievement: a basic inconsistency. In J. M. Bardwick, E. Douvan, M. S. Horner, & D. Guttman, **Feminine personality and conflict.** Monterey, Ca.: Brooks/Cole, 1970.

34. Kerckhoff, A. C., & Davis, K. E. Value consensus and need complementarity in mate selection. **American Sociological Review,** 1962, **27,** 295–303.

35. Kohlberg, L. Continuities in childhood and adult moral development revisited. In P. B. Baltes & K. W. Schaie (Eds.), **Life-span developmental psychology: personality and socialization.** New York: Academic Press, 1973.

36. Kohlberg, L. From is to ought: how to commit the naturalistic fallacy and get away with it in the study of moral development. In T. Mischel (Ed.), **Cognitive development and epistemology.** New York: Academic Press, 1971.

37. Kohlberg, L., & Kramer, R. Continuities and discontinuities in childhood and adult moral development. **Human Development,** 1969, **12,** 93–120.

38. Laws, J. L. A feminist review of marital adjustment literature: the rape of the Locke. **Journal of Marriage and the Family,** 1971, **33,** 483–516.

39. LeMasters, E. E. Parenthood as crisis. **Marriage and Family Living,** 1957, **19,** 352–355.

40. Lewis, R. A. A longitudinal test of a developmental framework for premarital dyadic formation. **Journal of Marriage and the Family,** 1973, **35,** 16–25.

41. Luckey, E. G., & Bain, J. K. Children: a factor in marital satisfaction. **Journal of Marriage and the Family,** 1970, **32,** 43–44.

42. Mace, D., & Mace, V. **Marriage east and west.** Garden City, N.Y.: Dolphin, 1960.

43. Macklin, E. Heterosexual cohabitation among unmarried college students. **The Family Coordinator,** 1972, **12,** 463–471.

44. Marcia, J. E. Ego identity status: relationship to change in self-esteem, "general maladjustment," and authoritarianism. **Journal of Personality,** 1967, **35,** 118–123.

45. Maslow, A. H. **Motivation and personality** (2nd ed.). Harper & Row, 1970.

46. Murstein, B. I. Person perception and courtship progress among premarital couples. **Journal of Marriage and the Family,** 1972, **34,** 621–626.

47. Oppenheimer, V. K. **The female labor force in the United States,** (Population Monograph Series, No. 5). Berkeley: University of California Institute of International Studies, 1970.

48. Perry, D. K. Validities of three interests keys for U.S. Navy Yeomen. **Journal of Applied Psychology,** 1955, **39,** 134–138.

49. Prather, J. E. When the girls move in: a sociological analysis of the feminization of the bank teller's job. **Journal of Marriage and the Family,** 1971, **33,** 777–782.

50. Ramey, J. W. Communes, group marriage, and the upper-middle class. **Journal of Marriage and the Family,** 1972, **34,** 647–655.

51. Ramey, J. W. Emerging patterns of innovative behavior in marriage. **The Family Coordinator,** 1972, **21,** 435–456.

52. Rees, B. J. (Ed.) **Modern American prose selections.** New York: Harcourt, 1920.

53. Rettig, S., & Pasamanick, B. Changes in moral values among college students: a factorial study. **American Sociological Review,** 1959, **24,** 856–863.

54. Rogers, C. R. A theory of therapy, personality, and interpersonal relationships. In S. Koch (Ed.), **Psychology: a study of a science.** Vol. III. New York: McGraw-Hill, 1959.

55. Rossi, A. S. Transition to parenthood. **Journal of Marriage and the Family,** 1968, **30,** 26–39.

56. Rubin, Z. Do American women marry up? **American Sociological Review,** 1968, **33,** 750–760.

57. Saxton, L. **The individual, marriage, and the family** (2nd ed.). Belmont, Ca.: Wadsworth, 1972.

58. Sheehy, G. **Passages.** New York: Dutton, 1976.

59. Sindberg, R. M., Roberts, A. F., & McClain, D. Mate selection factors in computer matched marriages. **Journal of Marriage and the Family,** 1972, **34,** 611–614.

60. Strong, E. K., Jr. **Vocational interests 18 years after college.** Minneapolis: University of Minnesota Press, 1955.

61. Strong, E. K., Jr. **Vocational interests of men and women.** Stanford: Stanford University Press, 1943.

62. Sullivan, J. A. **Selection of dates and mates.** Columbus, Ohio: Ohio State University Libraries, 1972.

63. Sussman, M. Parental participation in mate selection and its effects upon family continuity. **Social Forces,** 1953, **32,** 76–81.

64. Suter, L. E., & Miller, H. P. Components of differences between the incomes of men and career women. **American Journal of Sociology,** 1973, **79,** 962–974.

65. Tapp, J. L., & Levine, F. J. Compliance from kindergarten to college: a speculative research note. **Journal of Youth and Adolescence,** 1972, **1,** 233–249.

66. Tangri, S. S. Determinants of occupational role innovation among college women. **Journal of Social Issues,** 1972, **28,** 177–199.

67. Toder, N. L., & Marcia, J. E. Ego identity status and response to conformity pressure in college women. **Journal of Personality and Social Psychology,** 1973, **26,** 287–294.

68. Toffler, A. **Future shock.** New York: Random House, 1970.

69. Udry, J. R. **The social context of marriage** (2nd ed.). Philadelphia: Lippincott, 1971.

70. Udry, J. R. **The social context of marriage** (3rd ed.). Philadelphia: Lippincott, 1974.

71. Van Dusen, R. A., & Sheldon, E. B. The changing status of American women: a life cycle perspective. **American Psychologist,** 1976, **31,** 106–116.

72. Veroff, J., & Feld, S. **Marriage and work in America.** New York: Van Nostrand Reinhold, 1970.

73. Waterman, A. S., Geary, P. S., & Waterman, C. K. Longitudinal study of changes in ego identity status from the freshman to the senior year at college. **Developmental Psychology,** 1974, **10,** 387–392.

74. Waterman, A. S., & Waterman, C. K. A longitudinal study of changes in ego identity status during the freshman year in college. **Developmental Psychology,** 1971, **5,** 167–173.

75. White, M. S. Psychological and social barriers to women in science. **Science,** 1970, **170,** 413–416.

76. White, R. W. **Lives in progress** (3rd ed.). New York: Holt, Rinehart and Winston, 1975.

77. Wiegand, E. **Use of time by full-time and part-time home-makers in relation to home management.** Ithaca, N.Y.: Cornell University Agricultural Experiment Station, 1954. Cited in Blood, R. O. **The Family (5).**

78. Winch, R. F. **Mate selection: a study of complementary needs.** New York: Harper, 1958.

79. Yankelovich, D. **Generations apart.** New York: CBS News, 1969.

80. Yankelovich, D. **The new morality: A profile of American youth in the 1970's.** New York: McGraw-Hill, 1974.

CHAPTER II
The Middle Years

The middle years are almost always the most productive of our lives. We raise our children and launch them into lives and families of their own. Our careers flourish; income, opportunities, and responsibilities are likely to reach their highest points. At the same time, of course, the middle years bring anxieties commensurate with the increased family and career responsibilities. We worry about our children and often about our parents, who are growing old and may need more assistance. We worry about our work more than we used to, because now we have a greater say; we are more involved. But even as our major concerns in life—our family, our work—reach a zenith, we begin to notice a decline. Physical strength and stamina slowly lessen, and our memory does not seem quite as sharp as it once was. We begin to worry about our health. We begin to realize, perhaps for the first time, that someday we are going to die.

When does a person become middle-aged? Most people define "middle age" as beginning about 40 and extending to 50 or 55 (12, 49). But it is clear that this age range defines only the central core of middle age, for these same respondents define two other adult stages: "young adults," ages 18–25, and "old people," who are 65 or older. These definitions leave a couple of unnamed periods before and after middle age, transition periods of sorts. From 25 to 40, people are "developing"; some seem young and still struggling, while others seem middle-aged at 30—conservative and well along in their careers. From 50 to 65, some people are just reaching their peak, while others appear to be aging rapidly (all their friends comment on it). Acknowledging the considerable individual differences that exist at both ends of the middle years of adulthood, we will focus on the period that begins at age 35–40 and ends at 60–65.

In this chapter, we will first discuss personality development in the middle years. The individual's concerns about work, advancement, and family, of course, play a major role in this development. Another concern is about intellectual ability, and we will next review the research evidence on intellectual development, both its growth and decline. The increasing concern about health and physical abilities in the middle years will be briefly discussed in terms of menopause, heart attacks, and sexual "prowess." Finally we will explore the family in the middle years—relations with children and with aging parents, determinants of marital satisfaction, and, finally, the emotional impact of family disruption caused by separation or divorce.

Before turning to these topics, however, we should review the difference between longitudinal and cross-sectional studies of age-related phenomena. As defined in Chapter 1, a longitudinal investigation involves the observation of the same individuals at two or more ages; a cross-sectional study compares different groups of people varying in age (see Figure 11.1). Thus, for example, one could study age-related changes in health either by examining the same individuals every five years as they age from 35 to 65 or by examining, all at once, a group of 35-year-olds, a group of 40-year-olds, a group of 45-year-olds, and so on. Often longitudinal and cross-sectional studies yield similar results, but

● Figure 11.1   Cross-sectional and longitudinal studies. A cross-sectional study tests different groups of different ages (born in different years). A longitudinal study tests the same group at different ages (tested in different years).

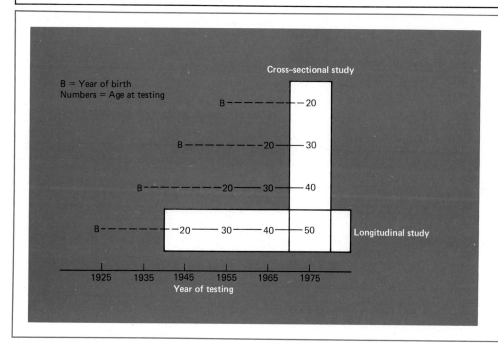

sometimes there are considerable differences, especially when the time period investigated is as extensive as the middle years of life. If there are differences, they are usually attributable to the fact that cross-sectional studies test people who not only are different ages but also were born in different years. Thus, if a cross-sectional investigation in 1979 discovers that the average 65-year-old is less healthy than the average 35-year-old, this difference may be due to normal aging processes. On the other hand, it may reflect, at least in part, improved nutrition and health care for people born in 1944, compared to people born in 1914.

Longitudinal studies are not free from problems of interpretation either—they are subject to bias, for example, if a large number of participants die, move away, or otherwise "get lost" over the period of the investigation—and they are generally quite expensive. Developmental psychologists feel most comfortable when they have data from both cross-sectional *and* longitudinal studies. The common state of affairs, however, is to have only cross-sectional data, and thus some of the conclusions in the pages that follow should be viewed with caution.

PERSONALITY DEVELOPMENT IN THE MIDDLE YEARS

The major developmental dilemma of the middle years of adulthood, according to Erik Erikson (18), is *generativity versus stagnation.* Generativity is a very broad concept in Erikson's theory, encompassing parenthood—having children and educating them—as well as most of what we mean by terms such as "productivity" and "creativity"—being competent, making a contribution. Generativity, therefore, is a concept similar to *self-actualization,* which Maslow (41) has defined as the motive to become the best one can be. Self-actualizing people try to be the best parents possible. In their chosen professions, they strive to do their best and to improve until they have reached the highest level of competence of which they are capable. They try to be loyal friends, active and concerned citizens, reliable tennis partners. They work to develop their virtues and to eliminate their faults, to become as nearly perfect as it is possible for them to be.

To the extent that a person fails to develop generativity, there is an absence of personal growth and enrichment, a negative quality that Erikson calls stagnation. In severe cases, "regression to an obsessive need for pseudo-intimacy takes place, often with a pervading sense of . . . personal impoverishment. Individuals, then, often begin to indulge themselves as if they were their own . . . one and only child; and where conditions favor it, early invalidism, physical or psychological, becomes the vehicle of self-concern" (18, p. 267).

Of course, everybody "stagnates" a bit now and then; everybody acts childish and self-indulgent at times. Successful resolution of the conflict between generativity and stagnation in middle adulthood means only that the person shades toward optimism over pessimism and prefers problem-solving to complaining. Erikson (19) identifies *care* as the human virtue most closely associated with generativity; mature adults are those who care for their children whom they have created, for their work which they have produced, or for the welfare of others in the society in which they live.

Stages of Personality Development

Erik Erikson's theory focused on childhood stages of development; his discussion of the middle years of life is brief and phrased in very general terms. Theorists who have focused on the adult years have tried to elaborate some of the concerns of the middle years, describing more of the prominent issues and defining a few more stages. It is important to note that these stages were developed almost entirely from studies of white, middle-class people; it is quite possible that the stages represent critical periods in middle-class careers and lifestyles and that different stages may have to be defined for different populations. Nevertheless, it is interesting that enough people have "life crises" at roughly the same age for researchers to identify and describe these adult stages.

Let us first recall the stages of young adulthood that precede those of the middle years. In their 20s people are generally concerned with the selection of a mate and a career, shaping a dream and starting out to achieve it. Somewhat later, around the age of 30, many people reevaluate their early choices about mates, careers, and dreams; in some cases they divorce their spouses and resign from their jobs. Finally, the early 30s is typically a time of settling down with new or reaffirmed choices.

The mid-life crisis   The first stage of the middle years begins around the age of 35 and extends into the early forties. This stage has been called the "deadline decade" (62) and the "mid-life crisis" (30). Its primary characteristic is an evaluation of the difference between one's dreams and goals in life and the actuality of one's existence. Since people's dreams about themselves almost always have some unrealistic aspects, even fantastic, magical "Cinderella" aspects, evaluations at this stage are more likely to be negative and emotionally depressing. The time left to make up the difference between dream and actuality suddenly appears frightfully short. On questionnaires, people around the age of 35 or 40 begin to disagree with items such as "There's still plenty of time to do most of the things I want to do"; instead, they find themselves concerned that it's "too late to make any major change in my career" (24). In one's 20s and 30s, one can be "promising"—people might say a young man or woman is a "promising young artist, executive, psychologist, or manager"—but after the age of 40, one is no longer young; it is time to fulfill one's promise. The individual may have to accept the fact that he or she is never going to become the president of the company, the senator from Minnesota, the acclaimed novelist, and, what's more, he or she may not even become a vice-president or state senator or minor writer.

The disillusionment that is not uncommon around the age of 35 or 40 can be dangerous for a person's ego. Dante, author of *The Divine Comedy,* described his own psychological turmoil at the beginning of this deadline decade: "Midway upon the journey of our life I found myself within a forest dark, for the straightforward pathway had been lost" (1, p. 15). Eleanor Roosevelt (Figure 11.2), six days shy of her thirty-fifth birthday, was less poetic but no less intense: "I do not think I have ever felt so strangely as in the past year. . . . All my self-confidence is gone. . . ." (39, p. 237). Attorney Oliver Wendell Holmes, Jr., at 35, was bored to death with his law practice: "Was this, he asked himself, to be his life, forever, year after year?" (9, p. 251).

In an intensive review of the lives of artists (30), some kind of dramatic change in their creativity around the age of 35 was found in almost every case. Some artists (e.g., Gauguin) began their creative work at this age. Others, however, seemed to lose their creative abilities or motivations around 35, and many died; the death rate for artists between 35 and 39 shows an abnormal increase. These artists who survived the deadline decade with creative powers intact usually demonstrated some significant change in their work. Often the change was one of intensity, as impulsive brilliance gave way to a mellowed and more

●Figure 11.2   Eleanor Roosevelt: "I don't think I ever felt as strangely as in the past year. . . . All my self-confidence is gone."

deliberate creativity. Indeed, one of the reasons for the mid-life crisis in artists is that the "impulsive brilliance" of young adulthood requires a stamina, which is at least partly physical, that no one can maintain forever. At 35 or 40, the hard-driving artist (or executive or professor) must change his or her pace or "burn out." Thus the issue of decreasing physical powers is typically raised in the lives of artists as well as laborers.

Major issues   How to deal with declining physical strength, stamina, and attractiveness is one of several major issues that an individual must confront, in one way or another, during the years of the mid-life crisis and beyond (53). For those who relied heavily on their physical advantages when younger, middle age can be a very depressing period. Stories of handsome men and beautiful women fighting the "ravages of time" are commonplace. Distress about decreasing stamina affects people in a surprising range of occupations, including, as we have seen, artists. University professors recall with some sense of loss their former ability as college students to go without sleep for days if so required by an important project. Many people simply complain about being tired too often. Although a thoughtful program of daily exercise and proper diet is beneficial, most people in the middle years begin to rely more and more on "brains" rather than "brawn." They find new and often more satisfying advantages in the accumulated knowledge from life's experience; they have "wisdom."

A second major issue of the middle years is sexuality. In the average person, there is some decline in interest, ability, and opportunity, especially as children grow older. Many people are surprised to realize how large a role sexuality played in interpersonal relationships when they were younger. We have numerous examples in fiction of the rather sad, middle-aged man or woman who continues to view each member of the opposite sex as a potential sexual partner, interacting with them on the single dimension of "attraction–rejection," and who "competes" with members of the same sex. Successful aging involves accepting others as individuals, as potential companions. "Socializing" replaces "sexualizing" in interpersonal relationships, and the relationships often "take on a depth of understanding which the earlier, perhaps inevitably more egocentric, sex drive would have tended to prevent to some degree" (53, p. 89).

Adjustment in middle age requires considerable flexibility. One valuable type of flexibility involves "the capacity to shift emotional investments from one person to another, and from one activity to another" (53, p. 89). Emotional flexibility, of course, is necessary at all ages, but in the middle years it becomes especially important, as parents die and children grow up and leave home. Inability to make emotional investments in new people (and new activities) leads to the kind of stagnation Erikson described.

Another kind of flexibility required for successful aging is "mental flexibility." There is a tendency among aging individuals to become increasingly rigid in their opinions and actions, closing their minds to new ideas. This mental

●Figure 11.3   For many people, the 50s are a period of new stability.

rigidity must be avoided or it will grow into intolerance or fanaticism. In addition, rigid attitudes lead to errors and an inability to perceive creative solutions to problems.

Stabilization   Successful resolution of the mid-life crisis usually involves a reformulation of goals with a more realistic and modest vision and an acceptance of one's limited time in this life. Spouse, friends, and children become more important, while self becomes less important (23). There is an increasing attempt "to be satisfied with what I have and not to think so much about the things I probably won't be able to get." There is a sharp increase in the feeling that "my personality is pretty well set." These changes mark the next stage of personality development, a period of "new stability" (24).

For many, the process of renewal that began when they confronted their disillusionments and declining physical abilities eventually results in a more peaceful and even happier life (62). In the 50s, health problems become more likely, and there is a growing awareness that time is "running out." Barring major health or economic tragedies, however, the 50s usually continue the new forms of stability achieved during the late 40s (see Figure 11.3).

Personality Traits

Although most people face similar developmental tasks and environmental pressures as they grow older, they do not always react to them in similar ways. Some face the "crises" of the middle years with optimism; after reevaluation of their goals, they become less anxious and depressed, more self confident, more cheerful. Other people find the same "crises" devastating and never seem to recover from the disillusionments; they become more anxious and depressed, less self confident, less cheerful. As one reviewer put it, "older people, like younger people, have differing capacities to cope with life stresses and to come to terms with their life situations . . . chronological age is not the decisive factor" (47, p. 324).

Suppose we ask, then, how personality changes with age. For the most part, we would have to say that some people change in one way; others change in the opposite way; and still others stay the same. We would expect that if we researched "age trends" in anxiety (or depression or self-confidence or cheerfulness or other personality traits), we would find very few *general* trends. In fact, this is a fair description of the results of research on personality change in the adult years.

In an early longitudinal study (33), about 500 people were tested, first around the age of 25, then again (in 1953 and 1954) when most of the subjects were in their early 40s. These people had not only survived World War II, but they had presumably passed through the mid-life crisis described above. In spite of such general social and psychological disturbances, the absence of general changes in personality was clearly in evidence. Very few of the 38 variables in the study showed significant differences in average scores from the first testing to the second.

The particular variables that did change with age did not fall into neat categories that were readily interpretable. Religious values and interests generally increased, and men developed a more positive attitude toward gardening. Both men and women saw themselves as less peppy, less neat, and less good-natured than they had been in their youth. It is hard to attribute these differences entirely to age. It may be, for example, that people are simply more willing to admit to an ill temper when they are older. And do the increases in religious values reflect a change that occurs with age? An alternative explanation is that people were generally more religious in 1953–1954 than they were in the late 1930s, during the last years of the Great Depression.

A more recent investigation (72) suggests that people tend to *perceive* more personality change than actually exists. Personality test scores of people first tested in 1944, when they were about 20 years old, were compared with their scores in 1969, when they averaged 45 years of age. The test yielded an overall score purported to be a measure of personal and social adjustment. There were no significant differences over the 25-year period, supporting the notion that age affects personality in few general ways. In the later testing, however, people were asked to take the personality test again, this time answering as they thought they probably had answered when they took it the first time, in 1944. These "remembered" scores were significantly lower than the real scores for the first testing, indicating that the people thought of themselves as less well-adjusted than they actually were 25 years previously. They thought their personalities had "improved," but the true test scores showed no evidence of such a change.

A large-scale series of investigations known collectively as the Kansas City Studies of Adult Life (47) also showed few personality traits to be age-related. For example, although individuals vary widely in personality traits related to ego functions (that is, the adaptive, goal-directed, and purposive thoughts and actions that are typically under conscious control), older people, on the average, do not differ from younger adults. Similarly, measures of satisfaction with life did not show age trends. The investigators concluded that, although stressful life situations such as poor health or inadequate income may become more likely with increasing age, people react differently to such stresses; personality might well change as a result, but the direction of change is difficult to predict from age alone.

Changes   Although most personality traits show no age trends, there are a few major exceptions. In the Kansas City Studies, the age-related changes occurred primarily in "inner-life processes" and were reflected in an increasingly less active and more fatalistic orientation toward the external world, together with an increasing preoccupation with self and a growing introversion. Specifically, the average 40-year-olds saw their environment as something they could influence with bold action, while the average 60-year-olds were more likely to see the world as controlling them and to see their role as one of conformity and accommodation—a defensive posture that psychologists sometimes call "passive mastery." Along with the increasing passivity comes increasing introspection; "contemplation and reflection and self-evaluation become characteristic forms of mental life. The reflection of middle-age is not the same as the reminiscence of old age; but perhaps it is its forerunner" (46, p. 140). In general, the heightened focus on the inner life has been called the "increased interiority of the personality" (46).

These changes in mental attitudes and orientations were determined primarily by projective tests. In the stories told about ambiguous pictures, there was a significant turn away from concern with the world-out-there and toward interest in self. One would think that this mental change would have some effect on the individuals' behavior in relationships to their social world. Their decreasing interest in the external environment might be expected to make them less involved socially or less competent, at least at tasks that require sensitive monitoring of the needs and desires of other people. But, as we have mentioned, there were no age-related changes in adaptive, purposive behaviors, and social contacts did not begin to thin out until the late 60s or later. Certainly one cannot argue that people become more introverted and introspective *because* they have withdrawn from society.

The changes in mental attitude from active mastery to passive mastery have been demonstrated in a number of different cultural settings around the world, including Kansas City, Mexico, and Israel, and among the Navajo Indians of Arizona (25, 26). Finding this age-related change in different cultures adds weight to the conclusion that it is a basic developmental change and not simply one dictated by specific events in a particular culture (47).

Sex roles   Carl Jung (32) many years ago suggested that "balance" between opposing forces is the key to understanding human personality. On the dimension of age, youth is a period of extraversion, a time to deal with the environment. This early preoccupation with the external, however, creates an imbalance, for a person must also deal with his or her inner life, with needs for introspection and reflection. Eventually this imbalance will be corrected; the individual will inevitably become more introverted with age. Jung's theory, of course, fits well with the research we have just described.

Another imbalance of youth, according to Jung, is the exaggerated sex roles that young men and women play. Men emphasize their aggressive nature, while women are nurturant. This denial of "feminine" qualities by men and of "masculine" qualities by women will eventually lead to a shift. With age, men will become more tender-hearted and emotional, and women will become less emotional and more openly aggressive.

Whether or not it occurs for the reasons Jung believes, there is evidence that such a shift in sex-role behaviors begins in the middle years. In one of the Kansas City Studies (48), subjects ranging from 40 to 70 years of age were asked to tell a story about a picture that depicted a young man and woman and an old man and woman, the four apparently in conversation. As shown in Figure 11.4, subjects over the age of 55 were likely to see the old man as passive instead of authoritative and the old woman as assertive rather than submissive or under the control of husband and children. From this and other studies, one reviewer concluded that "older men seemed more receptive than younger men of their affiliative, nurturant, and sensual promptings; older women, more receptive than younger women of aggressive and egocentric impulses" (47, p. 320). These data support the hypothesis that men begin to develop "feminine" qualities in the late stages of middle age and that women begin to show evidence of traits generally considered "masculine." Perhaps a better way of saying this is that

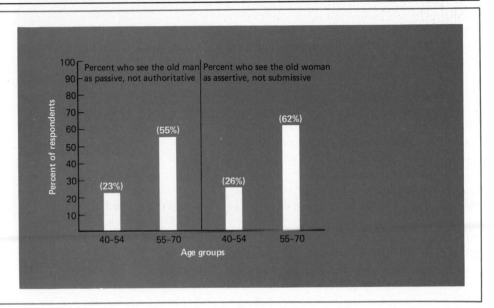

● Figure 11.4 Percent of subjects who, in a projective test, perceived an old man and an old woman behaving contrary to the traditional sex-role stereotypes. (Percentages computed from B. L. Neugarten and D. L. Gutmann. Age–sex roles and personality in middle age. In B. L. Neugarten (ed.). *Middle Age and Aging.* Chicago: University of Chicago Press, 1968.)

the exaggerated sex roles of young adulthood are no longer played, perhaps because they are no longer necessary, and the balanced personality, with both emotional–nurturant and assertive–aggressive qualities, can express itself.

The Potential for Change

Although some general modifications in personality seem to occur in most people as they grow older, the most general conclusion from the evidence collected so far is that there are few character changes that can be attributed solely to aging. In addition, apparent personality differences between young and old people can often be shown to be differences between the experiences and attitudes of different generations and not the result of age at all. For example, older people are typically more rigid in their opinions and behaviors; they seem to be unable to adapt as readily as younger people to changes in their environment. But longitudinal studies (60) show that the old people who now seem rigid were rigid all their lives; they did not become *more* rigid as they grew older. Instead, each new generation has been slightly less rigid than the preceding generation; on the average, people of less recent generations are more rigid than young people of more recent generations. These cross-sectional data were often misinterpreted as indicating an increase in rigidity with age.

To say that there are few age-related trends in personality, however, does not mean that personality change is impossible or even infrequent in the middle years and beyond. In fact, personality change is quite common throughout life. The absence of age trends simply indicates that different people change in different ways and that age, by itself, is not the major factor.

Suppose, for illustration, we reconsider the "early longitudinal study" (31) we discussed on page 415, which found little evidence of significant change with age. This conclusion was properly based on *average* personality test scores by the same people 15 to 20 years apart. Suppose, however, we consider the *correlations* of the scores on tests taken 15 to 20 years apart. This will tell us something different from the averages: whether the people who scored high (or low) in the 1930s were the same people who scored high (or low) in the 1950s. A low correlation suggests change, the highs becoming lows and the lows increasing, even though the average remains the same.

The correlations of scores of people around the age of 25 with scores of the same people in their early 40s were generally moderate for personality variables, ranging from 0.30 to 0.50. In statistical terms, the earlier scores, if used to predict the later scores, would account for less than 25 percent of the variability of the later scores—a fair but certainly not perfect job of prediction. Thus, there is good reason to expect individual personality change, even though these changes do not commonly correlate with age. Some people soften with age; others harden. Middle and old age are not much different from other periods of life in this respect; different people change in different ways.

Some characteristics of personality are more stable than others. Correlations of an individual's vocational interests over the years tend to be relatively high. Studies of people's *perceptions* of themselves—for example, self-ratings of morality or dependency—find reasonable consistency, but studies of actual behavior—for example, moral behavior, dependency behavior—produce much lower correlations. The picture is of real behavioral change over the years combined with a much less rapidly changing perception of oneself (44).

Perhaps the important result of the research on personality and aging is a renewed appreciation of the potential for personality change at any point in the life span. More and more researchers are concluding that "the search for 'invariant' and 'unidirectional' developmental functions in adulthood and aging is not a useful approach" (2, p. 721). Instead, the approach to adult development should emphasize the potential for change—indeed, the inevitability of change (55)—and individual differences. This conclusion has been applied, as we shall see, even to intellectual abilities. It is to the topic of intellectual development in the adult years that we now turn.

INTELLECTUAL DEVELOPMENT

What happens to the intellect during the middle years of adulthood? Common social beliefs have it both ways. Many people believe that the older individual, as long as he or she has not become senile, possesses a valuable combination of intellect and information that we call wisdom. Others believe that intellectual decline begins about the same time most people begin to decline physically, around the age of 30 or so, maybe sooner than that. Which version is nearer the truth?

There are a number of approaches to the study of intellectual development during middle adulthood. One is to examine changes in intelligence test scores over the years. Another approach is to record the products of intellect—the scholarly papers, the great inventions and discoveries—to see if most of them, or the most significant of them, occur at certain ages.

Age and Intelligence

If we ask whether the average 50-year-old has a lower IQ than the average 20-year-old, the answer is, of course, no. Both have an IQ of 100, the average by definition for any age group. This automatic adjustment for chronological age disguises the fact that once an individual enters the adult years, the same (uncorrected) test score earns higher and higher IQ scores with age. For example, in the Wechsler-Bellevue test, an overall score of 80 yields an IQ of 87 for a 20-year-old, an IQ of 92 for a 30-year-old, 97 for a 40-year-old, and 101 if the person is 50 (21). If we compare directly the test scores of different age groups, the average score is highest for 20-year-olds and systematically declines over the older groups. Figure 11.5 depicts an early study of this type.

The initial interpretation of such data was that an individual's intellectual abilities gradually but inexorably decline with the years. David Wechsler, who devised the famous Wechsler scales of intelligence for children and adults, believed that the "decline of mental ability with age is part of the general senescent process of the organism as a whole" (70, p. 30). In other words, Wechsler believed that mental ability deteriorated in ways similar to those of lung capacity, reaction time, and other physical abilities.

Longitudinal studies Wechsler's conclusions about the relationship of age and intelligence were generally accepted until the surprising results of the first longitudinal studies were published in the early 1950s. Longitudinal studies, as we have mentioned, are typically expensive and difficult, and few researchers enjoy waiting 40 years or so for the final results of a single investigation. By the 1950s, however, there existed a large number of people who had previously taken intelligence tests when entering a university, a practice that began in 1919; by finding them and retesting them, a researcher had a ready-made longitudinal study requiring less expense and trouble than usual. In one such investigation (52), people who were first tested in 1919, at the average age of 19, were retested again in 1950, at the average age of 50. The results showed a quite sizable *increase* in average test scores from 19 to 50—the exact *opposite* of results found in cross-sectional studies. In a still later follow-up, the same people were tested again in 1961, when their average age was 61. There was essentially no change

●Figure 11.5   An early cross-sectional study showing apparent decline in intelligence test scores with age. (From C. C. Miles and W. R. Miles. The correlation of intelligence scores and chronological age from early to late maturity. *American Journal of Psychology*, 1932, *44*, 44–78.)

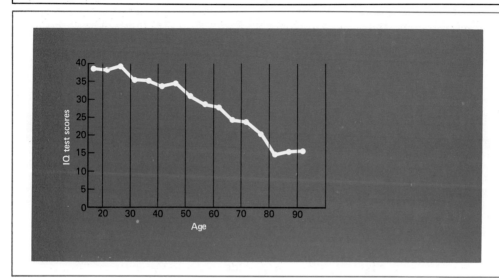

in average test scores from age 50 to 61. Other longitudinal studies published about the same time (e.g., 4) reported similar findings.

Most of the early longitudinal studies tested highly educated people whose professional careers required the use of academic skills—mathematics, extensive reading, abstract reasoning. Later studies, using samples more representative of the general population, indicate that the *increase* in intellectual performance was due to the special groups used in the first investigations; raw scores of the average person do not increase with age, but then neither do they decline (3). In one large-scale study (60), features of both cross-sectional and longitudinal designs were combined. A 1956 cross-sectional study of various age groups (24–70) was repeated, with as many of the same people as could be found, in 1963 and again in 1970. Thus, in effect, the researchers had three cross-sectional studies, but they could also observe the longitudinal changes for people over a period of 14 years. Each of the cross-sectional studies, considered separately, showed the typical declining curve of intellectual performance with age. But the individuals, on the average, maintained their levels well into their 70s (see Figure 11.6).

How can we account for these striking differences between the cross-sectional studies of different people of different ages and the longitudinal studies of the same people as they grow older? The major factor appears to be differences

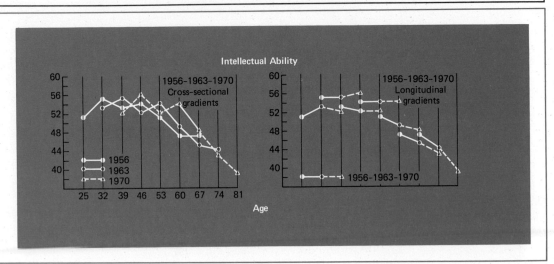

● Figure 11.6 Cross-sectional and longitudinal age gradients for a composite measure of intellectual ability. (Adapted from K. W. Schaie and G. Labouvie-Vief. Generational versus ontogenetic components of change in adult cognitive behavior: A fourteen-year cross-sequential study. *Developmental Psychology*, 1974, *10*, 305–320.)

between generations. For illustration, suppose we traced the intellectual development of a group of people born in 1927 and found them at roughly the same level of functioning in 1947 (when they were 20) and in 1977 (when they were 50). In 1977, however, suppose we also tested a group of people born in 1957 and found these 20-year-olds superior to the older group. Looking at just the 1977 data, it appears that intelligence declines from age 20 to age 50. But considering the fact that our 50-year-olds were really no smarter when they were 20, it is more plausible to conclude that people born in 1957, on the average, perform at a higher level of intellectual functioning than do people born in 1927. "In other words, there is strong evidence that much of the difference in performance on intellectual abilities between young and old is *not* due to decline in ability on the part of the old, but due to higher performance levels in successive generations" (59, p. 804).

Many factors have been suggested to explain why the average test scores are generally higher in successive generations; among them are better education, better nutrition, and more familiarity with tests in the later generations. It should be mentioned that there is some evidence that the steady upward march of intelligence test scores may have recently slowed or even reversed. For example, on the Scholastic Aptitude Test, which correlates highly with standard IQ measures, average scores for high-school seniors have been declining since 1962 (73). Part of this decline seems due to an increase in applications by less well-prepared students, who, in the past, would not have applied to college.

However, this is clearly not the only factor, and the recent decrease in intellectual performance has also been attributed to poorer education, poorer nutrition, and less interest in academic achievement—and even to a temporary decrease in the percentage of first-born children among those applying to college, on the basis of data showing that the eldest children typically score higher on IQ tests than their younger siblings (73).

Specific Intellectual Abilities

The early cross-sectional studies indicated an overall intellectual decline with age, but some investigators made a distinction between "hold" and "don't hold" subtests of specific intellectual abilities (70). The average scores on "don't hold" subtests seemed to decline rather rapidly after the age of 20 or 30, but the abilities measured by the "hold" subtests seemed to fare better with age, declining less rapidly or sometimes not at all until the final decades of life. Such a distinction can also be made in longitudinal studies, although in these investigations the scores on the "don't hold" subtests show only moderate decline if any, and the scores on the "hold" subtests may actually increase.

The intellectual abilities least likely to decline are those that most people would attribute to formal or informal educational experiences. These abilities are best represented by tests of vocabulary and general information and by some tests of reasoning, especially those that rely on acquired knowledge and practiced problem-solving strategies. In contrast, the abilities most likely to decline with age are those that do not benefit significantly from previous learning, such as the ability to recall a series of numbers immediately after they are presented. Older subjects are particularly poor at repeating numbers backwards (10) and at repeating numbers while performing some other task simultaneously (69). They also tend to perform more poorly than young people at tasks that reward a speedy response (8). For example, many subtests of the various IQ tests are scored for the number of correct answers in a given time period; older people tend to answer fewer questions in that time period and therefore earn a lower score than young subjects, even though their percentage of correct answers may be the same or even higher (14). There is evidence of a slowing of motor performance with age, especially in "the redirecting of movement in response to new information" (6, p. 812).

Psychologists since Wechsler have been inclined to explain the difference between abilities that "hold" and those that "don't hold" in terms of "acquired knowledge," which is maintained or even increased until very late in life, versus "native ability," which declines as the body ages and becomes less efficient. For example, one current hypothesis holds that the slower responses of older people "reflect a basic change in the speed with which the central nervous system processes information" (6, p. 808). Changes in the ability of the central nervous system to process information efficiently could also explain a gradual decline in basic intellectual abilities such as memory and attention. General information would be relatively unaffected by such a physical decline, and most intellectual tasks would not be expected to show deficits—providing older people are given enough time to respond.

A more formal theory of two types of intelligence has been constructed from mathematical analyses of the correlations among many different tests of intellectual functioning (28). Two broad factors emerged from these analyses. The first is called *crystallized intelligence*, which reflects mental abilities heavily influenced by formal education and general experience. The second is *fluid intelligence*, presumably the native-ability aspect of intelligent behavior. Crystallized intelligence generally increases with age in cross-sectional studies, and fluid intelligence systematically decreases, as shown in Figure 11.7. General

●Figure 11.7 Performance on tests of "fluid," "crystallized," and "general" intelligence. (From J. L. Horn. Organization of data on life-span development of human abilities. In L. R. Goulet and P. B. Baltes (eds.). *Life-Span Developmental Psychology: Research and Theory.* New York: Academic Press, 1970.)

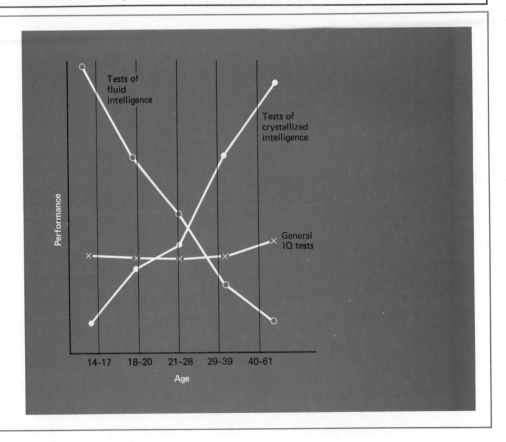

IQ tests include measures of both crystallized and fluid intelligence and show little change with age, for the increase in one type of intelligence is balanced by a decrease in the other.

The theory of crystallized and fluid intelligence is an intriguing one, but it is still not much more than theory, supported by only a few cross-sectional studies. Objections to the theory (2) center on the hypothesized decline in fluid intelligence; it is claimed that such a decline in cross-sectional studies may be misleading (for the reasons we have reviewed). More generally, many psychologists investigating the relationship between age and intelligence now believe that the search for the curve of "normal" deterioration in the physical basis of intelligence (which fluid intelligence presumably reflects) is a fruitless task (2). In the view of such psychologists, there is too much variability in age trends in intellectual ability to postulate one of these trends as normal or basic. Some people decline in intellectual ability, some increase; some abilities seem to be increasing in succeeding generations, some seem to be decreasing; an environmental event (e.g., the development of television) can change age trends for some people and have little effect on others. In this view, the search for the "normal" age changes in intelligence is "anachronistic," "reactionary," and "apt to retard progress in the field of intelligence in adulthood and old age" (2, pp. 724–725).

Environmental Influences

There are a number of important environmental influences on intellectual functioning, influences that profoundly affect the course of intellectual development. (One need not abandon the investigation of basic, underlying abilities in order to admit this fact, of course.) One environmental factor of great significance is disease. The older one gets, the more probable are diseases of various sorts, and many of these illnesses may affect intelligence, directly or indirectly. The distractions of pain and economic worries that accompany illness in the later years often lead to poorer performance on tests of intellectual functioning. In addition, a number of diseases can result in mild or severe brain injury and thus affect intelligence directly.

Perhaps the most important diseases affecting the relationship of age and intelligence are those classified as cardiovascular—having to do with the heart and blood vessels. When the blood flow to the brain is affected (cerebrovascular diseases), mental abilities usually decline to some degree, either temporarily or permanently. A "stroke"—a blocking of blood vessels in the brain—may result in permanent impairment, depending on the areas of the brain affected, but even mild cardiovascular disease has been shown to be related to deficits in memory (37) and lower scores on the Wechsler Adult Intelligence Scale (67). Apparently the lowered blood flow has its effects by decreasing the oxygen supply to brain cells, resulting in temporary "malnutrition" or "starvation" and death of tissue in affected brain areas (31).

Disease, of course, is more common later in life than earlier. Older people are significantly more likely to have health problems that affect their intellectual performance; cardiovascular disease, for example, increases rather systematically with age, at least after the age of 45 (34). Some of the intellectual decline that has been attributed to aging can no doubt be more properly attributed to the advent of chronic disease in older people. In a classic study of older men (average age 71 years) judged to be extremely healthy on the basis of intensive medical examinations (7), cerebral blood flow was no worse than for the average 21-year-old male, and these elderly subjects were equal or superior to young men on most of the intellectual tests. Another group of old men were believed to be healthy until the intensive examination turned up evidence of mild disease. Compared to the healthy old subjects, these men scored lower on most of the intellectual tests, indicating that "even a mild degree of chronic disease has major consequences for the aged on a wide variety of functions" (34, p. 366). Disease probably also accounts for much of the *terminal decline,* a relatively rapid loss of intellectual powers in the period preceding death (31, 56).

The social environment of adults and old people also affects their intellectual functioning (2, 3, 59). The degree to which the individual participates in social activities is related to whether he or she shows an increase or decrease in IQ scores over the years. Those adults who are fully engaged socially tend to gain in intellectual ability or to show no change, while those who are socially isolated tend to decline. Studies comparing older people who have been given special training on intellectual tasks with otherwise similar people given no special training show that "an old dog can learn new tricks." They also suggest that the opportunities and motivation for learning may decrease more with age than the actual ability to learn.

Age and Achievement

Another approach to the study of the relationship between age and intelligence is to investigate the end product of intelligent behavior, the "creative products" of scientists, philosophers, artists, businesspeople, politicians, chess players, and other people who rely primarily on their intelligence to earn their living. Do most achievements occur when people are young and their intellect presumably sharp, or when they are older and wiser?

Major creative works—the one or two accomplishments for which the person is best known—tend to occur relatively early in life (40). There are, of course, notable individual exceptions—Goethe completed *Faust* after the age of 80—and major achievements in some fields, such as philosophy, seem to occur later than in other fields. But most scientists, scholars, and artists produce their most notable works in their 30s. Especially when one considers the years of education and training that are often necessary before a major contribution is possible, these figures suggest that most major achievements occur quite early indeed.

The total output of creative people, however, is spread more evenly across the life span. In a study of 738 persons who lived to age 79 or beyond (15), the 60s were the most productive years for four groups: historians, philosophers, botanists, and inventors (see Figure 11.8). Scholars (history, philosophy, literature) were generally more productive in the later years—including the 70s. Scientists were most productive in their 40s, 50s, and 60s, and artists slightly earlier, in their 30s, 40s, and 50s.

Creative people are clearly capable of producing significant works throughout their lives. Although most important contributions tend to come earlier in a career, this does not necessarily mean the person is more creative or has a superior intellect at the younger age. Youth is a time of ambition, a time to make one's mark. Numerous studies have demonstrated a greater degree of achievement needs in the early adult years (38). Once status and recognition are forthcoming, some aspects of the motivation to achieve may diminish. Also, the first presentation of a new, creative set of ideas is often noted as the "most significant work," even though the later elaborations may be equally brilliant. Sigmund Freud's early publication, *The Interpretation of Dreams,* is generally considered his most important work, but he continued to expand, clarify, modify, and improve his psychoanalytic theory until his death at the age of 83.

BIOLOGICAL CONCERNS IN MIDDLE ADULTHOOD

The middle years of adult life bring an awareness of a gradually aging body, of a physical self that has begun its decline. A person confronts his mortality, often for the first time. Once in a while he will think about death, and he begins to worry about his health. The "sins" of his youth, such as smoking and drinking, begin to exact their toll, and he may give up smoking and reduce his intake of alcoholic beverages. He may take up jogging, concerned about his lack of exercise. Despite his desperate attempts to diet, his stomach seems to grow larger every year. His hair shows a little gray or begins to recede. He is growing older.

Biological concerns become a major issue in old age, but these concerns have their beginnings in the middle years. In this chapter we will briefly discuss three such concerns. The first is menopause, an inevitable biological event that affects women around the age of 50. The second is a frequently preventable, disease-related event whose victims are usually middle-aged men—heart attack. And third we will note some of the biological and social factors in the decrease in sexual behavior over the adult years, a concern, of course, of both men and women.

Menopause

Menopause is the time in the life of the adult female when menstruation ceases; at the same time, her ovaries stop producing a monthly ovum (egg). Usually there is a period of about two years before menopause during which menstrua-

Figure 11.8   Graph showing productivity for certain professions, expressed as a percentage of the output of the most productive decade (designated as 100 percent). Poets, architects, and chemists usually achieve maximum professional productivity during their forties, whereas inventors and historians do so during their sixties. The data summarized here are illustrative because the subjects were not uniform in degree of eminence, and the units of productivity (for example, a poem versus a history of Rome) are not equivalent. (Adapted from W. Dennis. Creative productivity between the ages of 20 and 80 years. *Journal of Gerontology*, 1966, *21*, 1–8.)

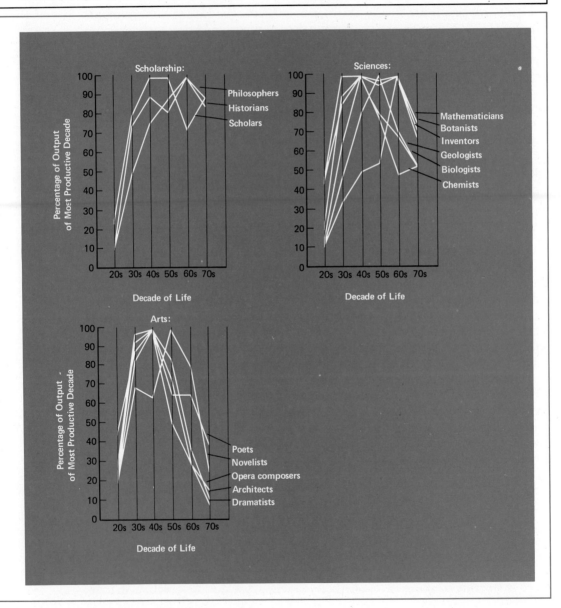

tion becomes irregular and a number of physical symptoms appear. The final menstruation occurs, in most women, sometime between the ages of 48 and 52 (5).

For many women, menopause and the year or two directly preceding it are times of both physical and psychological turmoil. The most common physical symptoms are "hot flashes" and dryness of the vagina. Hot flashes are sudden feelings of heat; they may involve sweating and redness of the skin and they are often followed by chills. Hot flashes last for a minute or less and occur four or five times a day in women who experience them at all. (About a third of the women in one survey (5) did not report hot flashes.) The other symptom, dryness of the vagina, is usually experienced as discomfort or pain during sexual intercourse, and many women begin using a lubricating jelly at this time. Both of these symptoms are apparently the results of decreasing levels of the hormone estrogen. If the symptoms are unusually severe, doctors may prescribe "estrogen replacement therapy," which generally alleviates or eliminates the symptoms (but which also has potentially harmful side effects).

A number of other symptoms are associated with menopause, although in some cases their relationship to menopause may be primarily psychological rather than physical. Many women report frequent dizzy spells, headaches, and heart palpitations, which may be physical or psychosomatic (34). Psychological complaints such as anxiety, irritability, impatience, and depression could result from hormonal imbalances or from the woman's psychological reaction to menopause and its symptoms; probably there is an element of both. For example, hot flashes often occur at night, disturbing sleep. If this happens, the woman is understandably tired and irritable during the day. In any case, most textbook descriptions of the frequency and severity of these symptoms appear to be exaggerated; about one out of five women will experience no unusual symptoms at all during menopause, and many of those who do have symptoms report no more than occasional hot flashes (5). Probably the unpleasantness of menopause is usually exaggerated because most of our information comes from women who have sought a doctor's help because their symptoms are extreme.

Nevertheless, the myths of menopause are many, and they have a real effect on women facing or undergoing this natural phenomenon. "I was afraid we couldn't have sexual relations after the menopause," said one woman (50), "and my husband thought so, too." Another woman thought "menopause would be the beginning of the end . . . gradual senility closing over, like the darkness." Mental stability is another concern: "I knew two women who had nervous breakdowns and I worried about losing my mind." Most women (and men) have at least a few distorted ideas about menopause, in conjunction with a lot of uncertainty and anxiety. A group of women who were experiencing or had experienced menopause, when asked what was the worst thing about menopause, most frequently said: "Not knowing what to expect" (50).

When menopause does occur, therefore, it is typically much less disruptive than the woman expects, and many women are pleasantly surprised by a number of desirable consequences. Simply not menstruating is a benefit, and not worrying about pregnancy can result in a happier sex life. Many women report increased vigor after menopause; "I'm just never tired now," said one (50). In this study, almost half of the women aged 45 to 55 agreed with the statement, "Many women think menopause is the best thing that ever happened to them."

The discomfort of menopause—especially the anxiety and depression—can make this a bad period for some women. Many psychoanalysts have suggested that the loss of child-bearing ability is especially traumatic—it is the "closing of the gates" (16)—but research evidence suggests otherwise. Only 1 woman in 25 mentioned "not being able to have children" as the worst thing about menopause (50). Instead, there is an abstract concern about menopause as a "sign of getting older"—about being considered dried up and useless. "I'll never forget a man's description of an elegant hotel in the Virgin Islands as 'menopause manor'! It made me glad at the time that I was still menstruating and didn't qualify for his derogatory observation" (5).

While there are definite physical and psychological symptoms experienced by most women at menopause, it appears that the actual experience is not as negative—and is in many respects much more positive—than popular belief would have it. Like any notable physical change—pregnancy, for example—menopause can affect women in different ways, benefiting some, increasing the problems of others. For most women, however, menopause has relatively little effect on their personalities or their lives. If society did not have a generally negative view of old people in general and old women in particular, menopause would deserve much less space in this book than it has received.

Heart Attack

In some respects, a heart attack may be to men what menopause is to women: It is considered a definitive sign of "old age" and the end to an "active and fun life." About 80 percent of all heart attack cases are male (8), and the probability of a heart attack increases sharply in the middle years of adult life (34). About one of every five males in the United States will have a heart attack before the age of 60 (64).

One of the best predictors of whether or not a man will have a heart attack is his "life style." In particular, medical researchers have identified a behavior pattern called "Type A," which is marked by competitive achievement striving, a constant feeling of time urgency, and hostility, often born of frustrations (20). Type A men have more than twice the incidence of heart disease as Type B individuals, who are relatively easy-going and patient (58). Why Type A men have more heart attacks is not fully understood, but several aspects of their lives probably play some role. Type A individuals are slightly more likely to be heavy cigarette smokers, for example. The single most important factor, however, is probably the situation of constant stress they create for themselves (Figure 11.9). Stress is known to result in increases in blood cholesterol, and cholesterol, in turn, has been associated with heart disease (22).

●Figure 11.9   Type A individuals are characterized by competitive achievement striving, constant impatience, and hostility born of frustration.

Men's reactions to an actual heart attack (acute myocardial infarction) appear to vary with age (57). Men who had a heart attack before the age of 40 seemed determined to demonstrate their virility and their ability to be active; they seemed almost to pooh-pooh the medical event. Nurses described them as cheerful, jovial, even "manic," and also flirtatious and seductive; the younger adult patients, more than any other age group, deliberately disregarded the prescribed medical regimen. The oldest patients—over 60 years of age—were also cheerful, but they were very cooperative, following instructions to the letter. Apparently the loss of abilities signaled by a heart attack is not as traumatic to the older male; perhaps such loss is even expected, in one form or another.

The reaction of the middle group, the 50-year-olds, however, is most interesting. These men should be in a period of transition between the active orientation of youth and the more passive orientation of later years. They "still cling to achievement-autonomy goals, feeling they must push on; . . . they have begun to doubt their ability to reach these goals, . . . (but) they are reluctant to retreat from the struggle" (57, p. 207). Empirically, the 50-year-old patients were most likely of all age groups to be "overtly depressed" and also "anxious and tense." The researchers conclude that a heart attack accentuates the normal life crises of a 50-year-old, making him especially vulnerable to its psychological impact; ". . . the immediate demands for passivity and dependence concretely represent the position toward which advancing age has begun to propel him, but which he is not yet prepared to accept" (57, pp. 207–208).

Sexual Behavior

The frequency of sexual intercourse between marital partners decreases as they grow older. According to a 1972 survey (29), the average man or woman between 35 and 45 had sexual intercourse about twice a week, while the average person over 45 had intercourse but once in the same time period. In contrast, young adults aged 18–24 reported an average of 3.25 sexual unions per week. People in all age groups were having sexual intercourse more frequently, however, than people their age in the early 1940s (35, 36). (See Figure 11.10.) Society is becoming more permissive about sexual matters in general, and this apparently affects marital sex, as it does sex before marriage.

●Figure 11.10 Marital coitus in the 1940s and the 1970s. Male and female estimates (medians) combined.

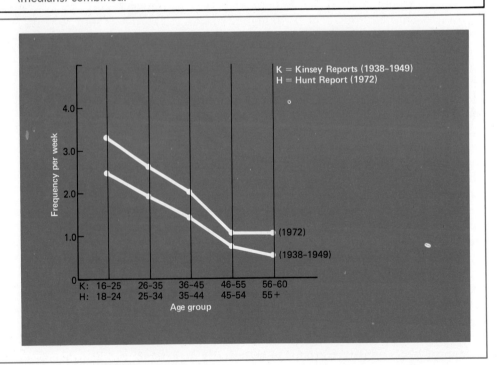

Biological factors may account for some of the decline in the average frequency of marital coitus with age. Masters and Johnson (42, 43) have found age decrements in the male's ability to have or maintain an erection and other sexual abilities. Sexual inadequacies—usually impotence—take "a sharp upturn about 50 years of age," although most of these incidents are apparently caused by psychological, rather than biological, problems. The fear of losing sexual ability is likely to become a self-fulfilling prophecy, causing that which is feared. However, even the normal male in middle age shows physical decrements, taking double or triple the young male's time to have an erection after sexual stimulation, ejaculating semen with about half the force of youth, and requiring up to 24 hours before another erection is possible. Females also show changes with age. These are age decrements in the lubrication and elasticity of the vagina, biological developments that become particularly prominent at menopause. As in men, the normal sexual reactions are present until very late in life, but they diminish in intensity; orgasmic contractions of the vagina, for example, continue for a shorter average duration with increasing age.

In addition to biological factors, there are a number of psychological and social factors that affect frequency of sexual intercourse. Performance anxiety can be a major problem for adult males, increasingly so with age (42). Some couples seem to become bored with each other, at least sexually. An important social factor in frequency of intercourse is children in the home; children limit the occasions for marital sex and may reduce spontaneity and vigor. The pressure of work is often greatest in the middle years; less time is spent at home, and work brought home spoils some of those precious hours. Thus, while biology may account for some of the decrease in the frequency of marital coitus, many nonbiological factors are also involved. About 40 percent of married men and 30 percent of married women report themselves to be dissatisfied with the frequency of sex in their marriage; they desire more (29). Half of the men over 45 said they would like more frequent sex. These figures suggest that motivation and probably ability exceed perceived opportunity.

The lack of an adequate sexual relationship at home, combined with doubts about declining physical abilities and physical attractiveness, leads some middle-aged men and women into extramarital sexual encounters. About half of all married men have at least one "affair" (29). The figure for married women is around 20 percent, but the differences between men and women are rapidly receding. Surprisingly, in light of the increasing permissiveness about sex, the great majority of Americans is still firmly opposed to extramarital sex. Magazine articles on mate-swapping notwithstanding, both young and old people view marital fidelity as essential to the marriage contract and infidelity as a serious moral offense. Even the people who have had affairs have similar attitudes; most of them keep their actions secret and experience considerable guilt; they also experience less pleasure, on the average, than in marital sex (29).

Dismayed by inadequate or infrequent marital sex and disinterested in extramarital outlets, many middle-aged couples set out to "renew" their physical relationship. By appraising the potentialities for an improved sex life, sometimes with the aid of a professional counselor, they often discover that the opportunities for enjoyable sex are much greater than they had imagined.

THE FAMILY IN THE MIDDLE YEARS

The middle years mark a period of many changes in the family. Most prominently, children grow up and depart to start their own lives and perhaps their own families, leaving behind a middle-aged couple known to family sociologists as the "postparental" family (65). In this section we will consider some of the adjustments to this new family status—"childless" once again. We will also discuss marital satisfaction, including the low ebb of satisfaction that leads some middle-aged people to consider an end to their marriage through separation or divorce.

The Postparental Family

The typical family of the early middle years is one with an adolescent child or two. When the mother is between the ages of 45 and 50, the youngest child leaves home, and thus the typical family of the late middle years is "childless" or "postparental." It has been suggested by some theorists that the transition from parental to postparental status is a particularly traumatic one for many people, especially for mothers who have defined their own identity in terms of their children. As one mother put it, "My daughters were both nineteen when they married. I didn't want them not to marry, but I missed them so much. I felt alone. I couldn't play golf. I couldn't even play bridge. I don't have a profession, and I couldn't take just any job. . . . I wanted my girls to wait until they were 30 before they got married" (17, p. 267).

Nevertheless, the evidence is that for most people the transition to postparental life is not overly difficult. In many respects life changes for the better. Many couples like being "childless" again, with time for travel, opportunities to do things spontaneously without considering the children, and a chance simply to be alone together. Adolescent children, from the point of view of the parents, can sometimes be a burden: They challenge authority, question traditional behaviors and values, and, over the years, become masters of the art of pitting one parent against the other for their own selfish purposes. A number of studies show average personal satisfaction with marriage decreasing steadily, reaching the lowest point just before the children leave home but then steadily increasing in the postparental years (34, 65) (Figure 11.11). These averages suggest that for most people the advantages of postparental life outweigh the loss of immediate, everyday contact with their children.

In one intensive study of people whose children had left home (17), over half saw the postparental period as better than preceding phases of family life, and most of the others saw it as about the same; only about 6 percent considered

● Figure 11.11   Marital satisfaction in various family situations. (Adapted from B. C. Rollins and H. Feldman. Marital satisfaction over the family life cycle. *Journal of Marriage and the Family*, 1970, *32*, 20–28.)

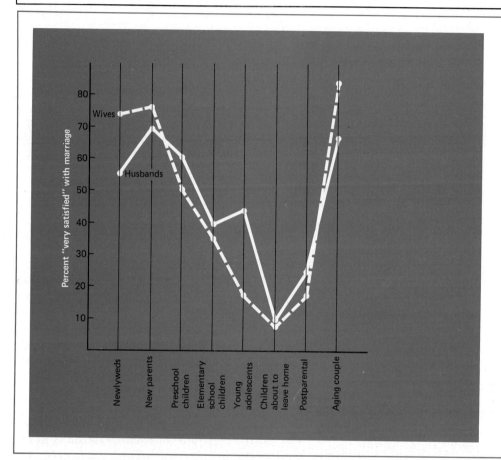

it worse. Such a study, of course, does not include couples who divorced after the children left home, but the data do not lend much support to the notion that the "empty nest" is an unhappy home. Among the reasons cited for saying life was improved was an improved financial situation; the expense of children, which tends to be greatest just before they go out on their own, had required sacrifices that were no longer necessary. Another pleasant surprise was the significant decrease in housework and other chores. "There's not as much physical labor," said one postparental mother (17, p. 265). "There's not as much cooking and there's not as much mending and, well, . . . for the first time that I can remember, my evenings are free." In addition to the freedoms granted by more money, more time, and fewer responsibilities, postparental couples often mention "satisfaction" and "contentment" from the fulfillment of another part of the life cycle: They have successfully raised children. Child-raising was a gratifying experience for them, but it was often quite difficult. A wife said, "My husband was a very nervous, jumpy man when the children were younger." Her husband said the same of his wife, "She's not as nervous since the children left home" (17, p. 265). Now they have completed their task; they can relax and enjoy life.

Relations with children Although it has been said of the United States and other industrial nations that the "extended family" has broken down, most Americans remain in fairly close contact with both their parents and their children (Figure 11.12). There is a considerable amount of economic interdependence, with parents providing at least emergency financial support for their children—and vice versa (65). In addition to money, parents often aid their "independent" children with gifts and services—help with moving or, of course, baby-sitting.

Emotional interdependence also continues. Approximately 85 percent of American parents over 65 report having seen at least one of their children within the previous week (61). The figure for middle-aged parents is probably less, since the geographical distance of parent from child is usually greatest during the postparental but pre-retirement stage of family life (65). But letters and phone calls provide contact among even the most distant of kin. Relations between mother and daughter are generally more important than those of mother–son, father–son, or father–daughter, in determining the amount of interaction between generations. If a young couple must decide where to go for the holidays, for example, more often than not they choose the home of the wife's mother. Although close positive ties between mother and daughter can account for this tendency in most cases, conflicts between the young wife and her mother-in-law may sometimes influence the decision *not* to visit the husband's mother. Some researchers (63) believe that interactions in the home—traditionally the "turf" of the female—force the young wife and her mother-in-law to demonstrate often conflicting opinions and behaviors.

Relations with parents When the children move out of the postparental family, it may be a time for the parents to relax and enjoy the peace and quiet. Not too long thereafter, however, some of these homes become two-generational once more, not because the children return but because one or more of the couple's own elderly parents move in. About a third of all people over 65 who have living children live with them (65). In most cases, this arrangement is not the preference of either the aging parent or the middle-aged couple; it is usually more of a last resort, when money is an unsurmountable problem or health problems make the arrangement necessary.

●Figure 11.12   Most Americans remain in fairly close contact with both their children and parents.

The adult individual's relationship to his or her parents is sometimes viewed as extremely negative, with the aged parents becoming more and more childish with age—in effect, reversing previous role relationships—and with the adult offspring trying to find a suitable "home" for the unwanted old people. Such a picture is accurate for only a few families. Instead most people develop what has been termed "filial maturity" (66), which is more a state of mutual respect than a reversal of parent–child roles. The adult child becomes "dependable," in a sort of mature identification with the parents as they were at the same age. The aging parents are directly involved, "first in a modeling capacity, and secondly in a rewarding capacity. In other words, the significance of the parent–child relationship does not end with launching but continues throughout life. The parent who continues to mature throughout his life—to accept his own development as meaningful and satisfying—is helping his children to mature in turn" (65, p. 277).

Marital Satisfaction

What makes one marriage unhappy and another a source of pleasure and great satisfaction? One factor is simply the stage of the family cycle, as we have mentioned above: Reported happiness is generally highest at the beginning of a marriage (honeymoon) and during the retirement years, and it is lowest when the children are about to leave the home. Another factor seems to be sexual satisfaction. There is ample evidence of a high correlation between marital adjustment and enjoyable marital sex (29, 66), but it is nearly impossible to say which causes which. One aspect that seems particularly important is an imbalance between the sexual desires of husband and wife; if one spouse consistently desires more sex than the other, constant frustration in this sphere of family life is likely to affect other spheres (11).

Marital satisfaction, usually assessed by self-reports of "happiness" or marital "success," reflects the quality of interaction between spouses and the fulfillment of personal needs in all aspects of family life. Global social variables have an influence on these everyday activities and thus affect marital satisfaction indirectly. For example, similarities in the spouses' age, race, religion, and socioeconomic status, factors that affect the initial choice of a marital partner, are also related to happiness after marriage (27). Similarity in these respects probably results in less conflict over values, role expectations, and other features of everyday marital interactions. In much the same fashion, a higher income (husband) and more education (husband and wife) mean a happier marriage, on the average. Money reduces one prominent source of stress in a marriage—financial worries—and an educated intelligence is a major resource for dealing with potentially divisive problems.

Role expectations—beliefs about how a "husband" and "wife" should act —are important for marital satisfaction in many respects. The role expectations of the man and the woman should not differ greatly, if the marriage is to be a satisfying one (66). No doubt the congruence of beliefs about the proper role of husband and wife will become an even greater factor in today's marriages, as variations from traditional roles become more numerous. And changes in role expectations (from "consciousness-raising" experiences in feminist discussion groups, for example) may result in discrepant views in a marriage that had previously been placidly congruent.

Marriages composed of two people from very conventional families are generally quite satisfying (71), at least partly because the husband and wife share detailed role expectations. In these conventional marriages, much depends on the ability of the husband to fill the role of breadwinner; one of the most important factors in the marital satisfaction of the wife is her husband's prestige or status in the community (27). The happiest of such unions occur when the husband has a self-concept strikingly similar to both that of his father *and* that of his wife's father.

Divorce

It is often thought that divorce represents the lowest point on a scale of marital satisfaction, but there are many factors other than satisfaction involved. Many very unhappy people stay married "for the sake of the children," for religious or economic reasons, or, in some cases, because an accommodation is reached that retains the name of marriage but very little of its substance. On the other hand, many couples who are not extremely dissatisfied may dissolve their union. One spouse might have found someone he or she loves more; the couple may decide that their "acceptable" marriage is too boring; or careers might split two good friends who think it is ridiculous for the husband to be living in New York while the wife works in Los Angeles. Government policies, such as easing divorce laws or increasing public assistance to unmarried or divorced parents of dependent children (45), can affect the divorce rate without changing the average level of marital satisfaction.

Whatever the causes, the divorce rate in the United States is rising rapidly —"skyrocketing" is the term aptly used by some journalists. The remarriage rate, which generally increases when the divorce rate increases, has been declining slightly since 1970 (51). Apparently more and more people are divorcing and then remaining single. Most of the divorced men in this country are in the group aged 35–44, with the 45–54 age group second; for women, the 45–54 group is first, with 35–44 second. Although divorce is becoming more common in all age groups, it is a particular problem in the middle years (13).

A listing of the social factors related to divorce would repeat those related to dissatisfaction and also those negatively related to the probability of getting married in the first place. In other words, people who are least likely to marry each other are most likely to have problems if they do (66). Marriages between people of two different faiths, races, social classes, levels of education, or even attitudes about life are more likely to end in divorce than marriages in which these differences do not exist. It should be noted, however, that as divorce becomes more common, the discriminating variables become less discriminating. For example, among men, low educational level, occupational status, and income have traditionally been associated with a higher probability of divorce. But in the last few decades, the divorce rate among more economically and socially privileged men has climbed more than the rate among the less fortunate (51). Among women, high income and status have long been associated with a *high* divorce rate, apparently because affluence lessens the financial obstacles to divorce. But a comparison of census data from 1970 and 1960 shows that the percentage of the poorer women divorced is rising more rapidly than the percentage of women with high incomes. "The important conclusion that can be drawn from these trends is that the recent increase in divorce has been pervasive with regard to social and economic level, . . . that socioeconomic differences in divorce are now smaller than they used to be" (51, p. 14).

Statistics and lists of relevant social factors do not do justice to the personal impact of divorce. Marriage is a commitment to an intimate relationship, and most people perceive divorce as a kind of failure. Even an unhappy marriage has some benefits. And the idea of living alone elicits considerable anxiety for many people. One woman said, "When the idea occurred to me that I could live without Dave and be happier, my immediate next feeling was just gut fear. It's really hard to explain. It was just terror" (68, p. 137). Another woman likened her continued yearning for her ex-husband, whom she did not like, to the feelings of a battered child: "You never find a battered child that does not want to be back with its parents, because they are the only parents it has. I just have very much this feeling" (68, p. 137). These feelings of anxiety and yearning, which appear whether the marriage has been happy or not and whether the divorce has been sought or not, are similar to those associated with the attachment bond between child and parent.

The stress of divorce or separation is apparently too much for a few people, who succumb to serious mental or physical disorders (34). Illnesses of almost every variety are more common among divorced people, probably because stress affects the body's resistance to disease. As a stressing event, divorce and separation are rated second only to death of a spouse—higher than being put in jail, being fired at work, and losing a close family member (other than spouse) by death (54). Alcoholism and suicide rates are higher among divorced people, and admission rates to mental hospitals are much higher than for comparable people who are married. In some cases, the alcoholism or the mental problems may have preceded the divorce, but there is no question that divorce itself is a traumatic event in the life of most who experience it.

Profound social changes are currently influencing marital satisfaction and the rate of divorce.

> There seems little doubt that a basic transformation of the institution of marriage is underway. . . . This transformation appears to be predicated largely on a restructuring of the roles which men and women play within the traditional boundaries of marriage and family living. Some people can confront this type of change and adapt to it without much difficulty; others find that the process of adjustment is much more difficult and leads ultimately to marital conflict and disruption (51, p. 17).

SUMMARY

The middle years begin at age 35 or 40 and run to 60 or 65. During this period, according to Erik Erikson, the question is whether or not one can deal with the responsibilities of being "generative." Generativity includes having and raising children and being creative and productive in one's job. If the individual does not "self-actualize"—strive to become the best he or she can be—there is a danger of "stagnation," marked by childish self-indulgences and the absence of personal growth.

The "mid-life crisis" has been identified as a period of reevaluation of one's goals in life, at least among many middle-aged, middle-class whites. It is characterized by perceived discrepancies between a person's "dreams" and his or her actual achievements and a sense that time is running out. Major adjustments include dealing with declining physical strength, stamina, and attractiveness and the decreasing role of sexuality in interpersonal relationships; emotional and mental flexibility is essential. Around the age of 45 or 50, many of the people who went through mid-life crises achieve a "new stability," more satisfied than before with their lot in life and willing to make the best of it.

Specific personality traits usually do not show age trends. Although personality change with age is not infrequent, some people change in one direction, and others change in the opposite way. There does seem to be an age trend, however, toward greater introspection and introversion. Also, men tend to become more emotional and nurturant with age, while women tend to become more aggressive; in other words, men and women tend to become more similar in sex-linked personality characteristics.

Cross-sectional studies compare different people of different ages; longitudinal studies compare the same people at different points of their lives. Cross-sectional studies of average IQ scores at different ages generally show lower scores for older age groups. Longitudinal studies, however, show that IQ scores of particular individuals do not usually decline with age. The apparent decline in cross-sectional studies can be accounted for by an increase in average IQ scores in successive generations. There is some evidence that "crystallized intelligence"—mental abilities influenced by formal education and life experiences, as measured by tests of vocabulary, general information, etc.—is affected less by age than is "fluid intelligence"—mental abilities often considered "native," uninfluenced by learning, as measured by tests of memory span, reaction time, etc. People who stay healthy and active tend to show no change or increases in IQ scores with age.

Major creative works by scientists, artists, and scholars tend to occur relatively early in life, but creative people are usually productive throughout their lives. That their most notable works occur early may be due to a sharper intellect during young adulthood, but it could also be due to increased motivation during this period. Another possible explanation is the tendency of others to consider the first in a series of related (but equally brilliant) achievements as the "most notable."

Biological concerns in the middle years include a growing awareness of physical aging. Menopause is rarely as bad as most women fear and is, in some respects, a positive experience. Heart attacks are a problem primarily for males. Younger victims (below the age of 40) tend to deny the severity of the disease, and 50-year-olds often become very depressed, as though the attack signifies their entry into "old age." Men over 60 are more philosophical and accepting of the necessary medical regimen. Sexual intercourse tends to decrease with age, partly for biological reasons but partly, too, because the increased responsibilities of the middle years—with careers, with growing children—leave less time and opportunity for sex.

The family in the middle years changes in many ways. Children grow up and leave home, but for most middle-aged couples, the "empty nest" is also a peaceful home; with more time for themselves, satisfaction with marriage typically improves. Relations with children continue, of course, even if the children move to distant cities. The middle-aged couple often has an elderly parent living with them. While both adult offspring and elderly parent might prefer more independent situations, the interdependencies of the two are rarely as negative as popular myths would have us believe.

The husband–wife relationship is often under stress during the middle years. Sexual satisfactions decrease, while pressures from jobs (including the self-generated pressures of the mid-life crisis) increase. Role expectations often change, especially as more and more women demand their share of authority in the family. People who can adjust to changes may create a much deeper and more satisfying marital relationship in the middle years, but increasing numbers of marriages end in divorce or separation. Marriages between people of different faiths, races, social classes, levels of education, or even attitudes about life are more likely to end in divorce than are marriages in which these differences do not exist, although these distinctions are becoming less apt, as divorce becomes more pervasive. Divorce is usually a negative experience, even if the marriage was unpleasant and unstable. As we mentioned in the previous chapter, profound changes in attitudes about marriage are occurring, and more and more people are moving to break up unhappy unions. Whether this trend will benefit individuals and society in the long run remains to be seen.

References

1. Alighieri, D. (Dante). **The divine comedy.** New York: Bigelow, Smith, 1909.
2. Baltes, P. B., & Schaie, K. W. On the plasticity of intelligence in adulthood and old age: where Horn and Donaldson fail. **American Psychologist,** 1976, **31,** 720–725.
3. Baltes, P. M., & Labouvie, G. V. Adult development of intellectual performance: description, explanation, and modification. In C. Eisdorfer & M. P. Lawton (Eds.), **The psychology of adult development and aging.** Washington: American Psychological Association, 1973.
4. Bayley, N., & Oden, M. H. The maintenance of intellectual ability in gifted adults. **Journal of Gerontology,** 1955, **10,** 91–107.
5. Berger, P. C., & Norsigian, J. Menopause. In The Boston Women's Health Book Collective (Eds.), **Our bodies, ourselves** (2nd ed.). New York: Simon & Schuster, 1976.
6. Birren, J. E. Translations in gerontology—from lab to life: psychophysiology and speed of response. **American Psychologist,** 1974, **29,** 808–815.
7. Birren, J. E., Butler, R. N., Greenhouse, S. W., Sokoloff, L., & Yarrow, M. R. (Eds.). **Human aging: a biological and behavioral study.** Washington, D.C.: U.S. Department of Health, Education, and Welfare, 1963.
8. Bischof, L. J. **Adult psychology** (2nd ed.). New York: Harper & Row, 1976.

9. Bowen, C. D. **Yankee from Olympus.** New York: Bantam, 1943.

10. Bromley, D. B. Some effects of age on short-term learning and remembering. **Journal of Gerontology,** 1958, **13,** 398–406.

11. Burgess, E. W., & Wallin, P. **Engagement and marriage.** Philadelphia: Lippincott, 1953.

12. Cameron, P. Age parameters of young adult, middle-aged, old, and aged. **Journal of Gerontology,** 1969, **24,** 201–202.

13. Carter, H., & Glick, P. C. **Marriage and divorce** (2nd ed.). Cambridge: Harvard University Press, 1976.

14. Christian, A. M., & Paterson, D. G. Growth of vocabulary in later maturity. **Journal of Psychology,** 1936, **1,** 167–169.

15. Dennis, W. Creative productivity between the ages of 20 and 80 years. **Journal of Gerontology,** 1966, **21,** 1–8.

16. Deutsch, H. **The psychology of women.** New York: Grune & Stratton, 1945.

17. Deutscher, I. The quality of postparental life. In B. L. Neugarten (Ed.), **Middle age and aging.** Chicago: University of Chicago Press, 1968.

18. Erikson, E. **Childhood and society** (2nd ed.). New York: Norton, 1963.

19. Erikson, E. **Insight and responsibility.** New York: Norton, 1964.

20. Friedman, M., & Rosenman, R. H. **Type A behavior and your heart.** New York: Knopf, 1974.

21. Garrett, H. E. **Great experiments in psychology.** New York: Appleton-Century-Crofts, 1957.

22. Glass, D. C. **Behavior patterns, stress, and coronary disease.** Hillsdale, N.J.: Erlbaum, 1977.

23. Gould, R. The phases of adult life. **American Journal of Psychiatry,** 1972, **129,** 521–531.

24. Gould, R. Adult life stages. **Psychology Today,** 1975, **8(9),** 74–78.

25. Gutmann, D. L. Aging among the highland Maya: a comparative study. **Journal of Personality and Social Psychology,** 1967, **7,** 29–35.

26. Gutmann, D. L. An exploration of ego configurations in middle and later life. In B. L. Neugarten (Ed.), **Personality in middle and late life.** New York: Atherton, 1964.

27. Hicks, M. W., & Platt, M. Marital happiness and stability: a review of the research in the sixties. **Journal of Marriage and the Family,** 1970, **32,** 553–574.

28. Horn, J. L., & Cattell, R. B. Age differences in fluid and crystallized intelligence. **Acta Psychologica,** 1967, **26,** 107–129.

29. Hunt, M. **Sexual behavior in the 1970's.** New York: Dell, 1974.

30. Jacques, E. Death and the mid-life crisis. **International Journal of Psychoanalysis,** 1965, **46,** 502–514.

31. Jarvik, L. F., & Cohen, D. A biobehavioral approach to intellectual changes with aging. In C. Eisdorfer & M. P. Lawton (Eds.), **The psychology of adult development and aging.** Washington: American Psychological Association, 1973.

32. Jung, C. G. The stages of life. In J. Campbell (Ed.), **The portable Jung.** New York: Viking, 1971.

33. Kelly, E. L. Consistency of the adult personality. **American Psychologist,** 1955, **10,** 659–681.

34. Kimmel, D. C. **Adulthood and aging.** New York: Wiley, 1974.

35. Kinsey, A. C., Pomeroy, W. B., & Martin, C. E. **Sexual behavior in the human male.** Philadelphia: Saunders, 1948.

36. Kinsey, A. C., Pomeroy, W. B., Martin, C. E., & Gebhard, P. H. **Sexual behavior in the human female.** Philadelphia: Saunders, 1953.

37. Klonoff, H., & Kennedy, M. A comparative study of cognitive functioning in old age. **Journal of Gerontology,** 1966, **21,** 239–243.

38. Kuhlen, R. G. Developmental changes in motivation during the adult years. In B. L. Neugarten (Ed.), **Middle age and aging.** Chicago: University of Chicago Press, 1968.

39. Lash, J. P. **Eleanor and Franklin.** New York: Norton, 1971.

40. Lehman, H. C. **Age and achievement.** Princeton, N.J.: Princeton University Press, 1953.

41. Maslow, A. H. **Motivation and personality** (2nd ed.). New York: Harper & Row, 1970.

42. Masters, W. H., & Johnson, V. E. **Human sexual inadequacy.** Boston: Little, Brown, 1970.

43. Masters, W. H., & Johnson, V. E. **Human sexual response.** Boston: Little, Brown, 1966.

44. Mischel, W. **Personality and assessment.** New York: Wiley, 1968.

45. Moles, O. C. Marital dissolution and public assistance payments: variations among American states. **Journal of Social Issues,** 1976, **32,** 87–101.

46. Neugarten, B. L. Adult personality: toward a psychology of the life cycle. In B. L. Neugarten (Ed.), **Middle age and aging.** Chicago: University of Chicago Press, 1968.

47. Neugarten, B. L. Personality change in late life: a developmental perspective. In C. Eisdorfer & M. P. Lawton (Eds.), **The psychology of adult development and aging.** Washington: American Psychological Association, 1973.

48. Neugarten, B. L., & Gutmann, D. L. Age-sex roles and personality in middle age: a thematic apperception study. In B. L. Neugarten (Ed.), **Middle age and aging.** Chicago: University of Chicago Press, 1968.

49. Neugarten, B. L., Moore, J. W., & Lowe, J. C. Age norms, age constraints, and adult socialization. In B. L. Neugarten (Ed.), **Middle age and aging.** Chicago: University of Chicago Press, 1968.

50. Neugarten, B. L., Wood, V., Kraines, R. J., & Loomis, B. Women's attitudes toward the menopause. In B. L. Neugarten (Ed.), **Middle age and aging.** Chicago: University of Chicago Press, 1968.

51. Norton, A. J., & Glick, P. C. Marital instability: past, present and future. **Journal of Social Issues,** 1976, **32,** 5–20.

52. Owens, W. A. Age and mental abilities: a second adult follow-up. **Journal of Educational Psychology,** 1966, **57,** 311–325.

53. Peck, R. C. Psychological developments in the second half of life. In B. L. Neugarten (Ed.), **Middle age and aging.** Chicago: University of Chicago Press, 1968.

54. Rahe, R. H. Subjects' recent life changes in their near-future illness susceptibility. **Advances in Psychosomatic Medicine,** 1972, **8,** 2–19.

55. Riegel, K. F. From traits and equilibrium toward developmental dialectics. In W. Arnold (Ed.), **Nebraska Symposium on Motivation** (Vol. 24). Lincoln, Nebraska: University of Nebraska Press, 1976.

56. Riegel, K. F., & Riegel, R. M. Development, drop, and death. **Developmental Psychology,** 1972, **6,** 306–319.

57. Rosen, J. L., & Bibring, G. L. Psychological reactions of hospitalized male patients to a heart attack: age and social-class differences. In B. L. Neugarten (Ed.), **Middle age and aging.** Chicago: University of Chicago Press, 1968.

58. Rosenman, R. H., and others. Coronary heart disease in the Western Collaborative Group Study: final follow-up experience of $8\frac{1}{2}$ years. **Journal of the American Medical Association,** 1975, **233,** 872–877.

59. Schaie, K. W. Translations in gerontology—from lab to life: intellectual functioning. **American Psychologist,** 1974, **29,** 802–807.

60. Schaie, K. W., & Labouvie-Vief, G. Generational versus ontogenetic components of change in adult cognitive behavior: a fourteen-year cross-sequential study. **Developmental Psychology,** 1974, **10,** 305–320.

61. Shanas, E., Townsend, P., Wedderburn, D., Friis, H., Milhhoj, P., & Stehouwer, J. **Older people in three industrial societies.** New York: Atherton, 1968.

62. Sheehy, G. **Passages.** New York: Dutton, 1976.

63. Sweetser, D. A. Asymmetry in intergenerational family relationships. **Social Forces,** 1963, **41,** 346–352.

64. Taylor, R. **Welcome to the middle years.** Washington: Acropolis Books, 1976.

65. Troll, L. E. The family of later life: a decade review. **Journal of Marriage and the Family,** 1971, **33,** 263–290.

66. Udry, J. R. **The social context of marriage** (2nd ed.). Philadelphia: Lippincott, 1971.

67. Wang, H. S., Obrist, W. D., & Busse, E. W. Neurophysiological correlates of the intellectual function of elderly persons living in the community. **American Journal of Psychiatry,** 1970, **126,** 1205–1212.

68. Weiss, R. S. The emotional impact of marital separation. **Journal of Social Issues,** 1976, **32,** 135–145.

69. Welford, A. T. **Aging and human skill.** London: Oxford University Press, 1958.

70. Weschsler, D. "Hold" and "Don't Hold" tests. In S. M. Crown (Ed.), **Human aging.** Middlesex, England: Penguin, 1972.

71. Whitehurst, R. N. Premarital reference-group orientations and marriage adjustment. **Journal of Marriage and the Family,** 1968, **30,** 397–401.

72. Woodruff, D. S., & Birren, J. E. Age changes and cohort differences in personality. **Developmental Psychology,** 1972, **6,** 252–259.

73. Zajonc, R. B. Family configuration and intelligence. **Science,** 1976, **192,** 227–236.

CHAPTER 12
Old Age

What is it to be? Will it be the "golden years"? Or will it be "statutory senility"? Life after 65 is a rather recent development, made possible by enormous advances in medicine and sanitation in the twentieth century, but now there promises to be a virtual stampede into old age. In 1975, there were 22 million people over 65 in the United States (8); by 2030, 52 million people will call themselves senior citizens—or will object to the term (Figure 12.1). The population explosion in the over-65 age group will undoubtedly have profound effects on many social and political institutions in our society. For example, social security and other pension systems will become a significant burden on younger workers. As one economist phrased it, "There is a danger that in the future workers will just say, 'We've had it. We will no longer support all these old people, these leeches'" (53, p. 52). Intergenerational conflicts may become severe, in part because the older generations will have the numbers, and hence the political influence, to make society respond to their needs.

On a personal level, most people anticipate old age with trepidation. There is a special and not unrealistic fear, shared by young and old, that many of the

●Figure 12.1 These age distribution and median age charts reflect the changing profile of the nation's population. If the birth rate stays low, the nation's demographic profile will change shape and the median age (half the population older, half younger) will rise. (The charts are based on U.S. Census projections assuming a fertility rate of 2.1 children per woman.)

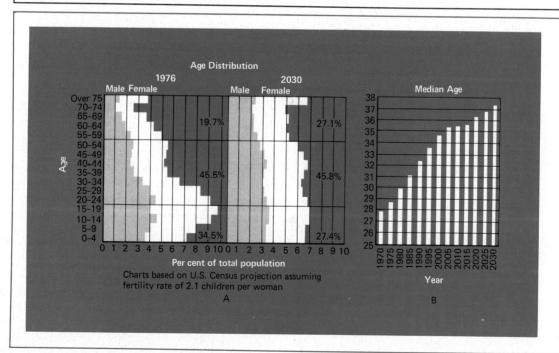

last years of life will be spent in ill health, with some chronic disease that will limit activity and possibly even impair reasoning abilities. History is replete with bizarre schemes for avoiding old age. The Bible reports the therapy used to keep David from the ravages of age: He was placed in bed between two nubile Hittite girls (40). Blood from young men and milk from young mothers were two popular remedies for aging in the past. These are replaced today by vitamins and other, more scientific-sounding potions—yogurt was the elixir of youth earlier in this century (29). Between the fears and the dreams, most of our popular attitudes toward aging combine "wishful thinking and stark terror"(7).

In a situation dominated by half-truths and wild speculation, the need for sound research is obvious. *Gerontology*—the study of the phenomena of old age —has been a rapidly growing specialty not only in psychology but in biology, zoology, anthropology, and other disciplines as well. In this chapter we will present some of the research in an attempt to dispel, substantiate, or clarify some of the myths of old age. First we will consider personality development, with major emphasis on the mental health of old people. Then we will turn to a consideration of social changes in old age, as most people retire from work and many other activities. A section on the family in old age includes discussions of grandparenting, marital relations, and widowhood. This will be followed by reviews of intellectual and biological development, including changes in memory, the nature of biological aging, and diseases of old age. Finally, perhaps appropriately in a book on the life span, the chapter concludes with a brief consideration of death and the processes of dying.

PERSONALITIES, ORDERED AND DISORDERED

There has not been much research on personality development in people over the age of 65. What little there is suggests that the trends of late middle age—toward a more introspective orientation, for example—continue into old age and that, as in any age group, differences among individuals are vast while similarities are few (see pp. 415–419). The one great similarity among old people is that each is coming to the end of life. Each must somehow deal with his or her life as a whole. Each, to some extent, reviews his or her personal history and is proud or disgusted, content or sad. For some, the accumulation of life's insults —physical and psychological—proves too much to bear, and their personalities fall into disorder. For most, fortunately, old age finds their personalities well-ordered and ready for the final experiences of life.

Ego Integrity

The eighth age of human life—old age—involves a central developmental issue Erik Erikson described as *integrity versus despair* (21). In Erikson's perspective of the life span, the four childhood psychosocial crises, if successfully resolved, should bring a basic sense of trust, individuality, initiative, and industriousness. In late adolescence and early adulthood, identity and intimacy crises are two more encountered; in middle adulthood, the issue is generativity versus stagnation. The eighth and final stage is one of integration, a last chance to "get it together." As Erikson has written: "Only in him who in some way has taken care of things and people and has adapted himself to the triumphs and disappointments adherent to being, the originator of others or the generator of products and ideas—only in him may gradually ripen the fruit of these seven stages. I know no better word for it than ego integrity" (21, p. 268).

Ego integrity is a very broad concept, involving the organization of many attitudes, beliefs, and motives. In essence, it involves a profound sense of order, "the acceptance of one's one and only life cycle as something that had to be and that, by necessity, permitted of no substitutions" (21, p. 268). There is a sense of satisfaction with a life well-lived (Figure 12.2). There is a maturity of spirit that is the same, and can be recognized, in "successful" old people of any culture—American or Chinese, millionaire or peasant. There is *wisdom*, a kind of detached (not selfish) knowledge of and concern for life (22).

In contrast, the lack (or loss) of ego integration is marked by despair. Despair involves the fear of time running out; time is too short to do this or try that; there is not enough time to integrate one's life. Despair means fear of death, for one's life is not accepted as good and proper or as a whole. Despair is often disguised as disgust, as "a thousand little disgusts" that reflect the disorganization and lack of integrity that produce the underlying despair.

Life Review Processes

The prospect of an end to life triggers a kind of retrospective of life, a life review process, in many old people (7). This process may be elaborate and organized, as in the writing of memoirs or an autobiography, but typically it is a haphazard collection of past-oriented activities: looking at scrapbooks, lingering with an old memory, comparing one's adolescent plans and dreams with the subsequent realities.

In some people, this life review is combined with a desire to leave a legacy, a wish to leave something behind when they die, to achieve at least a limited kind of immortality. Memoirs and autobiographies are legacies of experience and hard-earned wisdom. Wills may become toys, something to play with, a way to have an effect, a source of power, a means of threat, a meaningful promise. Some older people take strong stands—perhaps they withhold their blessings from the marriage of a grandchild—not with the goal of causing trouble, but of influencing another life cycle in a way they perceive is ultimately wise.

Life review can be used as a kind of therapy for old people (41). The therapist asks his or her elderly clients to construct their own autobiographies. They might use family albums, old letters, and even interviews with other family members to gain information about their own behavior and feelings at critical points in their lives. By elaborating and formalizing the life-review process, the

●Figure 12.2   A sense of satisfaction with a life well-lived.

therapist allows guilts, long-standing fears, and suppressed dreams to surface. In some cases, simply having someone who is willing to listen to regrets and unfulfilled dreams can have an "integrative" effect on the old person. In other, more involved cases, the surfacing of unresolved conflicts allows the therapist to deal with them directly.

Mental Health in Old Age

Old age has the potential for being an immensely interesting and emotionally satisfying period of life. But this potential is endangered by many forces. Change and loss are predominant themes. Loss of physical health and the death of important persons—spouses, close friends, colleagues, relatives—are occurrences in late life which tend to place enormous stress on human emotions. Crises of all kinds must be met, sometimes one after another, sometimes simultaneously—retirement, widowhood, major and minor illnesses, changes in bodily appearance, sensory losses, a feeling of decreasing social status and, for many elderly, a drastically lowered standard of living. There is much energy expended as the old go through the processes of mourning for their losses, resolving grief, adjusting to changes involved and recovering from the stresses. Multiple crises can leave people drained emotionally and weakened physically (7, pp. 225–226).

Mental illness is a significant threat in old age. The incidence of new cases among people over 65 is over twice as great as among people in the middle years and almost three times the incidence in young adulthood (7). Mental disorders are classified as either organic, if they have a physical cause, or functional, if there is no *known* physical cause. An organic disorder more common in older than in younger people is *cerebral arteriosclerosis,* in which fatty deposits accumulate in the blood vessels and decrease the flow of blood to the brain. Another common organic disorder is *senile brain disease,* marked by a depletion of brain cells and decreased brain function. The nature and origin of senile brain disease are poorly understood, but it is believed to account for about 65 percent of the cases of people over the age of 65 who suffer from mild to severe cerebral dysfunction (70). In addition to these chronic organic disorders, there are reversible organic disorders, caused by drugs or disease. Alcohol-induced dementia is not uncommon in old people, and many suffer from malnutrition, anemia, heart disease, and various infections; even extreme constipation can result in mental confusion (7). In one study (67), over half of the old patients admitted for mental illness were found to be suffering from reversible brain disorders that could be corrected by proper treatment.

Functional mental disorders include the psychoses and the neuroses which, although they may involve a genetic component, are influenced by personality factors and life's experiences. The psychoses, which include schizophrenia and manic-depressive psychosis, account for not quite 40 percent of the hospital admissions of people over the age of 75 (33). Many old people suffering from neuroses, which involve extreme anxiety or maladaptive reactions to anx-

iety, receive no treatment at all; "people will tolerate behavior in an old person that would send them rushing to the authorities if the same behavior occurred in a younger person" (33, p. 68). Clinical evaluations of "normal" old people often uncover evidence of functional psychopathology in a sizable percentage—62 percent in one investigation (60).

Suicide is more frequent among males over the age of 85 than among any other age group. There is, in fact, a steady increase with age in the suicide rate of white males, but not of males of other races (7, 36). Among women, the incidence of suicide increases to the age of 50 or so, then decreases to a very low rate among women over 85. No one has a completely adequate explanation of why aging white males should be particularly susceptible to the deep depressions that lead to suicide. Many theorists believe that white males, who tend to hold most of the high-status, high-income jobs in this society, are least able to handle the loss of status and income that comes with old age (7).

The treatment of old, mentally ill people in the United States is a national disgrace (7). Too often old people with emotional and mental problems are simply assumed to be "senile" and given only "custodial care," for "senility" is widely believed to be irreversible, even progressive. Many of the "senile" old people now "in custody" probably are suffering from functional emotional disorders (like neurosis) or reversible organic disorders (like those associated with alcoholism) and could return to a relatively normal life with even minimal treatment (67). Even people with irreversible, progressive brain disease can benefit from an informed, supportive therapeutic program that encourages them to "be the best they can be" within the context of their physical limitations; in fact, much of the current emphasis on self-actualization in normal people is based on the observed self-actualization of severely brain-injured soldiers (26). Yet the elderly receive care from outpatient mental health clinics and community mental health centers in far fewer numbers than would be expected from the incidence of mental illness in their ranks (33). Psychiatrists, clinical psychologists, and psychoanalysts tend to treat what one psychologist called the YAVIS—the young, attractive, verbal, intelligent, and successful clients (64). Therapists often have negative attitudes toward older patients, feeling that it is a waste of time to treat someone who may soon die (7). And, after all, "they are only senile."

If others believe the elderly are "hopeless," it is not surprising that many old people view themselves in the same way: hopeless and helpless. The ability to make one's own decisions, to have at least partial control over one's environment, is a major factor in the mental health of people in old age. The loss of job, income, and some degree of physical ability contributes to the sense of helplessness and hopelessness. Old people may begin to see themselves as passive objects manipulated by environmental events. If the feelings of helplessness are severe, the result can be psychological or physical disorders, even premature death (38).

In many respects, combating the sense of helplessness is one of the major tasks of old age. Old people living in nursing and retirement homes, where others "take care" of them, often deteriorate mentally and physically in a very short period of time. That a feeling of increasing uselessness is frequently involved was shown by a program in one nursing home where the elderly patients "were encouraged to make decisions for themselves, given decisions to make, and given responsibility for something outside of themselves" (a plant). Almost all of these patients showed improvement in mental alertness; they were rated as more active and happier, both by nurses and by themselves (38). This rather remarkable record of improvement contrasted sharply with the record of old people not involved in the "individual responsibility" program; 71 percent were rated as having become more "debilitated" in a three-week period.

The beneficial effects of having some measure of control over one's own activities were also shown by a study in which undergraduate students visited residents of a retirement home (49). The visits for the old people in one group were random (unpredictable, uncontrollable) but equal in frequency and duration to the visits to the old people in another group, who could specify when and for how long the visitor would come. Although the visits were equally enjoyable in both conditions, the elderly residents with a sense of control were happier, became more hopeful, and were rated by staff as having a greater "zest for life" than the old people whose visitors were "uncontrollable."

SOCIAL FACTORS IN AGING

Aging is a social as well as a biological process. When workers reach the age of 65, they cross a socially defined line between "mature employees" and old people who are expected to retire—in many organizations, *forced* to retire. They are then expected to build a new style of life, one acceptable for people their age. They must try not to be a burden. They should find something to interest themselves—a hobby, church work, perhaps travel. Death is on the horizon, so they should prepare for their funerals and the disposition of their estates; they should accept their mortality gracefully, "disengaging" gradually until the end comes. It matters little if the individual is vital, mentally and physically as alert as ever, destined to live another 30 years, or "worn out" and "old" for the previous 10 years, near death. The biological aspects of aging are, for the most part, ignored, and "old age," in this respect, is a socially defined period of the life span. One is old when others decide he or she has entered "old age."

Retirement

The concept of retirement has a surprisingly short but interesting history. In centuries past, few people lived to old age, and a general policy for old workers was unnecessary. Those who did survive into their 60s and 70s generally kept working until mental or physical incapacity made it impossible. Many merchants, farmers, and artisans took on apprentices to ease their work load in their later years (3). Incapacitated workers (of all ages) received care and support from their families or, in the less fortunate cases, they were sent to "poor farms" to live out the rest of their lives in squalid institutions. In the late nineteenth century, Chancellor Otto von Bismarck of Germany established a pension for people 65 and older; it was the beginning of our modern concept of retirement.

In the United States, the Social Security Act of 1935 confirmed the age of 65 as the "age of retirement." (Recent changes in federal and state laws have raised the retirement age to 70 for many occupations.) Coming during the Great Depression, Social Security was intended to provide: (1) financial support for old people, and (2) jobs for younger workers by encouraging the retirement of older employees (74). Before the Social Security Act, most men over 65 worked. In 1890, for example, 68 percent worked. Even after passage of the Social Security Act, the percentage of older people who work has continued to decrease. In 1950, the figure for men was 46 percent; in 1960, 32 percent; in 1970, 26 percent; in 1975, 21 percent (73). The percentages of women working are considerably lower for all time periods.

There is evidence that retirement is less than completely voluntary in the majority of cases (19), although what constitutes an involuntary retirement is often difficult to determine. Many workers—some estimates run as high as 50 percent (48)—retire because of poor health; are these retirements voluntary or involuntary? Some people find themselves retired by a series of events: Laid off or fired from one job, they reach the age of 65 and thus become eligible for full Social Security benefits. They would prefer working, but no one is interested in their services. They apply for Social Security benefits and tell their friends that they have decided to retire. A survey conducted in the summer of 1974 (27) asked a representative sample of retired persons if they had retired by choice or had been forced to retire. The majority—61 percent—claimed to have retired by choice, but 37 percent said they had retired against their will. The percentage "forced to retire" was even higher among certain subgroups, for example, men (41 percent), people with low incomes (46 percent), and blacks (50 percent). Considering that people generally try to describe their own decision processes in the most favorable light—in this case, as a voluntary decision—these percentages are probably underestimates of the number of people who feel coerced into retirement.

Many retired people face serious economic problems. On the average, the income of the retired family is half of the income before retirement. Some 4 or 5 million old people live in "poverty," which the government defines as less income than is necessary for survival (7). Nevertheless, especially since the advent of government programs such as Medicare and food stamps, the economic situation of the *average* old person is not one of desperation. The majority of old people see their income as adequate (69), and fears about crime and concerns about health were mentioned significantly more often than money worries in a recent national survey (27).

Psychological reactions to retirement It is commonly assumed that work is central to individuals' self-concepts and that retirement is a challenge to their views of themselves as worthwhile and useful. In a society "characterized by a religious devotion to work and peopled by individuals dedicated to conspicuous production as an important means of self-identification and self-justification" (38, p. 359), retirement could be expected to have serious psychological consequences. Perhaps unfortunately, however, there is very little evidence of such an emotional involvement with work on the part of the average American (16). Most workers are happy to quit working; if there is a sense of loss, it is purely economic (see Figure 12.3). Attempts to replace the "satisfactions of employment" with "activities that have the form and appearance of productive work" (48, p. 359) are generally unsuccessful—unless there is pay involved. The major satisfaction of most employment is money (10).

There are exceptions, of course. Some people are upset by retirement because their personal identities were defined largely by their jobs. More often than not, the people who miss their work are from the upper-middle and upper social classes. Their high-status jobs earn them respect, give them power and a

Figure 12.3　Although they may miss the income, most retired Americans prefer not working to working.

sense of responsibility. Typically, such jobs are quite demanding; so the individual devotes more time and energy to it. It is typically the high-salaried executives and professionals who become so involved with their jobs that they are called "workaholics." When these workers approach the age of 65, they are often reluctant to retire (69) and, in fact, are less likely to do so (19). This is true even though they have less economic need to continue working than people in lower-paying occupations. They have the resources (money, education) to enjoy retirement, but they find their jobs too interesting and involving. One reviewer notes the paradox that "the very individuals who, half a century ago, were considered to be candidates for a leisure class characterized by conspicuous leisure may now be the unexpected candidates for a 'working' class characterized by conspicuous occupational involvement" (48, p. 360).

Personality and retirement An individual's adjustment to retirement is directly determined by his or her attitudes and personality. Those who expect retirement to be traumatic or view it as an end of one's useful contribution to society are likely to find retirement difficult and unpleasant. An attitude that pictures retirement as part of a successful life cycle, the final stage of an orderly career, promotes positive adjustment (3). The personalities of men who were judged to have adjusted poorly to retirement were dominated by feelings of anger and resentment (62). These men were bitter about failure to achieve their goals in life and were unwilling or unable to accept an end to their strivings. In some cases, they blamed others for their failure—the anger was turned outward—and in other cases, they blamed themselves, turning their hostility inward. Good adjustment to retirement was found in men with healthy, mature personalities, as we would expect, but also in men who were judged "generally passive"—they liked the freedom from responsibility—and in those who were "armored" or protected from anxiety by defense mechanisms. The armored individuals tended to keep active, either in work or in some leisure activity, in efforts to ward off their feelings of uselessness.

Disengagement

How does one grow old gracefully? If you were to put this question to a number of people, chances are that most answers would fall into two categories. One type of answer would insist that, to age successfully, the person must keep active, finding new interests to replace work and new friends to replace those who die or move away. The second type of answer would portray old age as a time when the person "naturally" begins to slow down, curtailing activities and gradually reducing his or her circle of friends; in this view, the attempts of some elderly people to stay as active as ever are considered ridiculous or "desperate."

The theories of psychologists who study aging fall into roughly the same two categories: "activity theories" and "disengagement theories" (28). A short history of the most influential disengagement theory will show the advantages and disadvantages of both disengagement and activity theories and allow us to describe the aspects of aging that both theories seek to explain.

Disengagement as ideal   Almost all old people experience some reduction in social interaction and activities. In other words, there is some disengagement, whether the individual likes it or not. According to the original statement of the disengagement theory (15), the aging individual is at least accepting and probably desirous of the reduction. Social withdrawal "is accompanied by, or preceded by, increased preoccupation with the self and decreased emotional investment in persons and objects in the environment; . . . in this sense, disengagement is a natural rather than an imposed process" (28, p. 161).

Although this strong statement of the theory had the desirable effect of stimulating a great deal of research on the relationship between level of activity and life satisfaction in older people, the major feature of theory—that disengagement is natural and desirable—soon came under attack. Although research indicated that social disengagement in old age was often preceded by a psychological disengagement, an inward-turning of the personality, that began in late middle age (see pp. 416–417), the research evidence was clear that old people were not particularly fond of their decreasing social world. In fact, there is a rather sizable correlation between social *engagement* and satisfaction with life: the more activities and interactions, the happier the individual (47). Most old people regret the decreases in their activity levels, increasingly so with age (28).

It is possible that the relationship between disengagement and satisfaction becomes positive only later in life, not in the 60s, but later, after the age of 70 or so. To test this hypothesis, the correlation between activity level and satisfaction was computed separately for people under 70 and over 70; no significant difference was found (28). Older old people dislike the reduction in activity as much as the "youngsters" in this age group.

Disengagement as process   The hypothesis that elderly people are happiest if they disengage from society has not been supported by data; in fact, one could say the hypothesis appears to be untenable. Nevertheless, the research generated by the disengagement theory—much of it designed to refute the theory!—has added immensely to our understanding of the process of disengagement in old age. For most people, a decrease in activities and interactions is viewed as a change for the worse. Nevertheless, "most older persons accept this drop as an inevitable accompaniment of growing old; and they succeed in maintaining a sense of self-worth and a sense of satisfaction with past and present life as a whole" (28, p. 171).

Disengagement is a result of several factors (33). Most prominent is a change in the individual's position in the social structure. A woman was a worker; now she is retired. She was responsible for dependent children; now her children have responsibilities of their own. She was chairperson of the city planning commission; now her advice is solicited infrequently, although they call her a "valuable resource person." Many old people lose a spouse and do not remarry. A second factor is more psychological: "With an increasing awareness that his future is limited and that death is not only inevitable but no longer far distant, the older person may be more likely to attend to himself and to whatever is extremely important to him, simultaneously pushing away whatever is not extremely important" (33, p. 64).

A third factor in disengagement is biological. Most old people experience some of the phenomena associated with old age: a memory not quite so sharp or quick, a few chronic aches and pains, a reduced energy level. In addition, mild to severe health problems become more probable with age. Heart disease, crippling arthritis, eye cataracts, broken bones, and many other maladies of the old, all require at least some curtailment of activities. In one major study of fairly well-to-do aged people (45), the most clearly disengaging (or disengaged) among them were all unhealthy. Heavily involved in playing the role of "sick person," these people were withdrawing from other activities and interests, and they were very bitter about life.

There are undoubtedly other factors in disengagement, but even this short list points up some of the difficulties with making general statements about processes of aging. If people reduce their activities because they are forced to, by ill health or an unwanted retirement, chances are that they will be displeased with their state of affairs. Disengagement will not be related to high morale; rather it will be related to bitterness and dissatisfaction with old age. If, however, social disengagement is a natural consequence of an individual's desire to focus on those aspects of his or her life that are of central importance, disengagement can be satisfying and, for this individual at least, perhaps an optional pattern for dealing with aging.

Personality and disengagement   The significant individual differences in old people's reactions to disengagement can be attributed in part to personality differences. For example, a strong sense of personal adequacy (determined by psychiatric evaluation) predicts high morale in old age, even with low levels of social interaction (47). The unhealthy, disengaging, and bitter women in the study mentioned above (those involved in the "sick person" role) had what one would call unfortunate personalities (45). Compared to other old women, the average disabled-disengaging woman was rated as undependable, stingy, irritable, critical, aloof, moody, cold, unsympathetic, cheerless, devious, and generally negative. The discovery that she "does not arouse liking in others" is hardly surprising. In addition, the woman who was disengaging and hating it had another set of personality traits that served her poorly in her attempts to adjust to ill health and a reduction in activities: She was self-indulgent and self-pitying, with a tendency toward depression. She was bothered by demands made on her, and she withdrew in the face of threats.

An apt comparison of these unhappy old women can be made with another group of elderly women whose lot in life was, if anything, even worse. Their health, on the average, was almost as bad as that of the disabled-disengaging women; they had more physical disabilities. "Older, more often incapacitated, living alone, less well off economically, and widowed, . . . (these women) suffer just about all the woes that unfortunate elderly women can suffer" (45, p. 93). Yet, despite their obvious limitations, these women were much more active, with a more positive attitude. The personality traits that distinguished them from the average women in the study give an idea why: These women were rated straightforward, not self-defensive, and independent. Personally they were charming, interesting, not moralistic, and socially perceptive, and they aroused liking in others.

The degree of relationship between activity level and life satisfaction is fairly high, but it leaves room for many exceptions. In fact, while the combinations of high activity with high morale and low activity with low morale are the most common, many people with high activity levels are bitter about life, and many relatively inactive people are quite content. Personality factors help to explain both the common and the exceptional cases.

In one major study (51), interrelationships among personality type, amount of interpersonal activity, and degree of life satisfaction showed several interesting patterns. People with well-adjusted, integrated personalities were quite satisfied with life no matter what their level of activity. Some were quite active; some had become more selective and focused in their interests; and some were disengaging—by choice. The latter are "persons who have voluntarily moved away from role commitments, not in response to external losses or physical deficits, but because of preference. These are self-directed persons, not shallow, with an interest in the world, but an interest that is not imbedded in a network of social interactions" (51, p. 175). Their pattern of aging is calm, withdrawn but contented.

At the opposite extreme of personality type, people with unintegrated personalities were dissatisfied with life, no matter what their level of activity. Between these extremes of adjustment and personality integration, level of activity had its most significant effect on morale. People with "armored" personalities —ambitious and striving, but with an apparent need to keep their emotions and impulses under strict control—use high activity as a kind of defense against the idea that they are growing old. These are the people who say "I'll work until I drop," or "So long as you keep busy, you will get along all right" (51, p. 176). Low activity levels are disturbing to them. Similarly, passive-dependent personalities need interaction; they need people to "do for them," make decisions, talk for them, help them. Without activity, their predispositions result in extreme apathy.

Both the disengagement theory and the activity theory of successful aging were phrased in general terms, regardless of the personalities of the individuals involved. It is now the view of most gerontologists that probably both theories are correct, but for different people. No one pattern of aging is appropriate for all old people, just as no one life-style is right for all young adults.

THE FAMILY IN OLD AGE

An old person's family is often a source of great satisfaction. Typically his relationship with his wife has been improving since the youngest child has left the nest, and he finds grandparenting to have many of the advantages, without all of the disadvantages, of parenting. In a more abstract but no less important sense, he perceives a completeness in one of life's most significant endeavors: to find a mate, to raise a family, to see his children's children. His children and grandchildren are part of his legacy, his contribution to the world. He may consider his children to be a kind of "life after death," as these new human beings carry on his genetic and social influences even as he personally faces death.

While this idyllic picture of the old "family man" is accurate for a large number of men (and women) in the United States, many old people find their families, if they have any, a source of constant frustration. Their relationships with their spouses are unsatisfying, sometimes resembling open warfare, but financial considerations or apathy keep them from divorce or separation. Many old people, especially women, have lost their spouses through death; they face loneliness and economic hardships. Relations with children may be strained. One lonely old woman said, "I don't understand my son at all. But, worse than that, I can't stand him. And his wife treats me like I'm senile." So families are not always satisfying. Perhaps any institution that has the potential for producing deep contentment and happiness has also the potential for creating deep frustration and unhappiness.

Grandparenting

"Traditionally, grandma and grandpa are considered to be benign, gray-haired angels with enormous compassion and capacity for use and abuse. There seems to be evidence that this picture, if not fictional, is certainly changing" (3, p. 292) (see Figure 12.4). A number of studies suggest that grandparents are not quite as interested in their grandchildren as the traditional myth would have us believe (72). The typical grandparents are glad to see their grandchildren come— and glad to see them go. A significant factor in the relationship between grandparents and grandchildren is the age of the grandchildren. Grandparents enjoy younger children more than older children; the older children often do not want to bother with old folks.

In one extensive study of grandparents (52), about two-thirds found the role much to their satisfaction. The minority expressing discomfort often mentioned conflict with the parents of the grandchildren over child-rearing methods. Others (especially the grandparents still in their 50s) had no taste for the role; assuming a social status associated with "old age" threatened their self-concept. The most common style of grandparenting, characteristic of about one-third of the grandparents, was called *formal*. These people followed the traditional role of grandparent: occasionally indulgent, occasionally helping the

●Figure 12.4   The traditional picture of grandparents is changing.

parents with minor services like baby-sitting, constantly interested in the welfare of the grandchildren, but careful not to interfere with the duties of the parents. A second common type of grandparent was the *fun-seeker*, whose relationship to his or her grandchildren was marked by informal playfulness. These grandparents and the children were playmates, so to speak. The third common type was the *distant* grandparent, a shadowy figure who emerged on holidays and birthdays with ritual gifts. Although the distant grandparents typically liked their grandchildren, they were remote, interacting little with them. The last two types of grandparent were relatively uncommon. A few women (no men) were *surrogate parents*, usually because the mother worked. A few men (and one woman) were labeled the *reservoir of family wisdom;* usually this style was found in old-fashioned, patriarchal families, where the grandfather retained his authority as long as possible.

The age of the grandparents was a significant factor in determining the style of grandparenting they practiced. Of the three common styles, the formal style was most frequent among grandparents over the age of 65. Younger grandparents (50–65) were more likely to be either fun-seeking or distant. There are several possible interpretations of these data. One possibility is that they represent an age-related developmental trend; that is, people become more formal in social roles as they get older. It may be, on the other hand, that times are changing and that more recent generations value informal, fun-oriented interactions more than previous generations. A third possibility is that the age of the grandparents is simply correlated with the truly important factor, the age of the grandchildren. It may be that grandparents are playful with young children (or distant, if they relate poorly to children) and more formal with older grandchildren. The sparse research evidence (33) tends to support the third interpretation, but probably all three are partially correct.

Marital Relations

The relationship between husband and wife is an important one in old age. As children depart and friends and siblings die, one's spouse becomes more and more the single person with whom the individual can express intimate thoughts and emotional feelings. Sex becomes less urgent with age, although not unimportant by any means. But even the concept of sex begins to embrace more than simply intercourse, to include emotional responsiveness and affectionate acts such as touching (33). In general, the companionship aspect of marriage becomes more important with age.

The shift of focus by the marital partners from their children to each other is one of the major developmental events in marriage during later life (72). Another is the readjustment brought on by retirement; typically both spouses are now home during the day, and the amount of face-to-face interaction increases manyfold. Some strained marriages that were sustained because the partners could rather easily avoid each other while working become unbearable when avoidance is difficult (33). But most observers are struck by the feeling of peacefulness, the lack of stress, the general satisfaction with marriage in the average old couple (72). Elderly spouses value calmness, companionship, and conventionality. Their conversations tend to be impersonal, on general topics such as politics and religion and specific topics such as health and home repairs.

Widowhood   Over half of all women over the age of 65 (but less than 15 percent of men over 65) are widowed (11). Generally, husbands are older than wives, and generally women live longer than men; so the disproportionate number of widows is no surprise. The percentage of women still married at 75–79 years of age is about 25 percent; at 80–84 years it is roughly 15 percent; and over 85 years of age the figure drops close to 5 percent (72). It is no wonder that the "old widow" is considered by sociologists to be one of the common types of "family" in the United States.

Elderly women whose husbands have died (or have left them) encounter a number of economic, social, and psychological problems. Many of them face a continuing struggle to find a new focus for their lives after the loss of their husbands (45). There is also a constant concern about finances, met in a surprising number of cases by work. Widows (and widowers) also must struggle to reorganize their social life. Children, of course, remain a central concern, but some old friends, especially those whose social interactions are based on couple-to-couple relationships, find interactions with a single person awkward. One common research finding is that most older widows are socially better off than younger widows; if a woman loses her husband when most of her female friends are still occupied with their husbands, she is often left out; an older widow has a better chance to move into a social group of women in similar circumstances (4).

Psychologically, the year or so following the death of one's spouse is very stressful. The health of the widow or widower typically suffers; the death rate rises sharply (46, 57). These rather extreme effects reflect the grief, the loneliness, and the anxiety that accompany the loss of a loved one, especially someone who has played a central role in one's life for so many years. The most common symptoms in the first month of bereavement are crying, depression, and sleep disturbances (12). A sudden decrease in what we might call "interest in life" is often apparent in a lack of appetite, feelings of tiredness, and the loss of interest in "TV, news, friends, and clubs." About a fifth of the respondents in one survey felt some degree of guilt, believing that maybe there was something they could have done to prevent the death of their spouse. Gradually, however, the widowed person reorganizes his or her life. If his or her health is satisfactory and financial situation adequate, chances of leading a happy and satisfying life are good (14).

Remarriage   Many widowed persons over 65 remarry, preferring the conjugal state to living alone, living with relatives, or living in some sort of senior-citizen complex. Late-life marriages do not meet with general approval in this society, and in many cases the disapproval is open and direct. To remarry, the widow must face charges that she is acting childishly and that she is showing disrespect for her dear, departed husband. (The situation for widowers is comparable). Her children are likely to stand first in the ranks of the opponents to the

●Figure 12.5   This elderly gentleman, 89, and his bride, 86, are married at the home of the bride's daughter. A reception, attended by their grandchildren and great-grandchildren, followed the ceremony. The groom commented, "I was tired of running around and thought it would be a good time to settle down."

marriage. They find it "unfitting" that their elderly mother might have romantic notions, might even desire sex. Although it is rarely stated explicitly, another common reason for children's opposition to an elderly parent's remarriage is a fear that their inheritance will be lost or complicated. Over 25 percent of the respondents in one survey of late-life remarriages (50) confessed they almost decided to call off the wedding because of pressures from friends and relatives.

In spite of this lack of societal support, marriages in old age appear to be quite successful (Figure 12.5). In the above-mentioned survey (50), 100 marriages were observed; only 6 were rated unsuccessful. Most couples had known each other for a long time, usually before either had been widowed. In about 10 percent of the cases, the couple had been already related by marriage—for example, a woman would marry the widowed brother of her late husband—and there were even a few storybook romances, where childhood sweethearts had drifted apart and had been reunited late in life. In addition to their knowledge of their prospective partner, old persons about to remarry typically had well-reasoned views of the relationship. They had few notions that their new marriages would make them "a new person"—who has such dreams at 70? They expected "the pleasure and satisfaction of having someone nearby, someone to talk to, someone to make plans with," and they felt they could be "useful to someone," that they could make their new spouses happy and content. "The need to be needed does not fade in the later years" (50, p. 65).

INTELLECTUAL DEVELOPMENT

We have discussed the data on age-related changes in IQ in the previous chapter (pp. 419–426), and that discussion should alert us to the many problems in ininterpreting data on age changes in memory, problem-solving, and the other cognitive abilities we are about to review. Learning is likely to be a little slower, memory a bit dimmer, problems slightly more formidable for the old person compared to the young adult. Does this mean the average old person has slipped intellectually? Or has his or her generation been less fortunate in terms of educational opportunities and perhaps nutrition? We need to compare the results from cross-sectional and longitudinal studies before we can gain any confidence in our answers, and longitudinal studies in particular are hard to find. Let us proceed, then, with some caution and skepticism, beginning with an intriguing set of experiments on cognitive regression in old age.

Cognitive Regression in Old Age

In Piaget's view of intellectual development (see Chapter 3), children become less and less egocentric with age. "Egocentric" does not have the meaning of selfish or conceited in this usage; instead it refers to an inability to realize that, in addition to one's own point of view of an object or an event, there are other views as well. For example, preschool children often have great difficulty explaining things to a blindfolded adult (23). They seem to be unable to adjust to the fact that the adult cannot see, and they continue with worthless instructions such as "You must pick up this" (pointing) and "You must put it there" (pointing).

In recent years there has been increasing speculation that Piaget's stages of intellectual development may be repeated in old age—in reverse! It has been suggested that old people become more and more egocentric in their thinking with age (42). In support of this hypothesis, it is noted that, in children, egocentric thought supposedly decreases because of increased social interactions: "In the course of his contacts (and especially, his conflicts and arguments) with other children, the child increasingly finds himself forced to reexamine his own percepts and concepts in the light of those of others, and by so doing, gradually rids himself of cognitive egocentrism" (24, p. 279). If social engagement is the process by which egocentric tendencies in thought are overcome, cannot the social disengagement of old age lead to at least a partial return of these tendencies? So the speculation runs. Until recently, there has been very little research on the issue.

Recent studies (43, 63) do indeed find old people significantly more egocentric than young adults, as predicted, but the egocentrism may be of a somewhat different type than that observed in children. For example, in tasks where two people must instruct each other to achieve a mutually desired goal, "egocentric" old people are nearly as good as young adults who are low in egocentrism (43). Egocentric children have great difficulty with such tasks, presumably because they cannot see the problem from the perspective of another person. Old people, even those who are egocentric in nonsocial contexts, seem to retain the ability to communicate effectively with another person when it is to their mutual benefit.

On the other hand, although there were no significant differences in accuracy between old and young adults in the problem-solving task for pairs, old people took much longer—more than twice the time of the young subjects. This may be due in part to the well-known cautiousness of old people—they are generally more deliberate and less confident than young people, even when performing at the same level of skill and accuracy (6). Another factor, however, may be the intrusion of egocentric tendencies which, in this social task, are maladaptive. One sign of this was the kind of hand motions—pointing, describing something with a gesture—that are useless in a task where the partners cannot see each other. These worthless gestures are common among egocentric children, as we have mentioned. In this study, they were observed in old adults but not in young adults.

Conservation problems   Young children's reasoning is often dominated by superficial features of their perceptual experience, as shown in Piaget's famous conservation problems. In the conservation of quantity problem, children are shown two identical glasses filled with an identical quantity of liquid. Before the subject's eyes, the contents of one glass are poured into a third glass of a different shape, either taller and thinner or shorter and wider. Young children, under the age of 7 or so, are likely to say that the taller, thinner glass has more liquid, because the liquid rises to a higher level.

A number of rather startling studies (56) have shown that old people, like young children, are more likely than people in the middle age ranges to believe that the quantity of liquid changes when poured into a glass of a different shape and, in general, to do poorly on several conservation tasks. It is as if the basic cognitive abilities that are gained in youth are lost in old age. On the other hand, there is evidence that the mental abilities necessary for the understanding of conservation problems have not been lost, but for some reason are not used. To illustrate, consider a study of noninstitutionalized middle-class females aged 65–75 who were tested on a "conservation of surface" task: The women were shown two green cardboard rectangles, representing grass fields, with a little plastic cow in the center of each field and two small red barns close together along the top edge of the fields. They were asked a question such as "Do the two cows have the same amount of grass to eat or does one cow have more grass to eat than the other cow?" Then the two barns on one field were scattered —moved to other places on the field—and the question was repeated. This procedure was repeated with six and ten red barns. A "conserver" was defined as someone who, on at least two of the three trials, showed she understood that moving the barns made no difference in the exposed surface. Although this may not seem a difficult task, only 26 of the 60 women were able to satisfy the criterion for classification as a conserver. "These results support earlier findings that older adults perform poorly on Piagetian tasks of logical thought" (30, p. 71).

Then, however, women who failed the conservation-of-surface task were divided into two groups. Each woman was given 20 trials with a task similar to the one she had failed. Half of the women were given feedback—they were told when they were right or wrong—while the other women received no indication whether they were answering correctly or not. With feedback, the elderly women improved rapidly. On later tests with the original conservation-of-surface task, they performed nearly perfectly. The women in the comparison groups, without feedback, improved only slightly. The ease of training these old women suggests that they had the basic *competence* for the understanding of conservation problems but for some reason performed poorly. Among possible reasons for performance deficits in old subjects are lack of familiarity with the testing situation, lack of motivation (who cares about plastic cows and red barns?), problems with vision or memory, and a misguided desire to please the experimenter which, in this case, may result in silly answers to what the subjects perceive as silly questions. Or it may be that the relative isolation of old people leads them into egocentric modes of thought.

Whether one attributes poorer performance on Piaget's tests to inevitable neurological deterioration (44), social disengagement (42), or superficial performance factors (30), the evidence does suggest decreasing logical abilities in

●Figure 12.6   This picture, painted by an elderly woman in a nursing home, strikes one as childish. Has the woman regressed to a childlike way of perceiving the world? The director of nursing at the nursing home says "Maybe she has regressed. But she's had a hard life: little formal education, married early, many children, hard work on a farm, no time for 'artistic' things. I think she would have drawn the same picture at 35."

old age. We need longitudinal studies, of course, to evaluate the very real possibility that the cross-sectional findings reflect only generational differences in education, nutrition, and other factors, and not age differences at all (see Figure 12.6). But, in any case, differences between young and old adults in these very basic mental abilities may underlie some other research findings, such as those that suggest elderly subjects cannot solve problems as well as young people; we will examine this topic next. Finally, a number of studies have found that social interactions are important for successful aging. In particular, old people who have a *confidant*—a spouse, a child, a friend with whom they can discuss their dreams and fears—may be better able to avoid the egocentrism that disengagement appears to promote (42, 44).

Problem-solving

To solve the kinds of problems psychologists typically devise, one needs to "discover" some information and then to "utilize" that information to find a solution. The general finding of studies of old people is that they are apt to do poorly in both the discovery and the utilization phases of problem-solving (2). Since the average IQ of the older subjects is typically lower than that of younger participants, poorer problem-solving may be due simply to lower intellectual ability (75). However, deficits more specific than general mental ability have also been identified. For example, old subjects do particularly poorly with problems that require flexibility, that is, shifting from one possible solution to another (5). They also have trouble with redundant information: "A redundant example provides no information not already available from previous examples, but almost half of the old subjects performed as if they had new information" (2, p. 92). When searching for relevant information on their own, old subjects tend to ask again and again for the same information (32).

At least some of these specific deficits can be explained by a somewhat poorer memory in the average older subject. Old people tend to forget what they have already inquired about; so they appear to be asking for redundant information. They also appear to forget whether examples they have been given were positive or negative. ("X is *not* an example of what we're looking for" is a negative example.) Nevertheless, when memory demands are minimized by allowing subjects to take notes, old subjects still appear disorderly in their approaches to problem-solving; even special training in systematic note-taking does not help much (76).

Learning and Memory

Psychologists use memory to indicate learning and learning to instill memories. It is often difficult to distinguish between the concepts of learning and memory, especially in studies where the experimenters present lists of nonsense syllables, words, letters, or numbers to human subjects for later recall. Learning can be viewed as the introduction of new information into memory, that is, as one aspect of a concept of memory that also includes notions of storage and retrieval (25).

In general, old people perform poorly relative to young people on both learning and memory tasks. Most of the research has focused on variables that affect the magnitude of the differences between old and young, that is, that increase or decrease the performance of one group more than that of the other. "Pacing," the speed with which the task must be performed, is an important variable in this regard. Consider studies of paired-associate learning, in which typically the person learns pairs of words or letters and then is given one of the pair and is expected to retrieve the other; learning a list of foreign words and their paired English equivalents is a paired-associate task. Slowing the pace of presentation of the pairs (for learning) or increasing the time for response when one member of the pair is presented (as a test of learning) improves the performance of older people more than it helps younger people (2). When given unlimited time to study the pairs and, later, to respond—"self-pacing"—older people rarely increased their study time; it was the extra time to respond that helped them the most (9). Most of the improvement resulted from correct responses made in cases where, under fast pacing, the old people had made no response at all (errors of omission).

A major hypothesis about the effects of pacing (17) holds that old people become anxious and excited when fast-paced performance is demanded. As a result, they are unable to respond in time to avoid an error of omission. If allowed more time or unlimited time, they respond correctly. Interestingly, under these more relaxed circumstances, their reaction times (on the average) are shorter than the time allotted in the fast-paced conditions; this suggests they could have done much better in the demanding conditions if they had been less excited. In a test of this hypothesis, a drug that blocks physiological arousal resulted in significantly improved performance in old people (18).

In memory studies, current notions about various types of memory have been found useful in the study of age-related deficits. The research evidence, while not entirely consistent, suggests that *immediate memory* is not affected by aging (2, 13). This type of memory is indicated by tests of the *memory span*, in which strings of numbers, letters, or words are presented and the person is asked for immediate recall; the task is something like remembering a telephone number just received from "information." Most people, young or old, can recall a sequence with seven units or less. Longer strings—sequences that exceed the memory span—show age differences.

A typical test of memory used in laboratory experiments presents a list of words—usually more than the memory span—and then asks for recall ("What words were on the list?") or recognition ("Pick the words that were on the list: basket, tiger, daylight, . . ."). Such tasks presumably involve both an immediate memory (for some of the items presented last, for example) and another *intermediate memory*. Intermediate memory theoretically involves the storage of information for periods of time longer than the brief periods of immediate memory but shorter than those of long-term memory (discussed below). Recall of events in the last few hours, for example, would depend on intermediate memory. Old people typically perform poorly relative to younger adults on these tasks, leading many psychologists to focus on characteristics of intermediate memory in the search for age-related memory deficits.

Compared to young adults, old people appear to have difficulty encoding information for storage, a difficulty that probably affects both the amount stored and the ease with which stored information can be retrieved for later use. Old subjects do not spontaneously develop mediators—"mnemonic devices"—as well as young subjects (31). Thus, when mnemonic devices are provided by the experimenter, old people typically benefit more than young people. For example, if the words in the list are related in some way—perhaps they are all names of animals—old people improve more than young people, compared to their recall of lists of unrelated words (39). If the words on the list come from a small set of possible words—names of countries, for example—old people improve their relative position, presumably because searching memory for the words is easier (13). Old people often do as well as young adults if the test of memory involves recognition rather than recall (20); this suggests that old people may lack the encoding and retrieval strategies that make for efficient recall.

It is often said that very *long-term memory* is relatively unimpaired with age. Remembering the meanings of words and other general information is one of the intellectual tasks that show the least decrement with age (see pp. 423–425), and anecdotal evidence pictures the average old person as someone who can remember his or her first date, 50 years ago, in great detail but who cannot be certain what he or she did yesterday. Although empirical research on memory of long past events is difficult, the meager evidence supports folklore, that is, supports the notion that old people do not lose their long-established memories (52).

BIOLOGICAL CONCERNS IN OLD AGE

In the years following the 65th birthday, people naturally become concerned with biological aspects of life. Their eyesight may become poorer, and they may require a hearing aid. They may become chronically ill and thus fail in their fervent attempts to avoid being a burden to anyone. Death is closer, and this knowledge interests them in the general processes of aging. Some of their peers will desperately inquire about anything that might delay the inevitable end to life.

Biological Changes in Old Age

What cues do we use to identify someone as old? (See Figure 12.7.) If a man or woman has hair, it is often gray or white. Skin commonly exposed to the sun—on the face, on the hands—is wrinkled and sprinkled with dark spots. Since more than two-thirds of all people over 75 have lost all their teeth (3), we may recognize poor-fitting or too-beautiful dentures. The person moves slowly, without much evidence of agility, the result of muscle atrophy, bone degeneration, and possibly arthritis. His or her posture may be slightly stooped. And his or her voice is slightly higher in pitch than it used to be, and weaker, softer. A good young actor, with the help of make-up, uses cues such as these to create the impression of old age.

Vision becomes progressively poorer for most old people (3). Acuity—the ability that is tested in common eye charts—declines, and this is what old people usually mean when they say they can't see as well. But other aspects of vision also suffer. Old people, on the average, require more light; they adapt more slowly to changes in illumination; and they cannot distinguish colors as well as they once could. The lens in the eye tends to become less elastic with age, making it difficult for the older person to adjust to near objects. Although the indi-

● Figure 12.7   What are the clues to a person's age?

vidual over 65 who does not need eyeglasses for one reason or another is rare, compensatory lenses enable most people to live a normal life. About 10 percent of people over 65, however, have visual problems severe enough to limit their activities (73). About half of the 500,000 legally blind people in the United States are over 65. Even these severe problems can be alleviated in many cases —by replacing a cloudy lens from a cataract with a plastic one, for example, restoring nearly normal vision.

Hearing losses in old age are also common, especially in the higher frequencies (33). An unfortunate result of hearing loss is the further isolation of the old person, who cannot readily understand the conversations of the people around him or her. Communication becomes difficult. Again, mechanical devices—hearing aids—can alleviate some or all of the problem. An interesting study (49) compared the hearing deficits of old men in New York, Düsseldorf, and Cairo with those of old men in an African tribe living in the Sudan. The tribesmen could hear much better at all frequencies than their urban counterparts, leading some researchers to suggest that the "noise pollution" in large cities is responsible for at least a good part of the hearing loss in old age. Even in the United States, rural old people tend to have better hearing than people who have lived all their lives in the city (3).

Disease in Old Age

The probability of disease increases dramatically over the age of 65. The relevant statistics are endless: The elderly account for 25 percent of the nation's health expenditures; they are the main users of long-term care facilities and home-care services; they consume 25 percent of all drugs (7). Although they constitute only 10 percent of the population, they fill a third of the nation's hospital beds and account for 40 percent of physicians' office visits (53). Over 80 percent of old people are estimated to have at least one chronic disease, such as high blood pressure, arthritis, diabetes, heart disease, or kidney disease (7). Multiple ailments are common.

Disease has many effects on the life of the older person. There is often pain, for example, with diseases like arthritis. The financial effects, in spite of Medicare and other government programs, are still significant; about one-fourth of the medical expenses of the aged is still assumed by the old person involved (36). Many diseases lead to restrictions on activity. All of these effects —pain, expense, reduced activity—have psychological impacts as well, forcing the older person to be more dependent than he or she wants to be, lowering self-esteem or at least making "old age with integrity" a difficult achievement. When a national sample of people of all ages were asked for their opinion of the "worst things about being over 65 years of age," 62 percent cited poor health or poor physical condition (27).

Like younger people, the elderly react to illness in many different ways. Some of these individual differences are related to circumstances; people in the higher socioeconomic classes, for example, have fewer money worries and better medical attention than others less fortunate, and thus an illness is less disruptive for them. Personality is a factor, too. People with defensive and anxious personalities react to illness as a major threat to their self-esteem, often withdrawing from society with a defeated attitude, while less defensive people, similarly disabled, maintain a more positive and active orientation to life (45). Finally, there is an age-old question that William James phrased most poetically (35): "And our bodies themselves, are they simply *ours,* or are they *us?*" Old people who are able to distinguish between their bodies and their "selves" are best able to cope with illness (59).

There are also critical differences in reaction to illnesses (66). Old people in England are more likely to report their health as "good for their age" than their counterparts in the United States, in spite of the fact that, objectively, old people in Britain are less healthy than Americans. This finding is interpreted in terms of differing views of illness in the two countries. As sociologist Talcott Parsons noted (58), to be ill in the United States is "inherently undesirable." People are expected to be active and independent, and the sick person is "obliged" to recover as soon as possible. In England, on the other hand, illness is viewed as an unfortunate event which must be faced, as must all such events, with a "stiff upper lip." The emphasis is on self-control, and "whining" is discouraged.

Aging and Death

Why do people grow old? Apart from fatal accidents and illnesses, what determines how long a person will live? These questions have intrigued scientists for centuries, yet "the fundamental causes of biological aging are almost as much a mystery today as they have ever been" (29, p. 36).

Life expectancy has been increasing in the United States at a fairly rapid rate. A child born in 1900 could expect to live 47 years; the average child born in 1974 will live 25 years longer (73). (Women, on the average, outlive men by 8 years.) There are a number of reasons for this impressive increase in life expectancy, including improved nutrition, hygiene, and medical care. All of these reasons, however, have to do with illnesses and injuries that bring the person to an "untimely" end, that is, with factors that interrupt the "normal life span." There is no evidence that the potential life span of humans has increased in the slightest (29, 36). The death rates of young adults have decreased dramatically as medical discoveries reduce the impact of killer diseases, but the death rates of very old people have changed very little. If a cure for cancer were discovered, for example, the life expectancy of people aged 65 would increased by only 1.2 years (29). If medical science were able to eliminate heart disease and cancer, the major causes of death in old people, it would simply "reduce the possible ways in which the inevitability of our death will occur, and will allow accidents then to become the leading killer" (29, pp. 36–37) (see Figure 12.8).

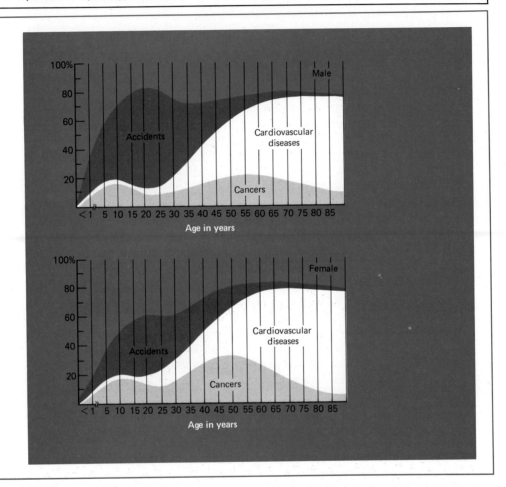

● Figure 12.8 Mortality from cancer, cardiovascular diseases (heart disease and cerebrovascular disease), and accidents in the United States, 1969, expressed as a percentage of total mortality by age group and sex. (Adapted from P. S. Timaras. *Developmental Physiology and Aging.* New York: Macmillan, 1972.)

Biological aging The potential life span of the average human is probably between 70 and 100 years, probably around 90 (29). As a person ages, biological
changes occur that affect his or her ability to survive, that is, to avoid accidents,
to fight off disease. Death occurs in a very old person not so much because of
the particular disease that happens to be involved but because of age-related biological decrements that make the disease more likely. For this reason, aging is
often defined as "a decline in physiologic competence" (71).

But why this decline? There are a vast number of theories of biological aging, but most of the serious contenders involve the genetic codes present in the body's cells (29). One theory proposes "aging genes" which program the biological changes we typically associate with aging—menopause, graying of the hair, and, at a more basic level, partial or complete loss of function of body cells. Another theory suggests, more simply, that our genetic apparatus is designed to promote growth and, eventually, reproduction; once this major task is completed, the organism runs out of useful genetic information and "runs down" like a clock that is no longer wound. Advocates of this theory point out that aging is an unusual and, in many respects, an abnormal phenomenon when viewed in terms of animal life in general. Animals in the wild, for example, rarely exceed more than half the life span of animals in zoos, because they are killed by disease and predators as their speed and strength diminish. No genetic code for later life is needed; except in the artificial environment we call civilization, "later life" doesn't exist.

Probably the most widely accepted theory of biological aging maintains that the genetic apparatus begins to use inaccurate, distorted information because the essential "information molecules" are damaged. The source of this damage may be inevitable injuries and accidents at the molecular level (inevitable in the sense that professional football players will be injured, if they play long enough). Or the damage may be due to natural tendencies of any system to become disordered over time (74); "self-poisons" manufactured (deliberately or otherwise) by other parts of the body are another possibility (68). In any case, as a result of the damage, replacement and repair of body cells comes to a halt or proceeds less rapidly and efficiently—or, perhaps, abnormal (cancerous) cells are produced instead.

Decreases in cell function lead to decreased function in various body organs necessary for survival. The thymus gland, for example, controls many important immune reactions; if it functions poorly, the body may lose its ability to fight off disease and to destroy cancerous cells. Or, for some reason, the immune system may lose its selectivity and begin to attack normal body cells as if they were foreign cells. These "autoimmune" reactions have been linked to certain diseases in old age such as arthritis and diabetes (36). Another important system in the body controls vital balances such as the level of sugar in the blood, acting to increase it when it is low and to lower it when it is elevated. Other "homeostatic" mechanisms keep the body temperature from becoming too high or too low, and water levels, salt levels, and acid levels in the normal range. To the extent that these self-regulating mechanisms become less efficient because of damaged "information molecules," the body loses its ability to react to stress. In many old people, death is due to relatively mild stress—like a change in the fluid balance caused by diarrhea—to which the aging body can no longer adapt.

Longevity   As we might expect from the discussion of biological aging in general, genetic factors play a major role in explaining why some people live longer than others. If your grandparents or parents lived to a ripe old age, your chances of doing the same are better than those of someone whose ancestors tended to die young. Environmental factors also predict individual differences in longevity. Heavy cigarette smoking lowers life expectancy, on the average, by about 12 years, and obesity lowers it by about a year and a half for every 10 percent overweight (36). Pollution of our air and our water, addition of dangerous chemicals to our food, overuse of pesticides and weed killers, and other side-effects of an industrial economy have a negative effect on longevity (74). A good marriage adds about five years to life (36).

Certain personality traits seem to be characteristic of people who live to be very old (55). Although the individual differences of people aged 90–100 are almost as great as those in any other age group, the general impression is one of a moderate and flexible approach to life. They are rarely extreme in their habits —they are neither health-food faddists nor gluttons, they are likely to enjoy a drink or two each day, and they exercise moderately each day. The lives they have lived tend to be quite varied—some full of stress, some relatively easygoing. It is not so much the presence or absence of pressure that marks them as their flexibility and adaptability to whatever comes their way. One woman, age 101, began her successive careers as a prostitute in western mining camps. After 12 years in this profession, she married and had three children. Her husband died; so she opened a bar in Missouri. Later she opened a foster home for homeless children. After the foster home burned down, she moved in with a widowed, tubercular daughter in Colorado. She contracted tuberculosis herself and spent two years in a sanitarium. At the age of 65, she married a man she met in the sanitarium. They moved to a ranch in New Mexico. At 101, she appeared to be making the best of her life in an old people's home and to be ready for whatever else might appear on the horizon (54).

DEATH AND DYING

Death is the biological end to life, but it is much more than that. It is a social event that affects many people, not simply the individual who died. Spouse, children, and friends are deeply affected, and, if the person is a leader of some note, his or her death may signal the end of a political era (e.g., Charles de Gaulle) or a religious beginning (e.g., Jesus). Death is also a personal event, something someone must somehow "come to grips with."

Although the time of death is determined primarily by biological factors, the "will to live" is a reality to most doctors who have treated dying patients. Some people seem to give up and die sooner than expected, while others "hold on," living months, even years, beyond "their time." An interesting study (61) began with the assumption that famous people who were dying would try to live until their birthdays, to experience one final public outpouring of praise and, perhaps, sympathy. By reviewing the vital statistics of several hundred prominent Americans, it was discovered that many fewer than would be expected (by an even distribution of deaths) died in the month before their birthday, while the death rate in the month following the birthday was much higher than normal. Among the most famous people—George Washington, Benjamin Franklin, Mark Twain, and others—78 percent of the deaths that were to be expected in the month preceding their birthday did not occur. Apparently many of these people were able to delay death, for a short time at least, to reap one final reward in life.

Perhaps the most influential research on the process of dying is by Elisabeth Kübler-Ross, a psychiatrist who observed and interviewed several hundred dying patients (37). Kübler-Ross identified five stages, each characterized by a particular attitude, between the time one knows "for sure" that death is imminent and death itself. The first stage is *denial.* Often ignoring obvious symptoms, the patient is saying, "No! Not me!" Denial is followed by *anger,* as the patient asks, "Why me? Why now?" Hostility toward doctors, nurses, and family is common; it is as if someone must be blamed.

In the third stage of dying, a *bargaining* attitude appears, as the patient seeks to cope with the inevitability of his or her death. God or even Satan is inundated by pleas for a pardon or at least a postponement. The patient may become very compliant, hoping to earn a few more months of life "for good behavior." Perhaps many of the extensions of life through one's birthday, noted above, are of the type, "Let me live until X, then I'll die peacefully."

The fourth stage is *depression,* as a sense of loss becomes unavoidable and pervasive. This "preparatory" sorrow is probably necessary for the final stage, *acceptance.* Stewart Alsop, the noted journalist, expressed his acceptance of his impending death in these words: "A dying man needs to die as a sleepy man needs to sleep, and there comes a time when it is wrong, as well as useless, to resist" (1, p. 299). Acceptance is not a happy stage, nor a sad one. "It is almost void of feelings. It is as if the pain had gone, the struggle is over . . ." (37, p. 100).

Kübler-Ross's seminal work has been responsible for an awakening of interest in the psychological aspects of dying and has undoubtedly been of help to many people who must interact with dying patients, friends, or relatives. As a scientific theory, however, it leaves much to be desired (34). Kübler-Ross's interviews were not very systematic; instead of statistical analyses, she presents examples of anecdotes. Other researchers do not find the same five stages; the only consistently reported stage is one of depression shortly before death (65).

Future research will undoubtedly show that the process of dying is modified by several factors (34). For example, the nature of the disease often affects the way a person dies—dying of cancer, many physicians note, is different from dying of emphysema or heart disease. There are probably sex differences and ethnic differences in the style of dying. A teenager dies in ways different from those of the elderly, and dying at home is different from dying at a hospital. Personality is also important: ". . . we approach our death to some extent as the type of person we have always been—reflective or impulsive, warm or aloof, whatever. A view of the dying process that excludes personality as such must also exclude much of reality" (34, p. 43).

In the period preceding death, the individual is likely to exhibit clearly the

●Figure 12.9   Senator Hubert H. Humphrey who, in Vice President Mondale's words, "taught us how to live—and how to die."

degree of ego integrity or despair that is the fruit of the life he or she has led (Figure 12.9). For some, death is part of the life cycle, and they are not afraid. For others, death means simply that time has run out; it is the ultimate frustration in a long series of frustrations. In addition, old people with integrity serve as a beacon for young people. In the words of Maggie Kuhn, founder of the Grey Panthers, they are the "elders of the tribe"; they present models to emulate; they personify goals; and they provide a basis for confidence in the future. Erik Erikson ties it all together:

> Webster's Dictionary is kind enough to help us complete this outline in a circular fashion. Trust (the first of our ego values) is here defined as 'the assured reliance on another's integrity,' the last of our values. I suspect that Webster had business in mind rather than babies, credit rather than faith. But the formulation stands. And it seems possible to further paraphrase the relation of adult integrity and infantile trust by saying that healthy children will not fear life if their elders have integrity enough not to fear death' (21, p. 269).

SUMMARY

The number of old people in the population is growing rapidly, and so is the number of scientists—called "gerontologists"—who study them. The central issue of old age, according to Erik Erikson, is integrity versus despair: whether there is a sense of satisfaction with a life well-lived or a feeling that one never quite achieved anything of value. These feelings often derive from a "life review," a retrospective look at one's hopes and fears, achievements and failures. In some old people, despair, combined with a series of personal losses—of loved ones, of an occupation, of bodily functions—leads to severe depression. Suicide, especially among white males, is a possibility. Although cerebral arteriosclerosis and senile brain disease are organic diseases resulting in mental disorders among some old people, many elderly mental patients suffer from reversible disorders such as alcoholism and neurosis. Even patients with "irreversible" disorders can be helped by giving them a sense of responsibility for their own destiny.

In the view of many people, the age of 65 marks the beginning of "old age." It also is the common age of retirement. Some people would prefer to keep working, if they had the choice; this is especially true of high-salaried executives and professionals who are very involved in their work. Most working-class people have little desire to continue working unless they need money. Personality factors are involved, too. Bitter, angry, resentful people ("despairing" people, in Erikson's terms) adjust poorly to retirement; "healthy" and "passive" personalities adjust better; "defensive" personalities adjust if they can keep active.

Successful aging involves an adjustment to decreased activities. Disengagement theories suggest that a gradual withdrawal from work and social interactions is natural and desired by the average elderly person. Research evidence, however, tends to support activity theories, which suggest that life satisfaction is positively correlated with social engagement. Personality factors are also important. Well-adjusted personalities can accept nearly any level of activity, while "unintegrated" personalities continue the distress of earlier life stages. In between these extremes, the moderately integrated personalities seem to rely on social activities for at least a part of their self-esteem and confidence.

Most old people are grandparents, but they do not always fill the roles in ways pictured in stories and movies. "Formal" grandparents follow the traditional script: occasionally indulgent, constantly interested, careful not to interfere. "Fun-seekers," who tend to be younger, are more like playmates to their grandchildren. "Distant" grandparents seem to relate poorly to children.

Marital relations in old age tend to be pleasant and satisfying, with an emphasis on companionship. Many women and a few men suffer the death of their spouses and, as a result, encounter financial and emotional problems. In addition to sadness, many widows and widowers feel guilty, believing that maybe there was something they might have done to prolong the life of their spouse. Some widows and widowers remarry. Often their adult children and society at large oppose these late-life marriages, but most of them are quite successful and satisfying.

There is evidence that the social isolation of some old people may lead to egocentric modes of thinking that hamper their performance in problem-solving tasks. Given proper incentive or brief retraining, however, most of them demonstrate that they have not lost their basic competence. Having at least one close friend or confidant helps prevent egocentric trends.

Compared to young adults, old people perform more poorly on problems that require flexibility, and they often respond to redundant information as if it were new. Memory deficits may account for some of these data. Old people show little or no deficit in immediate memory or in memory for events long since past, but they have difficulty with intermediate memory tasks. In particular, they seem less able than young people to use mnemonic devices or strategies to help them remember; thus, for example, organizing a list helps them more than it would young people. In learning tasks, the performance of old people is improved relative to that of young people if the pace is slowed, perhaps because a slower pace reduces anxiety or arousal.

Biological changes in old age include poorer vision and hearing, although eyeglasses and hearing aids can compensate for loss in all but the most extreme cases. Nearly three of four people over 65 have at least one chronic disease such as arthritis, diabetes, or heart disease. To some people, disease is a threat to their self-esteem because it makes them more dependent, but less defensive old people can maintain a positive and active orientation to life.

Although the maximum life span of humans does not appear to have increased, life expectancy is increasing because of fewer "early" deaths by disease or injury. Biological aging is still poorly understood. Many biologists define aging as a decline in the ability of the body to avoid disease and to recover from injury. This may be due to "aging genes" or to a "running down" of genetic programs designed only to promote early growth and, eventually, reproduction. On a more basic level, "information molecules" used by our bodies to replace injured tissue and to fight disease may themselves be damaged or poisoned with age. Short-lived ancestors, cigarette smoking, and obesity are factors that lower life expectancy, while a happy marriage and a flexible personality increase the chances of a long life.

According to Kübler-Ross, there are five stages of dying: denial, anger, bargaining, depression, and acceptance. Other researchers do not find the same stages, although depression has been found to be common. Some people seem to be able to put off their deaths for brief periods—until their birthdays, for example. The style of dying is probably affected by several factors, including age, sex, and the cause of death. The ego integrity of an old person facing death is often the basis of the self-confidence with which a child faces life.

References

1. Alsop, S. **Stay of execution.** Philadelphia: Lippincott, 1973.
2. Arenberg, D. Cognition and aging: verbal learning, memory, and problem solving. In C. Eisdorfer & M. P. Lawton (Eds.), **The psychology of adult development and aging.** Washington, D.C.: American Psychological Association, 1973.
3. Bischof, L. J. **Adult psychology** (2nd ed.). New York: Harper & Row, 1976.

4. Blau, Z. S. Structural constraints on friendships in old age. **American Sociological Review,** 1961, **26,** 429–439.

5. Botwinick, J. Behavioral processes. In S. Gershon & A. Raskin (Ed.), **Aging, Vol. II: Genesis and treatment of psychologic disorders in the elderly.** New York: Raven, 1975.

6. Botwinick, J. Cautiousness in advanced age. **Journal of Gerontology,** 1966, **21,** 347–353.

7. Butler, R. N. **Why survive?** New York: Harper & Row, 1975.

8. Bureau of the Census. **Demographic aspects of aging and the older population in the United States.** (Current Population Reports, P-22, No. 59.) Washington, D.C.: Government Printing Office, 1976.

9. Canestrari, R. E. Paced and self-paced learning in young and elderly adults. **Journal of Gerontology,** 1963, **18,** 165–168.

10. Carp, F. M. Differences among older workers, volunteers, and people who are neither. **Journal of Gerontology,** 1968, **23,** 497–501.

11. Carter, H., & Glick, P. C. **Marriage and divorce** (2nd ed.). Cambridge, Mass: Harvard University Press, 1976.

12. Clayton, P. J., Halikes, J. A., & Maurice, W. L. The bereavement of the widowed. **Diseases of the Nervous System,** 1971, **32,** 597–604.

13. Craik, F. I. M. Short-term memory and the aging process. In G. A. Talland (Ed.), **Human aging and behavior.** New York: Academic Press, 1968.

14. Cumming, E. The multigenerational family and the crisis of widowhood. In W. Donahue, et al (Eds.), **Living in the multigenerational family.** Ann Arbor, Mich.: Institute of Gerontology, 1969.

15. Cumming, E., & Henry, W. H. **Growing old.** New York: Basic Books, 1961.

16. Dubin, R. Industrial workers' world. **Social Problems,** 1956, **3,** 131–142.

17. Eisdorfer, C. Arousal and performance: Experiments in verbal learning and a tentative theory. In G. A. Talland (Ed.), **Human aging and behavior.** New York: Academic Press, 1968.

18. Eisdorfer, C., Nowlin, J., & Wilkie, F. Improvement of learning in the aged by modification of autonomic nervous system activity. **Science,** 1970, **170,** 1327–1329.

19. Epstein, L. A., & Murray, J. H. Employment and retirement. In B. L. Neugarten (Ed.), **Middle age and aging.** Chicago: University of Chicago Press, 1968.

20. Erber, J. T. Age differences in recognition memory. **Journal of Gerontology,** 1974, **29,** 177–181.

21. Erikson, E. **Childhood and society** (2nd ed.). New York: Norton, 1963.

22. Erikson, E. **Insight and responsibility.** New York: Norton, 1964.

23. Flavell, J. H. Role-taking and communication skills in children. **Young Children,** 1966, **21,** 164–177.

24. Flavell, J. H. **The developmental psychology of Jean Piaget.** Princeton, N.J.: Van Nostrand, 1963.

25. Geiwitz, J. **Looking at ourselves.** Boston: Little, Brown, 1976.

26. Goldstein, K. **Human nature in the light of psychopathology.** Cambridge: Harvard University Press, 1940.

27. Harris, L., & Associates. **The myth and reality of aging in America.** Washington, D.C.: The National Council on the Aging, 1975.

28. Havighurst, R. J., Neugarten, B. L., & Tobin, S. S. Disengagement and patterns of aging. In B. L. Neugarten (Ed.), **Middle age and aging.** Chicago: University of Chicago Press, 1968.

29. Hayflick, L. Why grow old? **The Stanford Magazine,** 1975, **3**(1), 36–43.

30. Hornblum, J. N., & Overton, W. F. Area and volume conservation among the elderly: assessment and training. **Developmental Psychology,** 1976, **12,** 68–74.

31. Hulicka, I. M., & Grossman, J. L. Age group comparisons for the use of mediators in paired-associate learning. **Journal of Gerontology,** 1967, **22,** 46–51.

32. Jerome, E. A. Decay of neuristic processes in the aged. In C. Tibbitts, & W. Donahue (Eds.), **Social and psychological aspects of aging.** New York: Columbia University Press, 1962.

33. Kalish, R. A. **Late adulthood: perspectives on human development.** Monterey, Calif.: Brooks/Cole, 1975.

34. Kastenbaum, R. Is death a life crisis? On the confrontation with death in theory and practice. In N. Datan & L. H. Ginsberg (Eds.), **Life-span developmental psychology: normative life crises.** New York: Academic Press, 1975.

35. Kent, D. P., & Matson, M. B. The impact of health on the aged family. **The Family Coordinator,** 1972, **21,** 29–36.

36. Kimmel, D. C. **Adulthood and aging.** New York: Wiley, 1974.

37. Kübler-Ross, E. **On death and dying.** New York: Macmillan, 1969.

38. Langer, E. J., & Rodin, J. The effects of choice and enhanced personal responsibility for the aged: a field experiment in an institutional setting. **Journal of Personality and Social Psychology,** 1976, **34,** 191–198.

39. Laurence, M. W. A developmental look at the usefulness of list categorization as on and to free recall. **Canadian Journal of Psychology,** 1967, **21,** 153–165.

40. Lee, R. V. The good old days. **The Stanford Magazine,** 1976, 4(2), 28–31.

41. Lewis, M. I., & Butler, R. N. Life review therapy. **Geriatrics,** 1974, **29,** 165–173.

42. Looft, W. R. Egocentrism and social interaction. **Psychological Bulletin,** 1972, **78,** 73–92.

43. Looft, W. R., & Charles, D. C. Egocentrism and social interaction in young and old adults. **Aging and Human Development,** 1971, **2,** 21–28.

44. Lowenthal, M. F., & Haven, C. Interaction and adaptation: intimacy as a critical variable. **American Sociological Review,** 1968, **33,** 20–30.

45. Maas, H. S., & Kuypers, J. A. **From thirty to seventy.** San Francisco: Jossey-Bass, 1974.

46. Maddison, D., & Viola, A. The health of widows in the year following bereavement. **Journal of Psychosomatic Research,** 1968, **12,** 297–306.

47. Maddox, G. L. Fact and artifact: evidence bearing on disengagement theory. In E. Palmore (Ed.), **Normal aging.** Durham, N.C.: Duke University Press, 1970.

48. Maddox, F. L. Retirement as a social event in the United States. In B. L. Neugarten (Ed.), **Middle age and aging.** Chicago: University of Chicago Press, 1968.

49. McFarland, R. A. The sensory and perceptual processes in aging. In K. W. Schaie (Ed.), **Theory and methods of research on aging.** Morgantown, W.V.: West Virginia University, 1968.

50. McKain, W. C. A new look at older marriages. **The Family Coordinator,** 1972, **21,** 61–69.

51. Neugarten, B. L., Havighurst, R. J., & Tobin, S. S. Personality and patterns of aging. In B. L. Neugarten (Ed.), **Middle age and aging.** Chicago: University of Chicago Press, 1968.

52. Neugarten, B. L., & Weinstein, K. K. The changing American grandparent. **Journal of Marriage and the Family,** 1964, **26,** 199–204.

53. **Newsweek,** February 28, 1977.

54. Overholser, R. V., & Randolph, E. Secrets of how to live longer. **Family Circle,** October, 1976.

55. Palmore, E., & Jeffers, F. C. (Eds.) **Prediction of life span.** Lexington, Mass: Heath, 1971.

56. Papalia, D., & Bielby, D. Cognitive functioning in middle and old age adults: a review of research based on Piaget's theory. **Human Development,** 1974, **17,** 424–443.

57. Parkes, C. M., Benjamin, R., & Fitzgerald, R. A. Broken heart: a statistical study of increased mortality among widowers. **British Medical Journal,** 1969, **1,** 740–743.

58. Parsons, T. Definitions of health and illness in the light of American values and social structure. In E. G. Jaco (Ed.), **Patients, physicians, and illness.** New York: Free Press, 1958.

59. Peck, R. F., & Berkowitz, H. Personality and adjustment in middle age. In B. L. Neugarten and associates (Eds.), **Personality in middle and late life.** New York: Atherton, 1964.

60. Perlin, S., & Butler, R. N. Psychiatric aspects of adaptation to the aging experience. In J. E. Birren et al. (Eds.), **Human aging.** Washington, D.C.: U.S. Government Printing Office, 1963.

61. Phillips, D. **Statistics: a guide to the unknown.** New York: Holden-Day, 1971.

62. Reichard, S., Livson, F., & Peterson, P. G. **Aging and personality.** New York: Wiley, 1962.

63. Rubin, K. H. The relationship between spatial and communicative egocentrism in children and young and old adults. **Journal of Genetic Psychology,** 1974, **125,** 295–301.

64. Schofield, W. **Psychotherapy: purchase of friendship.** Englewood Cliffs, N.J.: Prentice-Hall, 1974.

65. Schulz, R., & Alderman, D. Clinical research and the "stages of dying." **Omega,** 1974, **5,** 137–144.

66. Shanas, E., Townsend, P., Wedderburn, D., Friis, H., Milhoj, P., & Stehouwer, J. **Older people in three industrial societies.** New York: Atherton, 1968.

67. Simon, A., & Cahan, R. B. The acute brain syndrome in geriatric patients. In W. M. Mendel & L. J. Epstein (Eds.), **Acute psychotic reaction.** Washington, D.C.: American Psychiatric Association, 1966.

68. Strehler, B. L. A new age for aging. **Natural History,** February, 1973.

69. Streib, G. F., & Schneider, C. J. **Retirement in American society.** Ithaca, N.Y.: Cornell University Press, 1971.

70. Terry, R. D., & Wisniewski, H. M. Structural and chemical changes of the aged human brain. In S. Gershon & A. Raskin (Eds.), **Aging, Vol. II: Genesis and treatment of psychologic disorders in the elderly.** New York: Raven Press, 1975.

71. Timiras, P. S. **Developmental physiology and aging.** New York: Macmillan, 1972.

72. Troll, L. E. The family of later life: a decade review. **Journal of Marriage and the Family,** 1971, **33,** 263–290.

73. U.S. Bureau of the Census. **Statistical abstract of the United States: 1976** (97th ed.). Washington, D.C., 1976.

74. U.S. Department of Health, Education, and Welfare. **Working with older people, Vol. II: Biological, psychological and sociological aspects of aging.**

75. Wetherick, N. E. A comparison of the problem-solving ability of young, middle-aged and old subjects. **Gerontologia,** 1964, **9,** 164–178.

76. Young, M. L. Problem-solving performance in two age groups. **Journal of Gerontology,** 1966, **21,** 505–509.

Index

Ability, 37–38
Absence, parental, 244–245
Academic motivation, 256–259
Accommodation, in intellectual development theory, 19, 21
Achievement motivation
  age and, 426–427
  family and peer influences on, 256–259
  in preschool years, 220–222
Activism, 336–339
Activity level, infant, 76–79
Adaptability, infant, 78–79
Adler, Alfred, 372
Adolescence, 280–361
  alienation in, 9, 323, 333–343
    activism and, 336–340
    among privileged youth, 334–336
    social dropouts, 340–343
  biological factors in, 291–298
    physical maturation, 293–295
    psychological aspects of maturation, 294, 296–298
  cultural differences in, 117
  defined, 280
  drug use in, 343–350
    alcohol, 344–346
    amphetamines, 344, 349
    barbiturates, 349
    generation gap and, 343–344

    hallucinogens, 343, 349
    marijuana, 343, 344, 346–349
    opiates, 349–350
    reasons for, 350
  historical perspective on psychology of, 8–9
  independence in, 298–303
    in other cultures, 298–300
    in U.S., 300–303
  intellectual development in, 176–178
  juvenile delinquency in, 350–359
    deprivation and, 353
    incidence, 350–353
    parent-child relationships and, 357
    personality and, 353–357
    prevention and treatment of, 357–359
    social change and, 353
  moral development in, 309–316
    factors in, 309–311
    religious beliefs, 311–312
    values, 312–316
  peer relations in, 303
    conformity, 305–306
    influence of, 303–304
    juvenile delinquency and, 354
    marijuana use and, 348
    parental versus peer influences, 306–308
    social acceptance, 308

Adolescence (*Continued*)
  personality development in, 281–291
    identity, 281–288
    psychological effects of mental
      growth, 288–291
  psychoanalytic theory and, 25, 26
  sexual attitudes in, 323–333
    of contemporary Americans, 327–
      329
    cultural influences on, 326–327
    pregnancy and, 330–333
    sex differences in, 324–326, 328
  sexual behavior in, 326–327, 330
Adulthood, 9–11. *See also* Middle adult-
    hood; Old age; Young adulthood
Age
  dependency and, 212
  longitudinal and cross sectional stud-
    ies and, 408–409
  mate selection and, 377–378, 380
  memory and, 93–94
  perceptual development and, 155
Aging. *See* Middle adulthood; Old age
Aggression
  in preschool years, 204–211, 226–227
  in psychoanalytic theory, 22, 24
Alcohol use
  in adolescence, 344–346
  in old age, 451
  during pregnancy, 58–59
Alienation, adolescent, 9, 323, 333–343
  activism and, 336–340
  among privileged youth, 334–336
  social dropouts, 340–343
Alsop, Stewart, 479
Altruism, 228, 230
Amphetamine use, 344, 349
Anal stage of personality development,
    24–25
Androgens, 292
Angyal, Andras, 372
Animal behavior, 91, 104–106, 111,
    112–113, 116–117
Anxiety

  in infancy, 107–110
  memory and, 158, 160
  in preschool years, 213, 215, 218–220
  in psychoanalytic theory, 24, 25
  psychosomatic illness and, 266–267
  separation, 109–110
  about sex, 204
  stranger, 107–109
Approach/withdrawal dimension of in-
    fant temperament, 78–79
Aristotle, 280–281
Asceticism, 291
Assimilation, in intellectual develop-
    ment theory, 19, 21
Asthma, psychosomatic, 266–267
Attachment, 103–110
Attention, 80–81, 89–94
  discrepancy and, 92–93
  meaning and, 91–92
  memory and, 93–94
  schemata, formation of, 92
  stimulus determinants of, 89–91
Attractiveness, mate selection and, 376
Authoritarian control, 232
Authoritarian parents, 233–234, 241–
    242
Authoritative parents, 233, 241
Autistic children, 30, 34
Autocratic parents, 301
Autonomy, 212

Babbling in infancy, 99, 100, 106, 126,
    130
Baby biographies, 6, 8
Bandura, Albert, 32, 208
Barbiturate use, 349
Baumrind, Diana, 232–234
Bayley's Scale of Mental Development,
    183, 184
Bernstein, Basil, 147
Binet, Alfred, 179
Biological aging, 476–477
Biological factors
  in adolescence, 291–298

physical maturation, 293–295
  psychological aspects of maturation, 294, 296–298
heredity transmission, 43–52
  chromosomes, 44, 45, 47–48, 53–54
  determining extent of genetic influences, 45–47
  genes, 43–46
  of intelligence, 51–52, 187–192
  of mental defects, 49
  of mental disorders, 49–50
  of personality, 50–51
  of physical features, 48
  of sex, 47–48
in infancy, 43, 62–82
  basic needs, 74–76
  birth process, 62
  body growth, 65–66
  individual differences, 76–82
  premature births, 62–64
  response capabilities, 71–74
  sensory capacities, 66–71
in middle adulthood, 428–434
  heart attack, 430–432
  menopause, 428–430
  sexual behavior, 413, 432–434
during pregnancy, 53–62
  conception, 53–54
  embryonic development, 54, 55, 56
  environmental influences, 57–62
  fetal development, 55–57
in old age, 472–480
  biological changes, 472–474
  death and dying, 475, 478–480
  diseases, 474–475
  life expectancy, 475–478
Birth process, 62
Births, premature, 62–64, 100
Bismarck, Otto von, 454
Body growth in infancy, 65–66
Bottle feeding, 102–103
Brain
  blood flow to, 425
  in infancy, 68–69
  language development and, 129
  in old age, 451
Breast development, 294, 295
Broca's area, 129
Bryan, William Lowe, 390

California Preschool Schedule, 184
Care, 410
Careers, 389–401
  choosing, 391–394
  vocational values, 394–397
  of women, 397–401
Caretakers
  attachment to, 103–110
  interaction with, 103–117
  social responses to, 99–103
Caring, expansion of, 372
Castration complex, 25
Cerebral arteriosclerosis, 451
Child psychology, historical perspective, 4–8
Child rearing
  cultural differences in, 117–120
  dependency and, 214–215
Chomsky, Noam, 128–129
Chromosomes, 44, 45, 47–48, 53–54
Clark, Eve, 133
Classical conditioning, 28–30
Classifications, 176
Cognitive development
  adolescent, 289–291, 309–310
  cognitive activities, 153–165
  in infancy, 95–98
  language development and, 139, 143–146
  perceptual development. *See* Perceptual development
  units of cognitive activity, 151–153
Cognitive regression in old age, 466–469
Cohabitation, 383
College youth, 313, 316, 329, 368, 379, 396–397

Communal living, 383
Compensatory education, 190–198
Comprehension, speech, 129–130
Compulsions in middle childhood, 264–265
Conception, 53–54
Concepts, 152–153
Concrete operations stage of intellectual development, 21, 174–176
Conditioned response, 29
Conditioned stimulus, 29
Conditioning
  classical, 28–30
  operant, 30–31
Conformity to peer culture
  in adolescence, 305–306
  in middle childhood, 248–249
Conscience development
  in middle childhood, 259–262
  in preschool years, 228–230
Conservation, 174–176, 467–469
Consonant sounds, 130
Contour, response of infants to, 89–90
Contraception, 332–333
Controlled homes, 231–232
Conventional modes, 309
Cooing sounds in infancy, 99
Creativity, 161–162, 426–427
Creeping in infancy, 71, 72
Cross sectional approach to research, 15, 16–17, 408–409
Crying
  hunger and, 102, 103
  separation and, 109–110
  sex-typing and, 226
  strangers and, 107
Crystallized intelligence, 424–425
Cultural differences in child rearing, 117–120
Cultural influences on sexuality, 326–327

Dante, 411
Darwin, Charles, 6, 8

Death, 475, 478–480
Deductive reasoning, 165
Defense mechanisms
  of adolescents, 291
  of preschool children, 215, 218–220
  in psychoanalytic theory, 24
Demand feeding, 76, 103
Democratic home, 231, 232
Democratic marriage, 381–382
Democratic parents, 241, 301–303
Denial, 219
Deoxyribonucleic acid (DNA), 44
Dependency in preschool years, 211–215
Dependent variable, 14
Deprivation, juvenile delinquency and, 353
Depth perception in infancy, 94–95
Despair, 26
Developmental psychology, 2–39
  concerns of, 38–39
  goals of, 11–12
  historical perspectives, 4–11
    adult development and aging, 9–11
    child psychology, 4–8
    psychology of adolescence, 8–9
  as scientific discipline, 11–17
    explanation and theory, 12–13
    research methods, 13–17
  theory in, 17–38
    learning concepts, 34–38
    learning theories, 27–34, 126–128, 217
    Piaget's theory of intellectual development, 17–22, 95–98, 173–178, 466–469
    psychoanalytic theories, 22–27
  value of, 12–13
Differential Aptitude Test, 394
Directed cognitions, 153–154
Discrepancy, attention and, 92–93
Discrimination against women, 392–400
Discriminations, 35

Discriminative stimuli, 30–31
Disease
    in middle adulthood, 426
    in old age, 474–475
Disengagement, 457–460
Displacement, 219
Distant grandparent, 463
Distinctive-feature theory of perceptual
    development, 155–157
Distractibility, infant, 80–81
Distress, infant, 102
Divorce, 388–389, 439–440
Dominant genes, 44
Double-entendres, 289
Down's syndrome, 49
Dropouts
    school, 255–256
    social, 340–343
Drug use, 343–350
    alcohol
        in adolescence, 344–346
        in old age, 451
        during pregnancy, 58–59
    amphetamines, 344, 349
    barbiturates, 349
    generation gap and, 343–344
    hallucinogens, 343, 349
    marijuana, 343, 344, 346–349
    opiates, 349–350
    during pregnancy, 54, 58–59
    reasons for, 350
Dying, 478–480

Early Training Project of Peabody Col-
    lege, 196
Ego
    confusion, 281
    identity. *See* Identity
    integrity, 448–449
    in psychoanalytic theory, 22, 24
Eidetic imagery, 152
Elaborated language codes, 147
Embryonic development, 54, 55, 56
Emotional dependency, 212

Emotional expressiveness-reserve, 244
Emotional state of mother, effect on
    fetus, 60, 62
Empathy, 369
Environmental influences
    on fetus, 57–62
    on intellectual development in middle
        adulthood, 425–426
    on intelligence, 188–198
    in preschool years, 230–234
Equalitarian form of marriage, 382
Erikson, Erik, 24, 25, 26, 281, 283, 373,
    410, 448–449, 480
Estrogens, 292
Evaluation, 163–165
Executive process, 154
Experiment, 13–15
Explanation, 12–13
Extended family, 383
Extinction, 35
Extramarital sexual encounters, 433

Facial characteristics of infants, 66
Fallopian tube, 53
Familiarity, infant attention and, 91–92
Family
    in middle adulthood, 434–440
        divorce, 439–440
        marital satisfaction, 438
        postparental family, 434–437
    in old age, 461–466
        grandparenting, 461–463
        marital relations, 463–466
    in young adulthood. *See* Marriage, in
        young adulthood; Parenthood
Family influence in middle childhood,
    240–247
    on child's self-concept, 242–243
    parental absence, 244–245
    parent behavior, 240–242
    response to children's predispositions,
        243–244
    school achievement, 256–259
    siblings, 245–247

Father. *See also* Parent-child relationships; Parents
  absence of, 244–245
  adolescent identity and, 283
  of delinquents, 357
Fear. *See also* Anxiety
  of error, 163
  in middle childhood, 262–264
  in preschool years, 213, 215–218
Feeding situation
  attachment and, 104–105
  needs and, 76
  significance of, 102–103
Female reproductive system, 53, 55–56
Fertilization, 53–54
Fetus
  development of, 55–57
  environmental influences on, 57–62
Filial maturity, 437
Filter theory of mate selection, 375–377
First child crisis, 385–387
Fluid intelligence, 424–425
Food stamps, 455
Formal grandparent, 461, 463
Formal operations stage of intellectual development, 21, 176–178
Fraternal twins, 46–47, 52
Freud, Sigmund, 22–25, 27, 153, 154, 204, 427
Frustration, 205–206
Functional psychoses, 50
Fun-seeker grandparent, 463
Future Shock (Toffler), 390

Gauguin, Paul, 411
General Aptitude Test Battery, 394
Generativity, 25, 26, 410
Genes, 43–46
Genital stage of personality development, 25
Gerontology, 448
Gibson, Eleanor, 155
Goethe, Johann Wolfgang von, 426
Gottesman, I. I., 190

Grandparenting, 461–463
Grasping reflex, 67, 69, 74
Group marriage, 382–383
Growth spurt, 291, 293–295
Guilt, 228
Guthrie, Arlo, 49
Guthrie, Woody, 49

Habituation, 92
Halluginogens, 343, 349
Harlow, Harry, 104–105
Hayakawa, S. I., 340
Hayden, Tom, 340
Hearing
  in infancy, 70–71
  in old age, 474
Heart attack, 430–432
Hereditary transmission, 43–52
  chromosomes, 44, 45, 47–48, 53–54
  determining extent of genetic influences, 45–47
  genes, 43–46
  of intelligence, 51–52, 187–192
  of mental defects, 49
  of mental disorders, 49–50
  of personality, 50–51
  of physical features, 48
  of sex, 47–48
Heroin use
  in adolescence, 349–350
  during pregnancy, 58
Hierarchical sentence structure, 132
Hippies, 340–343
Holmes, Oliver Wendell, 411
Holophrastic speech, 130
Home environment. *See* Environmental influences; Family; Parent-child relationships; Parents
Hormones, 292–293
Hostility, 204, 241
Humanizing of values, 369–370
Humphrey, Hubert H., 480
Hunger in infants, 75
Hunt, J. McV., 197

Huntington's chorea, 45–46, 49
Hydrocarbon vapors, 344
Hypochondriasis, 265
Hypotheses, generation of, 160–165

Id, 22, 24
Identical twins, 46, 47, 51, 52, 188, 190
Identification in preschool years, 222–
    230, 283
  conscience development, 228–230
  defined, 222
  development of, 223
  sex-typing, 224–228
Identity, 25
  in adolescence, 281–288
  in preschool years. *See* Identification
    in preschool years
  in young adulthood, 368–369
Images, 152
Imitative aggression, 208, 209
Imitative learning, 126, 127–128
Imitative speech, 131
Immediate memory, 471
Impotence, 433
Imprinting, 105–107
Impulsive children, 163–165
Incorrigibility, 351
Independence, adolescent, 298–303
  in other cultures, 298–300
  in U.S., 300–303
Independent variable, 14
Individual differences among infants,
    76–82
Induction-phase of problem-solving,
    160
Infancy
  biological factors in, 43, 62–82
    basic needs, 74–75
    birth process, 62
    body growth, 65–66
    individual differences, 76–82
    premature births, 62–64
    response capabilities, 71–74
    sensory capacities, 66–71

  socioeconomic class and, 64
  defined, 64–65
  language development in, 130
  mental development in, 95–98
  perceptual development in, 89–95
    depth perception, 94–95
    discrepancy, 92–93
    meaning, 91–92
    memory, 93–94
    schemata, 92
    stimulus determinants of attention,
      89–91
  social development in, 98–120
    anxieties, 107–110
    attachment, 103–110
    cultural differences in child rearing,
      117–120
    interaction with caretakers, 103–
      117
    social responses, 99–103
Infantile amaurotic family idiocy, 49
Infant tests, 182–183
Informational value, 137
Institutional care, 113–116
Instrumental dependency, 212
Integrity, 26
Intellectual development, 11
  in adolescence, 176–178
  in middle adulthood, 419–428
    age and, 420–428
    environmental influences, 425–426
    specific abilities, 423–425
  in old age, 466–472
    cognitive regression, 466–469
    learning and memory, 470–472
    problem-solving, 469–470
  Piaget's theory of, 17–22, 95–98,
    173–178, 466–469
Intellectualization, 291
Intelligence, 172–200
  age and, 420–427
  career choice and, 394
  environment and, 188–198
  heredity and, 51–52, 187–192

Intelligence (*Continued*)
  Piaget's stages of, 173–178
  problem-solving and, 161
  social acceptance and, 308
  tests, 11, 172, 178–187
    infant tests, 182–183
    Stanford-Binet, 179–181, 184, 186–
      187, 194–195
    Wechsler, 181–182, 184, 420, 425
Intelligence quotients (IQ), 11, 51–52,
    64, 179
  age and, 426, 470
  career choice and, 394
  computation of, 179–180
  consistency of, 184–186
  heredity and, 187–190
  improvement of, 192–198
  juvenile delinquency and, 353
  race and, 190–192
  school dropouts and, 255
  usefulness of, 186–187
Interfaith marriages, 378–379
Intermittent reinforcements, 36–37
Interpersonal relationships in young
    adulthood, 369
Interpretation, 155–157
Interpretation of Dreams, The (Freud),
    427
Interracial marriages, 378–379
Interval schedules, 37
Intimacy, 25
  versus isolation, 373–375
Intimate alliances, 373
Introspection, 416–417
Introversion-extraversion, 51
Irradiation, effect on fetus, 59
Irritability, infant, 77–79
Isolation versus intimacy, 373–375

James, William, 67, 475
Jensen, Arthur, 190–191, 192, 197
Johnson, Virginia, 325, 433
Jung, Carl, 417
Juvenile delinquency, 350–359
  deprivation and, 353

incidence, 350–353
  parent-child relationships and, 357
  personality and, 353–357
  prevention and treatment of, 357–359
  social change and, 353

Kansas City Studies of Adult Life, 416
Kohlberg, Lawrence, 260–261, 309–
    310, 369–373
Kübler-Ross, Elisabeth, 479
Kuder interest inventories, 392
Kuhn, Maggie, 480

Language development, 38
  beginnings of speech, 129–130
  characteristics of early speech, 130
  cognitive development and, 139, 143–
    146
  first sentences, 130–132
  language universals, 128, 138–140
  in middle childhood, 140–143
  research on, 12
  semantic development, 132–138
  socioeconomic class and, 146–151
  theories of, 125–129
Language universals, 128, 138–140
Latency period of personality develop-
    ment, 25
Laughing, infant, 101–102
Learning
  aggression and, 206–210
  concepts, 34–38
  old age and, 470–472
Learning theories, 27–34, 126–128, 217
Life expectancy, 475–478
Life review processes, 449–451
Light intensity, response of infants to,
    89–90
Linguistic theories, 128–129
Linguistic universals, 128, 138–140
Locke, John, 6
Locomotion, infant, 71–74
Longevity, 477–478
Longitudinal approach to research, 15–
    16, 408–409

Long-term memory, 472
Looking, infant, 99
Lorenz, Konrad, 105–107
LSD, 343, 349
Luria, A. R., 143

Male reproductive system, 55
Manpower Report of the President, 397–398
Manus, 377
Marijuana use, 343, 344, 346–349
Marriage, 11
  in middle adulthood, 434–440
    divorce, 439–440
    marital satisfaction, 438
    postparental family, 434–437
  in old age, 463–466
  in young adulthood, 373–384
    choosing mates, 375–380
    choosing style of, 380–384
    intimacy versus isolation dilemma
      and, 373–375
    parenthood and, 387
Maslow, Abraham, 372, 410
Masters, William, 325, 433
Mastery, 220–222, 416–417
Masturbation, 204, 324, 326, 327
Matching Familiar Figures, 163–164
Mate selection, 375–380
Maturation, 43
  adolescent, 293–298
  infant, 70
Meaning, infant attention and, 91–92
Mediated generalization, 35
Medicare, 455
Memory, 155–160
  age differences in, 93–94
  attention and, 93–94
  defined, 157–158
  old age and, 470–472
  recall, 157–158, 160
  recognition, 157–158
Menopause, 427–430
Menstruation, 297

Mental defects, hereditary transmission
  of, 49
Mental disorders
  hereditary transmission of, 49–50
  in old age, 451
Mental flexibility, 413–414
Mental health in old age, 451–454
Mental representations, 174
Mental retardation, 37, 49, 98
Middle adulthood, 408–482
  biological factors in, 428–434
    heart attack, 430–432
    menopause, 428–430
    sexual behavior, 413, 432–434
  defined, 408
  family in, 434–440
    divorce, 439–440
    marital satisfaction, 438
    postparental family, 434–437
  intellectual development in, 419–428
    age and, 420–428
    environmental influences, 425–426
    specific abilities, 423–425
  personality development in, 410–419
    personality traits, 415–418
    potential for change, 418–419
    stages of, 410–415
Middle childhood, 240–272
  conscience development in, 259–262
  cultural differences in, 117
  defined, 240
  family influence in, 240–247
    on child's self-concept, 242–243
    parental absence, 244–245
    parent behavior, 240–242
    response to children's predisposi-
      tions, 243–244
    school achievement, 256–259
    siblings, 245–247
  language development during, 140–143
  peer relations in, 247–249
    academic achievement and, 258–259
    conformity, 248–249

Middle childhood (*Continued*)
　　peer subcultures, 247–248
　　social status, 248
　　psychological problems of, 262–270
　　　fears and phobias, 262–264
　　　minority groups, 267–270
　　　obsessions and compulsions, 264–265
　　　physical symptoms, 265–267
　　school, adjustment to, 249–256
　　　school dropouts, 255–256
　　　school size, 254–255
　　　teacher roles, 250–252
　　　teaching methods, 253
　　　textbooks, 253–254
Mid-life crisis, 411–413
Minority-group membership, problems of, 267–270
Models in observational learning, 32–34, 208–209
Moderate reformers, 338
Mongolism, 49
Moral development
　　in adolescence, 309–316
　　　factors in, 309–311
　　　religious beliefs, 311–312
　　　values, 312–316
　　in middle childhood, 259–262
　　in preschool years, 228–230
　　in young adults, 369–373
Moral realism, stage of, 259
Moral reasoning, 260–261
Moro reflex, 68
Mother. *See also* Parent-child relationships; Parents
　　attachment to, 103–110
　　career decisions of daughter and, 400
　　of delinquents, 357
　　dependency on, 211–215
　　interaction of infants with, 103–117
　　prenatal environmental influences and, 57–62
　　social responses of infants to, 99–103
　　substitute, 111–113, 250

Motivation, 38
　　academic, 256–259
　　achievement. *See* Achievement motivation
　　memory and, 158
Movement, response of infants to, 89–90

Nature versus nurture issue, 6
Needs
　　of infants, 74–76
　　mate selection and, 379–380
Neglectful parents, 242, 244–245
Neurosis, 265, 451–452
Newborn babies
　　attention and, 89
　　food needs of, 75
　　sensory capacities of, 66–71
　　sleep needs of, 75
Nightmares, 263, 264
Normative life crises, 11, 367–368
Nursing, 102

Object permanence, 97
Observational learning, 31–34, 126–127
Obsessions in middle childhood, 264, 265
Oedipus complex, 25
Old age, 447–482
　　attitudes toward, 447–448
　　biological factors in, 472–480
　　　biological changes, 472–474
　　　death and dying, 475, 478–480
　　　diseases, 474–475
　　　life expectancy, 475–478
　　family in, 461–466
　　　grandparenting, 461–463
　　　marital relations, 463–466
　　historical perspectives, 9, 11
　　intellectual development in, 466–472
　　　cognitive regression, 466–469
　　　learning and memory, 470–472
　　　problem-solving, 469–470
　　personality development in, 448–454

ego integrity, 448–450
   life review processes, 450–451
   mental health, 451–454
  psychoanalytic theory and, 25–26
  social factors in aging, 454–460
   disengagement, 457–460
   retirement, 11, 454–457
Olfaction in infants, 71
Operant conditioning, 30–31
Operations, in intellectual development
   theory, 18–19
Opiate use, 349–350
Oral stage of personality development,
   24
Ordinal position, 245
Outcomes, 35–37
Ovaries, 56, 292
Overdiscrimination in early speech, 133,
   135
Overgeneralization in early speech, 133,
   134
Ovum (egg), 44, 45, 46, 53

Pain sensitivity in infants, 71
Parent-child relationships
  in adolescence
   identity and, 283, 288
   independence and, 301–303
   juvenile delinquency and, 357
  historical perspective, 4–5
  in infancy, 99–117
   interactions, 103–117
   social responses, 99–103
  language development and, 137–138
  in middle childhood, 240–245
   child's self-concept, 242–243
   conscience development, 261–262
   parental absence, 244–245
   parent behavior, 240–242
   response to children's predisposi-
    tions, 243–244
  in old age, 461–466
  in postparental family, 436–437
  in preschool years, 228, 230–234

Parenthood, 383–389
  alternative styles of, 387–388
  first child crisis, 385–387
  single parents, 388–389
Parents
  absence of, 244–245
  achievement motivation and, 220–222
  adolescent marijuana use and, 348
  authoritarian, 233–234, 241–242
  authoritative, 233, 241
  autocratic, 301
  democratic, 241, 301–303
  hostile, 240–241
  identification with, 222–230
   conscience development, 228–230
   defined, 222
   development of, 223
   sex-typing, 224–228
  influences of
   on adolescents, 306–308
   on mate selection, 378
   on school-age children, 240–245
  neglectful, 242, 244–245
  permissive, 206, 207–208, 233, 234,
   301
  punishment by, 35–36
   for aggressive behavior, 209–210
   for early sex-play, 204
  rejection by, 240–242
  sexual attitudes of, 329
  single, 388–389
  surrogate, 463
Parsons, Talcott, 475
Passive mastery, 416–417
Patriarchal family, 381
Pavlov, Ivan, 28
Peer relations
  in adolescence, 303–308
   conformity, 305–306
   influence of, 303–304
   juvenile delinquency and, 354
   marijuana use and, 348
   parental versus peer influences,
    306–308

Peer relations (*Continued*)
  social acceptance, 308
  in middle childhood, 247–249
    academic achievement and, 258–259
    conformity, 248–249
    peer subcultures, 247–248
    social status, 248
Perception, defined, 155
Perceptual development, 155–157
  age differences in, 155
  distinctive-feature theory, 155–157
  in infancy, 89–95
    depth perception, 94–95
    discrepancy, 92–93
    meaning, 91–92
    memory, 93–94
    schemata, 92
    stimulus determinants of attention, 89–91
Perceptual salience, 137
Performance factors in learning, 37–38
Permissive parents, 206, 207–208, 233, 234, 301
Persistence, infant, 80–81
Personal growth in young adulthood, 368–372
Personality
  disengagement and, 459–460
  hereditary transmission of, 50–51
  illness and, 475
  longevity and, 478
  retirement and, 457
Personality development
  in adolescence, 281–291
    identity, 281–288
    juvenile delinquency and, 353–354
    psychological effects of mental growth, 288–291
  in middle adulthood, 410–419
    personality traits, 415–418
    potential for change, 418–419
    stages of, 410–415
  in middle childhood. *See* Middle childhood

  in old age, 448–454
    ego integrity, 448–450
    life review processes, 450–451
    mental health, 451–454
  in preschool years, 203–235
    achievement, 220–222
    aggression, 204–211, 226–227
    anxieties, 213, 215, 219–220
    conscience development, 228–230
    defense mechanisms, 215, 219–220
    dependency, 211–215
    fears, 213, 215–219
    home environment, 230–234
    identification, 222–230
    mastery, 220–222
    sex-typing, 224–228
    sexual motives and curiosity, 204
    socialization, 203
  in young adulthood, 367–373
Personality traits in middle adulthood, 415–418
Phallic stage of personality development, 25
Phenylketonuria (PKU), 49
Philosophers, child psychology and, 6
Phobias in middle childhood, 262, 264
Physical features, hereditary transmission of, 48
Physical maturation, 293–295
Piaget, Jean, 17–22, 95–98, 141–142, 146, 173–178, 240, 259, 466–469
Placidity-explosiveness, 244
Positive reinforcement, 35
Postparental family, 434–437
Posture, development in infants, 72
Preconventional modes, 309
Preconventional reasoning, 260–261
Predispositions of children, response to, 243–244
Pregnancy
  biological development during, 53–62
    conception, 53–54
    embryonic development, 54, 55, 56
    environmental influences, 57–62
    fetal development, 55–57

unwanted, 331–333
Prejudice, development of, 268–270
Premarital intercourse, 329, 330
Premature births, 62–64, 100
Preoperational stage of intellectual development, 21, 173–174, 240
Preschool children
  language development in. *See* Language development
  personality development in, 203–235
    achievement, 220–222
    aggression, 204–211, 226–227
    anxieties, 213, 215, 219–220
    conscience development, 228–230
    defense mechanisms, 215, 219–220
    dependency, 211–215
    fears, 213, 215–219
    home environment, 230–234
    identification, 222–230
    mastery, 220–222
    sex-typing, 224–228
    sexual motives and curiosity, 204
    socialization, 203
Privileged youth, alienation among, 334–336
Problem-solving
  language and, 145–146
  in old age, 469–470
  processes in, 155–165
Production, speech, 129–130
Projection, 219
Psychoanalytic theories of development, 22–27
Psycholinguist, 125
Psychological aspects
  of career choice, 390
  of maturation, 294, 296–298
Psychological control, 241
Psychological effects of mental growth, 288–291
Psychological factors affecting sexual behavior, 433
Psychological problems
  in menopause, 429–430
  of middle childhood, 262–270

    fears and phobias, 262–264
    minority groups, 267–270
    obsessions and compulsions, 264–265
    physical symptoms, 265–267
Psychological reactions to retirement, 455–457
Psychoses, 451
Psychosomatic illnesses, 266–267
Puberty, 291–298
Punishment, 35–36
  for aggressive behavior, 209–210
  for early sex-play, 204
Pupillary reflex, 70

Race
  intelligence and, 189–192
  mate selection and, 378
Race Differences in Intelligence, 190
Radical dissent, 338
Ratio schedules, 37
Reaching, development in infants, 74
Reaction intensity, infant, 80–81
Reasoning
  deductive, 165
  moral, 309–310
  preconventional, 260–261
Recall, 157–158, 160
Recessive genes, 44–45
Recognition, 157–158
Recovery, capacity for, 116–117
Reflective children, 163–165
Reflexes of newborn babies, 67–70
Regression, 37, 219
Reinforcement, 35–37, 126, 127
Relational terms, 176
Religion, 311–312, 378–379, 415
REM sleep, 75, 76
Repression, 22, 219
Research, 2, 11–17
Reservoir of family wisdom (grandparenting style), 463
Response hierarchy, 37

Responsiveness dimension of infant temperament, 80–81
Restricted language codes, 147
Retirement, 11, 454–457
Rewards, 35–37, 207
Rh factor, 60
Rhythmicity, 70–71, 78–79
Rise times, 70
Robins, Clarence, 148–150
Rogers, Carl, 369, 372
Roosevelt, Eleanor, 411, 412
Rooting reflex, 67, 68
Rousseau, Jean Jacques, 6
Rubella (German measles), 60
Rules, 153
Runaways, 342–343, 351

Schedules of reinforcement, 37
Schemata, 92, 151, 173
Schizophrenia, 50
School
    adjustment to, 249–256
        school dropouts, 255–256
        school size, 254–255
        teacher roles, 250–252
        teaching methods, 253
        textbooks, 253–254
    phobias about, 264
Self-actualization, 410
Self-concept, influences on, 242–243
Self-consistency, 294, 296
Self-images in minority groups, 267–268
Semantic development, 132–138
Senile brain disease, 451
Sensorimotor stage of intellectual development, 21, 96–97
Sensory capacities of infants, 66–71
Sentences, first, 130–132
Separation anxiety, 109–110
Sequences, 38
Serializations, 176
Serial marriage, 382
Sex chromosomes, 47–48

Sex differences
    in aggression, 210–211
    in body growth, 66
    in career opportunities, 397–400
    in delinquent behavior, 351–352
    hereditary transmission of, 47–48
    in life expectancy, 475
    in sexuality, 324–326, 328
Sex hormones, 292–293
Sex-linked chromosomes, 48
Sex-play in preschool years, 204
Sex roles, 224–228, 417–418, 438
Sex-typing, 224–228
Sexual attitudes in adolescence, 323–333
    of contemporary American adolescents, 327–329
    cultural influences on, 326–327
    pregnancy and, 330–333
    sex differences in, 324–326, 328
Sexual behavior
    in adolescence, 326–327, 330
    in middle adulthood, 413, 432–434
    in psychoanalytic theory, 22, 24
    in young adulthood, 373, 384
Sexual identity in adolescence, 284–288
Sexual intercourse, 324, 326, 329, 330, 432
Siblings, influence of, 245–247
Simon, Theodore, 179
Single parents, 388–389
Skinner, B. F., 30, 31, 37, 126
Sleep, infant, 74–76
Sleepwalking, 263–264
Slobin, Dan, 139
Smiling, infant, 100–102, 106, 107, 108, 111–112
Social acceptance, 308
Social change, juvenile delinquency and, 353
Social development in infancy, 98–120
    anxieties, 107–110
    attachment, 103–110
    cultural differences in child rearing, 117–120

interaction with caretakers, 103–117
social responses, 99–103
Social dropouts, 339–343
Social factors
in aging, 454–460
disengagement, 457–460
retirement, 11, 454–457
in mate selection, 378–379
Socialization, 203
Social responses of infants, 99–103
Social Security Act of 1935, 454
Social Security benefits, 454–455
Social status among peers, 248
Socioeconomic class
academic motivation and, 256, 258
adolescent sexual attitudes and, 329
infant intellectual development and,
114–117
infant vocalization and, 100
intelligence and, 188–189, 190
juvenile delinquency and, 352–353
language development and, 146–151
mate selection and, 379
memory and, 158
pregnancy and delivery and, 64
school dropouts and, 255–256
"Speed" (amphetamines), 344, 349
Sperm, 44, 45, 53
Stagnation, 25, 26, 410
Stanford-Binet Intelligence Test, 179–
181, 184, 186–187, 194–195
Stimulus determinants of attention, 88–
91
Stimulus factors in learning, 34–35
Stimulus generalization, 35
Stranger anxiety, 107–109
"Street people," 343
Stroke, 425
Strong-Campbell Interest Inventory,
392
Strong Vocational Interest Blank
(SVIB), 392–394
Subcultures, peer, 247–248
Suicide, 452
Superego, 22, 24

Surrogate parents, 463
Symbionese Liberation Army, 339
Symbols, 152
Syntactic Structures (Chomsky), 128
Syphilis, 59–60

Tabula rasa, 6
Teachers, role of, 250–252
Teaching methods, variations in, 253
Telegraphic sentences, 130–131, 132
Temperament, infant, 76–82
Terman, Lewis, 179
Testes, 55, 56, 292
Testosterone, 292
Textbooks, 253–254
Thalidomide, 58, 59
Thirst, infant, 76
Tics, 265–266
Toffler, Alvin, 390
Twins, 46–47, 51, 52, 188, 190

Umbilical cord, 54
Unconditional positive regard, 369
Unconditional stimulus, 28–30
Unconditioned response, 28–29
Unconscious mind in psychoanalytic
theory, 22
Underextension in early speech, 133,
135
Undirected cognitions, 153
Uterine environment, 43, 57–62
Uterus, 53–54

Values
of adolescents, 312–316
humanizing, 369–370
vocational, 394–397
Venereal disease, 330–331
Verbal Behavior (Skinner), 126
Verbal mediation, 144–146
Vietnam War, 339
Vision
in infancy, 70
in old age, 472, 474
Visual cliff, 94, 95

Visually directed reaching, 74
Visual pursuit, 70
Vocabularies, development of, 141, 142
Vocalizing, infant, 99–100
Vowel sounds, 130
Vygotsky, L. S., 143

Walking, development in infants, 71–72
Watson, John B., 29
Wechsler, David, 181, 420, 423
Wechsler Adult Intelligence Scale, 184, 425
Wechsler Intelligence Scale for Children (WISC), 181–182
Wechsler Preschool-Primary Scale of Intelligence, 181–182
Wernicke's area, 129
White, Robert, 368
Widowhood, 464
Wisdom, 449
Women, careers of, 397–401
Working youths, 314–316

X chromosomes, 47–48
X-rays, effect on fetus, 59

Y chromosomes, 47–48
Young adulthood, 367–401
    careers, 389–401
        choosing, 391–394
        vocational values, 394–397
        of women, 397–401
    defined, 367
    marriage, 373–384
        choosing mates, 375–380
        choosing style of, 380–384
        intimacy versus isolation dilemma and, 373–375
        parenthood and, 387
    parenthood, 384–389
        alternative styles of, 387–388
        first child crisis, 385–387
        single parents, 388–389
    personality development in, 367–373

78 79 80 81 82 9 8 7 6 5 4 3 2 1